INFORMATION SYSTEMS

PRINCIPLES, APPLICATIONS AND DESIGN

Dr. Ikvinderpal Singh

KHANNA BOOK PUBLISHING CO. (P) LTD.

::: *Publisher of Engineering and Computer Books* :::

Head Office	:	4C/4344, Ansari Road, Darya Ganj, New Delhi-110002	
		Phone: 011-23244447/48	Fax: 011-23244447
Regd. Office	:	1694-95, Nai Sarak, Delhi-110006	
		Phone: 011-23283211	Fax: 011-23256658
E-Mail	:	contact@khannabooks.com	
Website	:	www.khannabooks.com, www.khannapublishers.com	

INFORMATION SYSTEMS (Principles, Applications and Design)
Dr. Ikvinderpal Singh

ISBN : 978-93-82609-33-9

First Edition 2014

Published by:
KHANNA BOOK PUBLISHING CO. (P) LTD.
4C/4344, Ansari Road, Daryaganj, New Delhi-110 002
Phone: 011-23244448 Telefax: 011-23244447
E-mail: contact@khannabooks.com
Website: www.khannabooks.com, www.khannapublishers.com

Regd. Off: 1694-95, 1st Floor, Nai Sarak, Delhi-110006 (India)
Phone: 011-23283211 Telefax: 011-23256658

Cover Design & Layout by
Akriti Print & Graphics, Delhi

Printed in India by
S.P.S. Printers & Binders, Delhi

Dedicated

to

Meghanpreet kaur

and

Wahenoor kaur

Preface

This book provides a thorough coverage of the principles, applications and design of information systems in both private and public organisations. Suitable for students on professional and academic courses in Management and in Information Systems, this text covers all of the major topics including; systems; concepts; organisational structures and behaviour; management; leadership; planning; decision-making and information technology in general.

The organizations nowadays are operating in increasingly competitive and global marketplace. Hence the workers in all business areas, viz. accounting, finance, human resources, marketing, operations management, and production must be well prepared to make significant contributions which are required for success. They need to understand what information systems can and cannot do and be able to use them to help them accomplish their work. Further they are expected to discover opportunities to use these information systems and to participate in the design of solutions to business problems employing information systems. They are challenged to identify and evaluate information systems options. To be successful, the workers must be able to view the information systems from the perspective of business and organizational needs. For the solutions to be accepted, they must also recognize and address their impact on fellow workers, customers, suppliers, and other key business partners. For all these reasons, a course in information systems is essential for students in today's high tech world.

Our primary objective in this book is to provide the best information systems textbook for the information technology course required by all business students. The students are required to learn to use information technology to ensure their personal success in jobs and to improve the success of organizations. Through various inputs and feedback, this book has been developed to be the highest quality-set of teaching materials available to help the students achieve these goals.

This book stands proudly at the beginning of the IS curriculum and remains unchallenged in its position as being only IS principles text offering the basic IS concepts that every business student must learn to be successful. In the past, instructors of the introductory course faced a dilemma. On one hand, experience in business organizations allows students to grasp the complexities underlying important IS concepts. For this reason, many schools delayed presenting these concepts until students completed a large portion of the core business requirements. On the other hand, delaying the presentation of IS concepts until students have matured within the business curiculum often forces one or two required introductory IS courses to focus only on personal computing software tools and, at best, merely to introduce computer concepts.

This text prepares students for the constantly changing demands of using information systems as managers in today's fast-paced organizations first by relating MIS to management, the organization and technology, focusing on the importance of integrating these elements; second by tracking emerging technologies and organizational trends; and third by consistently using examples taken from real businesses, both domestic and foreign.

Current developments and experiences need interpretation and coalesence to provide the guidance that new and practicing managers need to further develop their knowledge edge and managerial skills.

DR. IKVINDERPAL SINGH

Contents

Information Concepts 1

1.1 DATA

Data can be defined as a representation of facts, concepts or instruction in a formalized manner which should be suitable for communication, interpretation or processing by human or electronic machine. It is defined as raw facts or observations, typically about physical phenomenon or business transactions. The word data is the plural of Latin datum, past participle of dare, "to give", hence "something given". Thus in general, data consists of propositions that reflect reality. A large class of practically important propositions are measurements or observations of a variable. Such propositions may comprise numbers, words, or images.

Data can also be known as objective measurements of attributes (the characteristics) of entities (such as people, place, things, and events). These measurements are usually represented by symbols such as numbers, words, codes composed of a mixture of numerical, alphabetical and other characters. For example, dates, weights, prices, costs, number of items sold, employees names, product names, a sale of machine tool etc. would generate a lot of data describing these events.

Thus, data is raw unprocessed facts and figures that have no context or purposeful meaning. For example, a computer operator may enter 36.41, which is data because we do not know why or in what context it is being used. However, if this number then appears on a bill to show that you owe a company £36.41 for goods received then this data has changed into information, because it has acquired a context (it's a bill) and meaning. The figures 36.41 will be held as binary data on some media such as a hard disk. It is the software which accesses this data and displays it in its context. It may also have some structure, if it is held in a program like a database for example, and a database will also give it structure. So, it is the software which turns the figures from data into information and gives them meaning. The binary patterns on backing storage devices such as a disk, CD or DVD, or memory stick, are all classed as data. For example, the binary patterns that describe an icon on your desktop are data. They become information after the operating system software has processed them, because then they become meaningful to you as the icons representative of your hard disk or Internet explorer.

Data item refer to an elementary description of things, events, activities, and transactions that are recorded, classified, and stored, but not organized to convey any specific meeting.

Data items can be numeric, alphanumeric, figures, sounds, or images. A student grade in a class is a data item, and so is the number of hours an employee worked in a certain week.

A single piece of data is called a **datum**. Unrelated items of data are considered to be essentially without meaning and are often described as 'noise'. It is only when data have been placed in some form of context that they become meaningful to a manager.

Data can exist *naturally* or can be created *artificially*. Naturally occurring data need only to be recorded. Managers have to put in place procedures and tools to ensure data are recorded. For example, to ensure a call centre operator includes the postcode of every customer this can be written into their script and a validation check performed to check these data have been entered into the system. Artificial data are often produced as a by-product of process. Processing an organization's accounts, for example, might produce the number of sales made in a particular month.

Computers represent data in the form of binary digits called **bits**. A bit is simply a number that has one or two values, 0 or 1. Computers use bits for storage because storage because they are easy to represent electronically. Bits can be used to represent data in a number of ways. To represent numbers, groups of bits are collected and a character code is used to translate the resulting group of bits into characters. For example, the bit pattern 01000001 represents the character A; 01000010 represent the character B. A group of bits that represents a character called a *byte*. Each byte represents a single character, bytes are grouped together to form fields or data items, a group of fields is called a record and a group of records is called a file.

Data	**Represented**	**By Example**
Alphanumeric Data	Numbers, letter, and other characters	A, B, C, ... 1, 2, 3, ... @, #, $, %, ^, &, (,), +, -, ...
Image Data	Graphic, images or pictures	 (Image of Books)
Audio Data	Sound, noise or tones	(The singing of birds.) (The honking of horns.)
Video Data	Moving images or pictures	(A visual presentation of college.) (A movie playing on television.)

Figure 1.1: Representation of data

Various types of data and their representation by various means are depicted in Figure 1.1.

1.1.1 Hierarchy of Data

Data is generally organized in a hierarchy that begins with the smallest piece of data used by computers (a bit) and progresses through the hierarchy to a database. Figure 1.2 shows the hierarchy of data.

- **Bit:** Smallest piece of data, a 0 or 1
- **Byte:** Eight bits make a byte. A character (a, A, p, P, 1, 9, $, #) is represented by a byte.
- **Field:** One or more characters make a field.
- **Records:** One or more fields make a record.
- **File:** One or more records make a file or table.
- **Database:** One or more files or tables make a database.

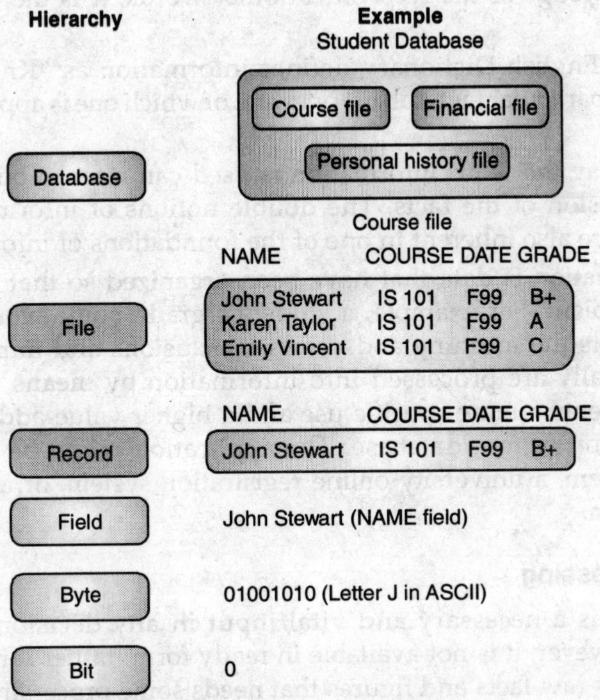

Figure 1.2: Hierarchy of Data

1.1.2 Quantitative and Qualitative Data

Some methods provide data which are quantitative and some methods provide data which are qualitative. Quantitative methods are those which focus on numbers and frequencies rather than on meaning and experience. Quantitative methods (e.g. experiments, questionnaires and psychometric tests) provide information which is easy to analyse statistically and fairly reliable. Quantitative methods are associated with the scientific and experimental approach and are criticised for not providing an in depth description.

Qualitative methods are ways of collecting data which are concerned with describing meaning, rather than with drawing statistical inferences. What qualitative methods (e.g.

case studies and interviews) lose on reliability they gain in terms of validity? They provide a more in depth and rich description.

Quantitative methods have come under considerable criticism. In modern research, most psychologists tend to adopt a combination of qualitative and quantitative approaches, which allow statistically reliable information obtained from numerical measurement to be backed up by and enriched by information about the research participants' explanations.

You will find that many of the core studies do collect both types of data.

1.2 INFORMATION

Information is the result of processing, manipulating and organising data in a way that adds to the knowledge of the receiver. In other words, it is the context in which data is taken.

The Oxford English Dictionary defines information as "Knowledge communicated concerning some particular fact, subject or event; of which one is apprised or told; intelligence, news."

Hence the way the word information is used can refer to both "facts" in themselves and the transmission of the facts. The double notions of information as both facts and communication are also inherent in one of the foundations of information theory.

Thus, information is data that have been organized so that they have meaning and value to the recipient. For example, a student's grade point average is information. The recipient interprets the meaning and draws conclusions and implications from the data. Data items typically are processed into information by means of an application. Such processing represents a more specific use and a higher value-added than simple retrieval and summarization from a database. The application might be a Web-based inventory management system, a university online registration system, or an Internet-based buying and selling system.

1.2.1 Data Processing

Information is a necessary and vital input in any decision-making process in an organization. However, it is not available in ready form; rather it has to be generated from data which acts as raw facts and figures that needs some processing. Figure 1.3 depicts the generation of information by data processing.

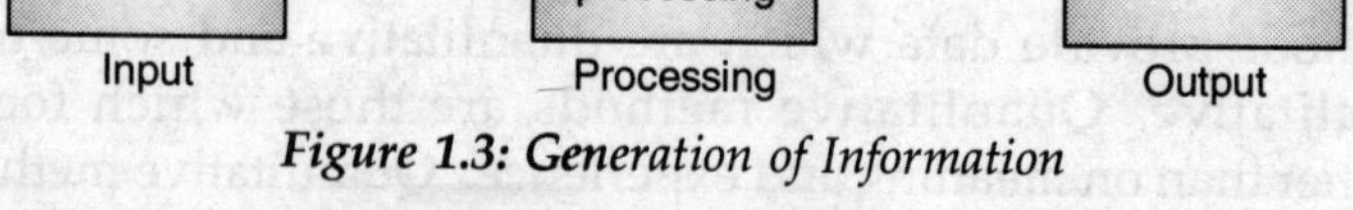

Figure 1.3: Generation of Information

Data processing is the re-structuring or re-ordering of data by people or machine to increase their usefulness & add values for particular purpose.

Data processing consists of basic steps input, processing and output. These three steps constitute the data processing cycle.

- **Input:** In this step the input data are prepared in some convenient form for processing.

The form will depend on the processing machine. For example, when electronic computers are used, the input data could be recorded on any one of several types of input medium, such as magnetic disks, tapes and so on.

- **Processing:** In this step input data are changed to produce data in a more useful form. For example, pay-checks may be calculated from the time cards, or a summary of sales for the month may be calculated from the sales orders.
- **Output:** Here the results of the proceeding processing step are collected. The particular form of the output data depends on the use of the data. For example, output data may be pay-checks for employees.

Thus, information in its unprocessed form is known as data, which is generated as a by-product of transactions taking place in the organization. Information on the other hand is processed data. Davis & Olson have defined information as data that has been processed into a form that is meaningful to the recipient and is of real or perceived value in current or prospective actions or decisions.

Processing data is necessary to place them into a meaningful context so that they can be easily understood by the recipient. Figure 1.3 illustrated the conversion of data into information.

A number of different data processes can be used to transform data into information. Data processes are sometimes also known as "**transformation processes**".

The conversion of facts into meaningful information is known as data processing. It is also called in general as information processing. It is the processing of data to make it more usable and meaningful, thus transforming into information.

Some examples of transformation processes include the following:

- **Classification:** This involves placing data into categories, for example categorizing an expense as either a fixed or a variable cost.
- **Rearranging/sorting:** This involves organizing data so that items are grouped together or placed into a particular order. Employee data, for example, might be sorted according to surname or payroll number.
- **Aggregating:** This involves summarizing data, for example by calculating averages, totals or subtotals.
- **Performing calculations:** An example might be calculating an employee's gross pay by multiplying the number of hours worked by the hourly rate of pay.
- **Selection:** This involves choosing or discarding items of data based on a set of selection criteria. A sales organization, for example, might create a list of potential customers by selecting those with incomes above a certain level.

It is worth noting that any action that serves to place data into a meaningful context can be considered a valid data process. In addition, several processes may be used in combination to produce information.

People often use the terms data and information interchangeably. However, it is better to view data as raw resources that are processed into finished information products. Then we can define information as data that have been converted into a meaningful and useful context for specific end users. Thus, data is usually not useful until subjected to a 'value-added' process, which we call data processing or information processing, where

(i) Its form is aggregated, manipulated and organized.
(ii) Its content is analysed and evaluated.
(iii) It is placed in a proper context for a human user.

So information should be viewed as processed data placed in a context that gives it value for specific end users.

We know now that information has a precise meaning & it is different from data. The information concept has a value in decision-making but the data has not. Information brings the clarity. Data is like raw facts and figures, while information is equivalent to the final product after processing the raw facts and figures. For example, in the report of IT students Roll number, Name, Class, Gender, Marks are the data attributes. But the actual information can be received by filling the records in respective data.

Some of the characteristics of information are as follows:

- Improves the representation of an entity.
- Updates the level of knowledge.
- Provides the surprise value.
- Reduces uncertainty.
- Helps in decision-making.

The information is said to be the basis for **decision making**. David and Olson define it as "Data that has been processed into a form that is meaningful to the recipient and is of real and perceived value in current decisions". The quality of the information can be decided depending on the above mentioned characteristics. The information is the meaningful representation of data to the recipient & is of real or perceived value in the current or the prospective actions or decisions of the recipient. Data can be a group of non-random symbol in the form of text, images or voice, actions & objects.

1.3 DECISION

A decision is a choice made from available alternatives. A decision is a final product of the specific mental/cognitive process of an individual or a group of persons/organisations which is called decision making; therefore it is a subjective concept. It is a mental object and can be an opinion, a rule or a task for execution/application.

1.3.1 Decision Making

Decision making is the cognitive process leading to the selection of a course of action among alternatives. Every decision making process produces a final choice. It can be an action or an opinion. It begins when we need to do something but we do not know what. Therefore, decision making is a reasoning process which can be rational or irrational, and can be based on explicit assumptions or tacit assumptions.

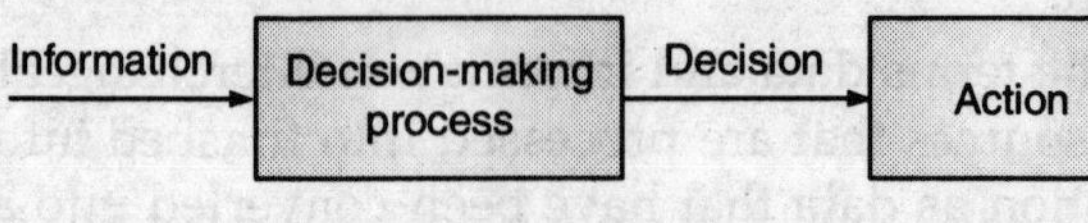

Figure 1.4: Decision making: transformation of information into action

1.4 KNOWLEDGE

Knowledge consists of data and/or information that have been organized and processed to convey understanding, experience, accumulated learning, and expertise as they apply to a current problem or activity. Data that are processed to extract critical implications and to reflect past experiences and expertise provide the recipient with organizational knowledge, which has a very high potential value.

Data, information, and knowledge can be inputs to an information system, and they can also be outputs. For example, data about employees, their wages, and time worked are processed as inputs in order to produce an organization's payroll information (output). The payroll information itself can later be used as an input to another system that prepares a budget or advises management on salary scales.

Humans have an endless thirst for knowledge, but how do we obtain knowledge? We can read books and magazines, study course materials, and of course we can gain knowledge from watching TV and listening to the radio. The knowledge about the weekend's sports matches can mean as much to one person as the latest advances in rocket science does to another.

We tend to gain knowledge from information and we use that information to make decisions.

Knowledge can be split into two categories: *explicit* and *tacit*.

- *Explicit* knowledge is rules or processes or decisions that can be recorded either on paper or in an information system.
- *Tacit* knowledge exists inside the minds of humans and is harder to record. It tends to be created from someone's experiences, so again it is based on a set of rules or experiences.

Knowledge acquisition involves complex cognitive processes: perception, learning, communication, association, and reasoning. The term knowledge is also used to mean the confident understanding of a subject, potentially with the ability to use it for a specific purpose. Knowledge doesn't exist until people are involved.

Epistemology is the theory of knowledge and is the branch of philosophy that studies the nature and scope of knowledge and belief. Much of the debate in this field has focused on analysing the nature of knowledge and how it relates to similar notions such as truth, belief, and justification. It also deals with the means of production of knowledge, as well as scepticism about different knowledge claims. In other words, epistemology primarily addresses the following questions: "What is knowledge?", "How is knowledge acquired?", and "What do people know?". The classical view of epistemology defines knowledge as being a product of both truth and belief as represented in Figure 1.5.

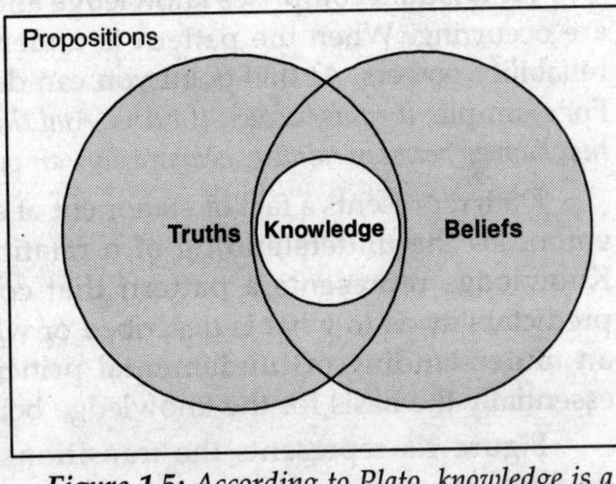

***Figure 1.5:** According to Plato, knowledge is a subset of that which is both true and believed*

1.5 WISDOM

Wisdom is an extrapolative and non-deterministic, non-probabilistic process. It callsupon all the previous levels of consciousness, and specifically upon special types of human programming (moral, ethical codes, etc.). It beckons to give us understanding about which there has previously been no understanding, and in doing so, goes far beyond understanding itself. It is the essence of philosophical probing. Unlike the previous levels, it asks questions to which there is no (easily-achievable) answer, and in some cases, to which there can be no humanly-known answers period. Wisdom is therefore, the process by which we also discern, or judge, between right and wrong, good and bad. Many scientists believe that computers do not have, and will never have the ability to posses' wisdom. Wisdom is a uniquely human state, requires one to have a soul, for it resides as much in the heart as in the mind.

1.6 DIKW HIERARCHY

DIKW refers to Data, Information, Knowledge and Wisdom; it is an information hierarchy where each layer adds certain attributes over and above the previous one. Data is the most basic level; Information adds context; Knowledge adds how to use it; and wisdom adds when to use it. This is the class of models for representing structural and functional relationships between data, information, knowledge, and wisdom, where the later is understood as ability to increase effectiveness and add value.

D: Data is the facts you will work with and they are without context. For example: *It is raining.*

I: Information comprises these facts with some context and perspective allowing you to see the relations between data. For example: *The temperature dropped 15 degrees and then it started raining.*

K: Knowledge comprises information and where you start to see patterns in those relations and begin to understand those patterns. Patterns give you predictability and repeatability (validity and reliability). For example: *If the humidity is very high and the temperature drops substantially the atmospheres is often unlikely to be able to hold the moisture so it rains.*

W: Wisdom comprises knowledge and occurs when you understand why these patterns are occurring. When the pattern is understood at this level you have high predictive and reliability powers. At this point you can determine the founding principles for the patterns. For example: *It rains because it rains. And this encompasses an understanding of all the interactions that happen between raining, evaporation, air currents, temperature gradients, changes, and raining.*

Data represents a fact or statement of event without relation to other things. Information embodies the understanding of a relationship of some sort, possibly cause and effect. Knowledge represents a pattern that connects and generally provides a high level of predictability as to what is described or what will happen next. Wisdom embodies more of an understanding of fundamental principles embodied within the knowledge that are essentially the basis for the knowledge being what it is. Wisdom is essentially systemic.

Figure 1.6 represents the transitions from data, to information, to knowledge, and finally to wisdom.

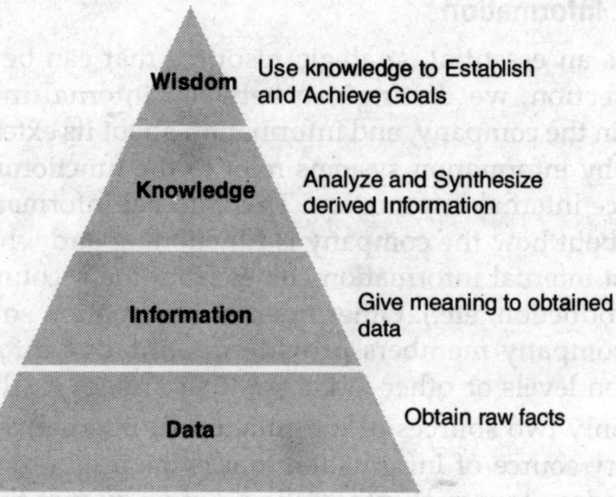

Figure 1.6: *Data, Information, Knowledge, and Wisdom Hierarchy*

As such, DIKW is a model that is useful to understanding analysis and the importance and limits of conceptual works. Evaluated understanding (wisdom) is the only stage of DIKW evolution dealing with the future; this is the tool for decision making.

Table 1.1 describes some of the distinctions between data, information, knowledge and wisdom.

Table 1.1: Distinctions between Data, Information, Knowledge and Wisdom

Level	Definition	Learning Process	Outcome
Data	Raw facts	Accumulating truths	Memorization (data bank)
Information	Meaningful, useful data	Giving form and functionality	Comprehension (information bank)
Knowledge	Clear understanding of information	Analysis and synthesis	Understanding (knowledge bank)
Wisdom	Using knowledge to esta blish and achieve goals	Discerning judgements and taking appropriate action	Better living/success (wisdom bank)

1.7 CATEGORIZATION OF INFORMATION

Information can be categorised under many headings that help us to determine its overall usefulness. The main categories are Source, Nature, Level, Time, Frequency, Use, Form, Type and Dimension. We will examine each of the categories and their sub-categories in some detail.

1.7.1 Sources of Information

Information is an essential, strategic resource that can be obtained from numerous sources. In this section, we distinguish between internal information relating to the environment within the company, and information about its external environment. Many of the data captured by information systems refer to the functioning of the organisation and are used to produce internal information. This internal information provides management with knowledge about how the company is functioning and whether or not it is achieving its objectives. Most internal information comes from the accounting system and statistical analyses (sales, production, etc.). Other internal information sources such as surveys and interviews with company members provide quantitative information on, for instance, workers' motivation levels or other indicators that are not easily quantified.

There are mainly two sources of information (i) internal, and (ii) external. Also there would be a primary source of information that is the origin of the data. In contrast, there can also be a secondary source of information. Let us discuss them in more detail here.

1.7.1.1 Primary Information

A primary source of information is one that provides data from an original source document. This may be as simple as an invoice sent to a business or a cheque received. It may be more complex, such as a set of sales figures for a range of goods for a tinned food manufacturer for one week, or it may be a set of sales figures over several weeks and several locations. There are many examples of primary sources in many walks of life, but generally a primary source is defined as being where a piece of information appears for the first time.

1.7.1.2 Secondary Information

A secondary source of information is one that provides information from a source other than the original. Secondary sources are processed primary sources, second-hand versions. Examples of secondary sources could be an accounts book detailing invoices received, a bank statement that shows details of cheques paid in and out. Where statistical information is gathered, such as in surveys or polls, the survey data or polling data is the primary source and the conclusions reached from the survey or the results of the poll are secondary sources.

1.7.1.3 Internal Information

The information generated through the internal sources of the organization is termed as internal information. The information generated by the managers of the organization, such as accounts manager, financial manager, sales manager, marketing manager, etc. is termed as internal information, as the sources of data are internal to the organization.

All organisations generate a substantial amount of information relating to their operation. This internal information is vital to the successful management of the organisation. The information may be available from a number of sources within the organisation, for example:

- Marketing and sales information on performance, revenues, markets shares, distribution channels, etc.
- Production and operational information on assets, quality, standards, etc.
- Financial information on profits, costs, margins, cash flows, investments, etc.
- Internal documentation such as order forms, invoices, credit notes, procedural manuals.

Users of internal information are within the organization such as:

- *Accounting:* The accounting department creates, maintains, processes and retrieves quantitative data related to the amount of profit or loss, cash flow, inventory control, payroll, cost allocation, and expense classification. Management seeks information relevant to its decision making such as data on investments in new projects, the current financial position of the firm and the control of expenses. Plant managers seek information relevant to material, labour and overhead costs. Sales managers are anxious to know the amount of contribution margin of different products.
- *Finance:* The finance department is in-charge of activities related to borrowing, funding and ascertaining necessary liquidity. Therefore, data related to capital structure, the number of outstanding shareholders, the degree of leverage, and the maturity dates of debits and treasury stocks must be available. Data related to prime interest rates, capital and each market condition must be constantly maintained. Top management seeks information relevant to decisions that would maximize the ultimate welfare of the outstanding shareholders.
- *Personnel:* Service contracts, fringe benefits, hourly/monthly rates, service seniorities and aptitude tests are a few examples of the duties of the personnel department. Personnel information is provided to other responsibility centres. For example, the payroll department is furnished with periodic reports containing names of current authorized employees and members; plant managers receive similar updated weekly reports. Management seeks information pertaining to the number of part-time and full-time employees, supervisor's reports and ethnic and sex manpower.
- *Public Relations:* The public relations department bridges the gap between the outside world and the organization. Union contract negotiations, scholarship and educational contributions and service rendered to the community are typical information aspects maintained by the public relations department.
- *Sales:* The sales department is the major revenue generating responsibility centre where efforts are geared towards sound planning and control of sales. Data in the sales department are used to produce a flow of indicative information pertaining to regional and total sales forecasts, actual sales, and performance reports. Sales managers use periodic sales reports with breakdown sales by products in evaluating the contribution margin of each territory. The management must be given information on any significant deviations from pre-determined forecasts along with justification for these differences. The accounting department receives daily documentary evidences and information related to cash and credit sales.
- *Market Research:* The market research department gathers information pertaining to the firm's market potential, consumer behaviour and competitive circumstances. Management must be furnished with information pertinent to market strategy and

trends. To illustrate, a manufacturer has designed software for the users of major hardware manufacturer. The firm's ability to achieve its sales forecasts was greatly hindered when the marketing research department failed to predict and account for major modification that took place in the hardware feature which made the firm's products quite obsolete.

- *Production:* In this department, data must be maintained relative to utilization, scheduling, priority, number of machines, equipments and facilities. Periodic reports are generated and provided to the plant managers to inform them of their production status. The control of manufacturing costs is a prime objective of the production department. Therefore, data concerning the physical flow of direct labour, and actual overhead costs are processed, maintained and transmitted to other responsibility centres involved in either the constant flow of input factors of production or the receipt of finished goods. The quality control department must be furnished with periodic reports containing the number of units produced and number of production batches in order to determine the sample size for quality inspection.
- *Purchasing:* The purchasing department is responsible for receiving a constant flow of raw materials, machinery, equipment, and office supplies. Purchasing departments are interested in information relevant to such areas as sources of supplies, favourable bids, terms of delivery, and quantity discounts. The accounts payable division needs documentary evidence supporting various supplier claims. Warehouse-keepers must be furnished with copies of purchase acquisition forms relating to the inflow of raw materials and supplies.

1.7.1.4 External Information

The information generated through the external sources of the organization is termed as external information. The information generate through government reports, the industry surveys, salesman, etc. is termed as external information, as the sources of data are outside the organization.

An external source of information is concerned with what is happening beyond the boundaries of the organisation. This covers any documentation relating to a subject area produced as a summary or detailed report by an agency external to an organisation. Such information may be obtainable from government agencies or private information providers.

Examples might include:

- census figures
- judgments on court cases
- legislation, for example the Data Protection Act
- trade journals
- professional publications
- industry standards
- telephone directories
- computer users' yearbook
- Gallup polls
- national opinion polls
- Ordnance Survey maps
- financial services agencies such as Dunn and Bradstreet
- the Internet

Users of external information are outside the organization, such as, a variety of external information users seek pertinent data from the firm as a business entity.

- *Government:* The government requires various reports from time to time about income tax matters and other regulations.
- *Auditor:* An external auditor or a certified public accountant is responsible for determining the validity of the firm's financial statements. He seeks multipurpose information to serve as supporting evidence in his course of investigation. Accounts receivable and accounts payable balance, petty cash vouchers, depreciation schedules and inventory evaluation sheets are some examples of processed data tailored to satisfy the auditor's needs.
- *Shareholders and Perspective Investors:* Outstanding shareholders and prospective investors are invested in information relating to the interim and annual earning, price earning ratios, earmarking of retained earnings, and projections for future expansion. Investors generally want to be informed of material decisions affecting the firm, asset valuation, and income determination.
- *Customer:* A customer requires unlimited amounts of information depending upon the type of business firm with which he deals. For example, a prospective airline traveller needs to know the timings and types of flights available and he may require the terms of excess luggage payments and types of flights available and the time of arrival. A customer of a savings bank wants to know the amount due to him and the interest accrued on his account at any given time. The purchaser of an automobile needs to know relevant information regarding warranty clauses, safety and economy features.

1.7.2 Nature of Information

According to its nature, information is characterized as formal and informal, or quantitative and qualitative.

1.7.2.1 Formal Information

This involves presenting information in a structured and consistent manner. It is usually defined, within an organisation, as the main way of communicating between and within parts of the organisation. It is also usually the main way of communicating externally from an organisation. The main methods of formal communication are still the formal letter, properly structured reports, writing of training materials, etc. Formal information is communicated in cogent, coherent, well-structured language.

1.7.2.2 Informal Information

This describes less well-structured information that is transmitted within an organisation or between individuals who usually know each other. It tends to be categorised as 'unofficial' information, and is communicated by casual conversations, e-mails, or text messages between colleagues. The language used is less well-structured than formal communication and tends to include colloquialisms and shorthand; and spelling is less important.

1.7.2.3 Quantitative Information

This is information that is represented numerically. Any event or object that can be represented as a set of numbers is an example of quantitative information.

1.7.2.4 Qualitative Information

This is information that is represented using words. Any event or object that is represented using words to describe its attributes is an example of qualitative information.

1.7.3 Levels of Information

The information needed by managers to make decisions and solve problems varies in accordance with their level in the organization, as depicted in Figure 1.7. Managers at the top of the organization's hierarchy have a unique need for information related to the formulation of strategy, policies, long-range plans, and long-term objectives. Middle managers tend to have greater need for information required to formulate tactical and operational plans and objectives, to implement strategies and to make operational decisions. Finally lower level managers have unique needs for information that will help them implement operational plans, control, make short-term decisions and conduct day-to-day information, predominantly from internal source.

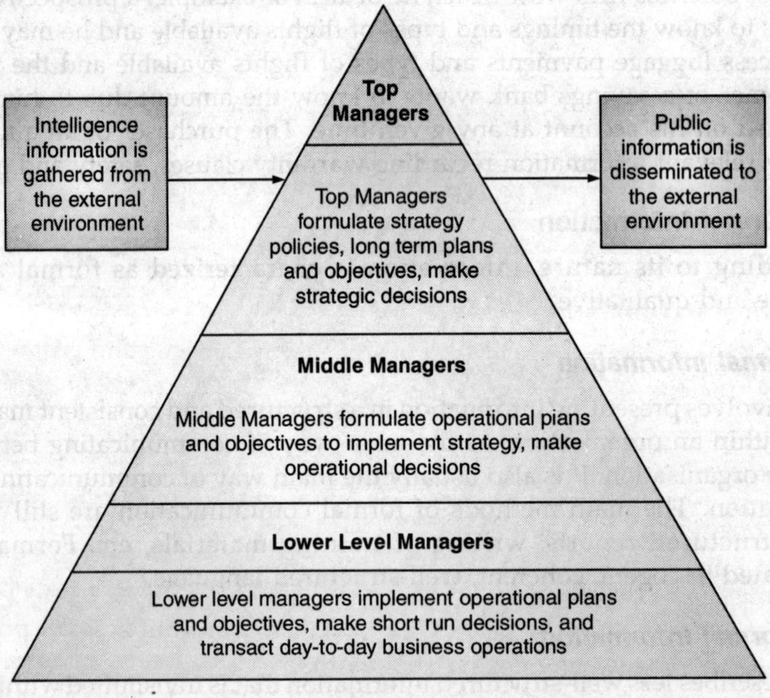

Figure 1.7: *Information Needs of Managers at Different Levels*

For the strategic roles performed by the top management, a great deal of information comes from external sources to the organization. Top management should have current information on such environment super-ordinates as the government, customers, creditors, suppliers, competitors, and so on. Conversely, lower level of managers need operational information from internal sources within the organization.

Although each level has critically different information needs, there is still a great deal of information that they must share. This fact reinforces the need to integrate and coordinate the overall information system. Broadly speaking, information could be classified on the basis of the purpose for which it is utilized. Information which are needed at different levels of management are *strategic, tactical* and *operational*. There is a direct correlation between the levels of importance of individuals or groups within an organisation and the level of information that is being communicated.

1.7.3.1 Operational Information

Operational information is such information that refers to the everyday needs to the organization which are needed for control over business activities; these are known as routine activities and are repetitive in nature. These activities are controlled at the lower level management i.e. decision-makers at the operational level. These may be section leaders or foremen in a large organisation or workers such as shop assistants, waiting staff, and kitchen staff, etc., in smaller businesses where there is no supervisory layer.

The timescale is usually very short, anything from immediately, daily or at most a week or month. Results of operational work will usually be passed upwards to let the tactical planners evaluate their plans.

Examples of operational information may include current stocks-in-hand, work-in-progress levels, outstanding orders from customers etc. The information regarding the cash position on day-to-day basis is monitored and controlled at the lower levels of management. Similarly, in marketing function, daily and weekly sales information is used by lower level manager to monitor the performance of the sales force. It is often required for taking immediate action. The source of such information is usually current activity data.

1.7.3.2 Tactical Information

Information in this category is used in short-term planning and is of use at management control level. Tactical information helps middle level managers in allocating resources and establishing controls to implement the top level plans and policies of the organization.

Tactical information will be mostly internal with a few external sources being used. Internal information is likely to be function related: for example, how much 'down time' a production line must allocate for planned maintenance.

Tactical information is used by middle management (employees) when managing or planning projects. The timescale is usually at least between 6 months and 5 years (depending on the scale of the strategic project). Circumstances vary but a small project may have a tactical timescale of between one and six months.

Tactical plans have a medium level of detail and will be very specific; they deal with such matters as who is doing what and within what specific budgets and timescales.

These plans have medium scope and will address details at the operational level. They will generally have specific objectives and be geared towards implementation by operational level employees.

For example, (i) information regarding the alternative source of funds and their uses in the short run, (ii) opportunities for the deployment of surplus funds in short-term securities, (iii) sales analysis and forecasts, production resource requirements, (iv) information regarding the annual financial statements etc.

The tactical information is generally predictive in nature, focusing on short-term trends of the business unit. This type of information is generally based on data arising from current activities of the organization. However, some of the tactical information, such as competitor information, may arise from sources external to the organization.

1.7.3.3 Strategic Information

Strategic information is used at the very top level of management within an organisation. These are chief executives or directors who have to make decisions for the long term.

Strategic information is required by the managers at the strategic level of management for the formulation of organizational strategies. This relates to long-term planning policies of the organization as a whole, for example, information pertaining to new technologies, new products, competitors, etc. Of course the operational information is needed to find out how the given activity can be performed better, strategic information is needed for making alternative choices among the business options. The strategic information helps in identifying and evaluating these options so that a manager makes informed choices which are different from the competitors and the limitations of what the rivals are doing or planning to do. Such choices are made by owners of the business. Strategic information is used by managers to define goals and priorities, initiate new programmes and develop plans and policies for acquisition and use of firm's resources.

Strategic information is broad based and will use a mixture of information gathered from both internal and external sources.

In general a timescale may be from one to five years or even longer depending on the project. Some oil related projects are planned from the outset to last for 25 or more years. A supermarket building a new superstore will look at a timescale of 20 years or so, whilst even a small business may have a five-year strategy.

Strategic plans will have little or no detail in them and more detailed strategic plans will be made slightly lower down the managerial ladder. A good strategic plan will be easier to flesh out lower down than a poor or vague strategic plan. Similarly, well-constructed and more detailed plans will be easier to implement than poorly constructed plans.

For example, information regarding the long-term needs of funds for on-going and future projects of the company may be used by top level managers in taking decision regarding public or approaching financial institutions for terms loan. Strategic information is predictive in nature, relies heavily on external sources of data, and has a long-term perspective. It is believed that strategic information is basically information regarding the external environment. However, it is now well recognised that the internal factors are equally responsible for success or failures of strategies and thus, internal information is also required for strategic decision making.

1.7.4 Time of Information

According to time dimension, information can be categorized as historic, present or future.

1.7.4.1 Historic Information

This is information gathered and stored over a period of time. It allows decision makers to draw comparisons between previous and present activities. Historic information can be used to identify trends over a period of time.

1.7.4.2 Present

This is information created from activities during the current work-window (day, week or month). In real-time systems this information would be created instantly from the data gathered (for example, the temperature in a nuclear power plant turbine), giving accurate and up-to-date information.

1.7.4.3 Future

This is information that is created using present and historic information to try to predict the future activities, trends and events relating to the operation of an organisation. An example would be sales figures for a company: if the sales figures are up 10% from those recorded this time last year it might be anticipated that next month's sales figures will also be up by 10%.

1.7.5 Frequency of Information

According to its frequency, information can be categorized as continuous or periodic.

1.7.5.1 Continuous

This is information created from data gathered several times a second. It is the type of information created by a real-time system.

For example, sensors may be set up to collect temperature and humidity readings in a large commercial greenhouse. It will be important for that information to be collected constantly because any variation in either the temperature or the humidity could point to the failure of some machinery and an alarm could be sounded to alert the staff. A very important system exists on modern aircraft where the navigation and flight-control systems are continuously monitoring and making adjustments; another is on a computerised production line where constant monitoring allows the system to correct faults. Obviously many other types of real-time systems exist but a feature of them all will be that they check data continuously.

1.7.5.2 Periodic

This is information created at regular timely intervals (hourly, daily, monthly, annually). Different examples of information generated by an organisation are needed at specific periods of time.

- *Annually:* On an annual basis a company must submit its report and accounts to the shareholders.
- *Monthly:* Banks and credit-card companies produce monthly statements for the majority of their customers.

- *Daily:* A supermarket will make daily summaries of its sales and use the product information to update its stock levels and to reorder stock automatically.
- *Hourly:* A busy call centre will often update totals for each operator on an hourly basis and give the top employee for the hour some reward.

1.7.6 Use of Information

According to its purpose it serves in various processes, information can be categorized as planning information, control information, or decision-making information.

1.7.6.1 Planning

Planning is the process of deciding, in advance, what has to be done and how it is to be done. Planning should be based on good information. Planning is not an end in itself; its primary purpose is to provide the necessary structure for decision-making and resulting actions, throughout the organisation.

The process of planning provides an opportunity to construct a sequence of actions that, when executed, will achieve the required aims and objectives.

Basically, planning means decisions by management about:

- what is to be done in the future
- how to do it
- when to do it
- who is to do it

An objective is something that needs to be achieved and a plan contains the activities or actions required to achieve the objective.

1.7.6.2 Control

Control can be defined as the monitoring and evaluation of current progress against the steps of a pre-defined plan or standard. If these tasks are not proceeding in line with expectations then action is taken to bring the project back in line with what had been planned.

Control is carried out at strategic, tactical and operational levels. The type of control changes according to the level of management as does the amount of time spent on control.

At an operational level the majority of the time of the manager or supervisor will be spent on control activities where the work of staff is compared to very specific financial or quantifiable terms (e.g. how many boxes have been packed).

At higher levels, planning and control are more closely linked, with management being concerned with the monitoring of progress against the plan, assessing the suitability of the plan itself and predicting future conditions.

Organisations and individuals must plan in order to operate effectively. Likewise they must also operate controls to ensure that progress is being made against the plan. These controls are needed because unexpected events can cause actual results to change from the expected planned results.

Control activities attempt to keep the organisation in line with the original plan or to enable the organisation to change to meet the new conditions. Unexpected events range from short delays in the completion of an element of a plan – which may be relatively minor – to major disturbances such as a large new competitor entering the marketplace.

Control measures actual progress against what is expected and provides information upon which remedial action can be taken, if required, either to change performance in order to conform to the original plan or to modify the plan.

1.7.6.3 Decision-making

Decision-making is the process of selecting an action or actions from those possible based on the information available. Decision-making involves determining and examining the available actions and then selecting the most appropriate actions in order to achieve the required results.

Decision-making is an essential part of management and is carried out at all levels of management for all tasks. All decisions are arrived at in the same way. The manager must choose, by some means, the result or results that s/he wishes to achieve and do some form of appraisal of the situation.

Decision-making is made up of four phases:

- finding occasions for decision making
- find possible courses of action (i.e. what choices are available)
- choosing among these courses of action
- evaluating past choices

1.7.7 Forms of Information

There can be various forms of available information, viz. written, aural, visual etc.

1.7.7.1 Written

The vast majority of information created within an organisation is in the written form. This can include hand-written or word-processed information and information in e-mails as well as reports produced from different classes of software, both general-purpose packages and bespoke software solutions. Examples of written information are reports, memos and tables, receipts, invoices, statements, and summary accounting information. The list is almost endless and different businesses will produce their own type of written information.

1.7.7.2 Aural

Another common form of information is aural, which is information presented as sound. The commonest form of aural information is of course speech and examples of this would be formal meetings (where minutes are taken), informal meetings, talking on the phone and voice-mail messages. Nowadays many organisations will have employees giving a presentation or talk to a group where there may be use made of music and sound effects as well as speech.

1.7.7.3 Visual

This form of information includes when pictures, charts and graphs are used to communicate information. Again, many presentations will make use of data projectors and presentation software that will include text, graphics and animations. Full video can also be projected via a data projector, and presentations can use video filmed with a digital video camera and then edited on a computer and distributed via CD or DVD now that DVD writers are quite common.

1.7.8 Types of Information

According to its contents, information can be categorized as detailed, sampled or aggregated.

1.7.8.1 Detailed

Detailed information might be an inventory list showing stock levels, actual costs to the penny of goods, detailed operating instructions, and so on. This information is most often used at the operational level within an organisation.

1.7.8.2 Sampled

This information usually refers only to selected records from a database: for example, only selected customers from a company's full customer list. In a supermarket this may be product and sales summaries given to departmental managers (bakery, fruit and vegetables, etc.). Sampled information is often used at a tactical level within an organisation. Depending on the size of the organisation it may also be relevant at a strategic level.

1.7.8.3 Aggregated

This is information that consists of totals created when detailed information is collated. An example of aggregated information is the details of all purchases made by customers totalled each month and displayed in a chart showing total sales for each month over a year.

In order to show all three types of information, here is an example that some of you should be familiar with. In a league of teams who play each other twice in a season, the *detailed* information would be the score line for each game played by all the teams in the league. *Sampled* information would be the details for a team in the league relating to their performance. *Aggregated* information would be the goals for, goals against and goal difference for a team in a league.

1.7.9 Dimensions of Information

Information may be understood to have various dimensions. However, for our purpose, the following three dimension of information will be of interest.

(i) Economic dimension,
(ii) Business dimension, and
(iii) Technical dimension.

1.7.9.1 Economic Dimension

This dimension of information refers to the cost of information and its benefits. Generation of information costs money. To decide about the money to be spent on information generation in an organization, a cost benefit analysis should be undertaken. Measuring costs and benefits of information is difficult because of intangible characteristics of information. However, the following aspects of information may be useful.

1. Cost of information

Information has a cost for its acquisition and maintenance. It may also include:

(i) cost of acquiring data
(ii) cost of maintaining data
(iii) cost of generating information
(iv) cost of communicating information

The cost is related to the response time required to generate information and communicate it. Thus, for a system with low response time, the cost is high. Similarly, cost also depends on the required accuracy, speed of generation etc. For more reliable and accurate systems, costs are higher as compared to the systems with low accuracy.

Information should be available within set cost levels that may vary dependent on situation. If costs are too high to obtain information an organisation may decide to seek slightly less comprehensive information elsewhere. For example, an organisation wants to commission a market survey on a new product. The survey could cost more than the forecast initial profit from the product. In that situation, the organisation would probably decide that a less costly source of information should be used, even if it may give inferior information.

2. Value of information

Information has a cost for its acquisition and maintenance. Thus, before a particular piece of information is acquired, decision makers must know its value. In decision theory, the value of information is the value of change in decision behaviour because of information. The change in behaviour due to new information is measured to determine the benefits from its use. To arrive at the value of new information, the cost incurred to get this information is deducted from the benefits. For example, if there are two products A and B to be developed with known pay-offs, as shown in Figure 1.8. The decision-maker will select the product which has got the maximum pay-off, i.e. product B.

A	25
B	35

(a)

A	40
B	30

(b)

Figure 1.8: (a) Decision=B (with existing information) (b) Decision=A (with new information)

However, if some additional information is made available to the decision-maker, according to which the pay-off distribution change as given in matrix (b), the decision maker will opt for product A. The additional of new information causes the decision-maker to choose product A, thereby increasing his gain from 30 to 40. Thus, the value of additional information is (40-30) = 10 unit. However, if the new information has some cost, the net value gain would be 10 units minus the cost of getting this new information.

In general, the value of the additional information making the existing information perfect is:

$$\text{Value of Perfect Information (VPI)} = (V_2 - V_1) - (C_2 - C_1)$$

where V_1 and C_1 is the value of the information and cost of obtaining the information relate to one set of information and V_2 and C_2 is the value of the information and cost of obtaining the information relate to other set of information.

The relative importance of information for decision-making can increase or decrease its value to an organisation. For example, an organisation requires information on a competitor's performance that is critical to their own decision on whether to invest in new machinery for their factory. The value of this information would be high. Always keep in mind that information should be available on time, within cost constraints and be legally obtained.

3. The Difference between Cost and Value

Many students in the past few years have confused the definitions of value and cost. Information gained or used by an organisation may have a great deal of *value* even if it may not have *cost* a lot. An example would be bookshops, who have used technology for many years now, with microfiche giving way to computers in the mid to late 1990s. Microfiche was quite expensive and what the bookshops received was essentially a list of books in print. By searching their microfiche by publisher they could tell you if a particular book was in print. Eventually this information became available on CD-ROM. Obviously this information has value to the bookshops in that they can tell you whether or not you can get the book. The cost of subscribing to microfiche was fairly high; subscribing to the CD-ROM version only slightly less so.

Much more valuable is a stock system which can tell you instantly whether or not the book is in stock, linked to an on-line system which can tell you if the book exists, where it is available from, the cost and delivery time. This information has far more value than the other two systems, but probably actually costs quite a bit less. It is always up-to-date and stock levels are accurate.

We are so used to this system that we cannot envisage what frustrations and inconvenience the older systems gave. The new system is certainly value for money.

1.7.9.2 Business Dimension

Information can also be understood from its business dimension. Different types of information are required by managers at different levels of the management hierarchy. The information needs of managers at strategic planning level are altogether different from those of operational control managers, as managers at different levels are required to perform different functions in the organization.

1.7.9.3 Technical Dimension

This dimension of information refers to the technical aspects of the database. Various aspects of the database, which are considered under this dimension, include the capacity of the database, response time, security, validity, data inter-relationship, etc. Technical dimension is covered under design of information systems and under the topic of database management system.

1.8 CHARACTERISTICS OF QUALITY INFORMATION

Good information is that which is used and which creates value. Experience and research shows that good information has numerous qualities.

The process of generation of information must focus on quality of information by aiming at improving the degree of each attribute of information. What characteristics would make information products valuable and useful to you? One way to answer this is to examine the characteristics or attributes of ***information quality***. People want information of high quality, i.e. information products whose characteristics, attributes, or qualities help make it valuable to them.

Quality information is that which accurately represents reality. It is the quality or accuracy of information that makes the information system function properly. If the managers come to know that the information is included of errors, they will avoid using it and its value to the decision making process is severely limited. Quality of information thus refers to its fitness for use and its reliability.

Quality information is **relevant** for its purpose, sufficiently **accurate** for its purpose, **completes** enough for the problem, **reliable** and **targeted** to the right person. It is also communicated **in time** for its purpose, contains the right level of detail and is communicated by an appropriate channel, i.e. one that is **understandable** to the user.

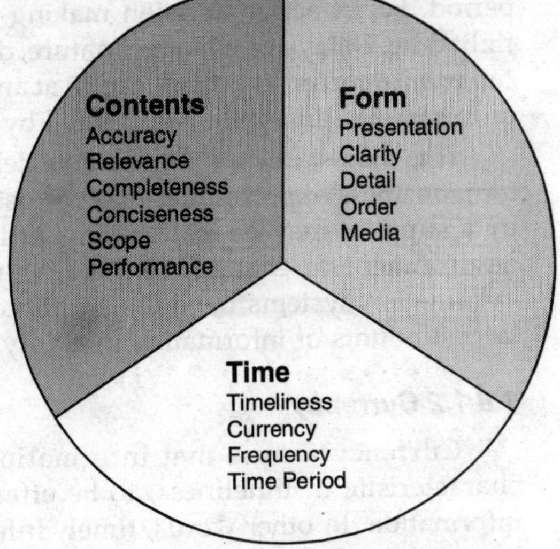

Figure 1.9: *Information as having three dimensions: Time, Content and Form*

It is useful to think of information as having the three dimensions of time, content and form, as shown in Figure 1.9. Quality, however, is not an absolute concept rather it is defined within a context.

1.8.1 Time Dimension

Time dimension specifies that information, if available when needed, has a greater value. Information must be on time for the purpose for which it is required. Information received too late will be irrelevant. For example, if you receive a brochure from a theatre and notice there was a concert by your favourite band yesterday, then the information is too late to be of use.

Information, like many organizational resources, can become old and obsolete. For example, if you want to make a stock trade today, you need to know the price of the stock right now. If you have to wait a day to view stock prices, you may not survive in the turbulent securities market. It's no wonder that over one-third of all stock transactions today occur over the Internet.

Your information is useful and relevant only if it describes the appropriate time period. For example, most utility companies provide you with a bill that not only tells you of your current usage and the average temperature but also compares that information to the previous month and perhaps the same month last year. This type of information can help you better manage your utilities or simply understand that this month's high utility bill was caused by inclement weather.

The time dimension describes the time period that the information deals with and the frequency at which the information is received.

1.8.1.1 Timeliness

Timeliness means that information must reach the recipients within the prescribed time-period. For effective decision making, information must reach the decision-maker at the right time, Delays, of whatever nature, destroy the nature of information. Timely information can ensure correct executive action at an early stage. The expected losses could be eliminated or minimized and gains maximized by proper management of operations.

It is also said that information delayed is information denied. Similarly, many short term business opportunities may be lost. For example, a discount on bulk purchases offered by a supplier may be lost because of late reports. Most managers function in a dynamic environment of change, demanding updated and current information. Computerized information systems have the ability to gather, sort, analyze, store, retrieve and transmit large amounts of information in a very short period of time.

1.8.1.2 Currency

Currency means that information must reach to the recipients up to date. The characteristic of timeliness, to be effective, should also include up-to-date, i.e. current information. In other words, timely information does not mean in-time information rather it means timely as well as up-to-date information.

1.8.1.3 Frequency

Frequency means that information should be provided as often as needed. Hence, in addition to being available when needed, information should also be available as often as needed. This normally means that information should be supplied at regular intervals, for example some organizations may require weekly sales reports whilst others need only monthly reports.

1.8.1.4 Time Period

Time period means that information can be provided about past, present and future time periods. The information should cover the correct time period. A sales forecast, for example, might include information concerning past performance, current performance and predicted performance so that the recipient has a view of past, present and future circumstances.

1.8.2 Content Dimension

Content dimension specifies the insides of the quality information. Quality information needs to be accurate, precise, unambiguous, relevant, adequate, complete, and concise.

1.8.2.1 Accuracy

Accuracy means that information is free from mistakes and errors, is clear and accuracy reflects the meaning of data on which it is based. It conveys an accurate picture to the recipient, who may require a presentation in graphical rather than tabular form. Accuracy also means that the information is free from bias.

Information needs to be accurate enough for the use to which it is going to be put. To obtain information that is 100% accurate is usually unrealistic as it is likely to be too expensive to produce on time. The degree of accuracy depends upon the circumstances. At operational levels information may need to be accurate to the nearest penny – on a supermarket till receipt, for example. At tactical level department heads may see weekly summaries correct to the nearest £100, whereas at strategic level directors may look at comparing stores' performances over several months to the nearest £100,000 per month.

Accuracy is important. As an example, if government statistics based on the last census wrongly show an increase in births within an area, plans may be made to build schools and construction companies may invest in new housing developments. In these cases any investment may not be recouped.

1.8.2.2 Precision

Precision is an important virtue of good quality information. Too much of information sometimes results in dumping of important information in the heap of details that may not be required at a particular time. Excessive detail of information results in information overload causing what is now being termed as Information Fatigue Syndrome. Only precise information is respected and used by the managers. Unnecessary and unwanted information are filed.

1.8.2.3 Unambiguity

Clarity of information is an important attribute of quality information. Information must be unambiguous and should be communicated in such a manner that it conveys the same meaning to different users. Modern databases maintain data dictionaries that clearly define the variable used in the information in order to standardize the terminology used in reports. There are other attributes such as quantifiability, verifiability, unbiasedness, etc. that one may attempt to incorporate to improve the quality of information.

1.8.2.4 Relevance

Information is said to be relevant if it should be related to the information needs of a specific recipient for a specific situation. In the other words, information system should serve the reports to managers which are useful and the information helps them make decisions. However, what is relevant information for one recipient is not necessarily relevant for another. The relevance of information from a specific customer order, for example, will vary among the employees of the company.

Information should be relevant to the purpose for which it is required. It must be suitable. What is relevant for one manager may not be relevant for another. The user will become frustrated if information contains data irrelevant to the task in hand. For example, a market research company may give information on users' perceptions of the quality of a product. This is not relevant for the manager who wants to know opinions on relative prices of the product and its rivals. The information gained would not be relevant to the purpose.

1.8.2.5 Adequacy

Adequacy means information must be sufficient in quantity, i.e. information system must provide reports containing information which is required in the deciding processes of decision-making. The report should not give inadequate or for that matter, more than adequate information, which may create a difficult situation for the decision maker.

Whereas inadequacy of information leads to a crisis, information overload results in chaos. Therefore, adequacy is a vital attribute of information which underscores that a report should cover all related aspects about a particular event or situation which the report is reporting.

1.8.2.6 Completeness

Information should contain all the details required by the user. Otherwise, it may not be useful as the basis for making a decision. For example, if an organisation is supplied with information regarding the costs of supplying a fleet of cars for the sales force, and servicing and maintenance costs are not included, then a costing based on the information supplied will be considerably underestimated.

Ideally all the information needed for a particular decision should be available. However, this rarely happens; good information is often incomplete. To meet *all* the needs of the situation, you often have to collect it from a variety of sources.

1.8.2.7 Conciseness

Information should be in a form that is short enough to allow for its examination and use. There should be no extraneous information. For example, it is very common practice to summarise financial data and present this information, both in the form of figures and by using a chart or graph. We would say that the graph is more concise than the tables of figures as there is little or no extraneous information in the graph or chart. Clearly there is a trade-off between level of detail and conciseness.

1.8.2.8 Explicitness

A report is said to be of good quality if it does not require further analysis by the recipient for decision making. On the other hand, a poor quality report requires further analysis or processing of its contents. Therefore, explicitness is a prominent attribute of management information procured through the information system of the organization. Thus, the reports should be such that a manager does not waste any time on the processing of the report rather he should be able to extract the required information directly.

1.8.2.9 Exception-based

Today more and more organizations are being run on the principle of management by exception. Top managers only need exception reports regarding the performance of the organization. Exception reporting principle states that only those items of information which will be of particular interest to a manager are reported. Usually, these items indicate that normal operations have gone awry. This approach results in saving precious time of the top management and enables the managers to devote more time in pursuit of alternatives for the growth of the organization. If reports do not follow the exception reporting principle, these will provide even those details which are not required by managers and thus a lot of their time would be wasted in sifting useful information, and as a result, they will not be able to spend much time on other important activities of the organization.

1.8.3 Form Dimension

In order to be of greater value, the form of information should closely match the requirements of the user or decision-maker's.

The form dimension of information has two primary aspects. The first is simply having information in a form that is most usable and understandable by you—audio, text, video, animation, graphical, and others. The second is accuracy. You need information that is free of errors. Think of information as you would think of a physical product. If you buy a product and it's defective, you become an unsatisfied customer. Likewise, if you receive information that is incorrect, you're very unhappy as well. The form dimension describes how the information is presented to the recipient.

1.8.3.1 Clarity

Information should be provided in a form that is easy to understand. Clarity of information can be achieved by discarding the irrelevant information and concentrating only on the relevant aspects of information.

1.8.3.2 Detail

Information should be provided in detail form. The information needs to be presented in such a detailed form that it helps in decision making, but care should also be taken not to include the unnecessary details, as it would only make the process of decision making more difficult and lengthy.

1.8.3.3 Order

Information can be arranged in a predetermined order required by the managers. Otherwise, they may not be able to interpret it in the correct manner and meaningful decisions may not be made.

1.8.3.4 Presentation

The presentation of information is important to the user. Information can be more easily assimilated if it is aesthetically pleasing. Information can be presented in narrative, numeric, graphic and other forms. For example, a marketing report that includes graphs of statistics will be more concise as well as more aesthetically pleasing to the users within the organisation. Many organisations use presentation software and show summary information via a data projector. These presentations have usually been well thought out to be visually attractive and to convey the correct amount of detail.

1.8.3.5 Media

Information can be provided in the form of printed paper documents, video displays, or other media. Proper media is chosen as per the requirements of the organization.

1.8.4 Additional Characteristics

In addition to the attributes described above, one might also add several others. Of particular importance is ***confidence*** in the source of the information received. Recipients are more likely to accept and trust the information they obtain if it is received from a source that has been accurate and reliable in the past.

A further attribute of information quality is that of ***reliability***. It can be argued that recipients should be confident that they can rely upon information being available when required and that the information will be of a consistent quality in terms of other attributes of information quality, such as accuracy and conciseness.

The widespread use of computer-based information systems raises a number of issues related to the sheer quantity of information that is freely available via sources such as the Internet. In addition, the use of computer-based information systems also raises concerns in relation to security. In view of this, one might suggest that a further attribute of information quality is that the information provided should be ***appropriate*** to the recipient's activities. This might restrict information from being supplied if it is of a confidential nature or beyond the duties or responsibilities of a person's role.

It also seems natural to suggest that some confirmation that the information has been ***received by the correct person*** is required. Unless the information has been received and acted upon, then it is of no value. Thus, it can be suggested that an additional attribute of information quality is that it can be verified that the information has been received and understood.

Finally, it can be argued that another attribute of information quality is that that information should be capable of being ***transmitted via the correct channels***. Most organizations have formal policies and procedures for dealing with particular situations. For example, a complaint against a member of staff is normally presented in a written form and travels upwards through the management hierarchy until it is received by the correct person. If the information were to be sent in any other way, for example by word of mouth, it might not reach its destination or might become garbled during the journey.

1.9 EVALUATION OF INFORMATION

Evaluation involves determining whether the expected value of the information exceeds the expected cost. It is the process of determining whether the acquisition of specified information is justified. Figure 1.10 shows the major steps of this process.

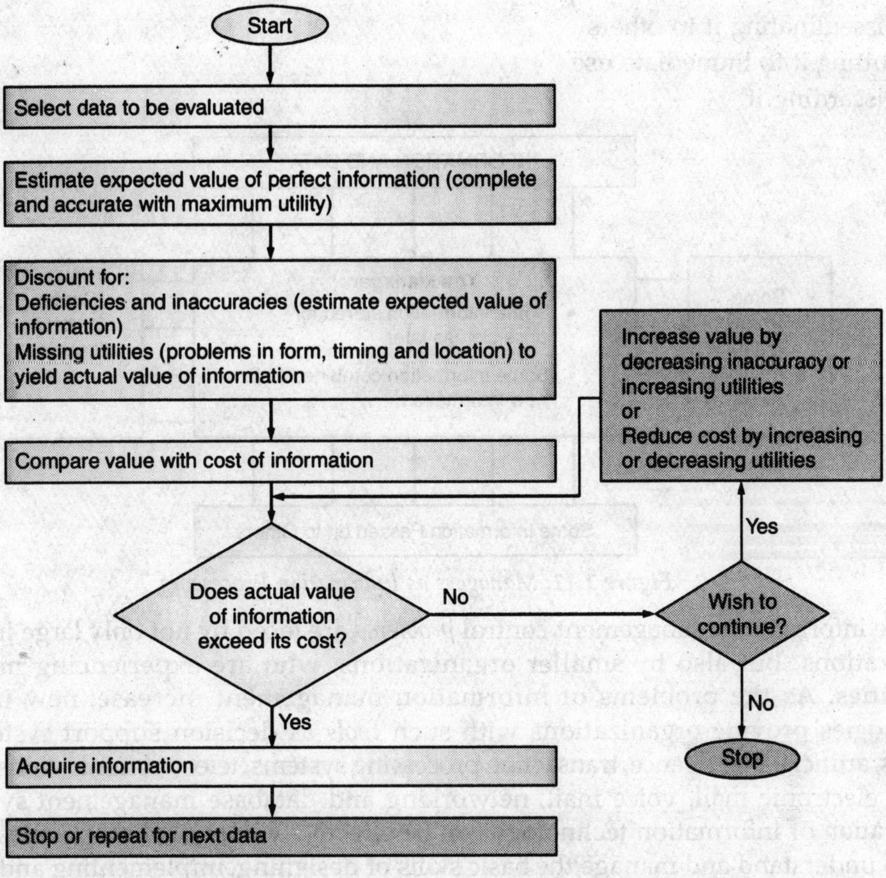

Figure 1.10: *Flow Chart for Evaluating Information*

The first step in evaluating information is determining the value of that information by selecting the data that needs to be analysed and then determining the expected value or return to be received from obtaining perfect information based on these data. Next, this expected value of perfect information should be compared with the expected cost of obtaining that information. Before this, an evaluation is to be done to ensure that this expected value should be reduced by the amount of benefit that will not be realised, because of deficiencies and inaccuracies expected to appear in the information.

If the expected cost does not exceed the expected value, the information should be gathered. If it does exceed, managers either must increase the information expected value, or decrease its expected cost before the information gathered can be justified.

1.10 MANAGERS AS INFORMATION PROCESSORS

Management needs only information but not data, to help them make effective decisions. Every manager is deluged with both data and information, sometimes to the point of information overload. The manager may do various things with that data and information including as shown in Figure 1.11:

(i) Storing it for further use
(ii) Disseminating it to others
(iii) Putting it to immediate use
(iv) Discarding it

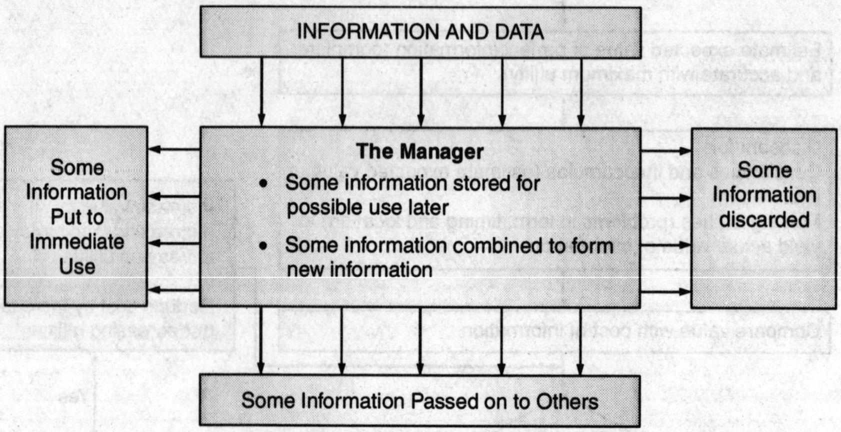

Figure 1.11: Managers as Information Processors

The information management control *problems* are faced by not only large international organizations, but also by smaller organizations, who are experiencing management difficulties. As the problems of information management increase, new information technologies provide organizations with such *tools* as decision support systems, expert systems, artificial intelligence, transaction processing systems, telecommunications, automated offices, electronic mail, voice mail, networking and database management systems. This proliferation of information technology can be effectively overwhelming, unless managers learn to understand and manage the basic skills of designing, implementing and controlling the information system.

1.11 INFORMATION UTILITY

Traditionally information has been accessed from a variety of libraries. Every university maintains a large library with diverse collection of books and other materials such as audio tapes, video tapes, microfilms, etc. Besides central library, departments maintain their own special libraries of interest to a small group of researchers. The library system is well developed; companies maintain libraries and most cities have public libraries too. It has been recognized that access to information is essential in modern civilization society and investment on libraries have grown over the years.

Scholarly as well as their information available in libraries is not only information people are concerned about. There is a variety of other information people need in their day-to-day life in a complex society. These include government rules and regulations, daily news, up-to-date information on prices of commodities, shares, etc., schedule to public transport, to cite a few.

The advent of computers half a century ago set in motion a new paradigm of information storage and retrieval. Early researchers worked on methods of classifying information for ease of retrieval in a computer based system. Research was impeded due to non-availability of large machine readable corpus of information as disks were of small capacity and manual transcription of information was slow and expensive.

The situation has changed now. There has been a convergence of a number of developments in computer technology in the last five years which has significantly affected the way computers can be used in libraries.

Some of these developments are described in what follows:

- Storage systems have become versatile and inexpensive. Compact Disk Read Only Memories (CDROMs) and now Digital Versatile Disk Read Only Memories (DVDROMs) with huge data storage capacity (7.5×10^9 bytes) are now widely available. To store a typical 500 pages book in uncompressed form requires about one M-bytes. Thus in one DVDROM we can store 7500 books. The cost of these storage devices is very low around ten paisa per M-bytes, and is falling.
- Computer network technology which has facilitated interconnecting computers not only within the world-wide computer network has matured. It is possible today to access any computer in the world connected to network from any place.
- Standard methods of digitizing, compressing and storing textual, audio, graphics, and video data have emerged. Compression and storage standards which are accepted widely allow easy interchange of these data.
- Very powerful processors which can process multimedia information very fast have now become inexpensive. Computer speeds have been doubling every 18 months for the past two decades. High speed processors allow cost-effective compression and decompression to be performed very fast allowing more data to be stored on-line.
- High resolution video terminals which can display information on multiple windows allow easy viewing of multimedia data.

When all the above developments are combined, we have a powerful technology to efficiently store multimedia information available in geographically dispersed locations, index them for easy retrieval and access the information from anywhere in the world using a Personal Computer (PC) connected to the international network of computers. These technologies have led to the concept of information utility. It is explained below, the concept of an information utility, its unique features and advantages, how the advent of such a utility affects the work, particularly of scientists and engineers and finally their relevance to India.

1.11.1 Attributes of An Information Utility

We can attempt to define the attributes of an information utility as:

- Information sources are geographically distributed and interconnected by high speed digital communication links.
- Access and storage methods are standardized to enable any user connected to the Internet to access information stored anywhere.
- Regulations are formulated to control storage and access of information and charges for usage.

Currently, the Internet and the World Wide Web (WWW) to some extent satisfy the first two conditions stated above. However, the last attribute is still being debated ad there is yet no consensus.

1.11.2 Components of Information Utility

The main components of an information utility are described below:

1.11.2.1 Information Resource

Information resource can be various types including textual data, numeric data, graphical data, audio data, video data and photographs.

- ***Textual Data:*** Textual data consist of books and journals and other useful information such as patterns, international standards, specifications, etc. stored in a digital form in a computer's disk store. There are two ways of storing this information. One way is to scan each page with the help of a scanner. A scanner works on a principle similar to a Xerox machine except that it digitizes the image, storing a 0 for white, and 1 for black spot in its local memory. For fairly good resolution, one page will be represented by (800 × 1000) bits (or 800 K-bytes). This form of storage is called a bit-mapped form. Bit patterns do not carry information for indexing. This is, however, the only practical way of storing old manuscripts, texts and journals, pictures and graphs. The image of a page may be retrieved and displayed on the video screen of the computer. Using this method of storage, a 500-page book will need 50 M-bytes. The bits, however, may be compressed to save space. Further, scanning is a human intensive task and it will be difficult to scan a large collection of material.

  The other way of storing a text is to represent each character by its ASCII code. Texts generated using word processors are already in this form. Most books and journals produced in the past few years will already be in this form. If a page has 6000 characters, it will need 6000 bytes of storage. Further it will be easy to index the document using arbitrary words in the text. If a table has numeric information, the numeric data would be stored in a coded form which allows it to be processed. Photographs or other complex figures in the text, however, will have to be scanned and stored as bit maps. Textual data in ASCII may also be compressed for storage.

  As it requires less storage to store text in ASCII coded form, software is becoming available to scan printed texts using a scanner and convert them to coded form. Conversion by such software is, however, not 100% accurate and manual correction is required before the text is stored. For old texts using non-standard or mixed fonts and for hand-written manuscripts, such conversion software is not available.
- ***Numerical Data:*** This type of data consists of tables of various types such as physical property data of various materials, data from experiments, astronomical tables, etc. Such numeric data stored digitally may be used (if required) by curve fitting programmes, spread sheet programmes, etc.
- ***Graphical Data:*** Graphics data may be photographs, maps, drawings, etc. The simplest way of storing such data is to scan the image and store it as a bit pattern. There are better ways of coding and storing maps, drawings, etc. which abstracts the information

contained in them. For example, maps may be stored using longitude/latitude as coordinates of cities, a linked list depicting road networks, etc. Data stored in this form ease retrieval.

- ***Audio Data:*** Audio data are digitized, compressed using a common accepted compression algorithm and stored. Musical scores may also be coded and stored along with the audio data, if required.
- ***Video Data:*** Video data require enormous storage space due to the need for repeating frames at least 30 times per second. Each frame of video is digitized using picture elements (or pixel) and requires 640 kilo pixels. Each picture element needs 3 bytes to code, various shades of colour and intensity. Thus 200 G-bytes are needed to store 1 hour of video if it is not compressed. Compression is thus essential. Common standards for compression have been evolved. The current standard is called MPEG-4 (Motion Picture Experts Group Version 4) which compresses a 90 minute video movie to occupy 7 G-bytes. The compressed video has to be decomposed using an appropriate algorithm.
- ***Photographs:*** Both colour and monochrome photographs are stored in bit mapped form using compression algorithms to reduce storage space.

1.11.2.2 Indexing

Indexing and interlinking multimedia data are extremely important for ease of retrieval. Keywords in textual documents are selected and linked to related words with logical links by appropriate software. This is called **hypertext**. For material in other media (audio, video) also, related elements are selected and linked in what is known as **hypermedia**. Such links will allow user to navigate through multimedia material. For example, from a multimedia encyclopaedia stored in a CDROM, one may request information on Taj Mahal. The computer would search the data and retrieve a page giving textual information about Taj Mahal which would be displayed on the video screen. If there is reference to music in the text, it may link to an audio clip giving recording of classical music of that time. Links may also be present to video clips on Mumtaz Mahal, Shah Jahan, Agra and any other related topics.

1.11.2.3 Linking

The information collection of the digital library will normally not be stored on one computer. It will be distributed in many computers known as **servers**. All these servers will be linked together by high speed communication links. The fact that the information is distributed need not be known to a user as it is not relevant from his point of view. A user gets a 'seamless' access to the information based on his request regardless of its geographical location.

1.11.2.4 Searching

As was pointed out, information resources are spread over many computers and it is not feasible for every user to keep a directory of available resources. Users require assistance from the system for retrieving information. This is done by **search engines**. These are pieces of software which accept keywords given by a user and search using it on all servers. The information in the servers is indexed using the keywords to facilitate search.

1.11.2.5 User

A user may access information from anywhere at any time using a terminal or a computer connected to network to which the information servers are connected. The information servers are available 24 hours a day. With the emergence of wireless networks, it would also become possible to access an information utility from a portable computer.

To summarize, the key components of an information utility are:

(i) A large collection of digitized and compressed multimedia data linked together logically and indexed with keywords (for elements) to enable easy search and retrieval.

(ii) The information collection is geographically distributed and stored on servers connected to a network, and

(iii) User can access this information collection from his computer which may be located anywhere provided it is connected to the network and has rights to access it.

1.11.3 Advantages of Information Utility

The fact that all types of data are in digital form and data are distributed and accessible from anywhere provides an information utility with some unique advantages. Unlike traditional libraries, documents are not physically handled by a user. A user views the necessary documents and prints the portion of interest to his location. Further, many users can simultaneously view a document. Thus, documents are not 'lost' due to theft or misplacing. Documents do not tear due to wear. Library need not have multiple copies of a popular journal. Rare manuscripts may be allowed to be viewed by many as only images are accessed by users.

Unlike printed text where tables of numbers can be studied but not easily processed, if they are in digital form the numbers in a table can be processed. In print, material numbers are 'passive' whereas in digital form the same numbers are 'active' as they can be processed and transformed. For instance, a table may be used in spread sheet program and we can find out how altering some entries change other entities. A user may also try to fit appropriate curves to a set of numbers in a table published in an article and give his own interpretation of the data.

An information utility can store unconventional information such as readings obtained from scientific instruments such as spectrometers. All modern instruments incorporate microprocessors and experimental data are already in digital form. A repository of experimental data can be stored in a server and made available to others to assist in their work.

Searching for information is much easier due to global indexing and use of hypertext and search engines. Fast communication networks provide widespread search for the required material.

The ability to digitally store and retrieve multimedia data allows one to effectively provide access to audio and video information. Providing such access is particularly difficult in current libraries due to difficulty in handling such material and wear and tear if many persons access the material. Information utility would also provide an effective method to preserve rare manuscripts, vintage movies, old music, etc. without denying access to users.

An information utility would provide users access to current information which normally takes a long time to reach a traditional library. For example, many authors store their latest research reports in their webpage and provide free access. Many conference papers may be found in the World Wide Web. An information utility provider can collect articles of interest to a research group and provide it in a local server thereby saving user time.

The internet allows easy access to discussion groups in specified subjects. Users of an information utility can find researchers working in similar areas and attempt collaborative work. An information scientist can enable this collaboration.

We are also seeing the emergence of journals published only in 'electronic form' with no print version. This reduces cost and allows prompt, wide dissemination of the journal. Some journals also provide means for readers to criticise the article and link them with the article. Such informal reviews are unorthodox but are very useful for a prospective reader.

Many other types of information not found in traditional library may be provided by an information utility such as computer-assisted learning aids, lecture demonstrations by musician dancers, and artists, lecture videos of important speeches, etc.

1.11.4 Features of Emerging Information Utility

The unique features of emerging information utility are as follows:

- Safe storage and multiple access of material
- Ability to process numerical data published in literature
- Ability to store variety of data such as audio, video, graphics, data output from experiments, computer-assisted learning aids, lecture demonstrations by artists, famous lectures, etc.
- Ability to access information
- Accessing information available anywhere in the world from anywhere else in the world; this alleviates to some extent the disadvantage felt by scientists living in remote areas
- Ease of search and retrieval
- Design data, drawings, etc.

Engineers and scientists will be deluged with information and have to find a technique of handling this 'information overload'. We will see the emergence of 'software agents' which can be tailored to satisfy the needs of individuals.

We have seen that the emergence of many technologies, both software and hardware, has led to a revolution in the way information is created, stored and disseminated. Rapid international access to a variety of information distributed across the world will, to some extent, alleviate problems faced by people in the developing world with regard to information availability. There are many new vistas being opened up by the digital mode of storing and retrieving information. At the same time, many problems need to be resolved before a world-wide information utility develops. Nevertheless, we are at the threshold of a new revolution in information dissemination.

1.11.5 Recent Trends Affecting Information Utility

Over the past decade, financial investors and entrepreneurs have advised companies to invest in Information Utility. The core idea of an Information Utility has remained the same, but evolved over the years.

Its characteristics include:

- Gathering, processing, or distributing information, which typically is digital.
- Providing services on a usage basis

Studies have found that the acceptance of outsourcing business functions such as software-as-a-service increases long-term growth. This includes functions from payroll to information technology to document management programs.

Following are the key trends affecting information utility in recent times:

- *Cloud Computing*: Sold as a product with configurable features. Provides capability of hardware and determines optimal physical configuration.
- *Social Networks:* A social utility that provides infrastructure to allow companies to interact with their customers. In turn, customers can then interact with each other.
- *Going Mobile:* By 2013, more than half of mobile phone users will be using a SmartPhone to access the internet over their home computer.
- *Information Processors:* As an information gatherer, Information Processors are known to create or aggregate information from other sources for business needs. Effective examples of information processors take advantage of customers' increased business and focus on functions and openness to outsourcing.
- *Software-as-a-Service (SaaS):* SaaS gives significant capacity for growth and operating leverage. As a subscription based utility, it reduces upfront costs due to not having to make a large upfront investment in hardware and software. SaaS also reduces the amount of IT Overhead, as it does not require internet IT resources. Lastly, customer satisfaction remains high as providers are motivated to continually improve processes with value-added services.
- *On-Demand Infrastructure:* By storing and securing data, these providers manage underlying communication networks that support distribution. On-Demand Infrastructure providers are known to offer value-added services that set them apart from commodity suppliers. Utilizing these includes the benefit of lessening the incremental capital investment over time.
- *How It Affects Paperless Offices:* More and more businesses are adopting the Information Utility principal of paying for what you use, and utilizing the products and services that are already available. Companies look at what they are currently doing and how they can make things more efficient, while still achieving a Return On Investment. Alternatives, such as the ones discussed in this blog entry, are growing because of the great impact they have made on companies throughout the most recent years

SUMMARY

Data can also be known as objective measurements of attributes (the characteristics) of entities (such as people, place, things, and events). These measurements are usually represented by symbols such as numbers, words, codes composed of a mixture of numerical, alphabetical and other characters. Information is the result of processing, manipulating and organising data in a way that adds to the knowledge of the receiver. A decision is a choice made from available alternatives. A decision is a final product of the specific mental/cognitive process of an individual or a group of persons/organisations which is called decision making; therefore it is a subjective concept. Knowledge consists of data and/or information that have been organized and processed to convey understanding, experience, accumulated learning, and expertise as they apply to a current problem or activity. Data that are processed to extract critical implications and to reflect past experiences and expertise provide the recipient with organizational knowledge, which has a very high potential value. Data, information, and knowledge can be inputs to an information system, and they can also be outputs. DIKW refers to Data, Information, Knowledge and Wisdom; it is an information hierarchy where each layer adds certain attributes over and above the previous one. Information can be categorised under many headings that help us to determine its overall usefulness. The main categories are Source, Nature, Level, Time, Frequency, Use, Form, Type and Dimension.

Traditionally information has been accessed from a variety of libraries. Every university maintains a large library with diverse collection of books and other materials such as audio tapes, video tapes, microfilms, etc. Besides central library, departments maintain their own special libraries of interest to a small group of researchers. The library system is well developed; companies maintain libraries and most cities have public libraries too. It has been recognized that access to information is essential in modern civilization society and investment on libraries have grown over the years. The situation has changed now. There has been a convergence of a number of developments in computer technology in the last five years which has significantly affected the way computers can be used in libraries.

EXERCISES

1. Describe the differences between data and information.
2. Explain various uses of data and information.
3. (a) Explain the relationship between knowledge and information.
   (b) Explain the difference between explicit and implicit knowledge, giving an example of each and of the kind of information that made that knowledge possible.
4. For each of the following situations say whether the information is primary or secondary and internal or external.
   - the minutes of a golf club committee meeting
   - a till roll showing the day's transactions in a corner shop
   - a university prospectus
   - the published accounts of a large public business
5. Describe the differences between:
   - formal and informal communication
   - quantitative and qualitative information

6. There are three levels of information, strategic, tactical and operational. State the characteristics of:
   - information used for decision making at the strategic level
   - information used for decision making at the tactical level
   - information used for decision making at the operational level
7. Explain the differences between information categorised by time:
   - historically
   - in the present time
   - in the future
8. 'Information can be used in planning, control and decision-making'. Describe how information can be used in:
   - planning
   - control
   - decision-making
9. There are three forms of information, written, aural and visual. Explain with the use of examples the difference between the three forms.
10. The type of information one may receive can be detailed, sampled or aggregated. Explain the differences between the three types of information with regard to the level of the information.
11. For each of the following characteristics of information explain why that characteristic affects the quality of the information:
   - availability or accessibility
   - accuracy
   - completeness
   - reliability or objectivity
   - timing
   - conciseness
   - presentation
   - value
12. What is the cost of information?
13. How to evaluate the value of information?
14. Explain the distinction between value and the cost of information.
15. How to evaluate the information?
16. Why managers need only information but not data?
17. How does the information needs differ at different management levels?
18. What do you mean by information utility? What are its main components? What are its attributes and unique features?
19. What are the advantages of an information utility?
20. What are the features of emerging information utility?
21. Explain the relevant trends affecting information utility?

❑

Information Capturing and Representation

2

2.1 CAPTURING OF INFORMATION

A strategy should be evolved by the analyst to gather information. The strategy consists of identifying information sources, evolving a method of obtaining information from the identified sources and using an information flow model of organization.

Qualitative researchers typically rely on four methods for gathering information: (a) participating in the setting, (b) observing directly, (c) interviewing in depth, and (d) analysing documents and material culture. These form the core of their inquiry—the staples of the diet. Several secondary and specialized methods of data collection supplement them. This chapter provides a brief discussion of the primary and the secondary methods to be considered in designing a qualitative study. This discussion does not replace the many excellent, detailed references on information collection. Its purpose is to guide the proposal writer in stipulating the methods of choice for his study and in describing for the reader how the data will inform his research questions. How the researcher plans to use these methods, however, depends on several considerations.

Before going into the details of each of the methods, let us have a brief introduction to the basic methods for capturing the information:

- ***Observation:*** Observation method depends on the observer and influenced by the bias. It is collecting information through "seeing" and "listening." Observations may be structured or unstructured.
- ***Experiment:*** Information can be collected through designing of the experiment where the quality of information depends on the experimentation technique. It is performed on trial basis of controlling the specific parameters.
- ***Survey:*** Survey method occurs through the questioners' session. According to the quality of question, quality of information can be decided. It is collecting standardized information through structured questionnaires to generate quantitative data. Surveys may be mailed (surface and electronic), completed on site or through interviews, either face-to-face or telephone. Sample surveys use probability or purposive sampling.
- ***Subjective estimation:*** Subjective estimation can be called as sub expert. If the above ways are unsuccessful then this applied to collect expert opinion.
- ***Transaction processing:*** This method consists of data processing leisure, representation throughout the organization.

- ***Purchased from outside:*** The information can be purchased from outside at the specific rate easily. It may be expensive and it may have a bias depending on the source.
- ***Publication:*** Publication provides various public forums. For example, Newspapers, government agencies, online information etc.
- ***Government agencies:*** It is available but cannot be directly used by all. For example, RBI Publications.
- ***Interviewing:*** Interviewing is the information collected by talking with and listening to people, either face-to-face or over the telephone. Interviews range on a continuum from those which are tightly structured (as in a survey) to free flowing, conversational interviews. It is a technique that is primarily used to gain an understanding of the underlying reasons and motivations for people's attitudes, preferences or behavior. Interviews can be undertaken on a personal one-to-one basis or in a group. They can be conducted at work, at home, in the street or in a shopping centre, or some other agreed location.
- ***Case study:*** The term case-study usually refers to a fairly intensive examination of a single unit such as a person, a small group of people, or a single company. Case-studies involve measuring what is there and how it got there. In this sense, it is historical. It can enable the researcher to explore, unravel and understand problems, issues and relationships. It is an in-depth examination of a particular case (program, group of participants, single individual, site/location). Case studies use multiple sources of information and methods to provide as complete a picture as possible.
- ***Group assessment:*** use of group processes to collect evaluation information such as nominal group technique, focus group, Delphi, brainstorming and community forums.
- ***Expert or peer review:*** It is an examination by a review committee, panel of experts or peers.
- ***Portfolio reviews:*** These are the collection of materials, including samples of work that encompass the breadth and scope of the program activity being evaluated.
- ***Testimonials:*** Testimonials are individual statements by people indicating personal responses and reactions.
- ***Tests:*** Use of established standards to assess knowledge, skill, performance such as in pen-and-pencil tests or skills tests also allow information collection.
- ***Photographs, slides, videos:*** Use of photography to capture visual images which result in collection of required facts.
- ***Diaries, journals:*** Diaries/journals present a recording of events over time revealing the personal perspective of the writer/recorder.
- ***Logs:*** Logs are the recordings of chronological entries which are usually brief and factual.
- ***Document analysis:*** Use of content analysis and other techniques to analyze and summarize printed material and existing information is also helpful in collection of information.
- ***Action cards:*** Action cards promote the use of index cards on which participants record what they did – the "action" – and when they reach their goal; primarily used in self-assessment.

- ***Simulations:*** Simulations present the use of models or mock-ups to solicit perceptions and reactions.
- ***Problem stories:*** Problem stories are the narrative accounts of past, present or future situations as a means of identifying perceptions using fictional characters to externalize the problem situation.
- ***Creative expression:*** Creative expression is the use of art forms to represent people's ideas and feeling as through stories, drama, dance, music, art.
- ***Unobtrusive measures:*** These measures represent the gathering of information without the knowledge of the people in the setting such as the wear and tear on a "planted" mat in front of a display.

The above mentioned methods are divided in two categories, viz. Primary Methods, and Secondary Methods. Let us discuss the details of some of the popular methods in each of the categories.

2.2 PRIMARY METHODS

Following are the primary methods for capturing of information:

2.2.1 Observation

Observation is way of gathering information by watching behavior, events, or noting physical characteristics in their natural setting. Observations can be overt (everyone knows they are being observed) or covert (no one knows they are being observed and the observer is concealed). The benefit of covert observation is that people are more likely to behave naturally if they do not know they are being observed. However, you will typically need to conduct overt observations because of ethical problems related to concealing your observation.

Observations can also be either direct or indirect. Direct observation is when you watch interactions, processes, or behaviours as they occur; for example, observing a teacher teaching a lesson from a written curriculum to determine whether they are delivering it with fidelity. Indirect observations are when you watch the results of interactions, processes, or behaviours; for example, measuring the amount of plate waste left by students in a school cafeteria to determine whether a new food is acceptable to them.

2.2.1.1 Covert Observation

Covert observation involves:

- The social researcher participating fully without informing members of the social group of the reasons for her presence, thus the research is carried out secretly or covertly.
- Contact with a *'gatekeeper'*, a member of the group under study who will introduce the researcher into the group.

Problems of covert observation include:

- The researcher having to become involved in criminal or dangerous activities, particularly where the research is studying a 'deviant' social group.
- Problems of negotiating and having to act out forms of behaviour which the researcher may personally find unethical or distasteful.

- The researcher having to employ a level of deceit, since the researcher is essentially lies about the nature of her presence within the group.
- Close friendships are often resulting from connections with members of the group under study and the covert nature of the research can put a tremendous strain on the researcher, both in and out of the fieldwork setting.
- The problem of *'going native'*, which refers to the fact that a researcher will cease to be a researcher and will become a full-time group participant.

Advantages of this type of covert participant role are:

- The researcher may gain access to social groups who would otherwise not consent to being studied.
- The avoidance of problems of *observer effect*, the conception that individuals' behaviour may change if they know they are being studied. However, there are problems of recording data.

2.2.1.2 Overt Observation

Overt observation involves:

- The researcher being open about the reason for her presence in the field of study since the researcher is given permission by the group to conduct her research.
- The use of a 'sponsor', who is an individual likely to occupy a high status within the group, therefore lessening any potential hostility towards the researcher.

Problems with overt observation include:

- *Observer effect*, where the behaviour of those under study may alter due to the presence of the researcher.

Advantages of the use of overt observation include:

- The avoidance of problems of ethics in that the group are aware of the researcher's role.
- The group is being observed in its 'natural setting'.
- Data may also be openly recorded.
- Problems of *'going native'* are avoided.

2.2.1.3 When Should You Use Observation?

- *When you are trying to understand an ongoing process or situation.* Through observation you can monitor or watch a process or situation that you are evaluating as it occurs.
- *When you are gathering information on individual behaviours or interactions between people.* Observation allows you to watch peoples' behaviours and interactions directly, or watch for the results of behaviours or interactions.
- *When you need to know about a physical setting.* Seeing the place or environment where something takes place can help increase your understanding of the event, activity, or situation you are evaluating. For example, you can observe whether a classroom or training facility is conducive to learning.
- *When information collection from individuals is not a realistic option.* If respondents are unwilling or unable to provide information through questionnaires or interviews, observation is a method that requires little from the individuals for whom you need information.

2.2.1.4 How Do You Plan for Observations?

- *Determine the focus.* Think about the evaluation question(s) you want to answer through observation and select a few areas of focus for your information collection. For example, you may want to know how well an HIV curriculum is being implemented in the classroom. Your focus areas might be interactions between students and teachers, and teachers' knowledge, skills, and behaviours.
- *Design a system for information collection.* Once you have focused your evaluation think about the specific items for which you want to collect information and then determine how you will collect the information you need. There are three primary ways of collecting observation information. These three methods can be combined to meet your information collection needs.
  - *Recording sheets and checklists* are the most standardized way of collecting observation information and include both preset questions and responses. These forms are typically used for collecting information that can be easily described in advance (e.g., topics that might be covered in an HIV prevention lesson).
  - *Observation guides* list the interactions, processes, or behaviours to be observed with space to record open-ended narrative information.
  - *Field notes* are the least standardized way of collecting observation information and do not include preset questions or responses. Field notes are open-ended narrative information that can be written or dictated onto a tape recorder.
- *Select the sites.* Select an adequate number of sites to help ensure they are representative of the larger population and will provide an understanding of the situation you are observing.
- *Select the observers.* You may choose to be the only observer or you may want to include others in conducting observations. Stakeholders, other professional staff members, interns and graduate students, and volunteers are potential observers.
- *Train the observers.* It is critical that the observers are well trained in your information collection process to ensure high quality and consistent information. The level of training will vary based on the complexity of the information collection and the individual capabilities of the observers.
- *Time your observations appropriately.* Programs and processes typically follow a sequence of events. It is critical that you schedule your observations so you are observing the components of the activity that will answer your evaluation questions. This requires advance planning.

2.2.1.5 What are the Advantages of Observation?

- Collect information where and when an event or activity is occurring.
- Does not rely on people's willingness or ability to provide information.
- Allows you to directly see what people do rather than relying on what people say they did.

2.2.1.6 What are the Disadvantages of Observation?

- Susceptible to observer bias.
- Susceptible to the "hawthorne effect," that is, people usually perform better when they know they are being observed, although indirect observation may decrease this problem.

- Can be expensive and time-consuming compared to other information collection methods.
- Does not increase your understanding of why people behave as they do.

2.2.2 IN-DEPTH INTERVIEWING

In-depth interviewing is a qualitative research technique that involves conducting intensive individual interviews with a small number of respondents to explore their perspectives on a particular idea, program, or situation. For example, we might ask participants, staff, and others associated with a program about their experiences and expectations related to the program, the thoughts they have concerning program operations, processes, and outcomes, and about any changes they perceive in themselves as a result of their involvement in the program.

2.2.2.1 When are In-depth Interviews Appropriate?

In-depth interviews are useful when you want detailed information about a person's thoughts and behaviours or want to explore new issues in depth. Interviews are often used to provide context to other data (such as outcome data), offering a more complete picture of what happened in the program and why. For example, you may have measured an increase in youth visits to a clinic, and through in-depth interviews you find out that a youth noted that she went to the clinic because she saw a new sign outside of the clinic advertising youth hours. You might also interview a clinic staff member to find out their perspective on the clinic's "youth friendliness."

In-depth interviews should be used in place of focus groups if the potential participants may not be included or comfortable talking openly in a group, or when you want to distinguish individual (as opposed to group) opinions about the program. They are often used to refine questions for future surveys of a particular group.

2.2.2.2 What are the Advantages and Limitations of In-depth Interviews?

The primary advantage of in-depth interviews is that they provide much more detailed information than what is available through other data collection methods, such as surveys. They also may provide a more relaxed atmosphere in which to collect information— people may feel more comfortable having a conversation with you about their program as opposed to filling out a survey. However, there are a few limitations and pitfalls, each of which is described below.

- *Prone to bias:* Because program or clinic staff might want to "prove" that a program is working, their interview responses might be biased. Responses from community members and program participants could also be biased due to their stake in the program or for a number of other reasons. Every effort should be made to design a data collection effort, create instruments, and conduct interviews to allow for minimal bias.
- *Can be time-intensive:* Interviews can be a time-intensive evaluation activity because of the time it takes to conduct interviews, transcribe them, and analyze the results. In planning our data collection effort, care must be taken to include time for transcription and analysis of this detailed data.

- *Interviewer must be appropriately trained in interviewing techniques:* To provide the most detailed and rich data from an interviewee, the interviewer must make that person comfortable and appear interested in what they are saying. They must also be sure to use effective interview techniques, such as avoiding yes/no and leading questions, using appropriate body language, and keeping their personal opinions in check.
- *Not generalizable:* When in-depth interviews are conducted, generalizations about the results are usually not able to be made because small samples are chosen and random sampling methods are not used. In-depth interviews however, provide valuable information for programs, particularly when supplementing other methods of data collection. It should be noted that the general rule on sample size for interviews is that when the same stories, themes, issues, and topics are emerging from the interviewees, then a sufficient sample size has been reached.

2.2.2.3 What is the Process for Conducting In-depth Interviews?

The process for conducting in-depth interviews follows the same general process as is followed for other research: plan, develop instruments, collect data, analyze data, and disseminate findings.

More detailed steps are given below:

1. Plan

- Identify stakeholders who will be involved.
- Identify what information is needed and from whom.
- List stakeholders to be interviewed. Identify stakeholder groups from national, facility, and beneficiary levels and then identify individuals within those groups—additional interviewees may be identified during data collection. Determine sample if necessary.
- Ensure research will follow international and national ethical research standards, including review by ethical research committees.

2. Develop Instruments

- Develop an interview protocol—the rules that guide the administration and implementation of the interviews. Put simply, these are the instructions that are followed for each interview, to ensure consistency between interviews, and thus increase the reliability of the findings. The following instructions for the interviewer should be included in the protocol:
- What to say to interviewees when setting up the interview;
- What to say to interviewees when beginning the interview, including ensuring informed consent and confidentiality of the interviewee;
- What to say to interviewees in concluding the interview;
- What to do during the interview (Example: Take notes? Audiotape? Both?); and
- What to do following the interview (Example: Fill in notes? Check audiotape for clarity? Summarize key information for each? Submit written findings?).
- Develop an interview guide that lists the questions or issues to be explored during the interview and includes an informed consent form. There should be no more than 15

main questions to guide the interview, and probes should be included where helpful. Please note that you will likely need interview guides for each group of stakeholders, as questions may differ.

- Where necessary, translate guides into local languages and test the translation.

Interview Question Tips

- Questions should be open-ended rather than closed-ended. For example, instead of asking "Do you know about the clinic's services?" ask "Please describe the clinic's services."
- You should ask factual question before opinion questions. For example, ask, "What activities were conducted?" before asking, "What did you think of the activities?"
- Use probes as needed. These include:
  - Would you give me an example?
  - Can you elaborate on that idea?
  - Would you explain that further?
  - I'm not sure I understand what you're saying.
  - Is there anything else?

3. Train Data Collectors

- Identify and train interviewers. Where necessary, use interviewers that speak the local language.

Training Tips for Data Collectors

Staff, youth program participants, or professional interviewers may be involved in data collection. Regardless of what experience data collectors have, training should include:

- An introduction to the evaluation objectives,
- A review of data collection techniques,
- A thorough review of the data collection items and instruments,
- Practice in the use of the instruments,
- Skill-building exercises on interviewing and interpersonal communication, and
- Discussion of ethical issues.

4. Collect Data

- Set up interviews with stakeholders (be sure to explain the purpose of the interview, why the stakeholder has been chosen, and the expected duration of the interview).
- Seek informed consent of the interviewee (written or documented oral). Re-explain the purpose of the interview, why the stakeholder has been chosen, expected duration of the interview, whether and how the information will be kept confidential, and the use of a note taker and/or tape recorder.
- If interviewee has consented, conduct the interview.
- Summarize key data immediately following the interview.
- Verify information given in interviews as necessary.

5. Analyze Data

- Transcribe and/or review data.
- Analyze all interview data.

Tips on Analyzing Interview Responses

- Read through the interview responses and look for patterns or themes among the participants.
- If you get a variety of themes, see if you can group them in any meaningful way, such as by type of participant. You may, for example, find that younger participants tend to think and feel differently from older ones or that men and women respond differently.
- You can also identify the responses that seem to have been given with enthusiasm, as opposed to those that the participants answered in only a few words.

6. Disseminate Findings

- Write report.
- Solicit feedback from interviewees and program stakeholders.
- Revise.
- Disseminate to interviewees, program stakeholders, funders, and the community as appropriate.

In addition to generic in-depth interviewing, there are several more specialized forms, including ethnographic interviewing, phenomenological interviewing, elite interviewing, focus-group interviewing, and interviewing children. We now describe each of these methods briefly.

2.2.2.4 Ethnographic Interviewing

Based on cognitive anthropology, ethnographic interviewing elicits the cognitive structures guiding participants' worldviews. Described as "a particular kind of speech event", ethnographic questions are used by the researcher to gather cultural data. Ethnographic interviewing is not simply doing an interview. Instead, it is an elaborate system of a series of interviews structured to elicit insiders' cultural knowledge. Three main types of questions are identified: descriptive, structural, and contrast. Descriptive questions allow the researcher to collect a sample of participants' language. Structural questions discover the basic units in the participants' cultural knowledge, and contrast questions provide the ethnographer with the meaning of various terms.

The value of the ethnographic interview lies in its focus on culture through the participant's perspective and through first-hand encounter. This approach is especially useful for eliciting participants' meanings for events and behaviours and for generating a typology of cultural classification schemes. It also highlights the nuances of the culture. The method is flexible in formulating working hypotheses and avoids oversimplification in description and analysis because of its rich narrative descriptions.

There are weaknesses in this method, however. The ethnographer can impose her values through the phrasing of questions or the interpretation of data (a concern with all forms of research but perhaps especially salient with qualitative methods). If the member of the cultural group chosen to participate does not represent that culture, the subsequent analysis will be impoverished. The success of this method, as in all interviewing, is highly dependent on the researcher's interpersonal skills.

2.2.2.5 Phenomenological Interviewing

Phenomenological interviewing is a specific type of in-depth interviewing grounded in a philosophical tradition. Phenomenology is the study of lived experiences and the ways we understand those experiences to develop a worldview. It rests on the assumption that there is a structure and essence to shared experiences that can be narrated. The purpose of this type of interviewing is to describe the meaning of a concept or phenomenon that several individuals share.

The three in-depth interviews compose phenomenological inquiry. The first focuses on past experience with the phenomenon of interest; the second focuses on present experience; and the third joins these two narratives to describe the individual's essential experience with the phenomenon. Prior to interviewing, however, the researcher using this technique has written a full description of her own experience, thereby bracketing off her experiences from those of the interviewees. This phase of the inquiry is referred to as ***epoche***. The purpose of this self-examination is to permit the researcher to gain clarity from her own preconceptions, and it is part of the "ongoing process rather than a single fixed event".

The next phase is called ***phenomenological reduction***; here, the researcher identifies the essence of the phenomenon. The researcher then clusters the data around themes that describe the "textures of the experience". The final stage, ***structural synthesis***, involves the imaginative exploration of "all possible meanings and divergent perspectives" and culminates in a description of the essence of the phenomenon and its deep structure.

The primary advantage of phenomenological interviewing is that it permits an explicit focus on the researcher's personal experience combined with those of the interviewees. It focuses on the deep, lived meanings that events have for individuals, assuming that these meanings guide actions and interactions. It is, however, quite labour-intensive and requires a reflective turn of mind on the part of the researcher.

2.2.2.6 Interviewing of Elites

An interview with an "elite" person is a specialized case of interviewing that focuses on a particular type of interviewee. Elite individuals are considered to be influential, prominent, and/or well-informed in an organization or community; they are selected for interviews on the basis of their expertise in areas relevant to the research.

Elite interviewing has many advantages. Valuable information can be gained from these participants because of the positions they hold in social, political, financial, or administrative realms. Elites can provide an overall view of an organization or its relationship to other organizations, albeit from their own limited and bounded perspectives. They may be quite familiar with the legal and financial structures of the organization. Elites are also able to report on an organization's policies, histories, and plans, again from a particular perspective. Interviewing religious or political leaders would be obvious examples. Less obvious examples include interviews with gang leaders, union bosses, or tribal chiefs.

Elite interviewing also presents disadvantages. It is often difficult to gain access to elites because they are usually busy people operating under demanding time constraints; they are also often difficult to contact initially. (This is also a consideration when requesting interviews with, for example, rural village women who have substantial work responsibilities.) The interviewer may have to rely on sponsorship, recommendations, and introductions for assistance in making appointments with elite individuals.

Another disadvantage in interviewing elites is that the interviewer may have to adapt the planned structure of the interview, based on the wishes and predilections of the person interviewed. Although this is true with all in-depth interviewing, elite individuals who are used to being interviewed by the press and other media may well be quite sophisticated in managing the interview process. (Sophistication and political astuteness are not exclusively the domain of elites, and we do not mean to suggest that they are.) They may want an active interplay with the interviewer. Well practiced at meeting the public and being in control, an elite person may turn the interview around, thereby taking charge of it. Elites often respond well to inquiries about broad areas of content and to open-ended questions that allow them the freedom to use their knowledge and imagination.

Working with elites often places great demands on the ability of the interviewer to establish competence and credibility by displaying knowledge of the topic or, lacking such knowledge, by projecting an accurate conceptualization of the problem through thoughtful questioning. The interviewer's hard work usually pays off, however, in the quality of information obtained. Elites may contribute insight and meaning to the interview through their specific perspectives. On the other hand, elites (just like other interviewees) may well have only vague understandings of a setting that is limited by a narrow viewpoint.

2.2.2.7 Interviewing Children

Children may be the primary focus of a study or one of many groups the researcher wants to interview. Increasingly, there are calls for including children's perspectives as relevant and insightful in learning more about aspects of their worlds. This is especially true in education where all too often those most affected by educational policy and programmatic decisions—the students—are absent from inquiry. There are special considerations, however, when the qualitative researcher proposes a study that involves children.

First are age considerations. Interviewing preschoolers, for example, is quite different from interviewing early adolescents. Young children are often active; early adolescents are frequently very self-conscious. Three-year-olds, exploring their emerging language skills, can drive one to distraction with their incessant questions (often quite sophisticated ones!), whereas early adolescents may be taciturn. It is unrealistic to expect young children to sit still for long, but joining them in some activity can create a climate for focused talk. Some adolescents may feel more comfortable with their peers in a focus-group interview, whereas others may prefer the intimacy of one-to-one interviews. Decisions about how to gather data with various age groups requires sensitivity to their needs, their developmental issues, and flexibility.

Second are role considerations. Some researchers note that the roles an adult researcher assumes when studying children vary along two dimensions: "(1) the extent of positive contact between adult and child, and (2) the extent to which the adult has direct authority over the child". They offer the roles of supervisor, leader, observer, and friend as appropriate. Of these, they find the role of friend the most fruitful, noting that the researcher then interacts with the children "in the most trusted way possible—without any explicit authority role". They caution, however, that age and power differences between adults and children are always salient.

2.3 BACKGROUND AND CONTEXT AND REVIEW OF DOCUMENTS

For every qualitative study, data on the background and historical context are gathered. This may not be a major part of data collection but at least, in proposing a particular setting, the researcher gathers demographic data and describes geographic and historical particulars. When she reviews old property transactions, skims recent newspaper editorials, or obtains information from a Web site, she is collecting data. Whether or not she counts this as data collection, she must proceed with caution.

Knowledge of the history and context surrounding a specific setting comes, in part, from reviewing documents. Researchers supplement participant observation, interviewing, and observation with gathering and analysing documents produced in the course of everyday events or constructed specifically for the research at hand. As such, the review of documents is an unobtrusive method, rich in portraying the values and beliefs of participants in the setting. Minutes of meetings, logs, announcements, formal policy statements, letters, and so on are all useful in developing an understanding of the setting or group studied. Research journals and samples of free writing about the topic can also be quite informative.

Archival data are the routinely gathered records of a society, community, or organization and may further supplement other qualitative methods. For example, marital patterns among a group of Mexicans, discovered through fieldwork in a community, could be tested through marriage records found in the offices of the county seat or state capitol.

Descriptions of articulated funding priorities by policymakers could be corroborated (or not) through an analysis of budgetary allocations. As with other methodological decisions, the decision to gather and analyze documents or archival records should be linked to the research questions developed in the conceptual framework for the study. Furthermore, documents must be viewed with the skepticism that historians apply as they search for truth in old texts.

The use of documents often entails a specialized analytic approach called content analysis. The raw facts and figures for content analysis may be any form of communication, usually written materials (textbooks, novels, newspapers, e-mail messages); other forms of communication— music, pictures, or political speeches—may also be included. Historically, content analysis was viewed as an objective and neutral way of obtaining a quantitative description of the content of various forms of communication; thus, counting the mention of specific items was important. As it has evolved, however, it is viewed more generously as a method for describing and interpreting the artifacts of a society or social group.

Probably the greatest strength of content analysis is that it is unobtrusive and nonreactive: It can be conducted without disturbing the setting in any way. The researcher determines where the emphasis lies after the data have been gathered. Also, the procedure is relatively clear to the reader. Information can therefore be checked, as can the care with which the analysis has been applied. A potential weakness, however, is the span of inferential reasoning. That is, the analysis of the content of written materials or film, for example, entails interpretation by the researcher, just as in the analysis of interactively gathered data: Numbers do not speak for themselves.

Care should be taken, therefore, in displaying the logic of interpretation used in inferring meaning from the artifacts.

Some combination of these primary research methods is typical for in-depth qualitative inquiry.

2.4 ISSUES WITH TRANSCRIBING AND TRANSLATING

Especially in the use of interviews, transcribing and translating text have become increasingly salient issues in the discourse on qualitative research. Neither is a *merely technical task;* both entail judgment and interpretation. In some way, when data have been translated and/or transcribed, they are not raw data any more—they are "processed data". Only recently has the methodological literature offered discussions about the issues in transposing the spoken word (from a tape-recording) into a text (a transcription), or in transposing the spoken word in one language (from a tape-recording) into another language (a translation) and then into a text (a transcription). Unfortunately, the literature has not problematized the challenges in these apparently transparent acts until very recently. Moreover, our review of the literature suggests that only issues with translation are currently being addressed.

2.4.1 Transcribing

If the researcher is fortunate enough to have interview partners who are comfortable with tape-recordings, she leaves the research encounter with spoken words, dutifully and seemingly unproblematically recorded on tape. Those who have then sat down to transcribe the tapes, however, know well the pitfalls of assuming that the spoken word closely parallels the written one. We do not speak in paragraphs, nor do we signal punctuation as we speak. The judgments involved in placing something as simple as a period or a semicolon are complex and shape the meaning of the written word and, hence, of the interview itself. Similarly, the visual cues that we rely on to interpret another's meaning are lost when we listen to a tape; the transcriber no longer has access to those important paralinguistic clues about meaning.

For example, a researcher conducted interviews for an evaluation of a systemic school reform initiative. One interviewee used a discursive style that could charitably be described as complex and dense. The interviewee would begin one topic, then loop to another midsentence, then on to another, finally saying, "Where was I?" and returning to the original topic after a prompt from the interviewer. While fascinating, this style was extremely difficult to transcribe—sentences were interrupted by the speaker herself, topics were left unfinished, and overall clarity was difficult to ascertain. The researcher struggled with this transcription, finally sharing it with the interviewee to be sure that the meaning was accurately rendered in the transcribed account of her words. In another study of women school superintendents, responses to questions were replete with long pauses, in which the subject was changed.

These gaps were, in the end, interpreted as indicators of a strong pattern of avoiding talking about and even denying experiences of sex discrimination—a major finding in her study. What if this researcher had made the mistake of simplistic transcription? But there is a cautionary note here: The meaning of pauses in conversation is not transparent; the researcher should use caution, as did Chase, in drawing inferences and offering interpretations of these linguistic patterns.

Experiences such as this are common. The implication is that the researcher needs to discuss the problematic nature of transcribing in the proposal and provide strategies for handling the judgments and interpretations inherent in such work.

2.4.2 Translating

Clearly, the issues associated with translating from one language into another are much more complex than transcribing because they involve more subtle issues of connotation and meaning.

As noted above, the methodological literature has recently grown to include essays discussing the difficult issues with translating. Writing in the context of the need for more sophistication in cross-language health research with refugee and immigrant populations, Esposito notes that translation is "the transfer of meaning from a source language . . . to a target language" and that the translator is "actually an interpreter who . . . processes the vocabulary and grammatical structure of the words while considering the individual situation and the overall cultural context". Thus the focus on generating *accurate and meaningful data* through translation processes is paramount.

Three primary issues about translating are addressed commonly: (a) whether to identify the translation act in the research report; (b) whether it matters if the researcher is also the translator; and (c) whether to involve the translator in analysis. These topics help move the field forward, but Rossman's experience in her graduate teaching, working intensively with students whose first language (or even second or third) is not English, critiques their discussion as naïve.

Addressing each of the issues in turn, she takes the position that none is problematic. First, she says that there is an ethical imperative to inform the reader that translation has occurred and to address how this will be (in the case of a proposal) or has been (in the case of a final research report) managed. Second, more issues of meaning and interpretation arise when *someone other than* the researcher translates spoken or written words. Third, since translation entails the construction of meaning, she believes that analysis is happening whether or not it is acknowledged.

So what are the important issues with translating the spoken or written word? Most important are the processes and procedures that the researcher/translator has used (or will use) to construct meaning through multiple transpositions of the spoken or written word from one language into another. Rossman and Rallis identify three others:

- If you have translated from one language to another, which language constitutes the direct quotes?
- Can you use translated words as a direct quote?
- How do you signal that a translation is accurate and captures the subtle meanings of the original language?

There are no simple strategies or blueprints for addressing these and other issues associated with translation. What is simple and clear, however, is that the reader of the proposal must know that the researcher understands the issues, will take an ethical stance on translating, and will make clear in the final report just what she has done.

Issues of transcribing and translating are subtle and complex; they are not merely technical tasks. The writer of a qualitative research proposal has an ethical obligation to discuss these issues and how she will approach them, especially since qualitative research generates words— the primary symbol system through which meaning is conveyed and constructed. Not all of the issues can be solved at the proposal stage; in fact, we are quite skeptical of those who write that they have them all wrapped up. Instead, the proposal should have a thoughtful discussion of the more generic issues of transcribing and translating, as well as the ones specific to the research site and participants.

2.5 SECONDARY AND SPECIALIZED METHODS

In addition to the primary data-gathering methods outlined above, the researcher can choose to incorporate several secondary and supplemental methods in the design of a study, as appropriate. Each of those described below is a full and complete method in and of itself and has a methodological literature explicating its nuances and subtleties. In some instances, the same terminology is used for data collection methods and for modes of reporting or presentation. For example, some speak of "doing case studies" as a way of collecting data, but, more often, an entire report, even a book, is a case study. Ethnographers talk of "doing an ethnography" to describe their approach to data collection when, in fact, an ethnography is a written product—*ethno = culture; graphy = writing* or an inscription.

The discussions that follow are necessarily simplified and brief and the list is not exhaustive. The methods discussed below, if used, should always be used with the understanding that observation and interviewing are the primary data collection methods for discovering context-laden patterns and understandings.

2.5.1 Focus Groups

A focus group is a group interview of approximately six to twelve people who share similar characteristics or common interests. A facilitator guides the group based on a predetermined set of topics. The facilitator creates an environment that encourages participants to share their perceptions and points of view. Focus groups are a qualitative data collection method, meaning that the data is descriptive and cannot be measured numerically.

2.5.1.1 When Should You Use Focus Groups?

- To get more in-depth information on perceptions, insights, attitudes, experiences, or beliefs. Focus groups are useful for gathering subjective perspectives from key stakeholders. For example, an evaluation of a CDC-funded asthma prevention program included focus groups of middle school students who had participated in the program. Data were collected on the students' perceptions about how well they were managing their asthma and how their asthma affects their school performance.

- To gather additional information as an adjunct to quantitative data collection methods. Focus groups, like other qualitative methods, are useful in providing interpretations of data collected through quantitative methods (quantitative data is numeric and measureable). For example, your program may use a log to track the number and type of teachers trained in an HIV-prevention curriculum and use a post-training questionnaire to measure knowledge gained immediately after the event. A focus group conducted several months later could provide additional information about how the teachers are using the new knowledge in their work, what they believe are the benefits of the training, and what insights they have about how the training could be improved.
- As part of a mixed method evaluation approach. Mixed methods approaches are used to increase validity of evaluation findings by using a variety of data collection techniques. Because focus groups are one of the few methods in which data is gathered from a group, it is useful as part of a mixed method approach.

2.5.1.2 How Do You Plan Focus Groups?

Successful focus groups start with thorough planning. Two key components of planning your focus groups include developing the focus group guide and deciding the number and type of participants.

- *Develop the focus group guide.* The focus group guide is a series a questions and prompts for the facilitator to use. Typically, the facilitator will ask questions of the group and allow time for participants to respond to each other's comments. The focus group guide serves as a "road map" and memory aid for the facilitator. When developing the focus group guide, identify from who you want to obtain information, what type of information you want to obtain, and what use you have for the information. The same focus group guide will be used for each focus group.
- *Select the number and type of participants for each focus group.* Once you have decided from whom you want to obtain information, you can decide what types of participants you will need for each focus group. Each individual focus group should be made up of similar individuals, so the number of focus groups will depend on how many different types of groups from which you want to gather information.

2.5.1.3 How Do You Conduct a Focus Group?

- *You will need a facilitator, note taker, and technician.*
  - The facilitator guides the group through the discussion and keeps the group focused on the topics for discussion.
  - The note taker is an observer and does not interact with the group. The notes should include a sense of what each person said; identify how comments were said; and record when transitions occurred from one topic to the next.
  - The technician is responsible for recording the focus group. The recording will be used to create a transcript of the event.
- *Focus groups can be conducted in person or via teleconference.* While it is ideal to conduct a focus group in person, it is possible to conduct a focus group by phone. Web conferencing is an additional technology that can be used for focus groups. When conducting focus

groups by phone or web conference, the facilitator has to work to ensure that everyone participates in the discussion.

- *Focus groups typically last about 60 to 90 minutes.* A focus group lasting more than 90 minutes probably includes too many questions or topics for discussion.
- *The focus group needs to be appropriate for the type of participants in the group.* The questions and the manner in which the focus group is facilitated will vary based on the type of participants. Planning for a focus group for third graders will be different than planning one for their parents or teachers and may require a facilitator skilled at working with children.

2.5.1.4 What are the Advantages Focus Groups?

- Quick and relatively easy to set up.
- The group dynamic can provide useful information that individual data collection does not provide.
- Is useful in gaining insight into a topic that may be more difficult to gather through other data collection methods.

2.5.1.5 What are the Disadvantages of Focus Groups?

- Susceptible to facilitator bias.
- The discussion can be dominated or sidetracked by a few individuals.
- Data analysis is time consuming and needs to be well planned in advance.
- Does not provide valid information at the individual level.
- The information is not representative of other groups.

2.5.2 Life Histories and Narrative Inquiry

Life histories and narrative inquiry are methods that gather, analyze, and interpret the stories people tell about their lives. They assume that people live "storied" lives and that telling and retelling one's story helps one understand and create a sense of self. The story is important but so is how the story is told. The researcher, working closely with the participant, explores a story and records it. Life histories and narrative analysis are used across the social science disciplines and are particularly useful for giving the reader an insider's view of a culture or era in history.

2.5.2.1 Life Histories

Life histories seek to "examine and analyze the subjective experience of individuals and their constructions of the social world". They assume a complex interaction between the individual understands of his or her world and that world itself. They are, therefore, uniquely suited to depicting and making theoretical sense of the socialization of a person into a cultural milieu. Thus, one understands a culture through the history of one person' development or life within it, a history told in ways that capture the person's feelings, views, and perspectives. The life history is often an account of how an individual enters a group and becomes socialized into it. That history includes the learning to meet the normative expectations of that society by gender, social class, or age peers. Life histories emphasize the experience of the individual—how the person copes with society rather than how society copes with the stream of individuals.

Life histories can focus on critical or fateful moments. Indecision, confusion, contradiction, and irony are captured as nuanced processes in a life. These histories are particularly helpful in defining socialization and in studying aspects of acculturation and socialization in institutions and professions. Their value goes beyond providing specific information about events and customs of the past—as a historical account might—by showing how the individual creates meaning within the culture. Life histories are valuable in studying cultural changes that have occurred over time, in learning about cultural norms and transgressions of those norms, and in gaining an inside view of a culture. They also help capture how cultural patterns evolve and how they are linked to the life of an individual. Often, this point of view is missing from standard ethnographies.

The term *life history* is sometimes used when, in fact, in-depth interviews are more focused on respondents' evolution or development over time. These parts of larger studies are particularly useful for identifying patterns in health, in the acculturation of immigrants, and the like. Scholars may also research family histories using parallel logics and methods.

The first strength of life history methodology is that, because it pictures a substantial portion of a person's life, the reader can enter into those experiences. The second is that it provides a fertile source of testable hypotheses, useful for focusing subsequent studies. The third strength is that it depicts actions and perspectives across a social group that may be analysed for comparative study. Life history as a methodology emphasizes the value of a person's story and provides pieces for a mosaic depicting an era or social group. This kind of research requires sensitivity, caring, and empathy by the researcher for the researched. Life histories are often used in feminist research as a way of understanding, relatively free of androcentric bias, how women's lives and careers evolve.

Five criteria have been offered for life histories. First, the individual should be viewed as a member of a culture; the life history "describe[s] and interpret[s] the actor's account of his or her development in the common-sense world." Second, the method should capture the significant role that others play in "transmitting socially defined stocks of knowledge." Third, the assumptions of the cultural world under study should be described and analysed as they are revealed in rules and codes for conduct as well as in myths and rituals. Fourth, life histories should focus on the experience of an individual over time so that the "processual development of the person" can be captured. And fifth, the cultural world under study should be continuously related to the individual's unfolding life story.

The major criticisms of the life history are that it makes generalizing difficult, offers only limited principles for selecting participants, and is guided by few accepted concepts of analysis. Once the researcher acknowledges the possible weaknesses in the method, however, he can circumvent them. Official records may provide corroborating information or may illuminate aspects of a culture absent from an individual's account. The researcher can substantiate meanings presented in a history by interviewing others in a participant's life.

A life history account can add depth and evocative illustration to any qualitative study. As with any qualitative genre, however, the abundance of data collected in a life history should be managed and reduced so that analytic headway can be made. Instead of using chronological order, the researcher can focus on (a) critical dimensions or aspects of the person's life, (b) principal turning points and the life conditions between them, and (c) the person's characteristic means of adaptation.

2.5.2.2 Narrative Inquiry

Closely related to life history is narrative inquiry, an interdisciplinary method that views lives holistically and draws from traditions in literary theory, oral history, drama, psychology, folklore, and film philosophy. The method assumes that people construct their realities through narrating their stories. The researcher explores a story told by a participant and records that story. Narrative analysis can be applied to any spoken or written account—for example, to an in-depth interview.

Narrative inquiry requires a great deal of openness and trust between participant and researcher: The inquiry should involve a mutual and sincere collaboration, a caring relationship akin to friendship that is established over time for full participation in the storytelling, retelling, and reliving of personal experiences. It demands intense and active listening and giving the narrator full voice. Because it is collaboration, however, it permits both voices to be heard.

This method is criticized for its focus on the individual rather than on the social context. Like life histories, however, it seeks to understand sociological questions about groups, communities, and contexts through individuals' lived experiences. Like any method that relies on participants' accounts, narrative may suffer from recalling selectively, focusing on subsets of experience, filling in memory gaps through inference, and reinterpreting the past. Crites cautions against "the illusion of causality"— the inference that the narrator's sequencing of the story uses cause and effect accurately. Narrative inquiry is also time-consuming and laborious and requires some specialized training. In the past decade, researchers have articulated criteria for good narrative inquiry.

As a qualitative research method for the social sciences and applied fields it is relatively new, but narrative inquiry has a long tradition in the humanities because of its power to elicit voice. Narrative analysis values the signs, the symbols, and the expression of feelings in language, validating how the narrator constructs meaning. It has been particularly useful in developing feminist and critical theory. Narrative inquiry is especially useful when exploring issues of social change, causality, and social identity.

Narrative inquiry may rely on journal records, photographs, letters, autobiographical writing, e-mail messages, and other data. Typically, field notes are shared with the narrator, and the written record may be constructed collaboratively. In the conduct of narrative inquiry, there is open recognition that the researcher is not just passively recording and reporting the narrator's reality. Researchers need to "be prepared to follow their nose and, after the fact, reconstruct their narrative of inquiry". This becomes, in effect, the recounting of methodology.

2.5.3 Historical Analysis

A history is an account of some event or combination of events. Historical analysis is a method of discovering what has happened using records and accounts. It is particularly useful in qualitative studies for establishing a baseline or background prior to participant observation or interviewing. Sources of historical data are classified as either primary or secondary. Oral testimony of eyewitnesses, documents, records, and relics are primary. Reports of persons who relate the accounts of eyewitnesses and summaries, as in history books and encyclopaedias, are secondary.

The researcher should consider the following sources of historical data: (a) contemporary records, including instructions, stenographic records, business and legal papers, and personal notes and memos; (b) confidential reports, including military records, journals and diaries, and personal letters; (c) public reports, including newspaper reports and memoirs or autobiographies; (d) questionnaires; (e) government documents, including archives and regulations; (f) opinions, including editorials, speeches, pamphlets, letters to the editor, and public opinion polls; (g) fiction, songs, and poetry; and (h) folklore.

Historical analysis is particularly useful in obtaining knowledge of unexamined areas and in re-examining questions for which answers are not as definite as desired. It allows for systematic and direct classification of data. Historical research traditions demand procedures to verify the accuracy of statements about the past, to establish relationships, and to determine the direction of cause-and-effect relationships. Many research studies have a historical base or context, so systematic historical analysis enhances the trustworthiness and credibility of a study.

There is a dialectical tension in this kind of analysis between contemporary and historical interpretations of events, even though texts representing either perspective are influenced by the social contexts in which they are produced. Historical analysis cannot use direct observation, and there is no way to test a historical hypothesis. There are also weaknesses in the classification of historical data. One must remember that documents may be falsified deliberately or may have been interpreted incorrectly by the recorder. Words and phrases used in old records may now have different meanings. The meanings of artifacts are perceived and interpreted by the investigator. Errors in recording, as well as frauds, hoaxes, and forgeries, pose problems in dealing with the past. The researcher should retain a modest scepticism about such data.

2.5.4 Films, Videos and Photography

Films and photography have a long history in anthropology. Called *visual anthropology* or *film ethnography,* this tradition relies on visual representations of the daily life of the group under study. Films are records of natural events and may be used as permanent resources. The concept and method of the research film have emerged and are now compatible with a variety of research methods to describe how people navigate in public places and how they use space, to present findings, and to empower participants. The various forms of photography can be used for data collection and for organizing, interpreting, and validating qualitative inquiry. Films of marriage ceremonies in different social strata in contemporary India, coupled with historical photos and documents, raised key questions in his search for cultural understanding of the interconnections between economics and tradition in handicrafts, dowries, and trousseaux.

Film has the unique ability to capture visible phenomena seemingly objectively—yet always from the perspective of the filmmaker, just as with other forms of observation. The filmmaker, the observer, must decide what to focus on while recording and then how to interpret the data in that recording (whether on film or in field notes). Research film methodology requires the documentation of the time, place, and subject of the filming, as well as the photographer's intent and interests. There is a great wealth of visual information in all natural events: To attempt a complete record of even a small event would be fruitless.

There are three kinds of sampling in films: opportunity, programmed, and digressive. Opportunity sampling documents unanticipated or poorly understood phenomena as they occur. Programmed sampling involves filming according to a predetermined plan—deciding in advance what, where, and when to film. Grounded in the research proposal's conceptual framework, programmed sampling stipulates which events are likely to be significant. It is guided by the research design rather than by intuition, as in opportunity sampling. Digressive sampling is deliberate searching beyond the obvious to the novel, to the places and events beyond typical public recognition.

Researchers choose to use ethnographic film for its obvious strengths. Visual samples enhance the value of any record. Film documents life crises and ceremonies, transmits cultural events to successive generations, and documents social conflicts (court proceedings, public speakers, Senate sessions, and so on). The film researcher is limited by what the mind can imagine and the camera can record— significant limitations because they involve ideology and other forms of cultural bias. But, of course, events can be documented in their natural setting.

Film is especially valuable for discovery and validation. It documents nonverbal behavior and communication such as facial expressions, gestures, and emotions. Film preserves activity and change in its original form. It can be used in the future to take advantage of new methods of seeing, analysing, and understanding the process of change. Film is an aid to the researcher when the nature of what is sought is known but the elements of it cannot be discovered because of the limitations of the human eye. It allows for the preservation and study of data from nonrecurring, disappearing, or rare events.

Film has certain weaknesses and limitations. There are always fundamental questions—What is the nature of truth? Does the film manipulate reality?—and concerns about professional bias and the interests of the filmmaker. Film is expensive, and most research budgets are minimal. Production can be problematic. The researcher needs technical expertise. And filming can be very intrusive, affecting settings and events. Film cannot be included in a book, journal, or dissertation. Finally, serious consideration must be given to the ethics of ethnographic filming.

2.5.5 Interaction Analysis

There are times when, since much is already known either because of much participant observation or good previous research, much focused data collection techniques can be deployed. At those times, researchers wanting finely focused data on verbal and nonverbal communication can use forms of interaction analysis to quantify patterns of interaction. An observer uses a predetermined coding scheme, often called a protocol, to produce a listing of the likely interactions. Then she samples duration at predetermined intervals. For example, the observer might sample blind-date eye contact for 5 seconds every 5 minutes or teachers' responses to student questions in a 30-minute lesson. First used as a method for studying small groups in organizations in the 1920s, interaction analysis gained prominence as a method for observing classrooms and for aiding teacher training. Now it is being used in research on couples to develop coding systems that can powerfully analyze an ongoing stream of dyadic behaviours.

One of the strengths of this approach is that systematic, quantified data are obtained. It is particularly useful for verifying patterns that emerged in early observations and interviews. Large amounts of focused data can be collected in a variety of settings, making statistical analyses useful.

Clearly, interaction analysis is only as good as the categories used to focus observations. When they are culturally biased, too reflective of the researcher's prejudgments, or not well designed for the setting, these categories are not particularly fruitful. There are two well-developed types of this method, kinesics and proxemics, which offer examples of finely focused analyses.

2.5.5.1 Kinesics

Learning about society can be enhanced if we study not only what people say but also what their body movements reveal. Kinesics is the study of body motion and its communicative messages. Motion is analysed systematically so that researchers can see and measure significant patterns in the communications process.

Some researchers assert that nonverbal body behaviours function like significant sounds that combine like words into single or relatively complex units. Body movements ranging from a single nod of the head to a series of hand and leg gestures can attach additional meaning to spoken words. All kinesics research rests on the assumption that individuals are unaware of being engaged constantly in adjustments to the presence and activities of other persons. People modify their behavior and react verbally and nonverbally. Their nonverbal behavior is influenced by culture, gender, age, and other factors associated with psychological and social development.

Four channels are labelled in the communicative process: vocal, visual, olfactory, and tactile. It is important that the researcher be aware of these channels because the verbal interaction between researcher and subject consists of a steady flow of nonverbal clues. Behind the words are messages both parties are communicating. Educated by this knowledge of nonverbal clues, the researcher can monitor subjects' behaviours, discovering their attitudes and giving their actions additional meaning. Body language can express unconscious thoughts that may be essential for observers to decode if they are to analyze situations accurately.

In the interpretation of body language lies one of the weaknesses of kinesics. Novice body readers who have a "pop-psych" understanding of the science of kinesics may make incorrect, perhaps damaging, interpretations of behavior. Related closely to this possibility of misinterpretation is that body language as an analytic tool can be trivialized. For example, many studies focus on frequency counts of isolated units of behavior that convey little meaning by themselves. The fact that a person blinked 100 times during a 15-minute interview is not significant unless the context of the situation is also apparent.

The strengths of kinesic analysis are that it provides a view into unconscious thoughts and a means for the triangulation of verbal data. A researcher can be more confident about the accuracy of information provided by a participant if the speaker's body language is congruent with his words. Also, the researcher can monitor her own nonverbal behavior to clarify messages sent to the subject and to stay in touch with her own feelings during data collection.

Kinesic analysis is limited because body language is not universal; researchers must be aware of cultural differences. Many gestures signal different meanings in different cultures. In some countries, moving the head up and down signifies no and moving it from side to side means yes. Body movements must be interpreted in context, and only experts can make fine-tuned kinesic interpretations. Pupil dilation or movements of tiny jaw or neck muscles should be interpreted cautiously.

2.5.5.2 Proxemics

This is the study of people's use of space in relation to culture. Many studies have been conducted on human activities in bars, airports, subways, and other public places where individuals have to deal with one another in a limited space. Using proxemics, the researcher focuses on space, from interpersonal distance to the arrangement of furniture and architecture. Anthropologists, for example, have used proxemics to determine the territorial customs of cultures. Proxemics has been useful in the study of the behavior of students in the classroom and of marital partners undergoing counselling.

There are several advantages to the use of proxemics. It is unobtrusive, and usually it is difficult for a subject to mislead the observer deliberately. Because it is concerned with nonverbal behavior, subjects would have to be skillful to "lie" about their feelings. Proxemics is useful for studying the way individuals react to the invasion of their territory. Likewise, proxemics can be used in cross-cultural studies because people's use of personal space varies greatly from one culture to the next. Finally, proxemic analysis is useful for studies in areas such as the effect of seating arrangements on student behavior or the effect of crowding on workplace productivity.

The greatest disadvantage of proxemics as a data collection method is that the researcher must be skilled in the interpretation of the observed behaviours. If the researcher is observing a conference or a business meeting, the manner in which the subjects take their seats can be of vital importance, but the data must be interpreted carefully. Exclusive reliance on proxemics could be misleading because relationships that do not exist might be suggested. Because proxemics is relatively new as a data collection method, few instruments to measure space in research are available, further limiting its diverse use. The use of proxemics is increasing throughout research arenas, however. It provides a revealing and interesting method of gathering information about individual social behavior.

2.5.6 Unobtrusive Measures

Unobtrusive measures are ways of collecting data that do not require the cooperation of the subjects and, in fact, may be invisible to them. Some researchers describe these measures as "nonreactive research" because the researcher is expected to observe or gather data without interfering in the on-going flow of everyday events. Data collected in this manner are categorized as documents, archival records, and physical evidence. Of these three, documents and archival records are the most frequently used in qualitative studies and were discussed earlier.

Physical evidence not produced specifically for the purpose of research often constitutes data. During the 1960s, the floor tile around the chick-hatching exhibit at the Museum of Science and Industry in Chicago had to be replaced every 6 weeks. Tile in other parts of the museum did not require replacement for years. The selective erosion of the tiles, indexed by the replacement rate, provided a measure of the relative popularity of exhibits.

Unobtrusive measures are particularly useful for triangulation. As a supplement to interviews, nonreactive research provides another perspective on a phenomenon, elaborating its complexity. These methods can be used without arousing subjects' notice and data collection is relatively easy because it often involves using data already collected by someone else (e.g., bills, archival records, sales records).

When used in isolation, however, unobtrusive measures may distort the picture. Erosion and survival may be affected by activities unknown to the researcher. For example, tiles near the chick-hatching exhibit may have worn out because it is close to the candy machine, not because of the exhibit's popularity. Some researchers consider the use of unobtrusive methods (e.g., monitoring exchanges on newsgroups or searching through garbage) to be unethical: They feel that those studied should be informed of the nature of the research.

When the researcher needs information for measures of frequency or attendance or when direct observation would be impossible or would bias the data, however, this method permits her to be quite creative. Unobtrusive data collection is often aided by hardware, such as audiotapes, hidden cameras, one-way mirrors, gauges, and infrared photos. Clearly, though, ethical issues abound in surreptitious observation.

2.5.7 Questionnaires and Surveys

Researchers administer questionnaires to some samples of a population to learn about the distribution of characteristics, attitudes, or beliefs. In deciding to survey a group of people, researchers make one critical assumption—that a characteristic or belief can be described or measured accurately through self-reporting. In using questionnaires, researchers rely totally on the honesty and accuracy of participants' responses. Although this limits the usefulness of questionnaires for delving into tacit beliefs and deeply held values, there are still many occasions when surveying can be useful.

Questionnaires typically entail several questions that have structured response categories; some open-ended questions may also be included. The questions are examined (sometimes quite vigorously) for bias, sequence, clarity, and face-validity. Questionnaires are usually tested on small groups to determine their usefulness and, perhaps, reliability.

In sample surveys, data are collected in a standardized format, usually from a probability sample of the population. The survey is the preferred method if the researcher wishes to obtain a small amount of information from a large number of subjects.

Survey research is the appropriate mode of inquiry for making inferences about a large group of people based on data drawn from a relatively small number of individuals in that group. Its basic aim is to describe and explain statistically the variability of certain features in a population. The general logic of survey research gives a distinctive style to the research process; the type of survey instrument is determined by the information needed. Surveys are conducted in three ways: by mail, telephone, and personal interview. Any method of data collection, however, from observation to content analysis, can be and has been used in survey research.

Most survey studies involve cross-sectional measurements made at a single point in time or longitudinal measurements taken at several different times. Other forms of survey research include trend studies that examine a population by studying separate samples at different points in time, cohort studies of a bounded population, and panel studies of a single sample of individuals at several points in time. Analysis of survey data takes the form of quantitative analysis that relies mainly on either descriptive or inferential statistics.

The relative advantages and disadvantages of survey research are weighed according to the following criteria: (a) appropriateness of the method to the problem studied, (b) accuracy of measurement, (c) generalizability of the findings, (d) administrative convenience, and (e) avoidance of ethical or political difficulties in the research process.

Surveys have definite advantages when the goals of research require obtaining quantitative data on a certain problem or population. They facilitate research in politically or ethically sensitive areas. They are used in programs for public welfare or economic development. Large surveys often focus on sensitive or controversial topics within the public domain.

The strengths of surveys include their accuracy, generalizability, and convenience. Accuracy in measurement is enhanced by quantification, replicability, and control over observer effects. Results can be generalized to a larger population within known limits of error. Surveys are amenable to rapid statistical analysis and are comparatively easy to administer and manage.

Surveys have weaknesses, however. They are of little value for examining complex social relationships or intricate patterns of interaction. Their strengths can also be weaknesses. Although controlling accuracy, a survey cannot assure without further evidence that the sample represents a broader universe. Thus, the method of drawing the sample and the sample size are critical to the accuracy of the study and its potential for generalizability. Also, even though surveys are convenient, they are generally a relatively expensive method of data collection. Finally, surveys may result in an invasion of privacy or produce questionable effects in the respondent or the community. Some research projects relying on these methods may enhance the position or resources of a particular group, and conflicts may arise between sponsors and research teams concerning how problems are defined. This problem is not specific to surveys and questionnaires, however.

2.5.8 Projective Techniques and Psychological Testing

Some types of interpretive psychological strategies were developed many years ago by clinical psychologists to obtain personality data. These strategies have been used fairly extensively in comparative studies about culture and for analysis of personality dynamics. Based on an internal, perceptual frame of reference, the techniques assume that one can get a valid picture of a person by assessing the way the individual projects his personality onto some standard, ambiguous stimuli.

Standardization and ambiguity are common elements in tests of this nature, although so-called clinical judgments form the primary interpretation bases of responses to these stimuli. Results are typically expressed in the form of a verbal report assessing the subject's dominant needs and ambitions, tolerance of frustrations, attitudes toward authority, major internal conflicts, and so on. The reputation and qualifications of the tester sometimes play a role in how the report is received and how much credibility is attached to the interpretation.

Two of the most well-known and frequently used psychological strategies of this notion are the *Rorschach inkblot test* and the *Thematic Apperception Test* (TAT). The original idea behind both includes the assumption that the stimuli are ambiguous so the subject has to be imaginative and projective in response. The Rorschach test uses pictures (symmetrical inkblots), usually presented in a predetermined order; the subject reports what each picture resembles or suggests. The number, quality, and variety of the subject's responses are compared with specific personality types and with the responses of other people to the same stimuli. In the TAT, the subject is asked to tell stories about a set of picture scenes. Test results are used to assess personality traits such as aggressiveness, dependence, and sexual conflicts.

Although projective instruments have been the object of considerable criticism for many years, they are still commonly employed in clinical contexts by psychologists. Questions remain as to their validity and reliability; environmental and cultural factors may also affect results. Today, concern focuses on the more concrete aspects of personality traits, such as self-esteem and styles of interpersonal behavior, rather than on the vague generalizations that characterized earlier interpretive schemes.

A number of other psychological tests and measurements have been developed for use in qualitative and anthropological research. Examples include the study of (a) the perception of illusions, in which optical and auditory illusions are examined for differences in perception related to differences in types of environments; (b) judgments of aesthetic qualities, in which pictures of art objects or musical stimuli are used to elicit opinions concerning aesthetic excellence; (c) psychomotor skills, in which physical activity measures indicate personality qualities, such as introversion and extroversion; (d) games people engage in, to provide significant information about community and social behavior; and (e) games as a laboratory device, in which a specific game involving family members is used to determine a relationship between communication patterns and socioeconomic differences. Attitude scales can be used in qualitative inquiry, as supplementary measures, and for triangulation. Other qualitative methods have been devised for studying entire communities, group living patterns, and the social integration of individuals in different residential contexts.

2.5.9 Using Computer and Internet Technologies

There is no question that the Internet and its associated hardware (desktop computers, most commonly) have changed the methodologies of social science research. Searching the Internet for resources (now called Googling), using software to manage citations and some aspects of data analysis, interviewing by means of e-mail or in dedicated chat rooms, and using dialogues and interactions online as sites for study are all now part and parcel of much scholarship in the social sciences and applied fields.

Using computers for data collection presents challenges and questions: Are data collected from an internet discussion board more or less authentic than data from, for example, interviews or focus groups? How can you guard the anonymity of sources if you collect data online? How do you manage the fact that your data come only from persons who are computer-savvy, comfortable with computers, and have computer access? Despite these challenges, computer-mediated data gathering may offer an alternative to face-to-face interviewing and be most appropriate for certain research projects. One major advantage is that one's sample can quite literally be a global one. Computers also provide access to populations uncomfortable with or unwilling to engage in face-to-face interactions.

2.5.10 General Principles For Designing Information Collection Strategies

In the proposal, the methods planned for data collection should be related to the type of information sought. Zelditch's chart, represented in Table 2.1, provides guidelines for three large categories of methods: enumerating, participant observation, and in-depth interviewing. Each broad category best yields a particular type of information. In determining which method to use, the researcher should carefully examine the questions guiding the study. Many *'how'* questions are really *'how many'* questions. For example, interviewing people in a program would not adequately answer the question of how many people drop out of the program.

Table 2.1: Information Types and Methods of Obtaining Information

	Method of Obtain Information		
Information Type	**Enumerations and Samples**	**Participant Observation**	**Interviewing Informants**
Frequency Distributions	Prototype and best form	Usually inadequate andinefficient	Often. but not always adequate; if adequate, efficient
Incidents, Histories	Not adequate by itself; not efficient	Prototype and best form	Adequate, with precautions, and efficient
Institutionalized norms and statuses	Adequate but inefficient except for unverbalized	Adequate but inefficient, best form norms	Most efficient and hence

The researcher should determine the most practical, efficient, feasible, and ethical methods for collecting data as the research progresses. He should also consider whether he can fashion and manage a role that works with the chosen data collection strategies. He might need to consider whether, in seeking approval or funding for the research, his chosen strategies will be seen as legitimate. He might start with participant observation as he seeks to identify questions, patterns, and domains. This strategy might change as the research becomes more focused and progresses toward more specific questions and clearer concepts that suggest the use of representative samples. Then the researcher could develop surveys and enumerate the findings. On the other hand, the findings might be descriptions, not numbers. If the research goal is a description of processes, concepts, categories, and typologies, then sampling and counting are merely tools of analysis, not necessarily part of the research findings. The proposal should demonstrate that the researcher is capable of designing and selecting data collection methods that are appropriate, well-thought-out, and thorough. Because the research question may change as the research progresses, the methods may change and the researcher must ensure this flexibility.

2.6 INFORMATION REPRESENTATION

In order to understand what happens inside a computer we must understand how a computer represents information internally. For example, the text you read on a computer screen is stored on a computer disk. It was entered into a computer system using, say, a word processing program. Inside the computer's memory and on the disk this text (and all other information) can be thought of as being represented by a very long sequence of ones and zeros, i.e. in **binary form**. It appears as text only on a computer's monitor or on printed output. A computer monitor's hardware receives binary information and transforms it to the symbols that are displayed. Similarly, a printer's hardware converts binary information to the text (or graphic) that is printed. Inside the CPU and the computer's memory, information is actually stored and transmitted in electrical form, while on disk it is stored in magnetic form. A particular electrical signal represents a one and another signal represents a zero. Similarly, a specific magnetic orientation represents a one and another orientation represents a zero. A group of these binary digits (bits) can be considered to form a binary code and information is encoded as a sequence of individual units each of which correspond to a distinct binary code.

The fundamental principle behind information representation in computers is as follows:

All information is represented by binary codes in a computer system.

2.6.1 CLASSIFYING INFORMATION

From a computing perspective, we can broadly classify the information we wish to store as either **numeric, textual, audio** (sound/music) or **image**. In this section, we only discuss numeric and textual information.

Numeric information refers to information with which we may wish to do arithmetic, i.e. numbers such as 23, 404, 3.14159, 0.96 and so on. Numbers without a decimal point are called **integers** and those that have a decimal point are called **reals**. Computer scientists often refer to real numbers as **floating-point** numbers. It is important to note that different techniques are used to represent integers and reals inside a computer system.

Textual information is made up of individual characters (e.g. a, b, c,.., A, B, C.., -, +, ; , &, %, #, 0,1,2,..9 etc.). Examples include a person's name, address, phone number, an essay, the information on the page you are reading. The term **alphanumeric** refers to text containing both alphabetic characters and numbers such as an address, e.g. *Rohini, New Delhi.* Fortunately international standards for information representation have been developed to make life easier for computer manufacturers and users. This means that we can easily transfer information from one make of computer to another. One such standard is the **ASCII** (American Standard Code for Information Interchange) standard. This standard is used for representing textual information and is described later.

2.6.2 Representing Numbers

Following sections explain the representation of numbers:

2.6.2.1 Integers

We are so familiar with the decimal number system that we might think that everything that uses numbers would, by default, use the decimal system. However, computers, as we have said, use a number system called **binary**, which involves only two digits: 0 and 1. In the decimal system, we represent numbers using 10 digits based on powers of 10. For example, the number 2376 may also be written as:

$$2*10^3 + 3*10^2 + 7*10^1 + 6*10^0$$

More formally, we say that the digits in a positive decimal number are weighted by increasing powers of 10. We say that they use the **base** 10. To illustrate this further, we could write the above number in the following form:

weighting	10^3	10^2	10^1	10^0
digits	2	3	7	6
decimal 2376 =	$2*10^3$ +	$3*10^2$ +	$7*10^1$ +	$6*10^0$

The leftmost digit, 2 in this example, is called the **most significant** digit. The rightmost digit, 6 in this example, is called the **least significant** digit. The digits on the left hand side are called the **high-order** digits (higher powers of 10) and the digits on the right hand side are called the **low-order** digits (lower powers of 10). The above system can be used to write numbers in any base **m** as follows, assuming we are dealing with a 4 digit number:

weighting	m^3	m^2	m^1	m^0
digits	d^3	d^2	d^1	d^0
base m $d^3d^2d^1d^0$ =	d^3*m^3 +	d^2*m^2 +	d^1*m^1 +	d^0*m^0

We refer to the digits making up a number by their position, starting from the right hand side with position **0** (i.e. we count from zero). As we have seen earlier, when the base is 10, we replace m by 10. In the binary number system the base is **2** so we can write the 8-bit binary number 0101 1100 as:

weighting	27	26	25	24	23	22	21	20
bits	0	1	0	1	1	1	0	0

01011100 = 0*27 + 1*26 + 0*25 + 1*24 + 1*23 + 1*22 + 0*21 + 0*20
= 0 + 6410 + 0 + 1610 + 810 + 410 + 0 + 0
= 9210

The leftmost bit is called the **most significant bit (MSB)**. The leftmost bits in a binary number are referred to as the **high-order** bits. The rightmost bit in a binary number is called the **least significant bit (LSB)**. The rightmost bits in a binary number are referred to as the **low-order** bits. In the case of a 16-bit number, we use the above scheme with the powers of 2 ranging from 0 to 15, with a 32-bit number, the powers of 2 range from 0 to 31.

1. Converting From Decimal to Binary

To convert from any number base to another, you repeatedly divide the number to be converted by the new base and the remainder of the division at each stage becomes a digit in the new base until the result of the division is 0. So to convert decimal 35 to binary we do the following:

	Remainder
35 / 2	1
17 / 2	1
8 / 2	0
4 / 2	0
2 / 2	0
1 / 2	1
0	

The result is read **upwards** giving $35_{10} = 100011_2$. The number 100011_2 is an unsigned binary number. We can convert any positive decimal number to binary using the above method. Signed numbers are represented differently, as described later.

Shortcuts

To convert any decimal number which is a power of 2, to binary, you simply write 1 followed by the number of zeros given by the power of 2. For example, 32 is 2^5, so we write it as 1 followed by 5 zeros, i.e. 10000; 128 is 2^7 so we write it as 1 followed by 7 zeros, i.e. 100 0000. Another thing worth remembering is that the largest binary number that can be stored in a given number of bits is made up of all 1's.

An easy way to convert this to decimal, is to note that this value is one less than 2 to the power of the number of bits. For example, if we are using 4-bit numbers, the largest value we can represent is 1111 which is 2^4-1, i.e. 15; with a 6-bit number the largest value we can represent is 11 1111, the decimal equivalent is 2^6-1, i.e. 63. The same techniques apply to decimal numbers, e.g. the largest value that a 3 digit decimal number can represent is 999 is 10^3-1.

2. Hexadecimal Numbers

One difficulty with binary numbers is that they tend to be composed of long sequences of bits and so it is easy to err in working with them. Thus, in writing them down we might arrange them in groups of 3 or 4. A 16-bit binary number such as 0110100011001010 could be written as 0110 1000 1100 1010 which is easier to read. However, it is still tedious to work with such numbers. For this reason we use other number systems. Because 10 is not an exact power of 2, it is not as convenient for working with binary numbers as a system using a base which is a power of 2. Two commonly used computer number systems are the **hexadecimal** (base **16**) and **octal** (base **8**) systems. It is easier to convert a binary number to hexadecimal or octal (and vice versa) than it is to convert a binary number to decimal.

With the hexadecimal system, we require 16 distinct digits (representing the numbers 0 to 15). Using the number digits alone only gives us ten digits, so we use letters as well. The decimal numbers 0 to 15 are represented by the hexadecimal digits 0 to 9 and the letters A to F. The hexadecimal digits correspond to their decimal equivalents. The letter A represents

10, B represents 11, C represents 12, D represents 13, E represents 14 and F represents 15. Hexadecimal numbers are weighted in powers of **16**, so the number 2FA can be converted to decimal as follows:

weighting:		16^2	16^1	16^0
digits		2	F	A
2FA	=	$2 * 16^2$ +	$F * 16^1$ +	$A * 160$
	=	$2 * 16^2$ +	$15 * 16^1$ +	$10 * 16^0$
	=	256 + 240 + 10		
	=	506_{10}		

A hexadecimal digit is represented by **4 bits** (since $2^4 = 16$ and we require 16 bit patterns for 16 digits). Thus, all 32-bit numbers can be written as 8-digit hexadecimal numbers, 16-bit binary numbers can be written as 4-digit hexadecimal numbers and 8-bit binary numbers can be represented by 2-digit hexadecimal numbers. This is the major advantage of using hexadecimal numbers, since computers tend to almost always use 32-bit, 16-bit or 8-bit numbers to represent information. So, if we wish to write down the contents of a processor register which can store 16-bits, we can write it as a 4-digit hexadecimal number. If we were to use decimal, we would have to write it as a number between 0 and 65,536 and this is not nearly so convenient or useful.

To convert a binary number to hexadecimal, you break the number into groups of 4 bits from the right hand side. Then you convert each group of 4 bits into its equivalent hexadecimal digit. This process gives you the hexadecimal equivalent of the original binary number. If there are fewer than 4 bits in the leftmost group, you still convert them to their hexadecimal equivalent (pad on the left with 0's). For example, the 16-bit binary number 0110100011001010 can be divided into the groups: 0110 1000 1100 1010. These are converted to the hexadecimal digits 68CA. Assembly language programmers make extensive use of the hexadecimal numbering system, so it is important to be familiar with it. For example, the letter 'A' is represented inside a computer by the binary code 0100 0001 which can be written in hexadecimal as 41. To convert from hexadecimal to binary, we simply convert each hexadecimal digit to its 4-bit equivalent, padding with 0's on the left, if necessary to make up the 4 bits. For example, hexadecimal digit 4 is written as 0100 in binary, hexadecimal digit 1 is written as 0001 in binary, thus, hexadecimal number 41 is 0100 0001 in binary.

When we write a number, we must indicate its base so that we know which number we are referring to. For example, the number 10 in binary represents two; in decimal it represents ten and in hexadecimal it represents sixteen. There are two common methods for indicating the base, when writing a number in an assembly language program, one method (used in 8086 programs) is to add a character to the end of the number to indicate the base, e.g. **H** for hexadecimal, **D** for decimal and **B** for binary. Thus, we can easily distinguish between the numbers 10H, 10D and 10B. Lowercase letters may also be used. The second method (used in M68000 programs) is to begin the number with a character which indicates the base. For example, hexadecimal numbers may be written so as to begin with the **'$'** character and binary numbers written so as to begin with the '%' character. Using this notation, the number $10 represents the hexadecimal number 10 and %10 represents the binary number 10. The absence of a leading character indicates a decimal number in an M68000 program. Table 2.2 displays the numbers 1 to 15 in the binary, hexadecimal and decimal bases.

Table 2.2: Representing numbers in binary, hexadecimal and decimal bases

Binary	Hexadecimal	Decimal
0000	0	0
0001	1	1
0010	2	2
0011	3	3
0100	4	4
0101	5	5
0110	6	6
0111	7	7
1000	8	8
1001	9	9
1010	A	10
1011	B	11
1100	C	12
1101	D	13
1110	E	14
1111	F	15

3. Negative Numbers

So far the only numbers we have looked at were **unsigned** numbers. It is important to be able to represent both unsigned and **signed** numbers, i.e. both positive and negative numbers. This raises the question of how to represent negative numbers. In our everyday representation of negative numbers, we use a **minus sign '–'** (hyphen on a keyboard) to indicate that a number is negative. Inside a computer we must represent the sign in binary, since all information is stored in binary form. There are a number of methods for representing negative numbers, two of which are the **signed magnitude** and **two's complement** representations.

(i) Signed Magnitude Numbers

In a signed magnitude number, the most significant bit is used as a **sign** bit to indicate whether the number is positive or negative. Thus for an 8-bit number, the most significant bit, bit number 7, acts as the sign bit. The value **1** is used to indicate a **negative** number and the value 0 indicates a positive number. The remaining bits are used to represent the **magnitude** of the number.

For example, the numbers 45 and -45 are represented in signed magnitude as:

+45 = 00101101B

-45 = 10101101B

If we are not interested in negative numbers we can represent numbers ranging from 0 to 255 using 8 bits. Such numbers are called **unsigned** numbers. Using signed magnitude the range that can be represented using 8 bits is from -127 to +127 and we should note that 0 is represented twice (as 1000 0000B and 0000 0000B, i.e. a positive and negative zero). This dual representation of zero causes problems when we wish to compare a variable with 0. In addition, the hardware to do arithmetic using signed magnitude numbers, is complex and slow when compared with using the two's complement representation of signed numbers. As a result, the signed magnitude representation is rarely used in computers.

(ii) Complementary Number Representation

We are used to the concept of a sign and a magnitude when dealing with decimal numbers. A positive sign is implicit (if not written) and negative numbers are written by preceding the positive number by a minus sign. The idea of a complementary number system is that each number has a unique representation. Two's complement is a complementary number system used in computers and is the most commonly used method for representing signed numbers.

Two's Complement Numbers

We still use a sign bit as an indicator of the sign of the number. In the case of positive numbers, the representation is identical to that of signed magnitude, i.e. the sign bit is 0 and the remaining bits represent the positive number. In the case of negative numbers, the sign bit is 1 but the bits to the right of the sign bit do not **directly** indicate the magnitude of the number. The number -1 for example is represented by 1111 if we use 4-bit two's complement numbers while it would represent the number -7 using a signed magnitude representation. Figure 2.1 shows the range of numbers that can be represented using a 4-bit two's complement representation.

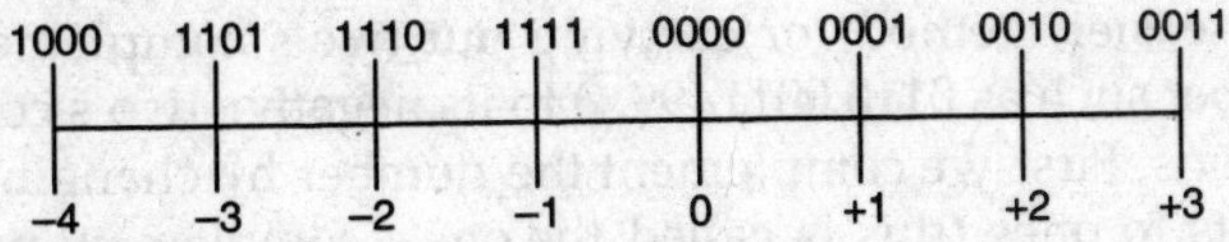

***Figure 2.1:** 4-bit two's complement numbers with their decimal equivalents*

In terms of digit weightings we can interpret two's complement numbers as using a negative weight for the most significant bit. In the case of a 4-bit two's complement number, the sign bit can be interpreted as having a weight of -23, i.e. -8 and the remaining bits have their usual positive weightings. In the case of an 8-bit two's complement number, the sign bit has a weight of -27, i.e. -128. Thus the weightings of an 8-bit two's complement number may be written as:

Bit position	7	6	5	4	3	2	1	0
Weighting:	-27	26	25	24	23	22	21	20
Signed equivalent:	-128	+64	+32	+16	+8	+4	+2	+1

The two complement number 1000 0000 (i.e. -128) is the largest negative number that can be represented using 8 bits. The two's complement number 0111 1111 (127) is the largest positive number that can be represented using 8 bits. In other words a total of 256 numbers can be represented using 8-bit two's complement numbers, ranging from -128 to 127. There is only one representation for zero. Table 2.3 lists the decimal equivalents of some 8-bit, 2's complement and unsigned binary numbers.

Table 2.3: Some 8-bit unsigned and two's complement numbers

Big Pattern	Unsigned	2's Complement
0000 0000	0	0
0000 0001	1	1
0000 0010	2	2
•	•	•
•	•	•
0111 1110	126	126
0111 1111	127	127
1000 0000	128	-128
1000 0001	129	-127
•	•	•
•	•	•
1111 1110	254	-2
1111 1111	255	-1

To convert a two's complement number such as 1000 0001 to decimal, we can use the weightings given above to compute the decimal equivalent, in this case, -128 + 1, i.e. -127. However, there is an easier method for carrying out two's complement conversions. To convert a binary number such as 0110 0011 (99_{10}) to its negative two's complement form, we carry out two operations. First we complement the number by changing all the one bits to zeros and the zero bits to ones (this is called the one's complement representation of the number). This step is also described as flipping the bits. The one's complement of 0110 0011, is 1001 1100. The second step in converting to two's complement, is to add 1 to the one's complement representation. The one's complement was 1001 1100, so the two's complement of this number is 1001 1100 + 0000 0001 giving 1001 1101 (-99_{10}).

In summary, to convert any unsigned binary number to its two's complement form, we flip the bits of the number and add 1.

In addition, to convert a two's complement number to its positive form we carry out the same steps, i.e. we flip the bits and add one. For example, converting 1001 1101 from two's complement yields 0110 0010 + 1 which gives 0110 0011 (99_{10}) and because the sign bit was 1 we know that the original number represented -99_{10}.

For example, to convert -89_{10} to two's complement,

	89_{10}	= 01011001
One's complement	89_{10}	= 10100110
Add one		+1
Two's complement	-89_{10}	= 10100111

Two's Complement Conversion Rule:

To negate a number to two's complement: Flip the bits and add 1.

A nice property of two's complement numbers is that we can add them together without concern for the sign. For example adding +89 to -89 is carried out as:

$$\begin{array}{rl} 01011001_2 & 89_{10} \\ +\,10100111_2 & -89_{10} \\ 00000000_2 & 0_{10} \end{array}$$

This means that to subtract one number from another number, we just negate the number to be subtracted and then add the two numbers. This operation is performed, whether the number to be subtracted is positive or negative. This means that using two's complement numbers, the processor can add and subtract, using the same hardware circuit, i.e. a separate circuit for subtraction is not required. This simplifies the design of the ALU and is one of the reasons why two's complement is the most commonly used method for representing negative numbers in microprocessors.

4. Number Range and Overflow

The range of numbers (called the number range) that can be stored in a given number of bits is important. Given an 8-bit number, we can represent unsigned numbers in the range 0 to 255 (2^8-1) and two's complement numbers in the range -128 to +127 (-2^7 to 2^7): Given a 16-bit number, we can represent unsigned numbers in the range 0 to 65,535 (2^{16} -1) and two's complement numbers in the range -32768 to 32767 (-2^{15} to 2^{15}-1). In general given an **n-bit** number, we can represent unsigned numbers in the range **0 to 2^n -1** and two's complement numbers in the range **-2^n-1 to 2^{n-1} -1.**

When we wish to know the maximum amount of memory that a processor can access, we look at the number of bits that the processor uses to represent a memory address. This determines the maximum memory address that can be accessed. For example, a processor that uses 16-bit addresses will be able to access up to 65,536 memory locations (64Kb), with addresses from 0 to 65,535. A 20-bit address allows up to 220 (1Mb) memory locations to be accessed, a 24-bit address allows up to 16Mb (224 bytes) of RAM to be accessed, a 32-bit address allows up to 4Gb (232 bytes) of RAM to be accessed.

What happens if we attempt to store a larger unsigned value than 255 (or a more negative signed value than -128) in an 8-bit register? For example, if we attempt the calculation 70 + 75 using 8-bit two's complement numbers, the result of 145 (1001 0001B) is a **negative** number in 2's complement! This situation, when it arises is called **overflow**. It occurs when we attempt to represent a number outside the range of numbers that can be stored in a particular register or memory variable. Overflow is detected by the hardware of the CPU and its occurrence is recorded in the CPU's status register. This register uses one flag called the overflow flag or O-flag to record the occurrence of an overflow. This allows the programmer to test for this condition in an assembly language program and deal with it appropriately. The 8086 provides the jo/jno instructions to branch (or not to branch) if overflow occurs. Figure 2.2 illustrates the relationship between number range and overflow for 8-bit two's complement numbers.

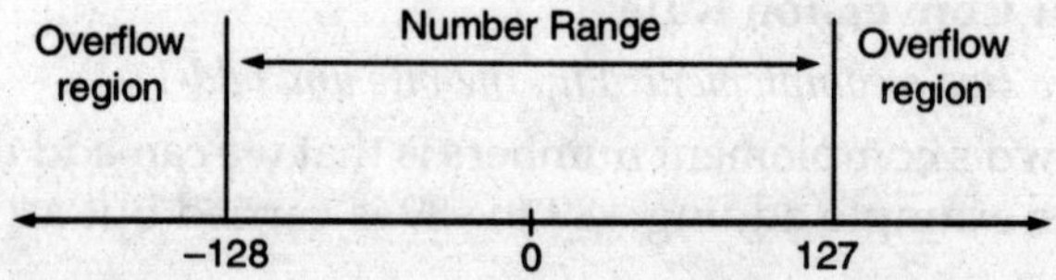

Figure 2.2: Number range and overflow regions for 8-bit two's complement numbers

2.6.2.2 Floating-point Numbers

So far we have described how to represent integers in a computer system, which is sufficient for the purposes of this text. We now briefly introduce methods for representing real numbers. A different representation is required for real (usually called floating-point) numbers. We sometimes write such numbers in scientific notation so that the number 562.42 can be written as 0.56242×10^3. We can express any floating-point number as: $\mathbf{m} \times \mathbf{r}^{\mathbf{exp}}$ where **m** is the **mantissa, r** is the **radix** and **exp** is the **exponent**. For decimal numbers the radix is 10 and for binary numbers the radix is 2. Since we use binary numbers in a computer system, we do not have to store the radix explicitly when representing floating-point numbers. This means that we only need to store the mantissa and the exponent of the number to be represented. Thus, for the number 0.11011011×23 only the values 11011011 and the exponent 3 (converted to binary) need to be stored. The binary point and radix are implicit.

A floating-point number is **normalised** if the most significant digit of the mantissa is **non-zero** as in the above example. Any floating-point number can be normalised by adjusting the exponent appropriately. For example, 0.0001011 is normalised to 0.1011 × 2-3. To represent 0, as a floating-point number, both the mantissa and the exponent are represented as zero.

There are various standards (IEEE, ANSI etc.) that define how the mantissa and exponent of a floating-point number should be stored. Most standards use a 32-bit format for storing single precision floating-point numbers and a 64-bit format for storing double precision floating-point numbers. A **possible** format for a 32-bit floating-point number is the following, which uses a sign bit, 23 bits to represent the mantissa and the remaining 8 bits to represent the exponent. The mantissa could be represented using either signed magnitude or 2's complement. The exponent could be in 2's complement (but another form called **excess notation** is also used).

Thus a 32-bit floating-point number could be represented as follows, where S is the sign bit:

S Exponent Mantissa

Using this format, the number 0.1101 1011 × 23 could be stored as:

0	0000 0110	000 0000 0000 0000 1101 1011

2.6.2.3 Binary Coded Decimal (BCD) Numbers

This form of number representation, allows us to represent numbers, in their decimal form in that each digit of the decimal number is translated to binary and the binary representations of the digits making up the decimal number are stored. This makes I/O operations for BCD numbers easier than if we represent decimal numbers as pure binary numbers as described earlier. For example, when we read a number like 254 from the keyboard, we convert it to binary if we wish to do arithmetic with it. This involves converting the '2' to its binary form, multiplying it by 100, converting the '5' to its binary form, multiplying it by 10 and adding it to the previous number (giving 250) and finally reading the '4', converting it to its binary form and adding it to the previous sum giving the number 254. The **BCD** method of representing numbers is used to get around this problem. Each digit is simply encoded into its equivalent 4-bit form and each digit is stored separately, instead of storing the binary equivalent of the whole number. Thus 254D would be stored as

0000 0010	0000 0101	0000 0100
2	5	4

in BCD form, using 8-bits per digit (**unpacked**) as opposed to representing it as

1111 1110

in unsigned binary form. The above BCD number can be **packed** so as to store two digits per byte:

0000	0010	0101	0100
0	2	5	4

The 8086 provides special instructions that allow addition, subtraction, multiplication and division to be carried out on BCD numbers.

2.6.2.4 Representing Characters: ASCII Codes

ASCII codes are uses to represent characters in a computer system. Each character we wish to use must be assigned a unique binary **code** or number to distinguish it from all other characters. There are over 100 characters to be represented, when we count the uppercase letters (A to Z), the lowercase letters (a to z), the digits (0 to 9), the punctuation (,;.'?!) and other characters. Using ASCII codes for example, the letter **A** is represented by the binary code 1000001, the letter **B** by 1000010 and so on. Because it is awkward to write these codes in binary form, we usually convert them to their **decimal** (or **hexadecimal, i.e.** base 16) equivalents. So the letter **A** may be represented by code **65** in decimal and **B** by code **66**. Inside the computer they are always represented as binary numbers.

The standard ASCII code uses 7 bits, i.e. each character is represented by 7 bits. As we have seen, the letter **A** is represented by the 7 bits 1000001, however we usually write them using 8 bits so we start with a leading zero i.e. 01000001. Because standard ASCII codes use 7 bits, a total of 128 different characters may be represented ($2^7 = 128$, the number of combinations of 7 bits). There are codes for the uppercase letters, lowercase letters, digits, punctuation and other symbols (e.g. ,;:?! *&%$#+-<>/[]{}\~() etc.).

In addition there are ASCII codes for a number of special characters called **control characters.** Control characters are used to control devices attached to the computer and to control communications between the computer and these devices. For example, one such character causes your computer to beep: the **Bel** character (ASCII code 7). The **Line-feed** (ASCII code 10) character causes a print head or screen cursor to go onto a new line. The **Carriage Return** (ASCII code 13) character causes the print head or screen cursor to go to the start of a line. The **Form-feed** (ASCII code 12) character causes a printer to skip to the top of the next page. Other control characters are used to control communication between devices and the computer.

Table 2.3 is a list of some commonly used ASCII codes and the full list of ASCII characters is given in Table 2.4. Remember, inside the computer it is the binary form of the ASCII code that is used. The decimal and hexadecimal values are useful for people to refer to a particular ASCII code.

Table 2.4: Some commonly used ASCII codes

Char	Binary	Hex	Decimal	Char	Binary	Hex	Decimal
NUL	000 0000	00	0	A	100 0001	41	65
BEL	000 0111	07	7	B	100 0010	42	66
LF	000 1010	0A	10	C	100 0011	43	67
FF	000 1100	0C	12	D	100 0100	44	68
CR	000 1011	0D	13	E	100 0101	45	69
SP	010 0000	20	32	F	100 0110	46	70
				G	100 0111	47	71
				H	100 1000	48	72
*	010 1010	2A	42	Y	101 1001	59	89
+	010 1011	2B	43	Z	101 1010	5A	90
,	010 1100	2C	44	[	101 1011	5B	91
-	010 1101	2D	45	\	101 1100	5C	92
.	010 1110	2E	46				
/	010 1111	2F	47	a	110 0001	61	97
0	011 0000	30	48	b	110 0010	62	98
1	011 0001	31	49	c	110 0011	63	99
2	011 0010	32	50	d	110 0100	64	100
3	011 0011	33	51	e	110 0101	65	101
4	011 0100	34	52	f	110 0110	66	102
5	011 0101	35	53	g	110 0111	67	103
6	011 0110	36	54	h	110 1000	68	104
7	011 0111	37	55				
8	011 1000	38	56	y	111 1001	79	121
9	011 1001	39	57	z	111 1010	7A	122

A non-standard 8-bit version of the ASCII codes is also used, which means that 256 characters may be represented. This allows Greek letters, card suits, line drawing and graphic characters to be represented. The 8-bit version is usually referred to as extended ASCII. When standard 7-bit ASCII codes are used, the 8th bit is available for other uses. One such use is as a **parity** bit. A parity bit is used for error detection. When data is transmitted over long distances, perhaps using telephone lines, there is a possibility that the data will be corrupted due to electrical noise. This means that a bit may be flipped, i.e. a 1 bit gets changed to a 0 bit or vice versa. A parity bit can give some protection to allow you detect that such corruption has occurred, i.e. a bit has been changed from 1 to 0 or 0 to 1. There are two parity schemes called **even parity** and **odd parity**. In an **even parity scheme**, the parity bit is used to ensure that the code for each character contains an **even number of 1's**. Thus, the parity bit would be set to 0 in the case of the letter 'A' whose ASCII code 100 0001 and the character would be transmitted as 0100 0001. The parity bit would be set to 1 in the case of the letter 'B' whose ASCII code is 100 0011 in order to make the number of 1's even and the character would be transmitted as 1100 0011. In an odd parity scheme, the parity bit is used in the same fashion, except that it is set to 0 or 1 in order to make the number of 1's transmitted, **odd**. Thus 'A' would be transmitted as 1100 0001 and 'B' as 0100 0011, if using an odd parity scheme.

When using parity bits, the receiver of a character can detect a single bit error, by computing the parity bit for the other 7 data bits and comparing it with the **actual** parity bit transmitted. If they are not the same, then an error has occurred. Parity checking cannot detect the corruption of a number of bits in the same byte, but this is relatively rare. Other methods may be used to detect such errors and they are studied in the field of data communications. The 8086 has conditional jump instructions for testing parity (**jpo** to jump on odd parity and **jpe** to jump on even parity).

ASCII is not the only such standard for representing information. IBM mainframe computers use **EBCDIC** (Extended Binary Coded Decimal Interchange Code) codes which are 8-bit codes, different from those used in the ASCII standard. In addition, there is a **16-bit standard code** referred to as **Unicode** for representing characters. The problem with ASCII codes is that a maximum of 256 characters can be represented. While this is fine for handling text in the English language, it is useless for handling other languages such as Chinese or Japanese where there are literally thousands of individual characters making up the language alphabet. Unicode allows excess of 65,000 characters to be represented and so is sufficient for the alphabet of almost any language. The first 256 Unicode codes correspond to the ASCII codes.

SUMMARY

In this chapter we have described various techniques of information capturing. Two categories of methods were discussed, viz. primary methods and secondary methods. We have also described how information is represented inside a computer system. We described how signed and unsigned numbers can be represented and we also discussed the use of ASCII codes for representing characters. Table 2.5 is a full listing of the ASCII codes.

Table 2.5: Standard ASCII Codes

Char	Binary	Hex	Decimal	Char	Binary	Hex	Decimal
NUL	000 0000	00	0	SP	010 0000	20	32
SOH	000 0001	01	1	!	010 0001	21	33
STX	000 0010	02	2	"	010 0010	22	34
ETX	000 0011	03	3	#	010 0011	23	35
EOT	000 0100	04	4	$	010 0100	24	36
ENQ	000 0101	05	5	%	010 0101	25	37
ACK	000 0110	06	6	&	010 0110	26	38
BEL	000 0111	07	7	'	010 0111	27	39
BS	000 1000	08	8	(	010 1000	28	40
HT	000 1001	09	9	)	010 1001	29	41
LF	000 1010	0A	10	*	010 1010	2A	42
VT	000 1011	0B	11	+	010 1011	2B	43
FF	000 1100	0C	12	,	010 1100	2C	44
CR	000 1011	0D	13	-	010 1101	2D	45
SO	000 1110	0E	14	.	010 1110	2E	46
SI	000 1111	0F	15	/	010 1111	2F	47
DLE	001 0000	10	16	0	011 0000	30	48
DC1	001 0001	11	17	1	011 0001	31	49
DC2	001 0010	12	18	2	011 0010	32	50
DC3	001 0011	13	19	3	011 0011	33	51
DC4	001 0100	14	20	4	011 0100	34	52
NAK	001 0101	15	21	5	011 0101	35	53
SYN	001 0110	16	22	6	011 0110	36	54
ETB	001 0111	17	23	7	011 0111	37	55
CAN	001 1000	18	24	8	011 1000	38	56
EM	001 1001	19	25	9	011 1001	39	57
SUB	001 1010	1A	26	:	011 1010	3A	58
ESC	001 1011	1B	27	;	011 1011	3B	59
FS	001 1100	1C	28	<	011 1100	3C	60
GS	001 1101	1D	29	=	011 1101	3D	61
RS	001 1110	1E	30	>	011 1110	3E	62
US	001 1111	1F	31	?	011 1111	3F	63

@	100 0000	40	64	‘	110 0000	60	96
A	100 0001	41	65	a	110 0001	61	97
B	100 0010	42	66	b	110 0010	62	98
C	100 0011	43	67	c	110 0011	63	99
D	100 0100	44	68	d	110 0100	64	100
E	100 0101	45	69	e	110 0101	65	101
F	100 0110	46	70	f	110 0110	66	102
G	100 0111	47	71	g	110 0111	67	103
H	100 1000	48	72	h	110 1000	68	104
I	100 1001	49	73	i	110 1001	69	105
J	100 1010	4A	74	j	110 1010	6A	106
K	100 1011	4B	75	k	110 1011	6B	107
L	100 1100	4C	76	l	110 1100	6C	108
M	100 1101	4D	77	m	110 1101	6D	109
N	100 1110	4E	78	n	110 1110	6E	110
O	100 1111	4F	79	o	110 1111	6F	111
P	101 0000	50	80	p	111 0000	70	112
Q	101 0001	51	81	q	111 0001	71	113
R	101 0010	52	82	r	111 0010	72	114
S	101 0011	53	83	s	111 0011	73	115
T	101 0100	54	84	t	111 0100	74	116
U	101 0101	55	85	u	111 0101	75	117
V	101 0110	56	86	v	111 0110	76	118
W	101 0111	57	87	w	111 0111	77	119
X	101 1000	58	88	x	111 1000	78	120
Y	101 1001	59	89	y	111 1001	79	121
Z	101 1010	5A	90	z	111 1010	7A	122
[	101 1011	5B	91	{	111 1011	7B	123
\	101 1100	5C	92	|	111 1100	7C	124
]	101 1101	5D	93	}	111 1101	7D	125
^	101 1110	5E	94	~	111 1110	7E	126
_	101 1111	5F	95	DEL	111 1111	7F	127

EXERCISES

1. What is meant by information capturing? Explain various information capturing techniques available.
2. Differentiate between primary and secondary techniques of information capturing.
3. Explain the observation technique of information capturing. Also explain covert and overt observations.
4. Explain the procedure of planning for information capturing through observation.
5. What is in-depth interviewing? Explain in detail the procedure of conducting an in-depth interview.
6. What are the various forms of specialized interviewing? Explain all of them in brief.
7. What is meant by transcribing and translating?
8. What are focus groups? Also give their advantages and disadvantages.
9. Explain the technique of information capturing through life histories.
10. How is historical analysis helpful in information capturing?
11. Explain the advantages of using videos and photography in information capturing.
12. What is meant by kinesics and proxemics?
13. How are questionnaires and surveys helpful in information capturing? Give the relevant advantages and disadvantages.
14. What are the general principles for designing information collection strategies?
15. How are integers represented in computer memory?
16. Explain the conversion of a decimal number to binary number.
17. How are hexadecimal numbers represented? Also explain the conversion of these numbers to decimal format.
18. What techniques are used to represent negative numbers in memory of a computer system?
19. What is signed magnitude?
20. What is two's complement representation?
21. How is floating point numbers represented in memory?
22. Explain the concept of BCD numbers?
23. What are ASCII codes?

❑

3 System Concepts

3.1 SYSTEM

A 'system' may be defined as a group of interrelated *components* working together towards a common goal by accepting inputs and producing outputs in an organized transformation process. The word 'components' may refer to physical parts (engines, wings of aircraft, computer hardware, etc.), managerial steps (planning, organizing, directing, coordinating, and controlling), or a subsystem in a multilevel structure. The components of a system are interrelated and interdependent.

The term system might even refer to a group of regulations which governs structure or behavior. The phrase System has a long record that could be traced back to Greek language.

In 19th century the 1st to establish the notion of the "system" in natural sciences was French physicist Nicolas who studied thermodynamics. In the year 1824 he studied what he called a working substance (system) that is normally a body of water vapour, in the steam engines, in regard to the ability of the system to work when heat is applied over it. The working substance can be put in contact with a boiler, or a cold reservoir (stream of cold water), or piston (where the working body can work by pressing on it). In the year 1850, German physicist Rudolf Clausius widespread this picture to comprise the concept of surroundings and started utilizing the term "working body" while referring to a system.

One of the initiates of the universal systems theory was biologist Ludwig von Bertalanffy. In the year 1945 he introduced principles, models as well as laws that apply to widespread systems or subclasses, irrespective of their exacting kind, nature of their constituent elements, plus the relation or 'forces' among them. Significant growth to the idea of a system was prepared by Ross Ashby and Norbert Wiener who pioneered the employ of mathematics to learn systems.

The word 'system' is used quite often in our day-to-day life. We talk about an educational system, political system, economic system, digestive system, solar system, computer system, and so on. The common feature that all these systems share is that they are a collection of elements integrated together to achieve the required goals. The three major components of a system are depicted in Figure 3.1.

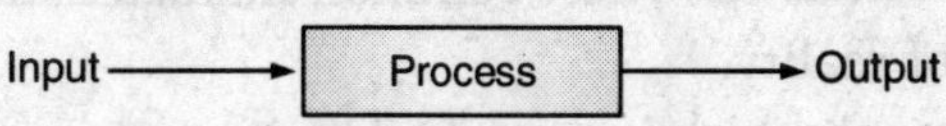

Figure 3.1: A Model of a System

Thus, a system may be regarded as a set of entities or elements interacting among themselves in a certain manner to process certain inputs to produce certain outputs (objectives) in a definite time period. The concept of multiple inputs and outputs is depicted in Figure 3.2.

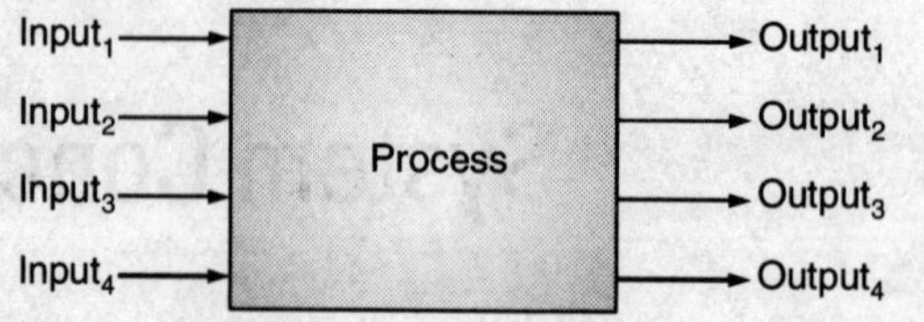

Figure 3.2: *A System with Multiple Inputs and Outputs*

For illustration, the main components that make up a typical computer system are the Processor, Memory, Input/ Output Devices and the Communication. The functional diagram of a typical computer system is depicted in Figure 3.3.

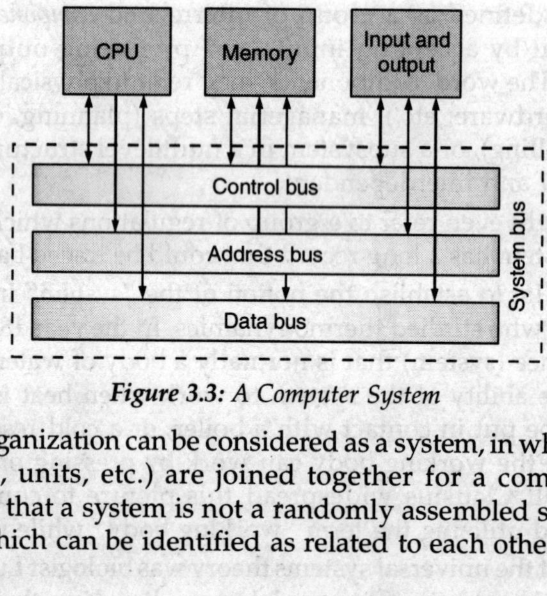

Figure 3.3: *A Computer System*

Also, a business organization can be considered as a system, in which the parts (divisions, departments, sections, units, etc.) are joined together for a common goal. In such an organization, it is clear that a system is not a randomly assembled set of elements; rather it consists of elements which can be identified as related to each other because of a common purpose.

Thus, systems are the set of interdependent or interacting entities, abstract or real, creating an incorporated whole. The notion of an incorporated whole could also be declared in terms of the system embodying a group of relationships that are differentiated from the relationships of a set to other elements, as well as from relationships among an element of a set as well as elements not the part of a relational regime.

The technical investigate field that is engaged in study of common properties of systems comprise systems science, systems theory and systemic. They examine the conceptual properties of organization and matter, searching concepts and values that are free of the particular domain, substance, kind, or chronological scales of survival. The majority of systems share the similar regular characteristics. These common characteristics comprise the following:

- Systems are concepts of reality.
- Systems have arrangement which is described by its parts as well as their composition.

- Systems have performance involving inputs, processing and outputs of material, energy or data.
- The different parts of a system have functional as well as structural relationships between each other.

3.2 ELEMENTS OF A SYSTEM

The important elements of a system are:

- Inputs
- Processor(s)
- Feedback
- Boundaries
- Outputs
- Control
- Environment
- Interface

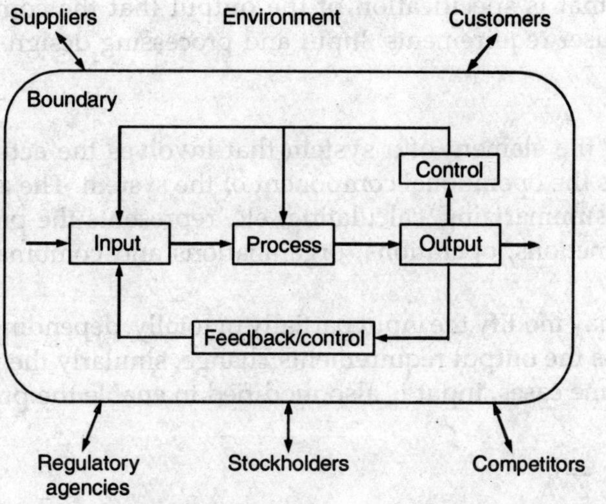

Figure 3.4: Elements of a System

3.2.1 Inputs

Input involves capturing and assembling components that enter the system to be processed. Input may be the start-up component on which the system operates. A system has one or multiple inputs; these inputs are processed through a transformation process to convert them into outputs.

For example, in a manufacturing organization, the raw facts and figures are input to a system which is processed by using various organizational processing facilities to convert it into finished products (i.e. output). Similarly, in an information system, data is input, which is processed to convert it into information.

3.2.2 Outputs

Output involves transferring elements that have been produced by the transformation process to their ultimate destination. Output is the end result of a system, and thus it represents the purpose or objectives of the system. The purpose or objective of the system (i.e. classifying, sorting, summarizing and calculating data) is to obtain information (about the number of customers, total sales, inventory status) so as to aid decision-making. For example, finished products, human services, and management information must be transmitted to their human users.

A major objective of a system is to produce an output that has value to its user. Whatever the nature of the output, it must be within the line with the explanations of the intended user. Inputs are the elements that enter the system for processing. Output is the outcome of processing. A system feeds on input to produce output in much the same way that a business brings in human financial, and material resources to produce goods and services. It is important to point out here that determining the output is a first step in specifying the nature, amount and regularity of the input needed to operate a system. For example in systems analysis, the first concern is to determine the user's requirements of a proposed commuter system – that is specification of the output that the computer is expected to provide for meeting user requirements. Input and processing design follow.

3.2.3 Processor(s)

The processor is the element of a system that involves the actual transformation of input into output. It is the operational component of the system. The actual classification of the data, its sorting, summarizing, calculating, etc. represents the processing of the data. People, machines, functions, operations, organizations and combinations of these act as processors.

Processing unit may modify the input partially or totally, depending on the requirements of the input. Hence, as the output requirements change, similarly the processing principles have to change. In some cases, input is also modified to enable the processor to handle the transformation.

3.2.4 Control

Control is defined as the system function that compares input to a predetermined standard. Control is achieved by correcting the deviation between output and standard. Control of accomplished by:

- Detecting feedback with sensors of some kind.
- Measuring the size, quantity, direction or intensity of the feedback.
- Comparing the results to the established standards of proper performance.
- Transmitting control signals that initiate corrective actions to adjust the activities of other system components.
- Bringing system performance 'under-control', i.e. back within an acceptable range of performance that leads to the attainment of system goals.

The control element guides the system. It is the decision-making sub-system that controls the pattern of activities governing input, processing and output. In an organizational context, management as a decision making body controls the inflow handling and outflow of activities that affects the welfare of the business. Output specifications determine what and how much input is needed to keep the system in balance.

In system analysis, knowing the attitudes of the individuals who control the area for which a computer is being considered can make a difference between the success and the failure of the installation. Management support is required for securing control and supporting the objective of the proposed change.

3.2.5 Feedback

Feedback is the function that provides information on the decision between outputs and the prescribed standards and delivers this information as input into the process from which the output was obtained.

Control in a dynamic system is achieved by feedback. Feedback measures output against standard in some form. After the output is compared against performance standards, changes can result in the input or processing and consequently, the output.

Feedback may be positive or negative, routine or informational. A system performing properly generates positive feedback, which signals the control function to maintain the system's current course towards the goal. The performance of such systems deteriorates over times, which have a negative feedback. This characteristic is called entropy, i.e. the tendency of a system to lose its homeostasis, which is a relatively stable state of equilibrium.

A system with feedback and control is sometimes called cybernetic system, i.e. self-monitoring, self-regulating system. Authors assumed here safely that a system has got different elements or components termed as subsystems. These subsystems have interaction. In general, any subsystem can be a system in itself, which has further subsystems.

Automation is introduced in engineering disciplines by involving the principles of feedback and control.

3.2.6 Environment

A system cannot exist in vacuum rather it exists and functions in an environment containing other systems. The environment is the "super system" within which an organization operates. If a system is one of the components of a larger system, it is called a subsystem, and the larger system is the environment.

It is the source of external elements that unhinge on the system. In fact, it often determines how a system must function. The organization's environment, consisting of vendors, competitions and others, may provide constraints and consequently influence the actual performance of the business. Also a system is separated from its environment and other systems by its system boundary. Several systems may share the same environment. Some of these systems may be connected to one another by means of a shared boundary or interface.

3.2.7 Boundaries

A system should be defined by its boundaries – the limits that identify its components, processes and interrelationships and interfaces with another system. For example, a teller system in a commercial bank is restricted to the deposits, withdrawals and related activities of customers checking and savings accounts. It may exclude mortgage foreclosures, trust activities and the like.

Each system has boundaries that determine its sphere of influence and control. Although in an integrated banking computer system design, a customer who has a mortgage and a checking account with the same bank may write a check through the "teller system" to pay the premium that is latter processed by the "mortgage loan system". Recently system design has been successful in allowing the automatic transfer of funds from the bank account to pay bills and other obligations to creditors, regardless of distance or location. This means that in systems analysis, knowledge of the boundaries of given system is crucial in determining the nature of its interface with other system for successful design.

3.2.8 Interface

Each system can have subsystems which in turn can be made up of units. The interconnections and inter-actions among the subsystems are known as interfaces. Typical scenario of an interface is depicted in Figure 3.5.

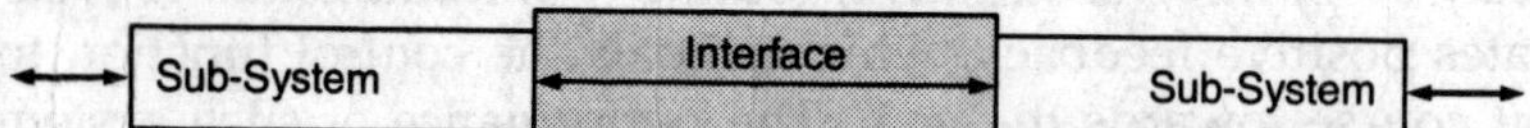

Figure 3.5: Interface

3.3 SYSTEM TERMINOLOGIES

Following are the different system terminologies:

- **Coupling:** This is close working together of subsystems such that there is close coordination. Decoupling is the reduction of the close interaction between the various components (subsystems). When there is coupling there is no need of stores hence the Just-in-time (JIT) system in Japan where there is no need of warehouses. Since the purchasing and supply systems are closely coupled, such that goods ordered are sufficient enough to go through the assembly units and be ready for shipment i.e. no stockholding or waste (muda). Decoupling necessitates the need for warehouses since the various systems are working without consultation e.g. since the CPU is faster than the printer, there is need for the job to be taken to a buffer in order for the printer to print at its pace.
- **Sub-optimality:** This is a situation in a system where a subsystem pursues objectives that are contrary to the overall objectives of the entire system
- **Synergy (holism):** This is a situation in a system where the product of two or more subsystems exceed the sum of the individual components
- **Redundancy:** This is a situation in system where a subsystem is removed for a system and the system is unaffected with its removal as a result of the existing duplication. Symbiosis is the opposite where a subsystem in removed and the entire system grinds to a halt.
- **Entropy:** This is a measure of randomness or disorderliness in a given system. There is need to apply negative entropy in order to bring the system to a state of equilibrium or stability or homeostatic
- **Filtering:** Is the removal of impurities for a given output

- **Factoring:** This is the breaking of the system into its constituent components or subsystems
- **Differentiation:** Its situation in a system where the different subsystems perform specialized tasks
- **Stress:** The amount of pressure exerted on subsystem by the main system so as to be consistent with overall aim of the main system

3.4 CHARACTERISTICS OF A SYSTEM

Our definition of a system suggests some characteristics that are present in all systems:

3.4.1 Organization

Organization implies structure and order. It is the arrangement of components that helps to achieve objectives. For example, a computer system is designed around an input device, a central processing unit, an output device, and one or more storage units. When linked together, they work as a whole system for producing information. Likewise, the hierarchical relationships in a business system, starting with the President on top and leading downwards to the blue-collar workers represent the organization structure. Such an arrangement portrays a system-subsystem relationship, defines the authority structure, specifies the formal flow of communication, and formalizes the chain of command.

3.4.2 Interaction

Interaction refers to the manner in which each component functions with other components of the system. In an organization, for example, purchasing must interact with production, advertising with sales, and payroll with the personnel. In a computer system, the central processing unit must interact with the input device to solve a problem. In turn, the main memory holds programs and data that the arithmetic unit uses for computation.

3.4.3 Interdependence

Interdependence means that parts of the organization or computer system depend on one another. They are coordinated and linked together according to a plan. One subsystem depends on the input of another subsystem for proper functioning, i.e. output of one subsystem is required as an input to another subsystem.

No system can function in isolation because it is dependent on the data, i.e. inputs it receives from other subsystems to perform its required task. For example, a decision to computerize an application is initiated by the user, analysed and designed by the analyst, programmed and tested by the programmer, and run by the computer operator.

3.4.4 Integration

Integration refers to the holism of systems. Synthesis follows analysis to achieve the central objective of the organization. Integration is concerned with how a system is tied together. It is more than sharing a physical part or a location. It means that parts of the system work together within the system even though each part performs a unique function. Successful integration will typically produce a synergistic effect and greater total impact than if each component works together.

3.4.5 Central Objective

The last characteristic of a system is its central objective. Objectives may be real or stated. Although a stated objective may be the real objective, it is not uncommon for an organization to state one objective and operates to achieve another. The important point is that users must know the central objective of a computer application early in the analysis for a successful design and conversion. This means that, the analyst must work around such obstacles to identify the real objective of the proposed amendment.

3.5 TYPES OF SYSTEMS

Various kinds of systems may be categorized as follows:

3.5.1 Formal Systems

Formal systems work on accepted and fixed definitions of data and procedures for collecting, storing, processing, disseminating, and using these data. Formal systems operate in conformity with predefined rules that are relatively fixed and not easily changed.

3.5.2 Abstract (Conceptual) Systems and Physical (Empirical) Systems

Systems can be categorized as abstract systems and physical systems. There can be misunderstandings if one system talks about an information system as a set of concepts, ideas, or characteristics (abstract) and his listener perceive it as an operational system of people, equipment and reports (physical).

An abstract system or conceptual system is concerned with theoretical ideas or constructs, which may or may not have any counterpart in the real world. For example, a system of theology is an example of abstract system, which is an orderly arrangement of ideas about God and the relationships of humans to God. Conceptual systems are typified by those of science, such as economic theory, non-Euclidian geometry systems, the general systems of relativity, or organization theory. Note that conceptual systems for organizations as composed of ideas are distinct from empirical organization systems made up of people.

Conceptual systems, then, are systems of explanation or classification. They may also appear in practical management affairs in the form of plans, accounting system structures and classifications of policies and procedures.

Physical systems are generally concrete operational systems made up of people, materials, machines, energy, and other physical things. Physical systems are more than conceptual constructs; they display some activity or behaviour. The elements in such a system interact to achieve a common objective, for example, the production system, the transport system, the computer system, and others.

3.5.3 Deterministic Systems and Probabilistic Systems

A deterministic system is one in which the occurrence of all events is known with certainty. In such a system, given a description of the system state at a particular point of time of its operation, the next state can be perfectly predicted. An example of such a system is a correct computer program which performs exactly according to a set of instructions.

A probabilistic system is one in which the occurrence of events cannot be perfectly predicted. Though the behaviour of such a system can be described in terms of probability, a certain degree of error will always be attached to the prediction of the behaviour of the system. An example of such a system is a set of instructions given to a person who may not follow the instructions as given. Another example is a warehouse and its contents. Given a description of the contents at a given point of time, the average demand, the length of time taken to process orders, etc., the contents at the next point in time could not be perfectly predicted. In our daily life, we usually have to deal with such probabilistic systems.

3.5.4 Open Systems and Closed Systems

Several systems may share the same environment. Some of these systems may be connected to one another by means of a shared boundary or interface. The concept of an open system is a system that interacts with the other systems in its environment system that can adjust their activities to acceptable levels and continue to function.

Hence, open system is a system that interacts with other systems in its environment system and thus exchanges information, material, or energy with the environment to adjust their activities to acceptable levels and continue to function.

The concept of interaction with the environment which characterizes open systems is essential for control. Receiving and evaluating feedback allows a system to determine how well it is operating. For example, if a business produces as output product or services that are high priced and of low quality, people probably will not continue to buy them. Low sales figures are feedback, telling management they need to adjust the products and the way they are produced to improve performance and bring it in line with expectations. Therefore, open systems can be called adaptive as they tend to react with the environment in such a way so as to favour their continued existence. Such systems are self-organizing in the sense that they change their organization in response to changing conditions.

All living systems, for example humans, plants, cells, etc. are open systems. They attempt to maintain equilibrium by homeostasis, the process of adjusting to keep the system operating within prescribed limits. An organization which is sensitive to changes in customer tastes, preferences, likings, disliking, demands, etc. and in consequence adjusts its prices, changes in product mix, or looks for new markets, is an open organization. All organizations essentially are open systems as they cannot work in isolation. Thus systems analyst usually deals with adaptive open systems.

A closed system is one which does not interact with its environment. In other words, we may say that a relatively closed system is one which controls its inputs and output and is protected from environmental disturbances. Such systems in business world are rare, but relatively closed systems are common. Thus, systems that are relatively isolated from the environment but not completely closed are termed as closed systems (which actually mean relatively closed systems). For example, a computer program is a relatively closed system because it accepts and processes previously defined inputs and provides outputs too in a previously defined way.

3.5.5 Adaptive Systems and Non-adaptive Systems

A system that reacts to its environment in such a way as to improve its functionality, achievement, or probability of survival is called an adaptive system. High-level living organisms such as animals and humans use adaptation in meeting threats of changes in the physical environment or changes in their societies. Evolution theory is based heavily on the concept of an adaptive system.

A system that does not react to its environment to change is called a non-adaptive system.

3.5.6 Subsystems and Supersystems

From the previous discussion it is clear that each system is nested in a larger system, the system in the hierarchy that we are most interested in studying or controlling the system. The business firm is viewed as 'the system' or the 'total system' when focus is on production, distribution of goods, and sources of profit and income. Smaller systems within the system are called subsystems. This distinction has important implications in practice with regard to optimization, people tend to optimize for the good of the system they are most closely related to rather than the whole system. Supersystem is opposed to subsystem. It is a part of the larger system. The larger system is called supersystem.

3.5.7 Permanent Systems and Temporary Systems

Permanent systems are those systems which are designed for a long period of time, without its modification. Permanent systems are isolated from the environment. Relatively few, if any, people-made systems are permanent. However, for practical purposes, systems enduring for a time span that is long relative to the operations of humans in the system may be said to be 'permanent'. Our economic system, which is gradually changing, is essentially permanent for our future plans. At another extreme, the policies of a business organization are 'permanent' as far as year-to-year operations are concerned. It is true that major policy changes may be made, but these will then last an indefinite and 'long' time relative to the daily activities of the employees.

Temporary systems are those which are designed to last for a specified period of time and then they dissolve. For example, the television system set up to record the proceedings of a national political convention is only a temporary system. Some systems that are temporary are not so by design. A company that is formed and quickly goes bankrupt is an example. Temporary systems are important accomplishment of specific tasks in business and for research in science.

3.5.8 Stationary Systems and Non-stationary Systems

A stationary system is one whose properties and operations either do not vary significantly or else vary only in repetitive cycles. For example, the automatic factory, the government agency that processes social payments, the super market store, high school, and the bus system are the examples of stationary system.

A non-stationary system is one whose properties and operations vary significantly. An advertising organization, a continental defence system, a research and development laboratory, and a human being are non-stationary systems.

3.5.9 Social, People-machine and Machine Systems

Systems that are made up of people are known to be purely social systems. Business organizations, government agencies, and technical societies are examples of social systems.

It is difficult to think of a system composed only of people who do not utilize equipment of some kind to achieve their goals. Even philosophers think and write. Most empirical systems fall under the category of people-machine systems. A small system that is purely mechanical, but is a part of a larger system involving people is also a common example.

Pure machine systems would have to obtain their own inputs and maintain themselves without any involvement of people. The development of a self-healing machine system would bring these systems closer to simulation of living organisms. Such systems would need to adapt to their environments.

3.5.10 Natural and Manufactured Systems

Natural systems are plenty in nature. The entire ecology of life is a natural system, and each organism is a unique natural system in its own. The water system of the world is natural system, as well as the solar system is also a natural system.

Manufactured systems were formed when people first gathered in groups to generate a system. One system may be concerned with national defence, while another may be a transportation system. A business organization is a system with many smaller systems included, such as production, sales, accounting, and so on.

3.6 SYSTEM DECOMPOSITION

A system can be divided into smaller systems known as sub-systems and a sub-system can further be divided into still smaller systems called sub-sub-systems, which in turn can be divided into still smaller systems. This process continues until the smallest sub-systems are of manageable size. The concept of sub-systems is an important aspect and is basic to the analysis and design of information systems, because it is difficult to comprehend a complex system when considered as a whole. Therefore, for the sake of convenience and clarity, a system is divided into smaller systems. The process of dividing or factoring a system into smaller systems is known as decomposing.

The subsystems resulting from this process usually form hierarchical structures. In the hierarchy, a subsystem is one element of a supra-system (the system above it). Such a hierarchy is depicted in Figure 3.6, where a system is divided into four smaller systems A, B, C, and D. A sub-system B is further divided into still smaller sub-systems B1 and B2.

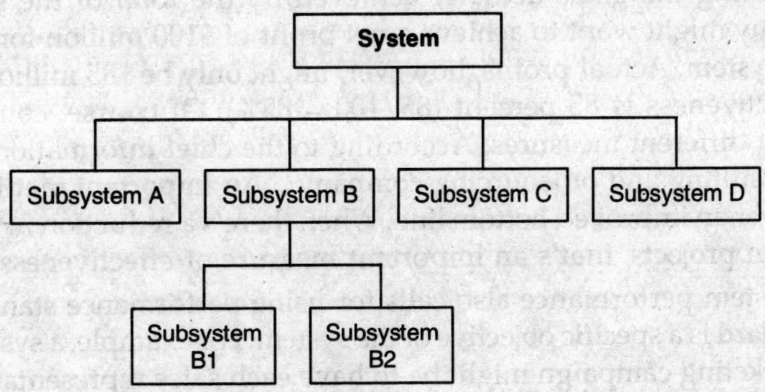

Figure 3.6: System Decomposition

The process of decomposition into smaller systems is used to both analyse an existing system and to design and implement a new system. On the basis of an objective, the system analyst has to draw boundaries and define the interfaces so that the sum of sub-systems constitutes the entire system.

3.6.1 Integration of Subsystems

A system is divided into subsystems only for the sake of clarity. However, it is the whole that dictates the overall role of the sub-systems. The concept of integration draws attention to the primary importance of the whole system. The whole system is a system, which behaves as if it is a single entity. Thus, one should not get lost amongst the smaller systems. Rather the sub-systems and their relationships among each other should evolve from the concept of the whole system. In other words, the whole should not be overlooked while trying to understand it through its parts.

As an example, a business system is a system where economic sources (inputs) are transformed by various organizational processes (processing) into goods and services (output). Information systems provide information (feedback) on the operation of the system to management for the direction and maintenance of the system (control), as it exchanges inputs and outputs with its environment.

3.7 System Performance and Standards

System performance can be measured in various ways. **Efficiency** is a measure of what is produced divided by what is consumed. It can range from 0 to 100 percent. For example, the efficiency of a motor is the energy produced (in terms of work done) divided by the energy consumed (in terms of electricity or fuel). Some motors have an efficiency of 50 percent or less because of the energy lost to friction and heat generation.

Efficiency is a relative term used to compare systems. For example, a hybrid gasoline engine for an automobile or truck can be more efficient than a traditional gasoline engine because, for the equivalent amount of fuel consumed, the hybrid engine travels more miles and gets better gas mileage. Many organizations can reduce their energy usage by investing in more energy-efficient computer systems.

Effectiveness is a measure of the extent to which a system achieves its goals. It can be computed by dividing the goals actually achieved by the total of the stated goals. For example, a company might want to achieve a net profit of $100 million for the year using a new information system. Actual profits, however, might only be $85 million for the year. In this case, the effectiveness is 85 percent (85/100 = 85%). Of course, companies measure effectiveness using different measures. According to the chief information officer (CIO) of Wipro, a large consulting and outsourcing company, "An important metric for us is when our people ... deliver an improved bottom line. When there's a reduction in people travelling for collaborating on projects, that's an important measure of effectiveness."

Evaluating system performance also calls for using performance standards. A **system performance standard** is a specific objective of the system. For example, a system performance standard for a marketing campaign might be to have each sales representative sell $100,000 of a certain type of product each year. A system performance standard for a manufacturing process might be to provide no more than 1 percent defective parts. After standards are established, system performance is measured and compared with the standard. Variances from the standard are determinants of system performance.

3.8 SYSTEMS DEVELOPMENT

Systems development is the activity of creating or modifying systems. Systems development projects can range from small to very large and are conducted in fields as diverse as stock analysis and video game development.

People inside a company can develop systems, or companies can use outsourcing, hiring an outside company to perform some or all of a system development project. Outsourcing allows a company to focus on what it does best and delegate other functions to companies with expertise in systems development. Any outsourcing decision should depend on the company and the project being considered for outsourcing.

Some system development efforts fail to meet their cost or schedule goals. Systems development failures can be a result of poor planning and scheduling, insufficient management of risk, poor requirements determination, and lack of user involvement. One strategy for improving the results of a systems development project is to divide it into several steps, each with a well-defined and set of tasks to accomplish. These steps are depicted in Figure 3.7.

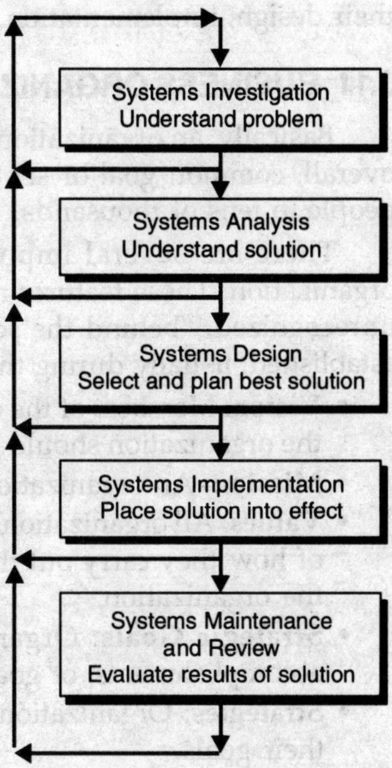

Figure 3.7: An Overview of Systems Development

3.9 SYSTEMS INVESTIGATION AND ANALYSIS

The first two steps of systems development are systems investigation and analysis. The goal of the systems investigation is to gain a clear understanding of the problem to be solved or opportunity to be addressed. After an organization understands the problem, the next question is 'Is the problem worth soling?'. Given that organizations have limited resources, i.e. people and money, this question deserves careful consideration. If the decision is to continue with the solution, the next step, systems analysis, defines the problems and opportunities of the existing system. During systems investigation and analysis, as well as design maintenance and review, discussed next, the project must have the complete support of top-level managers and focus on developing systems that achieve business goals.

3.10 SYSTEMS DESIGN, IMPLEMENTATION, MAINTENANCE AND REVIEW

Systems design determines how the new systems should be developed to meet the business needs defined during systems analysis. For some companies, this involves environmental design that attempts to use systems development approaches that are kind to the environment and make a profit. Systems implementation involves creating or acquiring the various systems components (hardware, software, databases, etc.) defined in the design step, assembling them, and putting the new system into operation. For many organizations, this includes purchasing software, hardware, databases and other components. The purpose of systems maintenance and review is to check and modify the system so that it continues to meet changing business needs. Increasingly, companies are hitting outside companies to do their design, implementation, maintenance, and review functions.

3.11 BUSINESS ORGANIZATIONS

Basically, an organization is a group of people intentionally organized to accomplish an overall, common goal or set of goals. Business organizations can range in size from two people to tens of thousands.

There are several important aspects to consider about the goal of the business organization. These features are explicit (deliberate and recognized) or implicit (operating unrecognized, "behind the scenes"). Ideally, these features are carefully considered and established, usually during the strategic planning process.

- **Vision:** Members of the organization often have some image in their minds about how the organization should be working, how it should appear when things are going well.
- **Mission**: An organization operates according to an overall purpose, or mission.
- **Values:** All organizations operate according to overall values, or priorities in the nature of how they carry out their activities. These values are the personality, or culture, of the organization.
- **Strategic Goals**: Organizations members often work to achieve several overall accomplishments, or goals, as they work toward their mission.
- **Strategies**: Organizations usually follow several overall general approaches to reach their goals.

Systems and Processes that are aligned with achieving the Goals:

Organizations have major subsystems, such as departments, programs, divisions, teams, etc. Each of these subsystems has a way of doing things to, along with other subsystems; achieve the overall goals of the organization. Often, these systems and processes are defined by plans, policies and procedures. How you interpret each of the above major parts of an organization depends very much on your values and your nature. People can view organizations as machines, organisms, families, groups, etc.

3.12 ORGANIZATION AS A SYSTEM

It helps to think of organizations are systems. As we know that a system is an organized collection of parts that are highly integrated in order to accomplish an overall goal. The system has various inputs which are processed to produce certain outputs that together, accomplish the overall goal desired by the organization. There is on-going feedback among these various parts to ensure they remain aligned to accomplish the overall goal of the organization. There are several classes of systems, ranging from very simple frameworks all the way to social systems, which are the most complex. Organizations are, of course, social systems. Systems have inputs, processes, outputs and outcomes.

Inputs to the system include resources such as raw materials, money, technologies and people. These inputs go through a **Process** where they're aligned, moved along and carefully coordinated, ultimately to achieve the goals set for the system. **Outputs** are tangible results produced by processes in the system, such as products or services for consumers. Another kind of result is outcomes, or benefits for consumers, e.g., jobs for workers, enhanced quality of life for customers, etc. Systems can be the entire organization, or its departments, groups, processes, etc. **Feedback** comes from, e.g., employees who carry out processes in the organization, customers/clients using the products and services, etc. Feedback also comes from the larger environment of the organization, e.g., influences from government, society, economics, and technologies. The inputs, outputs, process and feedback is depicted in Figure 3.8.

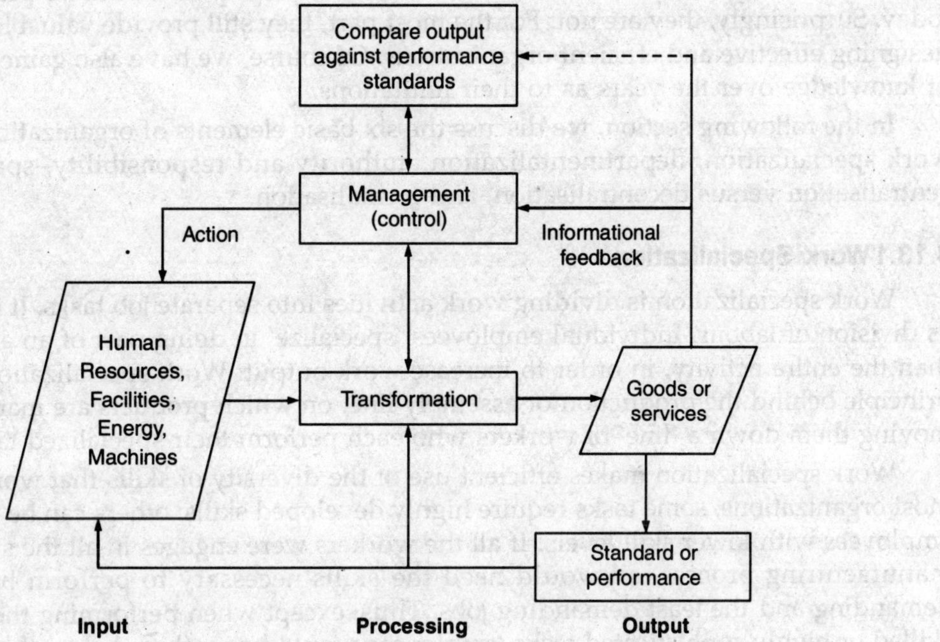

Figure 3.8: Inputs and Outputs in a Business Organization

Each organization has numerous subsystems, as well. Each subsystem has its own boundaries of sorts, and includes various inputs, processes, outputs and outcomes geared to accomplish an overall goal for the subsystem. Common examples of subsystems are departments, programs, projects, teams, processes to produce products or services, etc. Organizations are made up of people — who are also systems of systems of systems — and on it goes. Subsystems are organized in a hierarchy needed to accomplish the overall goal of the overall system.

The organizational system is defined by, e.g., its legal documents (articles of incorporation, bylaws, roles of officers, etc.), mission, goals and strategies, policies and procedures, operating manuals, etc. The organization is depicted by its organizational charts, job descriptions, marketing materials, etc. The organizational system is also maintained or controlled by policies and procedures, budgets, information management systems, quality management systems, performance review systems, etc.

3.13 KEY ELEMENTS IN ORGANIZATIONAL DESIGN

Few topics in management have undergone as that of organizing and organizational structure. Managers are re-evaluating traditional approaches and exploring new structural designs that best support and facilitate employees' doing the organization's work, designs that can achieve efficiency but are also flexible.

The basic concepts of organizational design formulated by management writes offered structural principles for managers to follow. Almost 80 years have passed since many of those principles were originally proposed. Given that length of time and all the changes that have taken place, you would think that those principles would be pretty worthless today. Surprisingly, they are not. For the most part, they still provide valuable insights into designing effective and efficient organizations. Of course, we have also gained greater deal of knowledge over the years as to their limitations.

In the following section, we discuss the six basic elements of organizational structure: work specialization, departmentalization, authority and responsibility, span of control, centralisation versus decentralisation, and formalisation.

3.13.1 Work Specialization

Work specialization is dividing work activities into separate job tasks. It is also known as division of labour. Individual employees 'specialize' in doing part of an activity, rather than the entire activity, in order to increase work output. Work specialization is the basic principle behind the production or assembly line, on which products are manufactured by moving them down a 'line' of workers who each perform their specialized tasks.

Work specialization makes efficient use of the diversity of skills that workers have. In most organizations, some tasks require highly developed skills; others can be performed by employees with lower skill levels. If all the workers were engages in all the steps of, say, a manufacturing process, all would need the skills necessary to perform both the most demanding and the least demanding jobs. Thus, except when performing the most highly skilled or highly sophisticated tasks, employees would be working below their skill levels. In addition, skilled workers are paid more than unskilled workers, and, because wages tend to reflect the highest level of skill, all workers would be paid at highly skilled rates to do easy tasks, which is an inefficient use of resources. This concept explains why you rarely find a cardiac surgeon closing up a patient after surgery. Once the surgeon has finished the surgery, doctors who are learning open-heart surgery stitch and staple the patient.

Early proponents of work specialization believed that it could lead to great increases in productivity. At the beginning of the twentieth century, that generalization was reasonable. Because specialization was not widely practiced, its introduction almost always generated higher productivity.

3.13.1.1 What is Today's View of Specialization?

Most managers today see work specialization as an important organizing mechanism because it helps employees to be more efficient. For example, McDonald's uses high specialization to get its products made and delivered to customers efficiently. However, managers also have to recognize its limitations. At some point, the lack of routine and repetitive nature of work which results from division of labour causes boredom, fatigue, stress, low productivity, poor quality, increased absenteeism, and high turnover, and exceed the economic advantages.

3.13.2 Departmentalisation

Early management writes argued that after deciding what job tasks will be done by whom, common work activities needed to be grouped back together so work gets done in a coordinated and integrated way. How jobs are grouped together is called departmentalisation. There are five common forms of departmentalisation as depicted in Table 3.1, although an organization may use its own unique classification. The methods or methods used should reflect the grouping that would best contribute to the attainment of the goals of the organization and the individual units.

Table 3.1: Type of Departmentalisation

Type	Description
Functional	Groups employees based in work performed (e.g. engineering, accounting, information systems, human resources)
Product	Groups employees based in major product areas in the corporation (e.g. women's footwear, men's footwear, apparel, and accessories)
Customer	Groups employees based on customer's problems and needs (e.g. wholesale, government)
Geographical	Groups employees based on location served (e.g. New Delhi, Mumbai, Chennai, and West Bengal)
Process	Groups employees based on the basis of work or customer flow (e.g. testing, payment)

3.13.2.1 What is Today's View of Departmentalisation?

Most large organizations continue to use most or all of the departmental groups suggested by the early management writers. However, today's competitive environment has refocused the attention of management of its customers. To better monitor the needs of customers and to be able to respond to changes in those needs, many organizations give greater emphasis to customer departmentalisation. Finally, we also see more organizations using teams especially as tasks have become more complex and diverse skills are needed to accomplish those tasks. A recent trend is the use of cross-functional teams, which are teams made up of individuals from various departments and that cross traditional departmental lines.

3.13.3 Authority and Responsibility

Authority refers to the rights inherent in a managerial position to give orders and expect the orders to be obeyed. Authority was a major concept discussed by the early management writers as they viewed it as the glue that held an organization together. It was delegated downward to lower-level managers, giving them certain rights while prescribing certain limits within which to operate. Each management position had specific inherent rights that incumbents acquired from the position's rank or title. Authority, therefore, is related to one's position within an organization and has nothing to do with the personal characteristics of an individual manager. When a position of authority is vacated, the person who has left the position no longer has any authority. The authority remains with the position and its new incumbent.

When managers delegate authority, they must allocate commensurate responsibility, i.e. when employees are given rights; they also assume a corresponding obligation to perform. And they should be held accountable for their performance. Allocating authority without responsibility and accountability creates opportunities for abuse. Likewise, no-one should be held responsible or accountable for something over which he or she has no authority.

To understand authority and responsibility, you also have to be familiar with the chain of command, the line of authority extending from upper organizational levels to lower levels, which clarifies who reports to whom. Managers need to consider it when organizing work because it helps employees with questions such as 'Who do I report to?' or 'Who do I go to if I have a problem?'.

3.13.3.1 Types of Authority Relationships

The early management writers distinguished between two forms of authority: line authority and staff authority. Line authority entitles a manager to direct the work of an employee. It is the employer-employee authority relationship that extends from the top of the organization to the lowest echelon, according to the chain of command as depicted in Figure 3.9. As a link in the chain of command, a manager with line authority has the right to direct the work of employees and so make certain decisions without consulting anyone. Of course, in the chain of command, every manager is also subject to the direction of his/her superior.

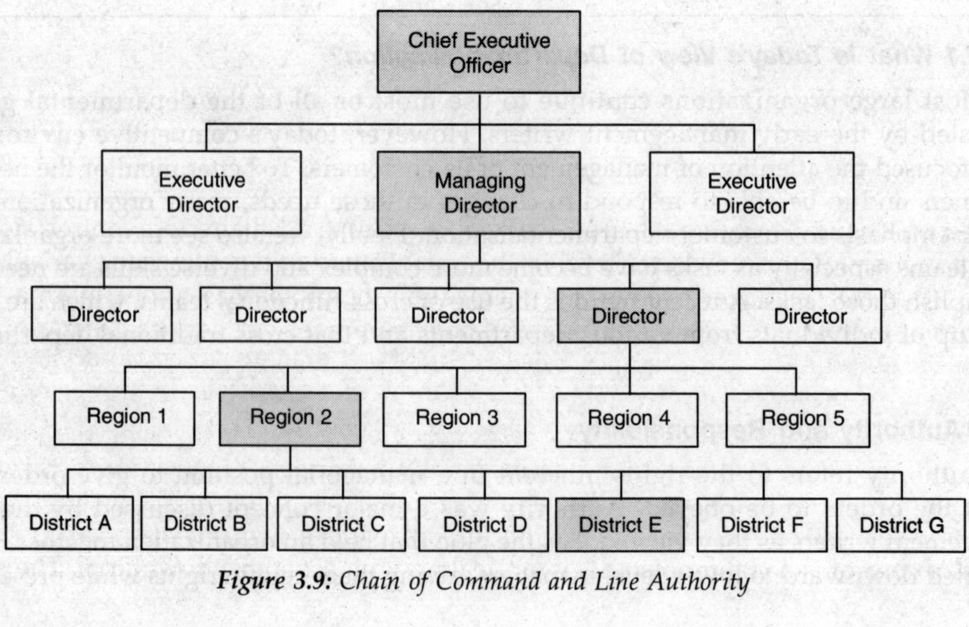

Figure 3.9: Chain of Command and Line Authority

An organization gets larger and more complex, line managers find that they do not have the time, expertise or resources to get their job done effectively. In response, they create staff authority functions to support, assist, advise and generally reduce some of their information burdens. The distinction between line and staff authority refers to whether the work that is performed contributes directly to organizational outputs. For example, in a manufacturing organization a manager with line authority has the authority to direct staff directly involved in making and selling the company's products. A manager with staff authority has the authority to direct employees whose work indirectly supports the manufacture and sale of company products, such as accountants who ensure the company can pay for product components. Figure 3.10 illustrates line and staff authority.

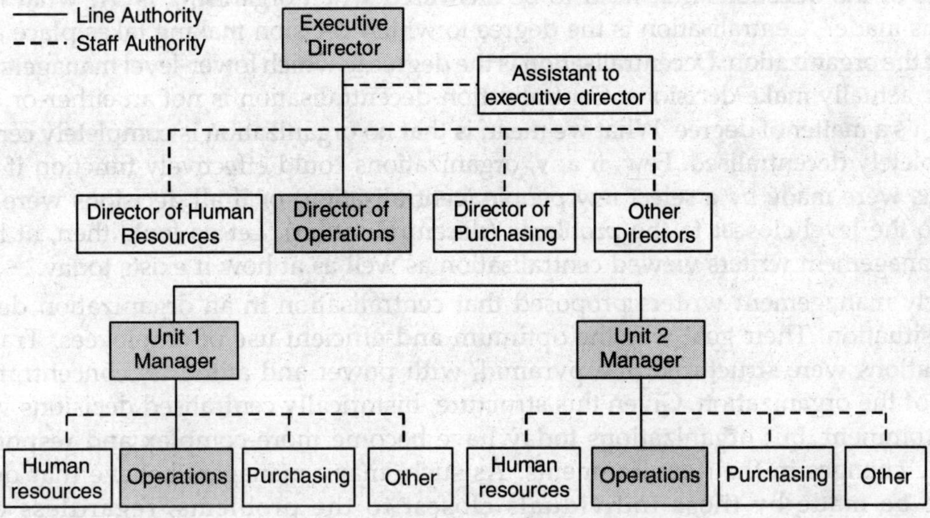

Figure 3.10: Line versus Staff Authority

3.13.4 Span of Control

Span of control refers to the number of employees reporting to a manager. It determines how closely a manager can monitor employees. The question of how many employees a manager can efficiently supervise received a great deal of attention from early management writers. Although early writes came to no consensus on a specific number, most favoured small spans, typically no more than six workers, in order to maintain close control. However, several writers did acknowledge level in the organization as a contingency variable. They argued that as a manager rises in an organization, he or she has to deal with a greater number of unstructured problems, so top managers need a smaller span than do middle managers, and middle managers require a smaller span than do supervisors. Over the last decade, however, we have seen some changes in theories about effective spans of control.

Many organizations are increasing their spans of control by reducing the number of managers they employ and making each remaining manager responsible for overseeing more employees. This has meant that they can reduce the number of managerial staff in their organizations and reduce costs. For this reason, reducing managerial staff and increasing spans of control is a common strategy for dealing with economic downturns. The span of control is increasingly being determined by looking at contingency variables. Managers who have well-trained and experienced employees can function with a wider span because the more training and experience employees have, the less direct supervision they need. Other contingency variables that determine the appropriate span include similarity of employee tasks, the complexity of those tasks, the physical proximity of employees, and the degree to which standardised procedures are in place, the sophistication of the organization's management information system, the strength of the organization's value system and the preferred managing style of the manager.

3.13.5 Centralisation and Decentralisation

One of the questions that need to be answered when organising is 'At what level are decisions made?' Centralisation is the degree to which decision making takes place at upper levels of the organization. Decentralisation is the degree to which lower-level managers provide input or actually make decisions. Centralisation-decentralisation is not an either-or concept. Rather, it's a matter of degree. What we mean is that no organization is completely centralised or completely decentralised. Few, if any, organizations could effectively function if all their decisions were made by a select few people (centralisation) or if all decisions were pushed down to the level closest to the problems (decentralisation). Let us look, then, at how the early management writers viewed centralisation as well as at how it exists today.

Early management writers proposed that centralisation in an organization depended on the situation. Their goal was the optimum and efficient use of employees. Traditional organizations were structured in a pyramid, with power and authority concentrated near the top of the organization. Given this structure, historically centralised decisions were the most prominent, but organizations today have become more complex and responsive to dynamic changes in their environments. As such, many managers believe that decisions need to be made by those individuals closest to the problems, regardless of their organizational level.

3.13.5.1 What is Today's View of Centralisation-decentralisation?

Today, managers often choose the amount of centralisation or decentralisation that will allow them to best implement their decisions and achieve organizational goals. What works in one organization, however, won't necessarily work in another, so managers must determine the amount of decentralisation for each organization and work units within it. Empowering employees and delegating to them the authority to make decisions in those things that affect their work and to change the way that they think about work. That is decentralisation. But when employees face dilemmas, they need to clearly understand what they have authority to do. We should note that decentralisation does not mean that top-level managers no longer make decisions. Rather, decentralisation frees top-level managers to focus on making decisions about unstructured problems.

3.13.6 Formalisation

Formalism refers to how standardised an organization's jobs are and the extent to which employee behaviour is guided by rules and procedures. In highly formalised organizations such as police services or hospitals, there are explicit job descriptions, numerous organizational rules and clearly defined procedures covering work processes. Employees have little discretion over what's done, when it is done, and how it is done because deviating from organizational procedures could have harmful or even tragic consequences. However, where formalisation is low, employees have more discretion in how they do their work. Early management writers expected organizations to be fairly formalised, as formalisation went hand-in-hand with bureaucratic-style organizations.

SUMMARY

This chapter explains the concept of a system. Definition of systems follows with the basic elements of the system which are inputs, outputs, processor(s), control, feedback, environment, boundaries and interface. All these elements work in sync for the proper functioning of the system. Organization, Interaction, Interdependence, Integration and a Central Objective are the characteristics that are common to all systems. Various types of systems are also explained.

System decomposition is dividing a system into subsystems for the sake of convenience. The subsystems can be further divided until the smallest subsystems are of manageable size.

Efficiency and Effectiveness measure the performance of a system. Evaluating a system is by system standards is also one of the objectives of the system.

System development process is divided into five phases namely, Systems Investigation, Systems Analysis, Systems Design, Systems Implementation and Systems Maintenance and Review.

The concept of Business Organizations is also important from the point of view of information systems. The organization is viewed as a system having some inputs, processing the inputs, and providing outputs in the form of finished goods and services. There are six basic elements of organizational structure: work specialization, departmentalization, authority and responsibility, span of control, centralisation versus decentralisation, and formalisation.

EXERCISES

1. What is system?
2. What is computer system?
3. What are the elements of a system?
4. Explain the system terminologies?
5. What are the characteristics of a system?
6. Explain the types of systems?
7. What is system decomposition?
8. Explain the system performance and standards?
9. What is systems development?
10. Explain the systems investigation and analysis?
11. Explain the systems design, implementation, maintenance and review?
12. What is a business organization?
13. Explain the organization as a system?
14. What are the key elements in organizational design?

❑

Information Systems

4

4.1 INFORMATION SYSTEMS

An information system is an organized combination of people, hardware, software, communication networks, and data resources that collects, transforms, and disseminates information in an organization. People (end users and IS specialists) have relied on information systems to communicate with each other in a variety of physical devices (hardware), information processing instructions and procedures (software), communication channels (networks), and stored data (data base resources). See Figure 4.1.

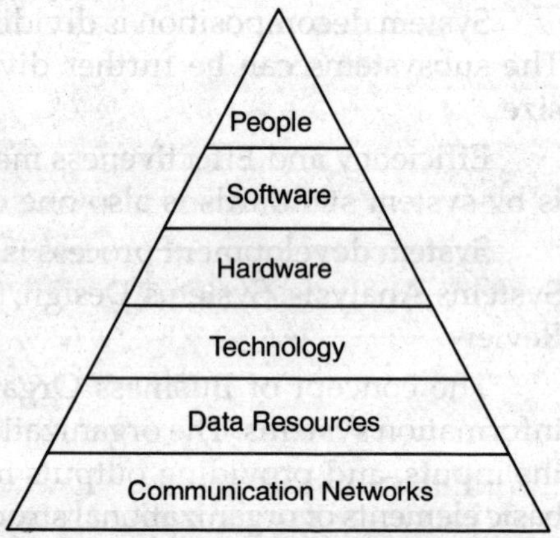

Figure 4.1: An Information System

An information system can be defined technically as a set of interrelated components that collect (or retrieve), process, store, and distribute information to support decision making and control in an organization. In addition to supporting decision making, coordination, and control, information systems may also help managers and workers analyze problems, visualize complex subjects, and create new products.

Information systems contain information about significant people, places, and things within the organization or in the environment surrounding it. By information we mean data that have been shaped into a form that is meaningful and useful to human beings. Data, in contrast, are streams of raw facts representing events occurring in organizations or the physical environment before they have been organized and arranged into a form that people can understand and use.

A brief example contrasting information and data may prove useful. Supermarket checkout counters ring up millions of pieces of data, such as product identification numbers or the cost of each item sold. Such pieces of data can be totalled and analyzed to provide meaningful information, such as the total number of bottles of dish detergent sold at a particular store, which brands of dish detergent were selling the most rapidly at that store or sales territory, or the total amount spent on that brand of dish detergent at that store or sales region (see Figure 4.2).

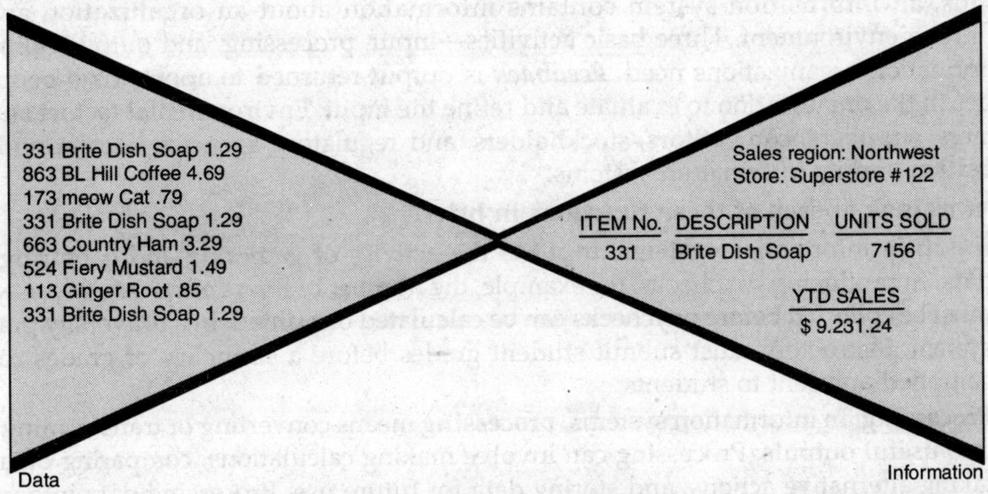

***Figure 4.2:** Data and information*

Raw data from a supermarket checkout counter can be processed and organized to produce meaningful information such as the total unit sales of dish detergent or the total sales revenue from dish detergent for a specific store or sales territory.

Three activities in an information system produce the information that organizations need to make decisions, control operations, analyze problems, and create new products or services. These activities are ***input, processing,*** and ***output*** (see Figure 4.3). Input captures or collects raw data from within the organization or from its external environment. Processing converts this raw input into a more meaningful form. Output transfers the processed information to the people who will use it or to the activities for which it will be used. Information systems also require feedback, which is output that is returned to appropriate members of the organization to help them evaluate or correct the input stage.

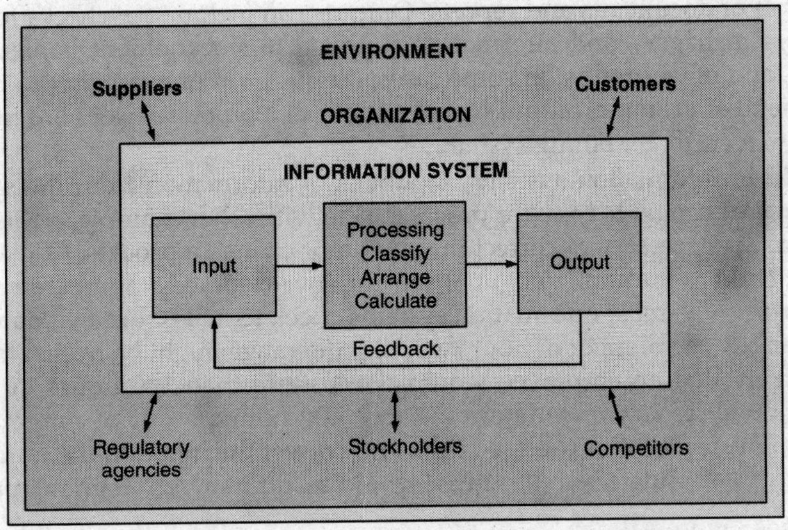

***Figure 4.3:** Functions of an information system*

Thus, an information system contains information about an organization and its surrounding environment. Three basic activities—input, processing, and output—produce the information organizations need. ***Feedback*** is output returned to appropriate people or activities in the organization to evaluate and refine the input. Environmental factors such as customers, suppliers, competitors, stockholders, and regulatory agencies interact with the organization and its information systems.

Let us look at each of these functions in brief.

- **Input:** In information systems, **input** is the activity of gathering and capturing raw data. In producing paychecks, for example, the number of hours every employee works must be collected before paychecks can be calculated or printed. In a university grading system, instructors must submit student grades before a summary of grades can be compiled and sent to students.
- **Processing:** In information systems, **processing** means converting or transforming data into useful outputs. Processing can involve making calculations, comparing data and taking alternative actions, and storing data for future use. Processing data into useful information is critical in business settings.

Processing can be done manually or with computer assistance. In a payroll application, the number of hours each employee worked must be converted into net, or take-home, pay. Other inputs often include employee ID number and department. The processing can first involve multiplying the number of hours worked by the employee's hourly pay rate to get gross pay. If weekly hours worked exceed 40, overtime pay might also be included. Then deductions—for example, federal and state taxes or contributions to insurance or savings plans—are subtracted from gross pay to get net pay.

After these calculations and comparisons are performed, the results are typically stored. *Storage* involves keeping data and information available for future use, including output, discussed next.

- **Output:** In information systems, **output** involves producing useful information, usually in the form of documents and reports. Outputs can include paychecks for employees, reports for managers, and information supplied to stockholders, banks, government agencies, and other groups. In some cases, output from one system can become input for another. For example, output from a system that processes sales orders can be used as input to a customer billing system.
- **Feedback:** In information systems, **feedback** is information from the system that is used to make changes to input or processing activities. For example, errors or problems might make it necessary to correct input data or change a process. Consider a payroll example. Perhaps the number of hours an employee worked was entered as 400 instead of 40. Fortunately, most information systems check to make sure that data falls within certain ranges. For number of hours worked, the range might be from 0 to 100 because it is unlikely that an employee would work more than 100 hours in a week. The information system would determine that 400 hours is out of range and provide feedback. The feedback is used to check and correct the input on the number of hours worked to 40. If undetected, this error would result in a very high net pay.

Feedback is also important for managers and decision makers. For example, a furniture maker could use a computerized feedback system to link its suppliers and plants. The output from an information system might indicate that inventory levels for mahogany and oak are getting low—a potential problem. A manager could use this feedback to decide to order more wood. These new inventory orders then become input to the system. In addition to this reactive approach, a computer system can also be proactive—predicting future events to avoid problems. This concept, often called **forecasting**, can be used to estimate future sales and order more inventory before a shortage occurs.

Although computer-based information systems use computer technology to process raw data into meaningful information, there is a sharp distinction between a computer and a computer program on the one hand, and an information system on the other. Electronic computers and related software programs are the technical foundation, the tools and materials, of modern information systems. Computers provide the equipment for storing and processing information. Computer programs, or software, are sets of operating instructions that direct and control computer processing. Knowing how computers and computer programs work is important in designing solutions to organizational problems, but computers are only part of an information system.

A house is an appropriate analogy. Houses are built with hammers, nails, and wood, but these do not make a house. The architecture, design, setting, landscaping, and all of the decisions that lead to the creation of these features are part of the house and are crucial for solving the problem of putting a roof over one's head. Computers and programs are the hammer, nails, and lumber of Computer-Based Information Systems (CBIS), but alone they cannot produce the information a particular organization needs. To understand information systems, you must understand the problems they are designed to solve their architectural and design elements, and the organizational processes that lead to these solutions.

4.2 COMPUTER-BASED INFORMATION SYSTEMS

Today's end users rely on many types of information systems. It might be simple manual hardware devices (paper-and-pencil) and informal communication channels (word-of mouth). However, in this book, we will concentrate on computer-based information systems (CBIS) that use computer hardware and software, telecommunication networks, computer-based data management techniques, and other forms of information technology (IT) to transform data resources into a variety of information products.

Thus a CBIS is an information system that uses computer technology to perform some or all of its intended tasks. Although not all information systems are computerized, today most are. For this reason the term 'information system' is typically used synonymously with 'computer-based information system'. The basic components of computer-based information *systems* are listed below. The first four are called information technology components. Figure 4.4 shows how these four components interact to form a CBIS.

- **Hardware** consists of devices such as the processor, monitor, keyboard, and printer. Together, these devices accept, process, and display data and information.
- **Software** is a program or collection of programs that enable the hardware to process data.

- A **database** is a collection of related files or tables containing data.
- A **network** is a connecting system (wireline or wireless) that permits different computers to share resources.
- **Procedures** are the instructions for combining the above components in order to process information and generate the desired output.
- **People** are those individuals who use the hardware and software, interface with it, or utilize its output.

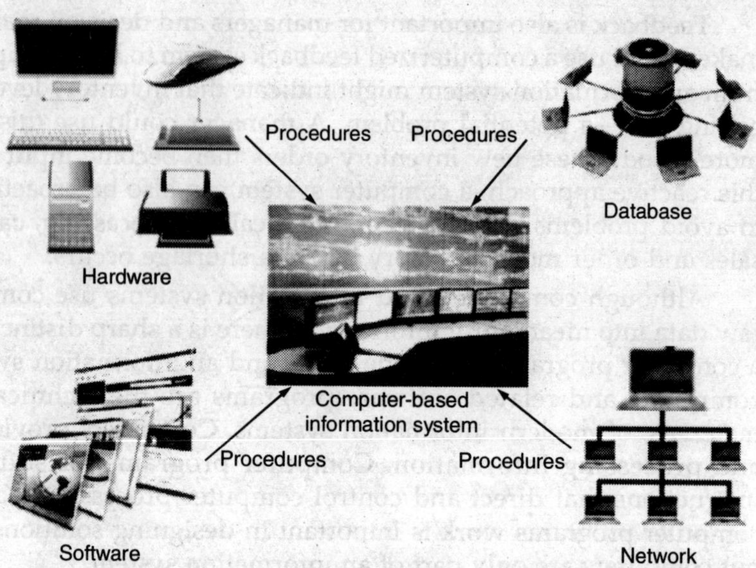

Figure 4.4: It takes technology (hardware, software, databases, and networks) with appropriate procedures to make a CBIS useful for people.

4.3 INFORMATION SYSTEM RESOURCES

Our basic information system model shows that an information system consists of five major resources: people, hardware, software, data and networks as depicted in Figure 4.5.

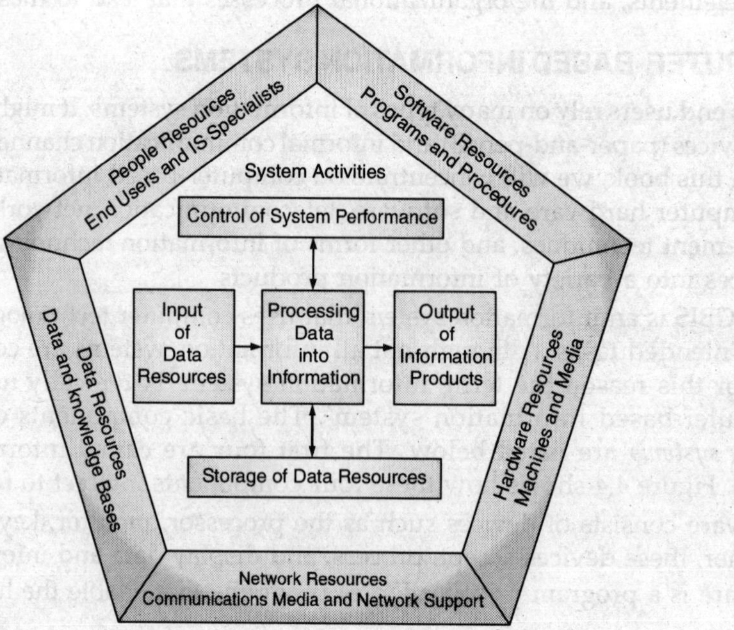

Figure 4.5: Information Systgem Resources

The following are the resources of basic information system model.

1. People Resources

People are required for the operation of all information systems resources. These include end users and Information System (IS) Specialists.

End users (also called users or clients) are people who use an information system or the information it produces. They can be accountants, salespersons, engineers, clerks, customers, or managers. Most of us are information system end users.

IS Specialists are people who develop and operate information system. They include system analysts, programmers, computer operators, and other managerial, technical and clerical IS personnel. Briefly, system analysts design information systems based on the information requirements of the end users, programmers prepare computer programs based on specifications of system analysis, and computer operator operate computer systems.

2. Hardware Resources

The concept of hardware resources includes all physical devices and material used in information processing. Specifically, it includes not only machines such as computers and calculators, but also all the data media, i.e. all tangible objects on which data is recorded from sheets of paper to magnetic disks. Examples of hardware in CBIS are:

Computer Systems consist of central processing units (CPUs) and a variety of interconnected peripheral devices. Examples are large main frame computer systems, midrange computer systems and micro-computer systems.

Computer Peripherals are devices such as keyboard or electronic mouse for input of data and commands, a video screen or printer for output of information, and magnetic or optical disks for storage of data resources.

3. Software Resources

The concept of software resources includes all sets of information processing instructions. this generic concept of software includes not only the sets of operational instructions called programs, which direct and control computer hardware, but also the sets of information processing instructions needed by people, called procedures. Therefore, even information systems that do not use the computers have a software resource component. The following are the examples of software resources:

System Software controls and supports the operations of a computer system, for example, operating system program.

Application Software are programs that direct processing for a particular use of computers by end users. Examples are a sales analysis program, a payroll system, and a word processing program.

Procedures are operating instructions for the people who will use an information system. Examples are instructions for filling out a paper form or using a software package.

4. Data Resources

Data is more than the raw facts and figures for information systems. The concept of data resources has been broadened by manager and the information systems professionals. They realize that data constitutes a valuable organizational resource. Thus, you should view data as data resources that must be managed effectively to benefit all end users in an organization.

Data can take many forms, including traditional alphanumeric data, composed of numbers and alphabetical and other characters that describe business transactions and other events and entities. Text data, constituting of sentences and paragraphs used in written communications, image data, such as graphic shapes and figures, and audio data, the human voice and other sounds, are also important forms of data.

The data resources of information systems are typically organized into:

- ***Data Bases*** that hold processed and organized data.
- ***Knowledge Bases*** that hold knowledge in a variety of forms such as facts and rules of inference about various subjects.

For example, data about sales transaction may be accumulated and stored in a sales database for subsequent processing that yield daily, weekly, and monthly sales analysis reports for management. Knowledge bases are used by information systems called expert systems to give end users advice on specific subjects.

5. Network Resources

Telecommunication networks have become essential to the successful operations of modern organizations and their computer-based information systems. Telecommunication networks consist of computers, end user terminals, communication processors, and other devices interconnected by communication media and controlled by communication software.

The concept of network resources emphasises that communication networks are a fundamental resource component of all information systems. Network resources include:

Communications Media is the physical media through which information (data) flow from source machines to the required destination machine. For example, twisted-wire cable, fibre-optic cable, microwave system and communication satellite system.

Network Support includes all of the people, hardware, software, and data resources that directly support the operations and use of a communication network. Examples include communications processors such as, modems and internetwork processors, and communications control software such as network operating systems, and internet access packages.

4.4 A BUSINESS PERSPECTIVE ON INFORMATION SYSTEMS

Managers and business firms invest in information technology and systems because they provide real economic value to the business. The decision to build or maintain an information system assumes that the returns on this investment will be superior to other investments in buildings, machines, or other assets. These superior returns will be expressed as increases in productivity, as increases in revenues (which will increase the firm's stock market value), or perhaps as superior long-term strategic positioning of the firm in certain markets (which produce superior revenues in the future).

There are also situations in which firms invest in information systems to cope with governmental regulations or other environmental demands. In some cases, firms are required to invest in information systems simply because such investments are required to stay in business. For instance, some small banks may be forced to invest in automatic teller machine (ATM) networks or offer complex banking services requiring large technology investments simply because it is a "cost of doing business." Nevertheless, it is assumed that most information systems investments will be justified by favourable returns.

We can see that from a business perspective, an information system is an important instrument for creating value for the firm. Information systems enable the firm to increase its revenue or decrease its costs by providing information that helps managers make better decisions or that improves the execution of business processes.

For example, the information system for analyzing supermarket checkout data illustrated in Figure 4.6 can increase firm profitability by helping managers make better decisions on which products to stock and promote in retail supermarkets and as a result increase business value.

Every business has an information value chain, illustrated in Figure 4.6, in which raw information is systematically acquired and then transformed through various stages that add value to that information. The value of an information system to a business, as well as the decision to invest in any new information system, is, in large part, determined by the extent to which the system will lead to better management decisions, more efficient business processes, and higher firm profitability.

Although there are other reasons why systems are built, their primary purpose is to contribute to corporate value.

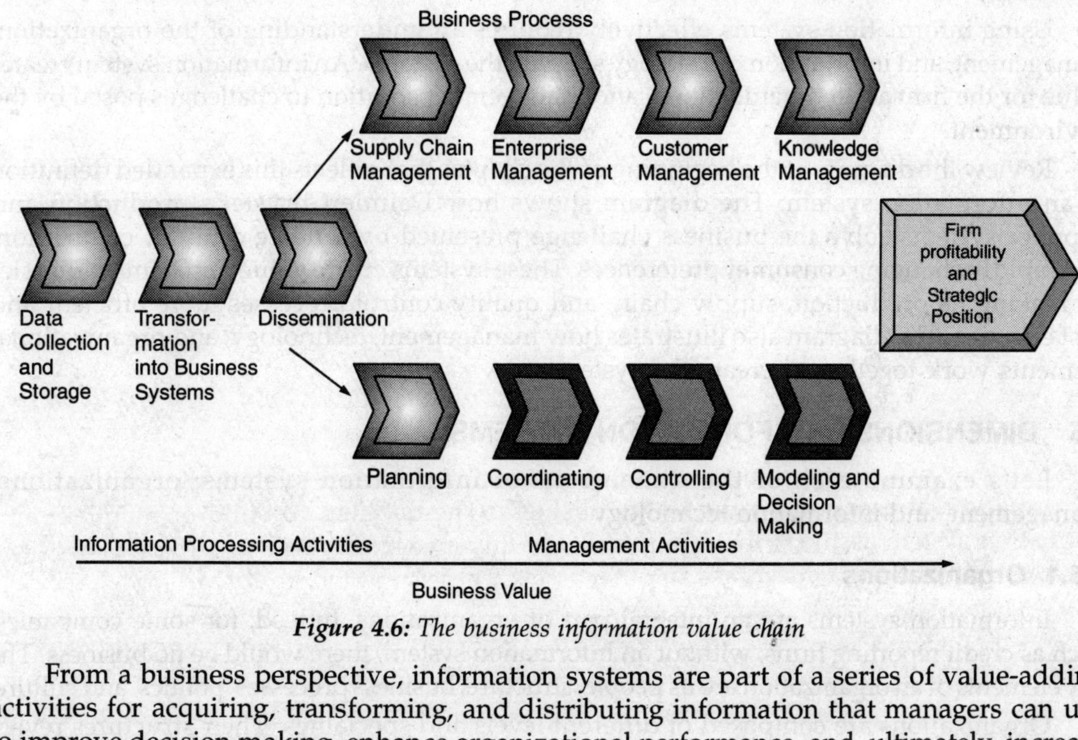

Figure 4.6: The business information value chain

From a business perspective, information systems are part of a series of value-adding activities for acquiring, transforming, and distributing information that managers can use to improve decision making, enhance organizational performance, and, ultimately, increase firm profitability.

The business perspective calls attention to the organizational and managerial nature of information systems. An information system represents an organizational and management solution, based on information technology, to a challenge posed by the environment. Every chapter in this book begins with short case study that illustrates this concept. A diagram at the beginning of each chapter illustrates the relationship between a changing business environment and resulting management and organizational decisions to use IT as a solution to challenges generated by the business environment.

To fully understand information systems, a manager must understand the broader organization, management, and information technology dimensions of systems (see Figure 4.7) and their power to provide solutions to challenges and problems in the business environment. We refer to this broader understanding of information systems, which encompasses an understanding of the management and organizational dimensions of systems as well as the technical dimensions of systems, as information systems literacy. Information systems literacy includes a behavioural as well as a technical approach to studying information systems. Computer literacy, in contrast, focuses primarily on knowledge of information technology.

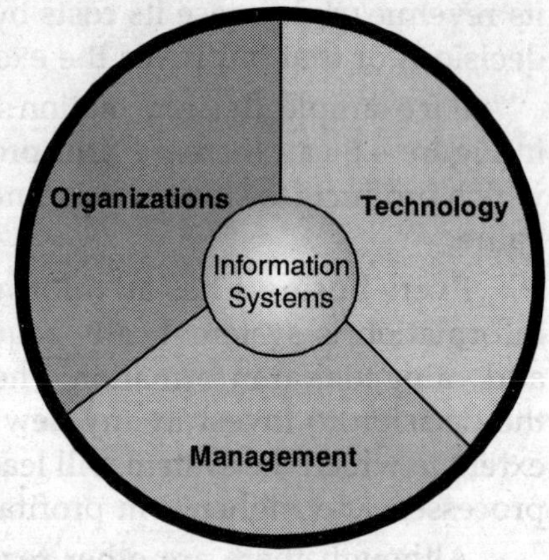

Figure 4.7: Information systems are more than computers

Using information systems effectively requires an understanding of the organization, management, and information technology shaping the systems. An information system creates value for the firm as an organizational and management solution to challenges posed by the environment.

Review the diagram at the beginning of the chapter that reflects this expanded definition of an information system. The diagram shows how DaimlerChrysler's production and supplier systems solve the business challenge presented by a fierce array of competitors and rapidly changing consumer preferences. These systems create value for DaimlerChrysler by making its production, supply chain, and quality control processes more efficient and cost effective. The diagram also illustrates how management, technology, and organizational elements work together to create the systems.

4.5 DIMENSIONS OF INFORMATION SYSTEMS

Let's examine each of the dimensions of information systems: organizations, management, and information technology.

4.5.1 Organizations

Information systems are an integral part of organizations. Indeed, for some companies, such as credit reporting firms, without an information system, there would be no business. The key elements of an organization are its people, structure, business processes, politics, and culture.

Organizations are composed of different levels and specialties. Their structures reveal a clear-cut division of labour. Experts are employed and trained for different functions. The major business functions, or specialized tasks performed by business organizations, consist of sales and marketing, manufacturing and production, finance and accounting, and human resources (see Table 4.1).

Table 4.1: Major Business Functions

Function	Purpose
Sales and Marketing	Selling the organization's products and services
Manufacturing and Production	Producing products and services
Finance and Accounting	Managing the organization's financial assets and maintaining the organization's financial records
Human Resources	Attracting, developing, and maintaining the organization's labour force; maintaining employee records

An organization coordinates work through a structured hierarchy and through its business processes. The hierarchy arranges people in a pyramid structure of rising authority and responsibility. The upper levels of the hierarchy consist of managerial, professional, and technical employees, whereas the lower levels consist of operational personnel.

Most organizations' business processes include formal rules that have been developed over a long time for accomplishing tasks. These rules guide employees in a variety of procedures, from writing an invoice to responding to customer complaints. Some of these procedures have been formalized and written down, but others are informal work practices, such as a requirement to return telephone calls from co-workers or customers, that are not formally documented. Many business processes are incorporated into information systems, such as how to pay a supplier or how to correct an erroneous bill.

Organizations require many different kinds of skills and people. In addition to managers, knowledge workers (such as engineers, architects, or scientists) design products or services and create new knowledge, and data workers (such as secretaries, bookkeepers, or clerks) process the organization's paperwork. Production or service workers (such as machinists, assemblers, or packers) actually produce the organization's products or services.

Each organization has a unique culture, or fundamental set of assumptions, values, and ways of doing things, that has been accepted by most of its members. Parts of an organization's culture can always be found embedded in its information systems. Different levels and specialties in an organization create different interests and points of view. These views often conflict. Conflict is the basis for organizational politics. Information systems come out of this cauldron of differing perspectives, conflicts, compromises, and agreements that are a natural part of all organizations.

4.5.2 Management

Management's job is to make sense out of the many situations faced by organizations, make decisions, and formulate action plans to solve organizational problems.

Managers perceive business challenges in the environment; they set the organizational strategy for responding to those challenges; and they allocate the human and financial resources to coordinate the work and achieve success. Throughout, they must exercise responsible leadership. The business information systems described in this book reflect the hopes, dreams, and realities of real-world managers.

But managers must do more than manage what already exists. They must also create new products and services and even re-create the organization from time to time. A substantial part of management responsibility is creative work driven by new knowledge and information. Information technology can play a powerful role in redirecting and redesigning the organization.

It is important to note that managerial roles and decisions vary at different levels of the organization. Senior managers make long-range strategic decisions about what products and services to produce. Middle managers carry out the programs and plans of senior management. Operational managers are responsible for monitoring the firm's daily activities. All levels of management are expected to be creative, to develop novel solutions to a broad range of problems. Each level of management has different information needs and information system requirements.

4.5.3 Information Technology

Information technology is one of many tools managers use to cope with change. Computer hardware is the physical equipment used for input, processing, and output activities in an information system. It consists of the following: the computer processing unit; various input, output, and storage devices; and physical media to link these devices together.

Computer software consists of the detailed, pre-programmed instructions that control and coordinate the computer hardware components in an information system.

Storage technology includes both the physical media for storing data, such as magnetic disk, optical disc, or tape, and the software governing the organization of data on these physical media.

Communications technology, consisting of both physical devices and software, links the various pieces of hardware and transfers data from one physical location to another. Computers and communications equipment can be connected in networks for sharing voice, data, images, sound, or even video. A network links two or more computers to share data or resources such as a printer.

The world's largest and most widely used network is the Internet. The Internet is an international network of networks that are both commercial and publicly owned. The Internet connects hundreds of thousands of different networks from more than 200 countries around the world. More than 900 million people working in science, education, government, and business use the Internet to exchange information or business transactions with other organizations around the globe.

The Internet is extremely elastic. If networks are added or removed, or if failures occur in parts of the system, the rest of the Internet continues to operate. Through special communication and technology standards, any computer can communicate with virtually any other computer linked to the Internet using ordinary telephone lines.

The Internet has created a new "universal" technology platform on which to build all sorts of new products, services, strategies, and business models. This same technology platform has internal uses, providing the connectivity to link different systems and networks within the firm. Internal corporate networks based on Internet technology are called intranets. Private intranets extended to authorized users outside the organization are called extranets, and firms use such networks to coordinate their activities with other firms for making purchases, collaborating on design, and other inter-organizational work.

Because it offers so many new possibilities for doing business, the Internet service known as the World Wide Web is of special interest to organizations and managers. The World Wide Web is a system with universally accepted standards for storing, retrieving, formatting, and displaying information in a networked environment. Information is stored and displayed as electronic "pages" that can contain text, graphics, animations, sound, and video. These Web pages can be linked electronically to other Web pages, regardless of where they are located, and viewed by any type of computer. By clicking on highlighted words or buttons on a Web page, you can link to related pages to find additional information, software programs, or still more links to other points on the Web. The Web can serve as the foundation for new kinds of information systems.

All of the Web pages maintained by an organization or individual are called a Web site. Businesses have created Web sites with stylish typography, colourful graphics, push-button interactivity, and sound and video to disseminate product information widely, to "broadcast" advertising and messages to customers, to collect electronic orders and customer data, and, increasingly, to coordinate far-flung sales forces and organizations on a global scale.

4.6 NEED FOR INFORMATION SYSTEMS

Today, few if any medium- or large-sized companies can survive without computers and information systems. This section identifies some reasons why organizations need information systems.

4.6.1 Meeting Global Challenges

The world has become a small place; the competition faced by a business is no longer limited by national boundaries. Companies therefore strive to produce high-quality goods and services that can compete in world markets. Though globalization can bring many benefits, such as increased profits and market share, the challenges of running a global company are also significant. If the company is to be successful, it must effectively coordinate and control products, people, and procedures around the world. This requires a great deal of timely, reliable and accurate information.

4.6.2 Capturing Opportunities in the Marketplace

Successful companies are those that can identify and take advantage of opportunities in the marketplace and can continue to do so over the long run. Information systems that allow a company to identify strategic growth opportunities in the marketplace are known as strategic information systems (SIS). These systems have catapulted some companies to the top of their industries, leaving their company far behind.

4.6.3 Supporting Corporate Strategy

Companies use three basic strategies to compete successfully in marketplace:

- They stay ahead of the competition by providing goods and services at a lower price than their competitors.

- They produce highly specialised or unique goods and services that allow them to stand apart from their competitors.
- They find a market niche and focus on meeting the needs of this special group.

These three strategies are not mutually exclusive; a company can use them in combination. Regardless of the strategy, a company uses to stay ahead of the competition, information systems and technologies play an important role in the implementation of business strategies.

4.6.4 Linking Department Whose Functions are Different

Some years ago, departments or units with different functions in a business, such as accounting, finance, marketing, manufacturing, and human resources, were viewed as separate business entities. Often the efforts of these departments were not coordinated; this resulted in inefficiencies and lost opportunities for the company. Today, most companies treat these apparently different departments as parts of a cohesive unit whose members must work together to achieve the overall goals of the business. This is not always an easy task, because the goals of some units may conflict with those of others. However, information systems can bring different functioning units together by coordinating their tasks and functions.

4.6.5 Enhancing Worker Productivity

The pervasiveness of computers and information systems in business has made them essential tools in many tasks, such as managing the shop floor, evaluating the performance of employees, tracking customers, reordering items, and generating the payroll. Computers and information systems can therefore have significant impact on a company's bottom line.

4.6.6 Increasing the Quality of Goods and Services

Quality is a leading concern for top and middle managers around the world, regardless of the products or services that their companies produce. Total quality management (TQM) is one of the most popular and most widely used approaches for enhancing the quality in an organization. Quality-oriented efforts and decisions are highly information sensitive, so computers help a company achieve its quality goals by providing the right information to the right people at the right time. The enterprise-wide effort is required to improve quality; this often involves coordinating the tasks and decisions of many departments and units, sometimes located all over the world.

4.7 CATEGORIES OF INFORMATION SYSTEMS

Because there are different interests, specialties, and levels in an organization, there are different kinds of systems. No single system can provide all the information an organization needs. Figure 4.8 illustrates one way to depict the kinds of systems found in an organization. In the illustration, the organization is divided into strategic, management, knowledge and operational levels and then is further divided into functional areas, such as sales and marketing, manufacturing and production, finance and accounting, and human resources. Systems are built to serve these different organizational interests.

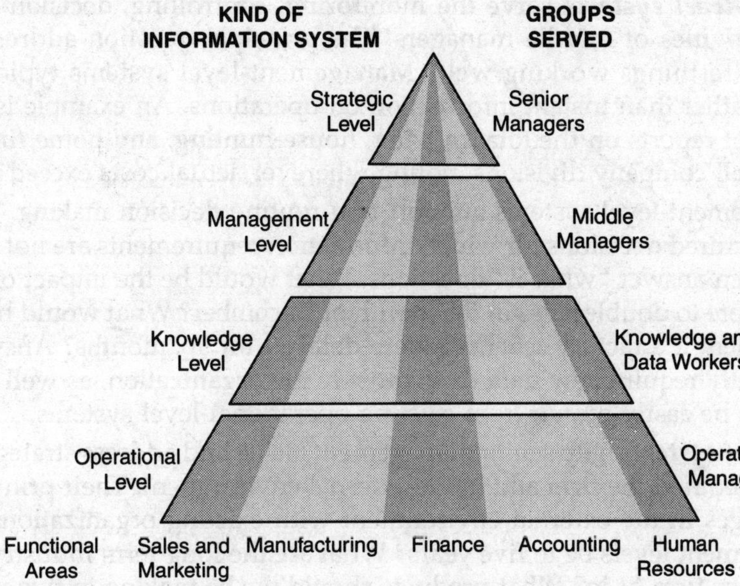

Figure 4.8: *Types of information systems*

Organizations can be divided into strategic, management, knowledge and operational levels and into four major functional areas: sales and marketing, manufacturing and production, finance and accounting, and human resources. Information systems serve each of these levels and functions.

4.8 DIFFERENT KINDS OF SYSTEMS

Four main categories of information systems serve different organizational levels: operational-level systems, knowledge-level systems, management-level systems, and strategic-level systems.

Operational-level systems support operational managers by keeping track of the elementary activities and transactions of the organization, such as sales, receipts, cash deposits, payroll, credit decisions, and the flow of materials in a factory. The principal purpose of systems at this level is to answer routine questions and to track the flow of transactions through the organization. How many parts are in inventory? What happened to Mr. Williams's payment? To answer these kinds of questions, information generally must be easily available, current, and accurate. Examples of operational-level systems include a system to record bank deposits from automatic teller machines or one that tracks the number of hours worked each day by employees on a factory floor.

Knowledge-level systems support organization's knowledge and data workers. The purpose of the knowledge-level systems is to help the business-firm integrate new knowledge into the business and to help the organization control the flow of paperwork. Knowledge-level systems, especially in the form of workstations and office systems are among the faster growing applications in business today.

Management-level systems serve the monitoring, controlling, decision-making, and administrative activities of middle managers. The principal question addressed by such systems is this: Are things working well? Management-level systems typically provide periodic reports rather than instant information on operations. An example is a relocation control system that reports on the total moving, house-hunting, and home financing costs for employees in all company divisions, noting wherever actual costs exceed budgets.

Some management-level systems support non-routine decision making. They tend to focus on less-structured decisions for which information requirements are not always clear. These systems often answer "what-if" questions: What would be the impact on production schedules if we were to double sales in the month of December? What would happen to our return on investment if a factory schedule were delayed for six months? Answers to these questions frequently require new data from outside the organization, as well as data from inside that cannot be easily drawn from existing operational-level systems.

Strategic-level systems help senior management tackle and address strategic issues and long-term trends, both in the firm and in the external environment. Their principal concern is matching changes in the external environment with existing organizational capability. What will employment levels be in five years? What are the long-term industry cost trends, and where does our firm fit in? What products should we be making in five years?

Information systems also serve the major business functions, such as sales and marketing, manufacturing and production, finance and accounting, and human resources. A typical organization has operational-, management-, and strategic-level systems for each functional area. For example, the sales function generally has a sales system on the operational level to record daily sales figures and to process orders. A management-level system tracks monthly sales figures by sales territory and reports on territories where sales exceed or fall below anticipated levels. A system to forecast sales trends over a five-year period serves the strategic level. We first describe the specific categories of systems serving each organizational level and their value to the organization. Then we show how organizations use these systems for each major business function.

4.9 SIX MAJOR TYPES OF SYSTEMS

Figure 4.9 shows the specific types of information systems that correspond to each organizational level. The organization has executive support systems (ESS) at the strategic level; management information systems (MIS) and decision-support systems (DSS) at the management level; knowledge work systems (KWS) and Office Automation Systems (OAS) at the knowledge level; and transaction processing systems (TPS) at the operational level. Systems at each level in turn are specialized to serve each of the major functional areas. Thus, the typical systems found in organizations are designed to assist workers or managers at each level and in the functions of sales and marketing, manufacturing and production, finance and accounting, and human resources.

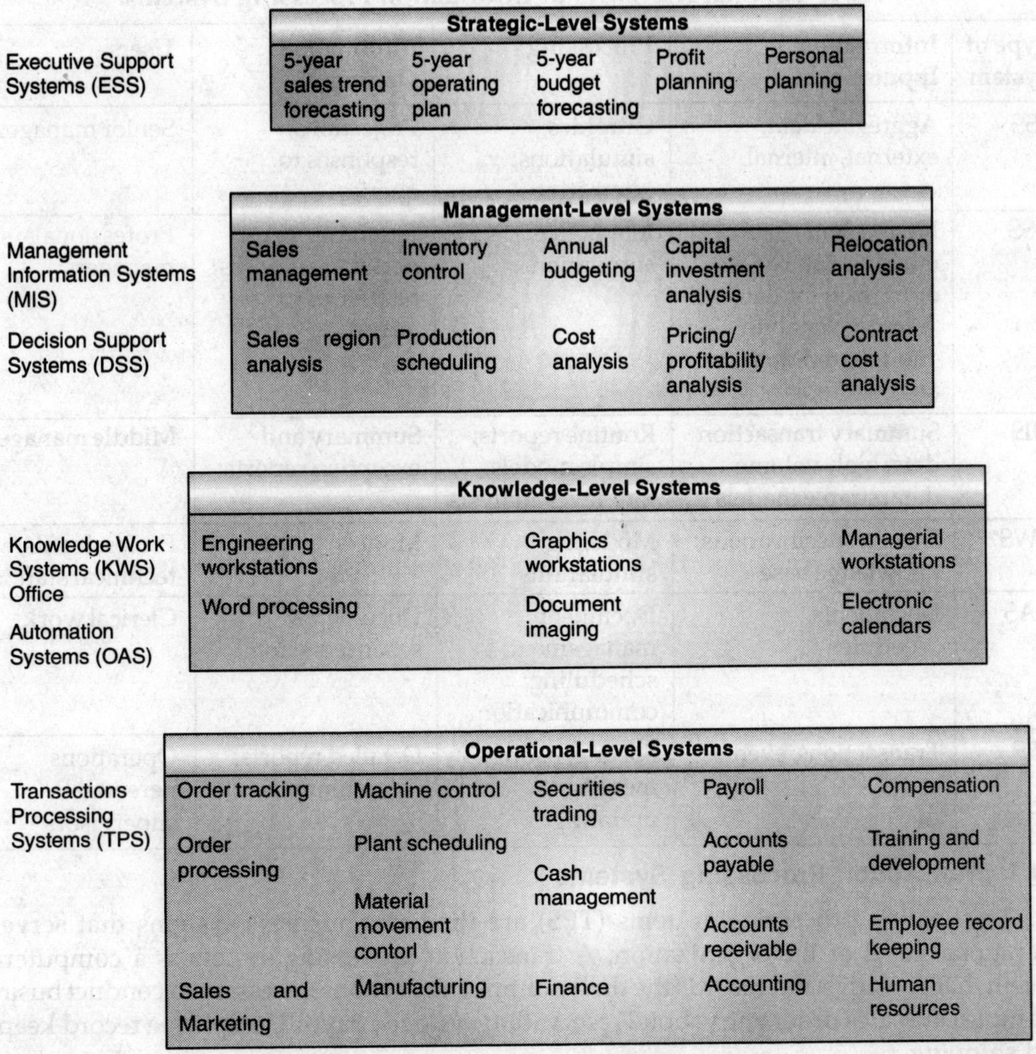

***Figure 4.9:** The six major types of information systems*

This figure provides examples of TPS, OAS, KWS, DSS, MIS, and ESS, showing the level of the organization and business function that each supports.

Table 4.2 summarizes the features of the six types of information systems. It should be noted that each of the different systems may have components that are used by organizational levels and groups other than its main constituencies. A secretary may find information on an MIS, or a middle manager may need to extract data from a TPS.

Table 4.2: Characteristics of Information Processing Systems

Type of System	Information Inputs	Processing	Information Outputs	Users
ESS	Aggregate data; external, internal	Graphics; simulations; interactive	Projections; responses to queries	Senior managers
DSS	Low-volume data or massive databases optimized for data analysis; analytic models and data analysis tools	Interactive; simulations;	Special reports; decision analyses; responses to queries	Professionals; staff managers
MIS	Summary transaction data; high-volume data; simple models	Routine reports; simple models; low-level analysis	Summary and exception reports	Middle managers
KWS	Design specifications; knowledge base	Modeling; simulations	Models; graphs	Professionals; technical staff
OAS	Documents; schedules	Document management; scheduling; communication	Documents; schedulers; mail	Clerical work
TPS	Transactions; events	Sorting; listing; merging; updating	Detailed reports; lists; summaries	Operations personnel; supervisors

4.9.1 Transaction Processing Systems

Transaction processing systems (TPS) are the basic business systems that serve the operational level of the organization. A transaction processing system is a computerized system that performs and records the daily routine transactions necessary to conduct business. Examples are sales order entry, hotel reservation systems, payroll, employee record keeping, and shipping.

At the operational level, tasks, resources, and goals are predefined and highly structured. The decision to grant credit to a customer, for instance, is made by a lower-level supervisor according to predefined criteria. All that must be determined is whether the customer meets the criteria.

Figure 4.10 depicts a payroll TPS, which is a typical accounting transaction processing system found in most firms. A payroll system keeps track of the money paid to employees. The master file is composed of discrete pieces of information (such as a name, address, or employee number) called data elements. Data are keyed into the system, updating the data elements. The elements on the master file are combined in different ways to make up reports of interest to management and government agencies and to send paychecks to employees. These TPS can generate other report combinations of existing data elements.

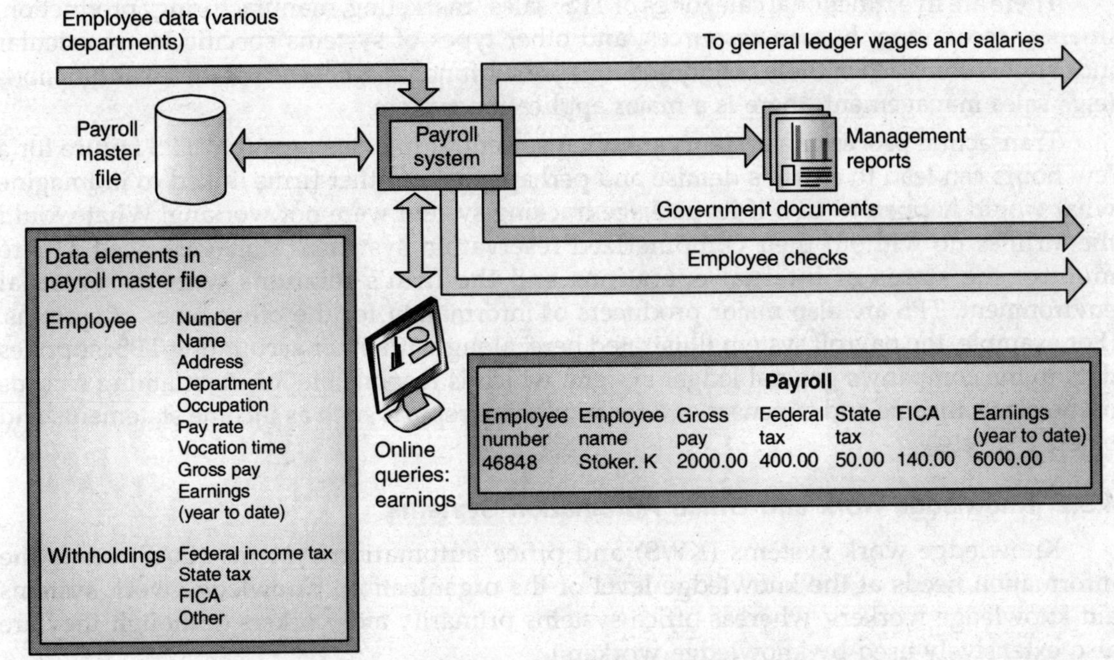

***Figure 4.10:** A symbolic representation for a payroll TPS*

A payroll system is a typical accounting TPS that processes transactions such as employee time cards and changes in employee salaries and deductions. It keeps track of money paid to employees, withholding tax, and paychecks.

Other typical TPS applications are identified in Figure 4.11. The figure shows that there are five functional categories of TPS: sales/marketing, manufacturing/production, finance/accounting, human resources, and other types of TPS that are unique to a particular industry.

Types of TPS Systems					
	Sales/ marketing systems	Manufacturing/ production systems	Finance/ accounting systems	Human resources systems	Other types (e.g., university)
Major functions of systems	Customer service Sales management Promotion tracking Price changes Dealer communications	Scheduling Purchasing Shipping/receiving Operations	General ledger Billing Cost accounting	Personnel records Benefits Compensation Labor relations Training	Admissions Grade records Course records Alumni records
Major application systems	Sales order information systems Sales commission systems Sales support system	Machine control systems Purchase order systems Quality control systems	General ledger Payroll Accounts receivable/payable Funds management systems	Employee records Benefits systems Employee skills inventory	Registration system Student transcript systems Curriculum class control systems Alumni benefactor systems

***Figure 4.11:** Typical applications of TPS*

There are five functional categories of TPS: sales/marketing, manufacturing/production, finance/accounting, human resources, and other types of systems specific to a particular industry. Within each of these major functions are subfunctions. For each of these subfunctions (e.g., sales management) there is a major application system.

Transaction processing systems are often so central to a business that TPS failure for a few hours can lead to a firm's demise and perhaps that of other firms linked to it. Imagine what would happen to UPS if its package tracking system were not working! What would the airlines do without their computerized reservation systems? Managers need TPS to monitor the status of internal operations and the firm's relations with the external environment. TPS are also major producers of information for the other types of systems. (For example, the payroll system illustrated here, along with other accounting TPS, supplies data to the company's general ledger system, which is responsible for maintaining records of the firm's income and expenses and for producing reports such as income statements and balance sheets.)

4.9.2 Knowledge Work and Office Automation Systems

Knowledge work systems (KWS) and office automation systems (OAS) serve the information needs at the knowledge level of the organization. Knowledge work systems aid knowledge workers, whereas office systems primarily aid workers (although they are also extensively used by knowledge workers).

Knowledge workers are people who hold formal university degrees and who are often members of recognized professions such as engineers, doctors, lawyers and scientists. Their job consists primarily of creating new information and knowledge. KWS, such as scientific or engineering design workstations, promote the creation of new knowledge and ensure that new knowledge and technical expertise are properly integrated into the business. *Data workers* typically have less formal advanced educational degrees and tend to process rather than create information. They consist primarily of secretaries, bookkeepers, filing clerks, or managers, whose jobs are principally to use, manipulate, or disseminate information. Office automation systems are information technology applications designed to increase data workers' productivity by supporting the coordinating and communication activities of the typical office. OAS coordinate diverse information workers, geographical units, and functional areas: The systems communicate with customers, suppliers, and other organizations outside the firm and serve as clearinghouses for information and knowledge flows.

Typical office systems handle and manage documents through word processing, desktop publishing, document imaging, and digital filing; scheduling through electronic calendars; and communication through electronic mail, voice mail, and video conferencing. Word processing refers to the software and hardware technology that creates, edits, formats, stores, and prints documents. Word processing systems represent the single most common application of information technology to office work, in part because producing documents is what offices are all about. Desktop publishing produces professional publishing-quality documents by combining output from word processing software with design elements, graphics, and special layout features. Companies are now starting to publish documents in the form of Web pages for easier access and distribution.

Document imaging systems are another widely used knowledge application. Document imaging systems convert paper documents and images into digital form so that they can be stored and accessed by the computer.

4.9.3 Management Information Systems

Management information systems are defined as the study of information systems in business and management. The term management information systems (MIS) also designates a specific category of information systems serving management-level functions. Management information systems (MIS) serve the management level of the organization, providing managers with reports and often online access to the organization's current performance and historical records. Typically, MIS are oriented almost exclusively to internal, not environmental or external, events. MIS primarily serve the functions of planning, controlling, and decision making at the management level. Generally, they depend on underlying transaction processing systems for their data.

MIS summarize and report on the company's basic operations. The basic transaction data from TPS are compressed and are usually presented in long reports that are produced on a regular schedule. Figure 4.12 shows how a typical MIS transforms transaction level data from inventory, production, and accounting into MIS files that are used to provide managers with reports. Figure 4.13 shows a sample report from this system.

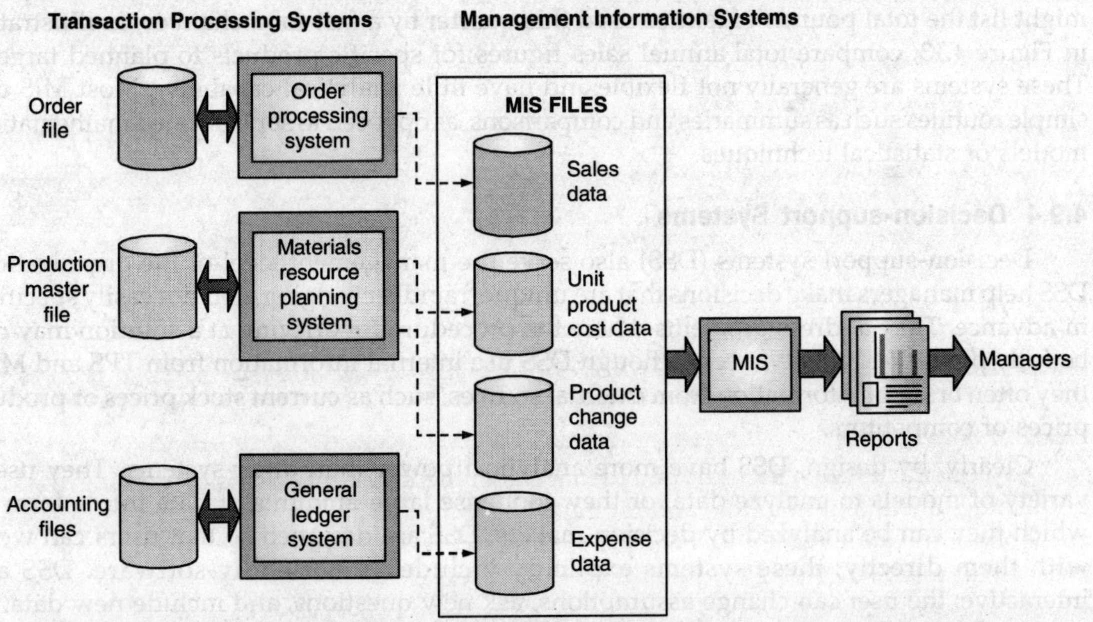

Figure 4.12: How management information systems obtain their data from the organization's TPS

In the system illustrated by this diagram, three TPS supply summarized transaction data to the MIS reporting system at the end of the time period. Managers gain access to the organizational data through the MIS, which provides them with the appropriate reports.

Consolidated Consumer Products Corporation Sales by Product and Sales Region : 2005

PRODUCT CODE	PRODUCT DESCRIPTION	SALES REGION	ACTUAL SALES	PLANNED	ACTUAL versus PLANNED
4469	Carpet Cleaner	Northeast	4,066,700	4,800,000	0.85
		South	3,778,112	3,750,000	1.01
		Midwest	4,867,001	4,600,000	1.06
		West	4,003,440	4,400,000	0.91
	TOTAL		16,715,253	17,550,000	0.95
5674	Room Freshner	Northeast	3,676,700	3,900,000	0.94
		South	5,608,112	4,700,000	1.19
		Midwest	4,711,001	4,200,000	1.12
		West	4,563,440	4,900,000	0.93
	TOTAL		18,559,253	17,700,000	1.05

***Figure 4.13:** A sample MIS report*

This report showing summarized annual sales data was produced by the MIS in Figure 4.12. MIS usually serve managers primarily interested in weekly, monthly, and yearly results, although some MIS enable managers to drill down to see daily or hourly data if required. MIS generally provide answers to routine questions that have been specified in advance and have a predefined procedure for answering them. For instance, MIS reports might list the total pounds of lettuce used this quarter by a fast-food chain or, as illustrated in Figure 4.13, compare total annual sales figures for specific products to planned targets. These systems are generally not flexible and have little analytical capability. Most MIS use simple routines such as summaries and comparisons, as opposed to sophisticated mathematical models or statistical techniques.

4.9.4 Decision-support Systems

Decision-support systems (DSS) also serve the management level of the organization. DSS help managers make decisions that are unique, rapidly changing, and not easily specified in advance. They address problems where the procedure for arriving at a solution may not be fully predefined in advance. Although DSS use internal information from TPS and MIS, they often bring in information from external sources, such as current stock prices or product prices of competitors.

Clearly, by design, DSS have more analytical power than other systems. They use a variety of models to analyze data, or they condense large amounts of data into a form in which they can be analyzed by decision makers. DSS are designed so that users can work with them directly; these systems explicitly include user-friendly software. DSS are interactive; the user can change assumptions, ask new questions, and include new data.

An interesting, small, but powerful DSS is the voyage-estimating system of a subsidiary of a large American metals company that exists primarily to carry bulk cargoes of coal, oil, ores, and finished products for its parent company. The firm owns some vessels, charters others, and bids for shipping contracts in the open market to carry general cargo. A voyage-estimating system calculates financial and technical voyage details. Financial calculations include ship/time costs (fuel, labor, capital), freight rates for various types of cargo, and port expenses. Technical details include a myriad of factors, such as ship cargo capacity, speed, port distances, fuel and water consumption, and loading patterns (location of cargo for different ports).

The system can answer questions such as the following: Given a customer delivery schedule and an offered freight rate, which vessel should be assigned at what rate to maximize profits? What is the optimal speed at which a particular vessel can optimize its profit and still meet its delivery schedule? What is the optimal loading pattern for a ship bound for the U.S. West Coast from Malaysia? Figure 4.14 illustrates the DSS built for this company. The system operates on a powerful desktop personal computer, providing a system of menus that makes it easy for users to enter data or obtain information.

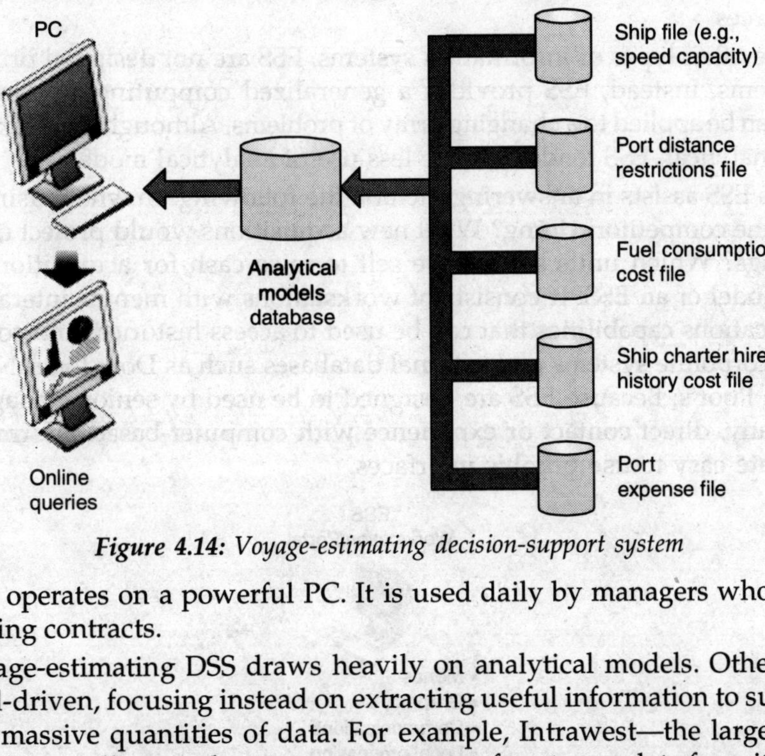

Figure 4.14: *Voyage-estimating decision-support system*

This DSS operates on a powerful PC. It is used daily by managers who must develop bids on shipping contracts.

This voyage-estimating DSS draws heavily on analytical models. Other types of DSS are less model-driven, focusing instead on extracting useful information to support decision making from massive quantities of data. For example, Intrawest—the largest ski operator in North America—collects and stores vast amounts of customer data from its Web site, call center, lodging reservations, ski schools, and ski equipment rental stores. It uses special software to analyze these data to determine the value, revenue potential, and loyalty of each customer so managers can make better decisions on how to target their marketing programs. The system segments customers into seven categories based on needs, attitudes, and behaviours, ranging from "passionate experts" to "value-minded family vacationers." The company then e-mails video clips that would appeal to each segment to encourage more visits to its resorts.

Sometimes you'll hear DSS systems referred to as business intelligence systems because they focus on helping users make better business decisions.

4.9.5 Executive Support Systems

Senior managers use executive support systems (ESS) to help them make decisions. ESS serves the strategic level of the organization. They address non-routine decisions requiring judgment, evaluation, and insight because there is no agreed-on procedure for arriving at a solution.

ESSs are designed to incorporate data about external events, such as new tax laws or competitors, but they also draw summarized information from internal MIS and DSS. They filter, compress, and track critical data, displaying the data of greatest importance to senior managers.

ESS employs the most advanced graphics software and can present graphs and data from many sources. Often the information is delivered to senior executives through a portal, which uses a Web interface to present integrated personalized business content from a variety of sources.

Unlike the other types of information systems, ESS are not designed primarily to solve specific problems. Instead, ESS provides a generalized computing and communications capacity that can be applied to a changing array of problems. Although many DSS are designed to be highly analytical, ESS tends to make less use of analytical models.

Questions ESS assists in answering include the following: In what business should we be? What are the competitors doing? What new acquisitions would protect us from cyclical business swings? Which units should we sell to raise cash for acquisitions? Figure 4.15 illustrates a model of an ESS. It consists of workstations with menus, interactive graphics, and communications capabilities that can be used to access historical and competitive data from internal corporate systems and external databases such as Dow Jones News/Retrieval or Standard & Poor's. Because ESS are designed to be used by senior managers who often have little, if any, direct contact or experience with computer-based information systems, they incorporate easy-to-use graphic interfaces.

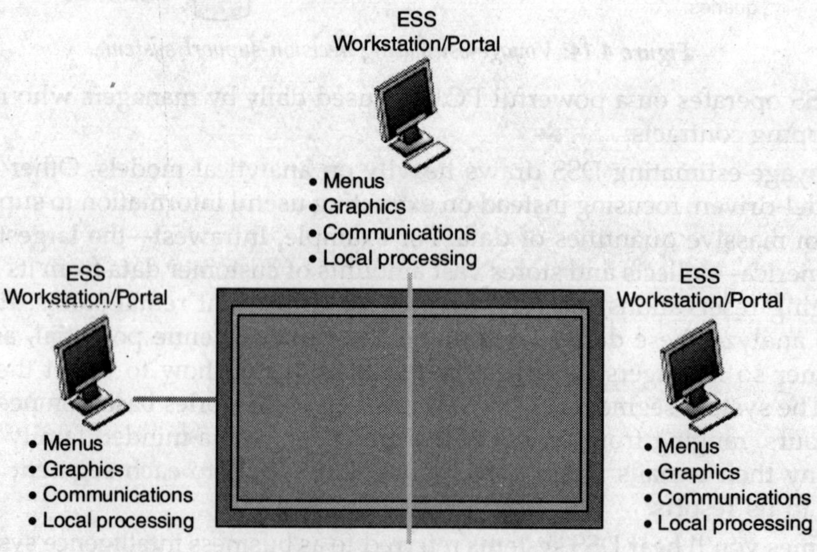

Figure 4.15: Model of a typical executive support system

This system pools data from diverse internal and external sources and makes them available to executives in an easy-to-use form.

4.9.6 Relationship of Systems to One Another

Figure 4.16 illustrates how the systems serving different levels in the organization are related to one another. TPS are typically a major source of data for other systems, whereas ESS is primarily a recipient of data from lower-level systems. The other types of systems may exchange data with each other as well. Data may also be exchanged among systems serving different functional areas. For example, an order captured by a sales system may be transmitted to a manufacturing system as a transaction for producing or delivering the product specified in the order or to a MIS for financial reporting.

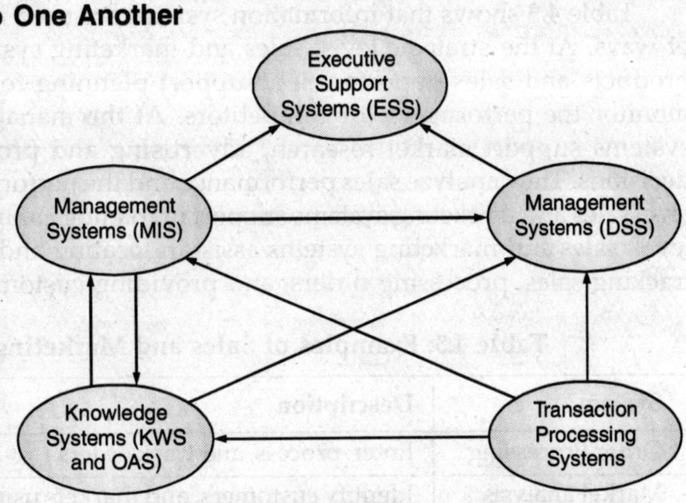

Figure 4.16: Interrelationships among systems

The various types of systems in the organization have interdependencies. TPS are major producers of information that is required by the other systems, which, in turn, produce information for other systems. These different types of systems have been loosely coupled in most organizations.

It is definitely advantageous to integrate these systems so that information can flow easily between different parts of the organization and provide management with an enterprise-wide view of how the organization is performing as a whole. But integration costs money, and integrating many different systems is extremely time consuming and complex. This is a major challenge for large organizations, which are typically saddled with hundreds, even thousands of different applications serving different levels and business functions. Each organization must weigh its needs for integrating systems against the difficulties of mounting a large-scale systems integration effort.

4.10 SYSTEMS FROM A FUNCTIONAL PERSPECTIVE

Information systems can be classified by the specific organizational function they serve as well as by organizational level. We now describe typical information systems that support each of the major business functions and provide examples of functional applications for each organizational level.

4.10.1 Sales and Marketing Systems

The sales and marketing function is responsible for selling the organization's products or services. Marketing is concerned with identifying the customers for the firm's products or services, determining what customers need or want, planning and developing products and services to meet their needs, and advertising and promoting these products and services. Sales are concerned with contacting customers, selling the products and services, taking orders, and following up on sales. Sales and marketing information systems support these activities.

Table 4.3 shows that information systems are used in sales and marketing in a number of ways. At the strategic level, sales and marketing systems monitor trends affecting new products and sales opportunities, support planning for new products and services, and monitor the performance of competitors. At the management level, sales and marketing systems support market research, advertising and promotional campaigns, and pricing decisions. They analyze sales performance and the performance of the sales staff. Knowledge level sales and marketing systems support marketing analysis workstations. At the operational level, sales and marketing systems assist in locating and contacting prospective customers, tracking sales, processing orders, and providing customer service support.

Table 4.3: Examples of Sales and Marketing Information Systems

System	Description	Organizational Level
Order Processing	Enter, process, and track orders	Operational
Market analysis	Identify customers, and markets using data on demographics, markets, consumer behaviour and trends	Knowledge
Pricing Analysis	Determine prices for products and services	Management
Sales trend forecasting	Prepare 5-year sales forecasts	Strategic

Review Figure 4.13. It shows the output of a typical sales information system at the management level. The system consolidates data about each item sold (such as the product code, product description, and amount sold) for further management analysis. Company managers examine these sales data to monitor sales activity and buying trends.

4.10.2 Manufacturing and Production Systems

The manufacturing and production function is responsible for actually producing the firm's goods and services. Manufacturing and production systems deal with the planning, development, and maintenance of production facilities; the establishment of production goals; the acquisition, storage, and availability of production materials; and the scheduling of equipment, facilities, materials, and labour required to fashion finished products. Manufacturing and production information systems support these activities.

Information systems can guide the actions of machines and equipment to help pharmaceutical and other types of firms monitor and control the manufacturing process.

Table 4.4 shows some typical manufacturing and production information systems arranged by organizational level. Strategic-level manufacturing systems deal with the firm's long-term manufacturing goals, such as where to locate new plants or whether to invest in new manufacturing technology. At the management level, manufacturing and production systems analyze and monitor manufacturing and production costs and resources. Knowledge manufacturing and production systems create and distribute design knowledge or expertise to drive the production process, and operational manufacturing and production systems deal with the status of production tasks.

Table 4.4: Examples of Manufacturing and Production Information Systems

System	Description	Organizational Level
Machine control	Control the actions of machines and equipment	Operational
Computer-aided design (CAD)	Design new products using the computer	Knowledge
Production planning	Decide when and how many products should be produced	Management
Facilities location	Decide where to locate new production facilities	Strategic

Most manufacturing and production systems use some sort of inventory system, as illustrated in Figure 4.17. Data about each item in inventory, such as the number of units depleted because of a shipment or purchase or the number of units replenished by reordering or returns, are either scanned or keyed into the system. The inventory master file contains basic data about each item, including the unique identification code for each item, a description of the item, the number of units on hand, the number of units on order, and the reorder point (the number of units in inventory that triggers a decision to reorder to prevent a stockout). Companies can estimate the number of items to reorder, or they can use a formula for calculating the least expensive quantity to reorder called the economic order quantity. The system produces reports that give information about such things as the number of each item available in inventory, the number of units of each item to reorder, or items in inventory that must be replenished.

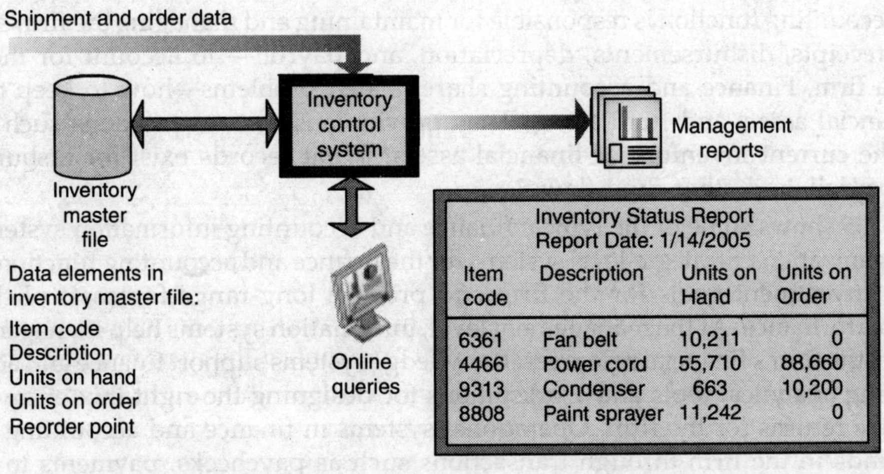

Figure 4.17: Overview of an inventory system

This system provides information about the number of items available in inventory to support manufacturing and production activities.

Product life cycle management (PLM) systems are one type of manufacturing and production system that has become increasingly valuable in the automotive, aerospace, and consumer products industries. PLM systems are based on a data repository that organizes every piece of information that goes into making a particular product, such as formula cards, packaging information, shipping specifications, and patent data. Once all these data are available, companies can select and combine the data they need to serve specific functions. For, example, designers and engineers can use the data to determine which parts are needed for a new design, whereas retailers can use them to determine shelf height and how materials should be stored in warehouses.

For many years, engineering-intensive industries have used computer-aided design (CAD) systems to automate the modeling and design of their products. The software enables users to create a digital model of a part, a product, or a structure and make changes to the design on the computer without having to build physical prototypes. PLM software goes beyond CAD software to include not only automated modeling and design capabilities but also tools to help companies manage and automate materials sourcing, engineering change orders, and product documentation, such as test results, product packaging, and postsales data. The Window on Organizations describes how these systems are providing new sources of value.

4.10.3 Finance and Accounting Systems

The finance function is responsible for managing the firm's financial assets, such as cash, stocks, bonds, and other investments, to maximize the return on these financial assets.

The finance function is also in charge of managing the capitalization of the firm (finding new financial assets in stocks, bonds, or other forms of debt). To determine whether the firm is getting the best return on its investments, the finance function must obtain a considerable amount of information from sources external to the firm.

The accounting function is responsible for maintaining and managing the firm's financial records—receipts, disbursements, depreciation, and payroll— to account for the flow of funds in a firm. Finance and accounting share related problems—how to keep track of a firm's financial assets and fund flows. They provide answers to questions such as these: What is the current inventory of financial assets? What records exist for disbursements, receipts, payroll, and other fund flows?

Table 4.5 shows some of the typical finance and accounting information systems found in large organizations. Strategic-level systems for the finance and accounting function establish long-term investment goals for the firm and provide long-range forecasts of the firm's financial performance. At the management level, information systems help managers oversee and control the firm's financial resources. Knowledge systems support finance and accounting by providing analytical tools and workstations for designing the right mix of investments to maximize returns for the firm. Operational systems in finance and accounting track the flow of funds in the firm through transactions such as paychecks, payments to vendors, securities reports, and receipts.

Table 4.5: Examples of Finance and Accounting Information Systems

System	Description	Organizational Level
Accounts receivable	Tracks money owned by the firm	Operational
Portfolio analysis	Design the form's portfolio of investments	Knowledge
Budgeting	Prepares short-term budgets	Management
Profit planning	Plans long-term profits	Strategic

4.10.4 Human Resources Systems

The human resources function is responsible for attracting, developing, and maintaining the firm's workforce. Human resources information systems support activities, such as identifying potential employees, maintaining complete records on existing employees, and creating programs to develop employees' talents and skills.

Human resources information systems reduce administrative costs, provide faster service to employees, and help firms manage their workforce.

Strategic-level human resources systems identify the manpower requirements (skills, educational level, types of positions, number of positions, and cost) for meeting the firm's long-term business plans. At the management level, human resources systems help managers monitor and analyze the recruitment, allocation, and compensation of employees. Knowledge systems for human resources support analysis activities related to job design, training and the modeling of employee career paths and reporting relationships. sHuman resources operational systems track the recruitment and placement of the firm's employees (see Table 4.6).

Table 4.6: Examples of Human Resources Information Systems

System	Description	Organization Level
Training and Development	Tracks employee training, skills, and performance appraisals	Operational
Career patching	Design career paths for employees	Knowledge
Compensation Analysis	Monitors the range and distribution of employee wages, salaries, and benefits	Management
Human Resources Planning	Plans the long-term labour force needs of the organization	Strategic

Figure 4.18 illustrates a typical human resources TPS for employee record keeping. It maintains basic employee data, such as the employee's name, age, sex, marital status, address, educational background, salary, job title, date of hire, and date of termination. The system can produce a variety of reports, such as lists of newly hired employees, employees who are terminated or on leaves of absence, employees classified by job type or educational level, or employee job performance evaluations. Such systems are typically designed to provide data that can satisfy federal and state record keeping requirements for Equal Employment Opportunity (EEO) and other purposes.

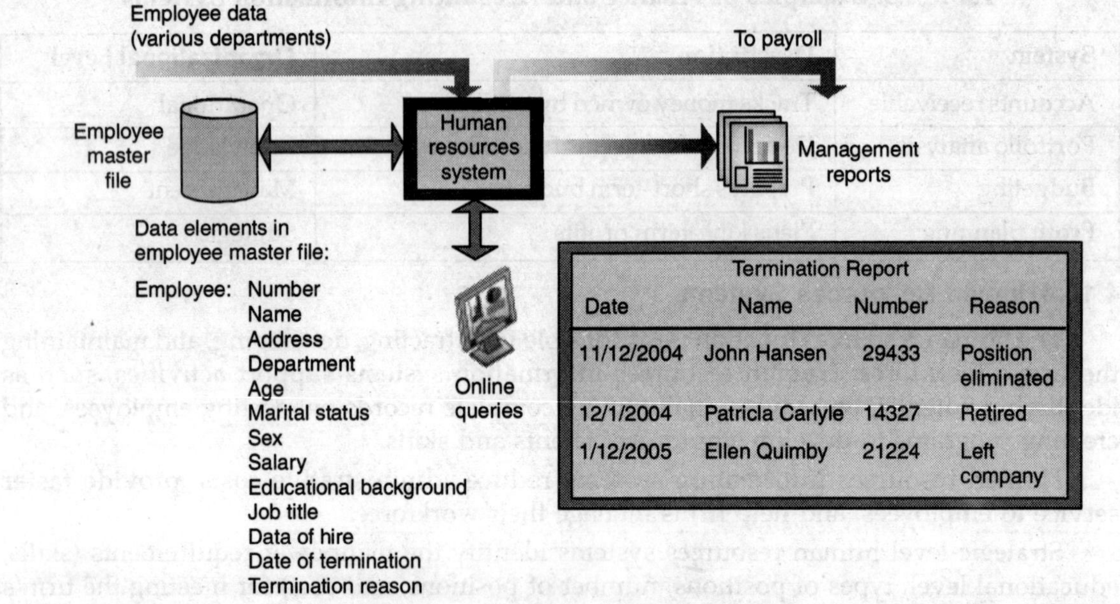

Figure 4.18: An employee record keeping system

This system maintains data on the firm's employees to support the human resources function.

4.11 DEVELOPMENT LIFE CYCLE OF INFORMATION SYSTEMS

Companies may also decide to custom-build an application. They can either perform this operation in-house or outsource the process. Although custom development is usually more time consuming and costly than buying or leasing, the results often fit better with the organization's specific requirements.

As the company goes through the development process, the mind-set changes. In systems investigation, the organization is trying to decide whether to build something: Everyone knows that it either may or may not be built. In later stages of the development process, the organization is fully committed to building the application, and although a project can be cancelled at any time, this change in attitude is still important.

The basic, backbone methodology for custom development is the systems development life cycle (SDLC), which we study in this section. Later we examine the methodologies that complement the SDLC: prototyping, joint application development, integrated computer-assisted systems development tools, and rapid application development. We also consider four other methodologies: agile development, end-user development, component-based development, and object-oriented development.

4.11.1 The Traditional Systems Development Life Cycle

The systems development life cycle (SDLC) is the traditional systems development method that organizations use for large-scale IT projects. The SDLC is a structured framework that consists of sequential processes by which information systems are developed. For our purposes (see Figure 4.19) we define six processes, each of which consists of clearly defined tasks:

- Systems investigation
- Systems analysis
- Systems design
- Programming and testing
- Implementation
- Operation and maintenance

Other models for the SDLC may contain more or fewer than the six stages presented here. The flow of tasks, however, remains largely the same. When problems occur in any phase of the SDLC, developers often must go back to previous phases.

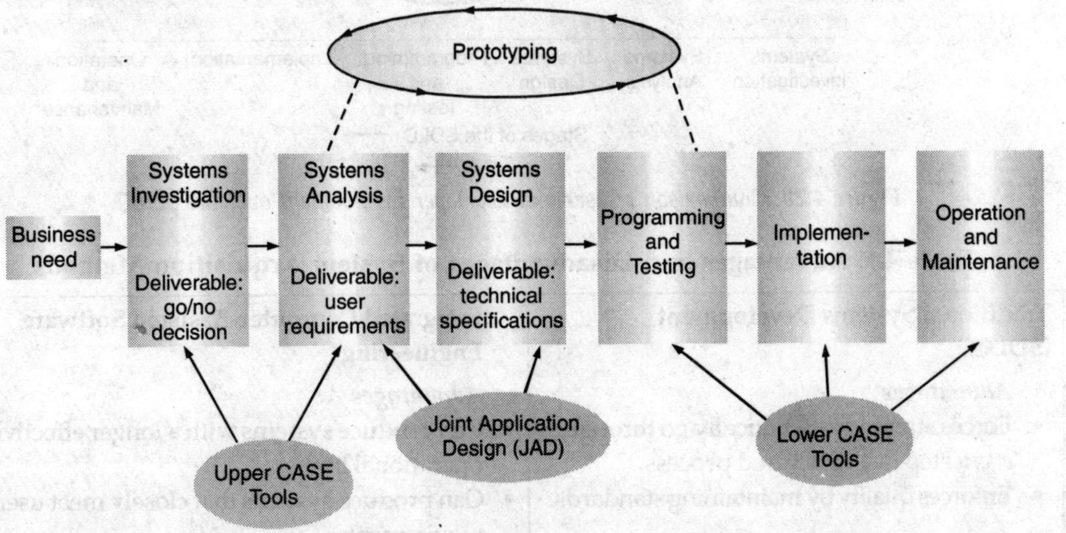

Figure 4.19: *A six-stage systems development life cycle (SDLC) with supporting tools.*

Systems development projects produce desired results through team efforts. Development teams typically include users, systems analysts, programmers, and technical specialists. Users are employees from all functional areas and levels of the organization who interact with the system, either directly or indirectly. **Systems analysts** are IS professionals who specialize in analyzing and designing information systems. **Programmers** are IS professionals who either modify existing computer programs or write new ones to satisfy user requirements. **Technical specialists** are experts on a specific type of technology, such as data bases or telecommunications. Finally, the **systems stakeholders** include everyone who is affected by changes in a company's information systems, for example, users and managers. All stakeholders typically are involved in systems development at various times and in varying degrees. Figure 4.20 indicates that users have high involvement in the early stages of the SDLC, lower involvement in the programming and testing stage, and higher involvement in the later stages. Table 4.7 discusses the advantages and disadvantages of the SDLC.

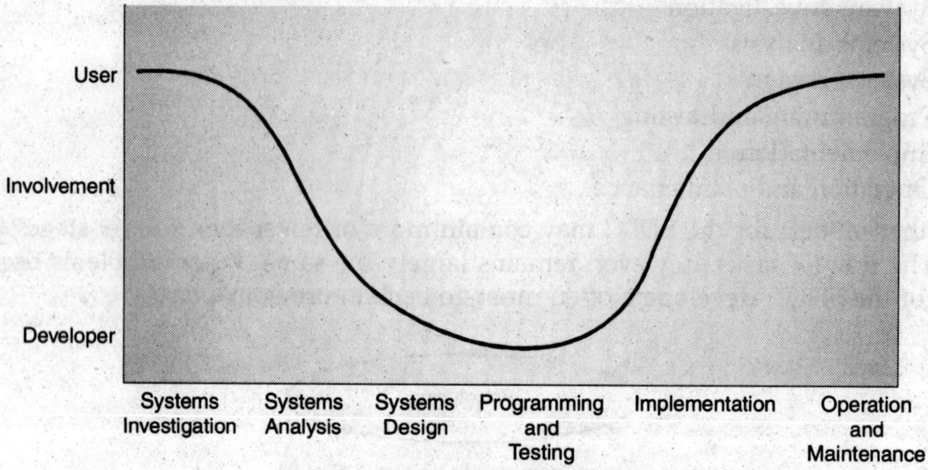

Figure 4.20: *Comparison of user and developer involvement over the SDLC.*

Table 4.7: Advantages and Disadvantages of System Acquisition Methods

Traditional Systems Development (SDLC)	**Integrated Computer-Assisted Software Engineering**
Advantages • Forces staff to systematically go through *every* step in a structured process. • Enforces quality by maintaining standards. • Has lower probability of missing important issues in collecting user requirements. ***Disadvantages*** • May produce excessive documentation. • Users may be unwilling or unable to study the specifications they approve. • Takes too long to go from the original ideas to a working system. • Users have trouble describing requirements for a proposed system.	***Advantages*** • Can produce systems with a longer effective operational life. • Can produce systems that closely meet user requirements. • Can speed up the development process. • Can produce systems that are more flexible and adaptable to changing business conditions. • Can produce excellent documentation. ***Disadvantages*** • Systems are often more expensive to build and maintain. • Requires more extensive and accurate definition of user requirements. • Difficult to customize.
Prototyping ***Advantages*** • Helps clarify user requirements. • Helps verify the feasibility of the design.	**Rapid Application Development** ***Advantages*** • Can speed up systems development. • Users are intensively involved from the start.

• Promotes genuine user participation. • Promotes close working relationship between systems developers and users. • Works well for ill-defined problems. • May produce part of the final system. ***Disadvantages*** • May encourage inadequate problem analysis. • Not practical with a large number of users. • Users may not *give* up the prototype when the system is completed. • May generate confusion about whether the system is complete and maintainable. • System may be built quickly, which may result in lower quality.	• Improves the process of rewriting legacy applications. ***Disadvantages*** • Produces functional components of final systems, but not final systems.
Joint Application Design ***Advantages*** • Involves many users in the development process. • Saves time. • Greater user support for new system. • Improved quality of the new system. • New system easier to implement. • New system has lower training costs. ***Disadvantages*** • Difficult to get all users to attend JAD meeting. • JAD approach has all the problems associated with any group meeting.	**End-User Development** ***Advantages*** • Bypasses the IS department and avoids delays. • User controls the application and can change it as needed. • Directly meets user requirements. • Increased user acceptance of new system. • Frees up IT resources. • May create lower-quality systems. ***Disadvantages*** • May eventually require maintenance from the IS department. • Documentation may be inadequate. • Poor quality control. • System may not have adequate interfaces to existing systems.
	Object-Oriented Development ***Advantages*** • Objects model real-world entities. • May be able to reuse some computer code. ***Disadvantages*** • Works best with systems of more limited scope; i.e., with systems that do not have huge numbers of objects.

4.11.1.1 Systems Investigation

The initial stage in a traditional SDLC is systems investigation. Systems development professionals agree that the more time they invest in (l) understanding the business problem to be solved, (2) specifying the technical options for the systems, and (3) anticipating the problems they are likely to encounter during development, the greater the chances of success. For these reasons, systems investigation addresses *the business problem* (or business opportunity) by means of the feasibility study.

The main task in the systems investigation stage is the feasibility study. Organizations have three basic solutions to any business problem relating to an information System: (1) do nothing and continue to use the existing system unchanged, (2) modify or enhance the existing system, or (3) develop a new system. The feasibility study analyzes which of these three solutions best fits the particular business problem. It also provides a rough assessment of the project's technical, economic, and behavioural feasibility.

- *Technical feasibility* determines whether the company can develop and/or acquire the hardware, software, and communications components needed to solve the business problem. Technical feasibility also determines whether the organization can use its existing technology to achieve the project's performance objectives.
- *Economic feasibility* determines whether the project is an acceptable financial risk and, if so, whether the organization has the necessary time and money to successfully complete the project. You have already learned about the methods commonly used to determine economic feasibility: NPV, ROI, breakeven analysis, and the business case approach.
- *Behavioural feasibility* addresses the human issues of the systems development project. Clearly, the developers will be heavily involved in this aspect of the feasibility study.

After the feasibility analysis is completed, a "Go/No-Go" decision is reached by the steering committee, if there is one, or by top management in the absence of a committee. The Go/NoGo decision does not depend solely on the feasibility analysis. Organizations often have more feasible projects than they can fund. Therefore, the firm must prioritize the feasible projects and pursue those with the highest priority. Unfunded feasible projects may not be presented to the IT department at all. These projects therefore contribute to the *hidden backlog,* which are projects of which the IT department is not aware.

If the decision is "No-Go," the project either is put on the shelf until conditions are more favourable, or it is discarded. If the decision is "Go" the project proceeds, and the systems analysis phase begins.

4.11.1.2 Systems Analysis

Once a development project has the necessary approvals from all participants, the systems analysis stage begins. Systems analysis is the examination of the business problem that the organization plans to solve with an information system.

The main purpose of the systems analysis stage is to gather information about the existing system in order to determine the requirements for an enhanced system or a new system. The end product of this stage, known as the *deliverable,* is a set of *system requirements.*

Perhaps the most difficult task in systems analysis is identifying the specific requirements that the system must satisfy. These requirements often are called *user requirements,* because users (meaning you) provide them. When the systems developers have accumulated the user requirements for the new system, they proceed to the systems design stage.

4.11.1.3 Systems Design

Systems design describes how the system will resolve the business problem. The deliverable of the systems design phase is a set of *technical system specifications,* which specifies the following:

- System outputs, inputs, and user interfaces
- Hardware, software, databases, telecommunications, personnel, and procedures
- A blueprint of how these components are integrated

The system specifications, when approved by all participants are "frozen"; that is, they should not be changed. Adding functions after the project has been initiated causes scope creep, which endangers the project's budget and schedule. Because scope creep is expensive, successful project managers place controls on changes requested by users. These controls help to prevent runaway projects.

4.11.1.4 Programming and Testing

If the organization dedcides to construct the software in-house, then programming begins. Programming involves translating the design specifications into computer code. This process can be lengthy and time consuming, because writing computer code is as much an art as a science.

Large systems development projects can require hundreds of thousands of lines of computer code and hundred s of computer programmers. These large-scale projects employ programming teams, which often include functional area users, who help the programmers focus on the business problem.

Thorough and continuous testing occurs throughout the programming stage. Testing is the process that checks to see whether the computer code will produce the expected and desired results. It is also intended to detect errors, or bugs, in the computer code.

4.11.1.5 Implementation

Implementation (or *deployment)* is the process of converting from the old system to the new system. The conversion process involves organizational change. Only end users, not the IS department, can manage organizational change. The IS department typically does not have enough credibility with the business users to manage the change process. Organizations use three major conversion strategies: direct, pilot, and phased.

In a **direct conversion**, the old system is cut off and the new system is turned on at a certain point in time. This type of conversion is the least expensive. It is also the riskiest because, if the new system does not work as planned, there is no support from the old system. Consequently, few systems are implemented using direct conversion.

A **pilot conversion** introduces the new system in one part of the organization, such as in one plant or one functional area. The new system runs for a period of time and then is assessed. If the assessment confirms that the system is working properly, the system is implemented in other parts of the organization.

Finally, a **phased conversion** introduces components of the new system, such as individual modules, in stages. Each module is assessed. If it works properly, other modules are introduced until the entire new system is operational. Large organizations commonly combine the pilot and phased approaches; that is, they execute a phased conversion using a pilot group for each phase.

A fourth strategy is *parallel conversion*, in which the old and new systems operate simultaneously for a time. This strategy is seldom used to day. One reason for this is that parallel conversion is totally impractical when both the old and new systems are online. Imagine that you are finishing an order on Amazon.com, only to be told, "Before your order can be entered here, you must provide all the same information again, in a different form, and on a different set of screens." The results would be disastrous for Amazon.

4.11.1.6 Operation and Maintenance

The new system, after it is implemented, will operate for a period of time, until (like the old system it replaced) it no longer meets its objectives. Once the new system's operations are stabilized, the company performs audits to assess the system's capabilities and to determine whether it is being utilized correctly.

Systems require several types of maintenance. The first type is *debugging* the program, a process that continues throughout the life of the system. The second is *updating* the system to accommodate changes in business conditions. An example is adjusting to new governmental regulations, such as changes in tax rates. These corrections and upgrades usually do not add any new functions. Instead, they simply help the system to continue meeting its objectives. In contrast, the third type of maintenance *adds new functions* to the existing system without disturbing its operation.

4.11.2 Alternative Methods and Tools for Systems Development

There are multiple alternative methods for systems development. These methods include joint application design, rapid application development, agile development, and end-user development.

4.11.2.1 Joint Application Design

Joint application design (JAD) is a group-based tool for collecting user requirements and creating system designs. It is used most often within the systems analysis and systems design stages of the SDLC. JAD involves a group meeting attended by the analysts and all of the users. It is basically a group decision-making process that can be con ducted manually or via the computer. During this meeting, all users jointly define and agree on the systems requirements. This process saves a tremendous amount of time. Table 4.7 lists the advantages and disadvantages of the JAD process.

4.11.2.2 Rapid Application Development

Rapid application development (RAD) is systems development methods that can combine JAD, prototyping, and CASE tools (discussed later in this section) to rapidly produce a high-quality system. In the first RAD stage, developers use JAD sessions to collect system requirements. This strategy ensures that users are intensively involved early on. The development process in RAD is iterative, similar to prototyping; that is, requirements, designs, and the system itself are developed and then undergo a series, or sequence, of improvements. RAD uses CASE tools to quickly structure requirements and develop prototypes. As the prototypes are developed and refined, users review them in additional JAD sessions. RAD produces the functional components of a final system, rather than prototypes. To understand how RAD functions and how it differs from SDLC, see Figure 4.21. Table 4.7 highlights the advantages and disadvantages of the RAD process.

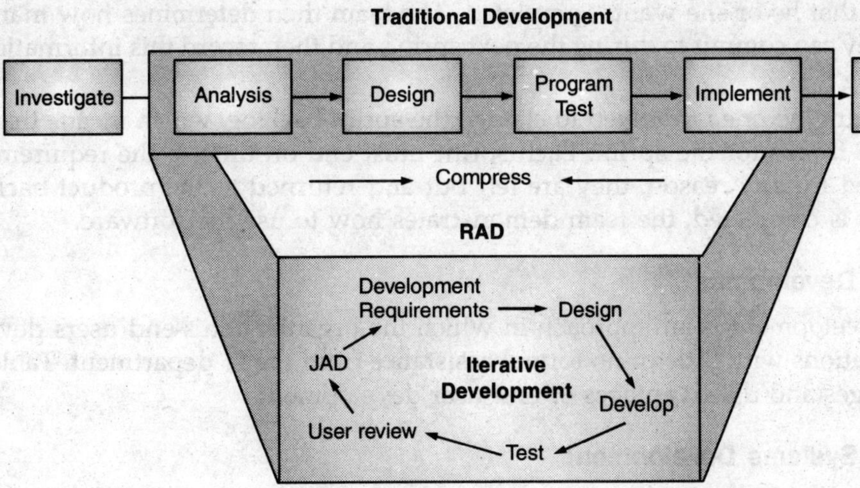

Figure 4.21: A rapid prototyping development process versus SDLC.

4.11.2.3 Agile Development

Agile development is a software development methodology that delivers functionality in rapid iterations, which usually are measured in weeks. To be successful, this methodology requires frequent communication, development, testing, and delivery. Agile development focuses on rapid development and frequent user contact to create software that addresses the needs of business users. This software does not have to include every possible feature the user will require. Rather, it must meet only the user's more important and immediate needs. It can be updated later to introduce additional functions as they become necessary. The core tenet of agile development is to do only what you have to do to be successful right now.

One type of agile development uses the *scrum approach.* A key principle of scrum is that during a project users can change their minds about what they want and need. Scrum acknowledges that a development problem cannot be fully understood or defined from the start. Therefore, scrum focuses on maximizing the development team's ability to deliver iterations quickly and to respond effectively to additional user requirements as they emerge.

Scrum contains sets of practices and predefined roles. The primary roles are:

- The *Scrum Master:* maintains the processes (typically replaces a project manager);
- The *Product Owner:* represents the business users and any other stakeholders in the project;

- The *Team:* a cross-functional group of about seven people who perform the actual analysis, design, coding, implementation, testing, etc.

Scrum works as follows: During each sprint- typically a two- to four-week period – the team creates a potentially shippable product increment, such as working and tested software. The set of features that go into each sprint come from the product backlog, which is a prioritized set of high-level work requirements to be completed.

The sprint planning meeting determines which backlog items will be addressed during a sprint. During this meeting, the product owner informs the team about the items in the product backlog that he or she wants completed. The team then determines how many of these projects they can commit to during the next sprint, and they record this information in the sprint backlog.

During a sprint, no one is allowed to change the sprint backlog, which means that the requirements are frozen for the sprint. Each sprint must end on time. If the requirements are not completed for any reason, they are left out and returned to the product backlog. After each sprint is completed, the team demonstrates how to use the software.

4.11.3 End-user Development

End-user development is an approach in which the organization's end users develop their own applications with little or no formal assistance from the IT department. Table 4.7 lists the advantages and disadvantages of end-user development.

4.11.4 Tools for Systems Development

Several tools can be used with various systems development methods. These tools include prototyping, integrated computer-assisted software engineering (ICASE), component-based development, and object-oriented development.

1. Prototyping: The prototyping approach defines an initial list of user requirements, builds a model of the system, and then refines the system in several iterations based on users' feedback. Developers do not try to obtain a complete set of user specifications for the system at the outset, and they do not develop the system all at once. Instead, they quickly develop a smaller version of the system known as a prototype. A prototype can take two forms. In some cases it contains only the components of the new system that are of most interest to the users. In other cases it is a small-scale working model of the entire system.

Users make suggestions for improving the prototype, based on their experiences with it. The developers then review the prototype with the users and use their suggestions to refine the prototype. This process continues through several iterations until the users approve the system or it becomes apparent that the system cannot meet the users' needs. If the system is viable, the developers can use the prototype to build the full system. One typical use of prototyping is to develop screens that a user will see and interact with. Table 4.7 describes the advantages and disadvantages of the prototyping approach.

There is a practical problem with prototyping: A prototype usually looks more complete than it is. It may not use the real database; it usually does not have the necessary error checking; and it almost never includes the necessary security features. Users who review a prototype that resembles the finished system may not recognize these problems.

Consequently, they might have unrealistic expectations about how close the actual system is to completion.

2. Integrated Computer-Assisted Software Engineering Tools: Computer-aided software engineering (CASE) is a group of tools that automate many of the tasks in the SDLC. The tools used to automate the early stages of the SDLC (systems investigation, analysis, and design) are called upper CASE tools. The tools used to automate later stages in the SDLC (programming, testing, operation, and maintenance) are called lower CASE tools. CASE tools that provide links between upper CASE and lower CASE tools are called integrated CASE (ICASE) tools. Table 4.7 lists the advantages and disadvantages of ICASE tools.

3. Component-Based Development: Component-based development uses standard components to build applications. Components are reusable applications that generally have one specific function, such as a shopping cart, user authentication, or a catalogue. Component-based development is closely linked with the idea of Web services and service-oriented architectures.

Many start-up companies are pursuing the idea of component-based application development, or less programming and more assembly. An example of these companies is Ning *(www.ning.com)*, which allows organizations to create, customize, and share their own social network.

4. Object-Oriented Development: Object-oriented development is based on a different view of computer systems than the perception that characterizes tradition al development approaches. Traditional approaches can produce a system that performs the original task but may not be suited for handling other tasks. This observation applies even when these other tasks involve the same real-world entities. For example, a billing system will handle billing but probably cannot be adapted to handle mailings for the marketing department or to generate leads for the sales force. This is true even though the billing, marketing, and sales functions all use similar data, including customer names, addresses, and purchases. In contrast, an *object-oriented (OO) system* begins not with the task to be performed, but with the aspects of the real world that must be modeled to perform that task. Therefore, in the above example, if the firm has a good model of its customers and its interactions with them, it can use this model equally well for billings, mailings, and sales leads.

The development process for an object-oriented system begins with a feasibility study and an analysis of the existing system. Systems developers identify the *objects* in the new system- the fundamental elements in OO analysis and design. Each object represents a tangible, real-world entity, such as a customer, bank account, student, or course. Objects have *properties*, or *data values*. For example, a customer has an identification number, a name, an address, account number(s), and so on. Objects also contain the *operations* (also referred to as *behaviours)* that can be performed on their properties. For example, operations that can be performed on the customer object may include "obtain-account-balance", "open-account", "withdraw-funds," and so on.

This approach enables object-oriented analysts to define all the relevant objects needed for the new system, including their properties and operations. The analysts then model how the objects interact to meet the objectives of the new system. In some cases, analysts can reuse existing objects from other applications (or from a library of objects) in the new system. This process saves the analysts the time they otherwise would spend coding these objects. In most cases, however, even with object reuse, some coding will be necessary to customize the objects and their interactions for the new system.

SUMMARY

In this chapter, an information system can be defined technically as a set of interrelated components that collect (or retrieve), process, store, and distribute information to support decision making and control in an organization. In addition to supporting decision making, coordination, and control, information systems may also help managers and workers analyze problems, visualize complex subjects, and create new products.

Information systems contain information about significant people, places, and things within the organization or in the environment surrounding it. By information we mean data that have been shaped into a form that is meaningful and useful to human beings. Data, in contrast, are streams of raw facts representing events occurring in organizations or the physical environment before they have been organized and arranged into a form that people can understand and use.

Four main categories of information systems serve different organizational levels: operational-level systems, knowledge-level systems, management-level systems, and strategic-level systems.

Information systems can be classified by the specific organizational function they serve as well as by organizational level. We now describe typical information systems that support each of the major business functions and provide examples of functional applications for each organizational level.

The basic, backbone methodology for custom development is the systems development life cycle. Later we examine the methodologies that complement the SDLC: prototyping, joint application development, integrated computer-assisted systems development tools, and rapid application development. We also consider four other methodologies: agile development, end-user development, component-based development, and object-oriented development.

EXERCISES

1. What is information system?
2. Explain the data and information?
3. What are the functions of an information system?
4. What are computer-based information systems?
5. Explain the various resources of information system?
6. Explain a business perspective on information systems?
7. What are the dimensions of information systems?
8. Explain the need of information systems?
9. What are the categories of information systems?

10. Explain the different kinds of systems?
11. Explain the six major types of systems?
12. What are characteristics of information processing systems?
13. Explain the systems from a functional perspective?
14. Explain the development life cycle of information systems?
15. Explain the traditional systems development life cycle in detail?
16. What are advantages and disadvantages of system acquisition methods?
17. What are the alternative methods for systems development?
18. Explain the tools for systems development?

❑

Technologies for Information Systems

5

5.1 HARDWARE

Hardware refers to the physical equipment used for the input, processing, output, and storage activities of a computer system. Decisions about hardware focus on three interrelated factors: appropriateness for the task, speed, and cost. The incredibly rapid rate of innovation within the computer industry complicates hardware decisions because computer technologies become obsolete more quickly than other organizational technologies.

In general, hardware is becoming smaller, faster, cheaper, and more powerful over time. In fact, these trends are so rapid that often it is difficult for companies to know when to purchase (or upgrade) hardware because, if they delay hardware purchases, they likely will be able to buy more powerful hardware for the same amount of money in the future. This means that buying more powerful hardware for the same amount of money in the future is a trade-off: An organization that delays purchasing computer hardware forgoes the benefits of the new technology it could buy today until the future purchase date arrives.

Hardware consists of the following:

- *Central processing unit (CPU).* Manipulates the data and controls the tasks performed by the other components.
- *Primary storage.* Temporarily stores data and program instructions during processing.
- *Secondary storage.* Stores data and programs for future use.
- *Input technologies.* Accept data and instructions and convert them to a form that the computer can understand.
- *Output technologies.* Present data and information in a form that people can understand.
- *Communication technologies.* Provide for the flow of data from external computer networks- for example, the Internet and intranets- to the CPU, and from the CPU to computer networks.

The next section discusses strategic hardware issues. The following sections address the various types of computers and input and output technologies. The final section takes a nuts-and-bolts look at the central processing unit and computer memory.

5.1.1 Strategic Hardware Issues

For most business-people the key issues with hardware are what it enables and how to keep up with rapid price/performance increases. In many industries, exploiting computer

4hardware is essential to achieving competitive advantage. Successful hardware exploitation comes from thoughtful consideration of the following questions:

- How will the organization keep up with the rapid price and performance advancements in hardware? For example, how often should the organization upgrade its computers and storage systems? Will upgrades increase personal and organizational productivity? If so, then how can the organization measure such increases?
- How should the organization determine the need for new hardware infrastructures, such as server farms, virtualization, grid computing, and utility computing?
- Portable computers and advanced communications technologies enable employees to work from home or almost any other location. Will these new work styles benefit employees and the organization? How do organizations manage such new work styles?

5.2 COMPUTER HIERARCHY

The traditional standard for comparing classes of computers is processing power. This section presents each class of computers, from the most powerful to the least powerful. It describes both the computers themselves and their roles in modern organizations.

5.2.1 Supercomputers

The term supercomputer does not refer to a specific technology. Rather, it indicates the fastest computers available at any given time. At the time of this writing, the fastest super computers boasted speeds exceeding one petaflop, or 1,000 trillion floating-point operations per second. (A floating-point operation is an arithmetic operation involving decimals.)

Because supercomputers are costly as well as fast, large organizations generally use them to execute computationally demanding tasks involving large data sets. In contrast to mainframes, which specialize in transaction processing and business applications, supercomputers typically run military and scientific applications? Although these machines cost millions of dollars, they are also being used for commercial applications where huge amounts of data must be analyzed. For example, large banks employ supercomputers to calculate the risks and returns of various investment strategies and healthcare organizations use them to analyze giant databases of patient data to determine optimal treatments for various diseases.

5.2.3 Mainframe Computers

Although mainframe computers are increasingly being viewed as just another type of server (albeit at the high end of the performance and reliability scales), they remain a distinct class of systems differentiated by hardware and software features. Mainframes remain popular in large enterprises for extensive computing applications that are accessed by thousands of users simultaneously. Examples of mainframe applications are airline reservation systems, corporate payroll programs, Web site transaction processing systems (e.g., Amazon and eBay), and student grade calculation and reporting.

Today's mainframes perform at teraflop speeds (trillions of floating point operations per second) and can handle millions of transactions per day. In addition, mainframes provide a secure, robust environment in which to run strategic, mission-critical applications.

5.2.4 Midrange Computers

Larger midrange computers, called minicomputers, are relatively small, inexpensive, and compact computers that perform the same functions as mainframe computers, but to a more limited extent. In fact, the lines between minicomputers and mainframes have blurred in both price and performance. Minicomputers are a type of server, that is, a computer that supports computer networks and enables users to share files, software, peripheral devices, and other resources. Note that mainframes are a type of server as well, because they provide support for entire enterprise networks.

5.2.5 Microcomputers

Microcomputers-also called *micros, personal computers*, or PCs- are the smallest and least expensive category of general-purpose computers. A PC is frequently defined as a computer that utilizes the Microsoft® Windows operating system. In fact, however, a variety of PCs are available, many of which do not use Windows. One well-known example is the Apple Macintosh, which uses the OS X operating system. The major categories of microcomputers are desktops, thin clients, notebooks and laptops, netbooks, and tablets.

1. Desktop PCs. The *desktop personal computer* is the familiar microcomputer system that has been a standard tool for business and the home. (Desktops are being replaced with portable devices such as laptops, netbooks, and tablets.) A desktop generally includes a central processing unit (CPU) - which you will learn about later-and a separate but connected monitor and keyboard. Modern desktop computers have gigabytes of primary storage, rewriteable CD-ROM and DVD drives, and up to a few terabytes of secondary storage.

2. Thin-Client Systems. Before we address thin-client systems, we need to differentiate between clients and servers. Servers are computers that provide a variety of services for clients, including running networks, processing Web sites, processing e-mail, and many other functions. *Clients* typically are computers on which users perform their own tasks, such *as* word processing, spreadsheets, and others.

Thin-client systems are desktop computer systems that do not offer the full functionality of a PC. Compared to a PC, or fat client, thin clients are less complex, particularly because they don't have locally installed software. When thin clients need to run an application, they access it from a server over a network rather than from a local disk drive. For example, a thin client would not have Microsoft® Office installed on it.

Thus, thin clients are easier and *less* expensive to operate and support than PCs. The benefits of thin clients include fast application deployment; centralized management; lower cost of ownership; and easier installation, management, maintenance, and support. The main disadvantage of thin clients is that, if the network fails, users can do very little on their computers. Users who have fat clients, in contrast, can still perform some functions when the network fails because the necessary software, such as Microsoft® Office, is installed on their computers.

3. Laptop and Notebook Computers. Laptop and notebook computers are small, lightweight microcomputers that fit easily into a briefcase. Notebooks and laptops are designed to be as convenient and easy to transport as possible. Just as importantly, they provide users with access to processing power and data outside an office environment. At the same time, they cost more than desktops for similar functionality.

4. Netbooks. A netbook is a very small, lightweight, portable computer that is energy efficient and relatively inexpensive. Netbooks are generally optimized for Internet-based services such as Web browsing and e-mailing.

5. Tablet Computers. A tablet computer, or simply a tablet, *is* a complete computer contained entirely in a flat touch screen that users operate via a stylus, a digital pen, or their fingertip instead of a keyboard or mouse. Examples of tablets are the Apple iPad 2, the HP Slate, the Toshiba Thrive, and the Motorola Xoom.

Figure 5.1: Laptop, notebook, and tablet computers.

5.3 INPUT AND OUTPUT TECHNOLOGIES

Input technologies enable people and other technologies to enter data into a computer. The two main types of input devices are human data-entry devices and source-data automation devices. *Human data-entry* devices, as their name implies, require a certain amount of human effort to input data. Examples are keyboard, mouse, pointing stick, trackball, joystick, touchscreen, stylus, and voice recognition.

An interesting development in input/output technologies is the Siri application released by Apple in October of 2011. This application allows users to simply speak to their phone and receive intelligent feedback. As this method of interaction develops, it will transform how and where we use computers as there will be far less need for traditional input/output devices.

In contrast, *source-data automation* devices input data with minimal human intervention. These technologies speed up data collection, reduce errors, and gather data at the source of a transaction or other event. Barcode readers, ATMs, and radio frequency identification are examples of source-data automation. Table 5.1 describes the various input devices.

The output generated by a computer can be transmitted to the user via multiple output devices and media. These devices include monitors, printers, plotters, and voice. Table 5.2 describes the various output devices.

Multimedia technology is the computer-based integration of text, sound, still images, animation, and digitized motion video. It typically represents a collection of various input and output technologies. Multimedia merges the capabilities of computers with televisions, VCRs, CD players, DVD players, video and audio recording equipment, and music and gaming technologies.

High-quality multimedia processing requires powerful microprocessors and extensive memory capacity, including both primary and secondary storage.

Table 5.1: Input Devices

Input Device Type	**Input Device**	**Description**
Human Data-Entry Devices	Keyboards	Most common input device (for text and numerical data).
	Mouse	Handheld device used to point cursor at a point on the screen, such as an icon; user clicks mouse button, instructing computer to take some action.
	Optical mouse	Mouse is not connected to computer by a cable; mouse uses camera chip to take images of the surface it passes over, comparing successive images to determine its position.
	Trackball	User rotates a ball built into top of device to move cursor (rather than moving entire device such as a mouse).
	Pointing stick	Small button-like device; cursor moves in the direction of the pressure you place on the stick. Located between keys near center of keyboard.
	Touchpad (also called a trackpad)	User moves cursor by sliding finger across a sensitized pad and then can tap pad when cursor is in desired position to instruct computer to take action (also called glide-and-tap pad).
	Graphics tablet	A device that can be used in place of, or in conjunction with, a mouse or trackball; has a flat surface for drawing and a pen or stylus that is programmed to work with the tablet.
	Joystick	Joystick moves cursor to desired place on screen; commonly used in workstations that display dynamic graphics and in video games.
		Touch screen Users instruct computer to take some action by touching a particular part of the screen; commonly used in information kiosks such as ATM machines. Touch screens now have gesture controls for browsing through photographs, moving objects around on a screen, flicking to turn the page of a book, and playing video games.

	Stylus	Pen-style device that allows user either to touch parts of a predetermined menu of options or to handwrite information into the computer (as with some PDAs); works with touch-sensitive screens.
	Digital pen	Mobile device that digitally captures everything you write; built-in screen confirms that what you write has been saved; also captures sketches, figures, etc. with on-board flash memory.
	Wii	A video game console by Nintendo. A distinguishing feature of the Wii is its wireless controller, which can be used as a handheld pointing device and can detect movement in three dimensions.
	Microsoft® Kinect	Enables users to control and interact with the Xbox 360 without the need to touch a game controller, through a natural user interface using gestures and spoken commands.
	Web camera (Webcam)	A real-time video camera whose images can be accessed via the Web or instant messaging.
	Voice-recognition	Microphone converts analog voice sounds to digital input for computer; critical technology for physically challenged people who cannot use other input devices.
Source-Data Automation Input Devices	Automated teller machine	A device that includes source-data automation input in the form of a magnetic stripe reader; human input via a keyboard; and output via a monitor, printer, and cash dispenser.
	Magnetic stripe reader	A device that reads data from a magnetic stripe, usually on the back of a plastic card (for example, credit or debit card).
	Point-of-sale terminals	Computerized cash registers that also may incorporate touchscreen technology and barcode scanners (see below) to input data such as item sold and price.
	Barcode scanners	Devices scan black-and-white barcode lines printed on merchandise labels.
	Optical mark reader	Scanner for detecting presence of dark marks on predetermined grid, such as multiple- choice test answer sheets.
	Magnetic ink character reader	Reads magnetic ink printed on a check that identifies the bank, checking account, and check number.
	Optical character recognition	Software that converts text into digital form for input into computer.

	Sensors	Collect data directly from the environment and input data directly into computer; examples include your car's airbag activation sensor and radio-frequency identification tags.
	Cameras	Digital cameras capture images and convert them to digital files.
	Radio frequency identification (RFID)	Uses active or passive tags (transmitters) to wirelessly transmit product information to electronic readers.

Table 5.2: Output Devices

Output Device Type	Output Device	Description
Monitors	Cathode ray tubes	Video display screens on which an electron beam illuminates pixels.
	Liquid crystal display (LCDs)	Flat displays that have liquid crystals between two polarizers to form characters and images on a backlit screen.
	Flexible displays	Thin, plastic, bendable computer screens.
	Organic light-emitting diodes (OLEDs)	Displays that are brighter, thinner, lighter, cheaper, faster, and take less power to run than LCDs.
	Retinal scanning displays	Project image directly onto a viewer's retina; used in medicine, air traffic control, and controlling industrial machines.
	Heads-Up displays	Any transparent display that presents data without requiring that the user looks away from his or her usual viewpoint; for example, see Microvision (www.microvision.com).
Printers	Laser	Use laser beams to write information on photosensitive drums; produce high-resolution text and graphics.
	Inkjet	Shoot fine streams of colored ink onto paper; usually less expensive to buy than laser printers, but can be more expensive to operate; can offer resolution quality equal to that of laser printers.
	Thermal	Produce a printed image by selectively heating coated thermal paper; when the paper passes over the thermal print head, the coating turns black in the areas where it is heated, producing an image.
Plotters		Use computer-directed pens for creating high-quality images, blueprints, schematics, drawings of new products, etc.

Voice output		In a speaker/headset, which can output sounds of any type, voice output is a software function that uses this equipment.
Electronic book	Amazon Kindle, Sony Reader, Barnes and Noble Nook.	A wireless, portable reading device with access to books, blogs, newspapers, and magazines. On-board storage holds hundreds of books.
Pocket projector		A projector in a handheld device that provides an alternative display method to alleviate the problem of tiny display screens in handheld devices. Pocket projectors will project digital images onto any viewing surface.
Pico projector		A very small projector incorporated into portable devices, such as the Nikon Coolpix S1000pj camera. Also incorporated into Samsung and LG mobile phones.

5.4 THE CENTRAL PROCESSING UNIT

The central processing unit (CPU) performs the actual computation or "number crunching" inside any computer. The CPU is a microprocessor, for example, Intel's Core i3, i5, and i7 chips, with more to come - made up of millions of microscopic transistors embedded in a circuit on a silicon wafer or *chip*. Hence, microprocessors are commonly referred to *as* "chips."

As shown in Figure 5.2, the microprocessor has different parts, which perform different functions. The control unit sequentially accesses program instructions, decodes them, and controls the flow of data to and from the ALU, the registers, the caches, primary storage, secondary storage, and various output devices. The arithmetic-logic unit (ALU) performs mathematic calculations and makes logical comparisons. The registers are high-speed storage areas that store very small amounts of data and instructions for short periods of time.

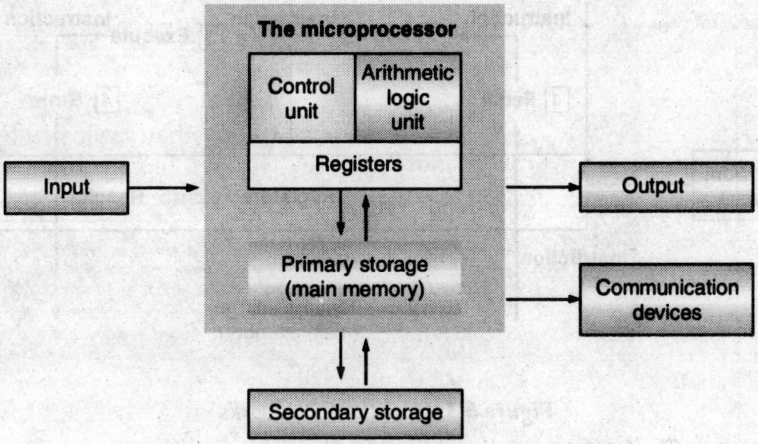

Figure 5.2: *Parts of a microprocessor*

5.4.1 How the CPU Works

Inputs enter the CPU and are stored until they are needed. At that point, they are retrieved and processed, and the output is stored and then delivered somewhere. Figure 5.3 illustrates this process, which works as follows.

- The inputs consist of data and brief instructions about what to do with the data. These instructions come into the CPU from random access memory (RAM). Data can be entered by the user through the keyboard, for example, or read from a data file in another part of the computer. The inputs are stored in registers until they are sent to the next step in the processing.
- Data and Instructions travel in the chip via electrical pathways called *buses.* The size of the bus- analogous to the width of a highway-determines how much information can flow at any time.
- The control unit directs the flow of data and instructions within the chip.
- The arithmetic-logic unit (ALU) receives the data and instructions from the registers and performs the desired computation. These data and instructions have been translated in to binary form, that is, only 0s and 1s. A "0" or a "1" is called a bit. The CPU can process only binary data. All types of data, such as letters, decimal numbers, photographs, and music, can be represented in binary form, and then be processed by the CPU.
- The data in their original form and the instructions are sent to storage registers, and then are sent back to a storage place outside the chip, such as the computer's hard drive (discussed below). Meanwhile, the transformed data go to another register and on to other parts of the computer (for example, to the monitor for display or to storage).

This cycle of processing, known as a *machine instruction cycle*, occurs billions of times per second.

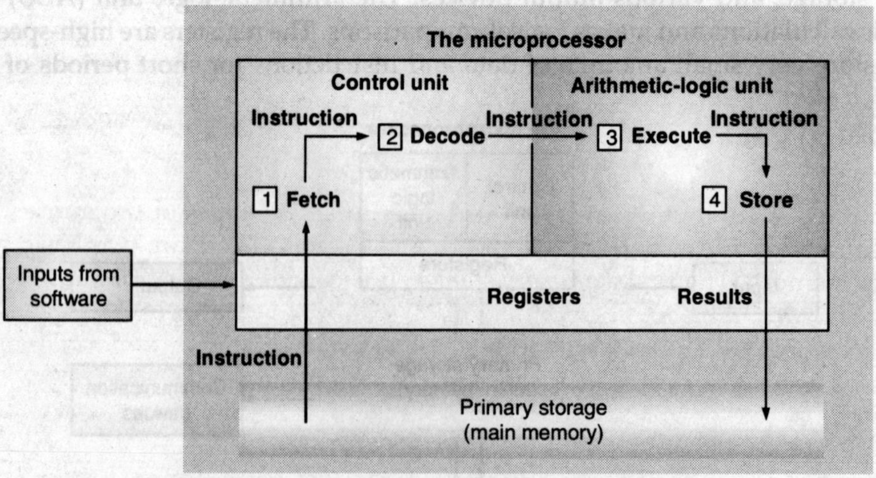

Figure 5.3: How the CPU works

5.5 ADVANCES IN MICROPROCESSOR DESIGN

Innovations in chip designs are coming at an increasingly faster rate, as described by Moore's Law. In 1965, Gordon Moore, a co-founder of Intel Corporation, predicted that microprocessor complexity would double approximately every two years. His prediction has been amazingly accurate.

The advances predicted from Moore's Law arise primarily from the following innovations:

- Increasingly miniaturized transistors.
- Multiple processors placed on a single chip. Chips with more than one processor are called *multicore* chips. For example, the Cell chip, produced by a consortium of Sony, Toshiba, and IBM, contains nine processors. Computers that use the Cell chip display very rich graphics. The Cell chip is also used in TV sets and home theatres that can download and show large numbers of high-definition programs. Intel *(www.intel.com)* and AMD *(www.amd.com)* offer multicore chips.
- In May 2011, Intel announced that its next generation of chips, which employ a three-dimensional design, will be introduced to the market early in 2012. These *3D chips* will require less power than Intel's current chips, while enhancing the performance of all computers. They will be particularly valuable in handheld devices, however, because they will also extend the device's battery life.

In addition to increased speeds and performance, Moore's law has had an impact on costs, as you can see in Table 5.3.

Table 5.3: Comparison of Personal Computer Components and Cost over Time

Year	Chip	RAM	Hard Drive	Monitor	Cost
1997	Pentium II	64 MB	4 GB	17-inch	$4,000
2007	Dual-Core	1 GB	250 GB	19-inch	$1,700
2011	Quad-Core	4 GB	1 TB	22-inch	$1,500

5.6 COMPUTER MEMORY

The amount and type of memory that a computer possesses largely determines its general utility. A computer's memory also determines the types of programs the computer can run, the work it can perform its speed, and its cost. There are two basic categories of computer memory. The first is *primary storage.* It is called "primary" because it stores small amounts of data and information that the CPU will use immediately. The second category is *secondary storage,* which stores much larger amounts of data and information - an entire software program, for example - for extended periods of time.

5.6.1 Memory Capacity

Recall that CPUs process only binary units- 0s and 1s- which are translated through computer languages. A particular combination of bits represents a certain alphanumeric character or a simple mathematical operation. Eight bits are needed to represent any given character. This 8-bit string is known as a byte. The storage capacity of a computer is measured in bytes. Bits typically are used as units of measure only for telecommunications capacity, as in how many million bits per second can be transmitted through a particular medium.

The hierarchy of terms used to describe memory capacity is as follows:

- *Kilobyte. Kilo* means 1 thousand, so a kilobyte (KB) is approximately 1,000 bytes. Actually, a kilobyte is 1,024 bytes. Computer designers find it convenient to work with powers of 2. When 2 is raised to the tenth power, the result is 1,024. This number is close enough to 1,000 that people use the standard prefix "kilo;' which means exactly 1,000 in familiar units such as the kilogram or kilometer.
- *Megabyte. Mega* means 1 million, so a megabyte (MB) is approximately 1 million bytes.
- *Gigabyte. Giga* means 1 billion, so a gigabyte (GB) is approximately 1 billion bytes.
- *Terabyte.* A terabyte is approximately 1 trillion bytes. The storage capacity of modern personal computers can be several terabytes.
- *Petabyte.* A petabyte is approximately 1,000 terabytes.
- *Exabyte.* An exabyte is approximately 1,000 petabytes.
- *Zettabyte.* A zettabyte is approximately 1,000 exabytes.

To get a feel for these amounts, consider the following example: A computer that has 1 terabyte of storage capacity on its hard drive (a type of secondary storage) can store approximately 1 trillion bytes of data. The average page of text contains about 2,000 bytes, so the hard drive could store approximately 10 percent of the entire print collection of the Library of Congress. That same 1-terabyte hard drive also could store 70 hours of standard definition compressed video.

5.6.2 PRIMARY STORAGE

Primary storage, or main memory, as it is sometimes called, stores three types of information for very brief periods of time: (1) data to be processed by the CPU, (2) instructions for the CPU on how to process the data, and (3) operating system programs that manage various aspects of the computer's operation . Primary storage takes p lace in chips mounted on the computer's main circuit board, called the *motherboard,* which are located as close as physically possible to the CPU chip. As with the CPU, all of the data and instructions in primary storage have been translated into binary code.

There are four main types of primary storage: (1) register, (2) cache memory, (3) random access memory (RAM), and (4) read-only memory (ROM). You learn about each type below.

(i) **Registers** are part of the CPU. They have the least capacity, storing extremely limited amounts of instructions and data only immediately before and after processing.

(ii) **Cache memory** is a type of high-speed memory that a processor can access more rapidly than main memory (RAM). Cache memory enables the computer to temporarily store frequently used blocks of data. Blocks used less often remain in RAM until they are transferred to cache; blocks used infrequently remain in secondary storage. Cache memory is physically located closer to the CPU than is RAM. Because the instructions travel a shorter distance to the CPU, cache is faster than RAM.

(iii) **Random access memory** (RAM) is the part of primary storage that holds a software program and small amounts of data for processing. When a software program (such as

Microsoft® Word) is started on your computer, the entire program is transferred from secondary storage into RAM. As you use the program, small parts of its instructions and data are sent into the registers and then to the CPU. Compared with the registers, RAM stores more information and is located farther away from the CPU. Compared with secondary storage, however, RAM stores less information and is much closer to the CPU.

RAM is temporary and, in most cases, is *volatile.* That is, RAM chips lose their contents if the current is lost or turned off, as occurs in a power surge, a brownout, or electrical noise generated by lightning or nearby machines.

Most of us have lost data at some time due to a computer "crash" or a power failure. The data lost are whatever was in RAM, cache, or the registers at the time, because these types of memory are volatile. Therefore, greater security is needed when certain types of critical data or instructions are stored. Cautious computer users frequently save data to non-volatile memory (secondary storage). In addition, most modern software applications have auto-save functions. Programs stored in secondary storage, although temporarily copied into RAM when they are being used, remain intact because only a copy is lost, not the original.

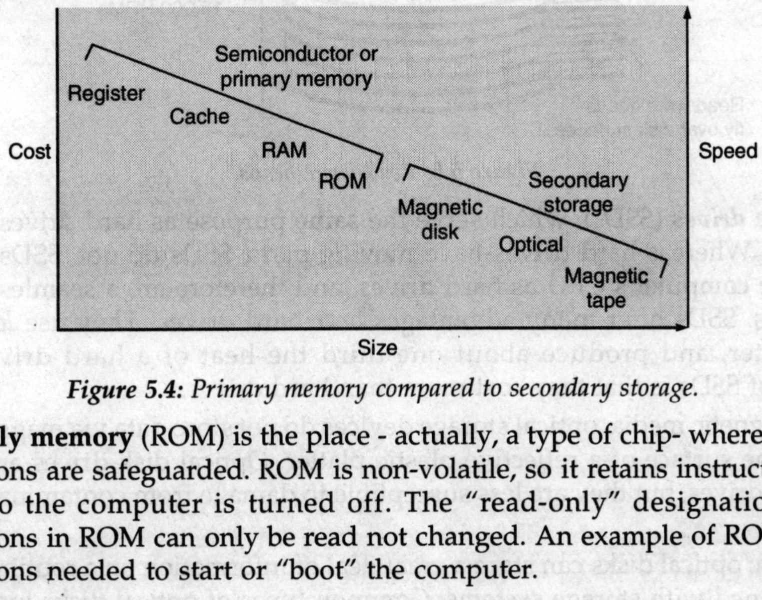

Figure 5.4: Primary memory compared to secondary storage.

(iv) Read-only memory (ROM) is the place - actually, a type of chip- where certain critical instructions are safeguarded. ROM is non-volatile, so it retains instructions when the power to the computer is turned off. The "read-only" designation means that instructions in ROM can only be read not changed. An example of ROM is the initial instructions needed to start or "boot" the computer.

5.6.3 Secondary Storage

Secondary storage is designed to store large amounts of data for extended periods of time. Secondary storage has the following characteristics:

- It is non-volatile.
- More time is needed to retrieve data from secondary storage than from RAM.
- It is cheaper than primary storage (see Figure 5.4).
- It consists of a variety of media, each with its own technology, as you will see next.

One storage device, ***magnetic tape***, is kept on a large open reel or in a smaller cartridge or cassette. Although this is an old technology, it remains popular because it is the cheapest storage medium, and it can handle enormous amounts of data. As a result, many organizations use magnetic tape for archival storage. The downside is that it is the slowest method for retrieving data, because all the data are placed on the tape sequentially. *Sequential access* means that the system might have to run through most of the tape before the desired piece of data appears.

Magnetic disks, called hard drives or *fixed disk drives*, are the most commonly used mass storage devices because of their low cost, high speed, and large storage capacity. Hard disk drives read from, and write to, stacks of rotating (at up to 15,000 RPM) magnetic disk platters mounted in rigid enclosures and sealed against environmental and atmospheric contamination (see Figure 5.5). These disks are permanently mounted in a unit that may be internal or external to the computer.

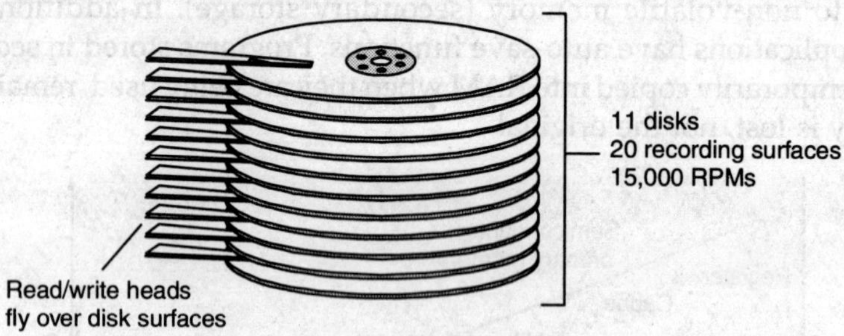

Figure 5.5: Read/write heads.

Solid state drives (SSDs), which serve the same purpose as hard drives, store data in memory chips. Whereas hard drives have moving parts, SSDs do not. SSDs use the same interface to the computer's CPU as hard drives, and therefore are a seamless replacement for hard drives. SSDs offer many advantages *over* hard drives. They use *less* power, are silent and faster, and produce about one-third the heat of a hard drive. The major disadvantage of SSDs is that they cost more than hard drives.

Unlike magnetic media, optical storage devices do not store data via magnetism. Rather, a laser reads the surface of a reflective plastic platter. Optical disk drives are slower than magnetic hard drives, but they are less susceptible to damage from contamination, and they are less fragile.

In addition, optical disks can store a great deal of information on a routine basis as well as when combined with storage systems. Common types of optical disks include compact disk read-only memory (CD-ROM), digital video disk (DVD), and Blu-ray disk.

Compact disk, read-only memory (CD-ROM) storage devices feature high capacity, low cost, and high durability. Because a CD-ROM is a read-only medium, however, it cannot be written on. A CD-R can be written to, but once this is done, the data written on it cannot be changed later. That is, CD-R is writeable (which CD-ROM is not) but is not rewriteable. In some applications, not being rewriteable is an advantage because it prevents some types of accidental data destruction. Compact disk, rewritable (CD-RW) adds rewritability to the recordable compact disk market.

The ***digital video disk*** (DVD) is a five-inch disk that can store about 135 minutes of digital video. DVDs can also perform as computer storage disks, providing storage capabilities of 17 gigabytes. DVD players can read current CO-ROMs, but current CD-ROM players cannot read DVDs. The access speed of a DVD drive is faster than that of a typical CD-ROM drive.

A dual-layer Blu-ray disc can store 50 gigabytes, almost three times the capacity of a dual=-layer DVD. The Blu-ray technology continues to develop, with 10-layered Blu-ray discs being tested.

Flash memory devices (or *memory cards)* are non-volatile electronic storage devices that contain no moving parts and use 30 times less battery power than hard drives. Flash devices are also smaller and more durable than hard drives. The trade-off is that flash devices store less data than do hard drives. Flash devices are used with digital cameras, handheld and laptop computers, telephones, music players, and video game consoles.

One popular Rash memory device is the ***thumb drive,*** also called *memory stick, jump drive,* or *flash drive.* These devices fit into Universal Serial Bus (USB) ports on personal computers and other devices, and they can store many gigabytes. Thumb drives have replaced magnetic floppy disks for portable storage.

5.7 SOFTWARE

Computer hardware is only as effective as the instructions you give it, and those instructions are contained in **software**. The importance of computer software cannot be overestimated. The first software applications for computers in business were developed in the early 1950s. At that time, software was less costly. Today, software comprises a much larger percentage of the cost of modern computer systems because the price of hardware has dramatically decreased, while both the complexity and the price of software have dramatically increased.

The ever-increasing complexity of software has also increased the potential for errors, or ***bugs***. Large applications today may contain millions of lines of computer code, written by hundreds of people over the course of several years. The potential for errors is huge, and testing and ***debugging*** software is expensive and time consuming.

In spite of these overall trends - increasing complexity, cost, and numbers of defects software has become an everyday feature of our business and personal lives. Your examination of software begins with definitions of some fundamental concepts. Software consists of computer programs, which are sequences of instructions for the computer. The process of writing or *coding* programs is called ***programming***. Individuals who perform this task are called ***programmers***.

Computer programs include ***documentation,*** which is a written description of the program's functions. Documentation helps the user operate the computer system, and it helps other programmers understand what the program does and how it accomplishes its purpose. Documentation is vital to the business organization. Without it, the departure of a key programmer or user may cause the organization to lose knowledge of the use and design of the program as well.

The computer can do nothing until it is instructed by software. Computer hardware, by design, is general purpose. Software enables the user to instruct the hardware to perform specific functions that provide business value. There are two major types of software: ***systems software*** and ***application software***. Figure 5.6 illustrates the relationship among hardware, systems software, and application software.

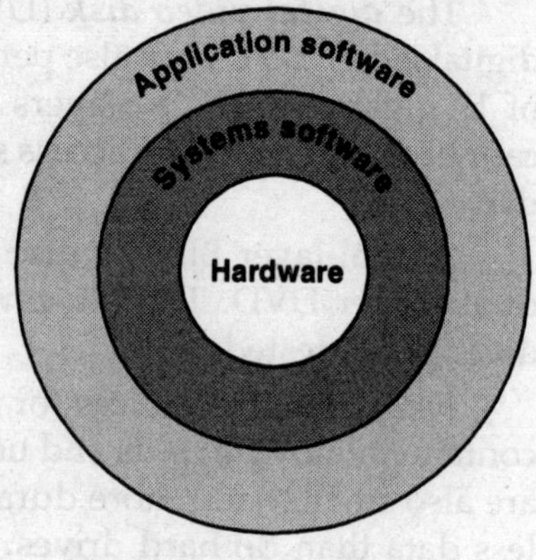

Figure 5.6: Systems software serves as an intermediary between hardware and functional applications.

Systems software is a set of instructions that serves primarily as an intermediary between computer hardware and application programs. Systems software enables computer systems to perform self-regulatory functions by loading itself when the computer is first turned on and providing commonly used sets of instructions for all applications. ***Systems programming*** refers to both the creation and the maintenance of systems software.

Application software is a set of computer instructions that provide more specific functionality to a user. This functionality may be broad, such as general word processing, or narrow, such as an organization's payroll program. Essentially, an application program applies a computer to a certain need. ***Application programming*** refers to the creation, modification, and improvement of application software. Application software may be proprietary or off-the-shelf. As you will see, modern organizations use many different software applications.

5.7.1 Software Issues

The importance of software in computer systems has brought new issues to the forefront for organizational managers. These issues include software defects (bugs), licensing, open systems, and open-source software.

5.7.1.1 Software Defects

All too often, computer program code is inefficient, poorly designed, and riddled with errors. The Software Engineering Institute (SEI) at Carnegie Mellon University in Pittsburgh defines good software as usable, reliable, defect free, cost effective, and maintainable. As dependence on computers and networks increases, the risks associated with software defects are getting worse.

The SEI maintains that, on average, professional programmers make between 100 and 150 errors in every 1,000 lines of code they write. Fortunately, the software industry recognizes this problem. Unfortunately, however, the problem is enormous, and the industry is taking only initial steps to resolve it. One critical step is better design and planning at the beginning of the development process.

5.7.1.2 Software Licensing

Many people routinely copy proprietary software, but making copies without the manufacturer's explicit permission is illegal. The Business Software Alliance (BSA) *(www.bsa.org)* has calculated that software piracy costs software vendors around the world billions of dollars annually. The BSA, a non-profit trade association dedicated to promoting a safe and legal digital world, collects, investigates, and acts on software piracy tips. Most tips come from current and past employees of offending companies.

To protect their investment, software vendors must prevent their products from being copied and distributed by individuals and other software companies. A company can copyright its software, which means that the U.S. Copyright Office grants the company the exclusive legal right to reproduce, publish, and sell that software.

The number of desktop computers continues to grow, and businesses continue to decentralize, so IS managers are finding it increasingly difficult to supervise their software assets. In fact, in a recent survey 70 percent of chief information officers (CIOs) were "not confident" that their companies are in compliance with software licensing agreements. For example, one medium-size company was fined $10,000 for unknowingly using Microsoft® Exchange mailbox licenses that had not been purchased. Worse, the company was also fined $100,000 for not having the necessary licenses for Autodesk, Inc.'s AutoCAD® design software.

To help companies manage their software licenses, new firms have arisen that specialize in tracking software licenses for a fee. Express Metrix *(www.expressmetrix.com)* and Software Spectrum, for example, will track and manage a company's software licenses to ensure compliance with U.S. copyright laws.

5.7.1.3 Open Systems

The open systems concept refers to a group of computing products that work together. In an open system, the same operating system with compatible software is installed on all computers that interact within an organization. A complementary approach is to employ application software that will run across all computer platforms. Where hardware, operating systems, and application software are designed as open systems, users can purchase the best software, called *best of breed*, for a job without worrying whether it will run on particular hardware.

5.7.1.4 Open-source Software

Within the software industry, the trend is away from proprietary software and toward open-source software. Proprietary software is purchased software that has restrictions on its use, copying, and modification. Companies developing such software spend money and time researching and developing their products, which are then sold in the marketplace. The proprietary nature of this software means that the company keeps the source code-the actual computer instructions- private (as Coca-Cola does with its formula).

In contrast, the source code for open-source software is available at no cost to developers or users. Open-source software is distributed with license terms that ensure that its source code will always be available.

Open-source software is produced by worldwide "communities" of developers who write and maintain the code. Inside each community, however, only a small group of developers, called *core developers,* is allowed to modify the code directly. All the other developers must submit their suggested changes to the core developers.

There are advantages to implementing open-source software in an organization. According to OpenSource *(www.opensource.org)*, open-source development produces high-quality, reliable, low-cost software. This software is also flexible, meaning that the code can be changed to meet users' needs. In many cases, open-source software is more reliable than commercial software. Because the code is available to many developers, more bugs are discovered early and quickly, and they are fixed immediately. Technical support for open-source software is also available from firms that offer products derived from the software. An example is Red Hat *(www.redhat.com)*, a major Linux vendor that supplies solutions to problems associated with open-source technology. Firms such as Red Hat provide education, training, and technical support, for a fee.

Open-source software also has disadvantages, however. The biggest is that companies that use open-source software depend on the continued good will of an army of volunteers for enhancements, bug fixes, and so on, even if there is a contract for support. Some companies will not accept this risk, although as a practical matter the support community for Linux, Apache, or Firefox is not likely to disappear. Further, organizations without in-house technical experts will have to purchase maintenance-support contracts from a third party. In addition, open-source software poses questions concerning ease of use, the time and expense needed to train users, and compatibility with existing systems either within or outside the organization.

There are many examples of open-source software, including the GNU (GNU's Not UNIX) suite of software *(www.gnu.org)* developed by the free Software foundation *(www.fsf.org)*; the Linux operating system *(www.linux-hq.com)*; Apache Web server *(www.apache.org)*; sendmail SMTP (Send Mail Transport Protocol) e-mail server *(www.sendmail.org)*; the Perl programming language *(www.perl.org)*; the Firefox browser from Mozilla *(www.mozilla.com)*; and Sun's StarOffice applications suite *(www.sun.com/software/star/staroffice/index.asp)*. In fact, more than 150,000 open-source projects are under way at Source Forge *(www.sourceforge.net)*, the popular open-source hosting site.

Open-source software is moving to the mainstream, as you see by the many major companies that use this type of software. For example, Japan's Shinsei Bank *(www.shinseibank.com)* uses Linux on its servers; SugarCRM *(www.sugarcrm.com)* for certain customer relationship management tasks; and MySQL *(www.mysql.com)* open-source database management software. Further, the *Los Angeles* Times use Alfresco *(www.alfresco.com)* to manage some of the images and video for the newspaper's Website.

5.8 SYSTEMS SOFTWARE

As you saw earlier, the programs in systems software control and support the computer system and its information-processing activities. Systems software also helps users and IT personnel program, test, and debugs their own computer programs. Systems software programs support application software by directing the computer's basic functions. For example, when the computer is turned on, the initialization program (a systems program) prepares and readies all devices for processing.

The major type of systems software with which we are concerned is the operating system. The operating system (OS) is the "director" of your computer system's operations. It supervises the overall operation of the computer by monitoring the computer's status, scheduling operations, and managing input and output processes. Well-known desktop operating systems include Microsoft® Windows *(www.microsoft.com)*, Apple Mac OS X *(www.apple.com)*, Linux *(www.linuxhq.com)*, and Google Chrome *(www.google.com/chrome)*. When a new version with new features is released, the developers often give the new version a new designation. For example, the latest version of Windows is Windows 7, and the latest version of OS X is Snow Leopard or OS X 1 0.6.

The operating system also provides an interface between the user and the hardware. This user interface hides the complexity of the hardware from the user. That is, you do not have to know how the hardware actually operates; you simply have to know what the hardware will do and what you need to do to obtain the desired results.

The ease or difficulty of the interaction between the user and the computer is determined to a large extent by the graphical user interface. The graphical user interface (GUI) allows users to exercise direct control of the hardware through manipulation of visible objects (such as icons) and actions that replace complex commands. Microsoft® Windows provides a widely recognized GUI.

The next generation of CUI technology incorporates features such *as* virtual reality, head-mounted displays, speech input (user commands) and output, pen and gesture recognition, animation, multimedia, artificial intelligence, and cellular/wireless communication capabilities. The new interfaces, called *natural user interfaces* (NUIs), will combine social, haptic, and touch-enabled gesture-control interfaces.

A social interface guides the user through computer applications by using cartoon like characters, graphics, animation, and voice commands. The cartoon like characters can be puppets, narrators, guides, inhabitants, or avatars (computer-generated humanlike figures). Social interfaces are hard to create without being corny. For example, the assistant "Clippy" was *so* annoying to users of Microsoft® Office 97 that the feature was eliminated from Office 2003 onwards.

Motion control gaming consoles are another type of interface. Three major players currently offer this interface: the Xbox 360 Kinect, the PS3 PlayStation Move, and the Nintendo Wii.

- Kinect tracks your movements without a physical controller, has voice recognition, and accommodates multiple players.
- The PlayStation Move uses a physical controller with motion-sensing electronics, making it the technological "cross" between Kinect and Wii. Move requires each player to use a wand.
- Wii uses a physical controller. Compared to Kinect and Move, Wii has been on the market longer, has the biggest library of motion-sensing games, and is the least expensive. Wii has the least accurate motion sensing of the three systems, however, and it is not available in high-definition, whereas Kinect and Move are.

Touch-enabled gesture-control interfaces enable users to browse through photos, "toss" objects around a screen, "flick" to turn the pages of a book, play video games, and watch movies. Examples of this type of interface are Microsoft® Surface and the Apple iPhone. Microsoft® Surface is used in casinos such as Harrah's iBar in Las Vegas and in some AT&T stores. The most visible use of Surface, however, was the touch wall used by CNN during its presidential election coverage in 2008.

5.9 APPLICATION SOFTWARE

As you saw earlier, application software consists of instructions that direct a computer system to perform specific information-processing activities and also provide functionality for users. Because there are so many different uses for computers, the number of application software programs is correspondingly large.

Application software may be developed in-house by the organization's information systems personnel, or it may be commissioned from a software vendor. Alternatively, the software can be purchased, leased, or rented from a vendor that develops applications and sells them too many organizations. This "off-the-shelf' software may be a standard package, or it may be customizable. Special-purpose programs or "packages" can be tailored for a specific purpose, such as inventory control or payroll. The word package refers to a computer program (or group of programs) that has been developed by a vendor and is available for purchase in a pre-packaged form.

General-purpose, off-the-shelf application programs designed to help individual users increase their productivity are referred to as personal application software. Some of the major types of personal application software are listed in Table 5.4. *Software suites* combine some of these applications and integrate their functions. Microsoft® Office is a well-known example of a software suite.

Table 5.4: Personal Application Software

Category of Personal Application Software	Major Functions	Examples
Spreadsheets	Use rows and columns to manipulate primarily numerical data; useful for analyzing financial information and for what-if and goal-seeking analyses.	Microsoft® Excel Corel Quattro Pro Apple iWork Numbers
Word Processing	Allow users to manipulate primarily text with many writing and editing features.	Microsoft® Word Apple iWork Pages
Desktop Publishing	Extend word processing software to allow production of finished, camera-ready documents, which may contain photographs, diagrams, and other images combined with text in different fonts.	Microsoft® Publisher QuarkXPress
Data Management	Allows users to store, retrieve, and manipulate related data.	Microsoft® Access FileMaker Pro
Presentation	Allows users to create and edit graphically rich information to appear on electronic slides.	Microsoft® PowerPoint Apple iWork Keynote
Graphics	Allows users to create, store, and display or print charts, graphs, maps, and drawings.	Adobe® PhotoShop Corel DRAW

Personal Information Management	Allows users to create and maintain calendars, appointments, to-do lists, and business contacts.	IBM Lotus Notes Microsoft® Outlook
Personal Finance	Allows users to maintain chequebooks, track investments, monitor credit cards, and bank and pay bills electronically.	Quicken Microsoft® Money Microsoft® FrontPage
Web Authoring	Allows users to design Web sites and publish them on the Web.	Macromedia Dreamweaver
Communications	Allows users to communicate with other people over any distance.	Novell Groupwise

Speech-recognition software is an input technology, rather than strictly an application, that can feed systems software and application software. Speech-recognition software, also called *voice recognition,* recognizes and interprets human speech, either one word at a time (discrete speech) or in a conversational stream (continuous speech). Advances in processing power, new software algorithms, and better microphones have enabled developers to design extremely accurate voice recognition software. Experts predict that, in the near future, voice recognition systems will be built into almost every device, appliance, and machine that people use. Applications for voice recognition technology abound. Consider these examples:

- Call centers are using the technology. The average call costs $5 if it is handled by an employee, but only 50 cents with a self-service, speech-enabled system. The online brokerage firm E-Trade Financial uses Tellme *(www.tellme.com)* to field about 50,000 calls per day, thereby saving at least $30 million annually.
- IBM's Embedded ViaVoice software *(www-306.ibm.com/software/voice/viavoice/)* powers CM's OnStar and other dashboard command systems, such as music players and navigational systems.
- Apple's Macintosh OS X and Microsoft's Windows 7 operating systems come with built-in voice technology.
- Nuance's Dragon NaturallySpeaking *(www.msance.com)* allows for accurate voice-to-text and e-mail dictation.
- Vocera Communications *(www.vocera .com)* has developed a communicator badge that combines voice recognition with wireless technologies. Among its first customers, medical workers used the badge to search through hospital directories for the right person to handle a patient problem or to find medical records.
- Vox-Tec's *(www.voxtec.com)* Phraselator, a handheld device about the size of a chequebook, listens to requests for a phrase and then translations it into any of 41 specified languages. U.S. troops in Iraq and Afghanistan are using it to provide translations in Arabic and Pashto.

5.10 CHOICE OF INFORMATION TECHNOLOGY: NATURE OF IT DECISION

A business enterprise or an organization requires making a decision of choosing appropriate information Technology (IT), as a vehicle, to handle the management information system. The choice of IT is a strategic decision, making long-term impact on the effectiveness of the MIS of the enterprise. The information technology affects the people, the processes and the productivity of the organization. It is a strategic business decision and not a financial decision to be taken on the least cost approach. Just as the MIS handles the decision support applications, the choice of the Information Technology makes a qualitative difference in the decision making process. Hence, a wrong choice of the IT would kill a good MIS design as the information technology would not support the user on the aspects and the requirements such as speed, response, access, security, autonomy and integration of the information processing on the different hardware software platforms. A wrong choice of the information technology would also kill the MIS designer's ability to develop a user-friendly end user computer system, providing all capabilities of the data and the information handling with flexibility and speed.

The choice of information technology can be compared to a decision of constructing a house. Through the cost of construction is a major decision parameter, many other factors such as the living comfort and convenience, accommodation of the family members with their respective living styles, etc. are equally important. Besides a house should have a privacy, should be aesthetic to look at, airy and well lit and also the maintenance of facilities and utilities should be easy. A wrong choice of house, therefore, affects the buyer for the lifetime, both, in terms of the cost and also in terms of comfort. The decision is usually irreversible and very costly, and may not satisfy all the needs of the members of the family.

The modern information technology offers a number of different system configurations, each being a candidate, as a solution to satisfy the needs of the MIS. The information technology decision, therefore, is a technical decision, where it is required to decide between the various configuration alternatives made of a variety of hardware and software option. The configurations are the LAN or the WAN, the Mini or the Superman, and the front end and the Back Office Systems, Internet/Intranet, OOT, Client Server Systems.

The configurations could be evolved on the basis of the approach to the information processing. It could either be distributed or centralized, local processing or centralized processing, etc. It could be a conventional data processing approach versus the database management approach.

Each configuration has certain technical merits and demerits, and, therefore, has to be weighed on some other criteria for its selection. Each one of them covers a wide cost spectrum. The wide cost spectrum results due to the different architecture options in the hardware such as the RISC, the CISC and the different processing chips such as the INTEL, the MOTOROLA or the PROPRIETARY Chip such as the Alpha of the Digital and the POWER PC of the IBM, etc.

The third reason is the different operating systems for the different platforms, i.e., the DOS, Windows NT, the UNIX, the OSF, the MOTIF, the OS2, the VMS and their proprietary versions such as the Ultrix, the HP UNIX, and the ORG UNIX, etc.

Several probable configuration options are further influenced by the available software running under each of the operating systems. The software options, an important dimension to the choice of the information technology, demand a certain operating system as a critical requirement. Some software option is efficient on one hardware platform and not on the other, so if the software is critical, then many times the hardware is critical, then many times the hardware becomes a no option decision.

Another important factor which influences the information technology decision is the organization and its infrastructural arrangement of the offices, warehouses, factories and the customers. Much organization would demand hardware typical to that particular location and also be able to communicate with other hardware-software platforms. In such situations, the communication requirement becomes a dominating factor in choice of the information technology.

For example, the warehouse may need just a PC or a PCLAN, the nearby factory may need a mini computer system and the corporate office would need a large Superman computer with special software suitable for its functioning. Each of these platforms may have different operating systems, and the MIS of such an organization requires data and information sharing between all these resources at various locations. The information technology decision must consider the communication problem and the interface between the two hardware options so that the data sharing is operationally feasible. Many a times, the operational feasibility problems are solved by writing the system utilities, the drivers, and the programmers so that these two platforms become ready to share each others resources effectively. The information technology decision is also influenced by people-related factors. The choice of the information technology is made on the basis of the ability of the people in the organization to run the hardware-software system. The place like warehouse may not have highly qualified computer literate personnel and, therefore, at such a location, PC systems would be an automatic choice or a dumb terminal of the main computer system. But at the factory location, since the personnel are of the higher skills, grade and qualifications, a Network or a mini system, capable of offering different software solutions, would be required. In such a place, hardware and software support in also required.

Though training the personnel to become computer literates is a solution to such problems it may not be always possible and operationally feasible to solve such problems and give a high-tech information technology solution which is uniform across the organization. The work culture and the people culture become the critical decision inputs for any information technology decision.

Finally the information technology choice is governed by the requirement of the mission critical application(s) of the organization. The hardware choice and its configuration in terms of memory, disk and communication are decided on the base of processing needs of the mission critical applications. The other requirement of the organization is to be fitted to this configuration.

For example, if the main business of an organization is service to the customer, then the mission critical application is the inventory management of a variety of items manufactured and distributed at different locations. Such an application would need resource sharing at different locations-of hardware, software and database. It could be a case of sharing between the UNIX DP network and the minis with different DBMS systems. The sharing of each other's resources may be for input acquisition and processing for integrating the data on a higher plane and sending the result to different locations, and for presenting on the different output devices such as the laser printers and plotter, and also on the storage devices available at the different locations.

The information technology decision is made for the current needs as well as for the futuristic needs of the organization. Hence, the decision is influenced by the technology forecast and the business forecast. It requires some valid assumptions about the growth of the business, the manner in which it will be conducted and the information needs of the organization to conduct the business. Such a probing in the futuristic needs helps to size up the various options and to weigh them critically on the various criteria.

The information technology decision, therefore, is a decision to be taken at a particular point of time and implemented over a period of time considering the various soft and hard options experienced from time to time. If the organization is under a financial pressure as the budget is not adequate to implement the best information technology opted for should be upgradeable, expandable and scalable. Such organizations can start with a smaller configuration and migrate to a bigger one with no risk of technological obsolescence no loss of development effort.

The nature of IT decision is complex and is governed by a number of factors. Since, this decision has long-term business and financial implications and affects the entire organization, it is a strategic decision.

5.10.1 Strategic Decision

The information technology choice is a strategic decision and, therefore, it should be taken after considering a number of factors. The information technology offers a number of alternatives which have varying costs. The costs differ due to the difference in the architecture of the hardware, capability of the software and different configurations but achieving more or less the same results. Apart from the cost factor there are other factors, such as data management, organization infrastructure and satisfying its information needs which influence the information technology decision. These factors are discussed at length in the following sections.

5.10.1.1 Management Process Or Style

The information needs of the people in the organization arise from the process or the style by which the management runs the business. The quality of management process depends on the people culture and the culture predominantly affects the decision making process.

If the decision processes are centralized at a higher level and the delegation of responsibilities and authorities is not proper, then the information technology choice will weigh heavily in favor of the distributed data acquisition systems and the centralized high end information processing systems for decision support. If the decision processes are decentralized, the information technology choice will weigh in favor of those systems, where the acquisition, processing, analysis and decision making will be at distributed nodal points. The organization which operates through a number of locations and on the basis of the Strategic Business Units (SBU) will opt for such an option. In such cases the typical nature of the concerned SBU will decide the hardware-software platform for the particular location. If the decisions in the organization are of the following types, then the information technology option would differ. These types are:

(a) The decisions affecting the operations management.
(b) The decisions affecting the execution and control of the business.
(c) The strategic business decisions.

In such cases, the information technology choice would be the Front End Processing System connected to the Bank Office Central System. Hotels, hospitals and large corporate bodies are the examples, where such a choice is desirable. The front end systems take care of the operations management, while the back office systems take care of the strategic and the operations planning and control of the business. There is other business situation where due to sensitive nature of the business, decision making is concentrated at one business location or in one of the business functions such as marketing, research and development, manufacturing, etc. The information technology choice is largely governed by the information needs of that particular location or function. In other words, every business has one or more mission critical applications serving the information needs of the critical strategic decision. The entire management process revolves around this application. The organizations information technology choice is, therefore, based on the requirement of these applications serving the critical business functions. Due to the organizations. infrastructure and also due to the nature of the business it so happens that there are data centers, where a large umber of transactions take place and these are the decision centers. In such cases the information technology choice will be in favor of the distributed high end data processing systems and the dedicated information processing system at the decision centre using the distributed data bases. Many service oriented business like the banks, the insurance companies, etc. fall into this category.

It is, therefore, important to note that the information technology choice considers the management process, the business organization, the decision making style and the mission critical applications as the important dominating factors. The choice of hardware details and the software mix will be decided on these factors.

5.10.1.2 Business Operations

There are many organizations, where the business operations are typical, voluminous and their information needs are largely transaction processed. The typical example is that of the banks where the banking operations are uniformly standard at almost all branch locations. The transactions are large in number and need to be processed very fast. The decision making process is rule based governed by the policy and the guidelines issued by the statutory bodies in the banking industry. The information technology choice in such cases would be the one which satisfies this need the best. In a Hospital, where the transaction processing is very low, the decision making need is satisfied by query type applications. The information needs here are largely the patient and doctor-oriented. The information technology choice, in such case, will be of the front end processing system supported by the back office mini or main frame system with a strong database system which is very powerful in data management and the query processing.

Suppose there is an organization the main business of which is marketing of a variety of product through a nationwide distribution channel system. The business here operates mainly on satisfying the needs of the buyers by providing them what they want. Hence, inventory management is the main business function here. The information technology choice in such case will be the one where the sales and the receipts data is processed very fast, the inventory related decisions are taken, stocks are adjusted and the procurement action is also taken quickly. The hardware details in such case will be decided based on the data volume, the speed and the communication systems.

There are certain business organizations the operations of which are such that if the organization takes care of one or two major functions, most of the information needs and the MIS needs would be satisfied. Many a times these functions are special and would be demanding special hardware and software. If the organization requires mix of such special hardware and software, then the information technology choice will be based on the integration possibility of the different information technology platforms satisfying the organizational information needs.

For example, in the high-tech engineering organizations, a lot of engineering and design activities, such as drafting, designing, modeling and analysis take place. Such a function would need special hardware such as work stations and special CAD/ CAM/ CAE software, etc. However the data processed by such hardware-software system needs to be integrated in the business and commercial systems of the organizations. The information technology choice in such cases would be based on the feasibility of sharing the resources and data of the two locations and having special application and information needs.

A number of such possibilities emerge and unless these factors are properly considered, the information technology choice may go wrong. The information technology choice therefore is strategic to the business performance. In all the business twenty per cent information set is critical and eighty per cent is not so critical. If the information technology choice does not satisfy the critical twenty percent need, then it can be said that the information technology choice is a strategic mistake with concurrent business and financial implications.

5.10.2 Configuration Design

The details of the information technology, such as architecture, communication, RDBMS, storage media, and operating system are also strategic to the success of the MIS. These details are carefully worked out for effective implementation of the information technology.

The details are worked out based on the following features:

1. Data type

Words, Numeric, Image and Voice. The hardware and software should be capable of handling these data types.

2. Data volume

The online storage capacity would be decided based on the processing needs. It will be further increased due to the disk mirroring.

3. I/O operations

These would decide the controllers and the speed of I/O processing.

4. Data sharing

If the data is to be shared across the databases, then the storage capacity will be decided based on the size of the databases.

5. Process speed

The speed needed for processing will decide the CPU, memory and the processing architecture.

6. RDBMS and 4GL

These will be chosen on the basis of the volume, special handling of the data, and the level of security and the integrity required. All RDBMS are not same and are not equally efficient on all the platforms.

7. Query processing

This decides the SQL or standard SQL and 4GL.

8. Communication protocols

If different platforms need to be connected, then the software such as the TCP/ IP needs to be considered.

9. Interface and gateways

These will be decided on the basis of data transfer needs between the locations and between the hardware-software platforms.

10. Security and Integrity

The level of security and integrity required will decide the hardware, the software and the operating system. All the hardware and software do not satisfy these needs fully.

11. Languages and packages

The requirement, often, is of a special language and packages besides the main software. The hardware and operating system will be decided based on this need. The information technology choice is translated into a variety of details based on the above factors. When all these factors and the associated choices of the information technology details are worked out, we can say that the configuration of the computer system is designed. Several configurations are possible and they need to be thoroughly evaluated before selection.

5.10.3 Evalution

As we develop different choices of information technology and its configurations, the decision making enters into the evaluation phase for selection. The selection criteria for evaluation would have different dimensions to be satisfied simultaneously. These dimensions are as follows:

1. Technical Evaluation
2. Operational Feasibility
3. Financial Consideration

5.10.3.1 Technical Evaluation (TE)

Technical evolution deals with the testing parameters, such as data transfer needs, the response level, the successful connectivity of the different hardware platforms, and the degree of meeting the overall system performance standards. Technical evaluation can be carried out first by studying the literature of the product in detail and then by conducting brain storming sessions with the vendor's specialists. In this phase a number of doubts are clarified and the vendor's claims in the areas of the system performance are confirmed.

Technical evaluation can then be planned by scheduling the activities such as the bench marking for a couple of key parameters. The bench marking studies could be at a raw level where you test the vendor's specifications. Once these are confirmed, the specifications are put to test on a live platform, i.e., the technical specification are tested by running live data in a particular format. Such an experiment would be a prototype model of your information processing need related to the mission critical applications. You may develop a mini representative processing application and run it on a model configuration of the system. Such experiment would confirm the vendor's claims and your expectations and needs. This would develop certain norms which can be used to configure the hardware details and building the architecture. The bill of material of hardware and software can be worked out with the help of these norms.

Following hardware software details are configured and the quality of each item is also decided using the norms developed in a live experiment. The decisions on the following points would facilitate the system configuration for a given requirement.

- Memory and Cache
- Disk Capacity, Features, Controllers
- CPU Speed, Processing Architecture and Capabilities
- Servers
- Terminals-PCs, X Terminals Work Station
- Network and Cabling, Internet and Intranet
- EDI, E-Mail
- Network Hardware
- Output Devices
- Monitors
- Operating System
- Standard: ASCII, ANSI, GUI
- Hardware Architecture
- System Software: OS, Gateways, Interfaces, Drivers, Utilities and Compilers
- Media, Copying Devices
- RDBMS, FEATURES
- Packages

Technical evaluation and confirm the information technology approach to the information processing needs of the organization. The issues like the centralized versus distributed, the online versus the batch versus the real time, the network versus the mini or the superman are also evaluated. Technical evaluation also helps in narrowing down the hardware choices as all the vendors may not satisfy the requirement of the organization.

Having narrowed down the hardware configurations to two or three options, the technical evaluation considers the performance related issues such as reliability, dependability, performance on the volume scale, security, integrity and autonomy, etc. All the option may not equally satisfy the evaluation standards set by the organization on these factors. The performance related issues will help fine tune the configuration details such as the memory, the number of ports, the specific input and output devices and the hardware infrastructure.

Technical evaluation also helps to break down the hardware on a time scale, i.e., the minimum required in the initial stage and subsequent add-ons, expansions and upgrades on a time scale.

In technical evaluation we are discussing information technology. The information technology is constantly under development and the scale on which such improvement takes place is phenomenal. Hence, it is necessary to select the latest technology in all areas of information processing as it would take you a long way and help you to protect the investment. The investment is protected, if the Information Technology choice is scalable, upgradeable and also expandable with the growth of the business.

5.10.3.2 Operational Feasibility

The options approved after the technical evaluation are tested on the operational feasibility. What the technology offers may not be possible to operate at the practical level and scale to obtain full benefits of the various inherent features. The operational feasibility evaluation considers the people-related issues and whether the systems and the procedures of the organization are complementary and conducive. In a number of situations, the choice of technology determines automatically the caliber, the competence, and the knowledge of the people in the organization. It is also observed that the organization does not provide people support to implement technology successfully. The shortcomings on people's side would be the lack of requisite qualification and the subject knowledge, the ability to absorb the technology, and use it effectively. Many a times, the organization would require appointing a new set of personnel to fulfill these needs.

Other areas affected would be the systems and the procedures currently operating in the company. The shortcoming is observed right from the absence to the inefficient systems and procedures. The modern information technology needs sophisticated back-up of the data at a requisite point and time. If such a data support is not available then the information technology would be underutilized or may not be worthwhile to implement. For example, the information technology offers a solution of fast data transfer and processing between the two platforms at two locations, i.e., the data source is at one location and its need is at two other locations. Due to the systems and the procedures prevailing at the source location, the arrival of the data at the required location is late and hence not useful. Hence, the information technology solution is operationally infeasible to obtain the best of the solution.

Most of the issues in the operational feasibility evaluation are related to the people and business processes (system and procedure). The environment must support proper implementation of a new information technology. If the environment does not support the new technology, it will be managerially prudent to choose next best option by obtaining full benefits in its successful implementation and further at a later date to switch over to the original best option.

5.10.3.3 Financial Evaluation

All the option can be evaluated in terms of the invested it calls for. It is always possible to rank the option on the basis of the basis of the investment. All business investment is evaluated in terms of return on the investment (ROI) or certain payback period. They are also judged from budget considerations.

The information technology investments are difficult to judge on the ROI basis as some aspect of the investment are intangible and are difficult to quantity in monetary terms. The best approach in such cases is to judge the investment in terms of the value of information it gives on an incremental scale. If the value of information in relation to its investment is not significant, then it could be advisable the consider the next best lower investment option.

In regard to the budget restrictions, it would be advisable to examine the possibility of scaling the hardware and the software options. It is then possible to have a solution implemented in terms of the budget provisions. The scaling can be done in terms of the quality of hardware required in the option. If may be possible to buy the requisite minimum in the first year and expand them in the subsequent period. It may be possible to configure the hardware in terms of the capabilities which are required now and which can be acquired later on. For example, one can start on 32MB memory and over to 64MB. One need not buy all the software in the first place. It can be phased out in terms of need, i.e., purchased the requisite software as and when required.

The budget restrictions can handle by taking the benefit of the scalable and the upgradeable technology. The scaling of the expansion can be done on two scales, viz. horizontal and vertical expansion. The horizontal expansion relates to the quantity while the vertical expansion relates to the quality and coverage.

1. Horizontal expansion

The memory, disk, terminals, peripheral equipment, etc. can be configured for the present needs and then expanded as the coverage increased.

2. Vertical expansion

The system integration, backward or forward, concentrates on the mission critical applications, covering only the main key business functionalities. However, in all these matters the total decision is to be taken first and then broken down into components and in terms of the budget provisions for the next two years or more.

In all these matters, a thought should be given to protect the information technology investment. If certain technological advances are round the corner, then it is better to defer the investment. The choice of hardware and software should be such that it should facilitate the integration of new technology into the old one. The new version of upgrades should be independent of the hardware. The application languages should be such that any open system can absorb it without many changes. The software choices should be independent of the hardware configurations such as the LAN, the WAN, the MINI etc.

Many a times, the packages cannot run on all the platforms because of the chip and the architecture of the hardware platform. The open system architecture is not always that .open. to accept all the software. These issues should be discussed squarely so that the investment though good at a point of time is not wasted at a later date.

5.10.4 Information Technology Implementation Plan

The implementation of the information technology is a complex task and needs a detailed and careful planning for successful implementation. It is necessary to prepare a plan of implementation covering the following features. These features are:

1. Site preparation
2. System development plan
3. Information technology installation schedule
4. Recruitment and training of computer personnel
5. Training of the users
6. Investment plan

5.10.4.1 Site Preparation

This is a major activity, wherein you prepare the site for the physical installation of the hardware i.e., the main computer system, the peripherals, the electrical and communication cabling, the air conditioning system, the tape-disk consumable storage, and the office layout for the professionals. The space allocation for each of these items is based on present need with some allowance for the future. The modern information technology needs site preparation at the user's end as well for the convenience and the ease of operations. Most of the information technology installations need infrastructural facilities, such as a conference room, and training-cum demonstration room with the modern aids of training. This process of site preparation takes away 10 to 12 per cent of investment. In all these matters, guidance is available from the hardware vendors. A committee consisting of the vendor's representatives, architect and interior designer, and in-change of the information technology implementation would be ideal for a planned site preparation activity.

5.10.4.2 System Development Plan

This is generally prepared while assessing the hardware and software needs. Such a plan gives the indication of the various locations of hardware in terms of quality and time when needed. System development plan priorities the various steps in the site preparation. One can make a site preparation plan for an immediate need and also for a later date. This would help to make a long-term financing plan. A system development plan also helps you in planning the other activities such as recruitment and training. It also helps in deciding the procurement plan of the hardware and software. A broad system development plan would go a long way preparing the operational and implementation plans of the information technology in the organization.

5.10.4.3 Information Technology Installation Schedule

This schedule gives the item-wise details of the hardware arrival and its installation, testing and acceptance. It also needs to be linked with the information system development plan to synchronize the installation with the user of the hardware and the software.

Many times the schedule also considers key issues like data conversion, switching over from an old system to a new system, rewriting programmer for new software environment and so on. Such schedule also helps in the smooth transition from old to the new. It may be from one information technology to another information technology environment or from the manual system to the computerized system.

5.10.4.4 Recruitment and Training of Information Technology Personnel

The implementation of the information technology needs specific skills in the manpower responsible for effective implementation. The skills may fall in the area of languages, tools of development and also acquiring the precise know-how on the emerging technologies and its application in the information systems.

The technology is changing at a very fast pace and it is necessary to upgrade the skills of the existing manpower by providing a need-based training. There are occasions where the skills are not available and a specific recruitment is called for. Such a recruitment and training then calls for restructuring of the information technology organization.

5.10.4.5 Training of Users

The latest development in the information technology requires its users to be well trained for its effective use. The training may range from awareness to learning of the specific tools. The users should be trained to accept the concept of end user computing. The users should be trained to use the various information technology facilities. The users should be trained to blend the information support in their day-to-day activities. It is a change in work culture and an appropriate attitude needs to be developed for the absorption of the new information technology solutions. Many software packages are available which need to be learnt for its appropriate use to become IT literate. With the support of the information technology, the user is becoming a knowledge worker. It is a qualitative cultural change and it is, therefore, necessary to prepare the user for this transformation through a comprehensive User Training Programme. Such training is imparted across the organization to the workers, officers, executives and the managers.

5.10.4.6 Investment Plan

When all the facets of the information technology implementation are ready, it is possible to work out the monetary implications such an implementation. Summarizing the estimates on the time scale would generate an investment plan. One can fit the investment in the budget provisions by suitable modifications in the implementation plan of the information technology. Since, the investment in the information technology is strategic; at the most it can be deferred but cannot be curtailed. It is important to note that the intermediate information technology solution to save on the investment is not effective. If there are any budgetary limitations, it is better to postpone the implementation. A carefully worked out investment plan should be submitted for approval with the implementation plan of the information technology. A presentation of an hour and a half to the top management highlighting the investment, the productivity gains and the competitive edge that the business of the organization acquires through the information technology, would help in obtaining the approval, its involvement and support in implementation of the information technology.

5.10.5 Choice of the Information Technology and The Management Information System

The choice of the information technology is a backbone of the Management Information System. It is a critical, strategic decision affecting the business operations and prospects. It affects the people, the processes and productivity and helps organization emerge with a new work culture. Since, it is a high investment decision; the management would look at it from the return it yields in the business.

The success of the MIS lies in how the information technology is implemented in the organization. A lot depends on the people and their ability to accept the new work style and the new work culture. All the implementation of the information technology leads to organizational transformation in the content and structure. If the human face of the organization is not properly aligned to the information technology, the best information technology would fail in its implementation, adversely affecting effective development of the MIS. There is a risk in manipulating the information technology beyond a limit to suit the personnel of the organization or the budget limitation. Hence, the implementation of the information technology could be slow on the time scale to accommodate a certain critical constraint, but it should not be allowed to adversely influence the information technology decision itself. The information technology changes are very rapid. To protect the investment in the information technology, the selection criteria should include features such as scalable architecture, upgradeable software, an open system environment, communication capability through gateways and interfaces and so on. A good management information system design requires a matching support from the information technology.

SUMMARY

Modern computer systems have six major components: the central processing unit (CPU), primary storage, secondary storage, input technologies, output technologies, and communications technologies.

Strategic issues linking hardware design to business strategy include: How do organizations keep up with the rapid price/performance advancements in hardware? How often should an organization upgrade its computers and storage systems? How can organizations measure benefits gained from price/performance improvements in hardware?

Supercomputers are the most powerful computers, designed to handle the maximum computational demands of science and the military. Mainframes, although not as powerful as supercomputers, are powerful enough for large organizations to use for centralized data processing and large databases. Minicomputers are smaller and less-powerful versions of mainframes that are often devoted to managing specific subsystems. Desktop personal computers (PCs) are the common, well-known personal and business computers. Laptop or notebook computers are small, easily transportable PCs. Tablet computers (or tablets) are complete computers combined entirely in a flat touch screen that uses a stylus, digital pen, or fingertip as an input device instead of a keyboard or mouse.

Principal human data-entry input technologies include the keyboard, mouse, optical mouse, trackball, touchpad, joystick, touchscreen, stylus, and voice-recognition systems. Principal source-data automation input devices are ATMs, POS terminals, barcode scanners, optical mark readers, magnetic ink character readers, optical character readers, sensors, cameras, radio frequency identification, and retinal scanning displays. Common output technologies include various types of monitors, impact and non-impact printers, plotters, and voice output.

The CPU is made up of the arithmetic-logic unit (ALU), which performs the calculations; the registers, which store minute amounts of data and instructions immediately before and after processing; and the control unit, which controls the flow of information on the microprocessor chip. After processing, the data in their original form and the instructions are sent back to a storage place outside the chip.

Microprocessor designs aim to increase processing speed by minimizing the physical distance that the data (as electrical impulses) must travel, increasing the number of transistors on the chip, increasing the number of CPUs on the chip, and using three-dimensional chip architecture.

There are four types of primary storage: registers, cache memory, random access memory (RAM), and read-only memory (ROM). Secondary storage includes magnetic media (tapes; hard drives; and thumb, or flash, drives) and optical media (CD-ROM, DVD, and Blu-ray disks).

Primary storage has much less capacity than secondary storage, and it is faster and more expensive per byte stored. It is also located much closer to the CPU. Sequential-access secondary storage media such as magnetic tapes are much slower and less expensive than hard drives and optical media.

Computer program code often contains errors. The industry recognizes the enormous problem of software defects, but only initial steps are being taken to resolve it. Software licensing is yet another issue for organizations and individuals. Copying proprietary software is illegal. Software vendors copyright their software to protect it from being copied. As a result, companies must license vendor-developed software to use it.

The advantages of open-source software include high quality, reliability, flexibility (code can be changed to meet users' needs), and low cost. Open-source software can be more reliable than commercial software. Because the code is available to many developers, more bugs are discovered early and quickly and are fixed immediately. Disadvantages include the cost of maintenance support contracts, ease of use, the time and expense needed to train users, and the lack of compatibility with existing systems both inside and outside the organization.

Software consists of computer programs (coded instructions) that control the functions of computer hardware. There are two main categories of software: systems software and application software. Systems software manages the hardware resources of the computer system; it functions between the hardware and the application software. The major type of systems software is the operating system. Application software enables users to perform specific tasks and information-processing activities. Application software may be proprietary or off-the-shelf.

Operating systems manage the actual computer resources (i.e., the hardware). They schedule and process applications (jobs); manage and protect memory; manage the input and output functions and hardware; manage data and files; and provide security, fault tolerance, graphical user interfaces, and windowing.

The major types of application software are spreadsheet, data management, word processing, desktop publishing, graphics, multimedia, communications, speech recognition, and groupware. Software suites combine several types of application software (e.g., word processing, spreadsheet, and data management) into an integrated package.

A business enterprise or an organization requires making a decision of choosing appropriate information Technology (IT), as a vehicle, to handle the management information system. The choice of IT is a strategic decision, making long-term impact on the effectiveness of the MIS of the enterprise.

EXERCISES

1. What do you mean by hardware?
2. Explain the different strategic hardware issues?
3. Explain the computer hierarchy?
4. Explain the different input and output technologies?
5. Explain the concept of central processing unit?
6. How the CPU works?
7. What are the advances in microprocessor design?
8. What do you mean by computer memory?
9. Explain the memory capacity?
10. Explain the primary storage devices?
11. What are the various secondary storage devices?
12. What is software?
13. Explain the various software issues?
14. Explain the concept of systems software?
15. What do you mean by application software?
16. The selection of information technology is a strategic decision in MIS development. Explain.
17. What are the technology decisions? And what is their relevance?
18. What is a configuration of IT platform when it comes to MIS? Why should the configurations be determined?
19. Which are the three parameters used in the evaluation of the IT before decision is made?
20. Why is the operational feasibility of the IT system important?
21. What methods are available to contain the investment in IT to the budget availability without compromise on the plan or quality of the MIS?
22. MIS implementation is use of IT in business processes is a cultural change in the organization. How would you handle it for smooth changes over from conventional to technology-based management?
23. Technology obsolescence is a fact of life when it comes to IT. While deciding configuration, what care should be taken so that the investment is protected for a reasonable period of time; application development effort is not wasted and organization is not required to learn a new technology again and again.
24. Top management always asks for return on investment (ROI) made in IT. How would you calculate ROI in IT? What other measures would you suggest for evaluating the investment in IT?
25. How does the work culture, management style and the organization's learning capability have a bearing on the IT or MIS decision?

❑

Transaction Processing Systems

6

6.1 INTRODUCTION

Since the 1950s, computers have been used to perform common business applications. Many of these early systems were designed to reduce costs by automating routine, labour-intensive business transactions. A **transaction** is any business-related exchange such as payments to employees, sales to customers, or payments to suppliers. Processing business transactions was the first computer application developed for most organizations. A **transaction processing system (TPS)** is an organized collection of people, procedures, software, databases, and devices used to perform and record business transactions. If you understand a transaction processing system, you understand basic business operations and functions.

6.2 THE PROBLEM

A **business transaction** is an interaction in the real world, usually between an enterprise and a person or another enterprise, where something is exchanged. For example, it could involve exchanging money, products, information, or service requests. Usually some bookkeeping is required to record what happened. Often this bookkeeping is done by a computer, for better scalability, reliability, and cost. Communications between the parties involved in the business transaction is often done over a computer network, such as the Internet. This is **transaction processing (TP)**—the processing of business transactions by computers connected by computer networks. There are many requirements on computer-based transaction processing, such as the following:

- A business transaction requires the execution of multiple operations. For example, consider the purchase of an item from an on-line catalog. One operation records the payment and another operation records the commitment to ship the item to the customer. It is easy to imagine a simple program that would do this work. However, when scalability, reliability, and cost enter the picture, things can quickly get very complicated.
- Transaction volume and database size adds complexity and undermines efficiency. We've all had the experience of being delayed because a sales person is waiting for a cash register terminal to respond or because it takes too long to download a web page. Yet companies want to serve their customers quickly and with the least cost.

- To scale up a system for high performance, transactions must execute concurrently. Uncontrolled concurrent transactions can generate wrong answers. At a rock concert, when dozens of operations are competing to reserve the same remaining seats, it's important that only one customer is assigned to each seat. Fairness is also an issue.
- If a transaction runs, it must run in its entirety. In a retail sale, the item should either be exchanged for money or not sold at all. When failures occur, as they inevitably do, it's important to avoid partially completed work, such as accepting payment and not shipping the item, or vice versa. This would make the customer or the business very unhappy.
- Each transaction should either return an acknowledgment that it executed or return a negative acknowledgment that it did not execute. Those acknowledgments are important. If no acknowledgment arrives, the user doesn't know whether to resubmit a request to run the transaction again.
- The system should be incrementally scalable. When a business grows, it must increase its capacity for running transactions, preferably by making an incremental purchase—not by replacing its current machine by a bigger one or, worse yet, by rebuilding the application to handle the increased workload.
- When an electronic commerce (e-commerce) web site stops working, the retail enterprise is closed for business. Systems that run transactions are often "mission critical" to the business activity they support. They should hardly ever be down.
- Records of transactions, once completed, must be permanent and authoritative. This is often a legal requirement, as in financial transactions. Transactions must never be lost.
- The system must be able to operate well in a geographically distributed environment. Often, this implies that the system itself is distributed, with machines at multiple locations. Sometimes, this is due to a legal requirement that the system must operate in the country where the business is performed. Other times, distributed processing is used to meet technical requirements, such as efficiency, incremental scalability, and resistance to failures (using backup systems).
- The system should be able to personalize each user's on-line experience based on past usage patterns. For a retail customer, it should identify relevant discounts and advertisements and offer products customized to that user.
- The system must be able to scale up predictably and inexpensively to handle Internet loads of millions of potential users. There is no way to control how many users log in at the same time or which transactions they may choose to access.
- The system should be easy to manage. Otherwise, the system management staff required to operate a large-scale system can become too large and hence too costly. Complex system management also increases the chance of errors and hence downtime, which in turn causes human costs such as increased stress and unscheduled night-time work.

In summary, transaction processing systems have to handle high volumes efficiently, avoid errors due to concurrent operation, avoid producing partial results, grow incrementally, avoid downtime, never lose results, offer geographical distribution, be customizable, scale up gracefully, and be easy to manage. It's a tall order. This chapter describes how it's done. It explains the underlying principles of automating business transactions, both for traditional businesses and over the Internet; explores the complexities of fundamental technologies, such as logging and locking; and surveys today's commercial transactional middleware products that provide features necessary for building TP applications.

6.3 TRANSACTION

Trans means "beyond," as in *transatlantic.* A transaction is the action that an entity performs beyond it-self, i.e., on another entity. Hence a transaction, at the simplest level, can be defined as an event involving the action of one entity on another. The word *exchange* is often used to characterize a transaction.

An **on-line transaction** is the execution of a program that performs an administrative function by accessing a shared database, usually on behalf of an on-line user. Like many system definitions, this one is impressionistic and not meant to be exact in all its details. One detail is important: A transaction is always the *execution* of a program. The program contains the steps involved in the business transaction—for example, recording the sale of a book and reserving the item from inventory.

We'll use the words **transaction program** to mean the program whose execution is the transaction. Sometimes the word "transaction" is used to describe the message sent to a computer system to request the execution of a transaction, but we'll use different words for that: a **request message**. So a transaction always means the execution of a program.

We say that a transaction performs an administrative function, although that isn't always the case. For example, it could be a real-time function, such as making a call in a telephone switching system or controlling a machine tool in a factory process-control system. But usually there's money involved, such as selling a ticket or transferring money from one account to another.

Most transaction programs access shared data, but not all of them do. Some perform a pure communications function, such as forwarding a message from one system to another. Some perform a system administration function, such as resetting a device. An application in which no programs access shared data is not considered true transaction processing, because such an application does not require many of the special mechanisms that a TP system offers.

There is usually an on-line user, such as a home user at a web browser or a ticket agent at a ticketing device. But some systems have no user involved, such as a system recording messages from a satellite. Some transaction programs operate **off-line**, or in batch mode, which means that the multiple steps involved may take longer than a user is able to wait for the program's results to be returned—more than, say, ten seconds. For example, most of the work to sell you a product on-line happens after you've entered your order: a person or robot gets your order, picks it from a shelf, deletes it from inventory, prints a shipping label, packs it, and hands it off to the shipping company.

In earlier, simpler times, when business operations were run on a small scale, it was not necessary to us information technology to get accurate status information about business processes. No technology was needed to mediate between the users and the physical reality they were trying to measure or manipulate. For instance, when a customer walked into a store and asked about the availability of a certain item, it would be possible for the clerk to go to the storage room, look up availability, and then report that information back to the customer in a matter of seconds. As this organization grew larger and larger, the size of its warehouse increased accordingly. Beyond some critical threshold point, it would take too long to check the item availability manually.

This is the point at which technology comes in to mediate between humans and the reality they are trying to control (Figure 6.1). In a computer-mediated environment, the relevant details of all the sales and shipments received are entered into a computer system. The computer system then automatically updates quantity on hand of any item sold or purchased. Hence, the old scenario would be replayed as follows:

When a customer walks into the store and asks about the availability of a certain item, the clerk has to look up its availability on the computer. In other words, the computer has now become the clerk's window into the real world. The picture of the world provided by the system is the only practical way of knowing what is happening in the world. What the system says is real-and only that-can be considered real.

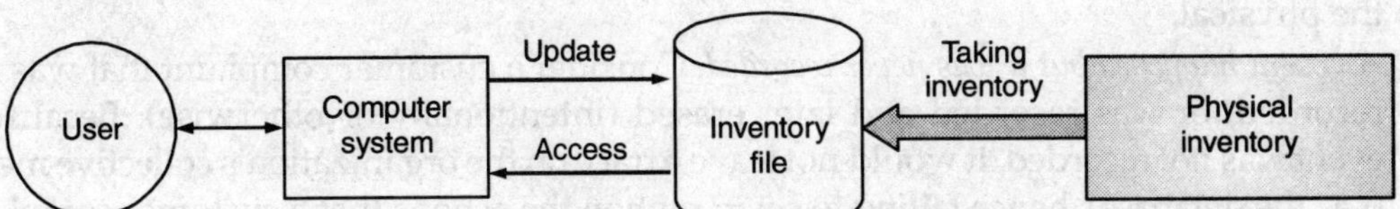

Figure 6.1: *The computer system mediating between the humans and physical reality in an inventory application*

From the above picture emerges the importance of capturing and recording events that impact other parts of the organization, and thus need to be retrieved at a later time. But an event has many different attributes. Only those attributes relevant to later retrieval and use need to be captured and stored. This is the basis on which the concept of transaction is defined as *a business event whose relevant attributes need to be recorded internally (in the corporate database) as well as externally (for a customer, a supplier, a business partner, etc.) due to the impact this information will later have on other operations of the organization and its stakeholders.* Being an event, a transaction takes place in time. It always has a date and time stamped on it. This is significant for reporting purposes, because management can later measure performance down to any unit of time desired ("How many burgers are sold per hour?").

Updates brought about by a transaction are of three types:

- ***Adding*** a new record, such as when a new customer signs up
- ***Changing*** an existing record, such as changes in credit available for a customer when that customer makes new purchases or returns already purchased products
- ***Deleting*** a record, such as when a product is discontinued

Thus defined, transactions are an ancient concept, as old as the beginning of writing. In the Fertile Crescent, archaeologists have found clay tablets written with cuneiform symbols that record commercial transactions such as sale of slaves. Some of these tablets are thousands of years old.

It really happened	1. OK Example: A rental Item is returned on time and is recorded as having been returned on time.	2. It did 'not happen' Example: A rental item is returned on time but is mistakenly stamped as having been returned late.
It really did not happen	3. It 'happened' Example A rental item is returned late but is mistakenly stamped as having been returned on time.	4. OK Example A rental item is returned late and it is stamped as having been returned late.

Figure 6.2: *What happened versus what was recorded. The event: Returning a rental item (such as a book or video CD) on time*

In a world in which the virtual is regarded as the image of the physical, what is beginning to matter more and more is not what actually happened, but what the system recorded as having happened. In Figure 6.2, four scenarios can be distinguished:

1. *An event happened and it was recorded.* This is a case in which the virtual accurately reflects the physical.
2. *An event happened but it was never recorded.* Consider a customer complaint that was never recorded, or was recorded and later erased (intentionally or otherwise). Because this event was not recorded, it would not leave a trace on the organization's collective memory (i.e., the database), hence failing to set in motion the actions that a customer complaint is supposed to trigger, such as a letter of apology to the customer and an investigation into the internal processes that were responsible for the complaint (defective product, discourteous employee, etc.). Unless the customer complained again, this information would not be acted on because of the organization not remembering it.
3. *An event that never happened was mistakenly recorded as having occurred.* This could take place due to fraud or forgery, but more often it may be due to incorrect processing. Hence, items may actually exist in stock but are shown by the computer system not to be there. Thus a salesperson, checking inventory on-line, could mistakenly see an item as not available and thus forego a sale while the item actually exists in inventory.
4. *An event that never happened was not recorded.* Again, in this case, the virtual accurately reflects the physical.

In short, in the TPS mind-set, if it was not recorded, it did not happen; if it was, it did.

Three important points need to be made about the concept of transaction. One subtlety associated with the concept of event is that *sometimes certain occurrences that do not happen but are expected to happen constitute events.* For instance, a customer's failure to make a payment on his credit card against an assigned deadline may appear as a non-event. Yet, because of the expectation of the receipt of the payment by the deadline, that non-event will become an event, triggering finance charges on the next account cycle.

The second subtlety is associated with the concept of relevance. Transactions record the relevant attributes of events, but relevant to what? Two types of relevance can be distinguished: operational and managerial.

The ***operational relevance*** of an event is derived from other operations in the organization that use the data captured about this event. The simplest way to bring out the operational relevance of an attribute of an event is to ask. "What operations in the organization will later use this piece of information, and how?" For instance, consider the business event in which a salesperson takes a prospective customer to lunch. The amount spent would be relevant because it will be used to later reimburse that salesperson.

The ***managerial relevance*** of an event is derived from controls set by management to assure that things go according to plan. Returning to the above example, the amount spent on lunch would also have a managerial relevance in that it should not exceed an upper limit preset by management. But more to the point would be the managerial relevance of the *purpose* of the lunch. If that piece of data is not captured, how will management be able to ascertain whether that expenditure was worth it?

The managerial type of relevance can be extended beyond control to include strategic objectives. It used to be that as soon as a customer walked through the door of the corner shop, the proprietor knew who he was and what he wanted. With the scale of business operations increasing immensely over time, organizations have become more impersonal. Strategic conceptions of TPS aim at bringing those days back. Retailers are trying to bring back the "personal touch" using technology to compensate for impersonal contact. Regardless of the scale of an organization's operations, it is good business to know who the organization's customers are and what they want. The problem for large organizations is that they do not even know who their customers are. A large supermarket might know how many units of which item it sold when, but it usually knows much less about the people who buy them. A strategically conceived TPS allows for *micro-marketing*- the ability to identify small groups of customers, even individuals, and sell them a product they need, or motivate them to buy such a product by sending them a customized coupon. In terms of customer recognition, this is possible through special-privilege cards that entitle the customer to discounts on selected items. When the customer swipes the card in the machine, his name comes up on the monitor, and he is greeted by the supermarket staff by name.

The third subtlety has to do with the notion of update versus access. Accessing a database to perform a query or produce a report does not ordinarily constitute a transaction because it does not involve an update to the database. However, *a query is considered a transaction if the query itself is meant to be tracked*. For instance, when a customer inquires into the availability of an item, this would ordinarily count as a read/access operation. However, management may at some point realize that the inquiries themselves are a way of tracking demand. At that point, each inquiry would be tracked in terms of the items requested and their availability. A high level of unavailability of an item would signal management to order or produce a higher level of it.

6.4 TRANSACTION PROCESSING SYSTEM

Having defined transaction, we can now proceed to define the term Transaction Processing System (TPS). TPS is a system that captures, enters, stores, retrieves, and processes the relevant details of business events, and generates the information/ documents necessary for running the organization and interfacing with external entities, such as customers.

The *processing* part of the TPS has to do with the various activities involved in running it, such as the following:

- Capturing the data as close to the source as possible
- Entering them into the system in a manner as effectively and efficiently as possible
- Storing them in the database
- Retrieving them from the database for further processing
- Transforming them from the raw form to information useful to the intended user.

The *systems* part of the TPS has to do with planning and designing the above elements so that they work in sync to produce the organizational objectives behind the TPS.

The *transaction* part of the TPS is somewhat more complicated. TPSs are characterized by

- Large amounts of input/output
- Large number of users
- Huge storage requirements
- Low computational complexity
- Fast input/output as well as processing capabilities
- A high degree of concern for potential security-related problems
- A high degree of concern for reliability and fault-tolerance.

A TPS is the lifeblood of an organization. For any business-related event occurring in an organization, a number of design decisions need to be made, such as these:

1. Is the event worth recording? If so, why? Customers calling to ask questions about their bill-is this event worth capturing? Yes, if (among other reasons) the organization is trying to find the most common reasons for customer calls, in order to automate responses to the most frequently asked questions.
2. If the event is worth recording, what attributes need to be captured, and why? Is the identity of the customer service representative (CSR) handling the customer's question in the above example worth documenting? Yes, if (among other reasons) the organization is trying to track customer satisfaction and train those CSRs who need more training.
3. In what form(s) should the event be documented? When a customer returns a product, there is a need to record this event not only internally (the database) but also externally (a credit memo issued to the customer).
4. How should the event be recorded? It used to be that prices were either stamped or tagged on products in supermarkets. The checker would then manually key this price into the cash register. This was both slow and prone to errors. With the advent of bar codes, this event was automated, thus making data capture faster as well as more accurate.

Picture the above design decisions being applied to the thousands and millions of events occurring in a large organization every day and you get a sense of the enormity and complexity of TPSs.

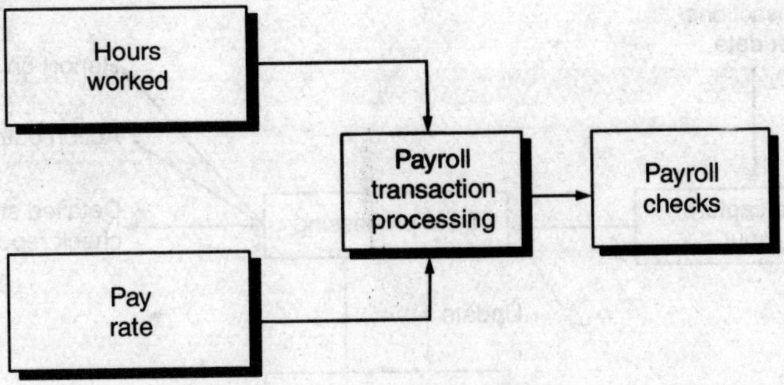

***Figure 6.3:** A Payroll Transaction Processing System*

One of the first business systems to be computerized was the payroll system (see Figure 6.3). The primary inputs for a payroll TPS are the number of employee hours worked during the week and the pay rate. The primary output consists of paychecks. Early payroll systems produced employee paychecks and related reports required by state and federal agencies, such as the Internal Revenue Service. Other routine applications include sales ordering, customer billing and customer relationship management, and inventory control.

The inner workings of a TPS are driven by the rules on which the organization runs. For instance, the inner workings of a hotel reservations system are dictated by the business rules and policies governing the reservation operation. Consider a hotel that has adopted the following policy: If a prospective guest cannot be accommodated in terms of the type of room requested, and if during the requested period a higher price room is available, then the guest will be accommodated in that higher price room while being charged the rate for the original room. The design of the reservations TPS of this hotel has to incorporate the above policy into it in order to work as desired. Not all rules are of an internal nature; they may be driven externally, such as by regulatory agencies.

The data captured and stored by a TPS serve two purposes: first, to support day-to-day routine operations by being made accessible to those parts of the organization (as well as to external entities), where they are needed; second, to feed the management reporting system and produce performance reports about the effectiveness and efficiency of the operations. The usefulness of transaction data goes beyond mere operations because large volumes of detailed data can be used as a historical reference for forecasting, identifying trends, and measuring performance.

Understanding a TPS can be accomplished along two different dimensions: externally versus internally and logically (what it does) versus physically (the technology based on which it works). Although a TPS is primarily concerned with day-to-day operations, it does play a critical strategic role in the organization, for it is with the operational level of the organization that customers and suppliers interact, and if the TPS is not working satisfactorily, then those external relations tend to suffer.

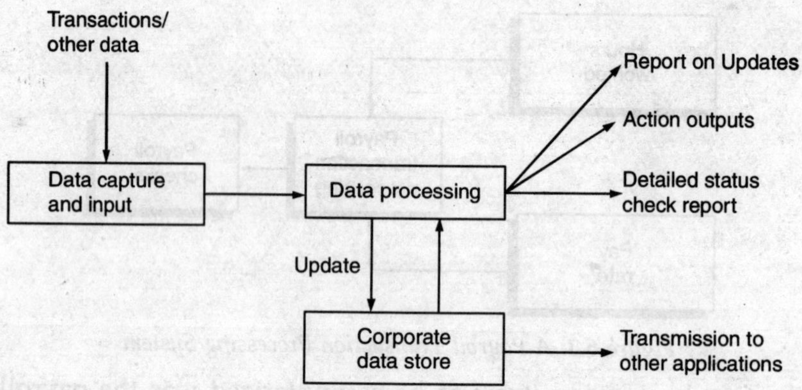

Figure 6.4: Basic TPS Model

A basic TPS model is depicted in Figure 6.4. TPS are also sometimes known as basic data gathering systems (BDS). Hence, TPS are the systems that capture, store and process data that are generated in the course of the day-to-day activities of organizations. Such systems help to address routine questions. The data can be categorized based on the two dimensions of *frequency* and *externality*.

- ***Frequency:*** Frequent data relates to the day-to-day, repetitive operations of the organisation, such as issuing payments. Non-frequent data relates to either one-off or infrequent operations of the organisation, such as hiring personnel.
- ***Externality***: External data relates to operations involving individuals or institutions outside the organisation's boundaries, such as the organisation's clients, suppliers. Internal data relates to operations involving individuals or institutions inside the organisation's boundaries, such as employees.

There are few absolutes when it comes to the inner workings of a TPS. Business process reengineering has challenged age-old assumptions about business practices. Consider the practice of issuing invoices to customers. Some redesigned processes have made this practice obsolete. Or consider the practice of issuing purchase orders to suppliers. Continuous replenishment processes have made this practice obsolete too.

6.5 THE LARGER FRAMEWORK

Any organization-regardless of size, industry, and profit orientation-exists to serve its clientele by adding value to the resources obtained from its external environment.

The operational level of the organization consists of those activities that perform the value-adding work on a day-to-day basis. The management control level consists of those activities that compare the results accomplished with the goals set by management in order to identify and correct any possible variances between the two.

Regardless of which purpose is served, a TPS stores the data it captures in a database for later use. As such, the database is a buffer (1) between the TPS and the management reporting system; and (2) between the TPS at one time and the TPS at a later time (Figure 6.5).

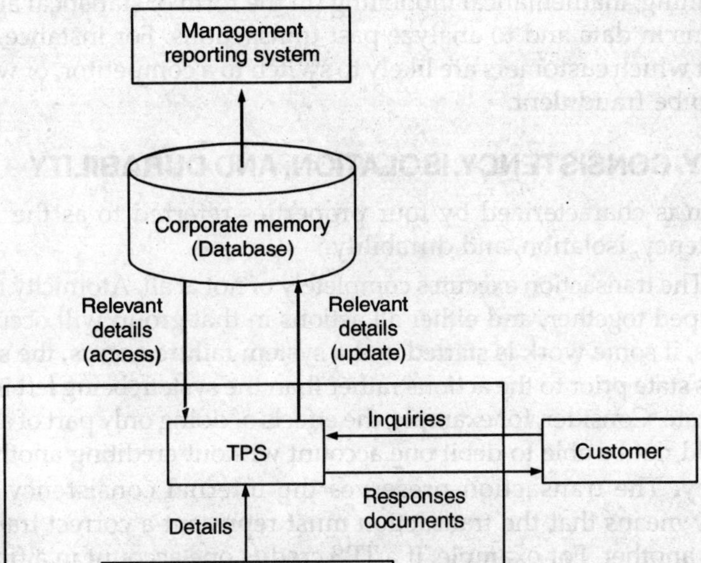

Figure 6.5: The larger framework of TPS

6.6 TPS AND DATABASE REQUIREMENTS

As pointed out earlier, a transaction captures the relevant attributes of an event for later use by other units in the organization or by external entities. This may be referred to as the *ripple effect* of transactions: Transaction data travel to all the other parts of the organization where they are needed. For instance, the news of customers returning the same defective product needs to travel to production, R&D, or purchasing, depending on where the cause of the defect may lie.

Transaction data are also used to update master files-where data about permanent entities (such as customers, products, suppliers, and employees) are stored. A customer returning a product will trigger a credit event that will update the field "credit available" in that customer's record in the customer file.

Because a transaction sets in motion the ripple effect discussed above, there must be a way to "de-ripple" those effects if the transaction is cancelled. That is why a transaction is sometimes defined as *a set of operations that must be executed together; of which none are performed if any one of them is not performed.* In other words, a transaction either *commits,* meaning the changes are all made, or *aborts,* meaning any changes in progress are undone. For instance, in the example of a customer returning a defective product, if later it turns out that the product was really not defective (the customer just didn't know how to use it) and it is returned to her, then any updates that may have already taken place need to be undone.

Two of the most exciting uses of transaction data stored in a database are data warehousing and data mining. To avoid endangering an organization's operations, data are pulled from the operational system and placed in a separate data warehouse for the users to access. In data mining, mathematical modelling (in the form of statistical algorithms) is used to identify patterns in data and to analyze past transactions. For instance, data mining can be used to predict which customers are likely to switch to a competitor, or which transactions are most likely to be fraudulent.

6.7 ATOMICITY, CONSISTENCY, ISOLATION, AND DURABILITY

A transaction is characterized by four properties referred to as the ACID properties: atomicity, consistency, isolation, and durability.

- **Atomicity:** The transaction executes completely or not at all. Atomicity means that actions can be grouped together, and either all actions in that group will occur or none will. In other words, if some work is started and a system failure occurs, the state of the system reverts to its state prior to the actions rather than the system being left in an intermediate, corrupted state. Consider, for example, the effects of doing only part of a financial transfer; a TPS should not be able to debit one account without crediting another.
- **Consistency:** The transaction preserves the internal consistency of the database. Consistency means that the transaction must represent a correct transformation from one state to another. For example, if a TPS credits one account in a financial transfer, it must debit the other by the same amount.
- **Isolation**: The transaction executes as if it were running alone, with no other transactions. Isolation means that actions do not interfere with each other. Multiple, simultaneous transactions must be made to appear as if they are actually a series of sequential transactions. If several users want to access the same bank account at the same time, the requests must be serialized and treated independently. Even if actions appear to happen simultaneously to the end users, they must be serialized and isolated internally.
- **Durability:** The transaction's results will not be lost in a failure. Durability means that once a change is made, it is not undone by a system failure. Changes to data must remain permanent once they are made.

This leads to an entertaining acronym, ACID. People often say that a TP system executes ACID transactions, in which case the TP system has "passed the ACID test."

6.8 VIEWS OF TPS

Having explained some of the basic concepts associated with a TPS, we will now discuss ways of viewing a TPS.

Table 6.1: The Two Dimensions of a TPS

	Logical	**Physical**
External	The information exchanged between the external entity (especially customer) and the organization	The technology (media) used for exchanging the information
Internal	The flow of the information within the organization	The technology (media) used for supporting the information flows within the organization.

A TPS can be viewed along two independent dimensions (Table 6.1). First is the external/internal dimension. From the outside, a TPS looks like a machine that takes certain inputs and produces certain outputs. The external view captures events taking place between the organization and its external environment. To understand how those inputs are converted to outputs, one needs to open up the box and look at the internal view. The internal view captures events taking place within the organization.

Second is the logical/physical dimension. The logical understanding of a TPS has to do with *what* information flows into/out of it, and *what* processes are performed on that information, and why. It is relatively stable and permanent. The physical understanding has to do with the technology used in entering the data, producing the information, and carrying out the processes. It is dynamic and transient due to rapid technological advances.

In what follows, we explore the logical and physical views and, within each, the external and internal views.

6.8.1 External Logical View of a TPS

This view is concerned with the interactions between the organization and its external environment. We will focus on the interaction between an organization and its customers only. The interactions between an organization and its suppliers are just the mirror image of the interactions between the organization and its customers. The following is a general model of the information exchanges between an organization and its customers (Table 6.2). It may be reminiscent of a game of ping-pong: For every action, there is a reaction.

Table 6.2: External Logical View of a Typical Sales TPS

Customer → TPS	TPS → Customer
eliminary request for information: Functionality • Price • Availability • Transaction alternatives	
	Preliminary information: • Functionality • Product name/number • Price • Availability • Transaction alternatives
Order details • Product • Quantity • Transaction specifics Customer details • Name • Address	

• Financial details	
	Confirmation of receipt of order Confirmation of details Request for payment • Amount • Payment alternatives
Payment	
	Confirmation of receipt of payment Confirmation of shipment • Order number • Date to be shipped • Date shipped
Request for delivery status	
	Delivery status

Typically, the interaction starts with the customer's preliminary request for functionality (i.e., whether the organization produces the types of products or services that would solve. the customer's problems), price, availability, and transaction alternatives (method of payment, delivery date, etc.). The organization's response, of course, would be to provide this detailed information for the customer. Once the customer has done sufficient "shopping around," the order is placed. This involves the specification of order details:

- Product
- Quantity
- Transaction specifics (expected delivery time, method of payment, etc.)

as well as customer details (for new customers):

- Name
- Address
- Phone
- Etc.

The organization's response to this is typically a confirmation (echoing) of the details received. The order is then processed and, as a result, the following may be communicated to the customer: order number, expected shipment date, and actual shipment date.

Depending on the details of the terms of trade, once the requested shipment is made, there is a request for payment (invoice). In response, the customer makes the payment. In response, the organization may produce a receipt of payment. In the process of waiting for the shipment, the customer may want to inquire into its status. The organization's response will be to provide this information.

The above model is generic. As pointed out earlier, not every organizational TPS involves those transactions. In fact, the proponents of business process reengineering would argue that some of the elements listed above, such as invoice, are unnecessary and may be reengineered out of existence.

6.8.2 Internal Logical View of a TPS

This view is concerned with the interactions within an organization that support the exchanges discussed above. It shows the various internal functions (processes) performed by the TPS as well as the data flows among them. As such, a data flow diagram is a suitable tool for showing the inner workings of a TPS. Figure 6.6 shows an example of the internal view of a TPS. It is meant to be representative, not complete.

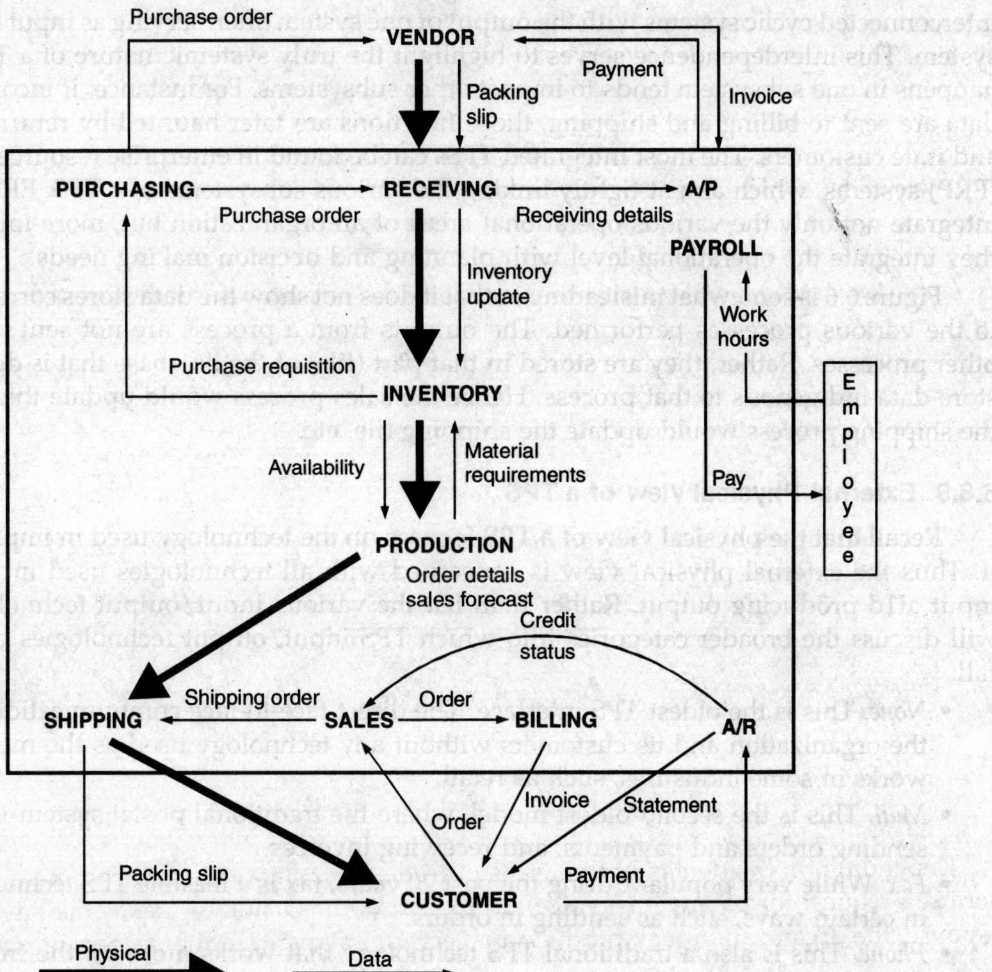

Figure 6.6: A partial view of the internal, logical views within a TPS

The major subsystems of this TPS are:

- Sales
- Shipping
- Billing
- Accounts Receivable *(A/R)*

- Production
- Inventory
- Purchasing
- Receiving
- Accounts Payable *(A/P)*
- Payroll.

As can be seen from Figure 6.6, an organization's TPS typically consists of several interconnected cyclic systems with the output of one system often serving as input to another system. This interdependence serves to highlight the truly systemic nature of a TPS: What happens in one subsystem tends to impact other subsystems. For instance, if incorrect sales data are sent to billing and shipping, those functions are tater haunted by returned goods and irate customers. The most integrated TPSs can be found in enterprise resource planning (ERP) systems, which aim at tightly linking the various subsystems of a TPS. ERP systems integrate not only the various operational areas of an organization but, more importantly, they integrate the operational level with planning and decision making needs.

Figure 6.6 is somewhat misleading in that it does not show the data stores corresponding to the various processes performed. The outputs from a process are not sent directly to other processes. Rather, they are stored in that part (file) of the database that is designed to store data indigenous to that process. Hence the sales process would update the sales file; the shipping process would update the shipping file, etc.

6.8.3 External Physical View of a TPS

Recall that the physical view of a TPS focuses on the technology used in implementing it. Thus the external physical view is concerned with all technologies used in providing input aI1d producing output. Rather than list the various input/output technologies, we will discuss the broader categories into which TPS input/output technologies commonly fall:

- *None.* This is the oldest TPS interface. The direct face-to-face communication between the organization and its customers without any technology used as the medium still works in some industries, such as retail.
- *Mail.* This is the second oldest model, where the traditional postal system is used for sending orders and payments, and receiving invoices.
- *Fax.* While very popular during the past 20 years, fax is a feasible TPS technology only in certain ways, such as sending in orders.
- *Phone.* This is also a traditional TPS technology that works more for the front end of the TPS cycle, namely, the cust6mer's preliminary request for functionality, price, availability, and transaction alternatives.
- *Electronic.* This is the most advanced form of communication. As such, it takes two different forms: free-format, and structured.
  - *Free-format.* E-mail communication falls in this category. Because e-mail contents are not governed by any standardized formatting rules, e-mail is not the optimal way of conducting customer-organization interactions.

– *Structured.* Electronic data interchange (EDI) and Internet-based electronic commerce (whether business to business or business to consumer) fall in this category. In either case, predesigned procedures are used to regulate the electronic flow of information between the customer and the organization. When the customer-organization communication is completely structured, it can be automated. Automated customer service representative systems and automated teller machines are examples of this principle.

6.8.4 Internal Physical View of a TPS

The internal physical view is concerned with all technologies used in converting the TPS inputs into outputs. In other words, they are processing technologies. Transaction volume is a major consideration in processor selection. An application that does not respond well to increased transaction volume is said to lack scalability. ***Scalability*** is defined as the ability of an application or platform to be expanded in terms of capacity to accommodate a larger number of users or transactions than originally planned without requiring significant changes in procedure.

Regardless of how technically advanced a processing technology is, if a TPS handles transactions one at a time immediately on request, then it is referred to as an on-line transaction processing (OLTP) system. The opposite of on-line transaction processing is batch processing. Instead of handling one transaction at a time, batch processing systems work on a group of transactions assembled for processing at a specific time, such as at the end of the day or the end of an accounting period. Payroll is a common batch processing application.

OLTP can also be viewed as a system of programs that facilitate and manage transaction-oriented applications, typically for data entry and retrieval in a number of industries, including banking, airlines, mail-order, supermarkets, and manufacturing. The classic example of a commercial OLTP product is IBM's CICS (Customer Information Control System).

Today's on-line transaction processing increasingly requires support for transactions that span a network and may include more than one company. For this reason, new OLTP software programs use client/server processing that allow transactions to run on different computer platforms in a network. Despite the recent shift to the client/server model, many legacy TPSs are still in use running on mainframe or midrange computers.

Regardless of the specific platform or architecture being used, the electronic medium has by itself revolutionized transaction processing. The difference between the electronic medium and the manual one is not just quantitative (faster, more accurate) but also qualitative (doing it versus not doing it). By hitting a single key on the specialized order entry keyboard of a point-of-sale system in a fast food chain, the order taker enters into the system a wealth of data (date, time, order details, employee ID, etc.) that are stored in the system for later use. Capturing this wealth of information in a low-tech, manual environment would not be feasible. A TPS that does not capture detailed data about the operation it is intended to support does not give its managers a clear picture of how effectively and efficiently that operation is performed.

6.9 FEATURES OF TPS

Transaction Processing is a system that processes the transactions of an organization. Online Banking and ATM is an example. A transaction Processing System is an exceptionally powerful and flexible transaction processing environment for both mobile and fixed-base data collection equipment. It provides the sophisticated connectivity needed in today's complex industrial, warehousing, distribution, and other environments.

Transaction Processing System has numerous features important in creating systems and solutions for demanding transaction processing requirements. With Transaction Processing System, you can:

- Develop high-performance data collection and bar code printing systems across client/server networks.
- Revitalize legacy software and hardware in a state-of-the-art transaction processing and bar code environment Interface with different types of host and network computers at the same time.
- Access multiple local and remote distributed databases, concurrently and simultaneously.
- Select and use terminals and printers from multiple leading manufacturers, all in one system.
- Run the same transactions on your radio-frequency devices that you run on fixed devices and PCs, including intelligent emulation.
- Select from a variety of automatic, dynamic servers and data backup schemes, which are available to ensure minimum downtime and maximum productivity.

6.10 TRANSACTION PROCESSING APPROACHES

There has been a trend for transaction processing systems to move through two stages as technology and perceived organisational needs change:

- **Batch systems:** Such systems collect the data to be processed over a certain period of time and then do the processing at some specified date or time.
- **Real time systems:** Real time systems on the other hand process the data as soon as the transaction occurs.

6.11 GENERIC EXAMPLES OF TPS

These are the generic examples of TPS:

- *Accounts Payable*. This keeps a record of money owed by the organisation.
- *Accounts Receivable*. This keeps a record of money owed to the organisation.
- *Personnel*. This keeps a record of all staff employed.
- *Customers*, This keeps a record of all the customers of an organisation
- *Payroll*. This calculates and records staff salaries and wages.
- *Inventory*. This tracks the movement of items in and out of a store.
- *General Ledger*. This keeps a central record of all financial transactions, drawn from accounts, payroll, inventory, etc.

Figure 6.7 depicts the interrelationships among these generic examples of TPS.

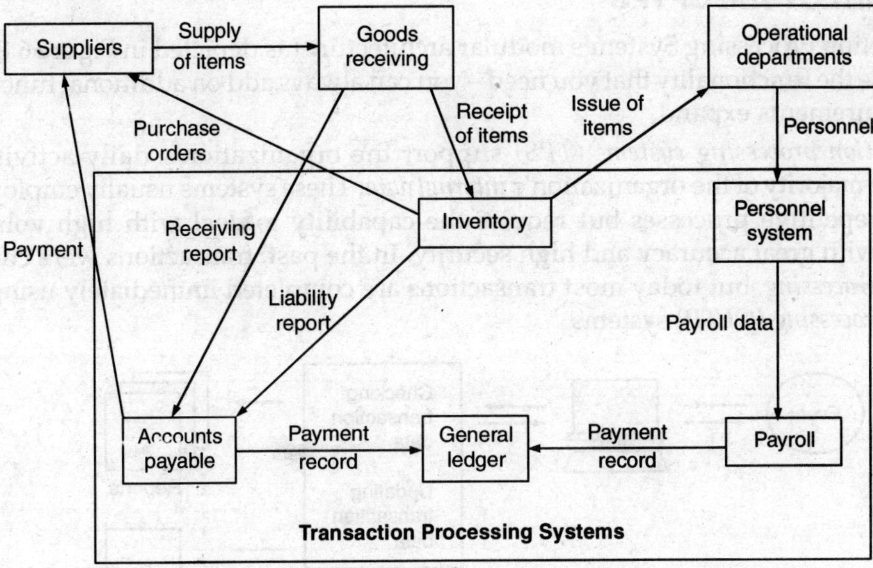

Figure 6.7: Interrelationships between Transaction Processing Systems

6.12 IMPORTANCE OF TPS

Because a TPS is used to capture, store and create information, it may look mundane to the casual viewer. However

- TPS is a mission critical system (example airline reservation system)
- Point of contact to customers and suppliers
- Data from the TPS is used to monitor organizational performance
- Relatively high cost if there is a system failure

6.13 COMPARING TPS WITH OTHER INFORMATION SYSTEMS

The specific capabilities of a basic data-gathering system, listed above, are what differentiate it from other information systems. However, there are other features, which are also typical of BDS/TPS that would tend to set them apart from information systems described elsewhere in this module, such as:

- Large hardware power requirement to cope with a high volume of data input, processing, storage and output.
- High reliability requirement to keep these fundamental systems operational (use fault-tolerant systems).
- High recoverability requirement to rebuild data files, ensure no transactions have been lost and become operational again after a system failure.
- Regular, structured format for data use. Routine, structured, pre-specified, regular and repetitive formats for data entry, processing and output.
- High levels of data detail within data inputs and outputs.
- Limited processing complexity. This is "number crunching".
- Use by operational/clerical levels of staff.

6.14 ARCHITECTURE OF TPS

Transaction Processing System's modular architecture (as depicted in Figure 6.8) allows you to choose the functionality that you need – you can always add on additional functionality as your requirements expand.

Transaction processing systems (TPS) support the organization's daily activities and maintain the majority of the organization's *internal data*. These systems usually employ simple but highly repetitive processes but require the capability to deal with high volumes of *transactions* with great accuracy and high security. In the past, transactions were completed using *batch processing*, but today most transactions are completed immediately using *on-line transaction processing (OLTP)* systems.

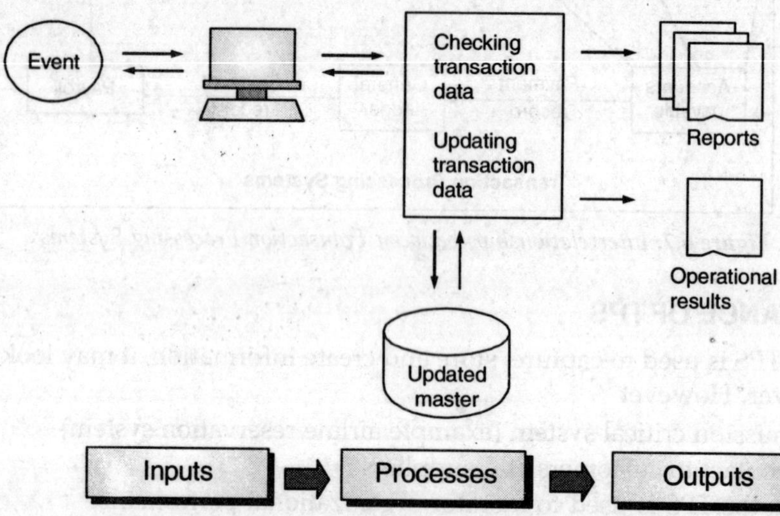

Figure 6.8: Transaction Processing Systems Architecture

To implement on-line transaction processing, *master files* containing key information about important business entities are placed on hard disk drives where they are directly accessible. The *transaction files* containing information about activity concerning these business entities, such as orders placed by customers, are also held in on-line files until they are no longer needed for everyday transaction processing activity. This assures that the transaction data is available to all applications, and that all data is kept up-to-the-minute.

Users with the proper *database permissions* may *download* data from the database to another location and *upload* changes to these on-line files as soon as changes are required. When the transaction files are no longer being "actively" used, they are not deleted. Instead they are archived in a special data storage facility called a data warehouse.

A Transaction Processing System (TPS) is designed for Operating Management. It is also called Electronic Data Processing (EDP). It has a limited area of functionality, and is designed for one area of the business.

It uses only data that is *internal* to the company. There are some possible exceptions, however. Inter -branch banking uses TPS as well as direct deposit of employee's pay from various companies and government institutions.

6.15 REPORTS AND OTHER OUTPUTS FROM TRANSACTION PROCESSING SYSTEMS

The outputs of TPS provide operational details, summary reports, and exception reports, which help supervise and control routine operations. *Exception reporting* provides a feedback loop to the operational manager about any unusual or unexpected activity that may require attention. Transaction processing systems may be divided into major functional areas. Accounting provides systems to handle general ledger, payroll, and accounts. Marketing has TP systems to handle sales, promotion and advertising activity. Manufacturing requires transaction processing systems and operational feedback from production processes. Manufacturing reporting systems must often be designed as *real-time systems* to allow operational managers and supervisors to closely monitor on-going operations. Human resources needs systems to support its daily operations in recruiting, maintaining employee records, providing benefits, and monitoring occupational conditions. Finance requires maintaining information on cash reserves and investment holdings, and the monitoring of changes to tax and fiscal regulations.

Many systems, such as order processing, may involve processes that cross functional boundaries in the enterprise. For example, an order may concern sales, manufacturing, distribution, and accounting. Transaction processing systems may depend upon each other in intricate ways that are not always apparent to the users of these systems.

When transaction data grows old, it can still be of value to the organization. However, it is not used frequently and takes up valuable disk space, so such data is often moved to other lower cost storage areas. In the past, *archived data* was difficult to access because the *data archives* were not well organized. Today, such archives are placed in *data warehouses*, which are data storage facilities that are managed by special database programs designed for that purpose. Analysts can then make use of *on-line analytical processing [OLAP]* tools to investigate either the current transaction data or the data that has been retired to the data warehouse facility. Using the company's data archives to determine trends and to extract other useful information is often referred to as *data mining*.

Steps in Transaction Processing are depicted in Figure 6.9.

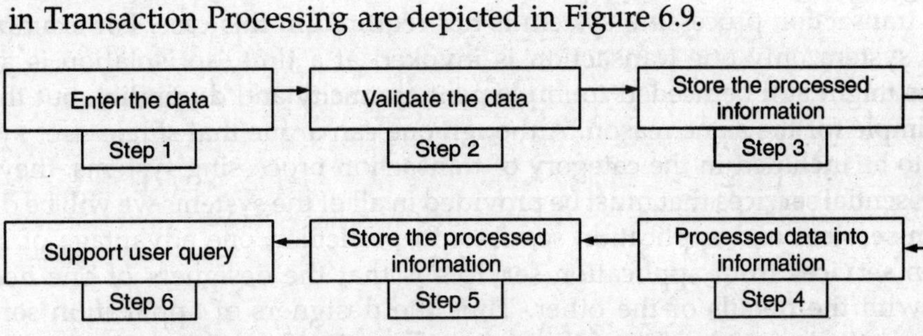

Figure 6.9: Steps in Transaction Processing System

6.16 TRANSACTION PROCESSING IN A CENTRALIZED SYSTEM

Due to hardware limitations, the earliest transaction processing systems were centralized. All modules resided on a single computer-for example, a single PC or workstation servicing a single user, or a mainframe computer with many connected terminals servicing multiple users concurrently. We consider these two cases separately.

6.16.1 Organization of a Single-user System

Figure 6.10 shows how a single-user transaction processing system might be organized on a PC or workstation. The user module performs presentation and application services. Presentation services display forms on the screen, and it handles the flow of information from and to the user through the forms. A typical cycle of activity might start with presentation services displaying a form on which the user enters information in textboxes and then submits a request for service by making an appropriate click. Presentation services recognize the click, and it calls application services to satisfy the request, passing to it the information that has been input. Application services checks the integrity constraints not specified in the schema and executes a sequence of steps in accordance with the rules of the enterprise.

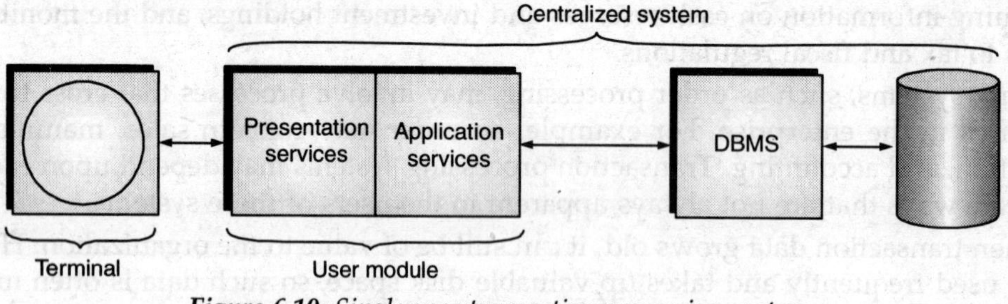

Figure 6.10: Single-user transaction processing system.

Application services must communicate with the database server. For example, the application service that registers a student for a course in the Student Registration System has to make sure that the student has taken the prerequisite courses and must add the student's name to the class roster. Its requests to access the database might be implemented in embedded SQL statements that are sent to the database server.

Although a program within application services can be viewed as a transaction, the full power of a transaction processing system is not required in this case. For example, with a single-user system only one transaction is invoked at a time, so isolation is automatic. Mechanisms might still be needed to implement atomicity and durability, but they can be relatively simple for the same reason. Although one can argue that single-user systems are too simple to be included in the category of transaction processing systems, they illustrate two of the essential services that must be provided in all of the systems we will be discussing: presentation services and application services. In particular, one advantage of separating presentation services from application services is that the designers of one need not be concerned with the details of the other. Thus the designers of application services can concentrate on the business rules of the enterprise and do not have to be concerned with the details of dealing with the presentation of the input and output. In fact the hardware or software drivers involved with presentation services can be changed without having any effect on the application services software (assuming the interface between the two services remains the same).

6.16.2 Organization of a Centralized Multiuser System

Transaction processing systems supporting an enterprise of any size must permit multiple users to have access to them from multiple locations. Early versions of such systems involved the use of terminals connected to a central computer. In situations in which the terminals and the computer were confined to a small area (for example a single building), communication could be supported over hard-wired connections. More frequently, however, the terminals were located at remote sites and communicated with the computer over telephone lines. In either case, a major difference between these early systems and current multi-user systems is that the terminals were "dumb." They had no computing capability. They served as I/O devices that presented a simple, generally textual interface to the user. In terms of Figure 6.10, presentation services (beyond those built into the terminal hardware) were minimal and had to be executed at the central site. While such systems could be spread over a substantial geographical area; they were not considered distributed since all of the computing and intelligence resided at a single site.

The introduction of multi-user transaction processing systems motivated the development of transactions and the need for the ACID properties. Since multiple users interact with the system concurrently, there must be a way to isolate one user's interaction from another. Because the system is now supporting a major enterprise, as contrasted with an individual's database, issues of atomicity and durability become important.

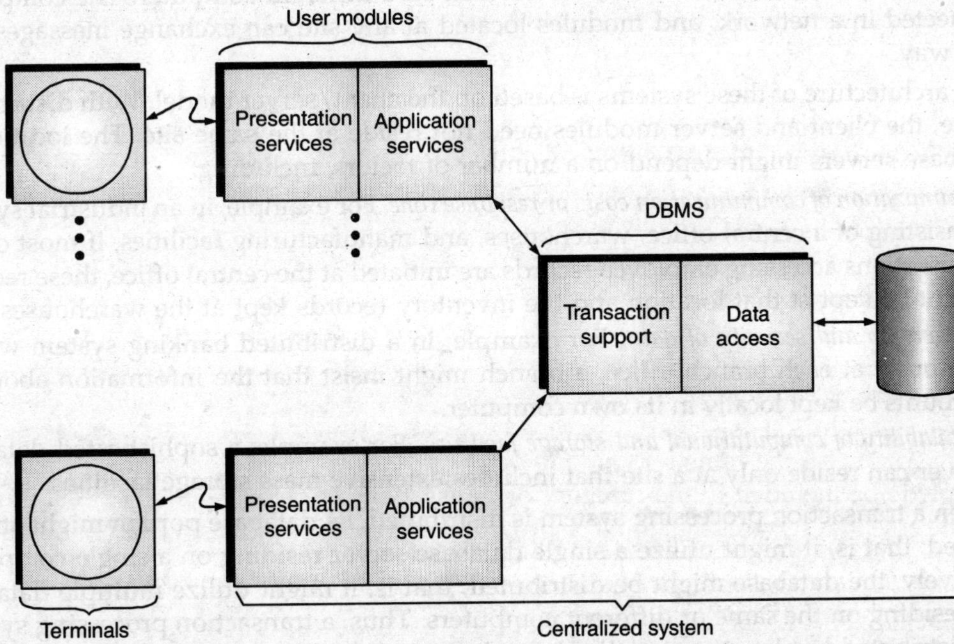

Figure 6.11: Multi-user centralized transaction processing system

Figure 6.11 shows the organization of early multi-user transaction processing systems. A user module, containing both presentation and application services, is associated with each user and runs at the central site. Since a number of users execute concurrently, each user module is executed in a separate process. These processes run asynchronously and can submit requests for service to the database server at any time. For example, while the server is servicing a request from one application to execute an SQL statement, a different application might submit a request to execute another SQL statement. Sophisticated database servers are capable of servicing many such requests simultaneously, with the guarantee that each SQL statement will be executed as an isolated and atomic unit.

As we have seen, however, such a guarantee is not sufficient to ensure that the interactions of different users are appropriately isolated. To provide isolation, the application program needs the abstraction of a transaction. A transaction support module is therefore provided within the database server to implement commands such as begin-transaction, commit, and rollback and to provide atomicity, isolation, and durability. This module includes the concurrency control and the log. Since presentation, application, and database services are all supplied at the same site, this organization is referred to as a single-tiered model.

6.17 TRANSACTION PROCESSING IN A DISTRIBUTED SYSTEM

Modern transaction processing systems are generally implemented on distributed hardware involving multiple independent computers at geographically distinct sites. The ATM machine is separate from the bank's computer, and a computer at a ticket agent's site is separate from the airline's main reservation system. In some cases, an application might communicate with several databases, each stored on a different computer. The computers are connected in a network, and modules located at any site can exchange messages in a uniform way.

The architecture of these systems is based on the client/server model. With distributed hardware, the client and server modules need not reside at the same site. The location of the database servers might depend on a number of factors, including:

- *Minimization of communication costs or response time.* For example, in an industrial system consisting of a central office, warehouses, and manufacturing facilities, if most of the transactions accessing employee records are initiated at the central office, these records might be kept at that location and the inventory records kept at the warehouses.
- *Ownership and security of data.* For example, in a distributed banking system with a computer at each branch office, a branch might insist that the information about its accounts be kept locally in its own computer.
- *Availability of computational and storage facilities.* For example, a sophisticated database server can reside only at a site that includes extensive mass storage facilities.

When a transaction processing system is distributed, its database portion might still be centralized; that is, it might utilize a single database server residing on a single computer. Alternatively, the database might be distributed; that is, it might utilize multiple database servers residing on the same or different computers. Thus, a transaction processing system can be distributed but have a centralized database.

6.17.1 Organization of a Distributed System

The organization of a distributed transaction processing system evolved from the multi-user system shown in Figure 6.11. As a first step, terminals are replaced by client computers, so the user module, responsible for presentation and application services, now resides on a client computer and communicates with the database server. This is referred to as a two-tiered model. Figure 6.12 shows the organization of a distributed transaction processing system with a centralized database. Application programs on client machines initiate transactions, which, as shown in Figure 6.11, are handled by the transaction support module on the database server to ensure atomicity and isolation.

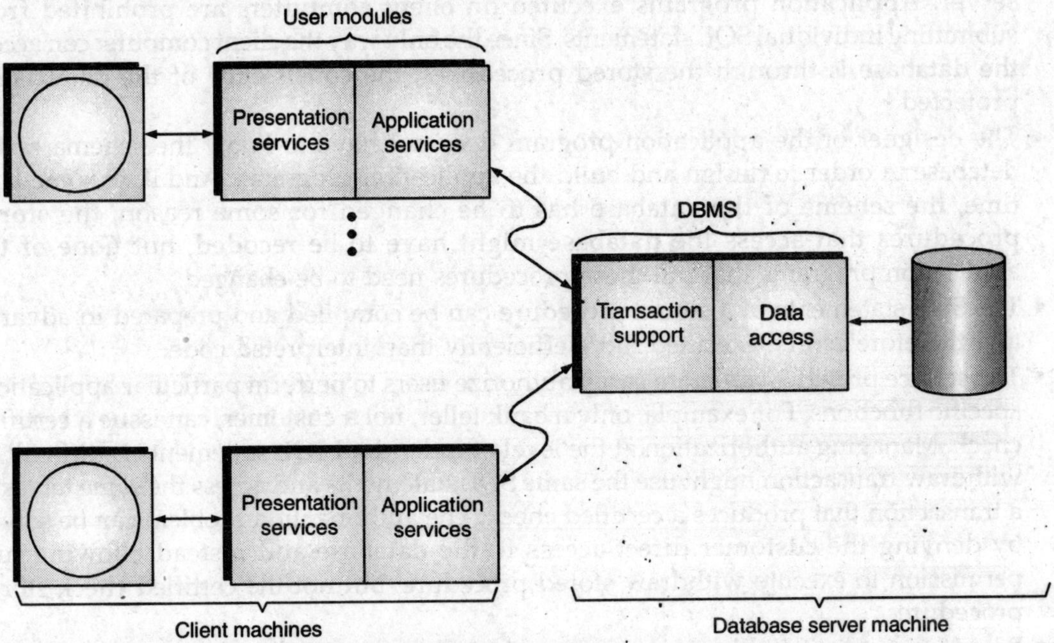

Figure 6.12: Two-tiered multi-user distributed transaction processing system

The database server might export an SQL interface so that an application program on the client computer can send a request to the database server to execute a particular SQL statement. However, several important problems arise when client machines directly use such an interface. One problem has to do with the integrity of the database. As with a single-user system, our concern is that the client machines, which reside at client sites, might not be secure and hence might not be trustworthy. An erroneous or malicious application program, for example, can destroy database integrity by submitting an improper update statement.

Another significant problem relates to network traffic and the ability of the system to handle a large number of clients. A user wishing to scan a table might execute SQL statements that cause all of the rows of the table to be transferred from the database server to the client machine. Since these machines can be widely separated, considerable network traffic might be required even though the result of the transaction might involve only a few of the rows transferred. Unfortunately, the network can support only a small number of clients if such requests have to be processed in this way.

Stored procedures: One way to address this problem is through stored procedures. Instead of submitting individual SQL statements, the application program on the client computer requests that a particular stored procedure be executed by the database server. In effect, the application program is now provided with a high-level, or more abstract, database interface. For example, a database server for a bank might make deposit () and withdraw () stored procedures available to application programs.

Stored procedures have several important advantages.

- They are assumed to be correct and their integrity can be maintained at the database server. Application programs executed on client computers are prohibited from submitting individual SQL statements. Since the only way the client computer can access the database is through the stored procedures, the consistency of the database is protected.
- The designer of the application program does not have to know the schema of the database in order to design and build the application programs. And if, at some later time, the schema of the database has to be changed for some reason, the stored procedures that access the database might have to be recoded, but none of the application programs that call those procedures need to be changed.
- The SQL statements of a stored procedure can be compiled and prepared in advance and therefore can be executed more efficiently than interpreted code.
- The service provider can more easily authorize users to perform particular application-specific functions. For example, only a bank teller, not a customer, can issue a certified check. Managing authorization at the level of individual SQL statements is difficult. A withdraw transaction might use the same SQL statements and access the same tables as a transaction that produces a certified check. The authorization problem can be solved by denying the customer direct access to the database and instead allowing him permission to execute withdraw stored procedure, but not the certified check stored procedure.
- By offering a more abstract service, the amount of information that must be communicated through the network is reduced. Instead of transmitting the intermediate results of individual SQL statements between the application program on the client machine and the database server, all processing of intermediate results is now done by the stored procedure at the database server, and only the initial arguments and final results pass through the network. This is how the table scan described above can be performed. Data communication is thus reduced, and a larger number of clients can be served. However, the database server must be powerful enough to handle the additional work that the execution of stored procedures entails.

The three-tiered model: The idea of providing higher-level services to the client computer can be carried one step further. Figure 6.13 shows a three-tiered model of a distributed transaction processing system, which contrasts with the two-tiered system of Figure 6.12. The user module has been divided into a presentation server and an application server that execute on different computers. Presentation services, at the client site, assembles the information input by the user, makes certain validity checks on the information (e.g., type checking), and then sends a request message to the application server, executing elsewhere in the network.

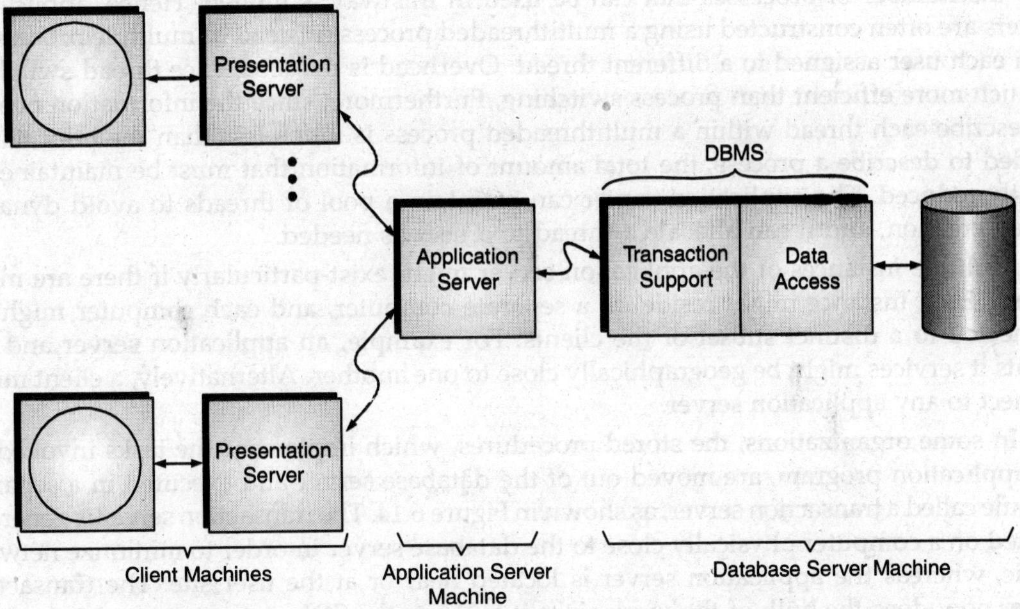

***Figure 6.13:** Three-tiered distributed transaction processing system.*

The application server executes the application program corresponding to the requested service. As before, this program implements the rules of the enterprise, checking conditions that have to be satisfied in order for the request to be executed and invoking the appropriate stored procedures at the database server to carry it out. The application program views the servicing of a user request as a sequence of tasks.

Each task might require the execution of a complex program, and each program might be a distinct stored procedure on the database server. The application program controls transaction boundaries by invoking begin-transaction and commit and hence can cause the procedures to be executed within a single transaction. Moreover, it encourages task reuse. If tasks are chosen to perform generally useful functions, they can be invoked as components of different application programs. In the general case, the transaction is distributed, having the application program as a root, and the stored procedures are the component subtransactions executing on different servers. In this case, more elaborate transaction support is required.

The application can be thought of as a workflow, consisting of a set of tasks that must be performed in some specified order (although all tasks in this case are computational). The application server can be thought of as a workflow controller, controlling the flow of tasks required to implement the user's request.

Figure 6.13 shows a single application server with multiple clients. Since the servicing of a single client request might take a substantial amount of time, a number of client requests might be pending at the same time. Hence, the application server must handle requests concurrently in order to maintain an adequate level of performance. It might do this by allocating a process for each user. Unfortunately, processes carry substantial overhead, and thus the number of processes that can be used in this way is limited. Hence, application servers are often constructed using a multithreaded process (instead of multiple processes), with each user assigned to a different thread. Overhead is reduced since thread switching is much more efficient than process switching. Furthermore, since the information needed to describe each thread within a multithreaded process is much less than the information needed to describe a process, the total amount of information that must be maintained is greatly reduced. The application server can maintain a pool of threads to avoid dynamic thread creation, and it can allocate a thread to a user as needed.

Multiple instances of the application server might exist-particularly if there are many clients. Each instance might reside on a separate computer, and each computer might be connected to a distinct subset of the clients. For example, an application server and the clients it services might be geographically close to one another. Alternatively, a client might connect to any application server.

In some organizations, the stored procedures, which implement the tasks invoked by the application program, are moved out of the database server and executed in a separate module called a transaction server, as shown in Figure 6.14. The transaction server is generally located on a computer physically close to the database server in order to minimize network traffic, whereas the application server is located near or at the user site. The transaction server now does the bulk of the work since it submits the SQL statements to the database server and processes the data returned. The application server is primarily responsible for sending requests to the transaction servers.

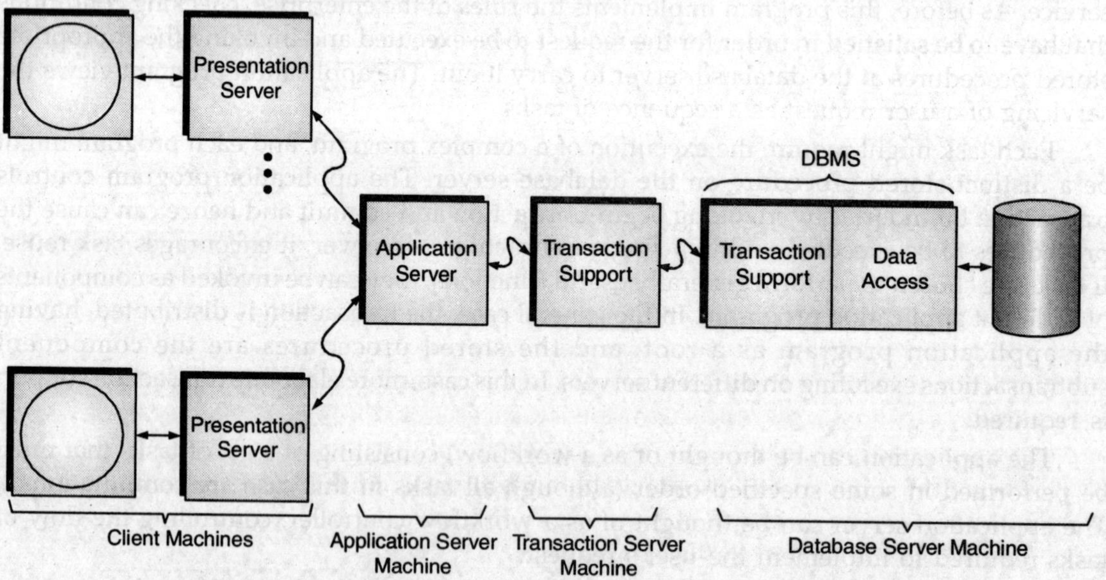

Figure 6.14: Three-tiered distributed transaction processing system with tasks executed in a transaction server

Although not shown in Figure 6.14, there might be multiple instantiations of the transaction server. This is an example of a server class, which is used when it is expected that the server will be heavily loaded. Instances of the class might run on different computers connected to the database server in order to share the transaction load arising from concurrently executing workflows. More generally, there might be multiple database server machines storing different portions of the enterprise's database-for example, a billing database on one server and a registration database on another. A particular transaction server might then be capable of executing only a subset of the tasks and be connected to a subset of the database servers. In that case, the application server must invoke the appropriate transaction server to get a particular task done. This selective invocation is frequently referred to as routing. An application program acting as a distributed transaction routes requests to multiple transaction servers, as shown in Figure 6.15.

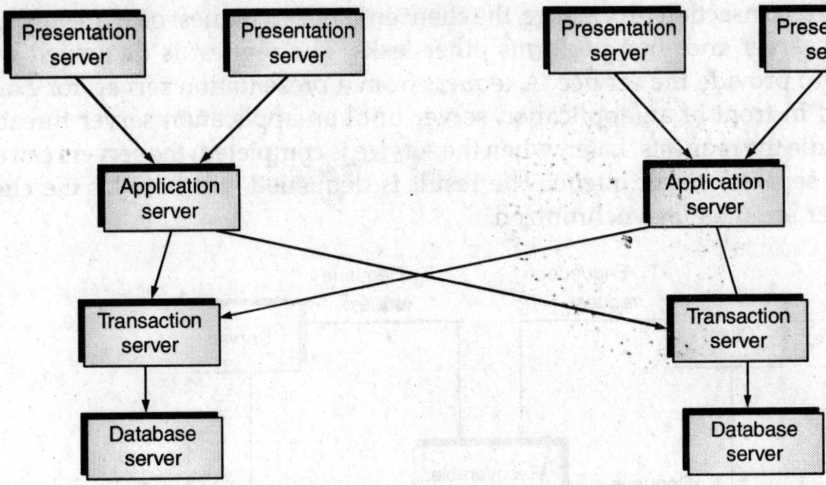

Figure 6.15: *Interconnection of presentation, application, and transaction servers in a three-tiered architecture*

Separating the transaction server from the database server is useful in the following situations:

1. Different components of an enterprise use different sets of procedures to access a common database. Separating these sets on different transaction servers allows each component to more easily control its own procedures. For example, the accounting system and the personnel system of a large corporation might use completely different procedures that access the same data.
2. A single procedure must access several different databases on different server machines.
3. The database server must handle requests arising from a large user population and hence can become a bottleneck. Moving stored procedures off the database machine eases this load.

Among the advantages of separating the client machines from the application server machine are these:

1. The client computers can be smaller (and hence cheaper). This is particularly important in applications involving hundreds, and perhaps thousands, of client machines.
2. System maintenance is easier since changes in enterprise rules (causing changes to the workflow program) can be localized to the application server computer instead of to all client computers.

3. The security of the system is enhanced since individual users do not have physical access to the application server computer and so cannot easily change the application programs.

6.18 QUEUED TRANSACTION PROCESSING

The two-tiered model shown in Figure 6.13 is referred to as data centered, whereas the three-tiered model shown in Figure 6.14 is referred to as service centered. In both, the client and server engage in direct transaction processing. The client invokes a server and then waits for the result. The service is provided as quickly as possible and a result is returned. The client and server are thus synchronized.

With queued transaction processing, the client enqueues a request on a queue of pending requests to the server and then performs other tasks. The request is dequeued when the server is ready to provide the service. A request from a presentation server, for example, is often enqueued in front of an application server until an application server thread can be assigned to handle the requests. Later, when the service is completed, the servers can enqueue the result on a separate result queue. The result is dequeued still later by the client. The client and server are thus unsynchronized.

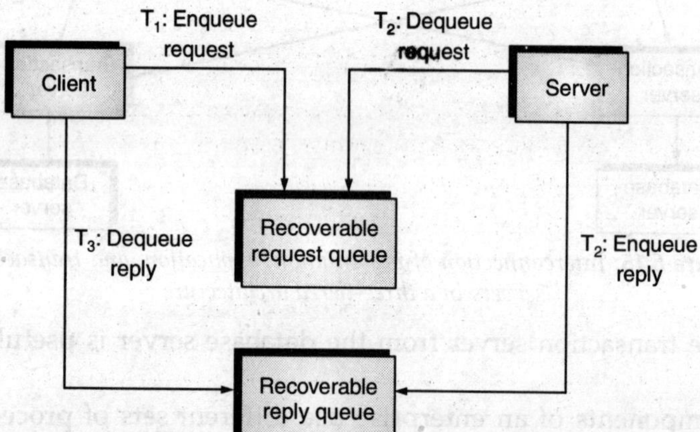

Figure 6.16: Queued transaction processing involves two queues and three transactions.

With recoverable queues, queue operations are transactional. The handling of a request in a queued transaction processing system might involve three transactions, as shown in Figure 6.16. The client executes transaction T_1 to enqueue the request prior to service; the server then executes transaction T_2, which dequeues the request, services it, and enqueues the result on the reply queue; and the client finally executes transaction T_3 to dequeue the result from the reply queue.

Queued transaction processing offers a number of advantages. The client can input a request at times when the server is busy or down. Similarly, the server can return results even if the client is unprepared to accept them. Furthermore, if the server crashes while the request is being serviced, the service transaction is aborted and the request is restored to the request queue. It is serviced when the server is restarted, without any intervention by the client. Finally, when multiple servers become available, the queue can be integrated into an algorithm that balances the load on all servers.

6.19 THE TP MONITOR

A TP monitor is a collection of software modules that augment the services provided by an operating system. An operating system creates the abstraction of concurrently executing processes that can communicate with one another using a message-passing facility, and provides them with shared access to the physical resources of the computer system. The TP monitor extends this to create the abstraction of transactions that execute concurrently in a distributed environment. As shown in Figure 6.17, a TP monitor can be viewed as a layer of software between the operating system and the application routines.

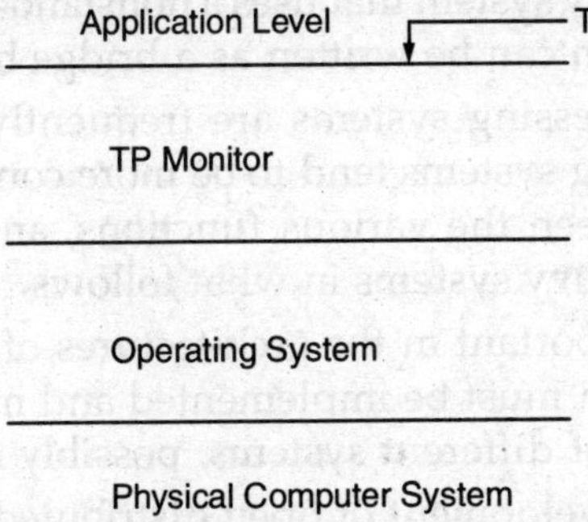

Figure 6.17: Layered structure of a transaction processing system

Examples of the services provided by a TP monitor are:

- Communication protocols of various kinds
- Security of distributed applications, including authentication and encryption
- Atomicity, isolation, and durability of distributed transactions

These services can be provided in an application-independent way; they have general utility and hence can be used in many different distributed applications.

A number of TP monitors exist. Tuxedo and Encina are early examples. Microsoft Transaction Server (MTS) is a more recent entry into the field, and Java Transaction Service QTS) is a specification of a Java-based TP monitor. All of them include or specify a set of application-independent services that, though needed in a transaction processing system, are not usually provided by an operating system.

Homogeneous and heterogeneous transaction processing systems: Early transaction processing systems were homogeneous, involving the hardware and software of a single vendor. Such systems utilized interfaces designed by the vendor - *proprietary interfaces* - that enabled its products to be interconnected in a variety of ways. Even when these interfaces were published, it was difficult to incorporate products from other vendors into the system because different vendors used different interfaces.

Many current transaction processing systems are heterogeneous, involving the products of multiple vendors: hardware platforms, operating systems, database managers, and communication protocols. Homogeneous systems have evolved into heterogeneous systems for the following reasons:

Newer applications often require the interconnection of older, legacy systems produced by different vendors that had previously operated independently. For example, over the years each department in a company might have developed its own purchasing system. Now the company requires a company-wide purchasing system that interconnects all local systems.

There are more vendors supplying hardware and software components, and users demand the ability to incorporate the best components available regardless of the supplier.

The implementation of heterogeneous systems requires vendors to agree on (1) standardized, nonproprietary interfaces-open interfaces-that define the content and format of the information that must be exchanged in an interaction and (2) communications software to transmit that information. If a legacy system that uses a nonstandard, proprietary interface is to be included, a wrapper program can be written as a bridge between interfaces.

Homogeneous transaction processing systems are frequently referred to as TP-Lite. Heterogeneous transaction processing systems tend to be more complex since there is more emphasis on strict boundaries between the various functions, and are referred to as TP-Heavy. We will be discussing TP-Heavy systems in what follows.

TP monitors are particularly important in the architectures of heterogeneous systems, where the abstraction of a transaction must be implemented and maintained in the context of the interconnection of a number of different systems, possibly from different vendors.

Middleware: To promote the development of open distributed systems in general-and transaction processing systems in particular-various software products have been developed that are frequently referred to as middleware. Middleware is software that supports the interaction of clients and servers, often in heterogeneous systems. Many of the modules provided by a TP monitor fall under the general heading of middleware.

JDBC and ODBC are two examples of middleware that allow an application to interact with database servers from a variety of vendors. CORBA, another example, allows applications to access objects distributed through a network.

6.20 TP SYSTEM CONFIGURATIONS

When learning the principles of transaction processing, it is helpful to have a feel for the range of systems where these principles are applied. In any given price range, including the very high end, the capabilities of TP applications and systems continually grow, in large part due to the steadily declining cost of computing and communication. These growing capabilities enable businesses to increase the functionality of classical TP applications, such as travel reservations and banking. In addition, every few years, these capabilities enable entirely new categories of businesses.

In the past decade, examples include large-scale Internet retailers and social networking web sites. There is no such thing as an average TP application or system. Rather, systems that implement TP applications come in a wide range of sizes, from single servers to data centers with thousands of machines. And the applications themselves exhibit a wide range of complexity, from a single database with few dozen transaction types to thousands of databases running hundreds of millions of lines of code. Therefore, whatever one might say about typical TP installations will apply only to a small fraction of them and will likely be outdated within a few years.

A low-end system could be a departmental application supporting a small number of users who perform a common function. Such an application might run comfortably on a single server machine. For example, the sales and marketing team of a small company might use a TP application to capture sales orders, record customer responses to sales campaigns, alert sales people when product support agreements need to be renewed, and track the steps in resolving customer complaints. Even though the load on the system is rather light, the application might require hundreds of transaction types to support many different business functions.

By contrast, the workload of a large Internet service might require thousands of server machines. This is typical for large-scale on-line shopping, financial services, travel services, multimedia services (e.g., sharing of music, photos, and videos), and social networking. To ensure the service is available 24 hours a day, 7 days a week (a.k.a. 24 × 7), it often is supported by multiple geographically distributed data centers. Thus if one data center fails, others can pick up its load.

Like hardware configuration, software configurations cover a wide range. The system software used to operate a TP system may be proprietary or open source. It may use the latest system software products or ones that were introduced decades ago. It may only include a SQL database system and web server, or it may include several layers of transactional middleware and specialized database software.

The range of technical issues that need to be addressed is largely independent of the hardware or software configuration that is chosen. These issues include selecting a programming model; ensuring the ACID properties; and maximizing availability, scalability, manageability, and performance.

6.21 STRATEGIC SIGNIFICANCE OF TPS

A customer's satisfaction with an organization is composed of two elements:

- The satisfaction with the *product* (service) acquired-its functionality/quality
- The satisfaction with the *process* involved in acquiring the product or service.

The latter is a function of the effectiveness and efficiency of the organization's TPS. An organization is typically represented in the form of a triangle/pyramid to show the management hierarchy. The TPS, being a subset of the operational system, is typically shown as the lowest level. Whether consciously or subconsciously, we associate more status and significance with higher levels and less with the lower ones. Most of those running the TPS, at the lowest level of the organization, are clerks of lower education and pay. But it is precisely with this level of the organization that customers interact in their day-to-day business dealings. It is this level-not the higher management levels- that customers "see" as the XYZ organization.

Even if the organization offers the highest quality product or service at the lowest price, the customers have to go through the labyrinth of the customer cycle (inquiry, ordering, paying, shipping, etc.) before they receive the actual product or service. With the slightest dissatisfaction occurring in this preliminary interaction, customers may change their minds, cancel the order, and switch to a competitor. At its best, the strategic significance of the TPS lies in its ability to offer a pleasant purchasing experience to customers; one that would satisfy them enough to make them want to come back again and again. At its worst, the strategic significance of the TPS is revealed when it fails to work, thus bringing the inner wheels of the organization to a disastrous halt.

The strategic significance of a TPS goes beyond mere efficiency in that a TPS can incorporate features aimed at attracting and keeping customers. The field of strategic information systems is replete with examples of mundane types of TPSs that were given a strategic thrust. An example of a mundane transaction processing subsystem is order processing. A typical order processing system is based on the following logic. Order data are received, verified, and entered into the system. The system then verifies the customer's credit status and product availability. If both are positive, the relevant information is sent to inventory (or production as the case may be), shipping, and billing. If the requested item is not in stock, the customer is asked if he wants to backorder the item. If he does, that sets in motion a whole series of actions. Along the way, some exception reports and documents are generated also. Regardless of the complexity and number of steps involved, there is a clear-cut structure to this process.

If most order processing systems follow the above logic, then how can one stand out as strategically superior to others? The classic example of revolutionizing order entry was the American Hospital Supply Corporation's ASAP (Analytic Systems Automatic Purchasing). Order entry terminals were placed in hospitals and linked to AHSC's computers. Using these terminals, hospitals could place orders with a great deal of peace of mind, being assured of cost, availability, and delivery in advance. With a system offering this level of service, it is unlikely that a client hospital would switch to AHSC's competition.

With the increasing popularity of the Internet and electronic commerce, this model has now become pervasive and improved *on* by pioneers such as Amazon.com and Drugstore.com. The more value a TPS offers the customer, the more customers will be attracted and kept loyal. There in lies the strategic promise of a TPS.

SUMMARY

Many of these early systems were designed to reduce costs by automating routine, labour-intensive business transactions. A **transaction** is any business-related exchange such as payments to employees, sales to customers, or payments to suppliers. Processing business transactions was the first computer application developed for most organizations. A **transaction processing system (TPS)** is an organized collection of people, procedures, software, databases, and devices used to perform and record business transactions. If you understand a transaction processing system, you understand basic business operations and functions.

TPS is a system that captures, enters, stores, retrieves, and processes the relevant details of business events, and generates the information/ documents necessary for running the organization and interfacing with external entities, such as customers.

A Transaction Processing System (TPS) is designed for Operating Management. It is also called Electronic Data Processing (EDP). It has a limited area of functionality, and is designed for one area of the business.

EXERCISES

1. Explain the concept of transaction.
2. What is a transaction processing system? Explain the features of such systems.
3. Explain the basic TPS model with the help of a diagram.
4. Explain ACID properties of transactions in brief.
5. What are various views of a TPS?
6. Explain the internal logical view of a TPS with the help of a diagram.
7. Give some generic examples of TPS. Also explain their interrelationship with the help of a diagram.
8. Explain the architecture of a TPS. Also explain the outputs of such a system.
9. Explain transaction processing scheme in a centralised system.
10. Explain transaction processing scheme in a distributed system.
11. How is a three-tier model implemented in designing TPS for distributed systems?
12. Explain queued transaction processing in brief.
13. Explain the concept of a TP monitor.
14. Give strategic significance of TP systems.

❑

Knowledge Work and Office Automation Systems

7

7.1 IMPORTANT DIMENSIONS OF KNOWLEDGE

There is an important distinction between data, information, knowledge, and wisdom. Chapter 1 defines data as a flow of events or transactions captured by an organization's systems that, by itself, is useful for transacting but little else. To turn data into useful information, a firm must expend resources to organize data into categories of understanding, such as monthly, daily, regional, or store-based reports of total sales. To transform information into knowledge, a firm must expend additional resources to discover patterns, rules, and contexts where the knowledge works. Finally, wisdom is thought to be the collective and individual experience of applying knowledge to the solution of problems.

Wisdom involves where, when, and how to apply knowledge. Knowledge is both an individual attribute and a collective attribute of the firm. Knowledge is a cognitive, even a physiological, event, that takes place inside peoples' heads, but it is also stored in libraries and records; shared in lectures; and stored by firms in the form of business processes and employee know-how. Knowledge residing in the minds of employees that has not been documented is called tacit knowledge, whereas knowledge that has been documented is called explicit knowledge. Knowledge can reside in e-mail, voice mail, graphics, and unstructured documents as well as structured documents.

Knowledge is generally believed to have a location, either in the minds of humans or in specific business processes. Knowledge is "sticky" and not universally applicable or easily moved. Finally, knowledge is thought to be situational and contextual. For example, you must know when to perform a procedure as well as how to perform it. Table 7.1 reviews these dimensions of knowledge.

Table 7.1: Important Dimensions of Knowledge

Knowledge Is a Firm Asset
Knowledge is an intangible asset.
The transformation of data into useful information and knowledge requires organizational resources.
Knowledge is not subject to the law of diminishing returns as are physical assets, but instead experiences network effects (law of expanding returns) as its value increases as more people share it.

Knowledge Has Different Forms
Knowledge can be either tacit or explicit (codified).
Knowledge involves know-how, craft, and skill.
Knowledge involves knowing how to follow procedures.
Knowledge involves knowing why, not simply when, things happen (causality).
Knowledge Has a Location
Knowledge is a cognitive event involving mental models and maps of individuals.
There is both a social and an individual basis of knowledge.
Knowledge is 'sticky' (hard to move), situated (enmeshed in a firm's culture), and contextual (works only in certain situations).
Knowledge Is Situational
Knowledge is conditional: Knowing when to apply a procedure is just as important as knowing the procedure (conditional).
Knowledge is related to context: You must know how to use a certain tool and under what circumstances.

We can see that knowledge is a different kind of firm asset from, say, buildings and financial assets; that knowledge is a complex phenomenon; and that there are many aspects to the process of managing knowledge. We can also recognize that knowledge-based core competencies of firms—the two or three things that an organization does best—are key organizational assets. Knowing how to do things effectively and efficiently in ways that other organizations cannot duplicate is a primary source of profit and competitive advantage that cannot be purchased easily by competitors in the marketplace.

For instance, having a unique build-to-order production system or customer relationship management system constitutes a form of knowledge and can be a unique asset that other firms cannot copy easily. With knowledge, firms become more efficient and effective in their use of scarce resources. Without knowledge, firms become less efficient and less effective in their use of resources and ultimately fail. Organizations differ in their abilities to apply knowledge, and firms that apply knowledge more effectively than competitors are more successful.

7.2 KNOWLEDGE MANAGEMENT

Knowledge management is the set of processes developed in an organization to create, gather, store, maintain, and disseminate the firm's knowledge. The major information systems that support knowledge management are office systems, knowledge work systems, group collaboration systems, and artificial intelligence systems.

Office systems are systems designed to increase the productivity of information workers in the office. Examples of office systems include word processing, desktop publishing, imaging and Web publishing, electronic calendars, and desktop database.

Knowledge work systems are information systems that aid knowledge workers in the creation and integration of new knowledge in the organization. Examples of knowledge work systems include CAD, virtual reality, and investment workstations.

Group collaboration systems facilitate communication, collaboration, and coordination. Examples of group collaboration systems include groupware, teamware, and intranets.

Artificial intelligence is the development of systems that behave as humans. Examples of artificial intelligence systems include expert systems, neural nets, fuzzy logic, genetic algorithms, and intelligent agents. Natural language, robotics, perceptive systems, expert systems, and intelligent machines are artificial intelligence initiatives.

Knowledge management promotes organizational learning as it defines and codifies the organization's knowledge base. Knowledge management enables the organization to learn from its environment and incorporate this new knowledge into its business processes. New Standard Operating Procedures can be created that reflect recent experiences within the organization. Knowledge management systems enable the creation and support of knowledge networks, knowledge repositories, and communities of practice. Knowledge networks enable people to be linked, so that experts in a given area can be easily identified and share tacit knowledge. Knowledge management streamlines the workflow and provides tools for creating a knowledge repository. A knowledge repository is a collection of internal and external knowledge stored in a single location for more efficient management and utilization by the organization. A community of practice is an informal group of people who may live or work in many different locations but who share a common professional interest.

In this chapter, we discuss knowledge work systems and office systems in further detail.

7.3 KNOWLEDGE WORK SYSTEMS

Firms have specialized systems for knowledge workers to help them create new knowledge for the firm.

7.3.1 Knowledge Workers and Knowledge Work

Knowledge workers include researchers, designers, architects, scientists, and engineers who primarily create knowledge and information for the organization. Knowledge workers usually have high levels of education and memberships in professional organizations and are often asked to exercise independent judgment as a routine aspect of their work. For example, knowledge workers create new products or find ways of improving existing ones. Knowledge workers perform three key roles that are critical to the organization and to the managers who work within the organization:

- Keeping the organization current in knowledge as it develops in the external world—in technology, science, social thought, and the arts
- Serving as internal consultants regarding the areas of their knowledge, the changes taking place, and opportunities
- Acting as change agents, evaluating, initiating, and promoting change projects

Most knowledge workers rely on office systems, such as word processors, voice mail, e-mail, videoconferencing, and scheduling systems, which are designed to increase worker productivity in the office. However, knowledge workers also require highly specialized knowledge work systems. These knowledge work systems (KWS) are specifically designed to promote the creation of knowledge and to ensure that new knowledge and technical expertise are properly integrated into the business. Moreover, knowledge work is segmented into many highly specialized fields, and each field has a different collection of knowledge work systems that are specialized to support workers in that field.

7.3.2 Requirements of Knowledge Work Systems

Knowledge work systems have characteristics that reflect the special needs of knowledge workers. First, knowledge work systems must give knowledge workers the specialized tools they need, such as powerful graphics, analytical tools, and communications and document management tools. These systems require great computing power to handle the sophisticated graphics or complex calculations necessary for such knowledge workers as scientific researchers, product designers, and financial analysts. Because knowledge workers are so focused on knowledge in the external world, these systems also must give the worker quick and easy access to external databases.

A user-friendly interface is very important to a knowledge worker's system. User-friendly interfaces save time by enabling the user to perform needed tasks and get to required information without having to spend a lot of time learning how to use the computer. Saving time is more important for knowledge workers than for most other employees because knowledge workers are highly paid—wasting a knowledge worker's time is simply too expensive, and knowledge workers can easily fall prey to information overload. Figure 7.1 summarizes the requirements of knowledge work systems.

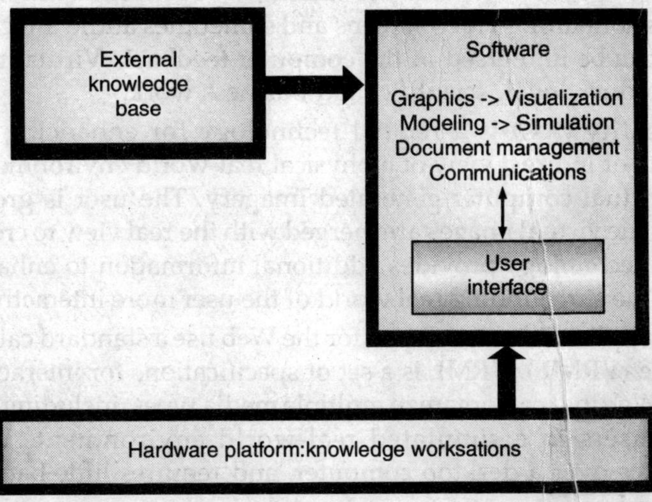

Figure 7.1: Requirements of knowledge work systems

Knowledge workstations often are designed and optimized for the specific tasks to be performed; so, for example, a design engineer requires a different workstation setup than a financial analyst. Design engineers need graphics with enough power to handle three-dimensional computer-aided design (CAD) systems. However, financial analysts are more interested in access to a myriad of external databases and technology for efficiently storing and accessing massive amounts of financial data.

7.3.3 Examples of Knowledge Work Systems

Major knowledge work applications include computer-aided design (CAD) systems, virtual reality systems for simulation and modeling, and financial workstations. Computer-aided design (CAD) automates the creation and revision of designs, using computers and sophisticated graphics software. Using a more traditional physical design methodology, each design modification requires a mould to be made and a prototype to be tested physically. That process must be repeated many times, which is a very expensive and time-consuming process. Using a CAD workstation, the designer need only make a physical prototype toward the end of the design process because the design can be easily tested and changed on the computer. The ability of CAD software to provide design specifications for the tooling and the manufacturing processes also saves a great deal of time and money while producing a manufacturing process with far fewer problems.

Virtual reality systems have visualization, rendering, and simulation capabilities that go far beyond those of conventional CAD systems. They use interactive graphics software to create computer-generated simulations that are so close to reality that users almost believe they are participating in a real-world situation. In many virtual reality systems, the user dons special clothing, headgear, and equipment, depending on the application. The clothing contains sensors that record the user's movements and immediately transmit that information back to the computer. For instance, to walk through a virtual reality simulation of a house, you would need garb that monitors the movement of your feet, hands, and head. You also would need goggles containing video screens and sometimes audio attachments and feeling gloves so that you can be immersed in the computer feedback. Virtual reality is starting to provide benefits in educational, scientific, and business work.

Augmented reality (AR) is a related technology for enhancing visualization. AR provides a live direct or indirect view of a physical real-world environment whose elements are *augmented* by virtual computer-generated imagery. The user is grounded in the real physical world, and the virtual images are merged with the real view to create the augmented display. The digital technology provides additional information to enhance the perception of reality and make the surrounding real world of the user more interactive and meaningful.

Virtual reality applications developed for the Web use a standard called **Virtual Reality Modeling Language (VRML)**. VRML is a set of specifications for interactive, 3-D modeling on the World Wide Web that can organize multiple media types, including animation, images, and audio to put users in a simulated real-world environment. VRML is platform independent, operates over a desktop computer, and requires little bandwidth.

The financial industry is using specialized investment workstations to leverage the knowledge and time of its brokers, traders, and portfolio managers. Firms such as Merrill Lynch and UBS Financial Services have installed investment workstations that integrate a wide range of data from both internal and external sources, including contact management data, real-time and historical market data, and research reports. Previously, financial professionals had to spend considerable time accessing data from separate systems and piecing together the information they needed. By providing one-stop information faster and with fewer errors, the workstations streamline the entire investment process from stock selection to updating client records. Table 7.2 summarizes the major types of knowledge work systems.

Table 7.2: Examples of Knowledge Work Systems

Knowledge Work System	Function on Organization
CAD/CAM (computer-aided design/ computer- aided manufacturing)	Provides engineers, designers, and factory managers with precise control over industrial design and manufacturing
Virtual reality systems	Provide drug designers, architects, engineers, and medical workers with precise, photorealistic simulations of objects
Investment workstations	High-end PCs used in financial sector to analyse trading situations instantaneously and facilitate portfolio management

7.4 OVERVIEW OF OFFICE AUTOMATION SYSTEMS

Office Automation Systems are computer based information systems that are new and expanding very quickly. In any work environment, people, tasks, equipment and resources are organised to accomplish specific objectives, generally some type of product. In the Office, the product is Information. Information is the product of data processing and is equivalent to finished goods produced after processing the raw material and also valuable in decision making. The purpose of this section is to show various consequences of Office automation systems and show how they will help increase the efficiency and productivity of office workers, typists, secretaries, administrative assistants, staff professionals, managers and others.

Office automation refers to the varied computer machinery and software used to digitally create, collect, store, manipulate, and relay office information needed for accomplishing basic tasks and goals. Office automation systems (OAS) are configurations of networked computer hardware and software. A variety of office automation systems are now applied to business and communication functions that used to be performed manually or in multiple locations of a company, such as preparing written communications and strategic planning. In addition, functions that once required coordinating the expertise of outside specialists in typesetting, printing, or electronic recording can now be integrated into the everyday work of an organization, saving both time and money.

The office is a part of business that handles the information dealing with various operations within an organisation that are performed to meet certain objectives. Such operations include accounting, payroll, billing, etc. Various activities that come under office work are document preparation, filling, performing simple computations, checking information, intra-office communication and external communication. Such processing within the office is usually stimulated by the arrival of a request for service such as an order, a bill, a complaint, a message to order more material, a message to change the order or the date changing to Friday etc. The office can be viewed as a mechanism that maintains the state of the business by means of a series of activities that cause a change in state. Therefore the term office automation refers to the use of integrated computer and communication systems to support administrative procedures in an office environment.

7.4.1 A Systems View of an Office

An office is an organizational unit that processes the information on which the functioning of an organization depends. Office system is a subsystem of its containing system– the organization. An office system contains:

- Layout
- Infrastructure
- Operators
- Services
- Activities

How the above components of an office system are brought together to serve and support the organisation constitutes the office configuration. The configuration of an office system is largely determined by the organization system that contains it and is mainly affected by (1) the nature of the organization, (2) size of the organization, (3) its requirement and (4) types of office technology employed. Taking the extent of office technology utilization, one can then have a continuum of offices ranging from *Traditional, Beginner, IT supported, Networked office, to Virtual offices.*

7.4.2 Office Automation

Office automation refers to the use of information technology to support routine office activities and functions. This work includes, but not limited to

- Document management: capturing, processing, producing, communicating, storing and sharing
- Collaborative work
- Management of project activities: time, money, idea, and other resources
- Personal organization,
- Other administrative tasks, organizing meetings, office record handling

7.5 OFFICE AUTOMATION SYSTEM

Office Automation systems (OAS) could therefore be defined as information systems intended to increase the productivity of office workers. As in most automation applications such systems would enable to do things faster, cheaper and better, i.e., in efficiency and effectiveness gains.

Further, OAS could be used organisationally to (1) coordinate and manage work of office workers within an organizational unit (2) link the work being performed across all levels and functions and (3) link the organization to its extended enterprises, i.e. customers, suppliers and other partners.

Office Automation System is the application of computers to handle the office activities. Different office activities can be broadly grouped into the following types of operations:-

- *Document Capture* - Documents originating from outside sources like incoming mails, notes, handouts, charts, etc. need to be preserved.
- *Recording utilization of resources* - includes record keeping in respect to specific resources utilized by office personnel.
- *Calculations* - Include the usual calculator functions like routine arithmetic operations for bill passing, interest calculations, etc.
- *Document Creation* - Consists of preparation of documents, dictation, editing of texts.

- Filing, Search, Retrieval and Follow up: related to filling, indexing, searching of documents which take up significant time.
- *Receipts and Distribution* - Includes distribution of correspondence to designated recipients.

In the automated office not only office work will be performed more efficiently but also the concept of office work will be altered. The greatest potential of office automation is not expected to be from the improvement of clerical and administrative tasks but from the ability of managers to gain increased control over their operations. The automation of everyday office tasks is one of the key results of the electronic revolution. No modern office can hope to survive without many of them.

Office Automation involves the planned application of integrated information handling tools and methods to improve the productivity of people in office operations. Although the handling of information by office people is the focus of this new technology, other aspects of the office will be affected. These include factors such as the organization of functions and lines of reporting, training for new methods, work space design, travel patterns, branch office location, home vs office work, hours of work, employee morale, and job classifications. Organizations that harness office automation products will need to deal with many more than just technological issues.

Office automation will impact industry and government organizations in very significant ways with both COST DISPLACEMENT and VALUE-ADDED results. These two terms are now being used by people who are considering the potential payoffs of office automation to their organizations.

Cost displacement applications have the objective of achieving overall reductions in support staff costs or of increasing work volumes without adding support staff. Such applications typically center around WORD PROCESSING and provide the base for the more advanced value-added applications.

Value-added applications are viewed as being directed toward improving managerial and professional staff productivity (and effectiveness) through use of more integrated office automation systems that can directly affect their work.

The value-added approach deals with far more fundamental issues than the replacement of some support staff positions with word processing pools. Its focus upon individuals and groups of managers and professionals as targets for productivity improvement brings with it opportunities for significant increases in organizational effectiveness and major cost benefits in the largest segment of the office cost spectrum.

For any organization, management choices at many levels will affect the balance between reducing total office costs (cost displacement) and increasing the total office effectiveness (value-added effects).

Office Automation is likely to become one of the fastest-growing and most significant new industries of the century. It will apply electronic technology to a broad new set of applications and bring significant change to many of the ways in which people and organizations work — AUGMENTING their capabilities and increasing both the quantity and quality of their contributions.

7.6 EVOLUTION OF OFFICE AUTOMATION SYSTEMS

Office automation is a process that started with the Industrial Revolution. The typewriter was introduced in the office in 1840s and was followed by stenotypes machines, duplicators, tabulating machines and many other types. Office automation is a gradual, evolutionary process of change. In many ways, the evolution of office automation parallels to data processing. Both evolved primarily in responses to the advancements in computer technology, experienced in using the technology, and changing business and market conditions. The changes are implemented in response to specific business needs and not merely for sake of introduction of most modern equipment. However, the term office system automation or office automation is the application of computer technology to processing and using information in the office. Automation provides more efficient and effective use of information, as well as faster processing of information, and it puts tools in the hands of workers in the office. Thus office automation tools are for managers, professionals and technical workers as much as they are for clerical workers.

At present the office automation concept of administrative support emerged along with the data processing concept of Management Information System (MIS). The objective is to use computers to support administrative and management activities.

7.7 TYPES OF OFFICE AUTOMATION SYSTEMS

Following are the types of office automation systems:

7.7.1 Personal OAS

Personal OAS includes the following systems:

- Word processing
- Database management
- Desktop Publishing
- Communication
- Spreadsheet
- Data Presentation
- Personal Schedulers

7.7.2 Group OAS

Groupware applications are the applications which assist teams of people within and/ or across an organisation in working together and help in achieving the three Cs – *Communication, Collaboration and Coordination*. Some groupware applications are summarised in the Table 7.3:

Table 7.3: Groupware Functions

Groupware function	Applications
Messaging	e-mail, electronic forms processing, group mail, electronic bulletin boards
Document management and information sharing	Document image processing, Electronic document management systems (EDMS): These are systems that allow the capturing, routing, storing and manipulation of documents electronically

Collaborative authoring	Systems that allow team development of designs Computer Aided Design (CAD) and documents. Their capabilities include shared access to documents, centralised spell-checking dictionary, commenting facility, file locking to ensure that two users do not try to alter the same original document at the same time, version control
Conferencing	Text conferencing, video conferencing, teleconferencing, data conferencing. Such systems facilitate meeting among physically distant people.
Time Management	Group scheduling system: The value of electronic diaries is considerably increased if they are made available over a network. An individual's schedule can then be accessed by other members of the work group. These other members can therefore easily find out where a staff member is now, and is going to be at some future point. They can also, perhaps subject to confirmation from the owner, write in appointments
Decision making	Group decision support systems provide data-gathering, structuring ideas and information, analysis and reporting functions to help a group of people make a decision in an ill-structured situation
Work management	Workflow systems: systems that enable to assign and manage work processes, tasks and information electronically among people

Groupware applications support collaboration and communication of groups in either synchronous or asynchronous basis. While synchronous systems support same time collaboration and communication, asynchronous modes support these across different times as depicted in Table 7.4.

Table 7.4: Synchronous and Asynchronous Systems

<table>
<tr><td rowspan="4">Location</td><td></td><td colspan="2">Time</td></tr>
<tr><td></td><td>Same</td><td>Different</td></tr>
<tr><td>Same</td><td>Synchronous, examples are meeting and group decision support systems, conferencing</td><td>Asynchronous: emails, discussion groups, bulletin boards, workflow systems, authoring systems</td></tr>
<tr><td>Different</td><td>Synchronous: teleconferencing, Internet chatting, group decision support systems, conferencing</td><td>Asynchronous: Email, Authoring systems</td></tr>
</table>

7.8 CLASSIFICATION OF OAS

We classify OAS in the following major categories:

7.8.1 Electronic Publishing

Electronic publishing systems include word processing and desktop publishing. Word processing software, (e.g., Microsoft Word, Corel Word-Perfect) allows users to create, edit, revise, store, and print documents such as letters, memos, reports, and manuscripts.

7.8.2 Electronic Communication

Electronic communication systems include electronic mail (e-mail), voice mail, facsimile (fax), and desktop videoconferencing.

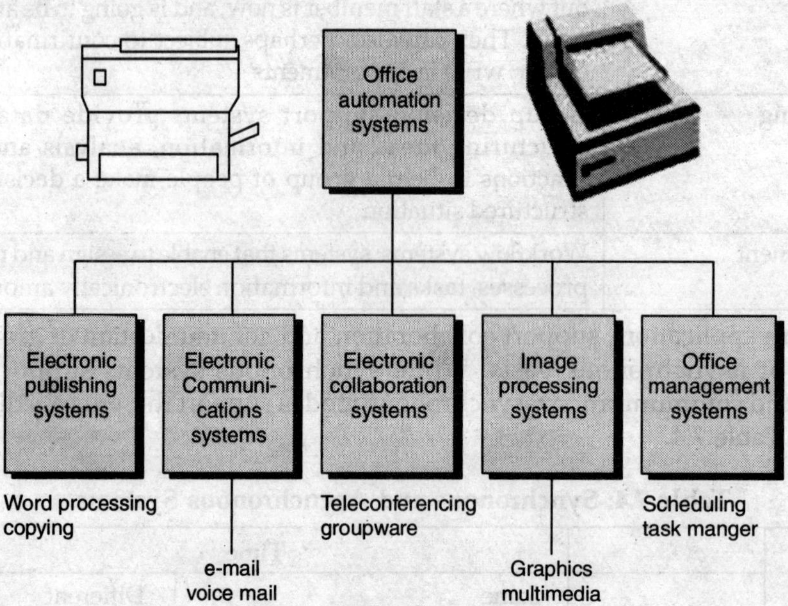

Figure 7.2: Classification of OAS

7.8.3 Electronic Collaboration

Electronic collaboration is made possible through electronic meeting and collaborative work systems and teleconferencing. Electronic meeting and collaborative work systems allow teams of co-workers to use networks of microcomputers to share information, update schedules and plans, and cooperate on projects regardless of geographic distance.

7.8.4 Image Processing

Image processing systems include electronic document management, presentation graphics, and multimedia systems. Imaging systems convert text, drawings, and photographs into digital form that can be stored in a computer system. This digital form can be manipulated, stored, printed, or sent via a **modem** to another computer. Imaging systems may use scanners, digital cameras, video capture cards, or advanced graphic computers. Companies use imaging systems for a variety of documents such as insurance forms, medical records, dental records, and mortgage applications.

7.8.5 Office Management

Office management systems include electronic office accessories, electronic scheduling, and task management. These systems provide an electronic means of organizing people, projects, and data. Business dates, appointments, notes, and client contact information can be created, edited, stored, and retrieved.

7.9 PROSPECTS OF OFFICE AUTOMATION

In the traditional office, secretaries and clerical worker support people who manage or supervise the operation of the enterprise, the boss/secretary team has been the basic organizational structure for offices in both public and the private sectors. Large enterprises are composed of multiple business units, each of which organized with one or more managers. Senior management personnel work together to co-ordinate these business units to accomplish the organization's basic goals. In every office, the requirements for shared information often result in considerable duplication of effort and for that additional costs are incurred. Today, the costs of computer technology have been falling at dramatic rates. Consequently, to capture the huge potential of this new technology, organizations have turned to office automation to increase their production.

Office automation is a process that requires understanding technology, business and people at work. It usually combines a large number of technologies including data processing, word processing, graphics and image processing, and communications. Office automation project will mainly focus the need to accomplish business objections. It is much more than selecting the right technology; the technology will help the organizations to achieve business goals.

7.10 CHARACTERISTICS OF OFFICE AUTOMATION SYSTEM

Office automation is a widely used term today. It generally means the application of computer and communication technology to improve the productivity of "knowledge works".

Office automation refers to the use of sophisticated electronic equipment and communication systems to carry out the "electronic tasks" the tasks include

- Text processing,
- Data processing
- Information storage,
- Information retrieval and updating,
- Message distribution,
- Document transmission and reproduction,
- Teleconferencing.

Office automation is a process that involves people, procedure and technology. Office automation technology include word processor, telecommunication, reprographics, e-mail, e-filing, facsimile transmission, micro-graphics and voice technologies.

Office automation involves the use of computers, in conjunction with other electronic-equipment to automate the basic secretarial and clerical the basic secretarial and clerical tasks of office.

Basic office automation consists of word processors connected to one another to means of a local area network.

Office automation should be designed as a multifunction information system to provide executives decision support tools such as:

- On-line access to databases,
- Model building and forecasting,
- Risk analysis,
- Sophisticated graphics,
- Integration of data and text,
- Data communication.

Some office automation systems go far beyond the function of providing word processing on networks. PCs or workstations are connected to a network.

- Office automation support a large number of software packages that could be used as decision support tools. Important ones are:
- Word processor, database management systems,
- Electronic spreadsheets,
- Graphics packages,
- Electronic mail systems.

Benefits of office automation include increased productivity, greater accuracy, lower clerical cost, continuously decreasing cost, decreasing size and increasing capabilities, quality and flexibility of outputs, and ease of operations.

7.11 WORKING OF OFFICE AUTOMATION SYSTEMS

Following are the approaches of office automation systems:

7.11.1 Traditional Approach

With Microsoft Office static templates can be produced by creating them individually beforehand.

With a high initial work effort, templates have thus to be created for each language, branch office, department, and for all employees.

Changes can only be made selectively. The creation of specific templates is therefore often left to the individual employees, which involves the risk that unwanted changes are made. There is no control and therefore no worldwide consistency.

This approach is depicted in Figure 7.3.

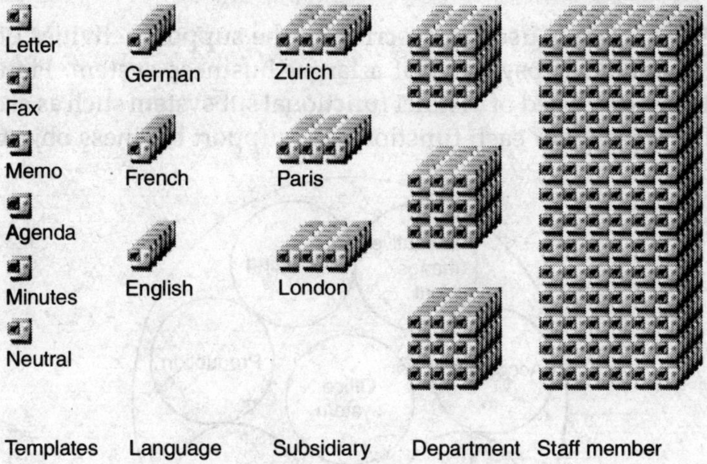

Figure 7.3: Traditional Approach

7.11.2 Automation Approach

With Office tools dynamic templates can be created in the form of master templates. After the first registration, they automatically adjust themselves to the different languages, subsidiaries, departments, and employees.

All the specific requirements incl. language changes can thus be covered with only one master template. The duplication of templates is no longer needed; the management of the templates is limited exclusively to a small number of masters. Changes are immediately effective in all relevant places. For the integration of address details of a new subsidiary or representative, in all correspondence only requires one additional entry in the database.

This approach is depicted in Figure 7.4.

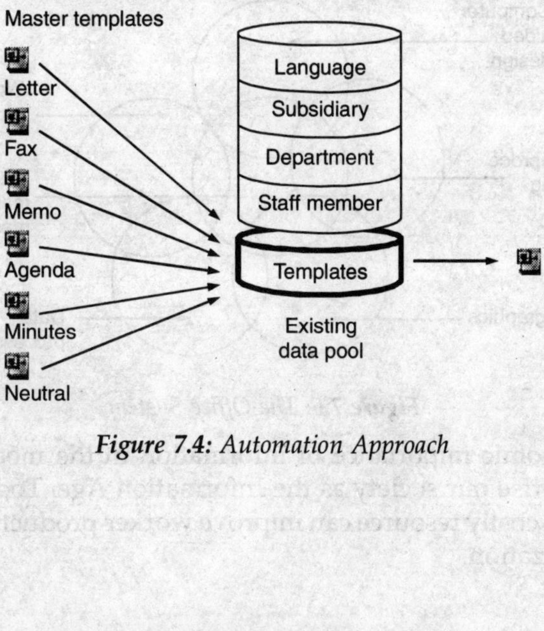

Figure 7.4: Automation Approach

7.12 OFFICE SYSTEMS OF A TYPICAL ENTERPRISE

The term office system is used to describe all the support activities of an organization. It may also be considered subsystems of a larger business system. Figure 7.5 shows the business system to be comprised of distinct functional subsystem such as accounting, finance, production etc. The mission of each function is to support business objectives.

Figure 7.5: The Business System

The functions overlap, but office system is common to all of them. Office system is a general term that describes the subsystem responsible for office automation.

Figure 7.6 shows that office systems are composed of subsystems. Office system support services such as word processing, data processing, reprographics or management facilities all work together for the completion of the common goal of office automation. The co-ordination of all subsystem is what makes office automation truly office system.

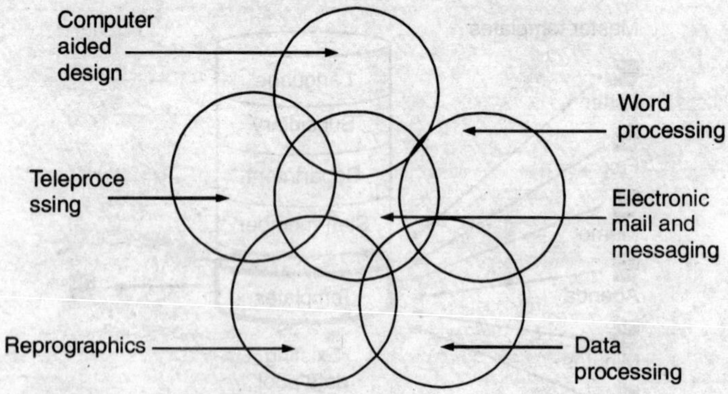

Figure 7.6: The Office System

The growing economic importance of information in the modern society has led the sociologists to characterise our society as the Information Age. Today, office automation is no longer a luxury; this costly resource can improve worker productivity, morale and overall operation of an organization.

According to our observation, to achieve maximum benefits from office systems automation, organizations should take the following measures:

1. Need to develop long-range strategic plans based on business requirements. Traditional Return-on-Investment (ROI) methodologies for justifying capital expenditure are not always applicable to office because many of the benefits for office work are difficult to quantify.
2. Old work force should be frequently trained to use the new technology and to adapt to change in occupation and the work environments. This should be a learning process that enables individuals to assimilate the new technologies.
3. To cope with the national and international competition, electronic information system should link globally enabling to move and share information.
4. The office automation manager should assume an active role as a change agent, collaborate effectively with various staff groups, co-ordinate the skills of the office automation team and understand the business requirements.

7.13 BENEFITS OF OFFICE AUTOMATION

Automation of office offers the following benefits:

- Brings tools and techniques into office and assists people as they process information.
- Alters the Quality of Work Life (QWL) which focuses on opportunities to workers job satisfaction by providing meaningful job as a supportive environment.
- Increase productivity because it enables work to be done quickly and/or easily.
- Makes information readily available to all who need it.
- Enable an enterprise to restructure entire operation in new ways.
- Can be used to gain strategic advantage.
- Creates new task, required to support the system or related to new products to new products or services. Existing job may be redesigned to incorporate these tasks or new jobs may be created.
- Large firms no longer have to employ typists
- Office employees become more flexible and several people
- Receptionists can spend more time with clients
- Managers need not necessarily delegate typing, to include more Public Relations work

7.13.1 BENEFITS FOR THE COMPANY

- Reduction of the number of templates
- Less administrative work for templates and contents
- Central data management, central management of multi-lingual contents
- Higher quality and productivity with Microsoft Office
- Saving of resources
- Personalized communication
- Constantly up-to-date contents, company or employee data
- Improvement of workflow and reduction of errors
- Worldwide consistent appearance of stationery and presentations
- Simplification of daily work

7.13.2 Benefits for the It Department

– No server software necessary
– Reduction of template maintenance work
– Use of existing user data from Directory Services (AD, NDS) or other databases
– Low to no need for training
– Simple and flexible access regulation
– Automatically correct printouts, automatic paper tray control
– Compatibility with all current Office versions
– Integrated user administration
– Flexible configuration
– Simple installation, only one installer for all versions

7.14 VARIOUS CHALLENGES

As we have seen that office automation offers new opportunities for improving the organizations and their employees, at all levels such as performance of work improve products and services etc. It also poses threat to the status quo and quality of work life. To take full advantage of the opportunities and avoid pitfalls, decision-makers should carefully integrate technology with business operations and goals. Capitalising the new opportunities requires foresight, careful planning and good magnet.

For most organizations office automation is a gradual process of change. The changes are accommodated in response to specific business necessities. However, not all impacts of technology have been beneficial. Poorly planned applications of office automation may produce some of the following undesirable results:

- Factory or assembly line approach of office work
- Displacement of people
- Reduced autonomy of employees
- Excessive monitoring of works
- Social isolation or lack of social support in work areas
- Poorly designed work areas, resulting in discomfort or health hazards
- Stressful work environments
- Low job satisfaction results, absenteeism and turnover

The above mentioned undesirable consequences of office automation results when decision makers ignore the potential impact of newly designed systems on individual workers and organization. Negative consequences also may result for inexperience with the technology, inadequate planning, lack of foresight, excessive focus on short term benefits, or management practices insensitive employees welfare. In the long term, ignoring these issues not only lowers the quality of work life, but productivity as well.

Automated office systems can provide a powerful mechanism for increasing productivity and improving the quality of work life by changing the fundamental nature of organizational information processing. According to our observation to achieve maximum benefits from office systems automation organisations should take the following measures:

- The office automation manager should assume an active role as a change agent, collaborate effectively with various staff groups, co-ordinate the skills of the office automation team and understand the business requirements.
- Old work force should be frequently trained to use the new technology and to adopt to change in occupation and the work environments.

7.15 OFFICE SYSTEM TOOLS

Office automation is more than a computer system or a specific software program, however, office automation offers new ways of organizing people, task and technology to meet business objectives. It also involves implementing various tools that solve specific problems. Some representative tools generally included under office automation are listed in the Table 7.5:

Table 7.5: Office System Tools

Tool name	Hardware/Software involved
Text handling tools	Electronic typewriters, dictation transcription systems, word processing, desktop publishing, electronic file and retrieval, optical character recognition (OCR), prints, photocopiers.
Data handling computing tools	Calculators, electronic spreadsheets, statistical packages, databases, decision support systems.
Communication tools	Telephones, Local Area Networks, electronic mail and messaging, voice mail messaging, videotext, and teleconferencing.
Image processing tools	Micrographics, computer output microfilm (COM), computer aided retrieval (CAR), optical disk.
Time management tools	Electronic calendars, project management software, electronic notebooks, and tracking systems.
Graphics tools	Computer graphics packages, computer-aided design, plotter, digitizers, scanners.
Artificial intelligence tools	Natural languages interface, expert systems, voice recognizers/ synthesis.

SUMMARY

Knowledge is generally believed to have a location, either in the minds of humans or in specific business processes. Knowledge is "sticky" and not universally applicable or easily moved. Finally, knowledge is thought to be situational and contextual.

Office Automation Systems are computer based information systems that are new and expanding very quickly. In any work environment, people, tasks, equipment and resources are organised to accomplish specific objectives, generally some type of product. In the Office, the product is Information. Information is the product of data processing and is equivalent to finished goods produced after processing the raw material and also valuable in decision making. The purpose of this chapter is to show various consequences of Office automation systems and show how they will help increase the efficiency and productivity of office workers, typists, secretaries, administrative assistants, staff professionals, managers and others.

EXERCISES

1. What are the important dimensions of knowledge?
2. What is knowledge management?
3. Explain the concept of knowledge workers and knowledge work?
4. What are the requirements of knowledge work systems?
5. Explain the examples of knowledge work systems?
6. Explain the concept of office automation systems?
7. What is office automation?
8. What do you mean by office automation system?
9. Explain the evolution of office automation systems?
10. What are the types of office automation systems?
11. Explain the classification of office automation systems?
12. What are the prospects of office automation?
13. What are the characteristics of office automation system?
14. Explain the working of office automation systems?
15. Explain the office systems of a typical enterprise?
16. What are the benefits of office automation?
17. What are the various challenges of office automation system?
18. Explain the various tools of office system?

❑

8 Management Information Systems

8.1 INTRODUCTION

Management Information System (MIS) is a system consisting of people, machines, procedures, databases and data models, as its elements. The system gathers data from internal and external sources of the organization; processes it and supplies Management Information to assist managers in the process of decision making. Here the word system implies that MIS follows a systems approach which means a holistic approach and is based on the concept of synergy where the output is greater than the sum of its parts. Thus, it clearly indicates that MIS is not a single system; rather it is an integrated system where parts (sub-systems) fit into an overall design.

The modern management needs more advance techniques for solving its basic requirements. The MIS is a new idea which is associated with men, machine, marketing and methods for collecting pertinent information from the internal and external source and processing this information for the purpose of facilitating the process of decision making of the business. The scope and purpose of MIS is better understood if each part of them is defined. Thus, we define each part as follows:

8.1.1 Management

Management has been defined in a variety of ways. To someone, it comprises the processes or activities that describe what managers do in the operation of their organization, such as plan, organize, initiate, and control operations. They plan by setting strategies and goals and selecting the best course of action to achieve these plans or goals. They organize the tasks necessary for operational plan, set these tasks up into homogeneous groups and assign authority delegation. They control the performance of the work by setting performance standards and avoiding deviation from standard.

The decision making is a fundamental prerequisite of each of the foregoing processes, the job of MIS is facilitating decisions necessary for planning, organizing and controlling the work and functions of the business so that specified goals of business are achieved.

8.1.2 Information

Information consists of data that have been retrieved, processed or otherwise used for information or as a basis for forecasting or decision-making regarding any business unit.

Information is knowledge that one derives from facts for effective functioning of systems placed in the right context with the purpose of reducing uncertainty regarding the alternative courses of action as they are based on description and management of attributes of various entities associated with the enterprise.

8.1.3 Systems

The systems can be defined simply as a set of elements joined together for a common objective. A subsystem is part of a larger system with which one is concerned. For our purpose, the organization is the system and the parts (i.e. division, department, functions, unit, etc.) are the subsystems.

The system concept of MIS is, therefore, one of optimizing the output of the organization by connecting the operating subsystems through the medium of information exchange. Management needs only information but not data, to help them make the effective decisions. Every manager is deluged with both data and information, sometimes to the point of information overload. A MIS is a network of communication channels and information processing centres collecting information from its sources of origin:

(i) Storing, updating, collecting and processing it.
(ii) Supplying processed information to the various users managing the organization.

8.2 DEFINITIONS OF MIS BY RESEARCHERS

Management Information System is generally defined as an integrated user-machine system for providing information for support operations, management and decision making function in an organization. The system utilizes computer hardware and software, manual procedure, models for analysis. Information is viewed as a resource much like land, labour, and capital. It must be obtained, processed, stored, manipulated, analysed, and distributed etc. An organization with a well-defined information system will generally have competitive advantage over organization with poor MIS.

The important definitions of MIS are as follows:

1. B. Davis defines Management Information System as:
   a. an integrated user machine system,
   b. for providing information,
   c. to support the operations, management analysis and decision making functions.

   The system utilizes:
   a. Computer hardware and software,
   b. Manual procedures,
   c. Models for analysis, planning, control, and decision making, and
   d. A database.
2. Jerome Kanter has defined Management Information Systems as:
   A system that aids management in making, carrying out, and controlling decisions.
3. Robert J. Thierauf and George W. Reynolds define MIS concept as:
   a. A collection of subsystems and related programme parts or modules that are interconnected, in a manner which fulfils the information requirements necessary to plan, organize, direct and control business activities.

   b. It is a system for producing and delivering timely information that will support management in accomplishing its specific task in an enterprise.

4. Robert G. Mudrick defines MIS as:
   A strategy which provides the information for making decisions regarding the integration of the organization through the process of management.
5. John G. Burch and Gary Gradnitsksi defines MIS in two ways:
   a. It is the development and use of effective systems in organizations.
   b. MIS is an information system that facilitates management by producing structured summarized reports on a regular and recurring basis. The output of such MIS are produced routinely and used primarily for controlling activities, although they can also be used for planning and organizing.
6. According to Institute of Management Accounts, UK:
   MIS is a system in which defined data are collected, processed, and communicated to assist those responsible for the use of resources.
7. T. S. Grewal says that:
   An organized method of providing each manager with all data and only those data which he needs for decisions, when one needs there and in a form which aids his understanding and stimulates his action.
8. James A. O'Brein has defined MIS as:
   To provide information to support management decision making, major types of MIS have the following goals:
   a. Pre-specified and pre-planned reporting to managers is accomplished by 'Information Reporting Systems'
   b. Interactive and ad hoc support for decision making by managers is accomplished by 'Decision Support Systems'
   c. Critical information for top management is provided by 'Executive Information Systems'

According to James A. O'Brein, MIS, also called Information Reporting Systems, were the original type of management support systems, and are still a major category of information systems. MIS produce information products that support many of the day-to-day decision making needs of the management. Reports, displays and responses produced by such systems provide information that managers have specified in advance as adequately meeting their information needs. Such predefined information products satisfy the information needs of managers at the operational and tactical levels of the organization who are faced with more structured types of decision situations.

8.3 MANAGEMENT INFORMATION SYSTEM

MIS can be defined as the systematic or organized way of providing informational support to the managerial functions of an organization. The system utilizes computer hardware, software, manual procedures, models for analysis, planning, control, and database in the decision-making. In other words, MIS is an automated system which presents information, both internal and external to the business that aids in making a specific set of routine decisions. There are a few aspects of the above definition that warrant closer scrutiny.

- MIS is an organized or planned effort and not the result of some sporadic attempts.
- Meaningful and interpreted information is the output of the system.
- The primary function of the MIS is to provide information.
- MIS is a facilitating or supporting system to aid managerial functions and not merely help operational tasks, that is, the MIS provides information that assists managers at different levels in the organization.
- MIS is formed from a number of components, including hardware, software, manual procedures, models and a database.
- MIS is a system of users and machines; the users are as important to the system as are the machines.

Thus, the purpose of the MIS is to aid in decision making and not to automate the decision making process itself. As a result, the decision maker is seen as having a dominant role, not the MIS. This in turn means that any attempt to design a system without the support and involvement of management is most often pointless. Another aspect of the definition is that the MIS should focus on routine decisions only. What this implies is that the determination of what should be included in a MIS is an economic decision by itself. The inclusion of any set of decisions, be they inventory, capital budgeting, scheduling, or line balancing, must be justified on a cost/benefit basis. There is a cost of including them in the system which consists of the model building cost, then the cost of collecting and maintaining the relevant database, and finally, the computer costs. The benefits, on the other hand, include the stream of savings that the new system will accrue over the old. Only those decisions whose cost/benefit ratio is attractive should be included.

The potential for MIS in an operational system is substantial. Generally the kinds of decisions that are made during the design, operation, and control of transformation process exhibit much more structure and are much more routine than decisions made elsewhere in the firm. For example, there would be less controversy over the conceptualisation, solution and implementation of a model designed to solve an inventory problem than of one of setting a marketing strategy. Consequently much of the effort in MIS has been directed at operational problems. There have, indeed, been countless successful applications. The record, however, has not been unblemished.

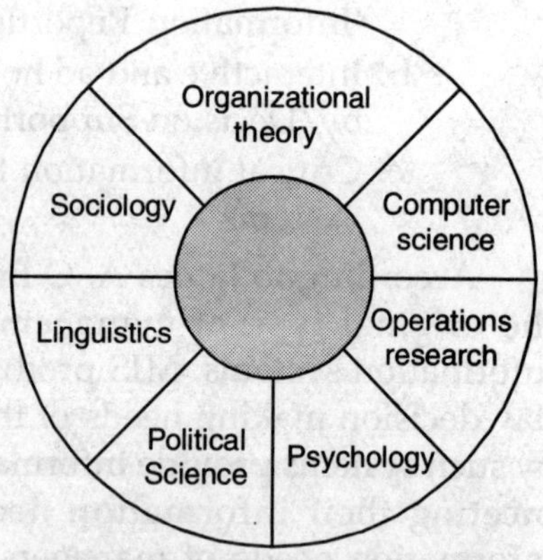

Figure 8.1: The field of MIS has been shaped and influenced by a number of other fields. Some of which are identified here.

The field of MIS is the study of information and its impact on the individual, the organization and society. Quite often, when we think about information systems we think of computers. Although computers are at the heart of today's information systems, a number of important social, organizational, behavioural, and ethical issues also surround the study of information systems. An appropriate analogy is the field of medicine. Medicine and its branches revolve around the human body and its various parts and functions. Similarly, today's information systems revolve around a business and its various components, such as people, products and procedures. MIS is an interdisciplinary field; many other fields of study influence it, as shown in Figure 8.1. Areas that contribute to influence the field of MIS include:

- *Computer Science:* theories and methods of computation, efficient data storage and access, and their impact on information
- *Political Science:* the political impact and uses of information, both within and outside the organization
- *Psychology:* cognitive models of human reasoning and behaviour as they relate to information
- *Operations Research:* scientific models that enhance decision making and make use of information to solve complex problems
- *Linguistics:* languages and human communications and their influences on the creation and use of information
- *Sociology:* principles governing society as it is related to shaping information policies and principles
- *Organization theory and behaviour:* the nature and characteristics of organizations and their effect on the way human beings use information to make decisions

MIS is a system that creates, processes, stores and generates information within and outside the organization. A system is a collection of parts that work together to achieve a common goal. The primary goal of MIS is to support organizational decision making, though it has many other uses, such as designing and developing new products, ensuring the quality of goods and services, preventing theft and pilferage, and so on. Table 8.1: presents the two common meanings of the term MIS.

Table 8.1: The two contexts in which term MIS is used

MIS as a field of study	MIS is an interdisciplinary field that is influenced by computer science, psychology, operations research, linguistics, sociology, and organizational theory.
MIS as an information system	MIS is a broad class of systems that provides information to facilitate organizational decision making.

8.3.1 Need of An MIS

The design, implementation and operation of an MIS are both expensive and difficult. This effort and expense must be justified. Several factors make such a system more necessary than it was just two or three decades ago.

One factor is that managers must deal with much more complex business environment than has existed before. One of the major reasons for this complexity is increased government regulation, which requires organizations to undertake many activities that were previously unnecessary; usually these involve filling a variety of regulatory reports. Another reason for this complexity is the wider variety of products and services that organizations offer customers; managing this greater variety requires more sophisticated information systems.

The business environment is not only more complex but also more dynamic. Managers have to make more decisions quickly, and typically less time must elapse between the emergence of management problem and its satisfactory solution. This is true partly because competitors have learned to adapt more rapidly to their environment. An MIS that provides both sophisticated and timely information is necessary part of the required adaptation. Indeed, a major trend in information systems is towards developing capabilities intended to facilitate the organization's rapid adaptation to change. On-call reports, ad hoc reports, and key-indicator reports are examples of these capabilities.

Another factor in the need for more sophisticated information systems cannot be overlooked. Schools of business and management have upgraded the quality of managers. Managers now understood and utilize more sophisticated management techniques than their predecessors did. Managers of today routinely use marginal analysis, standard costs, and direct-costing as well as traditional full costing, sensitivity analysis techniques, and a variety of other management methods not widely used two decades ago. Applying these techniques requires more sophisticated information than was previously needed, and this in turn requires a more sophisticated information system. This consideration will become even more important in the years ahead.

8.4 COMPUTER BASED MANAGEMENT INFORMATION SYSTEM

The notion Management Information System refers to the formal system installed in an organization for purposes of collecting, organizing, storing and processing data and presenting useful information to management at various levels. It serves as an aid to managerial functions of planning and control.

The specific features of computer-based MIS are outlined as follows:

1. *Organization and updating of huge mass of raw data*, or related and unrelated nature, derived from internal and external sources at different period of time.
2. *Ability to process data into information with high accuracy and high speed.* It involves making complex computations, analysis, comparisons and summarisations. Though humans can do the processing, the computer's ability to process huge data is phenomenal, considering its speed, reliability and faithfulness in perfectly following the set of instructions.
3. *Super-human memory, tremendous volume of data and information* and the large set of instructions can be stored in the computer and can be retrieved. Management can get any bit of stored information from the computer in a matter of seconds.
4. The input data in the computer can be processed into a number of different outputs and for a variety of purposes. The system is so organized that managers at different levels and in different activity units are in the position to obtain information in whatever form they want, provided that relevant 'programmes' or instructions have been designed for the purpose.
5. The information processing and computer technology have been so advanced that managers are able to obtain real time information on on-going activities and events without any waiting period.
6. *Speed of processing and retrieval of data has increased.* Modern business situations are characterised by high degree of complexity, keen competition and high risk and reward factors. This invariably calls for systems capable of providing relevant information with minimum loss of time. Manual systems howsoever well-organized often fail to match the demand for information for decision making. Computer with its unbelievably

fast computational capability and systematic storage of information with random access facility has emerged as an answer to the problems faced in modern-day management. Processing of data in relevant form and design and retrieval of them when needed in fact requires considerably less time and facilitate the management action and decision making. The speed of computer processing in nano second range, i.e. an operation takes only billionths of a second. This characteristic of computer has accounted for as a major factor in including MIS development. Computers today are capable of meeting varied type of information requirements of executives.

7. *Scope of use of information system* in business organizations was realised by most of the concerns, after the induction of computers for MIS development. Systems experts in business organizations developed areas and functions, where computerized MIS could be used to improve the working of the concern. This type of application hitherto was not feasible under the manual system. For example, it was made possible by using an online real time system to provide information to various users sitting at a remote distance from a centrally located computer system.
8. *Scope of analysis widened.* The use of computer can provide multiple type of information accurately and in no time to decision makers. Such information equips an executive to carry out a thorough analysis of the problem and to arrive at the final decision. Computers are capable of providing various types of sales reports, for example, area-wise sales, commission of each salesman, product-wise sales, etc. These reports are quite useful in analysing the sales department working and ascertain its weaknesses, so that adequate measures may be taken in time. In this way, the use of computer has widened the scope of analysis.
9. *Complexity of system design and operation increased.* The need for highly processed and sophisticated information based on multitudes of variable has made the designing of the system quite complex. During the initial years, after the induction of computer for MIS development, systems experts faced problems in designing systems and their operations. The reason at that time was the non-availability of experts required for the purpose. But these days, the situation is better. The computer manufacturers have developed some important programmes (software) to help their users. Besides, some private agencies are also there, who can perform the task of developing programmes to cater to the specialized needs of their customers, either on consultancy basis or on contract.
10. *Integrates the working of different information subsystems.* A suitable structure of management information system may be a federation of information subsystems, viz. production, material, marketing, finance, engineering, and personnel. Each of these subsystems is required to provide information to support operational control, management control, and strategic planning. Such information may be made available from a common database. This common database may meet out the information requirements of different information subsystems by utilizing the services of computers for storing, processing, analysing and providing such information as and when required. In this way, computer technology is useful for integrating the day-to-day working of different information subsystems.

11. *Increases the effectiveness of information system.* Information received in time is of immense value and importance to a concern. Prior to the use of computer technology for information purposes, it was difficult to provide the relevant information to business executives in time even after incurring huge expenses. The use of computer technology has overcome this problem. Now it is not difficult to provide timely, accurate and desired information for the purpose of decision making. Hence, we can conclude that the use of computers has increased the effectiveness of information system also.
12. *More comprehensive information.* The use of computer has MIS enabled systems expert to provide more comprehensive information to executives on business matters.
13. Computer-based MIS opens up new vistas for management to make efficient and timely decisions on vital operations of the enterprise and major strategic and tactical problems. It also helps organizations to gain substantial economies by reduction of clerical and computational time.

8.5 NATURE OF MIS

The nature of management information system can be discussed in the following points:

- The MIS is an orderly arrangement of data processing and information systems in order to enable the management in achieving the business objectives. MIS is well equipped in resourcing the data from external sources for the organizational usage. MIS is designed as a generalized model of a system based on the theory and gives output on the principle of feedback and control.
- MIS is designed to provide the information which is exceptional in nature from the point of view of business. To explain further, we can say that these exceptions could be abnormal events, surprising developments, and shocking news. The MIS must be well equipped to catch all such points and report to the concerned management. It should have the ability to recognize all such exceptions and in effect should provide a measure for comparison with the actual performance. In absence of this robust feature, the MIS will act merely as a data supplier and not information processor.
- The first stage of MIS activity is to concentrate on the quality of input. It should ensure that the input satisfies the parameters, such as impartiality, validity, reliability, consistency and age. This is imperative for ensuring the good quality of output, therefore a large amount of system effort is spent in this area.
- We know that MIS provides a system for data processing and data analysis. The stages are:
  - It uses a number of sources to produce information, such as applications and business models, operational research models, and application packages.
  - MIS is well designed to display the information and to print it in a report format.
  - It is also equipped with the feature of providing a facility to store the intermediate results, which are used in a number of other systems. The MIS is a combination of the deterministic (final outcome) and the closed systems, and the probabilistic (probably outcome) and the open systems.
- By nature, the MIS is an open system which interfaces between the internal and the external environment. It is self-organizing and sufficient in order to meet the ever increasing and changing information needs of the organization.

8.6 WORKING OF MIS

Many organizations design MIS to provide managers with the necessary information to make intelligent decisions. An MIS is used to collect data, store and process data, and present information to managers. MIS is a combination of computers and procedures for providing information to the managers for use in making decisions. Thus, MIS must perform the following functions in order to meet its objectives. Figure 8.2 depicts various functions performed by an MIS.

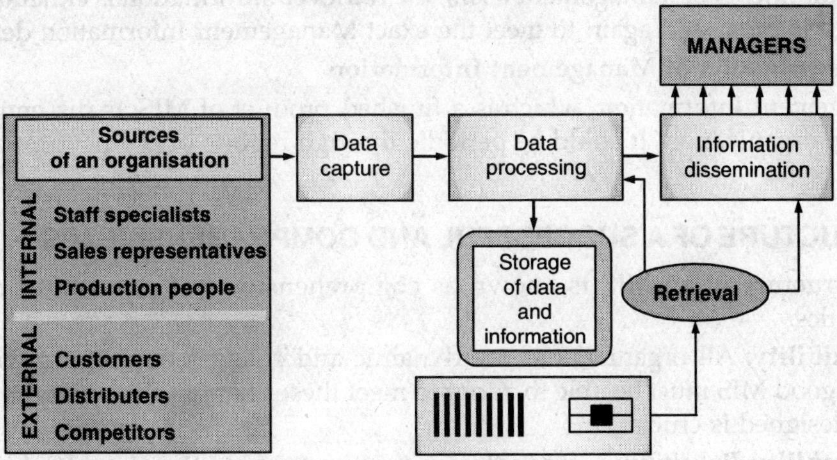

Figure 8.2: Working of MIS

1. Data Capturing

The first function of an MIS is to determine the information needed to make decisions and to organize it into a database. A 'database' is an integrated collection of data stored in one place for efficient access and information processing.

To obtain useful information, MIS captures data from various internal and external sources of an organization such as personnel records, information about customers, information about competitors, sales data, accounting data, and so on. Generally, most data collected for an MIS comes from internal sources such as company records or reports and information compiled by managers themselves. External sources include trade publications, customers and consultants. Data capturing may be manual or through computer terminals.

2. Processing of Data

The captured data is processed to convert it into the required management information. Processing of data (such as calculating, comparing, sorting, classifying, and summarising) is done through the application of computer software programs and judgement made by technical support staff and other system users. These activities organize, analyse and manipulate data using various statistical, mathematical, operations research and/or other successful business models.

3. Storage of Information

MIS stores processed or unprocessed data for future use. If any information is not immediately required, it is saved as an organization record. In this activity, data and information are retained in an organized manner for later use. Stored data is commonly organized into field, records, files, and databases, etc.

Data are generally stored on magnetic tape or hard disk when, mainframe computers are used and on hard disk or floppy (soft) disk, when minicomputers are used. The data can be loaded into computers in seconds for easy access by the user.

4. Retrieval of Information

MIS retrieves information from its stores as and when required by various users. As per the requirements of management users, the retrieved information is either disseminated as such or it is processed again to meet the exact Management Information demands.

5. Dissemination of Management Information

Management Information, which is a finished product of MIS, is disseminated to the users in the organization. It could be periodic through reports or online through computer terminals.

8.7 STRUCTURE OF A SUCCESSFUL AND COMPREHENSIVE MIS

The structure of an MIS is known as comprehensive if it possesses the following characteristics:

1. Flexibility: All organizations are dynamic and changes occur for a wide range of reasons. A good MIS must be able to adopt to meet these changes. Flexibility in the way the system is designed is crucial.

2. Reliability: Reliability is crucial to performance and can be ensured only by thorough checking and testing. Good standards help to make the MIS reliable as do validation and security routines.

3. Simplicity: Simplicity in design will find its way through the system. Anyone can design a complicated system but it takes real skill and experience to design simple systems which are easy to operate and control. Systems are abstract and therefore not apparent in complicated MIS.

4. Economy: The MIS should be cost-effective. There are many hidden costs in the design, development and operation of systems, the most important of which is the time the people involved. Costs should be carefully monitored once the system is working and compared with the original planned costs.

5. Helpfulness: Unless the MIS helps in the planning, operation and control of the business, it is superfluous.

6. Consistency: Information system should be consistent. There must be a link between all the data. Data should be collected by the same method and scale and should be presented at equal intervals. For example, if the data regarding sales of a particular concern is collected in lakh tonnes in one year then it should not be collected in terms of units for the next year. Thus there must be consistency in all the information given.

7. Management-oriented: It means that the development of the information system efforts should start from an appraisal of management needs and overall business objectives. Such a system is not necessarily for top management only. It may also meet the information requirements of middle level or operating levels of management as well.

8. Management-directed: Because of management orientation of MIS, it is necessary that management should actively direct the system's development efforts. Their mere one-time involvement is not enough. For system's effectiveness, it is necessary for management to devote their sufficient time not only at the stage of designing the system but for its review as well, to ensure that the implemented system meets the specifications of the designed system. In brief, management should be responsible for setting system specifications and it must play a key role in the subsequent trade-off decisions that occur in system development.

9. Integrated: Developed system of information should be an integrated one. It means that all the functional and operational information sub-system should be tied together into one entity. An integrated information system has the capability of generating more meaningful information to management. The word integration here means taking a comprehensive view or a complete picture look at the interlocking sub-systems that operate within a company.

10. Common data flows: It means the use of common input, processing, and output procedures and media whenever possible or desirable. Data is captured by system analysts only once and as close to its original source as possible. They then try to utilise a minimum of data processing procedures and sub-systems to process the data and strive to minimize the number of output documents and reports produced by the system. This eliminates duplication in data collection documents and procedures. It also avoids duplication, simplifies operations and produces an efficient information system. However, some duplication is necessary in order to ensure effective information systems.

11. Heavy planning element: An MIS usually takes 3 to 5 years and sometimes even longer to get established firmly within a company. Therefore, a heavy planning element must be present in MIS development. It means that MIS designer should keep in view future objectives and requirement of firm's information in mind. The designer must avoid the possibility of system obsolescence before the system gets into operation.

12. Sub-system concept: Even though the information system is viewed as a single entity, it must be broken down into digestible subsystems which can be implemented one at a time by developing a phasing plan. The breakdown of MIS is not meaningful subsystems sets the stage for this phasing plan.

13. Common data base: Data base is the mortar that holds the functional systems together. It is defined as a 'superfile' which consolidates and integrates data records formerly stored in many separate data files. The organization of a data base, allows it to be accessed by several information subsystems and thus eliminates the necessity of duplication in data storage, updating, deletion and protection. Although it is possible to achieve the basic objective of MIS without a common data base, thus paying the price of duplicate storage and duplicate file updating, more often than not the common data base is a definite characteristic of MIS.

14. Computerised: It is possible to have an MIS without using a computer. But its use increases the effectiveness of the system. In fact, its use equips the system to handle a wide variety of applications by providing quickly their information requirement. Other necessary attributes of the computer to MIS are accuracy and consistency in processing data and reduction in clerical staff. These needs in management information system make the computer a primary requirement.

15. Relevance: The information given to each manager should be relevant to his responsibilities and authorities. The flow of information should be from one level to another in the direction where the decision is to be taken. If information is being sent from top level to the middle level management then it should be sent to the proper responsibility centre so that the decision taken can be implemented.

16. Brevity: Information should not only be clear but also be brief. Brevity does not mean that certain matters be left out but it means that maximum information should be communicated in minimum words. Graphs, charts, tables, figures and other such media help in making the information brief.

17. Accuracy: Information should be accurate as far as possible and if not, then the level of inaccuracy should be within limits. For example, in reports if undue emphasis is laid on the accuracy then the reports cannot be submitted in time. Delayed submission increases its cost. Under such circumstances, it is better to permit tolerable inaccuracy.

Taking into consideration the above characteristics the suitable structure of a comprehensive MIS may be federation of information subsystems for different functions, viz. productions, material management, marketing, finance, engineering and personnel. Each subsystem of information system is supposed to provide information support to executives for operational control, management control and strategic planning. The information requirement of executives for operational control, management control and strategic planning itself depends upon operational function, level of management activity and type of decision making.

Different operational functions have different information requirements. Their requirements vary not only in content but in characteristics as well. In fact, the content of information depends upon the activities to be performed under an operational function. Also an operational function influences the characteristics, which particular information must possess. For example, the information used for preparing employees payroll by the accounts department should be highly accurate.

The level of management activity too influences the characteristics of information. For example, strategic planning requires more external information on the behaviour of relevant and likely future events. Management control requires more accurate, precise, current and repetitive information. Operational level requires information in detailed form about the performance.

The contents of information can be completely pre-specified in the case of programmed decisions. It is difficult to specify complete information requirements.

The information or data requirements of each subsystem of information system can be met by developing two types of data files, viz. unique and common. Unique data files meet the specific information requirements of each operational function at different levels of management activity for making programmed and non-programmed decisions. Common data files store data/information meant for general use in decision making process. The data stored in data files is usually in the raw form and thus, requires processing. Processing of data may be performed by using software and decision models kept under model base. The use of data, in data base, may be controlled by Data Base Management System. The structure of MIS thus evolved may be shown with the help of diagram in Figure 8.3.

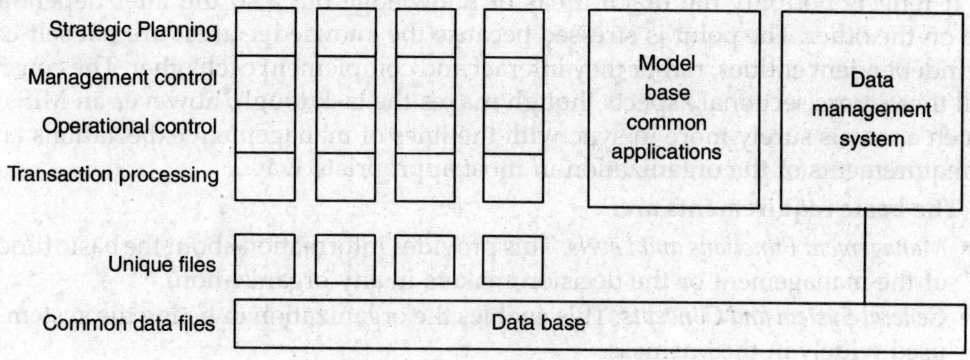

Figure 8.3: *Organizational MIS*

The terms data processing system and MIS are normally used interchangeably but there is a basic distinction between the two. A data processing system can be defined as a system which collects and processes data and estimates information in an organization. The management information system provides the necessary information to the managers, supervisors at various levels to enable them to discharge their functions of organizing, planning and control and decision making. A data processing system is hardware oriented, e.g. manual data processing, and electronic data processing etc. and hence it forms a subsystem of MIS in which additional men may be engaged in collecting data and dissemination of information derived from data processing system.

8.8 REQUIREMENTS OF MIS

In this section we categorically study about the requirements of MIS. We will depict this with the help of the Figure 8.4. This figure displays the major areas of knowledge which is a pre requisite for development and operation of the organizational MIS.

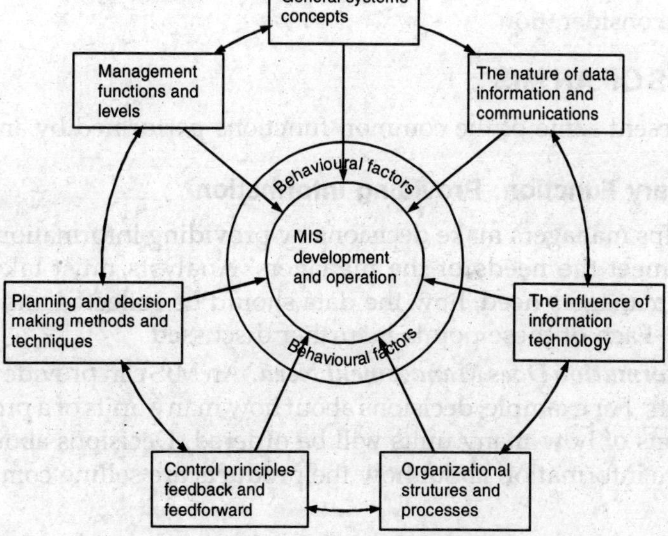

Figure 8.4: *Requirements for Development of MIS*

It reflects not only the major areas of knowledge but also the inter-dependability of each on the other. The point is stressed because the knowledge areas are not self-contained and independent entities; rather they interact and complement each other. The consideration of all these cross sectional aspects though makes the task tough, however an MIS designed in such a way is surely more in sync with the lines of management expectations and meets the requirements of the organization in most appropriate way.

The basic requirements are:

- *Management Functions and Levels:* This provides information about the basic functionality of the management or the decision makers in any organization.
- *General System and Concepts:* This enables the organization in listing the system which is used widely in the business.
- *Nature of Data Information and Communication:* The previous factor invariably also points out towards the nature of data information which may be required for an organization.
- *Influence of Information Technology:* Once the nature of data information requirement is assessed, the total impact of the information technology can be taken into account for developing the MIS.
- *Organizational Structures and Processes:* The influence of information technology helps in determining the structure of an organization and its processes. This in turn again is a deciding factor for developing MIS.
- *Control Principles, Feedback and Feed Forward:* Once the organizational structure is in place, it can substantially device the control factors and provide feedback and other required information for developing suitable MIS.
- *Planning and Decision Making Methods and Techniques:* Depending upon the feedback from the management, the planning can be done. Various decision making methods and techniques are then used for developing an effective MIS.
- *Behavioural Factors:* The core area is depicted here in the behavioural factors. This primarily reflects that even areas which are core quantitative areas, the reactions, motivations, aspirations, and capabilities of the people involved should very well be taken into consideration.

8.9 FUNCTIONS OF AN MIS

Here we present some of the common functions performed by an MIS.

8.9.1 The Primary Function: Providing Information

The MIS helps managers make decisions by providing information. The MIS must thus be designed to meet the needs of the managers. Analysts must take into account what information the managers need, how the data should be collected and analysed to provide to the managers. Each of these points is further discussed.

(a) What Information Does Management Need? An MIS can provide valuable information to decision makers. For example, decisions about how many units of a product to manufacture require projections of how many units will be ordered. Decisions about the tone of a sales campaign require information about how the products are selling compared to those in the competition.

In some cases, it is difficult to pinpoint exactly what information is needed to make a decision. Can managers decide how many units to manufacture on the basis of projections by salespeople, or should the decision be based on actual unfilled orders? Should workers be promoted solely on the basis of their volume of output, or should their attitudes and loyalty to the company also be considered? When planning the sales campaign, should a manager receive only historical summaries of his own company's sales, or should sales trends of other companies also be included?

These are not easy questions to answer. For this reason, an MIS can never be considered complete or infallible. An organization must continually update and upgrade its ways of handling information. However, certain factors are common to information systems in virtually all organizations: Data are collected from internal and external sources; Reports are generated from data; and The reports are distributed to the proper parties.

(b) Collecting the Data. The collection of data is a critical part of the system. Data comes from both internal and external sources. Generally, the data are in either human-readable or machine-readable form. Here are some examples of the forms of data.

Every time a small speciality clothing store makes a sale, the amount is written on a sales slip. The customer is given the original, and the clerk deposits the copy in the cash register along with the cash. At the end of each day, the cash register tape total and the pile of sales slips, both human-readable forms of data, are given to the store's accountant, who enters the amounts, item descriptions, and totals into the store's personal computer. When the information is needed, the computer can create graphics to show sales trends for each product line and print totals for income tax purposes.

A large, modern grocery store uses laser scanners at each checkout counter. The scanner 'reads' the Universal Product Code (UPC) from each item as it is passed over the laser beam. Clerks only use the cash register keyboard to enter the prices of produce, baked goods, and deli items. There is no need to record each sales on paper, since information about each item sold is automatically transmitted to a computer. All the data are in machine-readable form. At any time, the computer can generate reports about inventory levels, recorders, sales patterns, and sales summaries.

A large department-store mails credit card bills each month. Each bill contains a stub that is to be returned when the bill is paid. The stubs are printed in an Optical Character Recognition (OCR) font. When the stub is returned to the chain, an optical character reader quickly picks up the customer's account number and name (machine-readable data). A clerk then has only to enter the handwritten amount the customer chooses to pay (human-readable data).

Choosing how the data are to be collected and entered involves serious thought and a cost-benefit analysis. If the data will all be in machine-readable form, the benefits of this method should exceed its cost. For example, the costs of implementing a laser or OCR scanning system are very high. The benefits must also be calculated for the particular business. The clerks in the small speciality clothing store also serve as salespeople and often have an intimate knowledge of stock levels at any given moment. A computerised information system that uses machine-readable forms of data would not tell them they do not know already. It would not be worth the cost of purchasing sophisticated equipment in this case. In the grocery store, there are thousands of items and many cashiers. No one person can have total knowledge or control of the inventory. In this case there are many benefits of having a system that collects machine-readable data, and it may make sense to install one.

(c) Analysing the Data. After the data are collected, they are analysed, and the information is included in reports. These reports give managers the information they need to make their decisions, so they must be in useful form and must appear frequently enough so that the information is up-to-date. We now look at how reports are designed so that the information is useful and at how to decide how frequently a report should be issued.

(i) Designing Reports. Because the reports must provide information that is useful to managers, the managers work with the system designers to determine the best form for each report. Reports are meant to monitor operations, identify problems, request action, or support decisions. Such reports may appear on a video screen or be printed out on paper. Operations are monitored by designing regular reports in many areas. This is the most common type of report: a few examples include inventory lists, sales summaries, financial statements, and payroll cost summaries. An example of a payroll cost summary generally known as payroll register is shown in Figure 8.5. By reading this sort of report, managers can see how much each member is paid in various taxes.

Name		Hourly/ Salaried	Regular Pay	Overtime Pay	Gross Pay	Federal Pay	State Tax	Total Taxes	Net Pay
Jason	Kehl	Salaries	$490.00	$0.00	$490.00	$122.50	$14.70	$137.20	$352.80
Doreen	Marie	Hourly	$162.50	$0.00	$162.50	$24.38	$4.88	$29.26	$133.24
Louise	Marie	Hourly	$412.50	$96.25	$508.75	$50.88	$15.26	$66.14	$442.61
Fraink	Theodore	Hourly	$1,125.00	$112.50	$1,237.50	$123.75	$37.13	$160.88	$1,076.62
Jeffrey	Allan	Salaried	$325.00	$0.00	$325.00	$81.25	$9.75	$91.00	$234.00
Steven	James	Hourly	$325.00	$0.00	$325.00	$81.25	$9.75	$91.00	$234.00
Total			**$2,840.00**	**$208.75**	**$325.00**	**$81.25**	**$9.75**	**$1.00**	**$2,473.27**

Figure 8.5: *An example of a Report that Monitors Operations: A Payroll Report*

Problems are often identified by examining exception reports. Such reports usually exclude all information except that which shows an undesirable condition. For example, an inventory exception report may show only the items that are low or out of stock. Another example is an employee lateness report, which shows only the names of workers who have shown up late during the previous week.

Action reports are not usually thought of as reports. They are documents that imply or demand action. One example of this is a purchase order, a document sent to a supplier to request

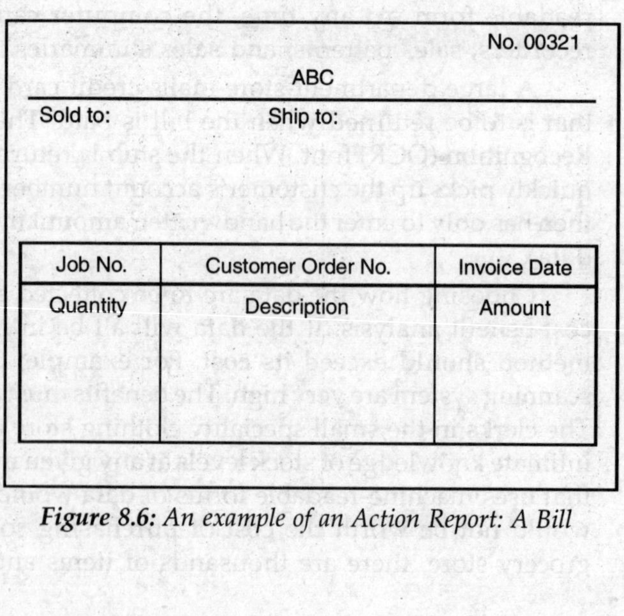

Figure 8.6: *An example of an Action Report: A Bill*

inventory or supplies. Another example is a production order, which gives instructions to the manufacturing department of a company to produce certain goods. Such reports may be generated by a computer when conditions demand them. Figure 8.ι shows the most familiar action report of all, a bill.

Decision support systems printed out on paper are usually not the most important product of processing to support decisions. Managers usually use computerized management information systems that can help them make decisions in interactive sessions. The user enters information about a certain problem, and the computer shows possible outcomes on the video screen, based on the information entered by the user. For example, a user may enter the price of a product; the cost of materials, labour and overhead, and estimates by market researchers of how the market would react to price changes. After the user enters this model, the computer can quickly calculate 'what if' revenue amounts if prices or costs change. Other examples include investigating the effects of dropping certain items from a company's product line, buying new equipment, and buying another company.

(ii) Frequency of Reports. Reports are produced either at regular intervals, whenever specific event requires one, or when demanded by a manager. The users and system designer together decide how frequently reports will be produced.

Reports produced at regular intervals are usually ones that monitor operations. These reports have the express purpose of documenting what goes on, and there is usually no immediate need to take action. A manager finds these on the desk shortly after the end of the week, month, or year.

Event-triggered reports are often related to problems or action. When inventory is low or employees are late, special reports are produced. Purchase orders are sent when supplies are needed, and bills are sent when there is an outstanding balance due.

Some reports, such as decision-support reports, appear only when specifically requested by the user. The decisions or actions relating to these reports come up irregularly. Pricing decisions never occur at fixed intervals. Companies do not consider dropping products, buying new equipment, or buying other companies all that frequently. The reports have to appear only when managers want to use them to make decisions.

(d) Distributing the Reports. The reports must be distributed, so they must match the needs and capabilities of the users. This is much more difficult than it appears on the surface. Matching the needs of users to reports requires that users specify those needs honestly and accurately. This is usually hard because managers often do not know what their needs are and often do not know what computers can do. Often a report has to be changed because a manager said, "This report is OK, but it would be nice if ..."

Besides matching a user's needs, reports should also match a user's capacity to process the information. Research in problem solving has established that human performance begins to decline when the mind is overloaded. This implies that if users are presented with many thick reports, the reports may not be useful. It is simply not possible for a human being to hold thousands of lines of computer output in mind while trying to make decisions based on that output. It is therefore very common to filter out much information from each manager. Filtering may be accomplished by using exception reports, by chopping off irrelevant parts of reports, or by summarizing. Summarizing is a particularly powerful method (as depicted in Figure 8.7). It involves recognizing what is of interest to a manager and presenting totals or subtotals for those items. A company chairman is not interested in how many hand towels were used in Building B's washroom, but certainly is interested in overall net profits. Though the number of hand towels used affects the net profit, it is only a small component. Therefore, the chairman needs to see only the bottom line, although he should have the ability to find out what contributed to the levels of net profits.

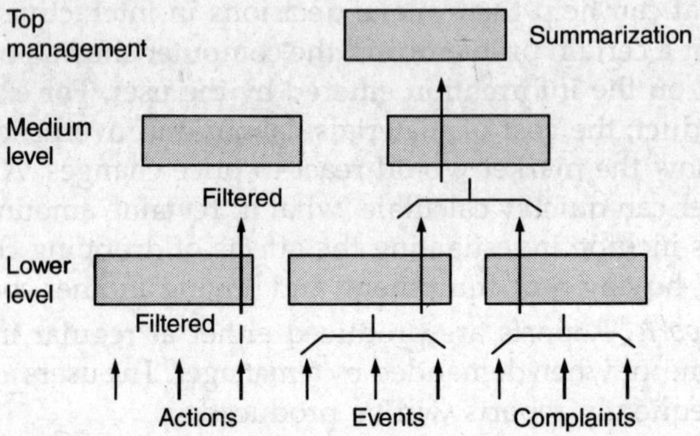

Figure 8.7: How Information is summarized in an Organization

An example of how this summarization can be used is shown in Figure 8.8. The Chairman's Monthly Responsibility Performance Report shows the Rs. 25,200 bottom-line unfavourable cost variance was the major cause of this problem. If the chairman wants to investigate further, he can examine the Production Vice-President's Monthly Responsibility Performance Report, which indicates that the machining department is responsible for Rs. 11,600 of the Rs. 20,600 budget overturn. Examination of the Machining Department Supervisor's Monthly Responsibility Performance Report shows that almost all of the $11,600 was caused by direct materials and direct labour. By tracing amounts to lower-level reports, it is possible for the chairman to discover reasons for unfavourable (or favourable) variances.

President's Monthly Responsibility Performance Report

	BUDGET		*VARIANCE FAVORABLE (UNFAVORABLE)*	
	This Month	**Year to Date**	**This Month**	**Year to Date**
President's Office	Rs. 6,000	Rs. 20,000	Rs.100	Rs.400
Controller	4,000	13,000	(200)	(1,000)
Production Vice President	1,16,000	3,77,000	(8,950)	(20,600)
Sales Vice President	40,000	1,30,000	(1,000)	(4,000)
Total Controllable Costs	Rs. 1,66,000	Rs. 540,000	Rs. (10,050)	Rs. (25,200)

Production Vice President's Monthly Responsibility Performance Report

	BUDGET		VARIANCE FAVORABLE (UNFAVORABLE)	
	This Month	Year to Date	This Month	Year to Date
Vice President's Office	Rs. 9,000	Rs. 29,000	Rs.(1,000)	Rs.(1,000)
Machining Department	72,000	236,000	(2,950)	(11,600)
Finishing Department	15,000	50,000	(2,000)	(3,000)
Assembly Department	20,000	62,000	(3,000)	(5,000)
Total Controllable Costs	Rs. 1,16,000	Rs. 377,000	Rs. (8,950)	Rs. (20,600)

Maching Department Supervisors Monthly Responsibility Performance Rreport

	BUDGET		VARIANCE FAVORABLE (UNFAVORABLE)	
	This Month	Year to Date	This Month	Year to Date
Direct Materials	Rs. 40,000	Rs. 1,40,000	Rs.(1,000)	Rs.(4,000)
Direct labor	25,000	75,000	(2,00)	(7,600)
Setup	4,000	12,000	400	100
Rework	2,000	6,000	(200)	(300)
Supplies	200	600	(40)	(100)
Small Tools	300	900	(50)	(100)
Other	500	1,500	(60)	(200)
Total Controllable Costs	Rs. 72,000	Rs. 236,000	Rs. (2,950)	Rs. (11,600)

Figure 8.8: An Example of Summarization

8.9.2 MIS Throughout the Organization

The second important function of an MIS is that it provides information to managers at various levels, in the organization. To see clearly how this works, we look at three views of how an MIS functions in an organization.

1. First View

One early view how an MIS functions within an organization can be seen in Figure 8.9. The organization is divided into four levels: strategic planning, management control, operational control and transaction processing.

(i) Strategic Planning Level. The top level in the figure is concerned with setting strategy and policy for the organization, and emphasis is on the distant future. Decisions are centered around what the organization should do. For example, in a large manufacturing firm, a typical 'top-level' decision may be 'produce automobiles and trucks'. Such a decision requires knowledge of customer needs, technology, legal issues, competitive forces and so forth. At this level, the MIS is usually referred to as a Decision Support System (DSS). This system should allow the kind of interaction discussed earlier, enabling a user to play 'what-if' games to discover the effects of certain decisions.

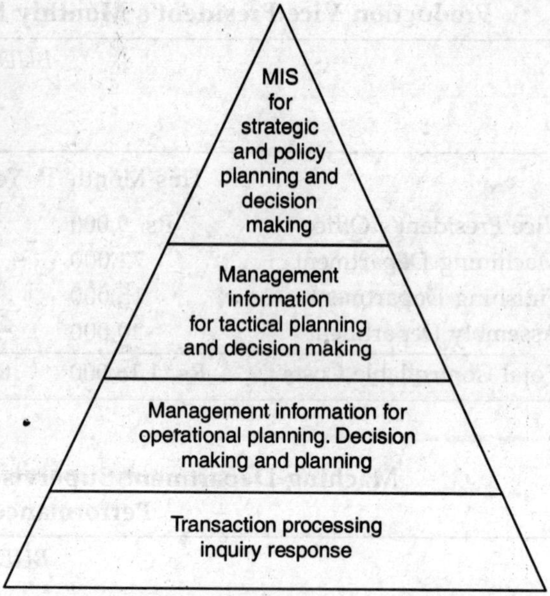

Figure 8.9: *The First View of an Organization*

(ii) Management Control Level. Decisions made at the second level concern the tactics through which the organization might best carry out the policy handed down from the top level. The focus is on the next year or two. A typical decision at this level might be to 'produce two (specified) types of subcompact cars, two styles of intermediate cars, and one full-sized car, as well as one pickup truck'. This is generally a high-level decision but, at the same time, it is more detailed than the top-level decision of producing automobiles and trucks. Making the decision requires more detailed knowledge of many areas, particularly consumer needs and the company's production capability, which can be provided by the MIS. To be useful to the managers, the MIS at this level must contain information about past performance and about policy decisions. This means that information is passed up to this level from low levels and passed down from the top level.

(iii) Operational Control Level. At the third level, decisions are made about how to produce or sell the automobile and trucks. The focus is on next few months. A typical decision at this level may be to 'offer a special SE option that includes a leather interior and fuel injection on the most popular subcompact cars'. This is indeed an important decision, but it is not nearly so critical as the decision made at the policy and tactical levels. Making decisions at this level requires knowing what is currently happening. The information must come from both upper and lower levels. Reports from below outlining inventory levels, current sales trends, and production costs are important. Reports from above communicate the more general tactical decisions that must be carried out.

(iv) Transaction Processing Level. The bottom level is concerned with recording transactions. The focus is on what has happened. Sales, purchases, labour hours, and so forth are recorded. Such information is necessary for doing the organization's bookkeeping. System developers have the easiest task when designing information systems at this level. It is easier to specify needs and suggest improvements for accounting-oriented systems, than for policy-related systems. This is because of the clarity of the job. A job description for a sales clerk is much

more tangible than one for a corporate vice-president. A sales clerk seldom wonders what is expected of him, but a corporate vice-president must often think about this.

To summarize this view: A strategic planning level develops policy and strategy; a management control level develops tactics to meet these objectives; an operational control level schedules tasks for carrying out the tactics; and the transaction processing level records the tasks as they are performed. Decisions at all levels are based on the information provided by the MIS.

2. Second View

The second view combines the ideas of the first view with the different functions in a typical organization and ties them together with a database management system (DBMS). The result is the grid, as shown in Figure 8.10. This view suggests that there are many functions in an organization, each of which contains tasks at the different levels of the management. In a manufacturing company, for example, there are strategic as well as transaction processing activities in each of the functional areas of the organization, such as marketing, production and personnel.

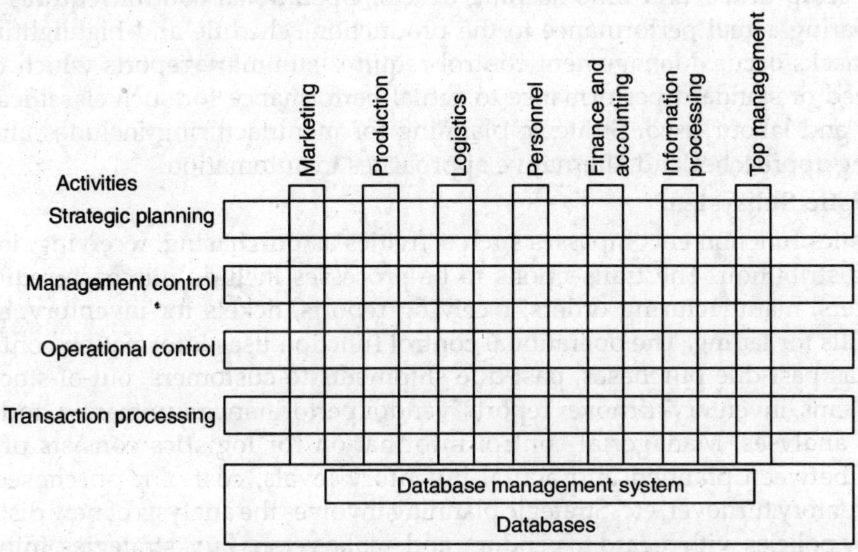

Figure 8.10: The Second View of MIS in an Organization

A management information system is essentially a federation of information systems that are designed to support the functional subsystems of the organization. Each functional system requires applications to perform all information processing related to the function, although this may involve calling upon a database, a model base, and some computer programs which are common to all functional subsystems. Within each functional subsystem, there will be applications for transaction processing, operational control, managerial control, and strategic planning.

(i) Sales and Marketing Subsystem

The sales and marketing functions generally include all activities related to the promotion and sales of products or services. The transitions are sales orders, promotion orders, etc.

The operational control activities include the hiring and training of the sales force, the day-to-day scheduling of sales and promotion efforts, and periodic analysis of sales volumes by region, product, customer, etc. Managerial control concerns comparisons of overall performance against a marketing plan. Information for managerial control may include data on customers, competitors, competitor products and sales force requirements. Strategic planning for marketing function involves consideration of new markets and new marketing strategies. The information requirements for strategic planning include customer analysis, competitor analysis, consumer survey information, income projection, demographic projections and technology projections.

(ii) Production Subsystem

The responsibilities of the production or manufacturing function include product engineering, planning of production facilities, scheduling and operation of production facilities, employment and training of production personnel, and quality control and inspection. Typical transactions to be processed are production orders (based on an explosion of sales orders and inventory requirements into component parts), assembly order, finished parts tickets, scrap tickets and time keeping tickets. Operational control requires detailed reports comparing actual performance to the production schedule and highlighting areas where bottlenecks occur. Management control requires summary reports which compare overall planned or standard performance to actual performance for such classifications as cost per unit and labour used. Strategic planning for manufacturing includes alternative manufacturing approaches and alternative approaches to automation.

(iii) Logistic Subsystem

The logistics function encompasses such activities as purchasing, receiving, inventory control and distribution. The transactions to be processes include purchase requisitions, purchase orders, manufacturing orders, receiving reports, tickets for inventory, shipping orders, and bills for lading. The operational control function uses information contained in reports such as past-due purchases, past-due shipments to customers, out-of-stock items, overstocked items, inventory turnover reports, vendor performance summaries, and shipper performance analyses. Managerial control information for logistics consists of overall comparisons between planned and actual inventory levels, costs for purchased items, stockouts, inventory turnover, etc. Strategic planning involves the analysis of new distribution strategies, new policies with regard to vendors, and 'make versus buy' strategies. Information on new technology, distribution alternatives, etc. is required.

(iv) Personnel Subsystem

The personnel subsystem includes hiring, training, record keeping, payment, and termination of personnel. The transactions result in documents describing employment requisitions, job descriptions, training specifications, personnel data (background skills, experience), pay rate changes, hours worked, paychecks, benefits, and termination notices. Operational control for personnel requires decision procedures for action such as hiring, training, termination, changing pay rates, and issuing benefits. Management control of the personnel function is supported by reports and analyses showing the variances resulting from differences between planned and actual performance for such classifications as number of employees hired, cost of recruiting, composition of skills inventory, cost of training (by employee, by program), salary paid, distribution of wage rates, and conformance with government equal opportunity requirements. Strategic planning for personnel is involved with evaluating alternative strategies for recruiting, salary, training, benefits, and building location to ensure that the organization obtains and retains personnel necessary to achieve its objectives. The strategic information required includes analyses of shifting patterns of employment, education, and wage rates by area of the country (or world).

(v) Finance and Accounting Subsystem

Finance and accounting are somewhat separate functions but are sufficiently related to be described together. Finance is responsible for ensuring adequate organizational financing at as low a cost as possible (in a manner consistent with other objectives). This function covers granting of credit to customer, collection processes, cash management, and financing arrangements (loans, sales of stock, leasing). Accounting covers the classification of financial transactions and summarization into the standard financial reports (income statement and balance sheet), the preparation of budgets, and classification and analysis of cost data. Budget and cost data are input for managerial control reports, which means that accounting provides input for managerial control applications in all functions. Among the transactions associated with finance and accounting are credit applications, sales, billings, collection documents (statements), payment vouchers, checks, journal vouchers, ledgers, and stock transfers. Operational control over the function itself requires daily error and exception reports, records of processing delays, reports of unprocessed transactions etc. The managerial control level for accounting and finance utilizes information on budgeted versus actual cost of financial resources, cost of processing accounting data, and error rates. The strategic planning level for accounting and finance involves a long-run strategy to ensure adequate financing, a long-range tax accounting policy to minimize the impact of taxes, and planning of systems for cost accounting and budgeting.

(vi) Information Processing Subsystem

The information processing function is responsible for ensuring that the other functions are provided the necessary information processing services and resources. Typical transactions for information processing are requests for processing, requests for corrections or changes in data and programs, reports of hardware and program performance, and project proposals. Operational control of information processing operations requires information on the daily schedule of jobs, error rates, and equipment failures; for new project development it requires daily or weekly schedules of programmer progress and test time. Managerial control over information processing requires data on planned versus actual utilization, equipment costs, overall programmer performance, and progress compared to schedule for projects to develop and implement new applications. Strategic planning for information systems involves the organization of the functions (such as centralized or decentralized), the overall information system plan, selection of strategic uses of information, and the general structure of the hardware and software environment. For example, a major strategic decision might be to implement microcomputer workstations for all analysts, planners, and managers.

Office automation may be defined as a separate subsystem or included within information processing. Office automation includes a wide range of support facilities for knowledge work and clerical activities. Examples are word processing, electronic mail, electronic filing, and data and voice communications.

(vii) Top Management Subsystem

The top management function (chief executive officer plus staff) operates from the functional areas, but also includes the functional vice president acting in a top management capacity such as in management committees. The transactions processed by top management are primarily inquiries for information and support of decisions. The transaction documents, therefore, tend to be letters and memoranda. Responding to the inquiries and making decisions requires wither access to the database and decision models of the organization or transmittal of the requests to other parts of the organization. The information for operational control in the top management function includes meeting schedules, correspondence files, and contract files. Managerial control by top management uses information which summarizes the management control being exercised by other functions to evaluate whether the functions are performing as planned. This requires access to the plans and actual performance of all the functions. Strategic planning activities relate to matters such as direction of the company (which business it should be in) and plans for ensuring necessary resources. The strategy determined by top management sets the framework for strategic planning within function and also coordinates planning to remove major inconsistencies. Strategic planning at the top management level requires a wide variety of summarized external and internal data. Information system support for strategic planning may include ad hoc retrieval of data, ad hoc analysis, and decision support systems.

An example of strategic decision making in manufacturing company's marketing department would include outlining a new general approach to marketing their products. Instead of emphasizing the fresh scent of the product, the decision makers may choose to stress the safety of the product's new packaging. The same marketing department also includes low-level transaction processing activities. It keeps careful track of how many advertisements are run by the competitor in each local newspaper.

The other departments also exhibit various levels of activity. For example, at one level, the production department makes general policy decisions about which methods to use to make the products; at the low level, it keeps a detailed record of how many hours were spent on a particular job by each employee. At the top level, the personnel department specifies the company's hiring philosophy, while at the low level, it actually conducts job interviews.

It is important that the team developing the information system for an organization recognize the different levels existing for each function. Having an understanding of the diversity of activities going on can help the team develop information systems that better meet the needs of the users. In this view, the database ties together all functions and levels by providing information to anyone in the organization who needs it. This ensures that data that are needed in an organization are stored and maintained in only one place, preventing redundancy. For example, the checking account department of a bank may have little to do with the loan department. A customer, however, may have accounts in both departments. If the two departments share information, the customer's name, address, employer, and credit history have to be stored only once. If the departments kept separate files, the information would have to be stored twice.

3. Third View

Like the other views, the third view also identifies the different levels of an organization. It then looks at the type of information required at the different levels and identifies the characteristics of the information. The characteristics include the source, scope, aggregation, time horizon, currency, required accuracy, and frequency of use. Figure 8.11 shows a model for this view, and defines each characteristic at each level.

Characteristics of Information	*Operational Control*	*Management Control*	*Strategic Planning*
Source	Largely Internal ◄──	──────────	──► External
Scope	Well-defined, Narrow ◄──	──────────	──► Very Wide
Level of Aggregation	Detailed ◄──	──────────	──► Aggregate
Time Horizon	Historical ◄──	──────────	──► Future
Currency	Highly Current ◄──	──────────	──► Quite Old
Required Accuracy	High ◄──	──────────	──► Low
Frequency of Use	Very Frequent ◄──	──────────	──► Infrequent

Figure 8.11: *The Third View of MIS in an Organization*

In the model one can see that at high organizational levels, most information comes from outside the organization. This is because the decisions made at this level are related to concerns about customers, government and competition. At low levels, most information comes from within the organization, with a focus on the actual performance of various functions. The scope of information about customers may be discovered through marketing surveys or through observations of buying habits. Information about the government may be tracked by a legal department or discovered in the local newspaper. Information about the competition may be discovered through discussion on the golf course or through articles in the trade journals.

The aggregation, or combining, of information is very high at the top and low at the bottom. This is a result of the filtering discussed earlier. At the lower level, managers must deal with a great amount of detailed data; at the top, managers see only selected data. Top level information emphasizes the future, while bottom level information is mostly about the past. New trends and technology are always important at the top level when making policy decisions, while actual (historical) transactions are the focus at the bottom.

Strangely enough, top level information is usually much older than low level information. Policy decisions are made on the basis of a lifetime about the business world's customers, competitors, and so on. Bottom level activity is usually based on records of current operations. Accuracy is not important at the top level, whereas it is crucial at the bottom. Guessing whether a competitor is trying to gain 30 percent or 35 percent of the market may not be important, even though an error may involve millions of dollars. The strategic decisions made would probably be the same in either case. However, while recording transactions, accuracy is a must. Ask any accountant of the financial records can be 'off' by a mere Rs. 100, and one may hear many reasons why they should be exact. Finally, low level information is used heavily; high level information is used infrequently. This is because a high level executive may not face the same problem twice in a month, while similar transactions at the lower level occur many times per day.

This view provides a richer look at information needs in an organization. All three views combine to provide an understanding of the levels, functions, and types of information needed throughout the organization. This understanding could be valuable for system developers in creating an MIS that meets all of the users of the system.

4. A System of Users and Machines

Since computers receive a great deal of attention in an organization, it is very easy to focus on the technology needed for data input, processing, and output and to ignore the users. Since most researchers agree that most MIS failures are caused by behavioural rather than technical problems, the user must receive some attention. Many employees facing their first computer system appear anxious when they discuss what is to come. This reaction is usually interpreted as fear of computers, but it can include resistance to change as well as resistance to the technology.

(i) Resistance to the Technology. Many people are afraid of computer systems. This is particularly interesting because computers do not pose any physical threats to people. In contrast, automobiles represent one of the greatest physical threats to people, yet few people ever speak of a fear of cars. Every day, several thousand very relaxed drivers and passengers casually neglect rules and regulations on the road, and the result is hundreds of injuries and deaths. Yet a box filled with electronics and attached to displays and keyboards can make people very anxious.

Obviously, anxiety and fear do not just arise from physical danger, an important difference between perceptions of cars and perceptions of computers is the level of understanding one has. People understand the use of automobiles very well. Automobiles have a clear, single function; transportation from one place to another. When people are asked to describe what computers do, they show by their wide range of answers that they have little understanding of computers.

Also it is easy for the average person to understand how an automobile works. Fuel is passed to combustion chamber, a spark ignites the fuel, and the explosion causes the shaft to turn. This shaft is connected to the wheels, making them turn also. Although most people do not know much more than that, this description is usually adequate to remove the element of mystery. It is much more difficult to describe how a computer works and how to use one. There are often very different tasks to accomplish and procedures to follow. Machine-readable information is invisible to the eye, and it is hard to visualise where it goes in the system.

Many studies suggest that understanding leads to greater feeling of control of a system. So it seems that people faced with a new computer system are unsure if they have the ability to learn how to use or control it. Rather than look stupid or feel inadequate, many resist the system. Top executives can resist a system by avoiding it, but lower-level workers do not have this option, they are forced to use the system. Their resistance often takes the form of aggression. People in middle management use the system, but project their emotions. The key of controlling such anxiety is proper training. It is not yet completely clear how new computer users should be trained. It may be most effective to tell users what a system will and would not do where data will move around in the system, and exactly what will be expected of them. By sticking to such issues, there is much less mystery and much more of a basis for viewing the computer as a useful tool.

(ii) Resistance to Change. Though resistance to technology may decrease as more and more people are exposed to computers, resistance to change remains a problem. Although a user may view computers as useful tools, the user's job will change, in some of the following ways:

- Less freedom, more pressure, and less responsibility
- The growth of feelings of not being needed
- Faster and more detailed reporting of job performance (and incompetence)
- Former competitors being forced to work together
- A greater need for understanding and thinking about the work rather than merely using intuition
- Changes in the formal and informal structure of the company
- Individual differences that can distort points of view

Even if the new MIS works better than the previous system, resistance may appear, since the system's implementation represents a change. The company may be able to minimize the resistance by providing realistic information before implementing a system. This information can be provided through formal training programs, by placing users on the development team, or by keeping very close contact with users while the system is being developed. The process is assisted by helping users to recognize that the new MIS helps them by making their work faster and less repetitive, as well as through training and development on a continuing basis.

8.10 MIS MODEL

MIS is a system which:

(i) Subserves managerial functions
(ii) Collects information systematically and routinely
(iii) Supports planning and controls decisions
(iv) Includes files, hardware, software and operations research models

MIS helps the organization to handle the required information by four common concepts namely:

- Management accounting
- Management science
- Management theory
- Data processing

MIS structure may be described by following a variety of approaches, such as:

- *Physical components,*
- *Information system processing functions,*
- *Decision support,*
- *Levels of management activities, and*
- *Organizational functions.*

8.10.1 MIS Structure Based On Physical Components

Structure of MIS may be understood by looking at the physical components of the information system in the organization. The physical components of an organizational information system may be hardware, software, database, manual procedures and operating persons.

A brief description of these components has been outlined as follows:

1. Hardware: Hardware refers to the physical data processing equipment and peripheral devices. For example, CPU, monitor, keyboard, printer, drives, communication devices etc.

2. Software: Software is a broad term given to the instructions or programs that direct the operation of the hardware. Software could be of two types, i.e. system software and application software.

3. Database: The database consists of all data utilised by application software. Data is stored in files.

4. Procedures: Formal operating procedures, which are required to operate a system, such as manuals, are also regarded as physical elements.

5. Operating Personnel: Personnel like Computer Operators, Computer Programmers, System Analysts, System Managers, etc. are the operating people of the information systems.

6. Input and Output: Various physical inputs and outputs from the information system existing in forms like printouts, reports, etc.

8.10.2 MIS Structure Based On Processing Functions

Information system structure can also be understood in terms of its processing functions. The function of an MIS explains what the system does. The main processing functions of information systems are described below and discussed through the following diagrams:

1. To Process Transactions: Information systems process transactions, where transaction may be defined as an activity taking place in an organization. For example, making a purchase or a sale or manufacturing a product. It may be within the organization or may be external in nature.

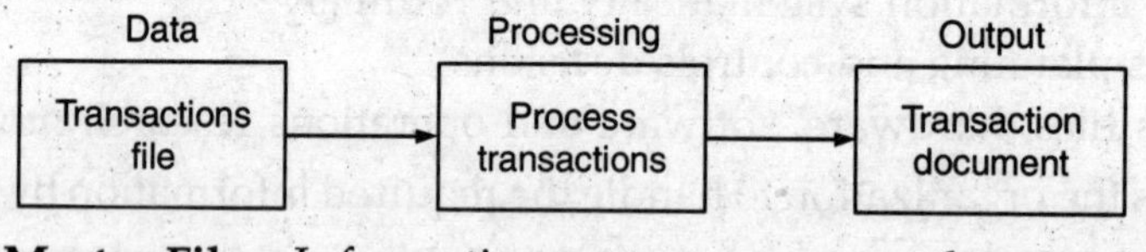

2. To Maintain Master Files: Information systems create and maintain master files in an organization. A master file stores relatively permanent or historical data about organizational entities. For example, data processing to prepare an employee's salary requires data items for the employee's basic pay, allowances, deductions, etc.

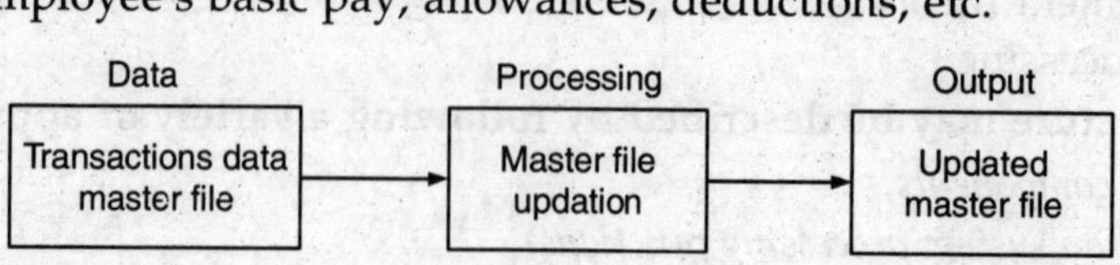

3. To Produce Reports: Reports are significant products of an information system. Many reports are purchased on a regular basis, which are called *scheduled reports.* An information system also produces reports on ad hoc requests, which are known as special or *ad hoc reports.*

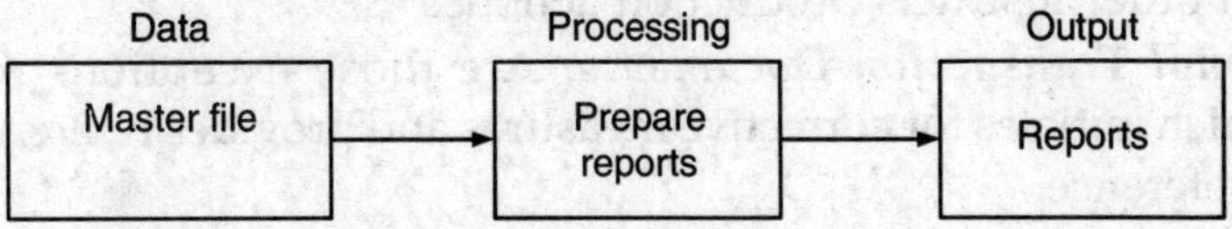

4. To Process Enquiries: An information system is used to process enquiries. For processing such queries, the information system uses its database. These may be regular enquiries with a predefined format or ad hoc enquires.

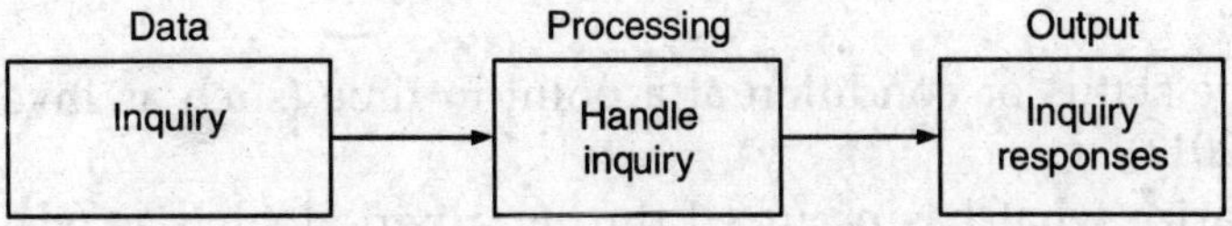

5. To Process Interactive Support Applications: The information system contains applications designed to support systems for planning, analysis and decision making. Various types of models are used for processing such applications. The mode of operation, as the name suggests, is interactive, in which the user responds to questions and requests for data and receives results so as to make changes in the inputs until an optimum solution is found.

8.10.3 MIS Structure Based On Output for Users

The user of a management information system provides inputs and receives outputs. The user's assessment of the information system is therefore dependent somewhat on the ease of input but is primarily based on the usefulness of the output the users see. The outputs thus form one description of an information system and can be classified as being of five major types:

1. Transaction Documents

Transaction documents record and process data resulting from business transactions. The results of transaction documents are used to update customer, inventory, and other organizational databases. These databases then provide the data resources that can be processed and used by management information systems, decision support systems and executive support systems.

Examples of transaction documents are items such as sales invoice, payroll checks, customer billing, and purchase orders. Transaction documents refer directly to the operations of the organization, while other types of outputs support management and control of those operations.

Transaction documents are of these three types:

- *Informational Transaction Documents:* Are those reports or confirms that action will be or has been taken. Examples are a sales order confirmation verifying reports of an order from a customer and a report describing receipt of goods previously ordered.

Their purpose is to provide feedback to persons connected in some way with action or later reference.

- *Action Oriented Transaction Documents:* Are those Requests or instructions for action. For example, a purchase order initiates a purchase, a cheque instructs the bank to pay, a production order instructs production actions.
- *Investigational Transaction Documents:* Are those exceptions reports and errors reporting which initiates for corrective measures and provides reference material control and future reference.

2. Pre-planned Reports

Pre-planned reports have a regular content and format and are usually run on a regularly scheduled basis. Examples are sales analysis, inventory stores, and budget variance reports. Prepared at a given time, they reflect one of the three conditions with respect to the time period they cover:

- They describe status or condition at a point in time (such as inventory status as of January 31, 2013).
- They summarize what has occurred during a period such as week, month, or year (such as sales during the month of January 2013).
- They present results to date and project to the end of the period (such as a year).

Pre-planned reports provide four types of information:

- *Monitoring Information:* The information confirms that actions have been taken and reports status in financial or other terms. The information also provides the recipient with background for understanding other reports and analysis. Monitoring information may provide a basis for problem finding and diagnosis and may lead to action, but no action is specified by the information itself.
- *Problem Finding Information:* The information is presented in a format that promotes identification of problems. Examples are comparisons between enterprises and standards (internal standards, industry averages, or competitor data and projections of current performance to the end of reporting period).
- *Action Information:* The information is presented with action specified or implied.
- *Decision Support:* The report, inquiry, result or dialog is oriented to performing analysis and making a decision.

3. Pre-planned Inquiry Responses

Pre-planned inquiries are generally associated with limited output like pay rate of an employee; balance due from a particular customer, etc.

4. Ad hoc Reports and Inquiry Responses

Ad hoc reports and inquiry responses occur at irregular intervals and require data or analysis whose format has not been pre-planned. If the data items needed are not available, a data collection procedure must be planned and implemented. If the data is already stored in the information system, the ad hoc request may be handled in two ways:

- The user may be provided with a means for preparing and processing the request. The inquiry may, for example, be formulated by use of an inquiry language using either an online terminal or special coding forms for subsequent transcription to machine-readable form.

- An information service (often called an information centre) may be available to process ad hoc requests. Specialists staffing the information service aid users to analyse requests and specify the retrieval and processing necessary to provide the requested data or analysis.

Regardless of how the request is handled, the capacity for the system to respond to the inquiry within a reasonable period of time (from a minute to a day) to support the current needs and activities of organization is crucial.

5. User-Machine Dialog Results

User-machine dialogue is a way in which a user can interact with a model to arrive at an analysis or a solution. User-machine dialogue differs from reports or inquiries. User-machine interaction employs a terminal such as visual display terminals or a stand-alone personal computer plus computer processing of a model such as analysis, planning, or decision model. Examples are site planning models, capital investment analysis models, and portfolio management models.

8.10.4 Development of Long Range Plans of MIS

We need MIS flexible enough to deal with, changing information needs of the organisation. It should be conceived as an open system to interact with the business environment, with a built in mechanism to provide desired information as per the new requirement. The designing of such open information is complex. Therefore the planning of MIS is necessary. The MIS plan is concurrent to the business plan of organisation. The development plan of MIS is linked with the steps of implementation in business development plan in the form of short range plan, long range plan.

Business Plan	MIS Plan
1. Business Goals and objectives	Consistent with the business.
2. Business plan & Strategy in MIS.	Business supports to strategy.
3. Strategic planning & decisions.	MIS itself is responsible for decision making.
4. Management plan for the execution & development.	MIS provides system development schedule & plan execution.
5. Operational plan for execution	Hardware & software plan for the procurement & the implementation.

8.10.4.1 Contents of MIS Plan Or Long Range Plan

MIS plan is linked to the business plan where it is necessary to develop the goal and the objective for MIS which will support the business goal. This will consider the management philosophy, policy, constraints, business risks, internal external environment of the organisation and the business.

MIS follows the following steps in the long range plan.

1. Strategy for plan achievements

The designer has to take numbers of decision for the achievement, goods & objectives such as development approach, online batch real time.

(a) system development:

It can operational v/s functional, accounting v/s db v/s conventional, distributed v/s centralised, SSAD v/s OOT.

(b) resources for system development:

Internal v/s external customized development.

(c) man power composition:

It considers the quality of manpower for analyst, programmer etc....

2. Architecture of MIS:

It provides the sub-system structure and their I/O with links. It can also provide the relationship and functionality.

3. System development schedule:

While preparing the schedule some considerations is given to the implementation of system in the overall information requirement. Schedule prepares the development steps against the timescale of execution of the system development.

4. Hardware and software plan:

Hardware investment is considered from lower configuration to higher level. The process is to match the technical decisions with the final decisions. The selection of h/w & s/w architecture is the strategic decisions. It is important to consider the following issues

1. Organisation strategic plan should be the basis for MIS strategic plan
2. The system development should match the implementation schedule of business plan.
3. The choice of I.T. is a strategic decision is not a financial decision.

5. General model of MIS plan:

(i) The corpor 'e information focuses on the current operations and the environment position

(ii) Corporate philosophy defines the policy, guidelines which form the work culture in the organisation.

(iii) Corporate mission, goals, objectives defines the long term aspects of the system.

(iv) Business risk and rewards defines the trade of between these factors to give the clear quantitative factors.

(v) Business strategy and policy focuses on the key areas of information system.

(vi) Information needs focuses on the critical information as well as how do we achieve the goals and the objectives in the system.

(vii) Architecture of plan focuses on the tools for the achievement.

(viii) System development schedule focuses on the details of system and sub-systems with their linkages charted against the timescale.

(ix) Organisation and execution of the plan focuses on the individual toll in the system.

(x) Budget focus on its cost investment schedule.

6. Ascertaining the class of information:

Organisational information: Information Entity	Manager Personnel	Production	Administration	A/C
Employee Attendance	n	n	n	y
Salary Ages/ Overtime	n	n	y	y
Human Resource Information	n	n	n	y

7. Functional information:

Functional information is defined as a set of information required by the functional head in conducting the administration and management function. It is purely local to that functional organisation and by the definition it does not has any use elsewhere except for the manager. Functional information is largely factual, statically and detail in multidimensional functional information is normally generated at equal time interval for understanding the trends and making the comparison against time scale.

The functional information can be accessed on the following three parameters:

- Working design
- Responsibility
- Functional Objective

Work design specifies procedure, work culture etc. The functional responsibility of individuals is used for accounting and decision making for achieving the target to identify the performance. Each function has its own objective which is delivered out of the corporate goals.

The functional goals and objective are necessary to achieve.

Overall corporate achievement such information can be collected from the manager and their functional head who together executes the business activities.

8. Knowledge information:

It shows the trend of the activity or the result against the time scale. It creates an awareness of those aspects of the business where the manager is forced to think, decide and act. It highlights the deviation from non-standards and also the abnormal level. The knowledge information supports the function of middle and top management. It is recorded in the graphical format for quick grasp. If the sales are declining the trend is likely to continue. The product is continuously failing the reason can be process of manufacture.

9. Decision-support information:

This information doesn't act as a direct input as the decision making information. Information issued in decision-support system & model building & problem solving in two ways justifying the need of decision. It aids in decision making:

e.g.: The information on non-moving inventory justifies the decision of disposal of item.

The demand forecast information aids in the decision on determining the orders quantity for orders & sales. The source of this information may be internal or external.

10. Operational information:

This information is required by the operator and the lower level of the management. The main purpose of this information is fact finding and taking such action and decision which will affect this operator at macro level.

The source of such information is largely internal through the transaction processing and the information relate to the small time span which is mostly current status.

8.10.5 Determining Information Requirement

Based on the uncertainty level following methods are used to handle the uncertainty.

- *Low knowledge (near certainty)*

  It is handled by operation management by determining the needs for the system.
- *Precise probabilistic knowledge(risk situation)*

  It is handled by middle level management which determines the existing system, methods of decision making & problem solving.
- *Not able to determine probabilistic term (very risky)*

  It is handled by the middle and the top level management which is determined through critical functions & decision making system.
- *High risk (Total uncertainty)*

  It is handled by top management which is determined by experimentation, modeling and sensitivity analysis.

Asking & interviewing, determine the information requirement when the user have to select one answer from finite set of answer. A closed question should be asked instead of open question which are the raw material used for making a product indicates a closed question, which are the raw materials used for a product indicates an open ques. the experts or the expertise users are supposed to give their best answers. This approach is called as Delphi method where the system designer has to check the validity separately.

The additional information required can be collected in minimum percent by decision making and problem solving where the other percent information is common to the existing.

For Example: payroll, accounting system etc.

Every business organisation performs successfully on the basis of certain critical factors which are important and the other plays a supportive role in functioning of the organisation. Many times a function is singularly critical to the successful function of business organisation. The experimentation would define the methodology for handling the complex situation. If the method is finalized information needs can be determined. Models are used for determining initial needs and they are modified, determined during the implementation on stage.

8.11 DEVELOPMENT OF MIS

When the system is complex the development strategy is prototyping the system. It is the progress of the information needs, development methodology trying it out in a smaller scale with respect to the data and complexity ensuring that it specifies the needs of the user and access the problem in development. This process identifies the problem area inadequacies in prototype the designer then takes the steps to remove inadequacies. The prototype approach brings the multiple users on same platform & changing their attitude towards a corporate goal is the managerial task of the system designer.

8.11.1 Life Cycle

There are many systems which have a life cycle that is starting and ending step which indicates that the system is very much structured and rule based. They have 100% clarity of input & their resources, definite set of output in terms of the contents and formats. This system can be developed in systematic manner, for example, accounting, payroll etc.

Prototype Approach	Life Cycle approach
1. It refers to open system with high degree of uncertainty of information.	It refers to open system with high degree of certainty of information.
2. The system design is unstable due to uncertainty.	The system design is stable due to certainty.
3. It is necessary to try for fixed ideas and complete information.	Here it is not necessary because it is already structured.
4. It is necessary to find the cost, scope and application of the system. Experimentation is necessary.	Scope, cost of the system is fully determined in clear terms. Experimentation is not necessary.
5. Information needs are not fixed.	Information needs are fixed.
6. It is Custom oriented system. is necessary.	Life cycle system is universal and governed by principles & practices

8.11.2 Implementation of MIS

For the successful implementation of the system, the system designer should:

(i) Satisfy all the information needs of the user
(ii) Offer the services to the user.
(iii) Respect the demands of the user
(iv) Not to recommend the modification of the needs unless technically feasible.
(v) Explain the nature of the system to the user to realise the information requirement of the current system.
(vi) Have a better decision making capability
(vii) Not expect the perfect understanding from the user as he may be the user of non-computerized system.
(viii) Conduct a periodical user meeting on system where it is easier to get the opportunities to know the on-going difficulties of the user.
(ix) Lewin's model suggest 3 aspects in implementation of MIS
  - *Unfreezing*: organisation to make people more receptive and interested in change.
  - *Choosing*: A course of action where the process begins & reaches to the desired level.
  - *Refreezing*: Where the changes are consolidated and equilibrium is reinforced.

8.11.3 Parameters of Management of Quality In MIS

Following are the parameters of management of quality in MIS:

(i) Complete data of all the transaction achieves the integrity of data with respect to the period.

(ii) Valid transaction input data ensures the validity of data and in turn assumes the valid information.

(iii) Accuracy & precision assures that results are accurate & precisely correct based on rules.

(iv) Relevance to user is appropriate in the quality of decision making.

(v) If the information is received late it becomes useless with the view of decision making.

(vi) Information should be complete & meaningful. It should be represented in proper format with references.

8.11.4 Organisation for Development of MIS

Organisation development consists of the following issues:

(i) Whether the function should be handled as centralised or decentralised activities. This can be resolved by accessing the information resources in the organisation i.e. information system management in centralised manner and information resource management in decentralised manner.

(ii) The allocation of h/w & s/w resources is available depending upon the functional resources. In a decentralised setup the allocation of h/w is a centralised decision but the data processing is user's responsibility.

(iii) The maintenance of service at an approximate level is needed.

(iv) Fitting the organisation of MIS in the corporate organisation, it's culture & management philosophy is the important issue in organisation.

8.12 PROBLEMS IN IMPLEMENTING MIS

Information is the input through which the mind expands its horizon and assesses and analyzes various data. There are many problems that stems from the nature of information itself. Information helps in increasing the capacity to achieve goals, often as the result of an input from another mind

8.12.1 Privacy

Privacy is of prime most concern when it comes to implementing management information system. The classification of information under categories as to what needs to be shared and what not needs to be shared is not an easy task. To top it up the expert may also have to filter the end users of any particular information. In other words all information should not be required by everyone in any organization and thus should be restricted in flow. This also raises the questions towards various safeguard measures which are essential for such filtering.

Mainly there are two types of forces which threaten our privacy:

- The rapid and extensive growth of information technology, with its enhanced capacity for surveillance, communication, computation, storage, and retrieval.
- The indispensable and increased value of information in decision making.

8.12.2 Accuracy

The accuracy of the information furnished is another most important question an organization is often faced with. The responsibility for the authenticity, fidelity, and accuracy of the information is hard to determine. This in turn raises the question as to who should be held accountable for the errors or misrepresentation in the information and how can the injured party redeemed for losses?

Misinformation can foul up with people's personal lives. This is more prone to happen when the party with inaccurate information has an upper hand in authority and power.

8.12.3 Property

This particularly talks about the ownership of the information. The information as everything else also has a price to pay for and is treated like a property. Once the information is derived from any source and processed logically, it becomes an intellectual and invaluable property. The allocation of this scares resources often is classified. Not everyone may have access to all kinds of information and in many cases it may come with a price tag.

The intellectual property right has raised many concerns in past. Who should have an access rightfully to the intellectual property? Can information be classified as property? There are substantial ethical concerns surrounding these rights. Any specific information can be quite costly to produce. However once it is produced, it possesses the illusive quality of being easily reproduced and to share with others. This particular attribute makes information hard to safeguard.

8.12.4 Accessibility

As we already said, all information may not require sharing with everyone. Contrary to this, particular information may have its own value for individual. In other words information flow normally should happen on the basis of requirements. Accessibility to certain kind of information should lie with specific departments or individuals. The question here is how to take appropriate safeguard measures?

In order to access information an individual should:

- Have the intellectual skills to deal with information.
- Have access to the information technologies which store, convey and process information.
- Have access to the information itself.

8.13 BENEFITS OF MIS

MIS no doubt have numerous benefits to offer to any organization. In today's world with so many fast moving technologies around it is impossible to imagine an organization which is not well equipped with effective MIS.

We will briefly take a tour through the benefits of an appropriately designed management information system.

- *Facilitates Planning:* MIS plays and imperative role in improving the quality of processes, by providing relevant information for sound decision making. Owing to their big sizes and complexity of organizational structure, most managers today have lost their touch with the operational facet; MIS provides them with a sight into these areas.

- *Minimize Information Overload:* MIS has the capability of processing raw and accumulated data into fine structured information, which is then utilized by respective departments. In other words, it plays an important role in transforming a massive pool of amalgamated data into fine summarized form. This helps in avoiding the confusion which is quite likely to arise when managers are flooded with detailed facts.
- *MIS Encourages Decentralization:* Decentralization of authority can solve many issues at ground level and can make the running of processes quite easy. However when thinking about decentralization, organizations are often faced with the tough task of how to impact it and still have the tap on it. MIS not only helps in monitoring operations at lower levels but also be used for measuring performance and making necessary change in the organizational plans and procedures.
- *Brings Co-Ordination:* MIS acts as an interface between all departments by facilitating integration of specialized activities. It helps in keeping each department aware of the problem and requirements of other departments.
- *Easier Control:* MIS serves as a vital link between managerial planning and control. It provides management with an upper hand in evaluating and improving performance.
- *Others:* Apart from all the above mentioned benefits, MIS is also quite useful for assembling, processing, storing, retrieving, evaluating, and disseminating the information.

8.14 LIMITATIONS OF MIS

Now that we have discussed the benefits of MIS, let us take a look at the limitations it has.

- *Highly Sensitive Requires Constant Monitoring:* MIS is highly sensitive for fraudulent activities. The information thus obtained can be used and manipulated to harm the particular organization in many ways. Bearing thus in mind, it requires continuous monitoring and filtering.
- *Budgeting of MIS Extremely Difficult:* Like all other department activities MISs cannot be budgeted. It is a highly sensitive and important function of an organization however it is not feasible to predict the budget of an MIS in any organization. Quite contrary, it is often unpredictable expense.
- *Quality of Outputs Governed by Quality of Inputs:* The information generated through MIS, is solely dependent on the raw data provided for the processing. The authenticity of the raw data will considerably access the quality of the information generated.
- *Lack of Flexibility to Update Itself:* Unlike many other applications, MIS does not have the feature of getting updated automatically. In order to update any information, the raw data has to be obtained and fed in for the processing and updating of the existing data.
- *Effectiveness Decreases Due to Frequent Changes in Top Management:* The effectiveness of information provided decreases owing to the frequent changes in middle or top level managements. The requirement of MIS substantially indicates towards the inputs given by these management levels. When the management changes, the requirements change

as well, therefore the resultant information produced till now may not be of much use to the new organization.

- *Takes into Account Only Qualitative Factors:* MIS has one big limitation of taking into account qualitative factors and completely ignoring the non-qualitative factors like morale of worker, attitude of worker, and motivation.

8.15 SIGNIFICANCE OF MIS

Importance of MIS is well known. It has come a long way, and enables any organization in achieving a particular function, objective or goal with the aid of a set of components. It not only provides a rational platform for decision making but also helps in operation of the sub-system of the firm and provides a synergistic organization in the process.

The absolute significance of a robust and effective MIS can be discussed as below:

- Technological revolutions in all spheres have made it imperative for the modern managers to have access to large amount of selective information for the complex tasks and decisions. It is almost impossible to arrive at a sound decision which is beneficial for the organization's growth without the help of effective and efficient MIS.
- MIS is very closely integrated with every organization's sales and marketing department. The average lifespan of any product is relatively becoming short in the volatile market. In order to increase the shelf life of their products, the managers have to be in complete tune with the current market trends, consumer demands and floating prices. MIS plays a vital role in sufficing all relevant information to the managers.
- Managers hugely rely on the MIS in order to access the relevant data which is specific to their requirements and functions. The organization's main research and development activities are based on the information provided by the MIS. It provides the accurate and up-to-date information to the managers, which is then used for processing and enhancing of various activities.
- The management information services are capable of taking advantage of the computational ability of the company like processing, storage capacity among others.

8.16 APPROACHES TO MIS DESIGN

MIS design should be specific to an organization, respecting its age, structure, and operations. Six strategies for determining MIS design have been suggested:

- *Organization-Chart Approach:* Using this approach, the MIS is designed based on the traditional functional areas, such as finance, administration, production, R&D and extension. These functional areas define current organizational boundaries and structure.
- *Integrate-Later Approach:* Largely a laissez faire approach, it does not conform to any specifies formats as part of an overall design. There is no notion of how the MIS will evolve in the organization. Such an MIS becomes difficult to integrate. In today's environment, where managers demand quick and repeated access to information from across sub-systems, the integrate-later approach is becoming less and less popular.
- *Data-Collection Approach:* This approach involves collection of all data which might be relevant to MIS design. The collected data are then classified. This classification influences the way the data can be exploited usefully at a later stage. The classification therefore needs to be done extremely carefully.

- *Database Approach:* A large and detailed database is amassed, stored and maintained. The database approach is more and more accepted for two main reasons: first, because of data independence it allows for easier system development, even without attempting a complete MIS; and second, it provides management with immediate access to information required.
- *Top-Down Approach:* The top-down approach involves defining the information needs for successive layers of management. If information required at the top remains relatively stable in terms of level of detail, content and frequency, the system could fulfil MIS requirements. The usefulness of this approach depends on the nature of the organization. It can be suitable for those organizations where there is a difference in the type of information required at the various levels.
- *Total-System Approach:* In this approach the interrelationships of the basic information are defined prior to implemenfation. Data collection, storage and processing are designed and done within the framework of the total system. This approach can be successfully implemented in organizations which are developing.

8.17 MIS FOR ORGANIZATIONS

Management is defined as the art of getting things done through people. A manager is the one who achieves the organization goals by motivating others to perform, not always doing things by him. Management in MIS is a process of planning, organizing, staffing, coordinating and controlling the efforts of the members of the organization to achieve stated goals of the organization.

8.17.1 Management Information System In Planning

An MIS for planning enables the corporation to have a central facility where large amounts of information can be gathered and stored. This information can be rapidly retrieved and updated to assist managers in making decisions. The management information system evaluates more alternatives than manual methods, can make better and faster decisions, and provides timely and accurate information for decision making. Perhaps if more companies are able to fully integrate the finance, marketing, production and personnel functions into an integrated corporate simulation model, they will be better able to determine the effects that changes in internal or external phenomenon will have on their organization.

Planning is nothing but the process of determining the goals and objectives and strategies fro achieving the goals of the organization. While planning, the managers need to:

- Write or review the organization's mission
- Identify and analyze opportunities
- Establish goals
- Select a course of action to achieve goals
- Determine resources needed

8.17.2 Management Information System In Organizing

A management information system in organizing includes grouping activities and establishing organizational structures and procedures to ensure that the activities are performed.

8.17.2.1 Organizing Information

Organizing information is at the heart of information science. Organizing information is important for establishing frameworks for thought and in assisting in the formation of useful concepts.

The design of a scheme for organizing information should be driven by the problems to be solved by the users. That is, information should be organized in such a way that it is easy to find information which is helpful in the solution of a given problem. This is not the same as a merely user-driven design. It is a problem-oriented design which is a process of joint problem analysis and problem solving in which the user and the information professional/ systems analyst each make their contribution.

This process starts with the preparation of an inventory of problems to be solved, decisions to be made, tasks to be performed. Each of these problems/ decisions/ tasks gives rise to one or more statements of information needed or search requests to be expected. These statements suggest the entity types and relationship types as well as specific entity types and relationship types and, for each entity type that requires it, a well-structured list of entity values (for example, a well-structured list of concepts). This scheme then serves as a framework for collecting and organizing information. It communicates the information needs to the operator of the information system (indexes, coders, data analysis).

The process of Organizing involves:

- Deciding what work needs to be done, assigning the tasks, and arranging them into a decision-making framework.
- Evolving the structure of the people working in the organization and their roles.
- Organizing is a process by which the structure and allocation of jobs is determined.
- Determining activities required to achieve the established company objectives, grouping these activities in a logical basis for handling by persons, managers and finally assigning persons for the job designed.

8.17.3 Management Information System In Staffing

The success or failure of an information services organization rests primarily on the quality of its people. Many firms consider IT staff planning, recruiting, training, and retaining qualified IS personnel, as one of their greatest challenges. Managing information services functions involves the management of managerial, technical, and clerical personnel. One of the most important jobs of information system services managers is to recruit qualified personnel and develop, organize and direct the capabilities of existing personnel.

Employees must be continually trained to keep up with the latest developments in a fast moving and highly technical field. Employee job performances must be continually evaluated, and outstanding performances must be rewarded with salary increases or promotions. Salary and wage levels must be set, and career paths must be designed so individuals can move to new jobs through promotions and transfer as they gain seniority and expertise.

In today's economic environment, employers devote a great deal of energy developing strategies so their organizations can retain a crystal sharp focus in vital business objectives such as acquiring new customers, beating the competition and raising revenue. With all of the needed focus on the bottom line, companies may be overlooking one of the most potentially serious and costly issues – Human Resources compliance. Certainly, the business of managing the workforce, HR administration, has become a very complex process indeed due to the ever changing economic, technical and legislative climate. It's no wonder that medium to large companies outsource their HR processes to Human Resources Information Systems (HRIS) firms.

HRIS is an overarching team for a suite of software products that help a firm manage very precise and tedious tasks, such as payroll administration, handling employee benefits, reviewing employee performance, and even employees training. In most cases, HRIS products have customizable user interfaces so employees can access their own HR information called Employee Self Service which greatly reduces calls to the HR department.

If you are planning to contract with a HRIS firm, you will need one that can align HR policies with your business objectives and goals in mind. The following is a list of best practice steps for transitioning your current Human Resources process to an HRIS Management System.

- *Evaluate the Personnel Needs:* During the initial analysis phase, the HRIS team should meet with the client for a discovery meeting and complete a comprehensive organizational analysis to understand the needs of the conversion. This is dependent on the sophistication of the client's record keeping. During this time, the HRIS firm begins to work with the client to document and improve their business processes.
- *Configure an HRIS Management System:* Once the client analysis is complete, the HRIS team sets up and configures the system based on the client's needs access during the initial phase.
- *Converting Legacy Data to the New HRIS Management System:* Human Resources, Performance Review, and Employee Training Records, to name a few, are migrated from the client's existing database to the HRIS technology platform. Once the database is transitioned, the data is tested for accuracy and validated.
- *Launching the New HRIS Management System:* The HRIS team ensures that the system has been appropriately configured to process transactions correctly by performing unit and payroll parallel testing. When the testing is complete and the issues are resolved, the team moves the database to production and the system becomes active.
- *Training for the new System:* This phase can begin any time during the Data Conversion and Testing/Deployment phases. End users attend the appropriate technical training sessions.

With the implementation of a new Human Resources Information System, business leaders can once again devote their energy to growing their business.

8.17.4 Management Information System In Directing

Directing is influencing people's behaviour through motivation, communication, group dynamics, leadership and disciples.

The process of directing involves:

- To channel the behaviours of all personnel to accomplish the organization's mission and objectives while simultaneously helping them accomplish their own career objectives.
- The complex task of implementing the process of management.

8.17.5 Management Information System In Controlling

Controlling is the management function, in which managers set and communicate performance standards for people, process and devices.

The four steps of the control process are:

- Establishing performance standards
- Measuring performance
- Comparing measured performance to established standards
- Taking corrective action

8.17.6 Management Information System In Coordinating

This function brings harmony and smoothness in the various group activities and individual efforts directed towards goals. Coordinating involves:

- The need of synchronizing efforts and actions which may differ.
- This is normally carried out by the authority of top level management.
- Communicating with others, providing directions and motivating people.

SUMMARY

Management Information System (MIS) is a system consisting of people, machines, procedures, databases and data models, as its elements. The system gathers data from internal and external sources of the organization; processes it and supplies Management Information to assist managers in the process of decision making. Here the word system implies that MIS follows a systems approach which means a holistic approach and is based on the concept of synergy where the output is greater than the sum of its parts. Thus, it clearly indicates that MIS is not a single system; rather it is an integrated system where parts (sub-systems) fit into an overall design.

MIS is a system that creates, processes, stores and generates information within and outside the organization. A system is a collection of parts that work together to achieve a common goal. The primary goal of MIS is to support organizational decision making, though it has many other uses, such as designing and developing new products, ensuring the quality of goods and services, preventing theft and pilferage, and so on.

Management in MIS is a process of planning, organizing, staffing, coordinating and controlling the efforts of the members of the organization to achieve stated goals of the organization.

EXERCISES

1. What do you mean by management?
2. What is information?
3. What is system?
4. Define MIS by researchers?
5. What do you mean by management information system?
6. Explain the areas that contribute to influence the field of MIS?

7. Why we need MIS?
8. Explain the concept of computer-based MIS?
9. Explain the nature of management information system?
10. Explain the working of MIS?
11. Explain the structure of an MIS?
12. What are the requirements of MIS?
13. What are the functions of an MIS?
14. Explain the model of MIS?
15. Explain the MIS structure based on physical components?
16. Explain the MIS structure based on processing functions?
17. Explain the MIS structure based on output for users?
18. Explain the development of long range plans of MIS?
19. Explain the information requirement of MIS?
20. Explain the development of MIS?
21. What the problems to implementing MIS?
22. What are the benefits of MIS?
23. What are the limitations of MIS?
24. What is the significance of MIS?
25. What are the approaches to MIS design?
26. Explain the MIS for organizations?

❑

Decision Support Systems

9

9.1 DECISION MAKING

Management is largely concerned with making decisions and any action originates from such decisions. Most decisions are made with two kinds of information – internal and external. Internal information normally comes from processed data from the organizational data bank or from the personal data bank. External information is obtained from sources external to the individual making decisions and the organization.

9.2 LEVELS OF DECISION MAKING

The well-known three-tier management pyramid, with transactional planning at the lower end, operational planning at the middle level, and policy planning at the top level, all need to use the computers for different purposes. People at the transactional planning level collect routine data generated within the organization and process it in well-defined, structured and static fashion to be converted to routine reports. At the transaction level, one is bothered only about what happens on a particular time-frame.

The middle level management does operational planning by retrieving data collected by lower level people mostly on an exception basis rather than on routine basis. They operate on information obtained by processing the data already collected. People at this level normally think of why and how things have happened. This can be categorised as semi-structured decision-making of the routine management type.

The top level management largely depends on external data – knowledge in the field, intuition and judgement. People at this level think mostly in terms of 'what if' situations. The top management extracts very little organizational data and relies more in external and personal data. The time-utilization, type of information and information sources for the three levels in the management hierarchy in any organization is shown in Figure 9.1.

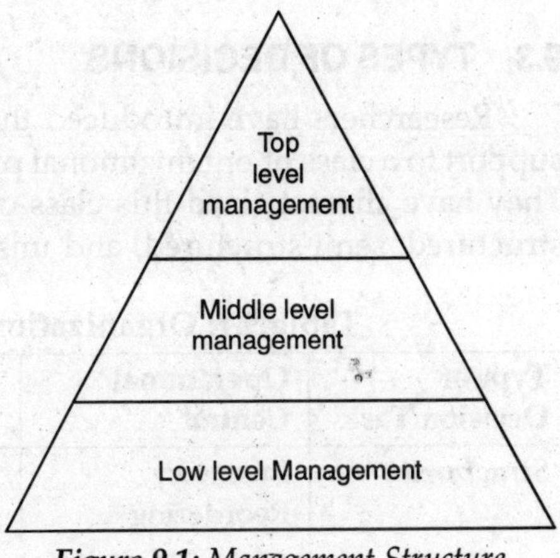

Figure 9.1: Management Structure

Figure 9.2 represents the interrelationship between the various levels of management and the internal and external data bases, through a flowchart.

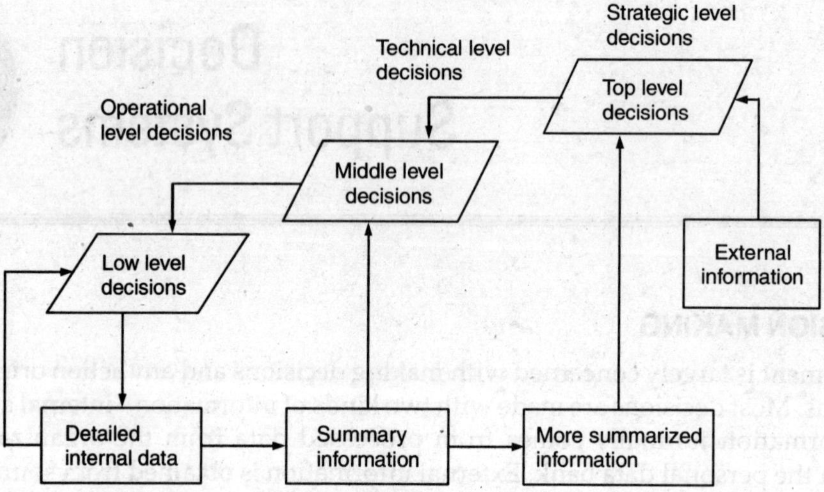

Figure 9.2: Inter-relationship between various management levels

Decision support is largely a concept, the reason being the lack of commercially available systems for the purpose. It may be worthwhile to compare the usage of computers for EDP, MIS, and DSS in terms of various factors such as the technology, applications, or environment. While MIS can be defined as computer-aided, decision-making based on information of a routine nature generated from a large pool of data through sophisticated processing. DSS can be defined as computer-aided selection of information in combination with the knowledge of persons using it, to arrive at decisions. While EDP and MIS are hardware-, data- and accounting-oriented; DSS can be thought of as opportunity-, decision- and function-oriented. DSS lays more emphasis on utilizing information to improve human effectiveness. Therefore, the objective of DSS is not to replace judgement but to support it in such a manner that the strength of both man and machine processes are utilized to the fullest.

9.3 TYPES OF DECISIONS

Researchers have introduced the concept of decision support by extending computer support to a class of organizational problems that elude EDP, MIS, and OR/MS approaches. They have characterized this class of problems by grouping organizational problems into structured, semi-structured, and unstructured categories as depicted in Table 9.1.

Table 9.1: Organizational Problems and Management Activity

Type of Decision/Task	Operational Control	Management Control	Strategic Planning	Support Needed
Structured	Inventory Reordering	Linear Programming for manufacturing	Plant location	Clerical, EDP, OR/MS Models

Semi-Structured	Bond Trading	Setting marketing budgets for consumer products	Capitalist Acquisition Analysis	DSS
Unstructured	Selecting a cover for TIME magazine	Hiring managers	R&D Portfolio Development	Human Intuition

The basis of differentiating between structured and unstructured decision situations is the amount of judgement and ad hoc evaluation as well as insights into problem definition the human decision maker must provide. Complex decision situations require a rich, subtle vocabulary to specify appropriate states and inter-relationships of decision elements. A decision situation that is verbalisable is understood well enough to be described accurately using words with precise meanings. At the other extreme, decision situations that are not well understood tend to be described in more general terms whose meanings, like understanding, are fuzzy. States and inter-relationships of elements are glossed over instead of being specified in precise expressions.

• **Structured Decisions:** Structured decisions are those for which a set of rules and procedures for the decision making process can be determined and utilised in subsequent decision situations. This implies that the decision model is essentially closed, because the outcomes and contingencies must be all known. Although structured decisions imply that the decision situations occur repetitively under the same sets of conditions, this is not necessarily true. The frequency is not the determining factor, the degree to which the contingencies and outcomes can be known in advance, and thus planned for, is the key. Payroll, production, accounts receivable, budget analysis, are examples of structured tasks.

These largely involve situations where no choice, or very little choice, or alternative, is possible. The decision situation here is largely self-evident once the facts and numbers are known. Managers make these decisions chiefly in areas of operations, rarely in cases of strategic planning. It is in dealing with the more highly structured decisions where MIS has been used mostly in the recent years.

• **Unstructured Decisions:** Unstructured decisions are those for which pre-planned rules and procedures cannot be completely specified. This implies an open decision model, because all possible outcomes and contingencies cannot be determined. This classification includes a very wide range of decision situations, from a one-time decision to terminate an organization to regular decisions on changing schedules for production based on changing economy. Even though decisions must be made regularly to deal with a recurring problem, the conditions are so different each time that no structured rules can be specified.

These involve data reference source. They represent decisions based entirely on a manager's intuition and judgement. These kinds of decisions are involved mostly in area of company strategic planning, not often in areas of management operations and control. Line managers face unstructured decisions chiefly in dealing with people – workers, other managers, bosses, and so on.

• **Semi-Structured Decisions:** The binary classification structured and unstructured is insufficient to business decision situations. It may not be possible to specify all conditions surrounding a decision situation, but it may be possible to specify a general set of guidelines to assist a decision maker. Such decision situations may be considered semi-structured, depending on the level of detail to which the process can be prespecified.

These involve both data and a manager's intuition and judgement and are the kind most commonly faced by line managers. For example, in operations control, decisions on expediting; in management controls, decisions on master scheduling; in strategic planning, decisions on optimum plant size and location. DSS can greatly assist line managers in making these kinds of decisions; MIS can help but little.

Thus, at one extreme is algorithmic, or completely structured decision making, and at the other extreme is heuristic, or completely unstructured, decision making and there exists a continuum between the two extremes based upon the degree of structure tree, as depicted in Figure 9.3.

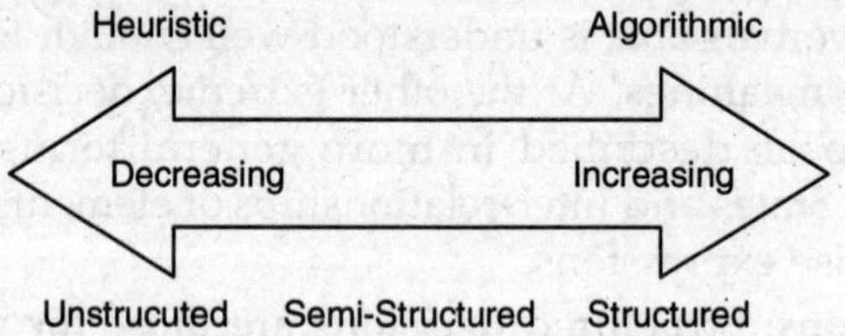

Figure 9.3: Decision Making Structure Continuum

The vast majority of an organization's business decisions lie somewhere between these extremes – some more or less structured, than others. For those decision situations that are somewhat more structured, routines, guidelines can be set up to assist the decision makers. For somewhat less structured decision situations, standards and policies may be used, but a decision maker must determine that a problem or opportunity exists, ascertain the possible alternatives, and select one. In other words, a decision maker must use judgement and ad hoc evaluation. The relationship of the decision structure topology to management functions is shown in Figure 9 4

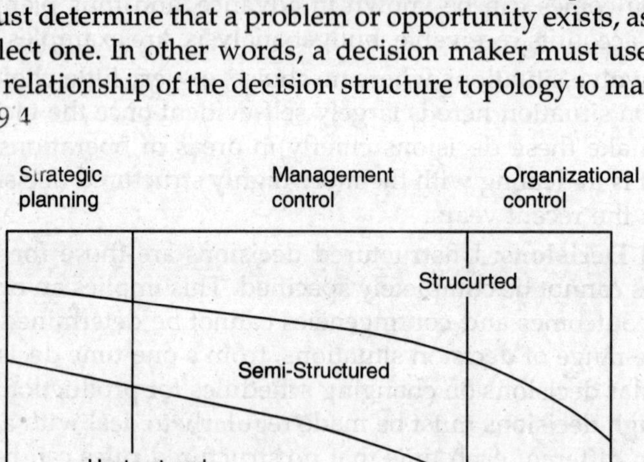

Figure 9.4: Decision making structure related to management functions

9.4 DECISION MAKING PROCESS

Decision making process model consists of four major phases: *Intelligence, Design, Choice* and *Implementation*. The decision making process is an important and integral part of the management process. Whatever a manager does, he does through decision making. So it is imperative on his part to take good decisions. This is possible only if he proceeds scientifically, step by step, analysing every relevant aspect of the problem, takes sufficient time within the limit and pays sufficient attention required to do so. The flow chart for decision making process is depicted in Figure 9.5.

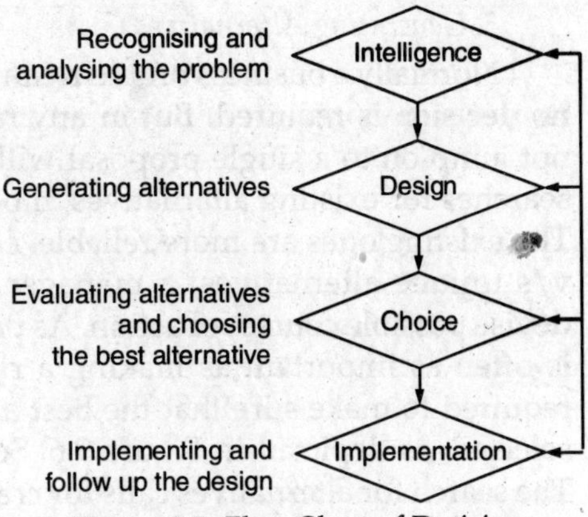

Figure 9.5: Flow Chart of Decision Making Process

The decision making will require a manager to go through the following steps:

9.4.1 Intelligence Phase

Intelligence consists of identifying the problems occurring in the organization. Intelligence indicates why, where, and with what effects a situation occurs. Intelligence activity is required to inform managers how well the organization has performed and let them know where problems exist. Intelligence phase of the decision making process involves:

1. Ascertaining or Recognising the Problem

Before deciding anything, it is important to know, define or recognise what actually the problem is. Problem is defined as the difference between something that is expected and reality.

Difference (Problem) = Desired/ Expected – Actually / Reality

In other words, before giving a solution to a particular problem as a decision, we must have a clear perception of what the problem is or where the trouble lies. With a wrong notion of the problem, we will take a decision just like a physician who prescribes a medicine for headache to a patient with stomach ache. For example, if decreasing sales of an enterprise are to be checked, it is important to know the basic or main cause of such a decrease in sales level. Thus, the manager has to identify critical or strategic factor of the problem. The critical factor determines the gap between the desired and the actual results. Proper emphasis on all relevant factors will greatly help in defining the problem, which amounts to half the solution to the same.

2. Analysing the Problem

After knowing the basic problem to be solved is, the decision maker must gather facts and separate them from beliefs, opinions and preconceived/lotions. According to Peter F. Drucker, 'To make a sound decision it is not necessary to have all the facts; but it is necessary to know what information is lacking in order to judge, how much risk the decision involves as well as how much precision and rigidity the proposed course of action can afford.' Knowing the extent of the gap which has forced him to guess will help at least in crystallising the problem correctly.

9.4.2 DESIGN PHASE

Design phase processes to understand the problem, to generate solutions, and the test solutions for feasibility. This activity may require more intelligence so that the manager can decide if a particular solution is appropriate.

3. Generating Alternatives

Normally a business problem can be solved in many ways. If there is only one alternative, no decision is required. But in any rational decision making process, the manager should not jump on to a single proposal without considering all the alternatives. At this stage, he searches for existing alternatives, modifies them and designs new alternatives as required. The existing ones are more reliable, easier to implement. Operating with extremes (existing v/s unique alternatives) a manager may well involve others in the exercise in order to devise possible courses of action. As pointed out by Koontz, the ability to develop alternatives is often as important as making a right decision. Research and creative imagination are required to make sure that the best alternatives are considered before a course of action is selected, as depicted in Figure 9.6. Sometimes, taking no action would itself be sufficient. The search for alternatives calls for creative abilities on the part of managers. The availability of two or three good alternatives enables managers to fully test the soundness of each and every alternative before it is finally translated into practice.

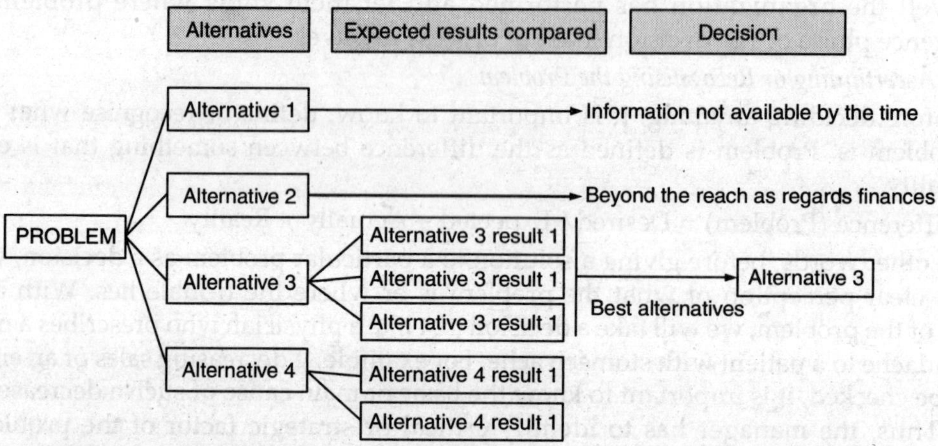

Figure 9.6: *Choose best alternative among different alternatives to solve a problem.*

9.4.3 Choice Phase

Choice stage selects an alternative course of action from those available to generate quality information. A choice is made and implemented. Choice phase of the decision making process involves:

4. Evaluating alternatives

The search for alternatives is an unending process. After having searched and enlisted a certain and sufficient number of alternatives, the decision maker should weigh alternative solutions against one another. The probable effects of each alternative must be outlined. Unfortunately, the consequences are not always clear. To reduce time and effort, he may well concentrate on really important facts of these alternatives by applying critical factor analysis. All pertinent facts must be collected, classified, the pros and cons must be considered and the important facts must be distinguished from the trivial ones. The basic purpose of evaluation should not be to find out one magical solution. The attempt should be to limit the alternatives to manageable (two or three) and economically feasible number. Evaluation must be made on the basis of values, i.e. desirable and undesirable aspects of every alternative listed and the conflicting values resolved in some satisfactory manner.

5. Choosing the best alternative

After having evaluated all the available alternatives, a comparison of all these is required to be made on the basis of profits, costs, production and quality as a pre-determined criteria. According to Peter F. Drucker, there are four criteria for picking the best from among the possible criteria:

(a) *Decision under risk:* The manager has to weigh the risk of each course of action against the expected gains. He must decide how much risk he can take and find out the alternatives that satisfy this criterion.

(b) *Decision under economy of efforts:* The alternative that will give the greatest output for the least input in terms of material and human resources is obviously the best one to be selected. Instead of picking up an elephant gun to chase sparrows, the manager may well select the one that ensures efficient utilization of scarce resources.

(c) *Decision under timing:* If the situation has great urgency, the best alternative is the one that warns the organization of the impending dangers. On the other hand, if consistent effort is needed a low start that gathers momentum may be preferable.

(d) *Decision under limitation of resources:* Physical, financial and human resources impose a limitation on the manager's choice. Of these, the most important resources whose limitations have to be considered are the human beings who will implement the decision. Their vision, skill, understanding and competence often determine how effectively the organization's efforts are carried out. If adequate human resources are not currently available, the decision should give effect to their development or acquisition from outside sources in the next plan.

9.4.4 Implementation Phase

At the implementation stage, managers can use a reporting system that delivers routine reports on the progress of a specific solution. Implementation phase of the decision making process involves:

6. Implementing the decision

A decision is not an end in itself. It is only a means to achieve an end. It is of no use to take even the best possible decision if it is not implemented. Therefore, every effort must be made to get the decision implemented. For such implementation, the following procedure may be adopted:

(a) Managerial executive should be delegated the required authority to implement the decision.

(b) Effective communication systems must be adopted to communicate the decision to the concerned employees.

(c) The acceptance of the employees must be obtained regarding the particular decision so that they may contribute their whole hearted efforts to implement it.

7. Follow up of the decision

Follow-up or feedback ensures whether the decision taken has brought the desired results. Managers should take the follow-up action in the light of the feedback from the concerned quarters about the results. If there is any gap between objectives and results, this should be analysed and factors responsible for this deviation should be identified. The feedback may also help in reviewing the decision when conditions change.

9.5 DECISION SUPPORT SYSTEMS

Decision Support Systems constitute a class of computer-based information systems including knowledge-based systems that support decision-making activities. Decision Support Systems (DSS) are a specific class of computerised information system that supports business and organisational decision-making activities. A properly-designed DSS is an interactive software-based system intended to help decision makers compile useful information from raw data, documents, personal knowledge, and/or business models to identify and solve problems and make decisions.

Typical information that a decision support application might gather and present would be:

- an inventory of all of your current information assets (including legacy and relational data sources, cubes, data warehouses, and data marts),
- comparative sales figures between one week and the next,
- projected revenue figures based on new product sales assumptions;
- the consequences of different decision alternatives, given past experience in a context that is described.

This chapter explains various terms related to DSS along with prominent types of DSS used in organizations. We also list some prominent future trends that DSS is most likely to follow in the years to come.

9.5.1 Decision Support Systems: Introduction

A decision support system is a way to model data and make quality decisions based upon it. Making the right decision in business is usually based on the quality of your data and your ability to sift through and analyse the data to find trends in which you can create solutions and strategies for. DSS or decision support systems are usually computer applications along with a human component that can sift through large amounts of data and pick between the many choices.

While many people think of decision support systems as a specialised part of a business, most companies have actually integrated this system into their day to day operating activities. For instance, many companies constantly download and analyse sales data, budget sheets and forecasts and they update their strategy once they analyse and evaluate the current results. Decision support systems have a definite structure in businesses, but in reality, the data and decisions that are based on it are fluid and constantly changing.

The key to decision support systems is to collect data, analyse and shape the data that is collected and then try to make sound decisions or construct strategies from analysis. Whether computers, databases or people are involved usually doesn't matter, however it is this process of taking raw or unstructured data, containing and collecting it and then using it to aid decision making.

Various attributes of decision support systems are as follows:

- ***Flexibility***: The systems are flexible so that any semi-structured or unstructured decision making situation can be tackled with ease and speed.
- ***Simple Models***: The systems use simple models of decision making.
- ***Database***: The decision supports the database.

Not all company decisions are recurrent, and some have to be taken infrequently or perhaps only once. Decision support systems (DSS) provide a tool to deal with less precisely structured or defined problems that arise sporadically. DSS help managers who have to take non-structured decisions. A decision is understood to be *non-structured* if there are no clear procedures in place to take the decision, and it is not possible to identify beforehand all the factors that need to be considered in the decision.

It must be said that all information systems support decision making, even if only indirectly. DSS have been expressly developed to support the decision-making process. These systems facilitate dialogue with the user when he or she is considering alternative solutions to a problem, and the system provides database access and models constructed to present information.

Decision support systems are interactive, and aim to expand human reasoning capacity to resolve specific non-structured decision-making problems. This type of system focuses on the decision-making processes and must provide relevant facts relating to the decision easily, quickly and accurately. It must also offer interactive access to processing media that can be used creatively and that allow the user to explore a range of alternatives, and provide the information necessary to respond to the problem. When managers use a DSS, they consider a number of possible scenarios by asking "What would happen if...?" For example, a manager who is deciding what price to set for a new product can use the marketing area of the decision support system. The system will have a model that combines various factors such as product price, the cost of materials, advertising costs, all of which affect profit forecasts for product sales over a five-year period. By varying the price of the product in the model, the manager can compare forecast results and select a price accordingly.

Unlike administrative information systems, decision support systems can help to make decisions for which a procedure cannot be fully programmed in a computer. To this end, some of the dependent relations between factors and their consequences are shown by computer models, and value judgements are introduced when the manager interacts with the system. Spreadsheets, which can help to manage data by representing them in columns and rows in a table, are frequently used to construct simple decision support systems.

The main purpose of decision support systems is to help the decision maker in the decision-making process. Unlike transaction processing systems and administrative information systems, DSS are not structured or formalised, since they are generally used for *ad hoc* processes and therefore they need to be flexible and adaptable. The key aspect of a DSS is that it supports decision making in situations where computer data processing capacity is needed in conjunction with the criteria or rationale of the decision maker.

The main emphasis of DSS lies in its support function, and not the automation of decisions. The computer's task is to provide access to data and offer the chance to test alternative solutions, but it must not replace the manager's criteria. In other words it does not attempt to offer responses or impose a sequence of predefined analyses; rather it is the user who chooses how to tackle the problem and in the final instance, takes the decision.

A DSS uses data from the organisation's transaction processing system and administrative information system as well as data from external sources. In fact, the data required to generate information can come from a range of sources, not only the database as in the case of the transaction processing system and the administrative information system. Moreover, a DSS can store and later reprocess previously obtained data. The user interacts with the system by making requests, creating or modifying models to adapt them to variations and to help understand the problem, managing data and designing the format and content of reports, which may include text, structured information or figures.

In using these systems it is essential to determine what information is necessary. In well-structured situations this information can be identified beforehand, but this becomes complicated in non- structured environments. Once the manager has certain information, he or she may realise that more information is necessary; in other words certain information reveals a need for further information.

In these cases neither the format nor the content of the system's reports can be designed previously. Decision support systems must therefore be more flexible than transaction processing systems or administrative information systems. The user must be able to define the content of each report he or she wants. The manager's own criteria therefore play an important role in taking decisions on non-structured problems. While DSS help managers, they are no substitute for the manager's own criteria.

One example of a non-structured decision is the decision banks had to take over whether or not to install ATMs. They had to calculate the cost of both manual and automatic services, the degree of customer acceptance, their competitors' response, etc.

9.5.2 Definitions of DSS by Researchers

Scott Morton defined Decision Support Systems as *Interactive computer based systems, which help decision makers utilize data and models to solve unstructured problems.*

Keen and Scott Morton stated that Decision Support Systems *couple the intellectual resources of individuals with capabilities of the computer to improve the quality of decisions. It is a computer-based support system for management decision-makers who deal with semi-structured problems.*

Earliest definition by Gerrity is one who described DSS as an *effective blend of human intelligence, information technology, and software which interact closely to solve complex problems.*

Other definitions are as follows:

A DSS is an interactive, flexible and adaptable computer-based information system that utilizes decision rules, models, and a model base coupled with a comprehensive database and decision-makers own insights. Using the DSS leads to specific implementable decisions in solving problems that would not be amenable to the management. Thus DSS supports complex decision-making and increases its effectiveness.

An information system that utilises decision models, a database, and a decision-makers own insights in an ad hoc, interactive analytical modelling process to reach a specific decision by a specific decision-maker.

9.5.3 Characteristics of DSS

Some of the key aspects of DSS can be made clearer with a discussion of the characteristics of DSS:

- Decision making supported by DSS must be in a semi-structured or unstructured environment. In every decision making situation, there are many factors to consider, conflict about the factors, insufficient information, complexity, and lack of clarity. While a computer cannot make an actual decision, it can help managers by analyzing the measurable factors.
- This sort of decision making occurs at all levels of management. Others in a company besides the chief executive officers can benefit from the use of DSS.
- A DSS should be able to help groups make decisions, rather than just individuals working on individual tasks. Decisions may be developed by many decision makers and then passed along to others as the company's new policy.
- The DSS should assist in all stages of decision making– including identifying problems, analysing and choosing a solution. How can a computer support all of these stages? Figure 9.7 shows the steps in the decision making process and how a computer can assist at the particular stage by providing a certain type of information.

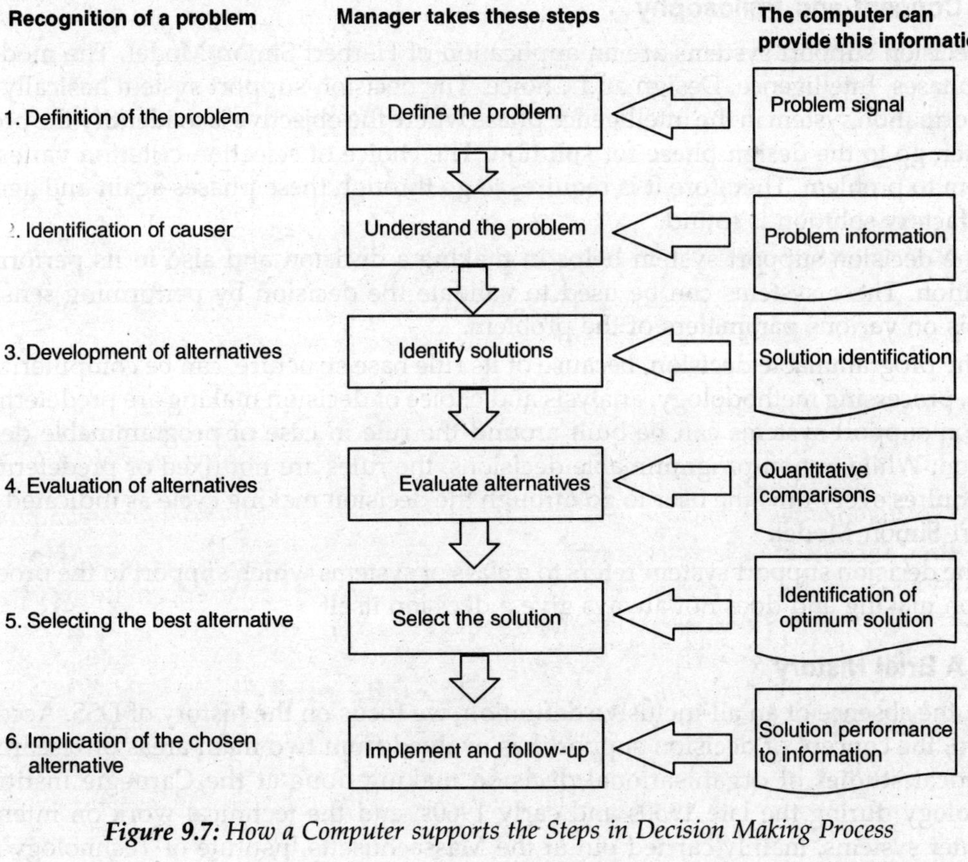

Figure 9.7: How a Computer supports the Steps in Decision Making Process

- A DSS should be flexible, fitting the style of a particular manager, and adaptable, accommodating changes in the environment. It is very different types of managers to be able to work with the DSS. If a particular manager places the greatest emphasis on mathematical comparisons, the DSS should be able to make comparisons. If a manager wants to spend more time identifying a problem, the DSS should have powerful report-writing, query, or graphics abilities.
- The DSS should be easy to use. A user should not be required to be a computer programmer to generate reports, answers to queries, or graphics. It must be convenient for the user to use the DSS. Otherwise, the DSS probably would not be used.
- DSSs are information systems whose focus is on decision making. In this sense they differ from EDP and MIS which focus on Data and Information respectively.
- They rely on the man and the machine working together for solving decision problems. In this sense they differ from EDP systems which focus on automating the routine processes, and MIS whose main objective is to provide information that can be useful to management.
- They are support tools under the control of managers. They do not attempt to automate decision making, predefine objectives, or impose solutions.

9.5.4 Concept and Philosophy

Decision support systems are an application of Herbert Simon Model. The model has three phases, Intelligence, Design and Choice. The decision support system basically helps the information system in the intelligence phase where the objective is to identify the problem and then go to the design phase for solution. The choice of selection criterion varies from problem to problem. Therefore it is requires to go through these phases again and again till a satisfactory solution is found.

The decision support system helps in making a decision and also in its performance evaluation. These systems can be used to validate the decision by performing sensitivity analysis on various parameters of the problem.

The programmable decision, because of its rule base structure, can be computerized, as inputs, processing methodology; analysis and choice of decision making are predetermined. Decision support systems can be built around the rule in case of programmable decision situation. While in non-programmable decisions, the rules are not fixed or predetermined, and requires every time the user to go through the decision making cycle as indicated in the Herbert Simon Model.

The decision support system refers to a class of systems which support in the process of decision making and does not always give a decision itself.

9.5.5 A Brief History

In the absence of an all-inclusive definition, we focus on the history of DSS. According to Keen, the concept of decision support has evolved from two main areas of research: the theoretical studies of organisational decision making done at the Carnegie Institute of Technology during the late 1950s and early 1960s, and the technical work on interactive computer systems, mainly carried out at the Massachusetts Institute of Technology in the

1960s. It is considered that the concept of DSS became an area of research of its own in the middle of the 1970s, before gaining in intensity during the 1980s. In the middle and late 1980s, executive information systems (EIS), group decision support systems (GDSS), and organisational decision support systems (ODSS) evolved from the single user and model-oriented DSS. Beginning in about 1990, data warehousing and on-line analytical processing (OLAP) began broadening the realm of DSS. As the turn of the millennium approached, new Web-based analytical applications were introduced.

It is clear that DSS belong to an environment with multidisciplinary foundations, including (but not exclusively) database research, artificial intelligence, human-computer interaction, simulation methods, software engineering, and telecommunications.

DSS also have a weak connection to the user interface paradigm of hypertext. Both the University of Vermont PROMIS system (for medical decision making) and the Carnegie Mellon ZOG/KMS system (for military and business decision making) were decision support systems which also were major breakthroughs in user interface research.

Furthermore, although hypertext researchers have generally been concerned with information overload, certain researchers, notably Douglas Engelbart, have been focused on decision makers in particular.

9.5.6 Problem Resolution With DSS

DSS are interactive information systems that help the decision maker deal with fairly unstructured problems by offering analytical models and access to databases. These systems are designed to help in the decision-making process. One of the main features of these systems is their flexibility. Personal DSS should be easy to use: the tools should be oriented to the final user for this purpose. On the other hand, an organisation's DSS, used widely by different members of a company, should be the result of a well-planned process. All DSS should be easy to use. Within its area of application, a DSS should offer the user a way to apply models and databases interactively that enhances the support it gives to deal with the problem the user faces.

So, what is the essence of DSS? In what type of business situations should the DSS approach be considered? The way people in an organisation tackle a problem will vary according to how structured the problem is; in other words, it will depend on the extent to which predefined procedures are in place to take decisions on the matter in hand.

Principally, DSS help to take decisions on semi-structured problems, where some phases in the decision process often require considerable computer support. This is because a model, which can contain hundreds of relationships, is applied to a database that frequently contains a large amount of data; the decision maker intervenes in the selection of this data. DSS can also be used to take decisions on non-structured problems. These decisions can also be taken with the support of expert systems, although with a very limited field, such as the decision to approve a loan application.

The main tasks facing managers involve a high level of ambiguity; in other words they generally have to deal with non-structured or semi-structured problems.

9.5.7 Possibilities of Decision Support Systems

A model is a representation of something, designed for a specific purpose. It is usually an abstraction or a simplification of a phenomenon. A model represents the relationships between the aspects resulting from the phenomenon. A model is constructed by adopting a series of suppositions or assuming a series of premises about the dependence between variables. Various alternatives can then be analysed by changing some variables and seeing what would happen if the premises were modified and then comparing the results (What would happen if...?"). For example, what would happen if we changed a product's sale price? What value would a variable need to have to achieve a certain result? What volume of sales would we need to obtain a given net profit?

9.5.8 Using a Spreadsheet as a Decision-making Support System

The spreadsheet program is widely used in the work environment and is now the standard software used to manage information in the business world. Despite this widespread use, we believe that a low percentage of users take full advantage of the spreadsheet's potential. The spreadsheet could be better exploited by applying the logic used to construct models with different scenarios. In many cases, poor use of the spreadsheet leads to considerable loss of time and on occasions, the program cannot be used to carry out some types of analysis.

The purpose of the spreadsheet is not to perform complicated mathematical operations; a calculator is sufficient for that. The spreadsheet comes into its own precisely when the result of the first calculation appears, which should lead on to an analysis of this result. The spreadsheet can also help achieve greater productivity when it is used to perform regular repetitive operations. The spreadsheet also includes logical functions and search functions that allow the user to delegate more mechanical decisions to the computer such as, for example "if this value is lower than that one, then multiply by x".

Hence, when we are about to start a task with the spreadsheet, we can have two aims:

- to construct a model for decision-making support, in which case our target should be to achieve maximum possible flexibility.
- to mechanise a repetitive process that we have to do on a regular basis, repeating the same calculations, which should aim to be both convenient and secure.

When constructing a spreadsheet, it is essential to know exactly what our objectives are; this will help us take the right approach to achieve our objectives.

9.5.9 Using a DSS in the Decision-making Process

The general, the decision-making process has four stages. During the first stage, known as the intelligence stage, the environment is explored in order to find or define the problem. During the second stage, the design stage, various alternatives are drawn up for comparison during the selection stage. The solution is then applied and improved where necessary. Each one of these stages can provide feedback to a previous stage in order to redefine the problem or select a better solution, for example.

DSS can help at different stages of the decision-making process. Spreadsheets are usually used to construct simple decision-making models. They do, however, have limitations. Their data-handling capacity is limited and they cannot work with very large databases.

9.5.10 Some More Facts About Decision Support Systems

Following are the facts about decision support systems:

- The decision support systems are developed by the users and system analysts jointly.
- The decision support systems use the principles of economics, science and engineering, and also the tools and techniques of management.
- The data used in the decision support system is drawn from the information systems developed in the company.
- The decision support systems are developed in isolation and form an independent system subset of the management information system,
- The most common use of the decision support system is to test the decision alternatives and also to test the sensitivity of the result to the change in the system and assumptions.
- The data and information for the decision support system are used from the internal sources such as the database and the conventional files, and from the external sources.

9.6 TAXONOMIES

Although computers and artificial intelligence are at work or at play with data, it is ultimately up to humans to execute these strategies or comprehend the data into a usable hypothesis. It is important to note that the field of DSS does not have a universally accepted model, meaning that there are many theories vying for supremacy in this broad field. Because there are many working theories on the topic of DSS, there are many ways to classify DSS. For instance, one of the DSS models available is with the relationship of the user in mind. This model takes into consideration passive, active and co-operative DSS models.

Decision support systems that just collect data and organise them effectively are usually called ***passive*** models, they do not suggest a specific decision, and they only reveal the data. An ***active*** decision support system actually processes data and explicitly shows solutions based upon that data. While there are many systems that are able to be active, many organisations would be hard pressed to put all their faith into a computer model without any human intervention.

A ***co-operative*** decision support system is when data is collected, analysed and then provided with a human component which helps the system revise or refine it. It means that both a human component and computer component work together to come up with the best solution.

While the above DSS model takes the relationship of the user in mind, another popular DSS model takes into consideration the mode of assistance as the underlying basis of the DSS model. This includes the Model Driven DSS, Communications Driven DSS, Data Driven DSS, Document Driven DSS, and Knowledge Driven DSS.

- **Model Driven DSS model** is when decision makers use statistical, simulations or financial models to come up with a solution or strategy. Keep in mind that these decisions are based on models; however they do not have to be overwhelmingly data intensive.

- **A Communications Driven DSS model** is when many collaborators work together to come up with a series of decisions to set in motion a solution or strategy. This communications driven DSS model can be in an office environment or on the web.
- **A Data Driven DSS model** puts its emphasis on collected data that is then manipulated to fit the decision maker's needs. This data can be internal, external and in a variety of formats. It is important that usually data is collected and categorised as a time series which is a collection of data that forms a sequence, such as daily sales, operating budgets from one quarter to the next, inventory levels over the previous year, etc.
- **A Document Driven DSS model** uses documents in a variety of data types such as text documents, spreadsheets and database records to come up with decisions as well as further manipulate the information to refine strategies.
- **A Knowledge Driven DSS model** uses special rules stored in a computer or used by a human to determine whether a decision should be made. For instance, for many days, traders stop loss limit can be seen as a knowledge driven DSS model. These rules or facts are used in order to make a decision.

You can also look at the scope in which decisions are made as a model of DSS. For instance, an organisational wide decision, department decision or single user decision, can be seen in the scope wide model.

9.7 DSS AS DETERMINISTIC SYSTEMS

There are a number of situations, where the management has to make a decision based on the analysis of business statistics. Most of these decision situations are fairly structured and therefore, can be put in the form of the business models.

If the management can design such models duly tested, they can be used by the decision makers, whenever the need arises. All such tools and models act as the support systems for decision making. The decision support systems based on such tools or models have found extensive use, as a number of computer based software tools and packages are available at a very reasonable price.

The origin of:these tools and models lie in the Business Management, the Management Science and the Operations Research.

Some are universally known and proven tools and have application in the Business Management.

1. The most significant advantage of the decision support system is its use in sensitizing the decisions and assessing its implications on the result or business performance.
2. The second advantage of such system is in focusing on the critical issues in business.
3. The third advantage of the decision support system is that it provides higher management ability to delegate decision making to the lower level once the tools and the models are tested.

9.8 TYPES OFTOOLS/ MODELS

The decision support system can be based on the different types of tools and models.

9.8.1 Behavioural Models

These models are useful in understanding the behaviour amongst the business variables. The decision maker can then make decisions giving due regard to such behavioural relationships; for example, the trends analysis, forecasting, and the statistical analysis models. The trend analysis indicates how different variables behave in trend setting in the past and hence in the future. A regression model shows the correlation between one or more variables. It also helps in identifying the influence of one variable on the other. These types of models are largely used in process control, manufacturing, agricultural sciences, medicines, psychology and marketing. The behavioral analysis can be used to set the points for alert, alarm and action for the decision maker.

9.8.2 Management Science Models

These models are developed on the principles of business management, accounting and econometrics. There are also management systems, which can be converted into the decision support system models; for example, the budgetary systems, the cost accounting systems, the system of capital budgeting for better return on the investment, the ABC analysis, the control of inventory through the maximum-minimum levels, the MRP systems, etc. are the examples of the use of the management science in the materials management. Production planning and control, scheduling and loading systems are the examples in Production Management. Manpower planning and forecasting is the example in Personnel Management.

Some of these models can be used straight away in the design of the decision support system. While some others require the use of management principles and practices, most of the procedure based decision making models belong to this category. Such models take away the personal bias of the decision maker.

9.8.3 Operations Research (OR) Models

The Operations Research (OR) models are mathematical models. These models represent a real life problem situation in terms of the variables, constants and parameters expressed in algebraic equations. Since, the models are mathematical; there are solutions to these problems. In arriving the solution, methods or calculus, matrix algebra, probability, and set theory are used. These models have clarity to the extent that each of them has a set of assumptions which must be true in real life. Further, if the assumptions are valid, the solutions offered are realistic and practical; the model represents the real life problem situation.

The OR models address themselves to two or more aspects of the decision situation. In business and industry, there are a number of situations where one type of cost is controlled, the other cost goes up. This play balanced at a point is an optimum point which finds a solution to minimize certain aspects of constraints.

In manufacturing business, the maximization of profit with an appropriate product mix, within the capacity and the market constraint; the allocation of an inventory to the various destinations with the least transportation costs; the minimization of capital blocked in the inventory and simultaneously meeting the market demand or the production requirement. The inventory control models offer an optimum solution, where the cost of inventory and the cost of ordering or set up is balanced. Some problems do not precisely fall in the category of the standard OR models. In such cases, the problems are solved by using a simulation approach. This approach uses a random occurrence of a large number of events, determines the status of the system and evaluates its cost of operations.

9.9 DSS SOFTWARE

This section discusses the basic modules and the corresponding structure of simple DSS software.

9.9.1 Modules of DSS Software

The important modules of DSS software are depicted in Figure 9.8.

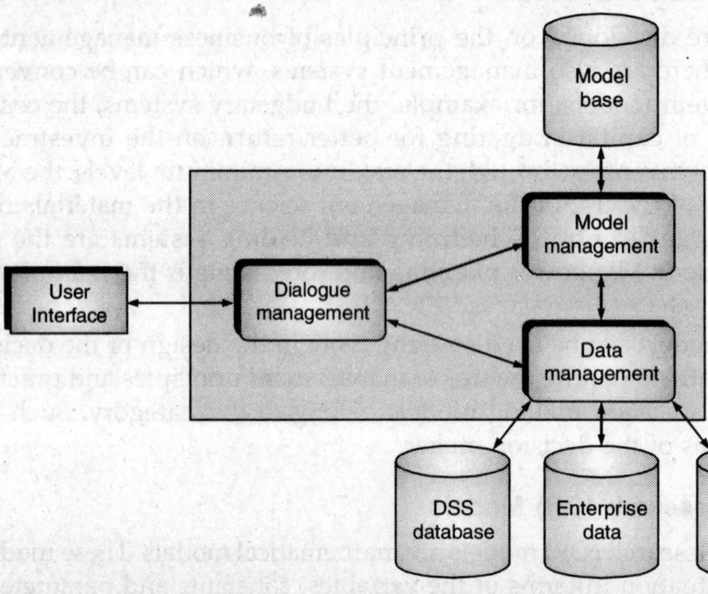

Figure 9.8: Components of a DSS software

1. **User Interface** with the dialogue management component, which is a set of programs that manages the user interface and translates the user's requests into commands for the other two components.
2. **The Model Management Component** maintains and executes models of business activity. Examples of models are spreadsheets, or models, financial models, or simulation models. It is used to create, store, and modify models and to cause them to be involved.
3. **The Data Management Component** maintains DSS data. Its tasks include managing the DSS database, which contains both intermediary and final results of DSS studies, and managing the interfaces to enterprise data, which is external to the DSS and data from external sources.

9.9.2 Structure of DSS Software

The basic structure of a DSS software/program through management processes is depicted in Figure 9.9.

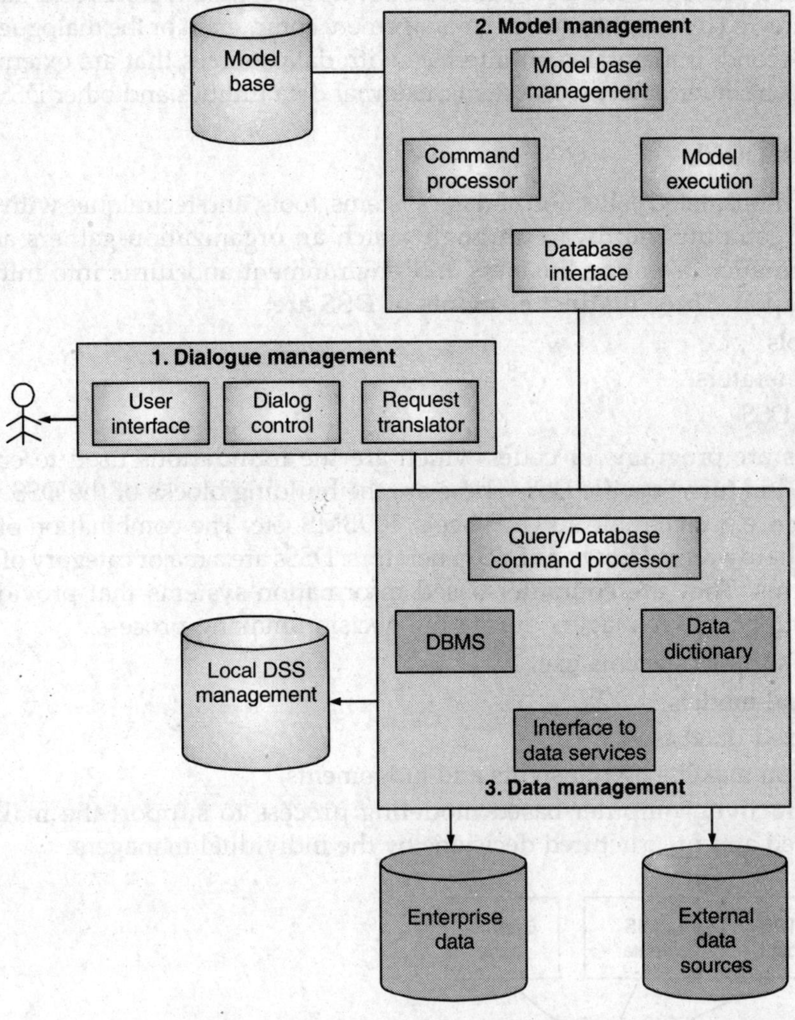

Figure 9.9: *Basic Structure of DSS Software*

1. Dialogue Management: It has three subsystems. The *user interface subsystem* manages the physical user interface. It controls the appearance if the screen accepts input from the user and displays the results. It also checks the user commands for the correct syntax. The *dialogue control subsystem* maintains a processing context with the user. The *request translator* is to translate the user command into actions for the model management or the data management components into a format and vocabulary understandable by the user. Since flexibility and ease of use are important in DSS, GUIs are becoming the standard for DSS applications. Database is normally through SQL.

2. Model Management: The command processor receives the commands from the dialogue management components and delivers those commands from the dialogue management component to either the model base management systems or the model execution system.

3. Database Management: Two functions for this are, first, it stores and manipulates the database as directed by either the model management component or the dialogue management component. Second, it maintains an interface with data sources that are external to the DSS viz. TPS database, inter-enterprise systems, external data utilities and other DSS applications.

9.10 A DSS MODEL

DSS is a co-ordinated collection of data, systems, tools, and techniques with the necessary software and computer hardware through which an organization gathers and interprets relevant information from the business and environment and turns into information that can be acted upon. **Three distinct elements of DSS are:**

(i) DSS Tools
(ii) DSS Generators
(iii) Specific DSS

DSS tools are programs or codes which are the foundations used to create the DSS generators and in turn Specific DSS. These are the building blocks of the DSS which acts as a user interface, e.g. electronic spread sheets, RDBMS, etc. The combination of DSS tools in the computer hardware is known as DSS generators. DSSs are a major category of management support systems. They are computer based information systems that provide interactive information support to managers during the decision-making process.

Decision support systems use:

(1) Analytical models,
(2) Specialized databases,
(3) A decision maker's own insights and judgements,
(4) An interactive, computer-based modeling process to support the making of semi-structured and unstructured decisions by the individual managers.

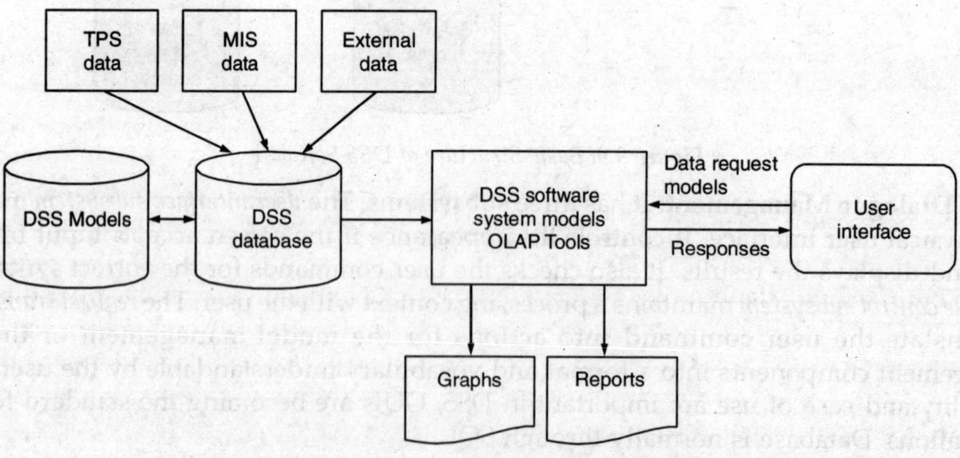

Figure 9.10: A Basic DSS Model

Decision support systems are thus able to directly support the specific types of decisions and the personal decision-making styles and needs of individual managers.

Figure 9.10 illustrates the components of a DSS. They include a database used for query and analysis, a hardware and software system with models, network, people resources needed to provide interactive decision support for managers a d other analytical tools and a user interface.

9.10.1 DSS Hardware and Network Resources

Personal computer workstations provide the primary hardware resource for a DSS. They can be used on a stand-alone basis, but are typically connected by a wide-area or local-area networks to servers and other computer systems for access to other DSS software, model and data resources.

9.10.2 DSS Software System

The DSS software system contains the software tools that are used for data analysis. It may contain various Online Analytical Processing (OLAP) tools, or a collection of mathematical and analytical models that easily can be made accessible to the DSS user.

9.10.3 DSS Database

A DSS database contains data and information extracted from the database of the organization, external databases, and a manager's personal databases. It includes summarised data and information most needed by manager for specific type of decisions. DSS database may be residing on a PC that contains a subset of corporate data that has been downloaded and possibly combined with the external data. Alternatively, the DSS database may be a massive data warehouse that is continuously updated by major organizational TPS (including enterprise systems and data generated by Web site transactions). The data in DSS databases are generally extracts or copies of production databases so that using the DSS does not interfere with critical operational systems.

9.10.4 DSS Model

A DSS model is an abstract representation that illustrates the components or relationships of a phenomenon. A model can be a physical model (such as a model airplane), a mathematical model (such as an equation), or a verbal model (such as a description of a procedure for writing an order). Each decision support system is built for a specific set of purposes and will make different collections of models available depending on those purposes.

Perhaps the most common models are libraries of statistical models. Such libraries usually contain the full range of expected statistical functions including means, medians, deviations, and scatter plots. The software has the ability to project future outcomes by analysing a series of data. Statistical modeling software can be used to help establish relationships, such as relating product sales to differences in age, income, or other factors between communities. Forecasting models are used to forecast sales. The user of this type of model might supply a range of historical data to project future conditions and the sales that might result from those conditions (entering, for example, a rise in raw materials costs or the entry of a new, low-priced competitor in the market) to determine how these new conditions might affect sales. Companies often use this software to predict the actions of the competitors. Model libraries exist for specific functions, such as financial and risk analysis models. Among the most widely used are Sensitivity Analysis Models that ask 'what-if' questions repeatedly to determine the impact of changes in one or more factors on outcomes, 'What-if' analysis working forward from known or assumed conditions allows the user to vary certain values to test results in order to better predict outcomes if changes occur in those values. 'What happens if' we raise the prices by 5% or increase the advertising budget by 20%? What happens if we keep the price and advertising budget the same? Desktop spreadsheet software, such as Microsoft Excel or Lotus 1-2-3 is often used for this purposely. Backward sensitivity analysis software is used for goal seeking. If I want to sell one million product units next year, how much must I reduce the price of the product?

9.10.5 DSS User Interface

The DSS user interface permits easy interaction between users of the system and the DSS software tools. A graphic, easy-to-use, flexible user interface supports the dialogue between the user and the DSS. The DSS users can be managers or employees with no patience for learning a complex tool, so the interface must be relatively intuitive. Many DSS today are being built with Web-based interfaces to take advantage of the Web's ease of use, interactivity, and capabilities for personalization and customization. Building successful DSS requires a high level of user participation to make sure the system provides the information managers need.

9.10.6 Working Principle

Data from organizations, TPS and MIS applications are input to the DSS software system models, along with the data from external sources and the DSS model data. As stated, the DSS may store and later reprocess its own model data as well. The user interacts with the DSS. Online requests are made, models are created, or adjusted, and data is manipulated etc. The outputs of the DSS program can be text, structured reports, or graphics. A variety of programs supported by the DSS include spreadsheet programs, personal database management systems, model base management systems (MBMS), word processing packages, graphics generators, statistical packages, and other special purpose programs.

Decision support systems are better viewed as facilities having data and data manipulation tools than as formalised systems. DSS are often used to respond on an ad hoc basis to problems and opportunities as they develop. As such, flexibility and adaptability are crucial. DSS often involves models of business activity. Sometimes DSS users build models as they use the system. Technology to support DSS is evolving.

9.11 ARCHITECTURE OF DSS

Figure 9.11 depicts the architecture of a DSS model. It shows that DSS architecture is composed of four major components:

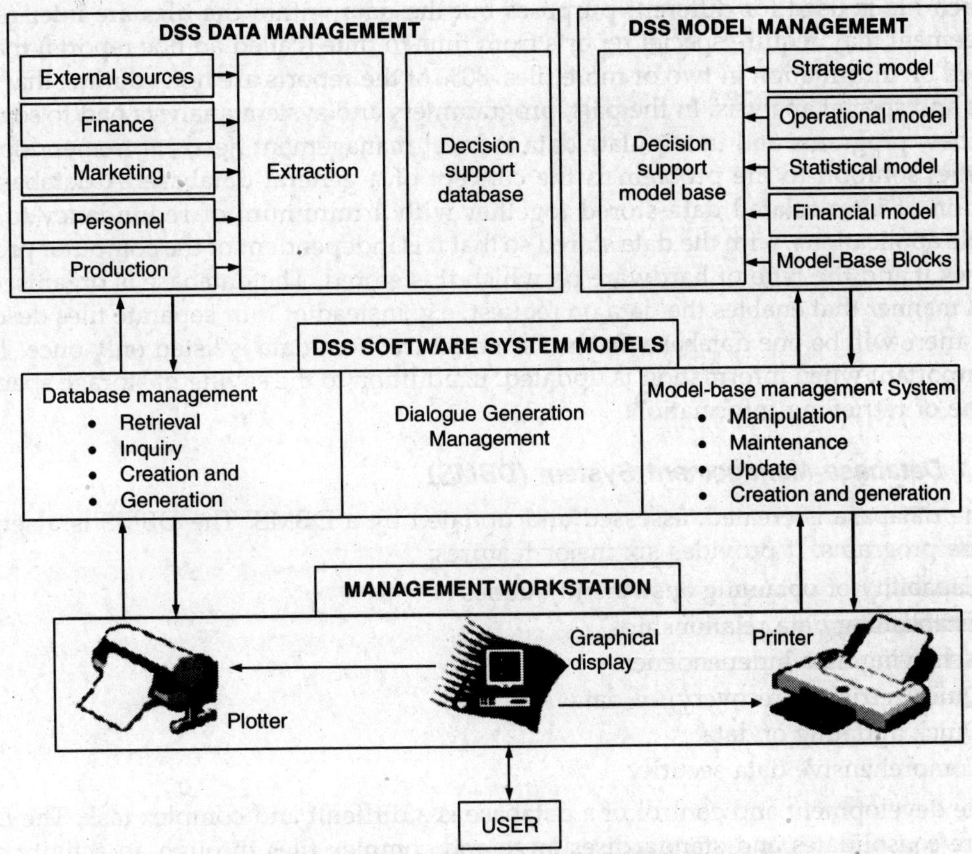

Figure 9.11: Architecture of a DSS Model

9.11.1 Database and Its Management

The database is a collection of data that is organized in such a way that it corresponds to the needs and structure of a company and can be used for more than one application. In order to understand a database, we should think of information kept in files. A file contains information regarding one application. For example, personnel file, listing all employees; a customer file, listing all customers; and so on. Each such file contains extensive information such as addresses, telephone numbers, and volume of purchases for each customer. In a computerised system, a file can be on an auxiliary device such as disk. Each file is used for a different purpose. Companies store thousands of files in the form of libraries. However, the data within each file may be interrelated. For example, a company has four files:

(i) a parts inventory file,

(ii) a parts usage file,

(iii) a product file, and

(iv) a customer file.

Each file is used for different purposes but the data within the files are inter-related. Management may require special reports from time to time (called ad hoc reports) that will be based on information in two or more files. 80% of the reports are non-routine, that is, for ad hoc and special analysis. In the past, programmers and system analysts had to sort files, create new programs and manipulate data to meet management needs at tremendous cost and time; solution to the problem is the concept of a general database. A database is a collection of inter-related data stored together with a minimum of redundancy to serve multiple applications, with the data stored so that it is independent of the computer program that uses it and the type of hardware on which it is stored. The database is organised in a special manner that enables the data on request, e.g. instead of four separate files described above, there will be one database. In the file structure, item data is listed only once. This is very important when information is updated, in addition to the saving of storage space and the time of retrieving information.

9.11.1.1 Database Management System (DBMS)

The database is created, assessed and updated by a DBMS. The DBMS is a series of software programs. It provides six major features:

- Capability of obtaining answers to queries
- Establishing data relationships
- Achieving data independence
- Quick retrieval (recovery) of data
- Quick updating of data
- Comprehensive data security

The development and control of a database is a difficult and complex task. The DBMS software consolidates and standardises large and complex files through an activity called extraction. DSS may include data from several databases, some of which are external to the company. In addition to internal and external files that are included in the DSS database, it is possible to add a manager's own files. A dialogue generation and management module provide an attractive use interface that supports interactive input and output by managers.

9.11.2 Model-base and Its Management

The model-base is divided into two major parts:

1. Pre-written computer programs (or packages): These may include standard mathematical and standard models such as linear programming or regression, as well as special programs developed for an individual manager, an organization, or an industry. Notable ones are strategic, long-range planning models, and tactical and operational models. In addition, the model-base includes the simulation program and sensitivity analysis routines.

2. Model building blocks: Some of the pre-written programs and sub routines can be used to construct ad hoc applications.

9.11.2.1 Model-base Management System (MBMS)

It is a software system that generates new routines and reports, model updates and changes and data manipulation. It is capable of inter-relating models with appropriate linkages through their database.

9.11.3 Hardware

It is typically used to run a large DSS in the mainframe computer. Many user-constructed DSS also run on micro-computers for managerial use, a graphic display is of tremendous value. Charts, graphs, diagrams and even three-dimensional pictures can be produced in color.

9.11.4 User System Interface

This component includes languages and devices with which information is entered into the computer and displayed. The following parts are included:

9.11.4.1 Query Language

A key factor for the development of a DSS is the communication between the manager and the computer. As many managers are not comfortable with procedural languages, such as BASIC and COBOL, communication should be in English like language. Today, there are several software packages that allow communication in fourth generation languages. Such languages have been developed mainly for the financial mode planning areas. These are:

- Interactive Financial Planning Systems (IFPS).
- EXPRESS developed by Tymshare Inc.
- Special purpose languages (developed for specific purposes. It is used in industries such as university administration – a language called EPPM, airlines and hospitals etc.)

These query languages are non-procedural which means that statements in the model describe results only (sum, delete, etc.) and they may be entered in any order, while the system itself decides the proper sequence. Problem with these languages is that currently, they are less efficient in execution than the procedural languages. DSS are not intended to have high efficiency, but it is expected to provide a convenient and effective tool for managers.

9.11.4.2 Entry and Display Procedure

DSS are constructed on-line with the computer and give:

- Immediate response to questions (interactive communication) and the timely preparation of analysis and reports, even during management meeting. Results can be displayed on a large CRT in the company's boardroom.
- Quick policy experimentation and sensitivity analysis.
- Monitoring and controlling production processes in real time. A key idea in DSS is that the user can play an active role in the development and implementation of the analysis. Emphasis is placed on case of use, flexibility and quick response all of which are necessary in practical decision-making situations.
- The manager communicates with the computer via a terminal. He turns on the terminal in the office and in English like language, commands the computer to execute some tasks. The computer accesses the database and uses the database as instructed. The results are then displayed.

9.12 COMPONENTS OF DSS

Once again, different authors identify different components in a DSS. For example, Sprague and Carlson identify three fundamental components of DSS: *(a)* the database management system (DBMS), *(b)* the model-base management system (MBMS), and *(c)* the dialogue generation and management system (DGMS).

- Haag *et al.* describe these three components in more detail: The Data Management Component stores information (which can be further subdivided into that derived from an organisation's traditional data repositories, from external sources such as the Internet, or from the personal insights and experiences of individual users); the Model Management Component handles representations of events, facts, or situations (using various kinds of models, two examples being optimisation models and goal-seeking models); and the User Interface Management Component is, of course, the component that allows a user to interact with the system.
- According to Power, academics and practitioners have discussed building DSS in terms of four major components: *(a)* the user interface, *(b)* the database, *(c)* the model and analytical tools, and *(d)* the DSS architecture and network.
- Hättenschwiler identifies five components of DSS:
  (a) users with different roles or functions in the decision making process (decision maker, advisors, domain experts, system experts, data collectors),
  (b) a specific and definable decision context,
  (c) a target system describing the majority of the preferences,
  (d) a knowledge base made of external data sources, knowledge databases, working databases, data warehouses and metadatabases, mathematical models and methods, procedures, inference and search engines, administrative programs, and reporting systems, and
  (e) a working environment for the preparation, analysis, and documentation of decision alternatives.
- Arakas proposes a generalised architecture made of five distinct parts:
  (a) the data management system,
  (b) the model management system,
  (c) the knowledge engine,
  (d) the user interface, and
  (e) the user(s).

9.13 CLASSIFYING DSS

There are several ways to classify DSS applications. Not every DSS fits neatly into one category, but a mix of two or more architecture in one. Holsapple and Whinston classify DSS into the following six frameworks: Text-oriented DSS, Database-oriented DSS, Spreadsheet-oriented DSS, Solver-oriented DSS, Rule-oriented DSS, and Compound DSS.

A compound DSS is the most popular classification for a DSS. It is a hybrid system that includes two or more of the five basic structures described by Holsapple and Whinston.

The support given by DSS can be separated into three distinct, interrelated categories:

- Personal Support,
- Group Support, and
- Organisational Support

Additionally, the build-up of a DSS is also classified into a few characteristics.

1. Inputs: This is used so the DSS can have factors, numbers, and characteristics to analyse.

2. User knowledge and Expertise: This allows the system to decide how much it is relied on, and exactly what inputs must be analysed with or without the user.

3. Outputs: This is used so the user of the system can analyse the decisions that may be made and then potentially.

4. Make a Decision: This decision making is made by the DSS; however, it is ultimately made by the user in order to decide on which criteria it should use.

DSS which perform selected cognitive decision-making functions and are based on artificial intelligence or intelligent agents' technologies are called Intelligent Decision Support Systems (IDSS).

9.14 APPLICATIONS

Some of the important applications where DSS have been effectively employed in business organizations are listed below:

- Accounting/Auditing for:
  - Auditing health insurance claims
  - Estimating pencil manufacturing costs
  - Analysing stochastic cost-volume-profit
- Finance for:
  - Asset-liability management
  - Cash management and debt planning
  - Capital budgeting
  - Evaluating financial risks
  - Financial analysis and diagnosis
  - Funding strategic product development
  - Locating banks
  - Managing portfolio
  - Planning in merges and acquisitions
  - Selecting R&D project
  - Structuring optimal lease
  - Real estate appraisal and investment
  - Setting interest rates for money market deposit accounts
  - Small business financial planning
- Human Resource Management for:
  - Manpower planning
  - Massive personal assignment
  - Resolving labour management dispute
  - Tracking critical human resources information

- International Business for:
  - Allocating investment funds in MNCs
  - Analysing international investment options
  - Planning global logistics
  - Planning global marketing/production/distribution
- Marketing for:
  - Allocating retail space in retail outlets
  - Competitive pricing and market share
  - Designing freight networks and integrated distribution systems
  - Distribution planning
  - Logistics planning and vehicle scheduling
  - Managing hazardous material shipments
  - Media-planning or advertising agencies
  - Measuring direct product profitability in retail merchandising
  - Selecting telemarketing sites
- Production and Operations Management for:
  - Demand forecasting
  - Master scheduling
  - Production planning
  - Process planning
- Strategic Planning for:
  - External environment and industry analysis
  - Strategic analysis of mergers and acquisitions, multi-level (corporate, division, department) and malfunctional corporate planning; production/market position
  - Managing a portfolio of new product development
  - Strategy control and evaluation

9.15 BENEFITS OF DSS

Following are the benefits of DSS:

- Improves personal efficiency
- Expedites problem solving
- Facilitates interpersonal communication
- Promotes learning or training
- Increases organisational control
- Generates new evidence in support of a decision
- Creates a competitive advantage over competition
- Encourages exploration and discovery on the part of the decision maker
- Reveals new approaches to thinking about the problem space

9.16 TYPES OF DSS

There are several types of decision support systems and many more are emerging. This goes to show the dynamic nature of the concept of decision support systems. In this section we shall examine the various types of decision support systems and their applications.

9.16.1 Group Decision Support System

This is an interactive computer-based system that facilitates users finding (partial) solutions to semi-structured problems. A GDSS uses a set of decision makers working together as a group.

Technical developments in electronic communication, computing, and decision support, coupled with new interest on the part of organisations to improve meeting effectiveness, are spurring research in the area of group decision support systems (GDSS). A GDSS combines communication, computing, and decision support technologies to facilitate formulation and solution of unstructured problems by a group of people. This unit presents a conceptual overview of GDSS based on an information-exchange perspective of decision making. Three levels of systems are described, representing varying degrees of intervention into the decision process. Research on GDSS is conceived as evolving over time from the study of simple "shell" systems, consisting of menus of features, available for selection by a group, to consideration of sophisticated rule-based systems that enable a group to pursue highly structured and novel decision paths. A multi-dimensional taxonomy of systems is proposed as an organizing frame- work for research in the area. Three environmental contingencies are identified as critical to GDSS design: group size, member proximity, and the task confronting the group. Potential impacts of GDSS on group processes and outcomes are discussed, and important constructs in need of study are identified.

9.16.1.1 Group Decision Support System Application

The first example or application for a groupware is **GDSS**, which stands for **G**roup **D**ecision **S**upport **S**ystem. There is such a GDSS system supported by the Faculty of Management at the University of Arizona. This kind of same-time-same-place conference is oriented toward business meetings and decision making.

The GDSS started originally from the Management Information System at University of Arizona. Some kind of problems has always been observed that are associated more with large meetings than with small meetings. By large meetings we mean meetings with generally more than 15 participants, but can go much beyond that, e.g. 40 or even 50.

Some of the identified problems are:

- time consuming;
- dominance over the meeting; and
- honesty and participation.

However, it is important to note that we are not trying to say that small meetings do not have the above problems; these problems mentioned exist in every kind of meetings, but we are just trying to stress that they are more commonly found in large meetings. Small meetings tend to be more easily controlled than large meetings.

In a GDSS environment, there is usually a big room with something like 40 seats, which means that 40 people can be at the meeting at any one time. There are not only 40 seats but also 40 microcomputers. This enables every participant to have the use of one microcomputer during the course of the meeting. The reason why each participant needs a microcomputer depends on how GDSS works.

In the GDSS, with special computer software, the facilitator of each meeting will first make the agenda of the meeting, which will be projected on to a big screen that everyone can see. The participants will type simultaneously their ideas of the topic of discussion on the individual microcomputers next to them. The computer will then sort the ideas, and the participants will then vote or comment on which ideas they like or dislike. In the course of the whole meeting, GDSS stores, categorises and prints out all the ideas, comments and vote tallies, so that each of the meeting participants will get a summary of the meeting when it ends.

What is so special about GDSS is that it enables meeting participants to simultaneously "talk", when the computer sorts and sends ideas to each of the terminal, all at the same time. That saves a tremendous amount of time, because all these are done electronically instead of manually, and the time saved will enable participants to spend more time manipulating and expressing their ideas. This can consequently increase the productivity and efficiency of the group. The time-saving benefit also has an added bonus: when productivity and efficiency in meetings increase, it is likely that the team spirit can be consolidated, resulting in an increase of the strength of binding among team members.

Besides, under this GDSS, no one can dominate the meeting. This is because of another feature of GDSS. GDSS provides an anonymous scheme, so that whatever you type in the terminal (i.e. your opinion) will be protected. Under this circumstance, no one really knows who is typing what. Because of this, not a single person can dominate the meetings. In the worst case, we might say "some ideas" are dominating the meeting, but this is perfectly fine because this is as a matter of fact an aim of the GDSS: to help meeting participants voice their opinions from an idea-oriented mindset. For example, simply because you have a prejudice against **person A** does not mean that you are going to reject the idea being proposed in the meeting, because you do not know who is proposing that idea!!

Besides, this anonymity scheme will also help those team members who are shy to voice opinions. And with the anonymity, people are likely to be more honest, just as you will say more, and more honestly on the professor's evaluation form if you know whatever you write will not affect your final grade on the course. This, of course, is because you know you do not have to worry about the consequences.

However, whether this anonymity is good or not can be very controversial. The success of meetings supported by GDSS depends largely on the conduct of the participants. If people are taking advantage of the anonymity system by typing obscene words or foul languages, this system may be banned for the good of the organisation.

9.16.2 Business Intelligence

Business Intelligence (BI) refers to technologies, applications and practices for the collection, integration, analysis, and presentation of business information and sometimes to the information itself. The purpose of business intelligence—a term that dates at least to 1958—is to support better business decision making. Thus, BI is also described as a decision support system (DSS). BI is sometimes used interchangeably with briefing books, report and query tools and executive information systems. In general, business intelligence systems are data-driven DSS.

BI systems provide historical, current, and predictive views of business operations, most often using data that has been gathered into a data warehouse or a data mart and occasionally working from operational data. Software elements support the use of this information by assisting in the extraction, analysis, and reporting of information. Applications tackle sales, production, finance, and many other sources of business data for purposes that include, notably, business performance management. Information may be gathered on comparable companies to produce benchmarks.

9.16.2.1 History

Prior to the start of the Information Age in the late 20th century, businesses had to collect data from non-automated sources. Businesses then lacked the computing resources necessary to properly analyse the data, and as a result, companies often made business decisions primarily on the basis of intuition.

As businesses automated systems the amount of data increased but its collection remained difficult due to the inability of information to be moved between or within systems. Analysis of information informed for long-term decision making, but was slow and often required the use of instinct or expertise to make short-term decisions. Business intelligence was defined in 1958 by Hans Peter Luhn who wrote that, *"business is a collection of activities carried on for whatever purpose, be it science, technology, commerce, industry, law, government, defence, et cetera".*

The communication facility serving the conduct of a business (in the broad sense) may be referred to as an intelligence system. The notion of intelligence is also defined here, in a more general sense, as "the ability to apprehend the interrelationships of presented facts in such a way as to guide action towards a desired goal."

In 1989 Howard Dresner, later a Gartner Group analyst, popularised BI as an umbrella term to describe "concepts and methods to improve business decision making by using fact-based support systems." In modern businesses the use of standards, automation and specialised software, including analytical tools, allows large volumes of data to be extracted, transformed, loaded and warehoused to greatly increase the speed at which information becomes available for decision-making.

9.16.2.2 Key Intelligence Topics

Business intelligence often uses key performance indicators (KPIs) to assess the present state of business and to prescribe a course of action. Examples of KPIs are things such as lead conversion rate (in sales) and inventory turnover (in inventory management). Prior to the widespread adoption of computer and web applications, when information had to be manually inputed and calculated, performance data was often not available for weeks or months. Recently, banks have tried to make data available at shorter intervals and have reduced delays. The KPI methodology was further expanded with the Chief Performance Officer methodology which incorporated KPIs and root cause analysis into a single methodology.

Businesses that face higher operational/credit risk loading, such as credit card companies and "wealth management" services, often make KPI related data available weekly. In some cases, companies may even offer a daily analysis of data. This fast pace requires analysts to use IT systems to process this large volume of data.

9.16.3 Land Allocation Decision Support System

LADSS or **Land Allocation Decision Support System** is an agricultural land use planning tool being developed at The Macaulay Institute.

LADSS is implemented using the programming language G2 from Gensym alongside a Smallworld GIS application using the Magik programming language and an Oracle database. LADSS models crops using the CropSyst simulation model. LADSS also contains a livestock model plus social, environmental and economic impact assessments.

LADSS has recently been used to address climate change issues affecting agriculture in Scotland and Italy. Part of this work has involved the use of General Circulation Models (also known as global climate models) to predict future climate scenarios. Other recent work has been a study into how Common Agricultural Policy reform will affect the uplands of Scotland, an assessment of agricultural sustainability and for rural development research within the AGRIGRID project.

9.16.4 Spatial Decision Support System

Spatial Decision Support Systems (SDSS) developed in parallel with the concept of Decision Support Systems (DSS). An SDSS is an interactive, computer-based system designed to support a user or group of users in achieving a higher effectiveness of decision making while solving a semi-structured spatial problem. It is designed to assist the spatial planner with guidance in making land use decisions.

For example, when deciding where to build a new airport many contrasting criteria, such as noise pollution versus employment prospects or the knock on effect on transportation links, which make the decision difficult? A system which models decisions could be used to help identify the most effective decision path.

An SDSS is sometimes referred to as a Policy Support System. A spatial decision support system typically consists of the following components.

1. A database management system - This system holds and handles the geographical data. A standalone system for this is called a Geographical Information System, (GIS).
2. A library of potential models that can be used to forecast the possible outcomes of decisions.
3. An interface to aid the users' interaction with the computer system and to assist in analysis of outcomes.

This concept fits dialog, data and modelling concepts outlined by Sprague and Watson as the DDM paradigm.

9.16.4.1 How Does An SDSS Work?

An SDSS usually exists in the form of a computer model or collection of interlinked computer models, including a land use model. Although various techniques are available to simulate land use dynamics, two types are particularly suitable for SDSS. These are Cellular Automata (CA) based models and Agent Based Models (ABM).

An SDSS typically uses a variety of spatial and non-spatial information, like data on land use, transportation, water management, demographics, agriculture, climate or employment. By using two (or, better, more) known points in history the models can be calibrated and then projections into the future can be made to analyse different spatial policy options. Using these techniques spatial planners can investigate the effects of different scenarios, and provide information to make informed decisions. To allow the user to easily adapt the system to deal with possible intervention possibilities an interface allows for simple modification to be made.

Here we present some examples where an SDSS has been used:

1. Community Viz: Community Viz is a land-use planning SDSS that works as an extension to ArcGIS Geographic Information System software produced by ESRI. It uses a scenario planning approach and calculates economic, environmental, social and visual impacts and indicators dynamically as users explore alternatives. Interactive 3D models and various tools for public participation and collaboration are also included. It has been commercially available since 2001.

2. Environment Explorer: The Environment Explorer (LOV) is a spatial, dynamic model, in which land use and the effects on social, economic and ecological indicators are modelled in an integrated way. Its primary goal is to explore future developments, combining autonomous developments with alternative policy options, in relation to the quality of the environment in which inhabitants of the Netherlands live, work and recreate. Various policy options from governmental departments are translated into a spatial, dynamic image of the Netherlands future with respect to issues such as: economic activity, employment, social well-being, transportation and accessibility, and the natural environment. The model covers the whole of The Netherlands.

3. LUMOCAP: LUMOCAP aims at delivering an operational tool for assessing land use changes and their impact on the rural landscape according to a Common Agricultural Policy (CAP) orientation. It focuses on the relations between the CAP and landscape changes and emphasises the spatiotemporal dimension of the former. The core of the tool is a dynamic Cellular Automata based land use model. Current usage areas – Poland (2 areas), Germany / The Netherlands (1 cross border area).

4. MOLAND: The aim of MOLAND is to provide a spatial planning tool that can be used for assessing, monitoring and modelling the development of urban and regional environments. The project was initiated in 1998 (under the name of MURBANDY – Monitoring Urban Dynamics) with the objective to monitor the developments of urban areas and identify trends at the European scale. The work includes the computation of indicators and the assessment of the impact of anthropogenic stress factors (with a focus on expanding settlements, transport and tourism) in and around urban areas, and along development corridors. Models now covering 23 European cities (map).

5. MURBANDY: The overall objective of MURBANDY is to provide datasets to study past and current land uses, to develop an Earth Observation based procedure to monitor the dynamics of European cities; to develop a number of "urban" and "environmental" indicators that allow to understand these dynamics and the impact these cities have on the environment, and finally to elaborate scenarios of urban growth. Initially this project covered 5 European cities, but the project has expanded into the MOLAND project.

6. Zero-M: Zero-M aims at concepts and technologies to achieve optimized close loop usage of all water flows in small municipalities or settlements (e.g. tourism facilities) not connected to a central wastewater treatment – the Zero Outflow Municipality (Zero-M).

9.16.5 Self Service Software

Self Service Software is a subset within the Knowledge Management software category and which contains a range of software that specialises in the way information, process rules and logic are collected, framed within an organised taxonomy, and accessed through decision support interviews. Self-service software allows people to secure answers to their inquiries and/or needs through an automated interview fashion instead of traditional search approaches.

9.16.5.1 Self Service Software Functionality

Self service software allows authors (typically subject matter experts) to readily automate the deployment of, the timeliness of, and compliance around a variety of processes with which they are involved in communicating without having to physically address the questions, needs, and solicitations of end users who are inquiring about the particular process being automated.

Self service software primarily addresses closed-loop inquiries whereby the author emulates a variety of known (finite) questions and related (known) responses on hand or required steps that must be addressed to derive and deliver a final answer or directive. Often the author using such software codifies such known processes and steps then generates (publishes) end-user facing applications which can encompass a variety of code bases and platforms.

Self service software is sometimes referred to as decision support software and even expert systems. It is typically categorised as a subtopic within the knowledge management software category. Self service software allows individuals and companies alike to tailor and address customer support, technical support and employee support inquiries and needs in an on-demand fashion where the person with a question (need) can interface with the author's generated application via a computer, a handheld device, a kiosk, register, or other machine type to secure their answers as if they were directly interacting (talking to) with the author.

9.16.6 Dashboards (Management Information Systems)

In management information systems, a **dashboard** is an executive information system user interface that (similar to an automobile's dashboard) is designed to be easy to read. For example, a product might obtain information from the local operating system in a computer, from one or more applications that may be running, and from one or more remote sites on the Web and present it as though it all came from the same source.

9.16.6.1 Types of Dashboards

Digital dashboards may be laid out to track the flows inherent in the business processes that they monitor. Graphically, users may see the high-level processes and then drill down into low level data. This level of detail is often buried deep within the corporate enterprise and otherwise unavailable to the senior executives.

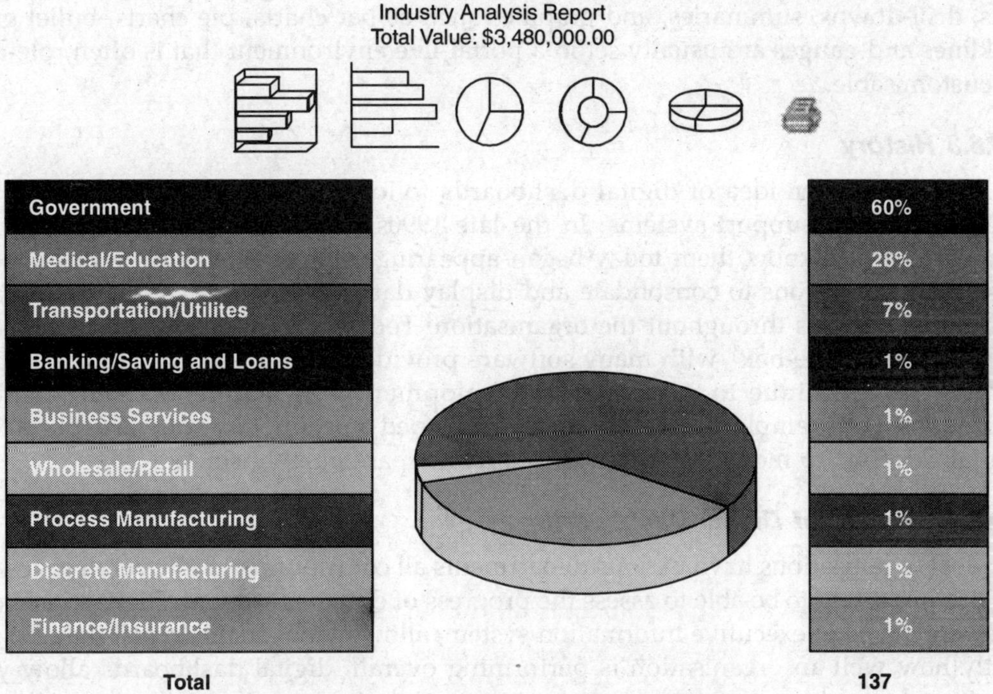

Figure 9.12: An example dashboard layout

Three main types of digital dashboard dominate the market today: stand-alone software applications, web-browser based applications, and desktop applications also known as desktop widgets. These latter would be driven by a Widget engine.

Specialised dashboards may track all corporate functions. Examples include human resources, recruiting, sales, operations, security, information technology, project management, customer relationship management and many more departmental dashboards.

Digital dashboard projects involve business units as the driver and the information technology department as the enabler. The success of digital dashboard projects often relies on the correct selection of metrics to monitor. Key performance indicators, balanced scorecards, sales performance figures — these are just some of the content appropriate on business dashboards.

9.16.6.2 Interface Design Styles

To some extent, most graphical user interfaces (GUIs) resemble an automobile dashboard. Although a computer dashboard is more likely to be interactive than an automobile dashboard, some product developers consciously employ this metaphor (and sometimes the term) in the interface design so that the user instantly recognises the similarity. Some products that aim to integrate information from multiple components into a unified display refer to themselves as dashboards. Based on the metaphor of the instrument panel in a car, the computer, or "digital" version of a dashboard provides a business manager with the input necessary to "drive" the business. Highlights with colors similar to traffic lights, alerts, drill-downs, summaries, and graphics such as bar charts, pie charts, bullet graphs, sparklines and gauges are usually set in a portal-like environment that is often role-driven and customisable.

9.16.6.3 History

Historically, the idea of digital dashboards follows the work in the 1970s with the study of decision support systems. In the late 1990s with the surge of the web, digital dashboards as we know them today began appearing. Many systems were developed in-house by organisations to consolidate and display data already being gathered in various information systems throughout the organisation. Today, digital dashboard technology is available "out-of-the-box" with many software providers on the scene. Certain companies however still continue to do in-house development and maintenance of dashboard applications. For example, GE Aviation has developed a proprietary software/portal called "Digital Cockpit" to monitor the trends in aircraft spare parts business.

9.16.6.4 Benefits of Digital Dashboards

Most organisations have various departments all contributing to its overall success and thus it is important to be able to assess the progress of each department. Digital dashboards, which are a type of executive information system, allow managers to do just that. To gauge exactly how well an organisation is performing overall, digital dashboards allow you to capture and report specific data points from each department within the organisation, thus providing a "snapshot" of performance.

Some benefits of using digital dashboards include:

- visual presentation of performance measures
- ability to identify and correct negative trends
- measures efficiencies/inefficiencies
- ability to generate detailed reports showing new trends
- increases productivity
- ability to make more informed decisions based on collected BI (business intelligence)
- aligns strategies and organisational goals
- saves time over running multiple reports

9.17 DECISION SUPPORT SYSTEM VERSUS MANAGEMENT INFORMATION SYSTEM

The Decision Support System (DSS) is a special class of system which is used as a support decision making. The basic characteristic of the decision support system is that it is based on some tool, technique or model. The DSS could be an internal part of the MIS. When the decision making need is in real time dynamic mode, all such systems are designed to read, measure, monitor, evaluate, analyze and act as per the decision guidance embedded in the system. The MIS designer has to look for all situations and design the DSS for integration in the system. The MIS would become more useful if the decision making is made person-independent and executed with well-designed DSS. When the decision situation requires multidimensional analysis using the internal and external data, then such decision support systems are kept out of the main MIS design scope. Most of these situations call for the use of models and the nature of decision is strategic, decision for planned activity.

Decisions like new product launch, price revision, appointing new dealers, change of product design or change in the manufacturing process are strategic decisions which require critical analysis of data, careful evaluation of various alternatives and selecting one of them for implementation on the given criteria.

The decision support system plays a dominant role in the management information system, as a support to decision making.

Sales managers typically rely on management information systems (MIS) to produce sales analytic reports. These reports contain sales performance figure by products line, sales person, sales region, and so on. A decision support system (DSS), on the other hand, would also interactively show a sales manager the effects on sales performance of changes in a variety of factors (such as promotion expenses and sales compensation). The DSS could then use several criteria (such as expected gross margin and market share) to evaluate and rank several alternative combinations of sales performance factors.

Table 9.2: Comparing DSS and MIS

	MIS	DSS
Decision Support Provided	Provide information about the performance of the organization	Provide information and decision support techniques to analyse specific problem or opportunities
Information form and Frequency	Periodic, exception, demand, and push reports and responses	Interactive enquiries and responses
Information Format	Pre-specified, fixed format	Ad hoc, flexible and adaptable format
Information Processing Methodology	Information provided by extraction and manipulation of business data	Information provided by analytic and modeling of business data

Using DSS involves an interactive modeling process. For example, using a DSS software package for decision support may result in a series of displays in response to alternative what-if changes entered by a manager. This differs from the demand response of MIS, since decision makers are not demanding pre-specified information. Rather, they are exploring possible alternatives. Thus, they do not have to specify their information need in advance. Instead they use a DSS to find the information they need to help make a decision. That is the essence of DSS concept.

9.18 THE FUTURE OF DECISION SUPPORT SYSTEMS

A host of new tools and technologies are adding new capabilities to DSS/ESS and will reshape DSS developments in organizations. They include hardware and mathematical software developments, artificial intelligence techniques, the data warehouse/ multidimensional databases (MDDB), data mining, online analytical processing (OLAP), enterprise resource planning (ERP) systems, intelligent agents, telecommunication technologies such as World Wide Web technologies, the Internet, and corporate intranets.

9.18.1 Single User Decision Support Systems

Ever-increasing computing power makes it possible to solve a large-scale mathematical optimization model in a fraction of a second. The size of the problem solvable by commercial software is virtually unlimited, only dependent upon the size of random access memory of computers and the user's patience.

Moreover, several solvers are built into the spreadsheet programs such as Microsoft Excel and Borland's Quattro-Pro, along with the capabilities of linking to databases and graphical user interfaces. With the increasing trend of national and global communication networking, single user DSS will increasingly become a part of organization-wide distributed decision-making (DDM) systems. The DDM system consists of several single user DSS that work together and independently to make a sequential decision such as joint production/ marketing decisions. DDM systems work as a mechanism for integrating a number of separate DSSs that coexist in an organization, facilitating group cooperation between several DSSs in a distributed environment, and meeting the specific needs of group planning and group decision making.

Notable developments that will significantly affect the future development of DSS are the data warehouse, data mining and intelligent agents. The data warehouse is a subject-oriented, integrated, time-variant, and non-volatile (read only) collection of a relational/ multidimensional database (MDDB) optimized for decision support, which is separated from operational databases. MDDB organizes data as an n-dimensional cube so that users deal with multidimensional data views such as product, region, sales, time, etc. with a faster query response time. Data mining, also known as Knowledge Data Discovery, refers to discovering hidden patterns/trends/classes/insights/relationships from data, and it attempts to automatically extract knowledge from the in large databases, either in the data warehouse or elsewhere (e.g., spreadsheets, transaction processing system files, etc.).

Intelligent agents (known also as intelligent interfaces, or adaptive interfaces) research is an emerging interdisciplinary research area involving researchers from such fields as expert systems, DSS, cognitive science, psychology, databases, etc. Intelligent agent's research has contributed to the emergence of a new generation of active and intelligent DSS and EIS. The active DSS will be equipped with the tools (stimulus agents) that will act as experts, servants, or mentors to decide when and how to provide advice and criticism to the user, while the user formulates and inquires about its problems under the continuous stimulus of electronic agents. The essence of active decision support activities includes monitoring decision making processes and stimulating creative ideas through carrying out insightful conversations with decision makers.

9.18.2 Knowledge-based Decision Support Systems (Intelligent DSS)

An increasing number of systems are incorporating domain knowledge, modelling, and analysis systems to provide users the capability of intelligent assistance. Knowledge base modules are being used to formulate problems and decision models, and analyse and interpret the results. Some systems are adding knowledge-based modules to replace human judgments. Managerial judgements have been used to ascertain (assess) future ur.certainty and to select assumptions on which decision models can be based.

Some decisions are both knowledge and data intensive. Consequently, a large amount of data usually requires considerable efforts for their interpretation and use.

The knowledge-based DSS include a knowledge management component which stores and manages a new class of emerging AI tools such as machine learning and case-based reasoning and learning. These tools can obtain knowledge from prior data, decisions and examples (cases), and contribute to the creation of DSS to support repetitive, complex real-time decision making. Machine learning refers to computational methods/tools of a computer system to learn from experience (past solutions), data and observations, and consequently alter its behaviour, triggered by a modification to the stored knowledge.

Artificial neural networks and genetic algorithms are the most notable approaches to machine learning. The role of knowledge-based DSS should be to allow experts to broaden and expand their expertise, not to narrow it down. Zeleny suggests the important future direction of knowledge-based DSS development in this way:

Trends toward narrow specialization of experts did take place in the society. The task of supportive expert systems should be to counteract such expertise-destructive trends, not to amplify them further. Observe that so-called 'knowledge explosion' (also 'information explosion' or 'information society') are misnomers limited to the structural ('surface') knowledge only. Even today we can aim for a 'renaissance man', especially with the help of expert systems constructed to move in the direction opposite of specialization, towards reintegration of knowledge, overcoming specialization, negating the 'experts' themselves.

9.18.3 The World Wide Web and Group/Organizational/Global DSS

The World Wide Web is increasingly being used as the client-server platform of many business organizations due to its network and platform-independence and very low software/installation/maintenance costs. More and more groupware will be inextricably tied to Internet technology. Especially, the World Wide Web is becoming an infrastructure for the next generation of decision support systems and groupware applications. Many groupware products, such as Lotus Development's Domino and Microsoft's Exchange, are integrating more Internet protocols into them.

Microsoft's next version of Office suite is expected to completely remove the boundaries between the World Wide Web and groupware. Many companies are applying groupware technology to increase business-to-business collaborations (e.g. collaborations among the company, its customers, and its suppliers, a.k.a. super workgroup software) over intranets and extranets. Another development in the information systems area is the growing importance of enterprise resources planning (ERP) systems. ERP systems are a new generation of information systems packages that integrate information and information-based processes within and across functional areas in an organization. ERP has focused primarily on processing of transaction data resulting in the creation of the extensive, organizational databases of an organization that may consist of individual business units across the globe. The extensive databases created by the ERP system provide the platform for decision support, data warehousing, data mining, and executive support systems.

Integrated solutions provided by the ERP system are attributable to the use of the common database. As we enter the age of the global village where geographical and temporal boundaries are shrinking rapidly, global DSS are emerging as the new frontiers in management information systems area. Over the next decade, DSS will focus on teams, work groups, and distributed, decentralized organizational structures. Consequently, many organizations will increasingly design and implement group/organizational/global DSS. Global management support systems (MSS) will emerge as a key element in management decision making and as an essential weapon against global competitors.

Supporting global business activities is becoming a most important and extremely complex task. To effectively cope with multinational managerial problems such as multiple currency management, foreign exchange risk management, global tax management and global consolidated reporting, global DSS are not enough. It is essential to develop an integrated global MSS which integrates EIS, artificial neural networks, ES with knowledge base captured from numerous experts in the same subject area as well as from a variety of specialists in international financial management, international accounting, international tax areas, and so forth.

9.18.4 Conclusion

Decision support systems are a form of management information systems used by management to aid decision making process. The complex problems that DSS are out to solve are often very poorly defined with a high level of uncertainty about the true nature of the problem, the various responses which the management could undertake or the likely impact of those actions. Many decision support systems have been developed so that they support implementation on a wide range of hardware. As there are several field in human endeavour so are there likely to be models and types of decision making systems. Aside from generalised decision support systems applicable to all, there are very specific decision support systems that address a particular subject or discipline. These types and models commonly have their strengths and weaknesses, but they all have the same concept of presenting a decision maker with variety of decisions to choose from based on the individual need of the managers.

SUMMARY

Decision Support Systems constitute a class of computer-based information systems including knowledge-based systems that support decision-making activities.

A decision support system is a way to model data and make quality decisions based upon it. Making the right decision in business is usually based on the quality of your data and your ability to sift through and analyse the data to find trends in which you can create solutions and strategies for growth.

According to Keen, the concept of decision support has evolved from two main areas of research: the theoretical studies of organisational decision making done at the Carnegie Institute of Technology during the late 1950s and early 1960s, and the technical work on interactive computer systems, mainly carried out at the Massachusetts Institute of Technology in the 1960s.

As with the definition, there is no universally-accepted taxonomy of DSS either. Different authors propose different classifications. Also, different authors identify different components in a DSS. DSS systems are not entirely different from other systems and require a structured approach.

There are several ways to classify DSS applications. Not every DSS fits neatly into one category, but a mix of two or more architecture in one.

DSS is extensively used in business and management. Executive dashboard and other business performance software allow faster decision making, identification of negative trends, and better allocation of business resources.

A GDSS is an interactive computer-based system that facilitates users finding (partial) solutions to semi-structured problems. A GDSS uses a set of decision makers working together as a group.

Business Intelligence (BI) refers to technologies, applications and practices for the collection, integration, analysis, and presentation of business information and sometimes to the information itself.

LADSS or **Land Allocation Decision Support System** is an agricultural land use planning tool being developed at The Macaulay Institute.

Spatial Decision Support Systems (SDSS) is developed in parallel with the concept of Decision Support Systems (DSS).An SDSS is an interactive computer.

Self Service Software (SSS) is a subset within the Knowledge Management software category and which contains a range of software that specialises in the way information, process rules and logic are collected, framed within an organised taxonomy, and accessed through decision support interviews.

In management information systems, a **dashboard** is an executive information system user interface that (similar to an automobile's dashboard) is designed to be easy to read.

Information documents confirm that a transaction has taken place or informs about one or various transactions. For example, a bank transfer slip with details of the transfer, or a breakdown of credit card payments that accompanies the credit card bill.

A wide variety of information can be extracted from a database using a database management system and user-oriented fourth generation languages. These queries can provide lists of all transactions processed during a specific time period, or error reports with a list of erroneously processed transactions.

EXERCISES

1. What is the relationship between information systems and decision making?
2. How does an IS support decision making?
3. What are different types of decisions?
4. How decision making process works?
5. Explain the various levels of decision making.
6. What is Decision Support System?
7. What are the various definitions of DSS by researchers?
8. What are the components of DSS software?
9. What is the structure of DSS software?
10. Explain the architecture of a generic DSS application.
11. What is Model-Based Management System?
12. What do you mean by query language and where is it used?
13. What are the features of Database Management System?
14. What is DSS? How does it differ from MIS?
15. How can DSS support unstructured or semi-structured decision making?
16. What are the basic characteristics of a DSS?
17. List various types of DSS.
18. What are various ways to classify DSS applications?
19. Explain various components of DSS in brief.
20. List some popular DSS applications.
21. What are group decision support systems (GDSS)?
22. What is business intelligence?
23. What are land allocation decision support systems?
24. Explain special decision support systems.
25. What is self service software?
26. Explain the concept of dashboards?
27. Explain some of the future uses of DSS.

❑

Executive Support Systems 10

10.1 INTRODUCTION

Many senior managers find that direct on-line access to organizational data is helpful. Information systems have long been used to gather and store information, to produce specific reports for workers, and to produce aggregate reports for managers. However, senior managers rarely use these systems directly, and often find the aggregate information to be of little use without the ability to explore underlying details.

An Executive Support System (ESS) is a tool that provides direct on-line access to relevant information in a useful and navigable format. Relevant information is timely, accurate, and actionable information about aspects of a business that are of particular interest to the senior manager. The useful and navigable format of the system means that it is specifically designed to be used by individuals with limited time, limited keyboarding skills, and little direct experience with computers. An ESS is easy to navigate so that managers can identify broad strategic issues, and then explore the information to find the root causes of those issues.

Executive Support Systems differ from traditional information systems in the following ways:

- are specifically tailored to executive's information needs
- are able to access data about specific issues and problems as well as aggregate reports
- provide extensive on-line analysis tools including trend analysis, exception reporting & "drill-down" capability
- access a broad range of internal and external data
- are particularly easy to use (typically mouse or touchscreen driven)
- are used directly by executives without assistance
- present information in a graphical form

These and other features of ESS are discussed in this chapter, along with the working and architecture of these systems.

10.2 EXECUTIVE SUPPORT SYSTEM

Executive Support System (ESS), also known as Executive Information System (EIS), is designed to facilitate senior management in making key strategic decisions. An ESS is software which allows companies to sort their data into summarised reports. These reports enable executive-level management access to reports from all area of the business including billing, cost accounting, staff, scheduling and more.

Executive level management need to be able to make informed decisions quickly and decisively and don't want to be wasting their time shifting through irrelevant information. An ESS can supply the summarized information executives need and yet provide the opportunity to **drill down** to more detail if necessary.

An executive's needs are always changing and new dilemmas emerge on a daily basis, thus it is crucial for the ESS to be flexible and easy to manage. ESS uses graphical presentation as it is much easier for the end user to understand the information.

An **Executive Information Systems** (EIS) is a type of management information system intended to facilitate and support the information and decision making needs of senior executives by providing easy access to both internal and external information relevant to meeting the strategic goals of the organization. It is commonly considered as a specialized form of a Decision Support System (DSS) and otherwise referred to as an ***Executive Support System*** (**ESS**).

ESS addresses non-routine decisions requiring judgement, evaluation, and insight because there is no agreed-upon procedure for arriving at a solution. Senior managers use ESS to make decisions. ESS serves at the strategic of the organization. ESS creates a generalized computing and communications environment rather than providing any fixed application or specific capability. ESSs are designed to incorporate data about external events such as new tax laws or competitors, but they also draw summarised information from internal MIS and DSS. It provides critical information in easy-to-use displays to top and middle management. They filter, compress, and track critical data, emphasizing the reduction of time and effort required to obtain information useful to executives. For example, top executives may use touch screen terminals to instantly view text and graphics displays that highlight key areas of organizational and competitive performance.

ESS are targeted at management needs to quickly assess the status of a business or section of business. These packages are aimed firmly at the type of business user who needs instant and up to date understanding of critical business information to aid decision making.

The idea behind an ESS is that information can be collated and displayed to the user without manipulation or further processing. The user can then quickly see the status of his chosen department or function, enabling them to concentrate on decision making. Generally an ESS is configured to display data such as order backlogs, open sales, purchase order backlogs, shipments, receipts and pending orders. This information can then be used to make executive decisions at a strategic level.

The emphasis of the system as a whole is the easy to use interface and the integration with a variety of data sources. It offers strong reporting and data mining capabilities which can provide all the data the executive is likely to need. Traditionally the interface was menu driven with either reports, or text presentation. Newer systems, and especially the newer Business Intelligence systems, which are replacing ESS, have a dashboard or scorecard type display.

10.3 PURPOSE OF ESS

The primary purpose of an Executive Support System is to support managerial learning about an organization, its work processes, and its interaction with the external environment. Informed managers can ask better questions and make better decisions. Firms with an ESS designed to maintain managers' "mental models" were less effective than firms with an ESS designed to build or enhance managers' knowledge.

A secondary purpose for an ESS is to allow timely access to information. All of the information contained in an ESS can typically be obtained by a manager through traditional methods. However, the resources and time required to manually compile information in a wide variety of formats, and in response to ever changing and ever more specific questions usually inhibit managers from obtaining this information. Often, by the time a useful report can be compiled, the strategic issues facing the manager have changed, and the report is never fully utilized.

Timely access also influences learning. When a manager obtains the answer to a question, that answer typically sparks other related questions in the manager's mind. If those questions can be posed immediately, and the next answer retrieved, the learning cycle continues unbroken. Using traditional methods, by the time the answer is produced, the context of the question may be lost, and the learning cycle will not continue.

A third purpose of an ESS is commonly misperceived. An ESS has a powerful ability to direct management attention to specific areas of the organization or specific business problems. Some managers see this as an opportunity to discipline subordinates. Some subordinates fear the directive nature of the system and spend a great deal of time trying to outwit or discredit it. Neither of these behaviours is appropriate or productive. Rather, managers and subordinates can work together to determine the root causes of issues highlighted by the ESS.

The powerful focus of an ESS is due to the maxim "what gets measured gets done." Managers are particularly attentive to concrete information about their performance when it is available to their superiors. This focus is very valuable to an organization if the information reported is actually important and represents a balanced view of the organization's objectives.

Misaligned reporting systems can result in inordinate management attention to things that are not important or to things which are important but to the exclusion of other equally important things. For example, a production reporting system might lead managers to emphasize volume of work done rather than quality of work. Worse yet, productivity might have little to do with the organization's overriding customer service objectives.

10.4 CONTENTS OF ESS

A general answer to the question of what data is appropriate for inclusion in an Executive Information System is "whatever is interesting to executives." While this advice is rather simplistic, it does reflect the variety of systems currently in use. Executive Information Systems in government have been constructed to track data about Ministerial correspondence, case management, worker productivity, finances, and human resources to name only a few. Other sectors use ESS implementations to monitor information about competitors in the news media and databases of public information in addition to the traditional revenue, cost, volume, sales, market share and quality applications.

Frequently, ESS implementations begin with just a few measures that are clearly of interest to senior managers, and then expand in response to questions asked by those managers as they use the system. Over time, the presentation of this information becomes stale, and the information diverges from what is strategically important for the organization. A "Critical Success Factors" approach is recommended by many management theorists. Practitioners such as Vandenbosch found that:

While our efforts usually met with initial success, we often found that after six months to a year, executives were almost as bored with the new information as they had been with the old. A strategy we developed to rectify this problem required organizations to create a report of the month. That is, in addition to the regular information provided for management committee meetings, the CEO was charged with selecting a different indicator to focus on each month.

While the above indicates that selection of data for inclusion in an ESS is difficult, there are several guidelines that help to make that assessment. A practical set of principles to guide the design of measures and indicators to be included in an ESS is presented below.

1. ESS measures must be easy to understand and collect. Wherever possible, data should be collected naturally as part of the process of work. An ESS should not add substantially to the workload of managers or staff.
2. ESS measures must be based on a balanced view of the organization's objective. Data in the system should reflect the objectives of the organization in the areas of productivity, resource management, quality and customer service.
3. Performance indicators in an ESS must reflect everyone's contribution in a fair and consistent manner. Indicators should be as independent as possible from variables outside the control of managers.
4. ESS measures must encourage management and staff to share ownership of the organization's objectives. Performance indicators must promote both team-work and friendly competition. Measures will be meaningful for all staff; people must feel that they, as individuals, can contribute to improving the performance of the organization.
5. ESS information must be available to everyone in the organization. The objective is to provide everyone with useful information about the organization's performance. Information that must remain confidential should not be part of the ESS or the management system of the organization.
6. ESS measures must evolve to meet the changing needs of the organization.

10.5 THE ROLE OF ESS IN THE ORGANIZATION

Executives often face information overload and must be able to separate the chaff from the wheat in order to make the right decision. On the other hand, if the information they have is not detailed enough they may not be able to make the best decision. An ESS can supply the summarized information executives need and yet provide the opportunity to drill down to more detail if necessary.

As technology advances, ESS are able to link data from various sources both internal and external to provide the amount and kind of information executives find useful. As common software programs include more options and executives gain experience using these programs, they're turning to them as an easy way to manipulate information. Many executives are also turning to the Web to provide the flexibility they need.

They provide executive information in a readily accessible, interactive format using graphics based queries on summarized and detailed data. They are also used to analyse, compare and highlight trends to help govern the strategic direction of a company. They are commonly integrated with operational systems, giving managers the facility to drill down to find out further information on a problem. It usually allows summary over the entire organisation and also allows drilling down to specific levels of detail. Thus they described as an MIS for executive use.

They are designed to the individual to let chief executive officers of organisations tie in to all levels of the organisation. They are very expensive to run and require extensive staff support to operate.

ESS helps managers with unstructured problems, focusing on the information needs of senior management. Combining data from internal and external sources, ESS creates a generalised computing environment that can be focused and applied to a changing array of problems. ESS helps senior executives monitor organizational performance, track activities of competitors, spot problems, identify opportunities, and forecast trends.

Contemporary ESS can bring together data from all parts of the organization and allow managers to select, access and tailor them as needed using easy-to-use desktop analytical tools and on-line data displays. Use of systems has migrated down several organizational levels so that the executive and any subordinates are able to look at the same data in the same way.

Today's systems try to avoid the problem of data overload so uncommon in paper reports because the data can be filtered or viewed in graphical format (if the user so chooses). ESSs have the ability to drill down (the ability to move from summary data to lower and lower levels of detail). The ability to drill down is useful not only to senior managers but also to employees at lower levels of organization who need to analyse data. OLAP tools for analysing large databases provide this capability.

A major challenge in building ESS has been to integrate data from systems designed for very different purposes so that the senior executives can review organizational performance from a firm-wide perspective. In the traditional firm, which typically had hundreds or even thousands of incompatible systems, pulling such information together and making sense out of it was a major task. Today, properly configured and implemented enterprise systems can provide managers with timely, comprehensive and accurate firm-wide information. ESS based on such data can be considered logical extensions of enterprise system functionality.

External data, including data from the Web, are now more easily available in many ESS, as well. Executives need a wide range of external data from current stock market news to competitor information, industry trends, and even projected legislative action. Through their ESS, many managers have access to news services, financial market databases, economic information, and whatever other public data they may require.

Contemporary ESS includes tools for modeling and analysis. With only a minimum of experience, most managers find that they can use these tools to create graphic comparisons by data, by time, region, product, price range, and so on.

ESS must be designed so that high-level managers and others can use them without much training. One area that merits special attention is the determination of executive information requirements. ESS need to have some facility for the environmental scanning. A key information requirement of managers at the strategic level is the capability to detect signals of problems in the organizational environment that indicate strategic threats and opportunities. The ESS needs to be designed so that both external and internal sources of information can be used for environmental scanning purposes.

ESS potentially could give top executives the capability of examining other manager's work without their knowledge, so there may be some resistance to ESS at the lower levels of organization. Implementation of ESS should be carefully managed to neutralize such opposition.

In recent years, the term ESS has lost popularity in and the terms "business intelligence" and "online analytical processing" are often used for these types of applications.

10.6 ESS COMPONENTS

The components of an ESS can typically be classified as:

1. Hardware: When talking about hardware for an ESS environment, we should focus on the hardware that meet executive's needs. The executive must be put the first and the executive's needs must be defined before the hardware can be selected. The basic computer hardware needed for a typical ESS includes four components:

(i) *Input data-entry devices.* These devices allow the executive to enter, verify, and update data immediately;

(ii) *The central processing unit* (CPU), which is the kernel because it controls the other computer system components;

(iii) *Data storage files.* The executive can use this part to save useful business information, and this part also help the executive to search historical business information easily;

(iv) *Output devices* which provide a visual or permanent record for the executive to save or read. This device refers to the visual output device or printer. In addition, with the advent of local area networks (LAN), several executive information system products for networked workstations became available. These systems require less support and less expensive computer hardware. They also increase access of the ESS information to many more users within a company.

2. Software: Choosing the appropriate software is vital to design an effective ESS. Therefore, the software components and how they integrate the data into one system are very important. The basic software needed for a typical executive information system includes four components:

(i) *Text base software.* The most common form of text is probably documents;

(ii) *Database.* Heterogeneous databases residing on a range of vendor-specific and open computer platforms help executives access both internal and external data;

(iii) *Graphic base.* Graphics can turn volumes of text and statistics into visual information for executives. Typical graphic types are: time series charts, scatter diagrams, maps, motion graphics, sequence charts, and comparison-oriented graphs (i.e., bar charts);

(*iv*) *Model base*. The executive information system models contain routine and special statistical, financial, and other quantitative analysis.

Perhaps a more difficult problem for executives is choosing from a range of highly technical software packages. Ease of use, responsiveness to executives' requests, and price are all reasonable considerations. Further, it should be considered whether the package can run on existing hardware.

3. *Interface:* An ESS needs to be efficient to retrieve relevant data for decision makers, so the interface is very important. Several types of interfaces can be available to the ESS structure, such as scheduled reports, questions & answers, menu driven, command language, natural language, and input & output.

It is crucial that the interface must fit the decision maker's decision-making style. If the executive is not comfortable with the information questions & answers style, the ESS will not be fully utilized. The ideal interface for an executive support system would be simple to use and highly flexible, providing consistent performance, reflecting the executive's world, and containing help information and error messages.

4. *Telecommunication:* As decentralizing is becoming the current trend in companies, telecommunications will play a pivotal role in networked information systems. Transmitting data from one place to another has become crucial for establishing a reliable network. In addition, telecommunications within an ESS can accelerate the need for access to distributed data.

10.7 ESS CHARACTERISTICS

ESSs are intended as decision support tools for senior managers. Since these strategic decisions are based on a wide range of input information, they always need to be well integrated with operational systems in a business.

A number of definitions have been put forward to describe ESS. While a definition is useful, in a complex area such as ESSs a better understanding is obtained by looking at their characteristics.

Some of these are given below:

- Executive support systems are end-user computerised information systems operated directly by executive managers. They utilise newer computer technology in the form of data sources, hardware and programs, to place data in a common format, and provide fast and easy access to information.
- They focus on helping executives assimilate information quickly to identify problems and opportunities. In other words, ESSs help executives track their critical success factors.
- Each system is tailored to the needs and preferences of an individual user, and information is presented in a format which can most readily be interpreted.
- They provide summary information to monitoring of business performance. This is often achieved through measures known as 'critical success factors' or 'key performance indicators' (KPIs). These will be displayed in an easy-to-interpret form such as a graph showing their variation through time. If a KPI falls below a critical preset value, the system will notify the manager through a visible or audible warning.

- They are used mainly for strategic decision making, but may also provide features that relate to tactical decision making.
- They provide a drill-down feature which gives a manager the opportunity to find out more information necessary to take a decision or discover the source of a problem. E.g. a manager with multinational manufacturing problem might find from the ESS that a particular country is underperforming in production. He could drill down to see which particular factory was responsible for this.
- They provide analysis tools.
- They must be integrated with other facilities to help manage the solving of problems and the daily running of the business. These include electronic mail and scheduling and calendar facilities.
- They integrate data from a wide range of information sources, including company and external sources such as market and competitor.
- They have to be designed according to the needs of managers who do not use computers frequently. They should be intuitive and easy to learn.

All these facilities require integration with operational data. Since this information is commonly stored in the ERP systems, these are often integrated with ESS or have ESS functions built in.

Although these characteristics apply to all ESSs, each individual system can potentially differ in scope, nature, purpose and content, depending on the environment in which it is implemented.

10.8 CAPABILITIES OF EXECUTIVE SUPPORT SYSTEMS

Most executive support systems offer the following capabilities:

- *Consolidation* – involves the aggregation of information and features simple roll-ups to complex groupings of interrelated information
- *Drill-down* – enables users to get details, and details of details, of information
- *Slice-and-dice* – looks at information from different perspectives
- *Digital dashboard* – integrates information from multiple components and presents it in a unified display.

10.9 WORKING OF ESS

Most executives have a number of extremely capable assistants who can produce written reports to meet the executive's information needs. The situation is now changing. Computer experienced business professionals may occupy a senior executive position and these professionals will be more open to and may even expect support from computer-based systems.

Top executives in the design of an executive information system for the chief executives, get the information they need from many sources including letters, memos, periodicals, and reports. Produced manually as well as by computer systems, other sources of executive information are meetings, telephone calls, and social activities. External information requirements are competitor information, regulatory information, regional economic indicators, customer preference to services, quality or service being produced etc. Much of the top executive information comes from non-computer sources. Company generated information has not played a primary role in meeting many top executive's information needs.

Many executives have a network of people to collect information. Secretarial assistance is also available to them to gather data, arrange meetings with experts, etc. They have staff to analyse problems, evaluate alternatives and make recommendations to them. ESS provides database support and interaction facility for the executive to try out his ideas and solutions.

The goal of Computer-Based ESS (CBESS) is to provide top executives with immediate and easy access to selective information about key factors that are critical to accomplishing a firm's strategic objectives. Hence, ESS is easy to operate and understand. Graphic displays are used extensively and immediate access to internal and external databases is provided. It provides information about the current status and projected trends for key factors selected by the top executives. ESS combines features of information reporting systems and DSS, but they are tailored to the strategic information needs of the top management. Top executives need information to support their strategic planning and control responsibilities. The goal of ESS is to provide the top management with immediate and easy access to information about a firm's critical success factors, i.e. key factors that are critical to accomplishing an organization's strategic objectives.

Software packages are now available that support ESS on mainframe, mini-computer and micro-computer systems. The use of ESS is expected to grow rapidly, as more top executives come to recognize their feasibility and benefits and as less expensive micro-computer based ESS become more available.

10.10 ARCHITECTURE OF ESS

Executive work stations depend on the mainframes or minicomputer systems for access to ESS software. This package works with DBMS and telecommunication software to provide easy access to internal, external and special database with almost instantaneous response times. A modeling capability to evaluate alternatives for decision support may also be provided, in the forms tailored to the preference of the executives using the system. Most ESSs stress on the use of graphics display that are easy to understand and communicate early and quickly.

Executives, through ESS can 'drill down' quickly to lower levels of detail in areas of particular interest to them. The drill down capability is related to the hypertext methodology, which allows end users to interactively retrieve related piece of information from text databases. Many ESS packages for microcomputers are based on hypertext technology. An ESS also stresses trend analysis and exception reporting. Thus, an executive can quickly discover the direction where the key factors are heading and the extent that critical factors are deviating from expected results.

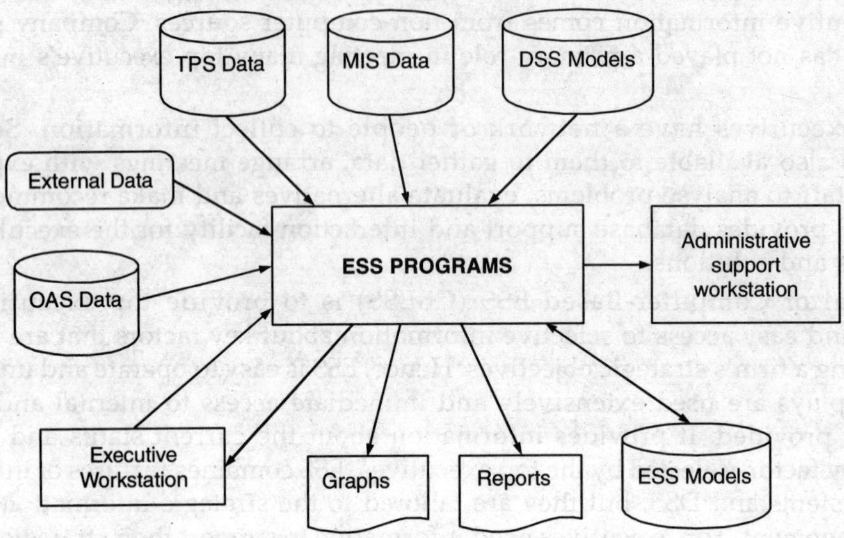

Figure 10.1: Architecture of Executive Support Systems

As depicted in Figure 10.1, an ESS accepts data from all of the other types of information systems. It also accepts from those who support the executive, such as administrative assistants. The primary goal of an ESS is to obtain data from variety of sources, integrate and aggregate that data, and display the resulting information in frequently standardised formats. Thus, an ESS integrates many sources of data. Timeliness and accuracy are vital in ESS.

10.11 IMPLEMENTATION OF AN EFFECTIVE ESS

Implementation of an effective ESS requires clear consensus on the objectives and measures to be monitored in the system and a plan for obtaining the data on which those measures are based. The sections below outline a methodology for achieving these two results. As noted earlier, successful ESS implementations generally begin with a simple prototype rather than a detailed planning process. For that reason, the proposed planning methodologies are as simple and scope-limited as possible.

10.11.1 Establishing Measures & ESS Requirements

Most organizations have a number of high-level objectives and direction statements that help to shape organizational behaviour and priorities. In many cases, however, these direction statements have not yet been linked to performance measures and targets. As well, senior managers may have other critical information requirements that would not be reflected in a simple analysis of existing direction statements. Therefore it is essential that ESS requirements be derived directly from interaction with the senior managers who will use the systems. It is also essential that practical measures of progress towards organizational objectives be established during these interactions.

Measures and ESS requirements are best established through a three-stage process. First, the ESS team solicits the input of the most senior executives in the organization in order to establish a broad, top-down perspective on ESS requirements. Second, interviews are conducted with the managers who will be most directly involved in the collection, analysis, and monitoring of data in the system to assess bottom-up requirements. Third, a summary of results and recommendations is presented to senior executives and operational managers in a workshop where final decisions are made.

10.11.1.1 Interview Format

The focus of the interviews would be to establish all of the measures managers require in the ESS. Questions would include the following:

1. What are the five most important pieces of information you need to do your job?
2. What expectations does the Board of Directors have for you?
3. What results do you think the general public expects you to accomplish?
4. On what basis would consumers and customers judge your effectiveness?
5. What expectations do other stakeholders impose on you?
6. What is it that you have to accomplish in your current position?

10.11.1.2 Senior Management Workshop

Since considerable variability is expected in the results of these interviews, analysis and synthesis are required to identify recurring themes and important differences of opinion. This information is brought forward to a senior management workshop.

The purpose of the senior management workshop is twofold. First, the workshop will be an opportunity to educate senior management on appropriate use of Executive Information Systems, to address some of the cultural issues raised earlier and to deal directly with resistance to the system. Second, managers at the workshop will be asked to reach agreement on an initial set of measures to be included in the ESS. The education component of the workshop is most effective if integrated with the work of creating measures.

The initial set of measures will be established within a framework derived from the interview process. Three to five categories of measures will be established prior to the workshop, and managers will be asked to select or create three to five technically feasible measures for each category. Each of the proposed measures will be subjected to the questions proposed by Meyer to determine if they are appropriate.

Technical staff will attend to respond to feasibility questions as they arise, and to improve their understanding of the ESS requirements.

10.11.1.3 Obtaining Critical Data Linking ESS Measures to Data Sources

Data to support the information requirements of senior managers will likely be dispersed across the organization's information systems and external sources. Some data may not be currently available at all, and collection mechanisms will have to be constructed.

The ESS project team, augmented by technical experts, and working from the requirements established in the senior management workshop will develop a list of required data elements and link them with appropriate data sources. The team will then establish requirements for data extraction from each of these systems and spin off appropriate systems development projects.

10.11.2 ESS Design, Prototyping & Evaluation

After information sources have been established, and projects are underway to permit ongoing extraction of that information, attention will turn to the design of the ESS itself. There are several components to consider.

1. Hardware: First, an inventory of computers used by executives must be taken to determine what upgrades are necessary and what hardware limitations will be imposed on the ESS design. Included in this inventory will be an assessment of network storage and communication facilities.

2. Data Repository: The second component is the design of the data repository in which summary data from all sources will be stored. The design of this repository is critical because it must allow managers to easily extract and explore data along numerous dimensions. Standard relational designs may not be sufficient or practical for this application.

3. ESS Interface Prototype: A third component is the design of the actual ESS interface that senior managers will interact with. Screens and commands must be exceedingly obvious and easy to use so that senior managers can quickly access the benefits of the system without wasting a lot of time learning how to use it. Ease of use can be ensured by developing a prototype system with "sample" data, and watching senior managers as they interact with the prototype. Two to three iterations of prototype redesign and testing with four senior managers would be sufficient to ensure that the system is easy to use.

10.11.3 Characteristics of Successful ESS Implementations

Following are the characteristics of successful implementations:

1. Find an Appropriate Executive Champion: ESS projects that succeed do so because at least one member of the senior management team agrees to champion the project. The executive champion need not fully understand the technical issues, but must be a person who works closely with all of the senior management team and understands their needs, work styles and their current methods of obtaining organizational information. The champion's commitment must include a willingness to set aside time for reviewing prototypes and implementation plans, influencing and coaching other members of the senior management team, and suggesting modifications and enhancements to the system.

2. Deliver a Simple Prototype Quickly: Executives judge a new ESS on the basis of how easy it is to use and how relevant the information in the system is to the current strategic issues in the organization. As a result, the best ESS projects begin as a simple prototype, delivered quickly, that provides data about at least one critical issue. If the information delivered is worth the hassle of learning the system, a flurry of requirements will shortly be generated by executives who like what they see, but want more. These requests are the best way to plan an ESS that truly supports the organization, and are more valuable than months of planning by a consultant or analyst.

One caveat concerning the simple prototype approach is that executive requests will quickly scatter to questions of curiosity rather than strategy in an organization where strategic direction and objectives are not clearly defined. A number of methods are available to support executives in defining business objectives and linking them to performance monitors in an ESS.

These are discussed further in the section on ESS and Organizational Objectives below.

3. Involve Your Information Systems Department: In some organizations, the motivation for an ESS project arises in the business units quite apart from the traditional information systems (IS) organization. Consultants may be called in, or managers and analysts in the business units may take the project on without consulting or involving IS. This is a serious mistake.

Executive Support Systems rely entirely on the information contained in the systems created and maintained by this department. IS professionals known best what information is available in an organization's systems and how to get it. They must be involved in the team. Involvement in such a project can also be beneficial to IS by giving them a more strategic perspective on how their work influences the organization.

4. Communicate & Train to Overcome Resistance: A final characteristic of successful ESS implementations is that of communication. Executive Support Systems have the potential to drastically alter the prevailing patterns of organizational communication and thus will typically be met with resistance. Some of this resistance is simply a matter of a lack of knowledge.

Training on how to use statistics and performance measures can help. However, resistance can also be rooted in the feelings of fear, insecurity and cynicism experienced by individuals throughout the organization. These attitudes can only be influenced by a strong and vocal executive champion who consistently reinforces the purpose of the system and directs the attention of the executive group away from unproductive and punitive behaviours.

10.12 BARRIERS TO EFFECTIVENESS OF ESS

There are many ways in which an ESS can fail. Dozens of high profile, high cost ESS projects have been cancelled, implemented and rarely used, or implemented and used with negative results. An ESS is a high risk project precisely because it is intended for use by the most powerful people in an organization. Senior managers can easily misuse the information in the system with strongly detrimental effects on the organization. Senior managers can refuse to use a system if it does not respond to their immediate personal needs or is too difficult to learn and use.

10.12.1 Unproductive Organizational Behaviour Norms

Issues of organizational behaviour and culture are perhaps the most deadly barriers to effective Executive Information Systems. Because an ESS is typically positioned at the top of an organization, it can create powerful learning experiences and lead to drastic changes in organizational direction. However, there is also great potential for misuse of the information.

The key barrier to ESS effectiveness, therefore, is the way in which the organization uses the information in the system. Managers must be aware of the dangers of statistical data, and be skilled at interpreting and using data in an effective way. Even more important is the manager's ability to communicate with others about statistical data in a non-defensive, trustworthy, and constructive manner. Argyris suggests a universal human tendency towards strategies that avoid embarrassment or threat, and towards feelings of vulnerability or incompetence. These strategies include:

- stating criticism of others in a way that you feel is valid but also in a way that prevents others from deciding for themselves
- failing to include any data that others could use to objectively evaluate your criticism
- stating your conclusions in ways that disguise their logical implications and denying those implications if they are suggested

To make effective use of an ESS, mangers must have the self-confidence to accept negative results and focus on the resolution of problems rather than on denial and blame. Since organizations with limited exposure to planning and targeting, data-based decision-making, statistical process control, and team-based work models may not have dealt with these behavioural issues in the past, they are more likely to react defensively and reject an ESS.

10.12.2 Technical Excellence

An interesting result from the Vandenbosch & Huff study was that the technical excellence of an ESS has an inverse relationship with effectiveness. Systems that are technical masterpieces tend to be inflexible, and thus discourage innovation, experimentation and mental model development.

Flexibility is important because an ESS has such a powerful ability to direct attention to specific issues in an organization. A technical masterpiece may accurately direct management attention when the system is first implemented, but continue to direct attention to issues that were important a year ago on its first anniversary. There is substantial danger that the exploration of issues necessary for managerial learning will be limited to those subjects that were important when the ESS was first developed. Managers must understand that as the organization and its work changes, an ESS must continually be updated to address the strategic issues of the day.

A number of explanations as to why technical masterpieces tend to be less flexible are possible. Developers who create a masterpiece ESS may become attached to the system and consciously or unconsciously dissuade managers from asking for changes. Managers who are uncertain that the benefits outweigh the initial cost of a masterpiece ESS may not want to spend more on system maintenance and improvements. The time required to create a masterpiece ESS may mean that it is outdated before it is implemented.

While usability and response time are important factors in determining whether executives will use a system, cost and flexibility are paramount. A senior manager will be more accepting of an inexpensive system that provides 20% of the needed information within a month or two than with an expensive system that provides 80% of the needed information after a year of development. The manager may also find that the inexpensive system is easier to change and adapt to the evolving needs of the business. Changing a large system would involve throwing away parts of a substantial investment. Changing the inexpensive system means losing a few weeks of work. As a result, fast, cheap, incremental approaches to developing an ESS increase the chance of success.

10.12.3 Technical Problems

Paradoxically, technical problems are also frequently reported as a significant barrier to ESS success. The most difficult technical problem — that of integrating data from a wide range of data sources both inside and outside the organization — is also one of the most critical issues for ESS users. A marketing vice-president, who had spent several hundred thousand dollars on an ESS, attended a final briefing on the system. The technical experts demonstrated the many graphs and charts of sales results, market share and profitability. However, when the vice-president asked for a graph of market share and advertising expense over the past ten years, the system was unable to access historical data. The project was cancelled in that meeting.

The ability to integrate data from many different systems is important because it allows managerial learning that is unavailable in other ways. The president of a manufacturing company can easily get information about sales and manufacturing from the relevant VPs. Unfortunately, the information the president receives will likely be incompatible, and learning about the ways in which sales and manufacturing processes influence each other will not be easy. An ESS will be particularly effective if it can overcome this challenge, allowing executives to learn about business processes that cross organizational boundaries and to compare business results in disparate functions.

Another technical problem that can kill ESS projects is usability. Senior managers simply have the choice to stop using a system if they find it too difficult to learn or use. They have very little time to invest in learning the system, a low tolerance for errors, and initially may have very little incentive to use it. Even if the information in the system is useful, a difficult interface will quickly result in the manager assigning an analyst to manipulate the system and print out the required reports. This is counter-productive because managerial learning is enhanced by the immediacy of the question - answer learning cycle provided by an ESS. If an analyst is interacting with the system, the analyst will acquire more learning than the manager, but will not be in a position to put that learning to its most effective use.

Usability of Executive Information Systems can be enhanced through the use of prototyping and usability evaluation methods. These methods ensure that clear communication occurs between the developers of the system and its users. Managers have an opportunity to interact with systems that closely resemble the functionality of the final system and thus can offer more constructive criticism than they might be able to after reading an abstract specification document. Systems developers also are in a position to listen more openly to criticisms of a system since a prototype is expected to be disposable. Several evaluation protocols are available including observation and monitoring, software logging, experiments and benchmarking, etc. The most appropriate methods for ESS design are those with an ethnographic flavour because the experience base of system developers is typically so different from that of their user population (senior executives).

10.13 MISALIGNMENT BETWEEN OBJECTIVES & ESS

The powerful ability of an ESS to direct organizational attention can be destructive if the system directs attention to the wrong variables. There are many examples of this sort of destructive reporting. Grant, Higgins and Irving report the account of an employee working under a misaligned reporting system.

I like the challenge of solving customer problems, but they get in the way of hitting my quota. I'd like to get rid of the telephone work. If (the company) thought dealing with customers was important, I'd keep it; but if it's just going to be production that matters, I'd gladly give all the calls to somebody else.

Traditional cost accounting systems are also often misaligned with organizational objectives, and placing these measures in an ESS will continue to draw attention to the wrong things. Cost accounting allocates overhead costs to direct labour hours. In some cases the overhead burden on each direct labour hour is as much as 1000%. A manager operating under this system might decide to sub-contract 100 hours of direct labor at $20 per hour. On the books, this $2,000 saving is accompanied by $20,000 of savings in overhead. If the sub-contractor charges $5,000 for the work, the book savings are $2,000 + $20,000 - $5,000 = $17,000. In reality, however, the overhead costs for an idle machine in a factory do not go down much at all. The sub-contract actually ends up costing $5,000 - $2,000 = $3,000.

10.14 ESS PROJECT TEAM

The process of establishing organizational objectives and measures is intimately linked with the task of locating relevant data in existing computer systems to support those measures. Objectives must be specific and measurable, and data availability is critical to measuring progress against objectives.

Since there is little use in defining measures for which data is not available, it is recommended that an ESS project team including technical staff be established at the outset. This cross-functional team can provide early warning if data is not available to support objectives or if senior manager's expectations for the system are impractical.

A preliminary ESS project team might consist of as few as three people. An ESS Project Leader organizes and directs the project. An Executive Sponsor promotes the project in the organization, contributes senior management requirements on behalf of the senior management team, and reviews project progress regularly. A Technical Leader participates in requirements gathering, reviewing plans, and ensuring technical feasibility of all proposals during ESS definition.

As the focus of the project becomes more technical, the ESS project team may be complemented by additional technical staff who will be directly involved in extracting data from legacy systems and constructing the ESS data repository and user interface.

10.15 FACTORS INFLUENCING THE FUNCTIONING OF ESS

Following are the factors influencing the functioning of ESS:

1. Organizational setup: The policies and procedures followed in an organization have a great impact in the manner management information systems are implemented in an organization. For e.g. If a company believes in centralization of authority and hesitates to delegate authority then ESS will be provided for the top most managers in the organization. On the contrary if the company is of the opinion that decentralization of authority will help in better governance then ESS will be introduced in a separate manner. They will be given to a couple of managers even at the junior level if it is believed that it will aid them in one way or the other.

2. Other factors: The internal and external factors connected directly or indirectly with the organization will have their own say in establishing executive information systems in an organization. For e.g. if matters relating to compliance of tax, audit and other statutory matters are handled by the senior managers only then ESS will be targeted to them alone.

On the other hand if clerical labour is also involved in the same procedures ESS they will also be able to access ESS and render the necessary supporting functions to the senior managers. Whatever be the case the role of men in an organization plays a crucial part in implementation and functioning of executive information systems.

The success of executive information systems lies in two issues. Firstly the information should properly reach the concerned executives. Secondly they should accord importance and act upon it. Above all whatever they say must be given due consideration by the decision making authority. The system must be a fool proof one. Only then the results will reveal the true picture.

10.16 ESS AND ORGANIZATIONAL OBJECTIVES

A number of writers have discovered that one of the major difficulties with ESS implementations is that the information contained in the ESS either does not meet executive requirements, or meets executive requirements, but fails to guide the organization towards its objectives. As discussed earlier, organizations that are comfortable in establishing and working towards Specific, Measurable, Achievable, and Consistent (SMAC) objectives will find it easier to create an ESS that actually drives organizational performance. Yet even these organizations may have difficulty because their stated objectives do not represent all of the things that are important.

Crockett suggests a four step process for developing ESS information requirements based on a broader understanding of organizational objectives. The steps are: (1) identify critical success factors and stakeholder expectations, (2) document performance measures that monitor the critical success factors and stakeholder expectations, (3) determine reporting formats and frequency, and (4) outline information flows and how information can be used. Crockett begins with stakeholders to ensure that all relevant objectives and critical success factors are reflected in the ESS.

Kaplan and Norton suggest that goals and measures need to be developed from each of four perspectives: financial, customer, internal business, and innovation and learning. These perspectives help managers to achieve a balance in setting objectives, and presenting them in a unified report exposes the tough tradeoffs in any management system. An ESS built on this basis will not promote productivity while ignoring quality, or customer satisfaction while ignoring cost.

Meyer raises several questions that should be asked about measurement systems for teams. Four are appropriate for evaluating objectives and measures represented in an ESS. They are:

- Are all critical organizational outcomes tracked?
- Are all "out-of-bounds" conditions tracked? (Conditions those are serious enough to trigger a management review.)
- Are all the critical variables required to reach each outcome tracked?
- Is there any measure that would not cause the organization to change its behaviour?

In summary, proper definition of organizational objectives and measures is a helpful precondition for reducing organizational resistance to an ESS and is the root of effective ESS use. The benefits of an ESS will be fully realized only when it helps to focus management attention on issues of true importance to the organization.

10.17 ESS AND ORGANIZATIONAL CULTURE

Henry Mintzberg has argued that impersonal statistical data is irrelevant to managers. John Dearden argued that the promise of real-time management information systems was a myth and would never be of use to top managers. Grant, Higgins, and Irving argue that computerized performance monitors undermine trust, reduce autonomy and fail to illuminate the most important issues.

Many of these arguments against ESSs have objective merit. Managers really do value the tangible titbits of detail they encounter in their daily interactions more highly than abstract numerical reports. Rumours suggest a future, while numbers describe a past. Conversations are rich in detail and continuously probe the reasons for the situation, while statistics are vague approximations of reality. When these vague approximations are used to intimidate or control behaviour rather than to guide learning, they really do have a negative impact on the organization.

Yet both of these objections point to a deeper set of problems — the assumptions, beliefs, values and behaviours that people in the organization hold and use to respond to their environment. Perhaps senior managers find statistical data to be irrelevant because they have found too many errors in previous reports? Perhaps people in the organization prefer to assign blame rather than discover the true root cause of problems. The culture of an organization can have a dramatic influence on the adoption and use of an Executive Information System. The following cultural characteristics will contribute directly to the success or failure of an ESS project.

10.17.1 Learning Vs Blaming

A learning organization is one that seeks first to understand why a problem occurred, and not who is to blame. It is a common and natural response for managers to try to deflect responsibility for a problem on to someone else. An ESS can help to do this by indicating very specifically who failed to meet a statistical target, and by how much. A senior manager, armed with ESS data, can intimidate and blame the appropriate person. The blamed person can respond by questioning the integrity of the system, blaming someone else, or even reacting in frustration by slowing work down further.

In a learning organization, any unusual result is seen as an opportunity to learn more about the business and its processes. Managers who find an unusual statistic explore it further, breaking it down to understand its components and comparing it with other numbers to establish cause and effect relationships. Together as a team, management uses numerical results to focus learning and improve business processes across the organization. An ESS facilitates this approach by allowing instant exploration of a number, its components and its relationship to other numbers.

10.17.2 Continuous Improvement Vs Crisis Management

Some organizations find themselves constantly reacting to crises, with little time for any proactive measures. Others have managed to respond to each individual crisis with an approach that prevents other similar problems in the future. They are engaged in a continual cycle of improving business practices and finding ways to avoid crisis.

Crisis in government are frequently caused by questions about organizational performance raised by an auditor, the Minister, or members of the Opposition. An ESS can be helpful in responding to this sort of crisis by providing instant data about the actual facts of the situation. However, this use of the ESS does little to prevent future crisis.

An organizational culture in which continual improvement is the norm can use the ESS as an early warning system pointing to issues that have not yet reached the crisis point, but are perhaps the most important areas on which to focus management attention and learning. Organizations with a culture of continuous improvement already have an appetite for the sort of data an ESS can provide, and thus will exhibit less resistance.

10.17.3 Team Work Vs Hierarchy

An ESS has the potential to substantially disrupt an organization that relies upon adherence to a strict chain of command. The ESS provides senior managers with the ability to micro-manage details at the lowest levels in the organization. A senior manager with an ESS report who is surprised at the individual results of a front-line worker might call that person directly to understand why the result is unusual. This could be very threatening for the managers between the senior manager and the front-line worker. An ESS can also provide lower level managers with access to information about peer performance and even the performance of their superiors.

Organizations that are familiar with work teams, matrix managed projects and other forms of interaction outside the chain of command will find an ESS less disruptive. Senior managers in these organizations have learned when micro-management is appropriate and when it is not. Middle managers have learned that most interactions between their superiors and their staff are not threatening to their position. Workers are more comfortable interacting with senior managers when the need arises, and know what their supervisor expects from them in such an interaction.

10.17.4 Data-based Decisions Vs Decisions in a Vacuum

The total quality movement, popular in many organizations today, emphasizes a set of tools referred to as Statistical Process Control (SPC). These analytical tools provide managers and workers with methods of understanding a problem and finding solutions rather than allocating blame and passing the buck. Organizations with training and exposure to SPC and analytical tools will be more open to an ESS than those who are suspicious of numerical measures and the motives of those who use them.

It should be noted that data-based decision making does not deny the role of intuition, experience, or negotiation amongst a group. Rather, it encourages decision-makers to probe the facts of a situation further before coming to a decision. Even if the final decision contradicts the data, chances are that an exploration of the data will help the decision-maker to understand the situation better before a decision is reached. An ESS can help with this decision-making process.

10.17.5 Information Sharing Vs Information Hoarding

Information is power in many organizations, and managers are motivated to hoard information rather than to share it widely. For example, managers may hide information about their own organizational performance, but jump at any chance to see information about performance of their peers.

A properly designed ESS promotes information sharing throughout the organization. Peers have access to information about each other's domain; junior managers have information about how their performance contributes to overall organizational performance. An organization that is comfortable with information sharing will have developed a set of "good manners" for dealing with this broad access to information. These behavioural norms are key to the success of an ESS.

10.17.6 Specific Objectives Vs Vague Directions

An organization that has experience developing and working toward Specific, Measurable, Achievable and Consistent (SMAC) objectives will also find an ESS to be less threatening. Many organizations are uncomfortable with specific performance measures and targets because they believe their work to be too specialized or unpredictable. Managers in these organizations tend to adopt vague generalizations and statements of the exceedingly obvious in place of SMAC objectives that actually focus and direct organizational performance. In a few cases, it may actually be true that numerical measures are completely inappropriate for a few aspects of the business. In most cases, managers with this attitude have a poor understanding of the purpose of objective and target-setting exercises. Some business processes are more difficult to measure and set targets for than others. Yet almost all business processes have at least a few characteristics that can be measured and improved through conscientious objective setting.

10.18 ADVANTAGES AND DISADVANTAGES OF ESS

Much of the value of ESS is found in their flexibility. These systems put data and tools in the hands of executives without addressing specific problems or imposing solutions. Executives are free to shape the problems as necessary, using the system as an extension of their own thinking processes. These are not decision-making systems; rather they are tools to aid execution in making decisions.

The most valuable benefit of ESS is their ability to analyse, compare, and highlight trends. The easy use of graphics allows the user to look at more data in less time with greater clarity and insight than paper-based systems can provide. In the past, executives obtained the same information by taking up days and weeks of their staff's valuable time. By using ESS, those staffs and the executives themselves are freed up for the more creative analysis and decision making in their jobs. ESS capabilities for drilling down and highlighting trends also may enhance the quality of such analysis and can speed up the decision making.

Executives are using ESS to monitor performance more successfully in their own areas of responsibility. Some companies are using these systems to monitor key performance indicators for the entire firm and to measure firm performance against changes in the external environment. The timeliness and availability of the data result in the needed actions being identified and taken earlier. Problems can be handled before they become too damaging; opportunities can also be identified earlier. These systems can thus help organizations move towards a 'sense and respond' strategy.

Some more advantages of ESS are as follows:

- As more executives come up through the ranks, they are more familiar with and rely more on technology to assist them with their jobs. Executive Support Systems don't provide executives with ready- made decisions. They provide the information that helps them make their decisions.
- Executives use that information, along with their experience, knowledge, education, and understanding of the corporation and the business environment as a whole, to make their decisions.
- Executives are more inclined to want summarized data rather than detailed data (even though the details must be available). ESS rely on graphic presentation of information because it's a much quicker way for busy executives to grasp summarized information
- It provides timely delivery of company summary information.
- It provides better understanding of information
- It filters data for management.
- It provides system for improvement in information tracking
- It offers efficiency to decision makers.

Some more disadvantages of ESS are as follows:

- Functions are limited, cannot perform complex calculations.
- Hard to quantify benefits and to justify implementation of an ESS.
- Executives may encounter information overload.
- System may become slow, large, and hard to manage.
- Difficult to keep current data.
- May lead to less reliable and insecure data.
- Small companies may encounter excessive costs for implementation.
- Highly skilled personnel requirement cannot be fulfilled by the small business.

10.19 ESS APPLICATIONS

ESS enables executives to find those data according to user-defined criteria and promote information-based insight and understanding. Unlike a traditional management information system presentation, ESS can distinguish between vital and seldom-used data, and track different key critical activities for executives, both which are helpful in evaluate if the company is meeting its corporate objectives. After realizing its advantages, people have applied ESS in many areas, especially, in manufacturing, marketing, and finance areas.

1. Manufacturing: Basically, manufacturing is the transformation of raw materials into finished goods for sale, or intermediate processes involving the production or finishing of semi-manufactures. It is a large branch of industry and of secondary production. Manufacturing operational control focuses on day-to-day operations, and the central idea of this process is effectiveness and efficiency. To produce meaningful managerial and operational information for controlling manufacturing operations, the executive has to make changes in the decision processes. ESS provides the evaluation of vendors and buyers, the evaluation of purchased materials and parts, and analysis of critical purchasing areas. Therefore, the executive can oversee and review purchasing operations effectively with

ESS. In addition, because production planning and control depends heavily on the plant's data base and its communications with all manufacturing work centres, ESS also provides an approach to improve production planning and control.

2. Marketing: In an organization, marketing executives' role is to create the future. Their main duty is managing available marketing resources to create a more effective future. For this, they need make judgments about risk and uncertainty of a project and its impact on company in short term and long term. To assist marketing executives in making effective marketing decisions, an ESS can be applied. ESS provides an approach to sales forecasting, which can allow the market executive to compare sales forecast with past sales. ESS also offers an approach to product price, which is found in venture analysis.

The market executive can evaluate pricing as related to competition along with the relationship of product quality with price charged. In summary, ESS software package enables marketing executives to manipulate the data by looking for trends, performing audits of the sales data, and calculating totals, averages, changes, variances, or ratios. All of these sales analysis functions help marketing executives to make final decisions.

3. Medical: Executive information systems are coming to hospitals a little later than they did to other industries, but there appears to be tremendous interest at the executive level. These systems provide information that is more timely, relevant, and concise than paper-based systems. With the changing environment in healthcare, the ability to monitor key areas of the operation in near real time is critical.

Hospitals are unusually information-rich environments. In fact, managements consider hospitals to be perfect models of information-based organizations. Within the hospital environment, ESS can gather up-to-the-minute information from all vertical areas of the enterprise—finance, nursing, clinical areas, medical staff—to provide executives with a high-level, real-time perspective on indicators and trends that affect business success.

In truth, all hospitals already have some type of executive information system; every paper report, procedural update, telephone message, fax, or memo that executives receive serves as part of an information system. At worst, the system may provide information that is outdated, inaccurate, or open to misinterpretation. At best, it offers a temporary, static analysis of data that cannot meet the needs of the fast-moving, highly competitive atmosphere of today's healthcare operation.

4. Financial: A financial analysis is one of the most important steps to companies today. The executive (Eddie Frame) needs to use financial ratios and cash flow analysis to estimate the trends and make capital investment decisions. An ESS is a responsibility-oriented approach that integrated planning or budgeting with control of performance reporting, and it can be extremely helpful to finance executives. Basically, ESS focuses on accountability of financial performance and it recognizes the importance of cost standards and flexible budgeting in developing the quality of information provided for all executive levels. ESS enables executives to focus more on the long-term basis of current year and beyond, which means that the executive not only can manage a sufficient flow to maintain current operations but also can figure out how to expand operations that are contemplated over the coming years. Also, the combination of ESS and EDI environment can help cash managers to review the company's financial structure so that the best method of financing for an accepted capital project can be concluded. In addition, the ESS is a good tool to help the executive to review financial ratios, highlight financial trends and analyze a company's performance and its competitors.

5. Government: Executive Information Systems in government have been constructed to track data about Ministerial correspondence, case management, worker productivity, finances, and human resources to name only a few. Other sectors use ESS implementations to monitor information about competitors in the news media and databases of public information in addition to the traditional revenue, cost, volume, sales, market share and quality applications.

10.20 FUTURE TRENDS IN ESS

The future of executive support systems will not be bound by mainframe computer systems. This trend allows executives escaping from learning different computer operating systems and substantially decreases the implementation costs for companies. Because utilizing existing software applications lies in this trend, executives will also eliminate the need to learn a new or special language for the ESS package. Future executive support systems will not only provide a system that supports senior executives, but also contain the information needs for middle managers. The future executive support systems will become diverse because of integrating potential new applications and technology into the systems, such as incorporating artificial intelligence (AI) and integrating multimedia characteristics and ISDN technology into an ESS.

SUMMARY

An Executive Support System (ESS) is a tool that provides direct on-line access to relevant information in a useful and navigable format. Relevant information is timely, accurate, and actionable information about aspects of a business that are of particular interest to the senior manager. The useful and navigable format of the system means that it is specifically designed to be used by individuals with limited time, limited keyboarding skills, and little direct experience with computers. An ESS is easy to navigate so that managers can identify broad strategic issues, and then explore the information to find the root causes of those issues.

Executive Support Systems meet the needs of corporate executives by providing them with vast amounts of information quickly and in graphical form to help them make effective decisions. ESS must be flexible, easy to use, and contain both internal and external sources of information.

EXERCISES

1. Explain executive support systems. What is the purpose of developing these systems?
2. What are the contents of executive support systems?
3. Explain the role of ESS in an organization's working.
4. What are various components in ESS?
5. Explain various characteristics of ESS.

6. Explain the working of ESS.
7. Explain the architecture of ESS.
8. How is an ESS implemented effectively?
9. What are the barriers to effective ESS implementation?
10. List the characteristics of an organization which determine the success of ESS.
11. What are various advantages and disadvantages of using an ESS?
12. Explain various ESS applications.

❑

CASE STUDY OF INFORMATION SYSTEMS 11

11.1 ACCOUNTING INFORMATION SYSTEMS

Accounting information systems (AIS) are the oldest and the most widely used information systems in business. AISs record and report business transactions and other economic events. These systems are based on the double-entry book-keeping concept, which is hundreds of years old than other, more recent accounting concepts such as responsibility accounting and profitability accounting. Computer-based accounting systems record and report the flow of funds through an organization on a historical basis and produce important financial statements such as balance sheets and income statements.

Operational accounting system emphasises legal and historical record keeping and the production of accurate financial statements. Typically, these systems include transaction-processing systems such as order processing, inventory control, accounts receivable, and accounts payable, payroll and general ledger systems. Management accounting systems focus on the planning and control of business operations. They emphasize cost accounting reports, the development of financial budgets and projected financial statements, and analytical reports comparing actual to targeted performance. In a nutshell, accounting information system that provides information related to the accounting activities in an organization. As a result of the important and spectacular development of informatics and information technology, wide-spread automatization can be observed relating to accounting work-processing. This is proved by the appearance and spread of the different user software. Nowadays accounting software packages have a quite wide market – there are numerous software programs supporting book-keeping, reporting, recording economic events or processing – and in many cases they support the activity of the enterprise as an organic part of a complex, up-to-date, integrated information system.

11.2 THE CONCEPT OF THE INFORMATION SYSTEM

Accounting, as a closed-system recording (which is the collection of procedures, methods, techniques, legal regulations, rules and experts), includes the identification, tracking, measuring, recording, processing, storing, systemizing, valuing, controlling and publishing of the phenomena influencing the property, financial and profit status of the enterprise, ensuring the conditions of continuous, undisturbed activity. In this regulated, closed system the accounting information system records the economic events influencing the enterprise, then processes them – according to the demands – and conveys them to the persons or units responsible for decisions. In addition, the system greatly contributes to preparing different reports, financial statements, working out an expense management system and compiling controlling reports.

Accounting is – at micro-level – i.e. the level of the enterprise – the sum of activities which are done within the framework of an accounting information system by the experts of the enterprise.

11.3 COMPONENTS OF AN ACCOUNTING INFORMATION SYSTEM

An accounting information system (AIS) is a structure that a business uses to collect, store, manage, process, retrieve and report its financial data so that it can be used by accountants, consultants, business analysts, managers, chief financial officers (CFOs), auditors and regulatory and tax agencies. In particular, specially trained accountants work with AIS to ensure the highest level of accuracy in a company's financial transactions and recordkeeping and to make financial data easily available to those who legitimately need access to it, all while keeping data intact and secure. This section will describe the primary components of an AIS and some of its real-life applications.

Accounting information systems generally consist of six main parts: people, procedures and instructions, data, software, information technology infrastructure and internal controls. Let's look at each component in detail.

11.3.1 People

The people in an AIS are simply the system users. Professionals who may need to use an organization's AIS include accountants, consultants, business analysts, managers, chief financial officers and auditors.

An AIS helps the different departments within a company work together. For example, management can establish sales goals for which staff can then order the appropriate amount of inventory. The inventory order notifies the accounting department of a new payable. When sales are made, sales people can enter customer orders, accounting can invoice customers, the warehouse can assemble the order, the shipping department can send it off, and the accounting department gets notified of a new receivable. The customer service department can then track customer shipments and the system can create sales reports for management. Managers can also see inventory costs, shipping costs, manufacturing costs and so on.

With a well-designed AIS, everyone within an organization who is authorized to do so can access the same system and get the same information. An AIS also simplifies getting information to people outside of the organization when necessary. For example, consultants might use the information in an AIS to analyze the effectiveness of the company's pricing structure by looking at cost data, sales data and revenue. Also, auditors can use the data to assess a company's internal controls, financial condition and compliance with the Sarbanes-Oxley Act (SOX).

The AIS should be designed to meet the needs of the people who will be using it. The system should also be easy to use and should improve, not hinder, efficiency.

11.3.2 Procedure and Instructions

The procedure and instructions of an AIS are the methods it u es for collecting, storing, retrieving and processing data. These methods will be both manual and automated, and the data can come from both internal sources (e.g., employees) and external sources (e.g., customers' online orders). Procedures and instructions will be coded into AIS software; they should also be "coded" into employees through documentation and training. Procedures and instructions must be followed consistently to be effective.

To store information, an AIS must have a database structure such as structured query language (SQL), a computer language commonly used for databases. The AIS will also need various input screens for the different types of system users and different types of data entry, as well as different output formats to meet the needs of different users and different types of information.

11.3.3 Data

The data contained in an AIS is all the financial information pertinent to the organization's business practices. Any business data that impacts the company's finances should go into an AIS. The data included in an AIS will depend on the nature of the business, but it may consist of the following:

- sales orders
- customer billing statements
- sales analysis reports
- purchase requisitions
- vendor invoices
- check registers
- general ledger
- inventory data
- payroll information
- timekeeping
- tax information

This data can then be used to prepare accounting statements and reports such as accounts receivable aging, depreciation/amortization schedules, trial balance, profit and loss, and so on. Having all this data in one place - in the AIS - facilitates a business's recordkeeping, reporting, analysis, auditing and decision-making activities. For the data to be useful, it must be complete, correct and relevant.

On the other hand, examples of data that would not go into an AIS include memos, correspondence, presentations and manuals. These documents might have a tangential relationship to the company's finances, but excluding the standard footnotes, they are not really part of the company's financial recordkeeping.

11.3.4 Software

The software component of an AIS is the computer programs used to store, retrieve, process and analyze the company's financial data. Before there were computers, AISs were manual, paper-based systems, but today, most companies are using computer software as the basis of the AIS. Small businesses might use Intuit's Quickbooks, Sage Peachtree Accounting, or Microsoft's Small Business Accounting but there are many others. Small to mid-sized businesses might use SAP's Business One. Mid-sized and large businesses might use Microsoft's Dynamics GP, Sage Group's MAS 90 or MAS 200, Oracle's Peoplesoft or Epicor Financial Management.

Quality, reliability and security are key components of effective AIS software. Managers rely on the information it outputs to make decisions for the company, and they need high-quality information to make sound decisions.

AIS software programs can be customized to meet the unique needs of different types of businesses. If an existing program does not meet a company's needs, software can also be developed in-house with substantial input from end users or can be developed by a third-party company specifically for the organization. The system could even be outsourced to a specialized company. For publicly traded companies, no matter what software program and customization options the business chooses, Sarbanes-Oxley regulations will dictate the structure of the AIS to some extent. This is because SOX regulations establish internal controls and auditing procedures that public companies must comply with.

11.3.5 Information Technology Infrastructure

Information technology infrastructure is just a fancy name for the hardware used to operate the accounting information system. Most of these hardware items are things a business would need to have anyway - they include personal computers, servers, printers, surge protectors, routers, storage media, and possibly a backup power supply. In addition to cost, factors to consider in selecting hardware include speed, storage capability and whether it can be expanded and upgraded. Perhaps most importantly, the hardware selected for an AIS must be compatible with the intended software. Ideally, it would be not just compatible, but optimal, a clunky system will be much less helpful than a speedy one. One way businesses can easily meet hardware and software compatibility requirements is by purchasing a turnkey system that includes both the hardware and the software that the business needs. Purchasing a turnkey system means, theoretically, that the business will get an optimal combination of hardware and software for its AIS.

A good AIS should also include a plan for maintaining, servicing, replacing and upgrading components of the hardware system, as well as a plan for the disposal of broken and outdated hardware so that sensitive data is completely destroyed.

11.3.6 Internal Controls

The internal controls of an AIS are the security measures it contains to protect sensitive data. These can be as simple as passwords or as complex as biometric identification. An AIS must have internal controls to protect against unauthorized computer access and to limit access to authorized users which includes some users inside the company. It must also prevent unauthorized file access by individuals who are allowed to access only select parts of the system. An AIS contains confidential information belonging not just to the company but also to its employees and customers. This data may include Social Security numbers, salary information, credit card numbers, and so on. All of the data in an AIS should be encrypted, and access to the system should be logged and surveilled. System activity should be traceable as well.

An AIS also needs internal controls that protect it from computer viruses, hackers and other internal and external threats to network security. Furthermore, it must be protected from natural disasters and power surges that can cause data loss.

11.4 TYPES OF ACCOUNTING INFORMATION SYSTEMS

Following are the types of accounting information systems:

(a) **General Ledger Systems** generate the company's income statements and balance sheets for the ledger entry data input and are responsible for managing new and old accounts in the company.

(b) **Asset Management Systems** maintain an inventory of the company's long-term assets and ensure that counting practices for the company assets comply with regulatory standards. The output of this system often becomes input to a general ledger system.

(c) **Order Entry Systems** capture and manage different kinds of data relating to a transaction, such as number of units sold, customer billing, credit history, sales tax and inventory levels. The output of this system is input to a number of other systems, such as accounts receivable and inventories management.

(d) **Accounts Receivable and Accounts Payable** capture and process data, such as creditor and customer billing information, payments received and owned, credit terms, account balances and payment schedules.

(e) **Inventory Control System** captures, processes and manages all data related to the company's inventory such as items in inventory, inventory levels and costs, accounting practices related to inventory maintenance, stock balance, and data on lost, damaged or returned goods.

(f) **Payroll Systems** capture and process data related to wages and salaries including taxes, other payroll deductions, employee benefits, overtime and like other functional systems.

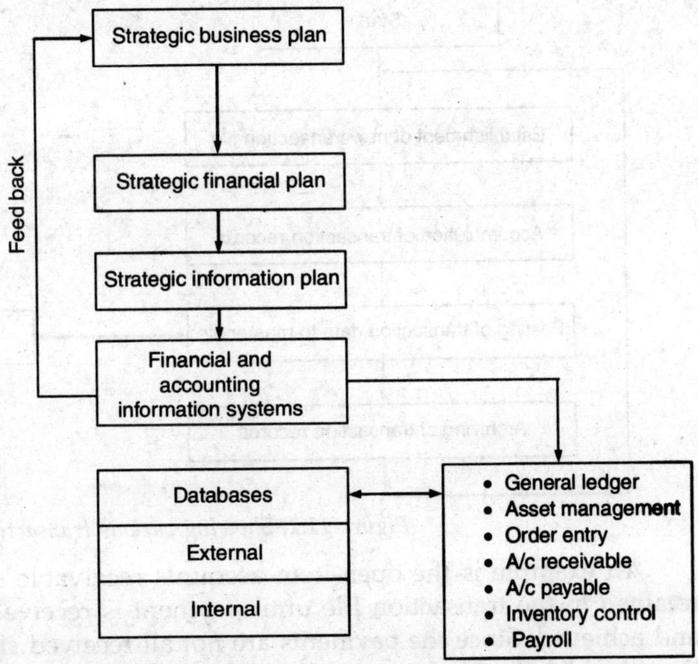

Figure 11.1: Process of Accounting Information Systems

In general the AIS is driven by strategic business plan and the strategic information plan related data as shown in Figure 11.1.

11.5 THE POSTING CYCLE

The posting is a regularly recurring operation. A general ledger system requires posting to be done at least once per year in time for closing of the books and the preparation of the annual financial statements, but often it is done more frequently to provide for interim statements and budget tracking. Other systems, such as accounts receivable and accounts payable require posting at least once per month, and possibly weekly. A payroll system would probably involve posting once per pay period such as weekly, or monthly, as the case may be. An inventory system would probably require the most frequent posting to control inventory levels properly; daily posting of inventory transactions is not uncommon.

Posting can usefully be understood in terms of a posting cycle as shown in Figure 11.2. It consists of the following steps:

- Establishment of a transaction file
- Accumulation of transaction records
- Posting of transaction data to the master file
- Archiving of the transaction records
- Purging of the transaction file

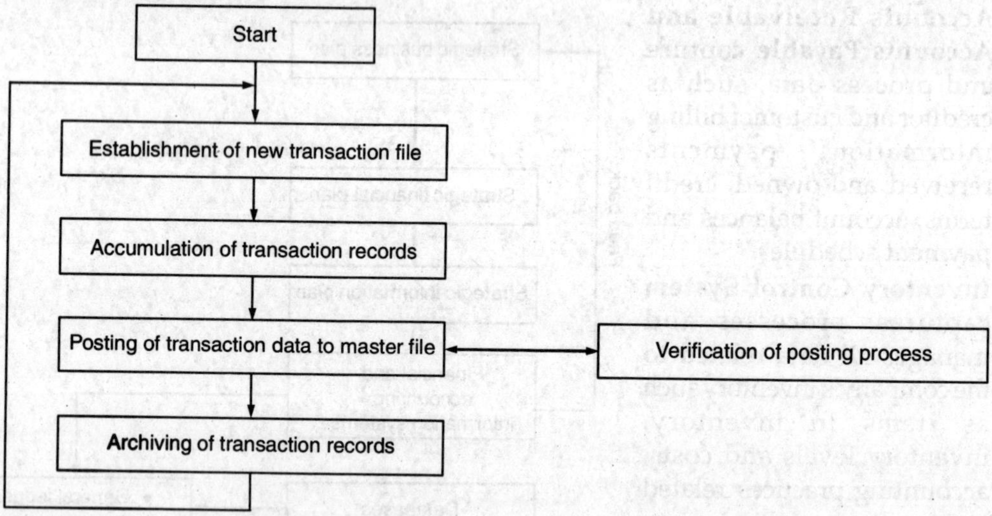

Figure 11.2: Showing various transaction processes

An example is the open-item accounts receivable system. Here, invoice records are retained in the transaction file until payment is received; at that point, they are detected and achieved. Since the payments are not all received simultaneously there is no point in time at which the whole transaction file could be purged and re-established. If the transaction remains open indefinitely posting to the master file takes on a somewhat different significance. In some cases, summarization of the transaction records is performed only when it is done each time from the transaction file, without any entry being made to the master file. In other cases, the summary figure is written to the master file; but only to provide a control balance and the detail remains in the transaction file. Individual transactions may remain in the transaction file during several postings, and some means is adopted for avoiding their being counted more than once; one commonly used technique is to 'flag' the transactions that they have already been included in the summary total. Open-item forward systems, which do conform to the classical posting pattern.

11.6 THE FUNCTION OF THE ACCOUNTING INFORMATION SYSTEM, ITS POSITION IN THE HIERARCHY OF THE ENTERPRISE

The accounting information system, i.e. the accounting process, can be defined as a subpart of the information system of the enterprise, and within it as a subpart of the information system of the management.

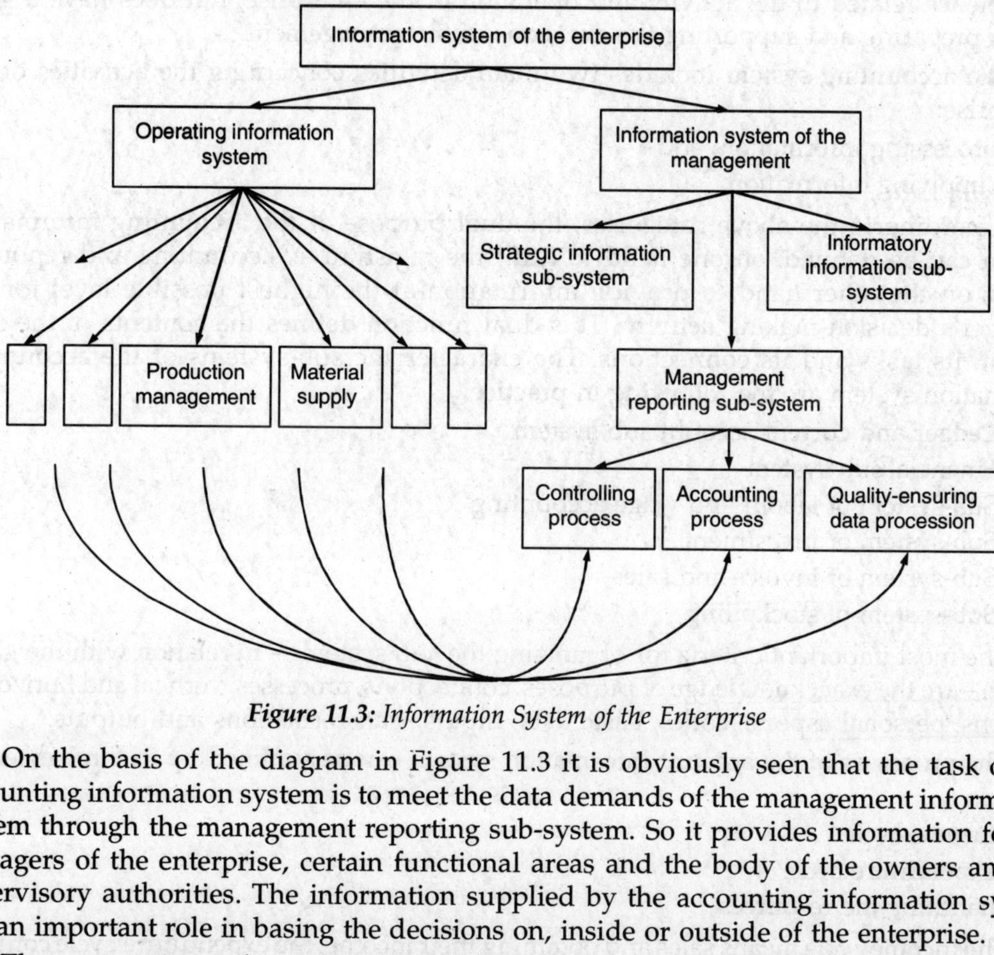

***Figure 11.3:** Information System of the Enterprise*

On the basis of the diagram in Figure 11.3 it is obviously seen that the task of the accounting information system is to meet the data demands of the management information system through the management reporting sub-system. So it provides information for the managers of the enterprise, certain functional areas and the body of the owners and the supervisory authorities. The information supplied by the accounting information system has an important role in basing the decisions on, inside or outside of the enterprise.

The accounting information system is in close connection with the management information department, the accounting and administration department, the inner control and the information technology team. The harmonic and efficient activity of these areas characterises the centre of the accounting information system, which provides for the basic data of the informational database.

The information system works within the enterprise and includes two, closely related sub-systems: a data-processing/information supplying sub-system and a decision-making sub-system. The data-processing system is responsible for acquiring, coding, storing, processing and forwarding the information necessary for the activity and operation. The task of the decisive sub-system is – on the basis of information from data-processing systems using them – to influence, directly or indirectly, with the management processes and the operation of the system. However, the decisive sub-system is special, as in practice it has "only" a pre-decisive, pro-decisive role.

Accounting, as the decisive sub-system of the information system, can have a special role because within the enterprise accounting as a functional area does not have decisive competence related to the activity and operation of the enterprise, but does have a great role in preparing and supporting the decisions of the management.

The accounting system includes two main activities concerning the activities of the enterprise:

- processing information; and
- supplying information.

According to the above categories, the dual purpose of the accounting information system can be defined: on one hand to fulfil the registrative, accounting and reporting duties; on the other hand to provide information at the highest possible level for the manager's decision-making activity. This dual function defines the contents of the sub-system, its tasks and its connections. The characteristic sub-systems of the accounting information system are the following in practice:

- Ledger and current account sub-system
- Financial sub-system
- Sub-system of labour and wage accounting
- Sub-system of investment
- Sub-system of invoice and sales
- Sub-system of stockpiling

The most important criteria for organizing the sub-systems – in relation with the given system – are the exact knowledge of purposes, connections, processes, vertical and horizontal relations, personal aspects, codes, basic data, inputs, transformations and outputs.

The processes of the account information system can be summed up in three essential groups:

- income cycle
- expenditure cycle
- handling the resources

The income cycle means sales and obtaining their income, the expenditure cycle contains the processes from getting the material to fulfilling the payment, and handling the sources means getting the sources, storing, using and optimizing them.

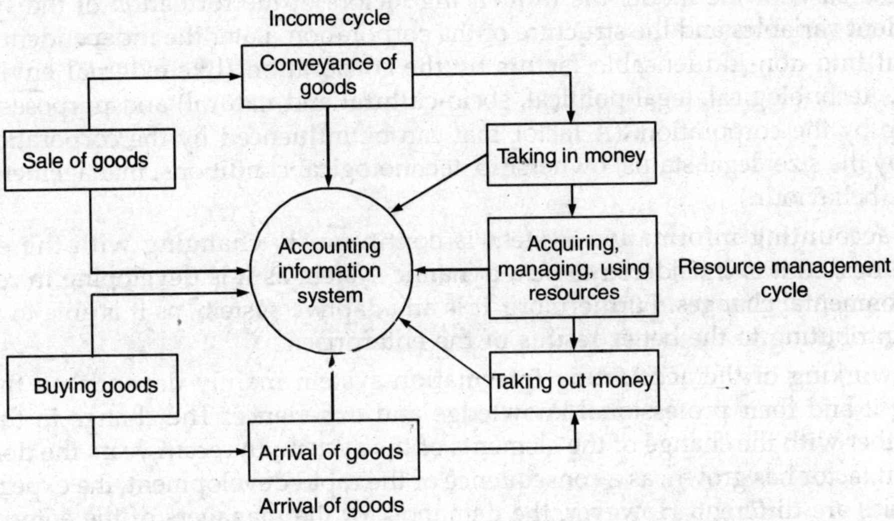

Figure 11.4: Process of Accounting Information System

The complete tracking of the economic processes can be realized if there is a complex and up-to-date database behind the above-mentioned processes.

11.7 THE ACCOUNTING INFORMATION SYSTEM AND ITS ENVIRONMENT

The accounting information system is the frame of practical accounting activity, as it tracks the events of the enterprise, supplies data for the managers' decisions, and organically contributes to the reports for the managers, to the financial statements, to compiling the expense management systems and last but not least to the controlling reports. The processes in the environment of the enterprise influence the elements of the accounting information system, too. Among the constituents of the accounting information system the human factor has an outstanding role (nowadays there are great demands concerning the employees' competence, expertness and experience) and those activities which belong to accounting (in brief, bookkeeping and reporting). The analysis of the system means the analysis of the system and also its environment for the sake of better and more complete knowledge.

Different models have been formed to illustrate the constituents of accounting information systems and the external effects influencing the system. The contingentalist attitude has been prevailing since the 1970s in the research of accounting and management control, as it was thought that an effort to form a situational explanation – starting from the analysis of the environment – can be useful in the research of these systems.

The early contingentialist model of the formation of accounting information systems was based on corporate theory:

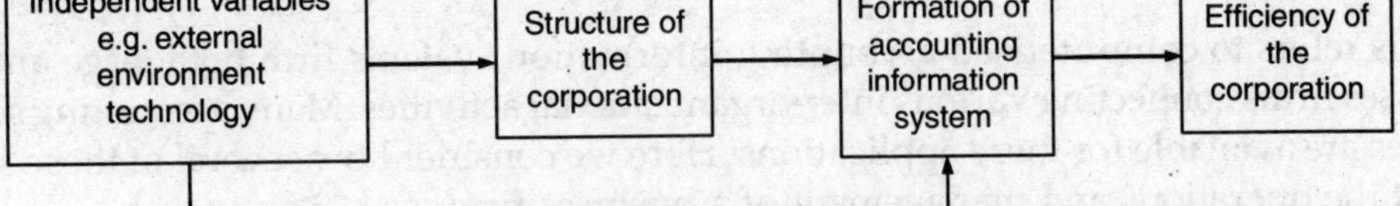

Figure 11.5: *The Early Contingentialist Model of Accounting Information Systems*

On the basis of the model the influencing factors of the formation of the system are independent variables and the structure of the corporation. Later the independent variables were split into non-influencable factors by the corporation (like external environment, economic, technological, legal-political, socio-cultural and natural) and purposes/strategy drawn up by the corporation. (A factor that can be influenced by the corporation can be defined by the size, legal status, ownership, technological conditions, management and the corporate behaviour.)

The accounting information system is continuously changing with the economic surroundings, so it is considered to be a dynamic system as it is developing in reaction to the environmental changes. Furthermore, it is an adaptive system, as it is able to react and adapt, contributing to the better results of the enterprise.

The working of the accounting information system mainly depends on the people operating it and their professional knowledge and experience. The change in the system goes together with the change of the elements of the system. In recent years the demand for the human factor has grown; as a consequence of the rapid development, the expected skills and abilities are different. However, the demands for the managers of the enterprises are not unified; they greatly depend on the special features of the enterprise.

The changes in the direct environment (processes within the enterprise) – and indirect (economic and social) have led to modifying the accounting information, the demands for it have also changed. New clients have appeared claiming the database created by the system and, in parallel, the contents of the required information have been modified, as well – the role of quality has risen.

In recent years the quality requirement has appeared more and more frequently in professional publications that define the requirements concerning accounting. The continuous development of the accounting information system usually does not belong to the primary purposes of the enterprise, as the management usually considers it too obvious that the information system is continuously increasing to meet the expectations. As a result, the development of the accounting information system is primarily defined from the side of requirements, so the quality demand changes concerning the accounting information, i.e. the output of the system, while newer demands may appear in relation with the process.

The development of the accounting information system is induced by the above-mentioned increase in demands, which may cause the modernization of the whole information system – if the enterprise can fulfil all necessary conditions. Regarding the increase and changes in demands, the primary purpose of development is improving quality; meeting this target is mainly supported by modern information technology. This is a serious job demanding time – and money – which is able to produce the required data at a newer and higher level.

11.8 INTERRELATIONSHIPS OF IMPORTANT ACCOUNTING INFORMATION SYSTEMS

This refers to computerised accounting information systems firm both large and small businesses firms connecting various inter-organizational activities. Many accounting software packages are available for these applications. Here we consider how several of these systems support the operations and management of a business firm.

(a) Order Processing. Order processing (or sales order processing) is an important transaction processing system, which captures and processes customer orders and produces invoices for customers and data needed for sales analysis and inventory control. In many firms, it also keeps track of the status of the customer orders until goods are delivered. Computer based sales order-processing systems provide a fast accurate and efficient method of reordering and screening customer orders and sales transactions. They also provide inventory control systems with information on accepted orders so that they can be filled as quickly as possible.

(b) Inventory Control. Inventory control systems process data reflecting changes to items in inventory. Once data about customer order is received from an order processing system, a computer-based inventory control system records changes to inventory levels and prepares appropriate shipping documents. Then, it may notify managers about items that need reordering and provides them with a variety of inventory status reports. Computer-based inventory control systems thus help a business to provide high-quality service to customers while minimizing the investment in inventory and inventory carrying costs. The integration of this system with other accounting information systems is based on the flow of transaction documents and also with other form of data files.

(c) Payroll. These systems receive and maintain data from employee time cards and other work records. Computer-based payroll systems help businesses to make prompt and accurate payments to their employees, as well as reports to management, employees and government agencies concerning earnings, taxes and other deductions. They also provide management with reports regarding labour costs and productivity.

11.9 THE ACCOUNTING INFORMATION SYSTEM IN PRACTICE

After the registration of a new firm at the court – which means the birth of the enterprise – in addition to the essential economic activity in close connection with it – the formation of the accounting information system has outstanding importance.

Concerning the accounting information system, the first important step is to decide how to realize the book-keeping of the enterprise:

- working within the enterprise (inner book-keeping)
- entrusting a book-keeping office (outer bookkeeping)

The choice is greatly influenced by the size of the enterprise, as well as its economic competence. A further emphatic aspect can be how to ensure the adequate flow of data, as the ability to react and decide thoughtfully greatly depends on the obtained information.

In the case of forming the accounting information system, among the requirements of the system I would draw attention to the conformity to the laws: both to the rules of accounting law and to conditions of the accounting policy (newly formed firms are obliged to prepare their accounting policy within 90 days after their formation) and to the registration and obligation to the tax authorities.

The most important purpose of the accounting information system is to promote the activity of the enterprise, to form a reliable and real picture of it. The accounting information system promotes the activity of the enterprise effectively in the case of the following points:

- preparing up-to-date statements,
- providing as much information as possible so that the data should be understandable not only for the experts (book-keepers),
- contributing to different statistics by means of the links of the system,
- tracking liquidity

Further questions may be asked in connection with the effective support of the economic activity concerning the accounting information system, e.g.:

- Does book-keeping support the system in controlling liquidity?
- What kind of income covers the expenses?

11.10 THE ACCOUNTING INFORMATION SYSTEM AND THE INFORMATION TECHNOLOGY

The spread of informatics has given rise to a completely new way of providing information. The development of information technology is a great help in accounting to manage the piles of data. In the 20th century the world-wide expansion of technology and informatics created the possibility of using the information obtained from the accounting information system consciously and efficiently.

As a consequence of automatization, nowadays accounting software (accounting software: a programme which makes accounting work processes easier and faster and which makes it possible to meet the information demand of the management) supports the accountants' work, helping to compile reports by recording and processing the events concerning the enterprise, (according to the law, since 30th April 2009 accounting statements/ reports must be published electronically) and preparing tax returns (the system of electronic tax returns was introduced on 1st January 2007; since then statements on paper have been largely abolished, with some exceptions). Besides supplying the basic information the accounting software should meet the demands for providing data that management can base its decisions on and for informing different sub-systems dealing mainly with planning.

One of the areas demanding extra information within the enterprise is management accounting, the efficient operation of which needs the working of the accounting system at a high level – its instruments are the modern computing programmes. Proper decisions made in proper time need accounting information which is produced by the information system supported by accounting software. In perceiving, recording, processing and forwarding information the accounting information system has indisputably a central role, which requires the quick and efficient processing and forwarding of data. Informational support is indispensable to reflect the economic changes in our globalized world; in its interest the accounting software efficiently assists the users to obtain the adequately transformed information in time. In respect of thoughtful decisions, obtaining information ensuring the adequate flow of data is very significant because it greatly determines the reactive ability of the enterprise. Nowadays (as a consequence of the economic crisis) the demand for "real and valid" data given by the accounting information system has risen, and their quality and feedback depend on the applied accounting software, the integrity of the database and the professional skills and flexibility of the accountants.

In the business world those enterprises and firms can be successful which are ready and able to renew. An essential element of this ability is applying modern software in the economic processes – connecting the modules supporting different areas for the sake of more efficient operation – which naturally concerns the accounting information system as well.

To automatize the processes of the enterprise it is usual to apply targeted software, i.e., complex solutions supporting the whole business processes have not spread yet, and the so-called island-like applications are dominant in the domestic market, too. The introduction of business software usually happens in cases of processes which can be easily automatized (usually accounting, book-keeping or wage-accounting) simply, isolated from other processes. Such software can be found even in smaller enterprises.

The well-chosen Resource Planning (ERP) system within it the proper accounting information system is a quickly recovering investment, by which the processes become transparent, the expenses can be planned, the managers' decisions are more supported; shortly, the firm is more capable of growth.

It is very advantageous if, besides the accounting system, the basic activity of the enterprise is supported by software modules which can be linked and are able to co-operate efficiently. In a complex system created like this it is important for the software to support the main activity, the different business processes in details, but in an integrated way. To realize this, it is essential to have a common database reflecting the whole activity of the enterprise, up-to-date data, and reliable information. The target of the complex information system is to support the planning and strategic decisions of the management (in which the management information system has an important role) and to support the inner mechanism of the enterprise and the inter-enterprise processes.

At the beginning of the formation of the system meeting the demands for the accounting and financial regulations and the management's expectations were essential Expectations appearing later included increasing efficiency, making the most of capacity, optimizing the supply processes, reducing the expenses, and the ability for planning. At that time the commercial and logistic areas were the primary areas of interest. Nowadays the main aspects are reducing risks, creating and keeping stability, and obtaining reliable data for the decisions of the management.

It is an important requirement to have a quickly, reliably operating system which can be used easily and can be complemented with further elements or functions, depending on the modifications, and therefore can react to changes. That is why the link among the different modules for automatic, efficient co-operation has become highly important, as it promotes the calculations, planning and decisions because the accounting information system is in direct connection with the relevant areas.

The old applications are inflexible. Their adaptation to changes is difficult, they are dissected vertically, and only certain areas are automatized, so the data relating to different areas must be entered separately, which is time- and work-consuming. It is indispensable to know the exact demand of the users so that the different levels of management can obtain the data relevant for them. Asking for the necessary information does not always give the expected results: giving the aggregated data takes too long because the proper links are missing from the databases A further fault of this management information system is that it fails to provide complex information with a strategic view.

The information of the enterprise has the following requirements:

- providing information for the management and creating a management information system which supports the decisions efficiently,
- besides the functional aspects it manages the processes outside the borders of the enterprise,
- for the sake of these, by forming an information technological environment for the whole enterprise which relies both on the inner and outer data, it creates links among the applications.

To meet the above-mentioned demands ERP systems have been produced. An ERP system is a package of complex software for realizing the planning of sources in the enterprise by which the firm completely electronizes its own inner management, from following the movement of material to comparing the bills and invoices. It is an application formed out of modules which offers an up-to-date, integrated software solution to manage the functional areas and operational processes of the enterprise.

With the formation of an ERP system both the accounting and controlling and management obtain a huge informational database. With the continuously widening functionality these systems are the bases of the informational support of the enterprise.

11.11 INVENTORY CONTROL/MANAGEMENT SYSTEM

Inventory refers to the stock of raw materials and finished goods available in the organization for production and sale. All organizations need an efficient system to maintain and control the optimum level of investment in all types of inventories. An inventory control system ensures that proper stock levels of each item are maintained. The improper stock levels (low or high) cause the following problems:

- Low inventory of raw materials leads to idle time in a production process and hence, causes wastage of resources like labour, power, equipments, etc. needed for production. It may also lead to decrease in sales due to out-of-stock especially during periods of peak demands.
- Low inventory of finished goods leads to backorder, lost sale and loss in goodwill of the company due to out-of-stock positions.
- High inventory of raw materials and finished goods leads to unnecessary investments and hence, causes a financial burden on the organization.

11.11.1 Inventory

Inventories occupy the most strategic position in the structure of working capital of most business enterprises. It constitutes the largest component of current asset in most business enterprises. In the sphere of working capital, the efficient control of inventory has passed the most serious problem to the cement mills because about two-third of the current assets of mills are blocked in inventories. The turnover of working capital is largely governed by the turnover of inventory. It is therefore quite natural that inventory which helps in maximize profit occupies the most significant place among current assets.

Meaning and Definition of Inventory:

In dictionary meaning of inventory is a "detailed list of goods, furniture etc." Many understand the word inventory, as a stock of goods, but the generally accepted meaning of the word 'goods' in the accounting language, is the stock of finished goods only. In a manufacturing organization, however, in addition to the stock of finished goods, there will be stock of partly finished goods, raw materials and stores. The collective name of these entire items is 'inventory'.

The term 'inventory' refers to the stockpile of production a firm is offering for sale and the components that make up the production.

The inventory means aggregate of those items of tangible personal property which

(i) are held for sale in ordinary course of business.

(ii) are in process of production for such sales.

(iii) they are to be currently consumed in the production of goods or services to be available for sale.

Inventories are expandable physical articles held for resale for use in manufacturing a production or for consumption in carrying on business activity such as merchandise, goods purchased by the business which are ready for sale.

It is the inventory of the trader who dies not manufacture it.

Finished Goods:

Goods being manufactured for sale by the business which are ready for sale are known as finished goods.

Materials:

Articles such as raw materials, semi-finished goods or finished parts, which the business plans to incorporate physically into the finished production.

Supplies:

Supplies are the articles which will be consumed by the business in its operation but will not physically as they are a part of the production.

The short inventory may be defined as the materials, which are either saleable in the market or usable directly or indirectly in the manufacturing process. It also includes the items which are ready for making finished goods in some other process or by comparing them either by the concern itself and/or by outside parties. In other words, the term inventory means the material having any one of the following characteristics. It may be

1. saleable in the market,
2. directly saleable in the manufacturing process of the business,
3. usable directly in the manufacturing process of the undertaking, and
4. ready to send to the outside parties for making usable and saleable productions out of it.

In the present study raw materials, stores and spare parts, finished goods and work-in-process have been included inventories. Firm also manufactures inventory to supplies.

Supplies included office and plant cleaning materials (soap, brooms etc. oil, fuel, light bulbs and the likes). These materials do not directly enter into the production process, but are necessary for production process. Inventory constitutes the most significant part of current assets of a large majority of companies in India. For example, on an average inventories are more than 57 per cent of current assets in public limited companies and about 60.5% in government companies in India. Therefore it is absolutely imperative to manage inventories efficiently and effectively in order to avoid unnecessary investment in them. An undertaking neglecting the management of inventories will be jeopardizing its long run profitability and may fail ultimately. It is possible for a company to reduce its level of inventories to a considerable degree *e.g.* 10 to 20 per cent without any adverse effect on production and sales.

11.11.2 The Functions Of Inventory

The functions that inventory performs can be summarised as follows:

First of all, the fundamental function for carrying inventories is to meet customer demand for a product. In fact, it is physically impossible and economically impractical for each stock item to arrive exactly where it is needed exactly when it is needed. Therefore, a reasonable level of inventory is normally maintained that will meet anticipated or expected customer or user demand.

Secondly, since demand is usually not known with certainty, additional amounts of inventory, called safety or buffer stocks, are often kept on hand to meet unexpected variations in excess of expected demand.

Thirdly, additional stocks of inventories are sometimes built up to meet demand that is seasonal or cyclical in nature. Companies will produce items when demand is low in order to meet high seasonal demand for which their production capacity is insufficient. Correspondingly, retailers might find it necessary to keep large stocks of inventory on their shelves to meet peak seasonal demand or for display purposes to attract buyers.

Finally, inventory can also be carried out to take the advantage of price changes. A company will often purchase large amounts of inventory to take advantage of price discounts, as a hedge against anticipated price increases in the future, or because they can get a lower price by purchasing in volume.

11.12 INVENTORY MANAGEMENT

Inventory Management is an enterprise-wide discipline concerned with the identification and tracking of Information Services (IS) hardware and software assets. Its three main areas of concern are:

- Acquisition
- Redeployment
- Termination

Acquisition procedures are established to assist personnel in procurement of software and hardware products. Its main purpose is to ensure that proper justifications are performed and that financial guidelines are followed.

Redeployment procedures are responsible for ensuring that assets are tracked when moved from one location to another and that budgetary considerations are adjusted as needed. Should a product be moved in conjunction with its original owner then the Inventory

System is updated to reflect the new location. Should a product location and owner change, then the Inventory System must be updated to reflect the new owner and their location. In this case, the old product is deleted from the original owner's budget and added to the new owner's budget.

Termination is responsible for deleting the asset from the inventory when it is discontinued, or replaced. The owner's budget will be updated to reflect the asset termination and the asset will no longer be listed when location reports are generated.

The **Inventory System** is maintained within a database that ties an asset to its owner and defines the location where the asset resides. The relative importance of the asset is added to the inventory record (i.e., Criticality = 1-5, where 1 is "Most Critical"). Based on this information the contingency planning specialist can plan asset recoveries needed to support critical business operations.

Like all databases, the Inventory System will only be effective if its information is kept current. To ensure the accuracy of the Inventory System, while not adding too great a burden to company personnel, every effort must be taken to implement processes that maintain inventory data with a minimum work effort from personnel

Inventory Management provides:

- Up-to-date information about data processing resources through the creation and archiving of records in a centralized repository.
- Financial records specific to a single component, or groups of components.
- Service records for all components in the inventory.
- Data used to support configuration diagrams of the hardware and software components contained within specific locations, or the entire data processing environment.

11.12.1 Objectives of Inventory Management

The primary objectives of inventory management are:

- To minimize the possibility of disruption in the production schedule of a firm for want of raw material, stock and spares.
- To keep down capital investment in inventories.

So it is essential to have necessary inventories. Excessive inventory is an idle resource of a concern. The concern should always avoid this situation. The investment in inventories should be just sufficient in the optimum level. The major dangers of excessive inventories are:

- the unnecessary tie up of the firm's funds and loss of profit,
- excessive carrying cost, and
- the risk of liquidity.

The excessive level of inventories consumes the funds of business, which cannot be used for any other purpose and thus involves an opportunity cost. The carrying cost, such as the cost of shortage, handling insurance, recording and inspection, are also increased in proportion to the volume of inventories. This cost will impair the concern profitability further.

On the other hand, a low level of inventories may result in frequent interruptions in the production schedule resulting in under-utilization of capacity and lower sales. The aim of inventory management thus should be to avoid excessive inventory and inadequate inventory and to maintain adequate inventory for smooth running of the business operations. Efforts should be made to place orders at the right time with the right source to purchase the right quantity at the right price and quality. The effective inventory management should

- maintain sufficient stock of raw material in the period of short supply and anticipate price changes.
- ensure a continuous supply of material to production department facilitating uninterrupted production.
- minimize the carrying cost and time.
- maintain sufficient stock of finished goods for smooth sales operations.
- ensure that materials are available for use in production and production services as and when required.
- ensure that finished goods are available for delivery to customers to fulfil orders, smooth sales operation and efficient customer service.
- minimize investment in inventories and minimize the carrying cost and time.
- protect the inventory against deterioration, obsolescence and unauthorized use.
- maintain sufficient stock of raw material in period of short supply and anticipate price changes.
- control investment in inventories and keep it at an optimum level.

11.12.2 Problems Faced By Management

Following are the problems faced by management:

- To maintain a large size inventories for efficient and smooth production and sales operation.
- To maintain only a minimum possible inventory because of inventory holding cost and opportunity cost of funds invested in inventory.
- Control investment in inventories and keep it at the optimum level.

Inventory management, therefore, should strike a balance between too much inventory and too little inventory. The efficient management and effective control of inventories help in achieving better operational results and reducing investment in working capital. It has a significant influence on the profitability of a concern.

11.13 INVENTORY MANAGEMENT SYSTEM

Inventory control is concerned with the acquisition, storage, handling and use of inventories so as to ensure the availability of inventory whenever needed, providing adequate provision for contingencies, deriving maximum economy and minimizing wastage and losses.

Hence Inventory control refers to a system, which ensures the supply of required quantity and quality of inventory at the required time and at the same time prevent unnecessary investment in inventories.

It is one of the most vital phases of material management. Reducing inventories without impairing operating efficiency frees working capital that can be effectively employed elsewhere. Inventory control can make or break a company. This explains the usual saying that "inventories" are the graveyard of a business.

Designing a sound inventory control system is in a large measure for balancing operations. It is the focal point of many seemingly conflicting interests and considerations both short range and long range.

The aim of a sound inventory control system is to secure the best balance between "too much and too little." Too much inventory carries financial rises and too little reacts adversely on continuity of productions and competitive dynamics. The real problem is not the reduction of the size of the inventory as a whole but to secure a scientifically determined balance between several items that make up the inventory.

The efficiency of inventory control affects the flexibility of the firm. Insufficient procedures may result in an unbalanced inventory. Some items out of stock, other overstocked, necessitating excessive investment. These inefficiencies ultimately will have adverse effects upon profits. Turning the situation round, difference in the efficiency of the inventory control for a given level of flexibility affects the level of investment required in inventory. The less efficient is the inventory control, the greater is the investment required. Excessive investment in inventories increase cost and reduce profits, thus, the effects of inventory control of flexibility and on level of investment required in inventories represent two sides of the same coin.

Control of inventory, which typically represents 45% to 90% of all expenses for business, is needed to ensure that the business has the right goods on hand to avoid stock-outs, to prevent shrinkage (spoilage/theft), and to provide proper accounting. Many businesses have too much of their limited resource, **capital**, tied up in their major asset, **inventory**. Worse, they may have their capital tied up in the wrong kind of inventory. Inventory may be old, worn out, shopworn, obsolete, or the wrong sizes or colors, or there may be an imbalance among different product lines that reduces the customer appeal of the total operation.

Inventory control systems range from eyeball systems to reserve stock systems to perpetual computer-run systems. Valuation of inventory is normally stated at original cost, market value, or current replacement costs, whichever is lowest. This practice is used because it minimizes the possibility of overstating assets. Inventory valuation and appropriate accounting practices are worth a book alone and so are not dealt with here in depth.

The ideal inventory and proper merchandise turnover will vary from one market to another. Average industry figures serve as a guide for comparison. Too large an inventory may not be justified because the turnover does not warrant investment. On the other hand, because products are not available to meet demand, too small an inventory may minimize sales and profits as customers go somewhere else to buy what they want where it is immediately available. Minimum inventories based on reordering time need to become important aspects of buying activity. Carrying costs, material purchases, and storage costs are all expensive. However, stock-outs are expensive also. All of those costs can be minimized by efficient inventory policies.

Inventory control involves the procurement, care and disposition of materials. There are three kinds of inventory that are of concern to managers:

- Raw materials,
- In-process or semi-finished goods,
- Finished goods.

If a manager effectively controls these three types of inventory, capital can be released that may be tied up in unnecessary inventory, production control can be improved and can protect against obsolescence, deterioration and/or theft, The reasons for inventory control are:

- Helps balance the stock as to value, size, color, style, and price line in proportion to demand or sales trends.
- Help plan the winners as well as move slow sellers
- Helps secure the best rate of stock turnover for each item.
- Helps reduce expenses and markdowns.
- Helps maintain a business reputation for always having new, fresh merchandise in wanted sizes and colors.

11.13.1 Typical Inventory Management System

The major objectives for implementing a computerised inventory management in an organization are:

- Maintaining an optimum level of raw materials and finished goods inventory.
- Preparation of purchase orders and inventory status reports accurately and on time.
- Preparation of various analysis reports.
- Generation of MIS reports that help management for making effective and timely decisions.

The various inputs to the system are:

- Data of vendors and buyers including code, name, address and other details of each one.
- Data of raw materials and finished goods including code, name, category, size, price and other details of each item along with their quantity.
- Good received note (GRN) indicates the quantity received of various items along with their details.
- Materials requisition slips indicate the quantity issued of various items to production departments or vendors along with their details.
- Materials rejection note indicates the quantity of items rejected to vendors/suppliers along with the reasons for rejection.

A typical inventory management system generates the following outputs:

- Purchase order (PO) includes PO number, PO date, supplier name, address, item code/name, category, quantity ordered, price, amount along with the terms and conditions.

- Purchase book includes the quantity and other details of items received.
- Inventory status reports (detailed and summary), includes the quantity and other details of items sold, received, issued and rejected with their closing balance.
- Materials return report indicates the quantity of items rejected along with other details.
- Materials transfer report indicates the quantity of items issued to other branches/ departments along with other details.
- Purchase analysis report (supplier and item wise) indicates the quantity and other details of items purchased during a period from various suppliers.

11.13.2 Functional Areas

The functional areas that interface with an Inventory Management System are:

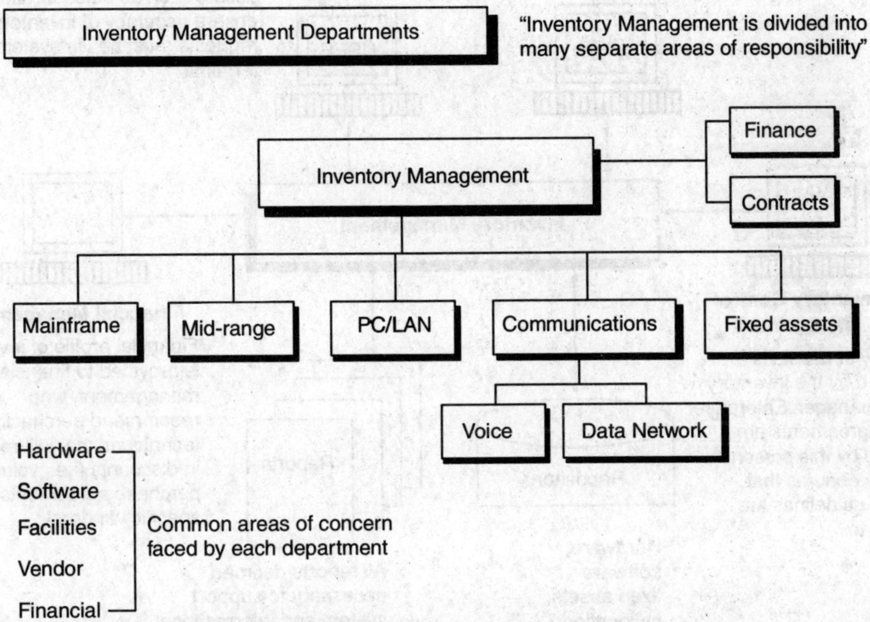

Figure 11.6: Overview of Inventory Management functional areas

All of the functional areas listed above can utilize the information contained within the Inventory Management System's Central Asset Repository of information. Additionally, the Recovery Management area could utilize inventory information to identify an assets criticality (especially when the asset's location and owner are identified within the Inventory Management System). Through the use of reports generated from the Inventory Management System's Repository, it would be possible to obtain a listing of all "Most Critical" resources, by location and group. This report would then serve as the basis of a Business Recovery Plan.

11.14 INTEGRATED INVENTORY MANAGEMENT SYSTEM

To successfully implement an Inventory Management System, it is necessary to integrate it within the everyday functions performed by company personnel. That is, when a user wants to order equipment or software, they would call up the Inventory Management System screen associated with Acquisition. The same types of processes should be available for Redeployment and Termination of assets. Should a user request the acquisition of a specific type of asset then it would be possible for the inventory system to determine if the asset is already in surplus, or if it should be purchased under an existing Volume Purchase Agreement with a vendor.

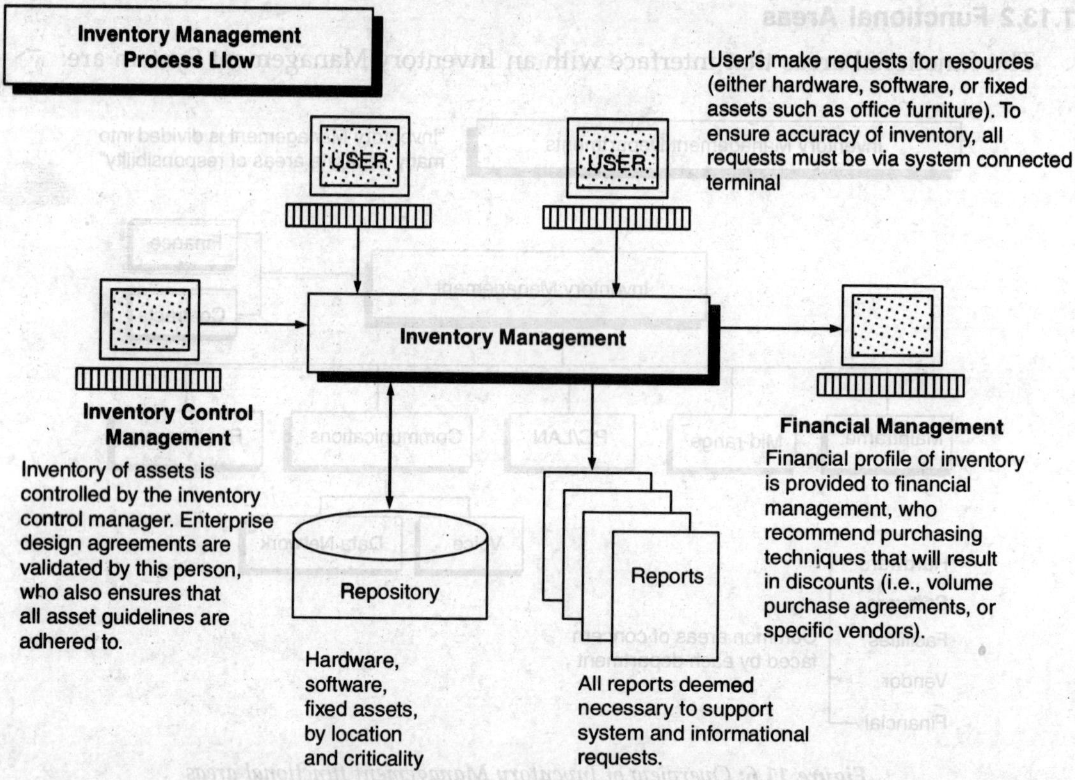

Figure 11.7: Overview of an integrated Inventory Management System

The utilization of Inventory Management Systems to control the purchase and installation of assets can aid in the control of the business environment, while assisting in the assignment of personnel to perform asset related work functions. This methodology will result in a workflow and asset management system that is optimized to the enterprise.

11.15 SMC DISCIPLINE INTERFACES

The Systems Management and Control (SMC) disciplines that will interface with the Inventory Management System are illustrated within the diagram listed below.

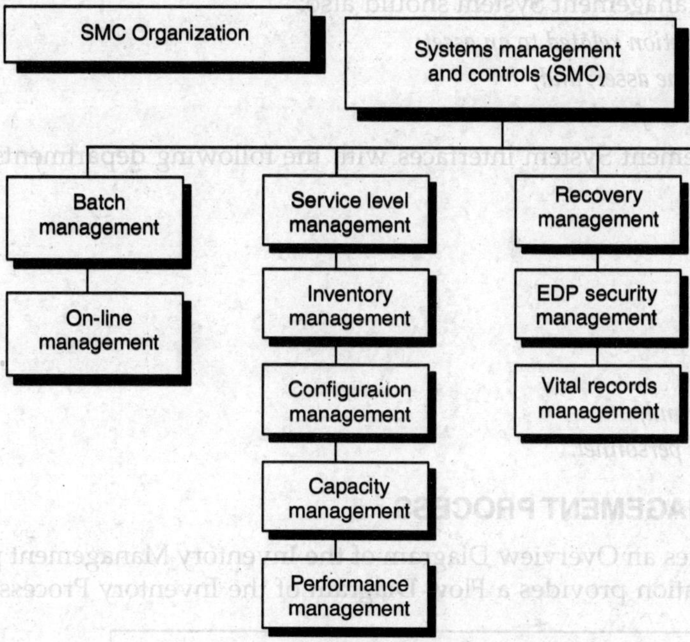

Figure 11.8: SMC Discipline Interfaces

The disciplines interfacing directly with Inventory Management and their functional responsibilities are:

- **Capacity Management** (i.e., PC memory and speed, DASD size, etc.).
- **Performance Management** (speed and usage information).
- **Change Management** (version and release information, benchmark, testing, etc.).
- **Recovery Management** (recovery planning for critical assets and sizing requirements for recovery facilities).
- **Service Level Management** (Service Level Agreements - SLA's and Service Level Reporting - SLR of user processing and service requirements).
- **Problem Management** (Change History, Problem History, troubleshooting, pathway, version and release information, etc.).
- **Configuration Management** (hardware, software, location, HVAC requirements, power, water, floor space, fixed assets, etc.).

11.16 INVENTORY MANAGEMENT DISCIPLINES AND INTERFACES

The Inventory Management function is responsible for tracking all assets, from Mainframe based to Data Network based, that are connected to the data center or data network. In each case, the Inventory Management Systems must be able to:

- *Identify the asset and its serial number;*
- *Associate the asset with its owner and location;*
- *Relate the asset to its vendor;*
- *Track the maintenance level of the asset; and,*
- *Provide the asset's Problem and Change history.*

The ideal Inventory Management System should also:

- *Provide financial information related to an asset;*
- *Define the criticality of the asset; and,*
- *Supply history information for the asset.*

The Inventory Management System interfaces with the following departments:

- *Finance;*
- *Contracts;*
- *Systems Software;*
- *Technical Support;*
- *Change Management;*
- *Production Services;*
- *Facilities Management; and,*
- *Enterprise Management personnel.*

11.17 INVENTORY MANAGEMENT PROCESS

The Figure 11.9 provides an Overview Diagram of the Inventory Management process, while the following illustration provides a Flow Diagram of the Inventory Process.

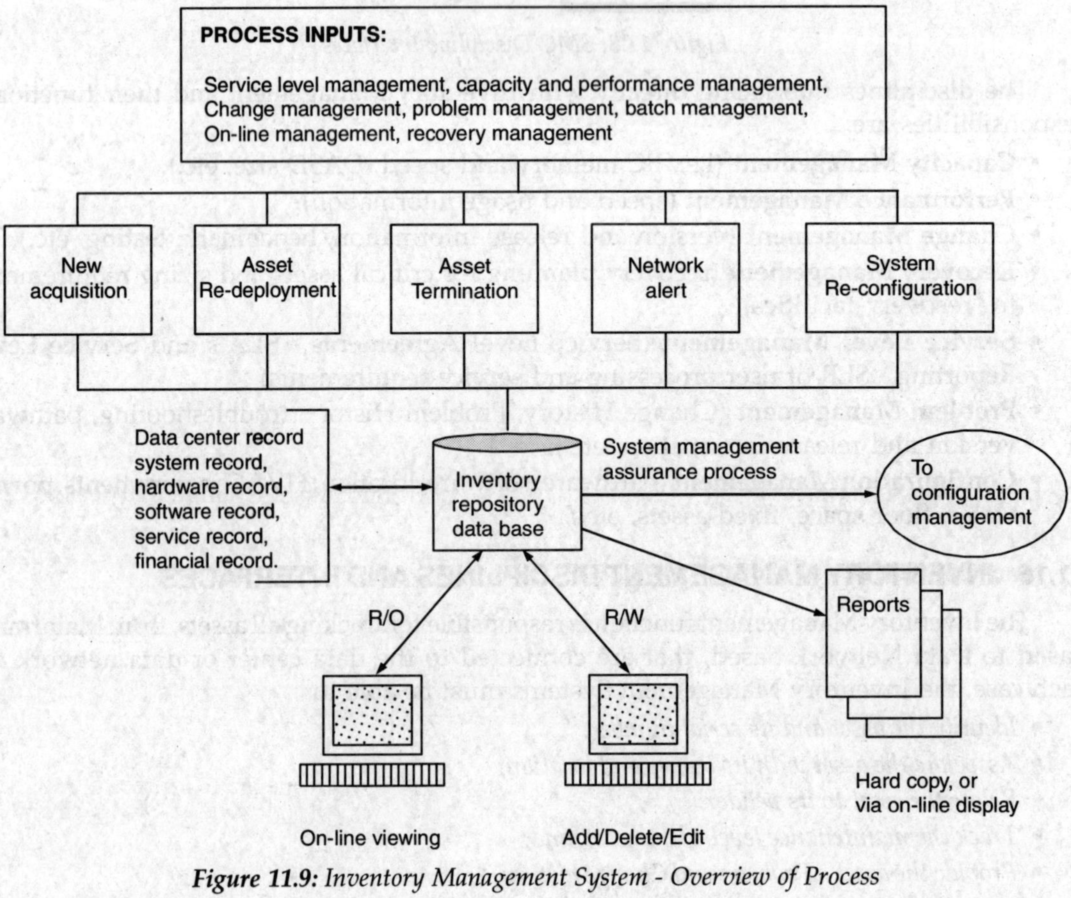

***Figure 11.9:** Inventory Management System - Overview of Process*

11.18 INVENTORY MANAGEMENT FLOW

The inventory process starts with Non-Controlled Entry, or Controlled Entry of an asset, then proceeds by generating an Asset Database Record, including: asset information, location, and financial information.

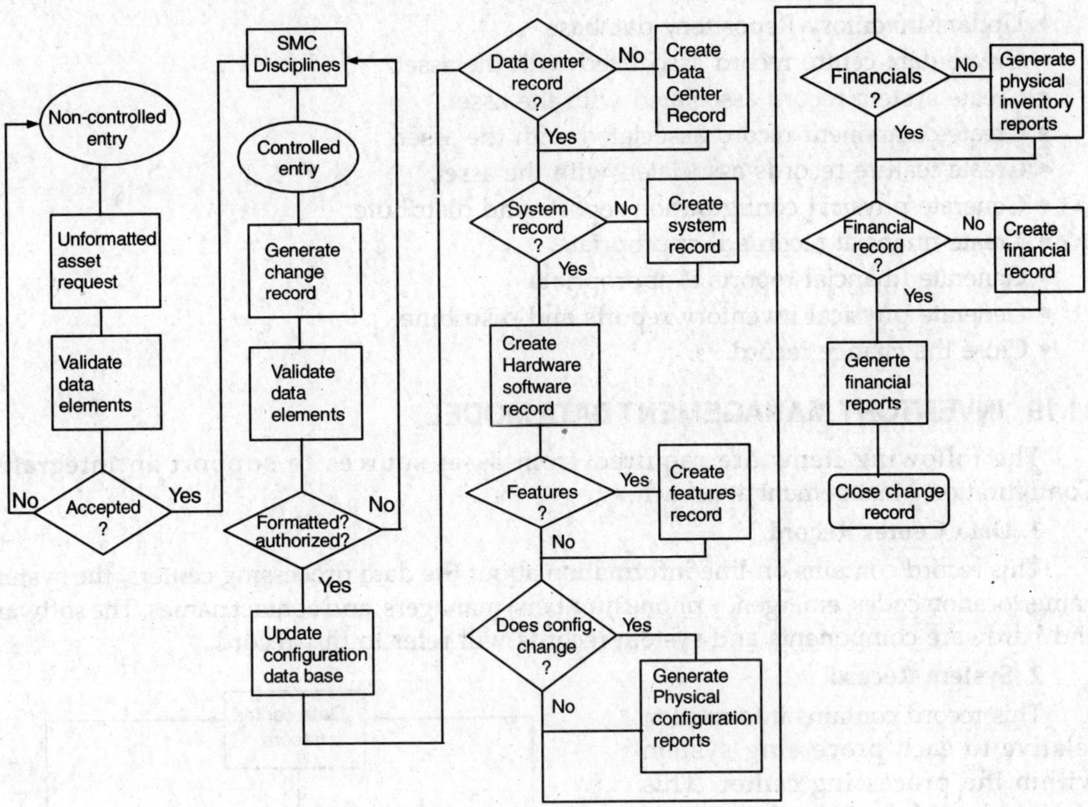

Figure 11.10: Inventory System Flow Diagram

11.18.1 Process Flow

The process is entered as a Controlled or Non-Controlled Asset Change Request (ACR) as follows:

Non-Controlled ACR Entry

- ACR received by any method other than the Change Control process.
  - Confirm all necessary information is available about the asset.
  - Request is reviewed locally for acceptance.
  - Problems documented and returned for resolution.
  - ACR accepted and authorized.
  - Request forwarded to Change Control process for input as a Controlled ACR.

Controlled ACR Entry

- Validate all data elements are present in the Change Record.
- Reviewed by all I/S organizations accountable for asset control.
- Problems documented and returned for resolution.
- ACR accepted and authorized.
- Update Inventory Repository database.
- Create data centre record associated with the asset.
- Create system record associated with the asset.
- Create component record associated with the asset.
- Create feature records associated with the asset.
- Generate physical configuration reports and distribute.
- Create financial records if appropriate.
- Generate financial reports if appropriate.
- Generate physical inventory reports and distribute.
- Close the change record.

11.19 INVENTORY MANAGEMENT DATA MODEL

The following items are required from asset sources to support an integrated Configuration Management approach.

1. Data Center Record

This record contains on-line information about the data processing centers, the system name, location codes, emergency phone numbers, managers, and contact names. The software and hardware components and system records will refer to this record.

2. System Record

This record contains information relative to each processing system within the processing center. This record should contain the system names by LPAR, location codes, operator names, and support numbers. Software and hardware components can refer to this record.

3. Service Record

This record contains the service organization's data. Maintaining service organization records is advantageous when a user is displaying a record of a failing component. This record should contain the name, location, prime-shift phone number, off-shift phone number, hardware and software

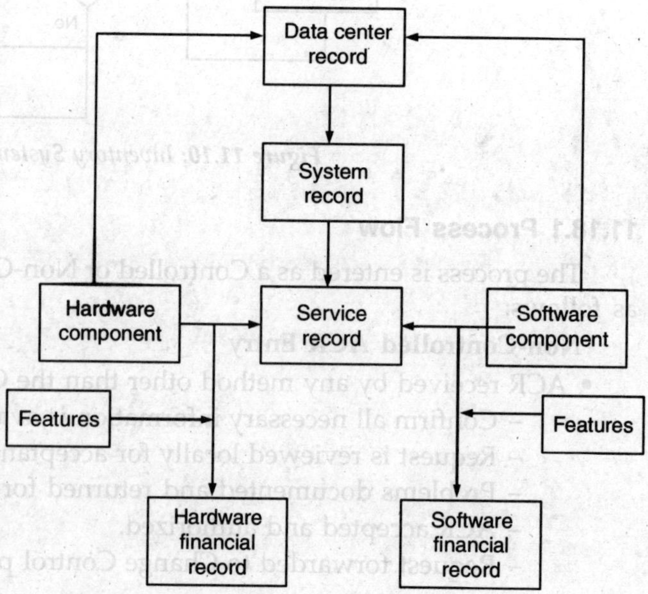

Figure 11.11: Inventory Management Data Model

representative's name, contact phone numbers, and a description of the service organization. Hardware and software components can refer to this record.

4. Financial Record

Helpful information in this record assists in warranty and service incidents. Hardware financial records contain a user financial id, a financial type, and a description. For software records the same information is required in addition to a license type record entry.

5. Hardware Components

For hardware component records a consensus must be reached on the hardware types to be managed. A hardware model record for each hardware type will be created and all common hardware components will be entered using this template. This record should contain the following information:

- Component ID,
- Serial Number,
- Generic device type,
- Model,
- Manufacturer,
- Owner,
- Install Date,
- Location,
- Maintenance Vendor,
- Contract type,
- Component status,
- Component description.

In some instances a hardware subcomponent record must be entered. A subcomponent can be thought of as a feature that can be a stand-alone component and has mobility in the inventory (for example, 3726, 3727, external hard disks). This will allow subcomponents to be removed or moved from their hardware component or attached to another component. This record should contain a subcomponent status code and a description.

6. Software Components

For software component records a consensus must be reached as to what level of installed software will be within the scope of the asset database. For example, is the workstation (PC-based) software to be managed? If so, are we to account for all application software or just operating system software?

The answers to these questions are linked to what kind of information the user support groups require to provide service to the client. In a centralized Help Desk environment, all user application software, including maintenance levels, are maintained. This provides up-to-date information to the Help Desk personnel about the user environment and adds greatly to their productivity.

A software model record for each component contains an ID, maintenance level, program type, status and a description. A typical software record should contain the following information:

- System (application runs on),
- Name,
- Model,
- Vendor,
- Serial Number,
- Renewal Date,
- License Type,
- Contract Type,
- Maintenance Level,
- Description.

7. Feature Components Record

This record identifies associated features and relates these features back to other records.

8. Model Component Record

The industry uses this type record as a productivity tool to greatly enhance the ability to build large data bases quickly with minimum data entry errors. Model records themselves do not hold configuration data, but they make the entry of data easier by allowing the creation of component records from models that hold information common to a number of components (or subcomponents) of the same type.

The model capability also provides the ability to build one or many relationships between model features and hardware or software components. Features that are common to many components can be contained in a single model feature record that is referred to by many component records.

11.20 MARKETING INFORMATION SYSTEM

The Internet is rapidly changing the way business views marketing information systems. New business models present challenges and opportunities as organizations seek to adopt "e-business" methodologies in the search for competitive advantage. Organizations of all sizes are feeling the "ripple effect" of Internet-enabled customers, supply chains and competitors. This pressure is particularly acute in the marketing function where information technology touches the customer and is increasingly becoming the key to creating superior customer value.

The importance of marketing information is particularly apparent as the economy continues to emphasize services as a primary source of value. Services are heavily information dependent. Information is rapidly becoming a service in its own right. Even in industries that are primarily manufacturing in nature, the information content of the final product is rapidly increasing. Mass customization, often described as "one-to-one" marketing or the customizing of products and services for individual customers, is heavily dependent on comprehensive and timely customer information. Modern marketing organizations, with their focus on the Internet, exhibit different characteristics than their "old economy" brethren. They create and manage the customer interface where interactions are more virtual than face-to-face. They leverage IT technology to integrate and coordinate with customers and business partners to rapidly achieve measurable business results. The emphasis in on the rapid conversion of knowledge into customer value which depends on the ability to develop, deploy, and manage powerful new marketing information systems (MkIS). The key to competitive advantage depends on the firm's ability to convert knowledge into customer relationships, reduced time to market and lower costs.

To survive in highly competitive markets, companies need to be able to develop the marketing function and scale it up on "Internet time" with best-of-class decision support solutions for customer relationship management, sales force automation, market research, marketing communications, logistics, and product development. The purpose of this paper is to provide an overview of the MkIS as it is evolving into an Internet-based system.

11.20.1 Definition—Marketing Information System (MkIS)

Simply put, an MkIS is a computerized system that is designed to provide an organized flow of information to enable and support the marketing activities of an organization. The MkIS serves collaborative, analytical and operational needs. In the collaborative mode, the MkIS enables managers to share information and work together virtually. In addition, the MkIS can enable marketers to collaborate with customers on product designs and customer requirements. The analytical function is addressed by decision support applications that enable marketers to analyze market data on customers, competitors, technology and general market conditions. These insights are becoming the foundation for the development of marketing strategies and plans. The MkIS addresses operational needs through customer management systems that focus on the day-to-day processing of customer transactions from the initial sale through customer service.

MkIS systems are designed to be comprehensive and flexible in nature and to integrate with each other functionally. They are formal, forward looking and essential to the organization's ability to create competitive advantage. The MkIS is the firm's "window on the world" and, increasingly, it is the primary customer interface. Figure 11.12 presents the basic architecture of the MkIS.

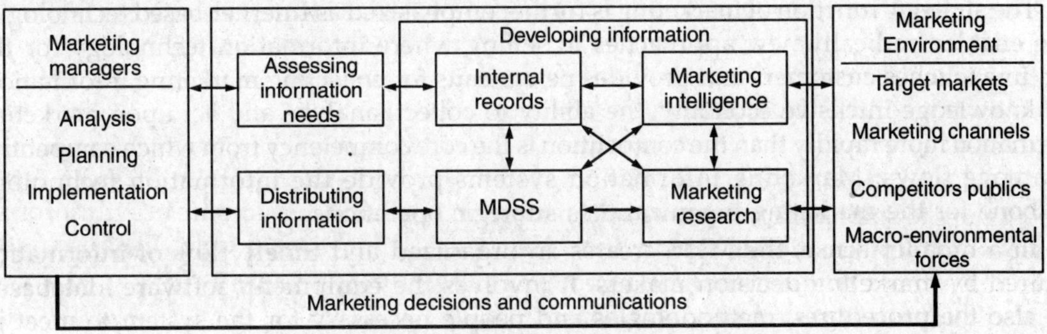

Figure 11.12: The Marketing Information System

11.20.2 History

Every firm organizes the flow of marketing information to its marketing manager as a support for his marketing interventions. Companies are studying their manager's information needs and designing Marketing Information Systems (MkIS) to meet these needs. Marketing

Information System is that part of Business Information System which meets the information needs of an organization in sales, distribution, advertising, market analysis, market intelligence, product research, service management, customer profile and other marketing functions. A Marketing Information System (MkIS) consists of people, equipment and procedures to gather, sort, analyse, evaluate and distribute needed, timely and accurate information to marketing decision makers.

The role of MkIS is to access the marketing manager's information needs, then develop the framework for collecting information and distribute the information gathered to the end-users in time. The MkIS is generally carried out marketing need analysis, planning, implementation and control functions of marketing managers. The needed information is developed through internal company records, marketing intelligence activities, marketing research and marketing decision support analysis. Robert J. Williams has been credited with creating the first marketing information system in 1961 at the Mead Johnson Division of Edward Dalton Company in Indiana, USA.

11.20.3 The Strategic Role of the Marketing Information Systems

Historically, the role of the marketing function has been to support "make and sell" business strategies that emphasized increases in market share over the creation of long-term customer value. This view started to change after World War II with the recognition that satisfying the customer's needs and wants should be the focus of a firm's business activities.

The emphasis on the customer elevated the importance of marketing as a core business function on a par with research and development and production. The marketing function has become the firm's window to the world in the sense that it must monitor the marketing environment for changes in buyer behavior, competition, technology, economic conditions, and government policies. Marketing is a "strategic" function in that marketing activities enable organizations to identify and adapt to changes in the market environment.

The strategic function of marketing is further emphasized as Internet-based technologies have enabled radically new approaches to selling where information technology for the first time touches customers and provides new means for collecting marketing information. In a knowledge-intensive economy, the ability to collect, analyze and act upon marketing information more rapidly than the competition is the core competency from which competitive advantage flows. Marketing information systems provide the information technology backbone for the marketing organization's strategic operations.

In a broader sense, the MkIS creates an organized and timely flow of information required by marketing decision makers. It involves the equipment, software, databases, and also the procedures, methodologies and people necessary for the system to meet its organizational objectives. MkIS encompasses a broad spectrum of activities from simple transaction processing complex marketing strategy decision making.

11.20.4 The Role of the Internet

Information technology has transformed how firms conduct business. For example, financial service providers such as banks, stockbrokers and insurance companies could not do business today without their client-server-based information technology. This technology has long supported marketing activities. However, it is the recent advent of the Internet, and especially the browser-based World Wide Web, which has ignited a revolution in MkISs.

The term "cybermarketing" is often used to describe the Internet's convergence of computers, information systems, telecommunications and the customer with the marketing process. Internet marketing is characterized by interactivity, graphical user interfaces, multimedia content, and one-to-one connectivity. Internet technologies are not only providing new ways to reach the customer, but also to enable the reengineering of the entire marketing process and, indeed, the entire enterprise. It is no longer acceptable to view marketing as a standalone activity with lengthy time lapses between product concept, marketing strategy and commercialization.

Marketing has become interactive and real time. The rapidly growing field of marketing automation encompasses customer management functions to support e-commerce. As depicted in Figure 11.13, customer management applications include marketing decision support systems, customer relationship management, sales force automation, customer service and e-commerce activities. These activities are often described as "front office" customer-oriented activities. "Back office" enterprise resource planning (ERP) activities include manufacturing, finance and human resources. "Supply chain management" (SCM) activities encompass electronic procurement, inventory management, quality management and logistics systems to link an organization with its suppliers. These three elements comprise the enterprise information system.

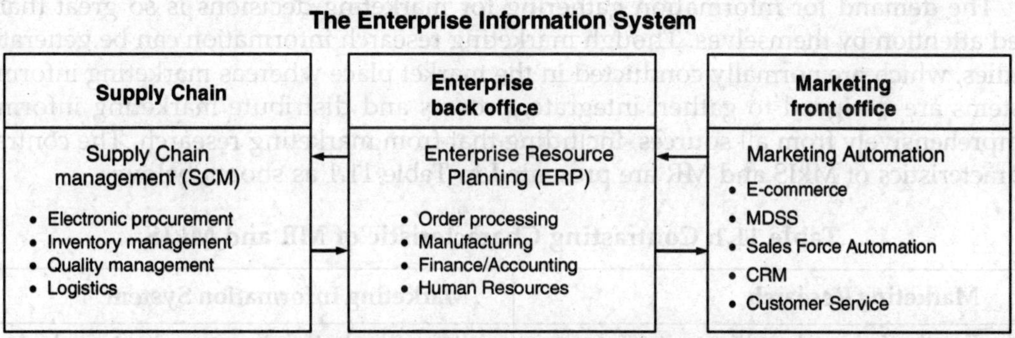

***Figure 11.13:** The Interfaces of MkIS*

Large integrated enterprise software companies such as Oracle, SAP, PeopleSoft, and IBM address all three major applications and they are beginning to use Web-based technologies to redesign business processes throughout the organization. The result is leaner organizations, faster response times, and lower costs. Decision-makers are able to integrate information from customers, suppliers, and the internal organization to obtain an enterprise-wide view of their ability to develop and execute marketing strategy. Until truly integrated browser-based systems are widely in use, the principal challenge for marketers is to tie e-commerce generated data with legacy information systems in order to create a unified view of each customer. Marketers will need to understand all the various ways that customers are touching the business through existing interfaces and e-commerce. Many of the older interfaces, such as telemarketing centers, point of sale (POS) systems, and the sales force are likely to be supported by legacy client-server technology. Marketers need to consolidate data from those systems with that from the Web-based ecommerce sources into a holistic view of the customer and make it available to decision-makers.

11.20.5 Relevance of MkIS

Three crucial developments render the need for MkIS. Firstly, when companies expand and diversify into new markets, the marketing managers have to necessarily deal with new situations both from the companies and from the customer's point of view. Therefore, there would be greater need for marketing information. Secondly, when there is a perceptible and significant increase in the level of income of the buyers, consumers tend to get more selective and discriminative in their buying process. The marketers should be fully aware of what makes a buyer prefer a brand and what distinguished his brand from that of the close competitors. This awareness is possible only with the help of a well-designed effective MkIS. Thirdly, as the markets develop and the competition moves from price to non-price grounds, it becomes increasingly important to find the moves adopted and implemented by the competitors and the response of the consumers towards them. Analysing the needs for MkIS from a third person's angle, three more factors come to the forefront viz., the information explosion, increasing complexity in decision making and the technological developments.

11.21 MARKETING RESEARCH AND MkIS

The demand for information gathering for marketing decisions is so great that they need attention by themselves. Though marketing research information can be generated by studies, which are normally conducted in the market place whereas marketing information systems are designed to gather, integrate, process and distribute marketing information comprehensively from all sources, including that from marketing research. The contrasting characteristics of MkIS and MR are presented in Table 11.1 as shown below:

Table 11.1: Contrasting Characteristic of MR and MkIS

Marketing Research	Marketing Information System
Emphasis is on handling external information	It handles both internal and external information
It is concerned with solving problems	It is concerned with preventing as well as solving problems
It operates in a fragmented fashion, i.e. on a project-to-project basis	It operates continuously as a system
It tends to focus on past information	It tends to be future oriented
It is a source of input for marketing information system	It includes other subsystems besides marketing research

The business function of marketing is concerned more with the planning, promotion and sale of products in existing markets and the development of new products and new markets. Thus marketing performs a vital function in the operation of a business enterprise.

Business firms who turned to computers have been able to perform vital marketing function effectively for organizations' growth in the face of global competition.

11.22 MARKETING INFORMATION SYSTEM FUNCTIONAL COMPONENTS

As shown in Figure 11.14, an MkIS consists of four major components: (1) user interfaces, (2) applications software, (3) databases, and (4) systems support.

1. *User Interfaces.* The essential element of the MkIS is the managers who will use the system and the interfaces they need to effectively analyze and use marketing information. The design of the system will depend on what type of decisions managers need to make. The interface includes the type of hardware that will be used, the way information is analyzed, formatted and displayed, and how reports are to be compiled and distributed. Issues to resolve are ease of use, security, cost, and access.

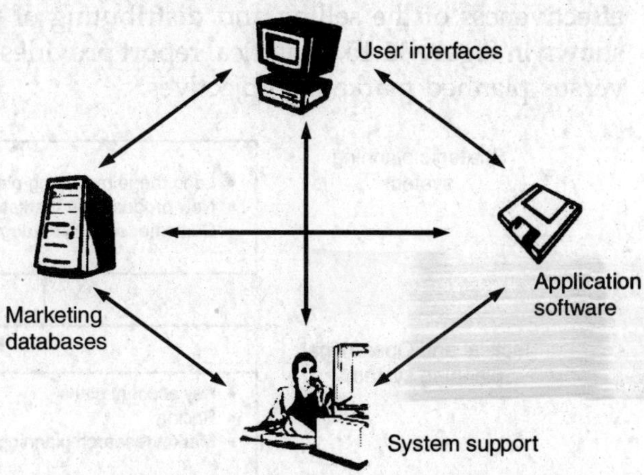

Figure 11.14: *MkIS Functional Components*

2. *Applications Software.* These are the programs that marketing decision makers use to collect, analyze, and manage data for the purpose of developing the information necessary for marketing decisions. Examples include the marketing decisions support software (MDSS) and customer management software for on-line sales and customer service.

3. *Marketing Databases.* A marketing database is a system in which marketing data files are organized d stored. Data may be collected from internal and external sources. Internal sources largely result from transactions. They provide data from e-commerce sites, sales results, shipping data, inventories, and product profitability. External sources include market research, competitor intelligence, credit bureaus, and financial institutions. Data can be organized in a *flat file* (Text file with one data record per line) or a *relational database* (Data is stored in tabular form where each row represents one entity and each column represents one characteristic of that entity). For instance, each row could represent a customer with the columns providing name, identification number, and purchase information.

4. *System Support.* This component consists of system managers who manage and maintain the systems assets including software and hardware network, monitor its activities and ensure compliance with organizational policies. This function may also include a help desk for system users.

11.23 WORKING OF MKIS

Strategic, Tactical and Operational information of MkIS will assist the managers in the following domains:

- Product Planning
- Pricing Decisions

- Advertising and Sales
- Promotional Strategies
- Promotional Expenditures
- Forecasting Market Potential for New and Existing Products
- Determining Channels of Distribution and so on.

Control Reporting Systems of MkIS will provide data for controlling the efficiency and effectiveness of the selling and distributing of products and services of the company. As shown in Figure 11.15, analytical report provides information on a firm's actual performance versus planned marketing objectives.

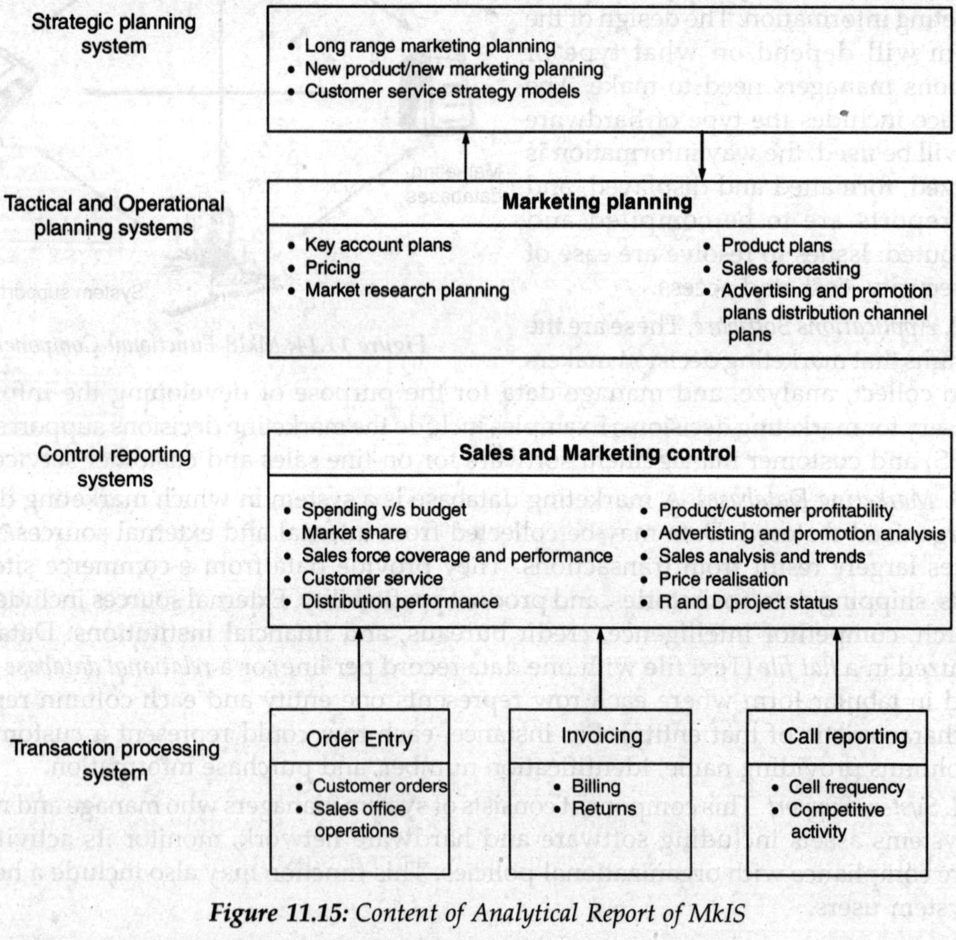

Figure 11.15: Content of Analytical Report of MkIS

MkISs are primarily customer-oriented information systems that work toward realising the strategic sales plan and the marketing plan of an organization.

Marketing systems, unlike other functional systems, need not be standardised and that every company has its own way in which it generates leads and prospects, prepares bids, fills orders and delivers goods to its customers. Therefore, MkIS must be tailored to match the marketing policies, procedures and practices of each company. Figure 11.16 shows sub-systems of a MkIS.

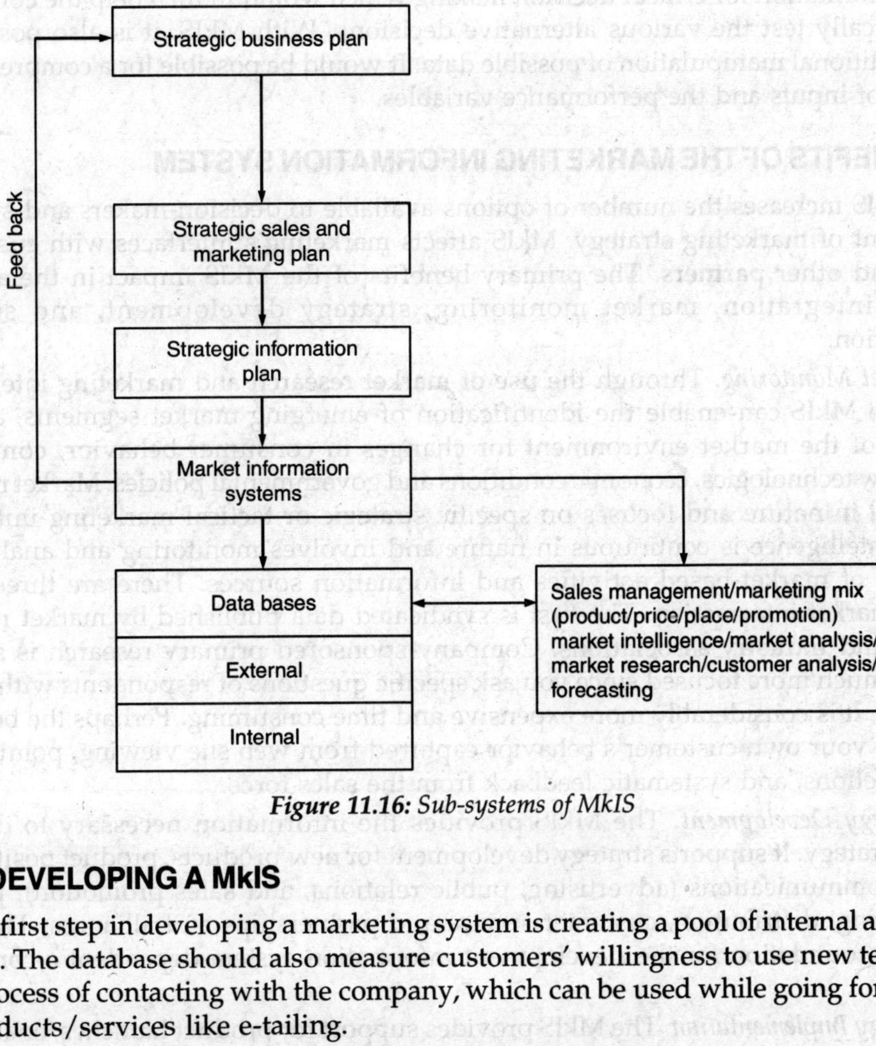

Figure 11.16: Sub-systems of MkIS

11.24 DEVELOPING A MkIS

The first step in developing a marketing system is creating a pool of internal and external database. The database should also measure customers' willingness to use new technologies in the process of contacting with the company, which can be used while going for launching new products/services like e-tailing.

An ideal database should provide the answers to the following queries:

- What is the best way to capture data at the point of sale?
- How can we ensure that marketing operations are run smoothly and efficiently?
- What are the goods and services that our customers want?
- How do customers define customer service?
- What kinds of services are important to customers?
- Are customers interested in and willing to use information technology?
- How much more customers afford to pay for higher quality service?
- What impact would higher quality customer service have on the profits of the company?
- How can we attract and retain customers' loyalty?

As regards benefits of MkIS, it may be noted that it would help the companies first by generating the necessary reports in time. The MkIS would help the companies to organize their vital information for critical decision making which would in turn help the companies to systematically test the various alternative decisions. With MkIS, it is also possible to generate additional manipulation of possible data. It would be possible for a comprehensive monitoring of inputs and the performance variables.

11.25 BENEFITS OF THE MARKETING INFORMATION SYSTEM

The MkIS increases the number of options available to decision-makers and supports every element of marketing strategy. MkIS affects marketing's interfaces with customers, suppliers and other partners. The primary benefits of the MkIS impact in the areas of functional integration, market monitoring, strategy development, and strategy implementation.

1. *Market Monitoring*. Through the use of market research and marketing intelligence activities the MkIS can enable the identification of emerging market segments, and the monitoring of the market environment for changes in consumer behavior, competitor activities, new technologies, economic conditions and governmental policies. Market research is situational in nature and focuses on specific strategic or tactical marketing initiatives. Marketing intelligence is continuous in nature and involves monitoring and analyzing a broad range of market-based activities and information sources. There are three major sources of market information. The first is syndicated data published by market research companies and industry associations. Company-sponsored primary research is another option. It is much more focused since you ask specific questions of respondents within your markets. But, it is considerably more expensive and time consuming. Perhaps the best data available are your own customer's behavior captured from web site viewing, point of sale (POS) transactions, and systematic feedback from the sales force.

2. *Strategy Development*. The MkIS provides the information necessary to develop marketing strategy. It supports strategy development for new products, product positioning, marketing communications (advertising, public relations, and sales promotion), pricing, personal selling, distribution, customer service and partnerships and alliances. The MkIS provides the foundation for the development information system-dependent e-commerce strategies.

3. *Strategy Implementation*. The MkIS provides support for product launches, enables the coordination of marketing strategies, and is an integral part of sales force automation (SFA), customer relationship management (CRM), and customer service systems implementations. The MkIS enables decision-makers to more effectively manage the sales force as well as customer relationships. Some customer management software companies are extending their CRM applications to include partner relationship management (PRM) capabilities. This has become increasingly important as many marketers are choosing to outsource important marketing functions and form strategic alliances to address new markets.

4. *Functional integration*. The MkIS enables the coordination of activities within the marketing department and between marketing and other organizational functions such as engineering, production, product management, finance, manufacturing, logistics, and customer service.

11.26 PERSONNEL INFORMATION SYSTEMS

The Personnel Information System (PIS) deals with the flow of information about people working in the organization as well as forecasting requirements of human resources. In most of the organizations, the system is concerned with the following five subsystems:

- Recruiting
- Placement
- Training
- Compensation
- Maintenance

Initially businesses used computer-based information system to produce paychecks and payroll reports, maintain personnel records and analyse the use of personnel in businesses operations. Now, computers dominated all spheres of personnel function.

11.26.1 Data, File Type and Structure of PIS

Following are the data, file type and structure of PIS:

(a) Performance Data: It is used for supervisory and work force planning purposes. An employee review system i.e., the immediate supervisor reviews the employees' performance periodically, rate them according to the evaluation schemes and set goals for the next period.

(b) Benefit Data: It is required to administer the employee benefit programs such as Life Insurance, Health Care Insurance, Pension Plans and so on.

(c) Skills Data: It is mainly used for employee promotion and project assignment purpose concerning the last job position held prior to the employee current position. Various skill codes are widely used in the employee file to summarise the employee skills.

(d) Payroll Data: As depicted in Table 11.2, payroll data which contains a combination of several data like pay scale, TA, DA, HRA and so on clubbed together for drawing meaningful breakup of the pay structure of an organization.

(e) Affirmative Action Data: Affirmative action data items are facts required to prepare a defence against charges of:

- Unfair hiring
- Promotion
- Termination practices

(f) Termination Data: Termination data is primarily of value in controlling employee welfare and insurance expense.

Table 11.2: Employee File Data Items

Data	Data Items
Identification Data	Employee number, name, address, telephone number, job code, location, shift and citizenship
Performance Data	Last review data, review type, rating, promotability date, next job, comment and so on

Benefit Data	Life insurance policy type, effective date, coverage, payroll deduction amount, and effective date
Skills Data	Last job title, location, reporting authority's name and designation
Payroll Data	Pay scale, HRA, DS, TA, IR, entertainment allowances and so on
Affirmative Action Data	Race, sex, age, religion
Termination Data	Position at the time of termination, department, pay rate, last day of work

A standard data and data items of employee file are demonstrated in Table 11.3.

Table 11.3: Data and Data Items of Job Files

Data	**Data Items**
Identification Data	Location code, job code, shift, cost centre account number, job title
Position Description Data	Summary statement of duties, specific duties, experience, educational qualifications
Budget Data	Labour hours, average labour cost/hour, average related expense/hour, total labour cost, total related expense and so on
Performance Data	Turnover rate, tardiness, absenteeism and so on

11.26.2 Major Files in PIS

Following are the major files in PIS:

(a) Job File: A job or position exists irrespective of employees filling it or not, within a workforce budget. It is usually defined by a job description that covers qualifications, duties, and responsibilities. The same job may exist in several places in a organization. To define the job specifically, a location code and job code is usually required. More than one employee may be required to perform a certain job in a particular location. Another important data item is number of full time and part time employees filling a particular job at a location.

The common data in this file includes:

- **(i) Identification Data:** the items serve to identify the location code, job code, account number, job title.
- **(ii) Position Description Data:** Widely used by the Personnel department in advertising and screening applicants for those positions.
- **(iii) Budget Data:** This file provides supporting data for other labour and labour related welfare expenses and total cost apportioned in various cost centres.
- **(iv) Performance Data:** This reviews the employees' performance as to the turnover rate, and absenteeism. Thus also checks how the productivity is and whether the employee is satisfied or dissatisfied with his job or not.

(b) Job Applicants File: The items included in this file are categorised under four heads such as:

- Application identification data
- Work history data
- Educational qualification data
- Application status data

Here also the data, classifications and other modes vary from company to company.

The applicant identification data identifies the data and the job for which he is applying. The pointer to the next name in alphabetical order is needed to efficiently access the file by applicant name. The complete job history of an applicant may be collected on a written applicant form for further processing. Table 11.4 shows a model job applicant file structure.

Table 11.4: A Model Job Applicant Files Structure

Data	Data Items
Applicant Identification Data	Covers location code, shift, job code, name, address, telephone number, e-mail id, and so on
Work History Data	Covers last job title, location, reporting authority's name and designation, duration
Educational Qualification Data	Covers various forms of educational qualification starting from the highest level to school level, major, technical skill code, and so on
Application Status Data	Initial screening results, interview

(c) Accident File: This file contains a record for each reportable accident within the factory. The organization may be held responsible for damages for an event, (a) either directly, or (b) through worker's compensation insurance.

The data items are grouped into three categories such as:

- ***Time and place data***
- ***Characteristics data***
- ***Effects data***

Table 11.5: A Model Accident Files Structure

Data	Data Items
Time and Place Data	Serial number, date of accident, time of accident, day of week
Characteristic Data	Accident type code, mechanical failure, vehicle number
Effects Data	Corrective actions taken , total property damage

(d) Claims and Injuries File: These may be insurance claims recorded by the organization under insurance policies or employee under group insurance policies managed by the organization themselves. These are organized as shown in Table 11.6.

Table 11.6: Claims and Injuries File Data and Data Items

Data	Data Items
To-data	Relation to organization (employee, customer, etc.), name
From-data	Insurance policy involved, general ledger account
Basis-data	Claim type, injury or damage code
When-data	Data claim filed
Amount-data	Expense type code, actual cost

11.26.3 SUBSYSTEMS OF PIS

Following are the subsystems of PIS:

1. Personnel Status Reporting System: These systems make available data in the employee and jobs files for supervisory purposes. The systems are designed to meet leave the needs of at least four groups.

- **Employment Control reporting System:** This system accesses the job file in 'Location Code' sequences so that all positions reporting to a particular Manager are together accessed on this report. The report hence produced periodically to serve different purposes. It may be run as a batch job at a computer centre. major purpose of this system is to control work force salary costs and to provide selected data items on each employee for various decision-making purposes.

2. Employee Profile System: This system produces a 'multi copy form' that displays key items in an individual employee file record. The concerned individual employee manager reviews each item and corrects or updates the database frequently. This includes employee name, address, job and organization codes, salary, education and training, work history and so on.

3. Personnel Data Retrieval System: This system is concerned with the procedures by which the personnel department obtains data from the employee file. In smaller organizations, this data may be supplemented from the employment control report. In larger organizations, this system provides efficient means to access and summarize employee data to the personnel department for various purposes.

4. Employee Practice Compliance Report: These reports will be based on many laws and regulations that are enforced by the government and other agencies from time to time and their requirements are in a state of evolution. Generally these reports cover employee population statistics, parity indices, applicant flows, and employee selections.

5. Personnel Action Systems: This system supports the activity of the Personnel department in taking actions on the following matters:

- *Filling job openings, and*
- *Recording and reporting promotions, transfers, terminations and other employee status changes.*

Generally systems involved during the above process are:

- *Placement data system, and*
- *Personnel activity reporting system*

6. Placement Data System: Placement data procedures centre on the development and use of more applicant files. Separate files are required for jobs that require new type of data items on job applicants. Usually files may be different for blue-collar and white-collar jobs.

The applicant file is linked to jobs file by having the same file key, so that the list of applicants for a desired job can be quickly retrieved. In the job file, one or more detail items to define how many openings are there and the cut-off date for receiving the applications indicates the available job openings. It also contains a description of job, experience, education pre-requisites, location, travel and other special requirements, if any, for the same.

When a manager needs an employee for an existing position, or for a new position he first fills out a job requisition form and sends it to the personnel department. If the status of an existing employee is changed due to promotion, transfer or termination action should be reported to the personnel department for updating the employee file. After receiving the requisitions and personnel action reports by the personnel department, the data is input to the job files and the employees file either through a remote on-line termination in the personnel department or submission of the data to a key entry section.

A skill search of the employee file may be performed to locate qualified candidates. This can be through DBMS that has a user-oriented retrieval language. Such language permits the user to define the characteristics required of an applicant for a specific job. The system examines each record of the employee and entered into the applicant file by the personnel department either on a remote data terminal or by sending the data to the processing department for key entry. The manager who has sent the requisition is the final authority to decide which applicants to be interviewed.

For those who were not qualified for interview, it should be stated in their application and these should be returned to personnel department for input of the reason into the applications file. The conclusion of each interview with manager's recommendations should be recorded and entered in the applicant's file. A formal interview report is produced or evaluation may be included on the application form. This can be an input to the applications file in the personnel department. The record of a successful applicant is placed in the employee master file. The records in an applicant file concerning a job that has been filled should be removed from the active applicant's file and placed in a history file.

7. Compensation Systems

These are the primary mechanisms by which organizations endeavour to influence employees' behaviour. Most compensation systems are developed with two broad goals in mind such as:

- *To produce the desired behaviour from the employees:* This includes motivating employee to join the organization, to remain with it and to perform well for it.
- *To accomplish the first goal within the limitations faced by the organization:* This may focus on the constraints or limitations faced by most organizations, including their ability to pay, legal constraints such as minimum wages, regulations, labour union, and external labour markets.

Components of Compensation System

The company's total compensation package includes a variety of economic rewards and non-monetary rewards such as autonomy, recognition and a sense of achievement. In return for their services, employees receive compensation, a combination of payments, benefits and employer service. Although it is not the only factor in motivating employees, proper compensation is crucial for retaining their loyalty. Few people will work for prestige and social status and many people use compensation as a yardstick for measuring their success in the job. Following two assumptions are valid in any PIS format.

- *Wages means cash payment based on a calculation of the number of hours/days the employee has worked or the number of goods produced, and*
- *Salaries period such as weekly, monthly, or yearly cash compensation for work.*

Table 11.7: Guidelines for selection at a HRIS

Get advice	Help from a reputable HR consulting firm minimizes the risk. These specialists have been through the process before.
Tests the payroll	High-volume transaction processing is the toughest job for client-server systems. Ask prospective human resources vendor to run your payroll for you.
Play the numbers	Do not ignore the benefits of outside service bureaus- especially in the area of payroll. Tax, retirement, and other legal conditions change. If you have got more than 500 employees, run cost-benefits analysis.
Get it in writing	Don't be afraid to ask your vendor for a guarantee.
Train, train, train	Provide plenty of project staffing and technology education for your HR staff on the new system.
Be prepared	A merger or acquisition can affect your business at any time. A firm might need to add 5,000 employees to benefits and payroll systems within 30 days.
Act like traditional IS	Today's human resources departments must worry about security and data integrity, taking over that responsibility in some cases from information systems departments.

11.27 QUALITY INFORMATION SYSTEM

Quality information systems are standalone systems or embedded systems that help an organization to achieve its quality goals. The quality plan is derived from the strategic information plan.

Figure 11.17 shows, how the strategic quality plan is derived from the strategic information plan. In some cases, a firm has no separate quality plan, but instead makes quality a component of other plans, such as marketing, manufacturing, and so on. The information systems (IS) department plays a major role in ensuring the success of TQM efforts in an organization. An information system can promote quality and provide tools and techniques to help the firm achieve its quality goals. Information systems also help firms achieve quality certification. There are many institutions and agencies that certify the quality efforts of an organization and provide guidelines to firms that plan to instil quality in all aspects of their operations.

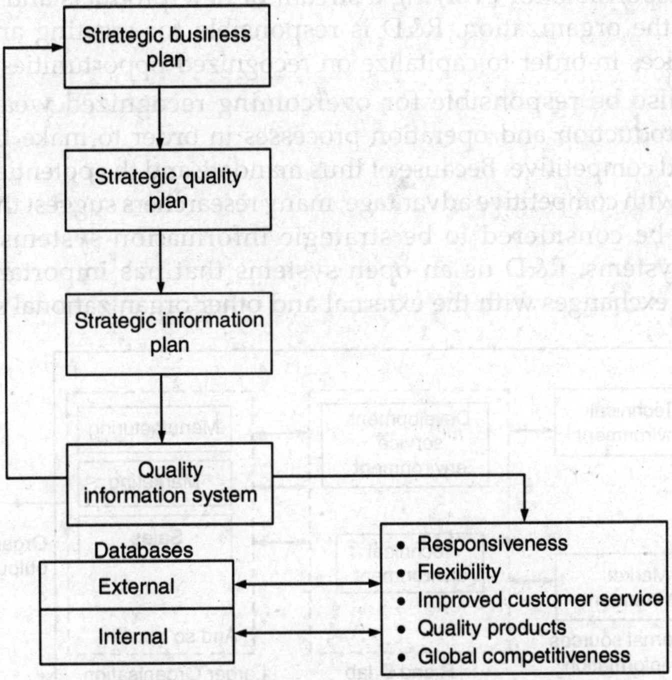

Figure 11.17: *Derivation of Quality Information Systems*

The role of IS may vary from one organization to the next, or even from one program to the next, but there are four major areas where IS plays an important role in the certification process. They are: partial systems overhaul, full systems overhaul, training, and oversight. In a partial systems overhaul, existing systems are partially revamped in order to update them and make them more responsive to the changing needs of decision makers. Partial systems overhaul may include providing users with better interfaces, better end-user support, or better integration of existing systems. In a full overhaul, the old system is replaced with a new system. Training is another area where IS can play an important role in quality certification. Users must be well-trained in systems that are partially or fully overhauled, because this has a direct impact on both quality and productivity. More important, good data comes from well-trained users and forms the basis of good decisions. Overall, the information systems should oversee the entire quality certification process; this is often a time consuming task. It requires coordination and cooperation among departments; IS can play a facilitating role by ensuring the free flow of information between decision makers. Often, organizational data and information have to be sent to external agencies and IS plays a critical role in getting the right data to the right people at the right time.

11.28 R&D INFORMATION SYSTEM

Advances in information technology have spawned specialized information systems in many other business areas. The significant area receiving considerable attention is Research and Development (R&D). R&D has long been recognised as an information sensitive activity that is usually responsible for evolving a stream of new products and production process innovations for the organization. R&D is responsible for creating and developing new products or services in order to capitalize on recognized opportunities.

R&D may also be responsible for overcoming recognized weaknesses in current organizational production and operation processes in order to make them more efficient, cost-effective, and competitive. Because of thus mandate and the potential of R&D to provide the organization with competitive advantage, many researchers suggest that R&D information systems should be considered to be strategic information systems. Like many other organizational systems, R&D us an open systems that has important information and communications exchanges with the external and other organizational subunits.

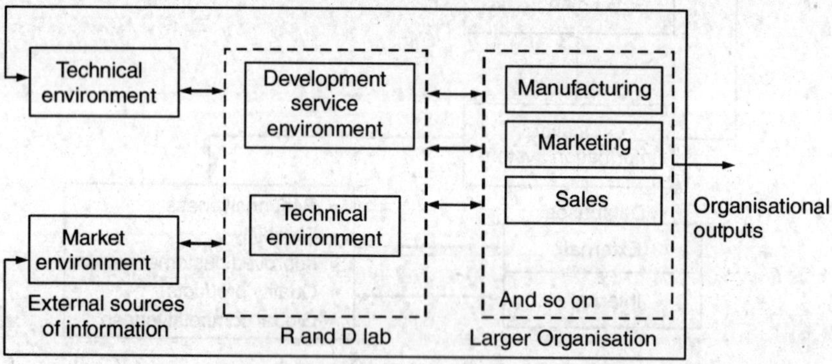

Figure 11.18: *Major Information Flow Crucial for R&D Effectiveness*

Figure 11.18 depicts the major information flows crucial for R&D effectiveness. This figure suggests that strong linkages should exist between R&D and the marketing/production subsystems of the organization. In most organizations, the proportion of spending in information technology for R&D is increasing and that integrated laboratory information management systems are gaining popularity. the productivity of R&D professionals has increased because of these changes, resulting in reduced product development time. Also, the access to external databases and to other sources of external information has increased dramatically over the past few years. However, linkage between R&D subunits that have online access to marketing or production databases IS far from expected level.

11.29 WORKGROUP INFORMATION SYSTEMS

Individuals in a business usually do not work entirely alone, but instead in teams, committees, departments, and other types of workgroups. To collaborate on common tasks, workgroup members can have meetings, talk on the telephone, send faxes, and distribute memos. Group members can also use workgroup information systems to help them collaborate. This type of system is also called a group support system because it supports the work of people in a group. This section looks at applications used in workgroup information systems, and shows how these applications affect group collaboration in businesses. First, we explain how workgroup information systems encourage group collaboration.

11.29.1 Workgroup

A Workgroup is an organized system of two or more individuals who are interrelated so that the system performs some function, has a standard set of relationships among members, and has a set of norms that regulate the functions of the group and each of its members.

Observe the three components of this definition of a workgroup function, role and norm. The workgroup function is the purpose for which the group exists. In formal organizations, this function generally is established explicitly organizational descriptions and tacitly in organizational budgets. Concerning the role component, there are two basic group types: homogeneous and heterogeneous. It is important to know these types because character of information system varies between them.

11.29.1.1 Homogeneous Workgroups

In homogeneous workgroups, everyone in the workgroup (except managers) fulfils the same role. Within a word processing department, for example, everyone works in the role of word processing operator and has the same job functions of creating, storing, and printing documents. All employees have the same level of training and skill. Work is assigned on a first available, first assigned basis. For example, a typical word processing group. This group works a schedule of two shifts, seven days a week. There is a group manager and two shift supervisor. Everyone else in the group is a word processing operator. As more employees are added to a homogenous workgroup, productivity increases at a nearly linear rate. The second, third, and fourth operators add about the same amount of productivity as do the tenth, eleventh and twelfth operator.

One challenge for such a workgroup concerns balancing the number of workers to the amount of work. This is especially true in businesses that involve seasonal changes such as a law firm at the end of the calendar year or a CPA firm during tax season. Another challenge concerns morale. Since such groups offer little work differentiation, task variety, autonomy, and promotional opportunities, workers can easily become discouraged.

Information systems tend to be easier to build and support for homogeneous workgroups than for heterogeneous workgroups. Since everyone does the same job, attention can be focused on information systems to support that single job. Further, a productivity improvement that helps one worker will generally help all workers.

11.29.1.2 Heterogeneous Workgroups

Heterogeneous workgroups involve a variety of different roles and job descriptions. In a customer support group, for example, there are people who specialise in particular products and people whose advanced level of knowledge and expertise qualify them to handle only certain difficult questions or key customers. Other specialists exist as well.

For illustration, organizational chart of Customer Support representatives are assigned to one of two groups, depending the level of the knowledge and experience. The more knowledgeable representatives are assigned to Speciality Requests group. In addition, one person is assigned full-time to training and another has the responsibility for producing the Customer Support newsletter. These specialists are assigned by other members of the workgroup as necessary.

As people are added to a heterogeneous workgroup, the productivity does not rise at a linear rate. The first person, who knows a great deal about a particular role, adds much more productivity than does the tenth. This phenomenon makes personnel hiring more difficult. When the workload increases, it is not possible to simply hire another typist. For Customer Support, a person must not only be a good communicator, but he must also possess the specialized knowledge needed to fill a role in the workgroup.

Two important challenges to heterogeneous workgroups concern communication and training. Since the group involves multiple roles, there is a tendency splinter into subgroups. This tendency reduces productivity and can also result in cliques and other forms of exclusivity than dampen morale. Training presents, another problem if the workgroup must expand and contract its size. It is more difficult to develop information systems for heterogeneous groups than for homogeneous groups. Since there are a variety of different jobs, there is often a need for a variety of different systems. Instead of 24 people using one system, there may be 6 people using four different systems. Consequently, development costs are higher. Further, the development cost of four systems must be amortized by the work of 24 people.

Additionally, since roles are specialized, information systems must be specialized as well. This means that a variety of different information systems technologies, and hence expertise, will be required to support the group.

11.29.1.3 Workgroup Norms

The third element of the structural definition of a workgroup if workgroup norms. A norm is a expectation, shared among workgroup members, that regulates member behaviour. For example, norms determine the pace at which members are expected to work, the hours they are expected to keep, and the values they are expected to hold. Norms are powerful influences, and groups find many overt and covert ways to enforce them.

One of the most important ways in which norms influence information systems concerns the group's attitude about the role of computer systems. If a workgroup norm implies that members are to gainfully utilize computer systems, then members of the group find ways to overcome computer phobia or other resistance when necessary. The group will provide support and assistance to new members to adapt to the systems. A typical statement to a new group member might be, "When I first came here, I didn't know how to use a computer either. But it really isn't that hard. Let me show you how I did it."

On the other hand, if the workgroup norm opposes the use of computer systems, then such systems will fail. Whoever desires the system to work must first address the changing of workgroup norms before proceeding with systems implementation. Computer systems never succeed if group norms oppose their use.

11.29.2 Objectives of Workgroup Information Systems

Fundamentally the purpose of a workgroup MIS is to facilitate the group's effectiveness. Nadler, Hackman and Lawler define such effectiveness in three dimensions. First, workgroups should produce output that meets or exceeds expectations. Second, they should provide for the personal need satisfaction of group members and third, the workgroup should function so as to facilitate the group's capacity for future cooperation.

By the same model, these dimensions of effectiveness are determined by three factors, namely, group effort, group knowledge and skill, and the approach and strategy used to perform work. While information systems influence all three of these factors, they are particularly important with regard to the last two. Workgroup information systems can facilitate workgroup communication and thus improve the group's knowledge and skills. Additionally, information systems can enable both discovery and implementation of new approaches and strategies for work.

11.29.3 Characteristics of Workgroup Information Systems

The primary difference between workgroup information systems and personal systems is that workgroup systems must support the controlled sharing of information, knowledge, data and other resources. To accomplish the objectives described in the last section increasing the workgroup's productive output through increased effort and knowledge and providing for better work strategies, members must be allowed to access each other's resources and to the workgroup's resources.

Observe the phrase controlled sharing. The workgroup's intellectual resources are shared, but the sharing must be done with care so that one person's work does not interfere with another's. For example, consider a word processing group. One operator may enter a document that is modified by a second operator on the next day, and by a third operator on the day after that. To make this possible, all three operators must have access to the pool of documents currently in process. Thus, that pool must be shared. At the same time, if two word processing operators modify the same document simultaneously, trouble will result. Thus, the information system must allow the operators to access from a shared pool, but carefully.

Additionally, controlled sharing also involves security. Often, not every member of the group needs or should have access to all of the group's information resources. In these cases, the information systems must provide passwords, account numbers, and other forms of security to restrict the access and activity in an appropriate way.

The term granularity refers to the size of the units of data or information that is shared. For example, the granularity of a shared word processing system could be a document. If so, this means that the entirety of a single document is checked out to an individual for processing. Alternatively, the granularity might be larger or smaller than this. A system might be designed to allocate an entire floppy disk to a word processing operator. In that case, the level of granularity is the collection of documents on that disk. For yet another alternative, the level of granularity might be major sections within a document. In this case, only a portion of a document is checked out to a particular user.

The level of granularity influences the throughput of the shared system. The larger the level of granularity, the greater the chance of delays due to contention, but greater is the ease of administering the system. On the other hand, the smaller the level of granularity, the smaller the chance of delays due to contention, but greater is the cost of administering the shared resources.

11.29.4 Survey of Workgroup Information Systems

In workgroups, there is often considerable overlap between the various types of systems defined in the previous chapters. For example, a single system may support TPS, MIS, and OAS applications.

Consider the Customer Call system used by Customer Support at AirTel. the system keeps track of customers who have paid for customer service. It also keeps records of the calls made by customers and records of the services that have been provided. Both of these functions facilitate operations, and the system that provides them could well be labelled a TPS.

On the other hand, the Customer Call system produces two reports that facilitate the management of Customer Support. One report, the Support Representative Call Summary ("Rep") report, lists the calls taken by each operator along with the operator's total time on telephone and the average time per call. This report can be used to gauge the work rate and the productivity of the support representatives. The second report, The Question Type Call Summary ("Question") report, lists the calls by call type. This report can be used to gauge the need for additional training or for specialization within the department. Considering these two reports, it would seem appropriate to classify the Customer Call system as an MIS.

If you reflect on the uses of information systems in workgroups, these multiple roles will not be surprising. The members of the workgroup process operational data to accomplish the operational goals of the groups. As that data is processed, the system also maintains data about the amount and flow of work in the group. This data is used to facilitate workgroup management. It may also facilitate strategic planning.

11.30 PERSONAL MANAGEMENT INFORMATION SYSTEMS

Personal MIS are computer-based information systems used by individuals to improve their personal productivity. They are employed by a wide range of business professionals, from managers to technical professionals, attorneys, accountants and other knowledge workers, politicians and so forth. They are also used in every business functional area.

In this section, we first describe the fundamental types of personal MIS. We will discuss the purpose and character of each type. After this survey, we will then discuss the professional needs that underlie each of these types. Finally, we will consider the impact of personal information systems on job quality and motivation.

There are three major categories of personal information systems: text processing, spreadsheet and database management. While these comprise the bulk of information systems applications, there are also a number of other important, but less prevalent categories of applications. We will discuss several of these other categories as well.

11.30.1 Text Processing

The fundamental purpose of a text-processing application is to prepare, store, and print documents. The documents can be simple text or they can include multiple type fonts, type sizes, and even graphics and graphical symbols. The foundation of all text processing is word processing, and we will begin with this topic.

1. Word Processing: Word processing was the first type of computer-based application. With word processing, documents are entered to a computer workstation, stored, and subsequently printed. Word processing is much more efficient than typing because for one, the mistakes are easily corrected. A mistake can be rekeyed, missing text can be inserted and undesired text can be readily removed.

In addition to easy error correction, other advantages of word processing include the ability to cut and copy large blocks of text, the capability to automatically search a document for particular letters, words, or phrases and the automatic replacement of one group of characters for another. Many word processing systems also include spelling checkers, which are programs within the word processing program that identify possible misspelled words and correct them when desired. With word processing, the keying and printing of a document are separate. Once a document has been entered, it is stored on a disk. Later the user can direct the word processing program to print the document. The printed document can be sent directly to a printer, or it can be save don another file and printed later. Much of the physical format of a document need be specified until print time. The width of margins, number of lines per page, the line spacing (e.g. single-spaced, double-spaced, etc.), and other similar format characteristics can be changed after the document has been keyed. With most word processors, page headings and footings and footnotes are automatically adjusted when the physical format of the document is altered.

Because keying is so much easier than typing and because of the separation between keying and printing, many professionals enter their own documents rather than relying on a typist. Once the document has been entered, the professional might give the file to a secretary who then formats it in accordance with office standards and practice and prints it. In accounting, consulting, and many types of law, the word processor has all but eliminated the use of dictating equipment, especially among the younger professional staff.

There are hundreds of different word processing program products. Several common products of this type are WordPerfect, WordStar, Microsoft Word, MultiMate, and XyWrite.

2. Mail/Merge Facilities: Many individuals and businesses have found it advantageous to conduct direct-mail sales and marketing activities. Often, these businesses produce personalized form letters to their customers.

Personalized form letters are written in a generalized form for a class of readers; then they are personalized by filling in the addressee's name, address, company name, and so forth, in the appropriate columns. Some of these letters print the personal data in both the address and the body of the letter.

3. Automated Document Production: Another word processing application is the production of boilerplate documents. A boilerplate is a standard document form into which someone inserts specific data.

4. Desktop Publication: Desktop publishing is a computer-based application that can be used to integrate text with graphics to produce professional-quality page layouts.

5. Electronic Spreadsheets: Electronic Spreadsheet programs are used to perform repetitive calculations of complicated data interrelationships. Such applications are common among business professionals, accountants and financial analysts.

11.30.2 Personal Database Application

A personal database application is a computer-based information system that keeps track of entities important to business professionals. A database application is used to record facts and figures about entities, to change those facts and figures as necessary, and to display results in a format convenient to user.

11.30.2.1 Components of a Database Application

The components of database application include the database, the data-entry forms, the reports, the query language, and a series of processing menus.

1. Database: A database is a collection of interrelated tables of data. Each table has data relevant to a particular theme.

2. Data Entry: Data-entry forms are video displays used to enter data.

3. Report: A report is a formatted presentation of data from the database. Reports are, by far, the most common way of displaying information from a database.

4. Query Language: Another, less frequently used, alternative is a query language, which is a general purpose language for obtaining data from the database on an ad hoc basis. Query languages are simpler than programming languages, and they can be learned by business professionals with no programming background.

5. Menus: Menus are lists of actions from which the user can choose to direct and control processing activity. Sometimes, one menu can involve another menu, and so forth, for several levels.

6. Application Programs: Finally, application programs are instructions for database processing that cannot be accomplished with generic DBMS functions.

11.30.3 Personal Database Management System

The database is processed by a program called a database management system (DBMS). Most DBMS products also include a number of easy-to-use tools for developing data-entry forms, reports, and menus. Often, too, there are default components that are created by the DBMS when tables are defined. Similarly, a default report is created for listing that data.

The defaults, while convenient, are often rough-hewn and not acceptable to end-users. Consequently, most D. MS products provide other tools to customize and tailor forms, forms, reports and menus. Most DBMS products also support a programming language so that application programs can be written to express unique or rare processing logic or other needs. The use of these tools and languages, however, requires programming and other advanced expertise.

The most popular microcomputer DBMS is dBASE (of which there are several varieties: dBASE II, dBASE III Plus, and dBASE IV). Other such products are ORACLE, Paradox, R:Base, and Sybase. Structured Query Language (SQL) is the standard query language adopted by the American National Standards Institute. Most DBMS products today include support for this language.

Strategic Planning: Strategic planning involves achieving personal objectives. Strategic planning issues tend to be unstructured. At the personal level, such issues only infrequently involve computer-based information systems.

11.30.4 Personal Management Control

Personal management control concerns the acquisition and effective use of resources. Personal management control involves the acquisition and use by an individual. Often the assigned asset is a monetary budget, but it also be equipment, personnel and consumable goods. In the case of an engineer, a designer, an attorney, or some other knowledge worker, the allocated asset is sometimes that person's own time. An attorney, for example, is told to spend five hours in the library and develop the best possible opinion on a legal question.

One of the ways that professional work differs from non-professional work is that the professional is given greater latitude in the use of his time and resources. The professional is expected to reflect on the use of those resources and to make changes when appropriate. Whereas the attitude of a non-professional can sometimes be "They tell me what to do and I do it.", the attitude of a professional is expected to be "There's a better way to do this job, and I'm going to find it and do it.". When a professional makes a change in the use of resources, often no one other than that individual is even aware that a change occurred. Higher output or better results are the only indication. Information systems are often of great help in personal management functions, especially spreadsheets and personal database applications.

11.30.5 Personal Operations Control

Personal operations control involves the execution of specific tasks. At the personal level, this means doing one's assigned job. For a product manager, it means developing a product plan; for an engineer, an engineering drawing or analysis; for a designer, a design, and so forth.

As with management control, operations control issues can be facilitated by spreadsheet and personal database applications. Word processing systems are also used, especially for professions such as law, accounting, and various types of consulting.

In addition to such general purpose applications, many professions developed special-purpose packages. Engineers use computer-aided design (CAD) and computer-aided manufacturing (CAM) applications to develop engineering drawings and submit them to manufacturing. Drafts people have a variety of drawing systems. Publishers use computer systems for typesetting and page layout. Attorneys use specialized packages for querying legal databases to locate particular cases and precedents. All of these systems are examples of control over one's own operations.

11.30.6 Personal Product Quality

Information systems facilitate the external functions by improving both product quality and product delivery. At the personal level, products are the output of a particular job. The product of an advertising copywriter is an advertising copy. The product of an auditor is an audit. The product of a quality control engineer is controlled product process.

Observe the relationship between an individual's products and an organization's products. The company produces a product, say clothes dryer that is assembly of many individual's products. In some cases, an individual's product relates directly to the organization's product, and in other cases, it does not. The work of a clothes dryer engineer relates directly to the clothes dryer. The work of an organizational behaviourist who recommends a new organization in the accounting department does not directly relate to its product. In both cases, however, the individual does produce a product.

Personal operations and personal products are similar, but there is an important difference. Operations concern activities that create the product. Operations concern activity with an individual's sphere that only the individual sees or knows about. The product is the entity referred from individual to someone else. It crosses the boundary from one individual's boundary to another's. Products have both a physical component and information component. For the clothes dryer, there is a physical component and the documentation and support component. Along with the clothes dryer engineer, there is a physical design (a blueprint, a CAD drawing, a specification, and a report) and there is also the information of that design, the design itself.

Obviously, the information content of the plan is also important. No matter how well it is presented, if the plan is inconsistent or incomplete, problems will occur. Now, for personal products, especially those for knowledge workers, information systems are sometimes used as the physical product component.

11.30.7 Personal Product Delivery

The final function that personal information systems can serve is improved personal product delivery. For one, individuals can perform their work faster. This means that information products can be provided more frequently and that they will be more current and up-to-date. Additionally, personal information systems can be made more accessible. For example, work results can be made immediately available to concerned workers via electronic mail. As another example, engineer identifies a problem with a product; the problem description can be quickly designated to concerned employees throughout the company.

Such rapid personal product delivery also has a downside. If an individual makes an error, it can be quickly communicated. Imagine the chaos and disruption that might occur if erroneous description of a product problem is broadcast through Sales and Customer later retracted, changed, and then retracted again.

SUMMARY

The six components of an AIS all work together to help key employees collect, store, manage, process, retrieve, and report their financial data. Having a well-developed and maintained accounting information system that is efficient and accurate is an indispensable component of a successful business.

In recent ERP systems accounting – from the book-keeping items to the instruments for reporting, controlling and output-management – is an highlighted area. ERP software should ensure a connected application for management and reporting, among which the elements (ledger, different analytics) supporting the accounting information system have special significance. These applications provide the necessary transparency and the access to the financial and accounting data for the employees concerned.

The book-keeping programmes mainly help the bookkeepers' and financial managers' work. Though their work has a crucial importance for the enterprise, it is limited to preparing tax returns and reports on the budget and finances.

Unfortunately it occurs in practice that the managers of the enterprise sign quarterly or yearly reports which are not transparent and representative, i.e. they are not understandable for them. The standardized statements are not made for top managers, rather for the operative leaders. By using ERP systems it is possible for those in the top management to view the financial and accounting indices and to understand their meaning, as it is possible to follow the indices and data to the lowest level.

Inventory refers to the stock of raw materials and finished goods available in the organization for production and sale. All organizations need an efficient system to maintain and control the optimum level of investment in all types of inventories. An inventory control system ensures that proper stock levels of each item are maintained.

Inventory control is concerned with the acquisition, storage, handling and use of inventories so as to ensure the availability of inventory whenever needed, providing adequate provision for contingencies, deriving maximum economy and minimizing wastage and losses.

Hence Inventory control refers to a system, which ensures the supply of required quantity and quality of inventory at the required time and at the same time prevent unnecessary investment in inventories. Control of inventory, which typically represents 45% to 90% of all expenses for business, is needed to ensure that the business has the right goods on hand to avoid stock-outs, to prevent shrinkage (spoilage/theft), and to provide proper accounting. Many businesses have too much of their limited resource, **capital**, tied up in their major asset, **inventory**. Worse, they may have their capital tied up in the wrong kind of inventory. Inventory may be old, worn out, shopworn, obsolete, or the wrong sizes or colors, or there may be an imbalance among different product lines that reduces the customer appeal of the total operation.

Inventory control systems range from eyeball systems to reserve stock systems to perpetual computer-run systems. Valuation of inventory is normally stated at original cost, market value, or current replacement costs, whichever is lowest. This practice is used because it minimizes the possibility of overstating assets. Inventory valuation and appropriate accounting practices are worth a book alone and so are not dealt with here in depth.

MkIS is a computerized system that is designed to provide an organized flow of information to enable and support the marketing activities of an organization. The MkIS serves collaborative, analytical and operational needs. In the collaborative mode, the MkIS enables managers to share information and work together virtually. In addition, the MkIS can enable marketers to collaborate with customers on product designs and customer requirements. The analytical function is addressed by decision support applications that enable marketers to analyze market data on customers, competitors, technology and general market conditions. These insights are becoming the foundation for the development of marketing strategies and plans. The MkIS addresses operational needs through customer management systems that focus on the day-to-day processing of customer transactions from the initial sale through customer service.

The Personnel Information System (PIS) deals with the flow of information about people working in the organization as well as forecasting requirements of human resources.

Quality information systems are standalone systems or embedded systems that help an organization to achieve its quality goals. The quality plan is derived from the strategic information plan.

Advances in information technology have spawned specialized information systems in many other business areas. The significant area receiving considerable attention is Research and Development (R&D). R&D has long been recognised as an information sensitive activity that is usually responsible for evolving a stream of new products and production process innovations for the organization. R&D is responsible for creating and developing new products or services in order to capitalize on recognized opportunities.

Individuals in a business usually do not work entirely alone, but instead in teams, committees, departments, and other types of workgroups. To collaborate on common tasks, workgroup members can have meetings, talk on the telephone, send faxes, and distribute memos. Group members can also use workgroup information systems to help them collaborate. This type of system is also called a group support system because it supports the work of people in a group.

Personal MIS are computer-based information systems used by individuals to improve their personal productivity. They are employed by a wide range of business professionals, from managers to technical professionals, attorneys, accountants and other knowledge workers, politicians and so forth. They are also used in every business functional area.

EXERCISES

1. What is accounting information system?
2. Explain the concept of the information system?
3. What are the components of an accounting information system?
4. What are the types of accounting information systems?
5. Explain the posting cycle in detail?
6. Explain the function of the accounting information system, its position in the hierarchy of the enterprise?
7. Explain the accounting information system and its environment?
8. What are interrelationships of important accounting information systems?
9. Explain the accounting information system in practice?
10. Explain the accounting information system and the information technology?
11. What is inventory control/management system?
12. What is inventory management?
13. What is inventory management system?
14. Explain the concept of integrated inventory management system?
15. Explain the SMC discipline interfaces?
16. Explain the inventory management disciplines and interfaces?
17. Explain the process of inventory management?
18. Explain the flow of inventory management?
19. Explain the data model of inventory management?
20. What is marketing information system?
21. Explain the marketing research and MkIS?
22. What are the functional components of marketing information system?
23. Explain the working of MkIS?

24. Explain the development of a MkIS?
25. What are the benefits of the marketing information system?
26. What is personnel information system?
27. Explain the data, file type and structure of PIS?
28. Explain the major files in PIS?
29. What are the subsystems of PIS?
30. What is quality information system?
31. What is R&D information system?
32. What are workgroup information systems?
33. What are the objectives of workgroup information systems?
34. Explain the characteristics of workgroup information systems?
35. What is personal management information system?
36. What is text processing?
37. What is personal database application?
38. Explain the components of a database application?
39. What is personal database management system?
40. Explain the concept of personal management control?
41. What is personal operations control?
42. Explain the personal product quality and delivery?

❑

OTHER USEFUL BOOKS BY THE AUTHOR

INTERNET APPLICATIONS

Salient Features

- Explains the basics of internet and its working, internet service provider (ISP), internet addressing (DNS) and IP addresses).
- Presents the structure and working of an E-mail message.
- Deals with the file transfer protocol (FTP), Gopher, Telnet, newsgroup, WWW.
- Deals with Web designing using HTML and DHTML.
- Describes the components and working of search engines.
- Explains the concept of intranet and extranet.

ISBN : 9789381068397 **Pages (Approx.) : 700**

COMPUTER FUNDAMENTALS AND PROGRAMMING IN C

Salient Features

- Explains the introduction to computers and operating system.
- Describes the concept of number systems, computer codes and arithmetic, logic gates and Boolean algebra.
- Deals with the building of different logic circuits.
- Introduces the concept of primary/secondary storage and Input/ Output devices.
- Complete introduction to C programming features are given in detail.
- Around 200 solved C programs and 100 objective type questions are included.

ISBN : 9789381068380 **Pages (Approx.) : 750**

COMPUTER ORGANIZATION AND ARCHITECTURE

Salient Features

- Extensive coverage of electronic basics, architectural advancement of computer systems.
- Presents the analysis and design of sequential and combinational circuits.
- Demonstrates the concept of register transfer language and CPU organization.
- Provide the description for machine and assembly language.
- Covers the concept of control unit and I/O organization.
- Provides the conceptual detail of pipeline and vector processing.
- Covers basic memory concepts and other alternative architectures that have emerged in recent years.

ISBN : 9789381068311 **Pages (Approx.) : 750**

Fundamentals of COMPUTERS, OPERATING SYSTEMS AND INFORMATION TECHNOLOGY

Salient Features

- Provides a comprehensive coverage of the subject.
- Explains the introduction to computers, computer generations, classification of computers and applications of computer in corporate environment.
- Presents the basic organization of a computer system and its internal working. It also explains different types of processors.
- Describes the concept of number systems, computer codes and arithmetic, logic gates and Boolean algebra.
- Deals with the building of different logic circuits like multiplexer, demultiplexer, encoder, decoder, generators, flip-flops, registers and counters etc.
- Introduces the concept of primary/secondary storage and Input/ Output devices.
- Describes the concept of operating system.

ISBN : 9789381068335 **Pages (Approx.) : 950**

WINDOWS BASED COMPUTER COURSES
A Visual Approach

Salient Features

- Computer Fundamentals summarizes the simple concepts of computer technology related to hardware and software advancements and IT gives the close look to data communication, networking and internet.
- MS DOS is single user operating system tell the beginners about the various useful internal and external commands.
- Windows Vista is the latest and greatest in the illustrious line of Windows operating systems from Microsoft.
- Microsoft Office is essential software for the beginners for the creation of documents, spreadsheets, presentation and databases using of Microsoft Word, Microsoft Excel, Microsoft PowerPoint and Microsoft Access.

ISBN : 9789381068359 **Pages (Approx.) : 1000**

ELECTRONICS - ANALOG AND DIGITAL

Salient Features

- Extensive coverage of electronic basics, architectural advancement of analog and digital systems.
- Presents analysis of semiconductor diodes and transistors.
- Provides description of Includes various network theorems: Thevenin's and Norton's Theorems.
- Provides various number system and codes, logic gates, flip-flops, registers and counters.
- Gives detailed description of semiconductor memories and AD and DA converters.
- Presents complex topic of logic families includes TTL, CMOS, ECL, RTL, IIL, etc.

ISBN : 9789380016955 **Pages (Approx.) : 639**

SOLVED PROGRAMMING IN C

Salient Features

- Includes 1600 solved programs.
- Includes system-level programming.
- Numerous examples are included to illustrate concepts and techniques.
- Each and every program given in the book is perfectly working.

ISBN : 9789380016191 **Pages (Approx.) : 530**

SOLVED PROGRAMMING IN C++

Salient Features

- Includes 2200 solved programs.
- Includes system-level programming.
- Numerous examples are included to illustrate concepts and techniques.
- Each and every program given in the book is perfectly working.

ISBN : 9789380016184 **Pages (Approx.) : 880**

C++ AND DATA STRUCTURES

Salient Features

- Extensive coverage of C++ and Data structure basics, pictorial representation of each and every Data Structures is given in detail.
- Includes numerous illustrative examples to understand the topic easily.
- Demonstrates the implementation of algorithm in a good programming style.
- Around 300 solved C++ programs are included.
- Around 300 objective type questions are included.
- Around 200 algorithms are included.

ISBN : 9789380016795 **Pages (Approx.) : 1260**

DATA STRUCTURES An Algorithmic Approach

Salient Features

- Extensive coverage of Data structure basics, pictorial representation of each and every Data Structures is given in detail.
- Demonstrates the development of algorithms in a lucid manner.
- Includes numerous illustrative examples to understand the topic easily.
- Demonstrates the implementation of algorithms in a good programming style.
- Objective-type questions have been provided.
- Around 300 algorithms are included.

ISBN : 9789380016702 **Pages (Approx.) : 680**

DATA STRUCTURES An Algorithmic Approach with C

Salient Features

- Extensive coverage of Data structure basics, pictorial representation of each and every Data Structures is given in detail.
- Demonstrates the development of algorithms in a lucid manner.
- Includes numerous illustrative examples to understand the topic easily.
- Demonstrates the implementation of algorithms in a good programming style.
- Objective-type questions have been provided.
- Around 200 solved C programs and algorithms are included.

ISBN : 9789380016696 **Pages (Approx.) : 960**

DATA STRUCTURES An Algorithmic Approach with C++

Salient Features

- Extensive coverage of Data structure basics, pictorial representation of each and every Data Structures is given in detail.
- Demonstrates the development of algorithms in a lucid manner.
- Includes numerous illustrative examples to understand the topic easily.
- Demonstrates the implementation of algorithms in a good programming style.
- Objective-type questions have been provided.
- Around 200 solved C++ programs and algorithms are included.

ISBN : 9789380016856 **Pages (Approx.) : 940**

EXPERT C PROGRAMMING

Salient Features

- Complete introduction to C programming features are given in detail.
- Includes numerous illustrative examples to understand the topic easily.
- Demonstrates every program in a good programming style.
- Around 300 solved C programs are included.
- Around 300 objective type questions are included.

ISBN : 9789380016764 **Pages (Approx.) : 718**

EXPERT C++ PROGRAMMING

Salient Features

- Complete introduction to C++ programming features are given in detail.
- Includes numerous illustrative examples to understand the topic easily.
- Demonstrates every program in a good programming style.
- Around 500 solved C++ programs are included.
- Around 300 objective type questions are included.

ISBN : 9789380016771 **Pages (Approx.) : 1105**

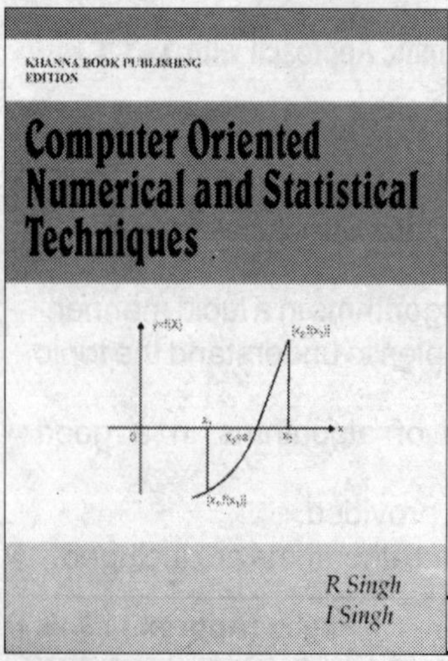

COMPUTER ORIENTED NUMERICAL AND STATISTICAL TECHNIQUES

Salient Features

- Extensive coverage of computer basics, numerical and error analysis and solution of transcendental and polynomial equations.
- Presents analysis of numerical differentiation, numerical integration, solution of ordinary and partial differential equations in enough detail.
- Provides description of interpolation formulae, and solution of linear equations.
- Detailed analysis of techniques like measures of central tendency and measure of dispersion.
- Covers all statistical techniques moment generating functions, Skewness and Kurtosis.
- Detailed analysis of Correlation, Linear, non-linear and multiple regression analysis.

ISBN : 9789380016788 **Pages (Approx.) : 860**